WILLIAM WORDSWORTH

Henry Edridge (1769–1821). Tinted pencil drawing of Wordsworth aged 36 (1806).

# WILLIAM WORDSWORTH

## *A Life*

═══❧═══

STEPHEN GILL

Oxford   New York
OXFORD UNIVERSITY PRESS
1990

Oxford University Press, Walton Street, Oxford OX2 6DP

Oxford New York Toronto
Delhi Bombay Calcutta Madras Karachi
Petaling Jaya Singapore Hong Kong Tokyo
Nairobi Dar es Salaam Cape Town
Melbourne Auckland
and associated companies in
Berlin Ibadan

Oxford is a trade mark of Oxford University Press

First published 1989
Reprinted 1989
First issued as an Oxford University Press paperback 1990

British Library Cataloguing in Publication Data
Gill, Stephen, 1941–
William Wordsworth: a life.—(Oxford lives)
1. Poetry in English. Wordsworth, William, 1770–1850
I. Title
821.7
ISBN 0–19–282747–2

Library of Congress Cataloging in Publication Data
Gill, Stephen Charles.
William Wordsworth: a life / Stephen Gill.
p. cm. Includes bibliographical references.
1. Wordsworth, William, 1770–1850—Biography. 2. Poets,
English—19th century—Biography. I. Title.
821'.7—dc20 PR5881.G55 1990 89–49325
ISBN 0–19–282747–2

Printed in Great Britain by
Courier International Ltd.
Tiptree, Essex

TO

ROBERT WOOF

# PREFACE

ALL previous biographies of Wordsworth were superseded by Mary Moorman's two-volume life (1957 and 1965). This substantial, yet very readable, biography was a splendid work of scholarship, but the publication of its first volume coincided with the beginning of a golden age in Wordsworth and Coleridge studies, which has greatly altered our perception of both poets. New editions have appeared of their letters, their prose works, of Coleridge's private notebooks, and of Wordsworth's poems. Mark Reed has assembled an invaluable day-by-day chronology of Wordsworth's life and writings to 1815. Scholarly monographs have shed new light on his school-days and early adult years. Articles, books, and every volume so far of the *Cornell Wordsworth* have transformed our understanding of the poet's manuscripts and his working methods. In 1977 the Wordsworth Library in Grasmere acquired a large and previously unknown cache of family papers.

The main purpose of this biography is to offer the general reader a life of Wordsworth that takes account of this new information. My subject is Wordsworth the writer. What follows *is* a biography, not an 'intellectual history' exegesis of specific works and phases of thought, but I have not hesitated to sacrifice domestic detail when other material about Wordsworth's writing and publication competed for space. Readers who want to know exactly what the poet did on 4 October 1798 can consult Reed's *Chronology*. Those who want a fuller picture of his domestic life will find it in Moorman's biography and in the volumes of the family letters.

This book, however, aims to be more than just a conduit for recent scholarship. It has been shaped by three convictions. The first is that in discussing the first thirty years of Wordsworth's life the biographer must not succumb to Wordsworth's own account of them. His strong self-representation must be assessed, not simply followed. Why resistance is necessary is explained in the Introduction.

The second is that some shift of emphasis is called for in approaches to the poet and his poetry. Like Blake, Wordsworth was a visionary poet. Unlike Blake, Wordsworth became increasingly determined that people should know it and that his voice should be heard. He cared about his publications, about reviews, about his audience and his public image. Excellent books have been written about Wordsworth the solitary visionary, communing, as Hazlitt put it, only with himself and the universe. Too little attention has been paid to the imperious, self-willed Wordsworth, who wanted to be recognized as an intellectual power.

My third conviction is that Wordsworth's later years cannot be dismissed as of 'merely biographical interest'. The modern critical consensus is that

Wordsworth's best poetry was written before he was 40 and that it would have been better for his reputation had he joined Keats, Shelley, and Byron in an early death. It is not likely that this literary-critical evaluation will be reversed. What needs to be recognized, however, is that as Wordsworth grew older he became a stronger, not a weaker, power in national culture. His later writings were increasingly well received at the same time as his earlier work was being discovered by many in the younger generation who were to contribute significantly to the culture of nineteenth-century Britain and America. Wordsworth began to matter to his contemporaries just as, in the judgement of most critics, he stopped being an important poet. I have tried to bring out the significance of this paradox.

A book of this kind is of necessity a collaborative project. I have relied upon the published and unpublished scholarship of a great many people, whose work is acknowledged in the bibliography. For particularly valued help I would like to thank the following: David Bentley-Taylor, Paul F. Betz, James Butler, Marilyn Butler, Jared Curtis, Beth Darlington, Donald E. Hayden, Alan G. Hill, Terry McCormick, Jerome McGann, Mary Moorman, W. J. B. Owen, Stephen Parrish, Mark L. Reed, Jonathan Wordsworth. The following have also given me kindly assistance, for which I am grateful: Anne Barton, Alan Bell, Olivia Bell, Sidney Chapman, Jeff Cowton, Jack and Marianne Hall, Dennis Kay, Paul Langford, Sally Woodhead.

For permission to consult and publish materials in their collections, I would like to thank the following: the librarians of: the Beinecke Library, Yale University; Bristol University Library; the Bodleian Library; the British Library, particularly Hilton Kelliher; Cornell University Library; the Houghton Library, Harvard University; Keble College Library, Oxford; New York Public Library, Astor, Lenox and Tilden Foundations, particularly the Director of the Henry W. and Albert A. Berg Collection; Northwestern University Library; the Pierpont Morgan Library, New York; Princeton University Library; the Wordsworth Library.

For permission to publish other copyright material I am particularly indebted to the Trustees of Dove Cottage and to Oxford University Press.

For assistance with illustrations and permission to publish I am indebted to the Trustees of the National Portrait Gallery; the Master and Fellows of St John's College, Cambridge; the Trustees of Dove Cottage; J. C. Hardy.

Grants from Lincoln College, Oxford, and from the funds of the English Faculty, Oxford University, greatly helped my research, for which I am very grateful.

I would also like to thank Kim Scott Walwyn and Frances Whistler of Oxford University Press, who could not have been more encouraging, and

Alison Marsland for uncomplaining labour at the word-processor. Clare Tilbury helped in every way throughout the writing of this book, but I am particularly grateful for her obstinate questionings of sense, which shaped my revision of it.

Finally, I would like to acknowledge that an inspiration for my own work has been the self-effacing labour and tireless dedication of the great Wordsworth scholar to whom this book is dedicated.

# CONTENTS

# LIST OF ILLUSTRATIONS

The author and publishers are grateful to the following for permission to reproduce the above:

The Trustees of Dove Cottage: Frontispiece, the Walter Scott manuscript, 2, 3, 5, 6, 7.

National Portrait Gallery: 1, 8, 10.

Birmingham Museums and Art Gallery: 4.

Dr J. C. Hardy: 9.

# SHORT FORMS OF CITATION

Place of publication is London unless otherwise noted.

*The Prelude*

In order to avoid multiplying short forms of citation the following are used to refer both to the poem as it was at various stages of composition and to the authoritative texts of the Cornell Wordsworth series:

*1799 Prelude*: *The Prelude, 1798–99*, ed. Stephen Parrish (Ithaca, 1977)

*1805 Prelude*: *The Thirteen-book Prelude*, ed. Mark L. Reed, is still forthcoming. Reference to the poem of 1805 is therefore to the text in *The Prelude 1799, 1805, 1850*, ed. Jonathan Wordsworth, M. H. Abrams, Stephen Gill (New York, 1979). This edition is also cited on occasion as *Norton Prelude*.

*1850 Prelude*: *The Fourteen-book Prelude*, ed. W. J. B. Owen (Ithaca, 1985)

*Other Citations*

| | |
|---|---|
| *Benjamin* | William Wordsworth, *Benjamin the Waggoner*, ed. Paul F. Betz (Ithaca, 1981) |
| *BJRL* | *Bulletin of the John Rylands University Library of Manchester* |
| *BL* | Samuel Taylor Coleridge, *Biographia Literaria*, ed. James Engell and W. Jackson Bate (2 vols., 1983) |
| *Blanshard* | Frances Blanshard, *Portraits of Wordsworth* (1959) |
| *BNYPL* | *Bulletin of the New York Public Library* |
| *Borderers* | William Wordsworth, *The Borderers*, ed. Robert Osborn (Ithaca, 1982) |
| *BRH* | *Bulletin of Research in the Humanities* |
| *BWS* | *Bicentenary Wordsworth Studies*, ed. Jonathan Wordsworth (Ithaca, 1970) |
| C | Samuel Taylor Coleridge |
| CC | Catherine Clarkson |
| *Chandler* | James K. Chandler, *Wordsworth's Second Nature: A Study of the Poetry and Politics* (Chicago, 1984) |
| *CL* | *Collected Letters of Samuel Taylor Coleridge*, ed. Earl Leslie Griggs (6 vols., Oxford, 1956–71) |
| *CN* | *The Notebooks of Samuel Taylor Coleridge*, ed. Kathleen Coburn (6 vols., continuing, 1957–) |
| *CPW* | Samuel Taylor Coleridge, *The Complete Poetical Works*, ed. Ernest Hartley Coleridge (2 vols., Oxford, 1912) |
| *Curry* | *New Letters of Robert Southey*, ed. Kenneth Curry (2 vols., New York and London, 1965) |
| CW | Christopher Wordsworth, the poet's brother |

| | |
|---|---|
| *Descriptive Sketches* | William Wordsworth, *Descriptive Sketches*, ed. Eric Birdsall (Ithaca, 1984) |
| *DQL* | *De Quincey to Wordsworth: A Biography of a Relationship. With the Letters of Thomas De Quincey to the Wordsworth Family*, ed. John E. Jordan (Berkeley and Los Angeles, 1962) |
| *DQR* | Thomas De Quincey, *Recollections of the Lakes and the Lake Poets*, ed. David Wright (Harmondsworth, 1970) |
| DW | Dorothy Wordsworth |
| *DWJ* | *Journals of Dorothy Wordsworth*, ed. E. De Selincourt (2 vols., 1941) |
| *EIC* | *Essays in Criticism* |
| EQ | Edward Quillinan |
| *Essays* | Samuel Taylor Coleridge, *Essays on his Times*, ed. David V. Erdman (3 vols., 1978) |
| *Evening Walk* | William Wordsworth, *An Evening Walk*, ed. James Averill (Ithaca, 1984) |
| *EY* | *Letters of William and Dorothy Wordsworth*, ed. E. De Selincourt; *The Early Years, 1787–1805*, revised Chester L. Shaver (Oxford, 1967) |
| *Farington* | *The Diary of Joseph Farington*, ed. Kenneth Garlick and Angus Macintyre (vols. I–VI); ed. Kathryn Cave (vols. VII–XVI continuing) (New Haven and London, 1978–) |
| *Friend* | Samuel Taylor Coleridge, *The Friend*, ed. Barbara E. Rooke (3 vols., 1969) |
| *Gill: Oxf. W.* | *William Wordsworth* [Oxford Authors], ed. Stephen Gill (Oxford, 1984) |
| *Goodwin* | A. Goodwin, *The Friends of Liberty: The English Democratic Movement in the Age of the French Revolution* (1979) |
| *Gray* | *Correspondence of Thomas Gray*, ed. Paget Toynbee and Leonard Whibley (3 vols., Oxford, 1935); reissued with corrections and additions by H. W. Starr (3 vols., Oxford, 1971) |
| *Grosart* | *The Prose Works of William Wordsworth*, ed. Alexander B. Grosart (3 vols., 1876) |
| *Haydon* | *The Diary of Benjamin Robert Haydon*, ed. Willard Bissell Pope (5 vols., Cambridge, Mass., 1960–3) |
| *Haydon: Corr.* | *Benjamin Robert Haydon: Correspondence and Table-talk*, ed. Frederic Wordsworth Haydon (2 vols., 1876) |
| *HCL* | *Letters of Hartley Coleridge*, ed. Grace Evelyn Griggs and Earl Leslie Griggs (1936) |
| HCR | Henry Crabb Robinson |
| *HCR* | *The Correspondence of Henry Crabb Robinson with the Wordsworth Circle*, ed. Edith J. Morley (2 vols., Oxford, 1927) |

| | |
|---|---|
| *HCR: Books* | *Henry Crabb Robinson on Books and their Writers*, ed. Edith J. Morley (3 vols., 1938) |
| *Home at Grasmere* | William Wordsworth, *Home at Grasmere*, ed. Beth Darlington (Ithaca, 1977) |
| *Howe* | *The Complete Works of William Hazlitt*, ed. P. P. Howe (21 vols., 1930–4) |
| IF | Isabella Fenwick |
| *JEGP* | *Journal of English and Germanic Philology* |
| *Johnston* | Kenneth R. Johnston, *Wordsworth and The Recluse* (New Haven and London, 1984) |
| *Journals* | *Journals of Dorothy Wordsworth*, ed. Mary Moorman (1971) |
| JW | John Wordsworth |
| *JWL* | *Letters of John Wordsworth*, ed. Carl H. Ketcham (Ithaca, 1969) |
| *Keats* | *The Letters of John Keats 1814–1821*, ed. Hyder Edward Rollins (2 vols., Cambridge, Mass., 1958) |
| LB | Lady Beaumont |
| *Lectures* | Samuel Taylor Coleridge, *Lectures 1795 on Politics and Religion*, ed. Lewis Patton and Peter Mann (1971) |
| *Lindop* | Grevel Lindop, *The Opium-eater: A Life of Thomas De Quincey* (1981) |
| *LY* | *The Letters of William and Dorothy Wordsworth*, ed. E. De Selincourt; *The Later Years, 1821–1853*, revised Alan G. Hill (4 vols., Oxford, 1978–88). |
| *Marrs* | *The Letters of Charles and Mary Lamb*, ed. Edwin W. Marrs (3 vols., continuing, Ithaca and London, 1975–) |
| *Memoirs* | Christopher Wordsworth, *Memoirs of William Wordsworth* (2 vols., 1851) |
| MH | Mary Hutchinson |
| *Moorman* | Mary Moorman, *William Wordsworth: A Biography; The Early Years: 1770–1803* (Oxford, 1957); *The Later Years: 1803–1850* (Oxford, 1965) (identified by volume number) |
| *MP* | *Modern Philology* |
| *Murdoch* | *The Discovery of the Lake District*, ed. John Murdoch (1984) |
| MW | Mary Wordsworth |
| *MWL* | *The Letters of Mary Wordsworth 1800–1855*, ed. Mary E. Burton (Oxford, 1958) |
| *MY* | *The Letters of William and Dorothy Wordsworth*, ed. E. De Selincourt; *The Middle Years, 1806–11*, revised Mary Moorman (Oxford, 1969); *The Middle Years, 1812–1820*, revised Mary Moorman and Alan G. Hill (Oxford, 1970) (identified by volume number) |

| | |
|---|---|
| *Peter Bell* | William Wordsworth, *Peter Bell*, ed. John E. Jordan (Ithaca, 1985) |
| *PMLA* | *Publications of the Modern Language Association of America* |
| PP | Pinney Papers, University of Bristol Library |
| *Prose* | *The Prose Works of William Wordsworth*, ed. W. J. B. Owen and Jane Worthington Smyser (3 vols., Oxford, 1974) |
| *PW* | *The Poetical Works of William Wordsworth*, ed. E. De Selincourt and Helen Darbishire (5 vols., Oxford, 1940–9) |
| *P2V: Curtis* | William Wordsworth, *Poems, in Two Volumes*, ed. Jared R. Curtis (Ithaca, 1983) |
| *Reed* | Mark L. Reed, *Wordsworth: The Chronology of the Early Years 1770–1799* (Cambridge, Mass., 1967); *Middle Years 1800–1815* (Cambridge, Mass., 1975) (identified by volume number) |
| *Reflections* | Edmund Burke, *Reflections on the Revolution in France*, ed. Conor Cruise O'Brien (Harmondsworth, 1968) |
| *RES* | *Review of English Studies* |
| *Roe* | Nicholas Roe, *Wordsworth and Coleridge: The Radical Years* (Oxford, 1988) |
| *The Ruined Cottage* | William Wordsworth, *The Ruined Cottage and The Pedlar*, ed. James Butler (Ithaca, 1979) |
| RW | Richard Wordsworth, the poet's brother |
| *Salisbury Plain Poems* | William Wordsworth, *The Salisbury Plain Poems*, ed. Stephen Gill (Ithaca, 1975) |
| SGB | Sir George Beaumont |
| SH | Sara Hutchinson |
| *Sheats* | Paul D. Sheats, *The Making of Wordsworth's Poetry, 1785–1798* (Cambridge, Mass., 1973) |
| *SHL* | *Letters of Sara Hutchinson*, ed. Kathleen Coburn (1954) |
| *SIB* | *Studies in Bibliography* |
| *SIR* | *Studies in Romanticism* |
| *SL* | *The Life and Correspondence of Robert Southey*, ed. Charles Cuthbert Southey (6 vols., 1849–50) |
| *Taylor* | *Correspondence of Henry Taylor*, ed. Edward Dowden (1888) |
| *Taylor Autobiography* | Henry Taylor, *Autobiography* (2 vols., 1885) |
| TP | Thomas Poole |
| *Tuft of Primroses* | William Wordsworth, *The Tuft of Primroses with Other Late Poems for The Recluse*, ed. Joseph Kishel (Ithaca, 1986) |
| *TWT* | T. W. Thompson, *Wordsworth's Hawkshead*, ed. Robert Woof (1970) |
| *UTQ* | *University of Toronto Quarterly* |
| W | William Wordsworth |

WL                    Wordsworth Library, Grasmere
*WLL*                 *The Love Letters of William and Mary Wordsworth*, ed.
                      Beth Darlington (Ithaca, 1981)
*Watchman*            Samuel Taylor Coleridge, *The Watchman*, ed. Lewis
                      Patton (1970)

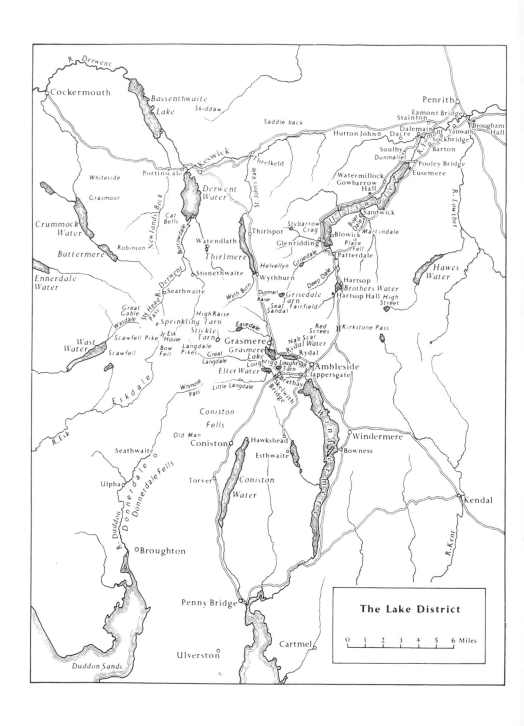

The Lake District

0  1  2  3  4  5  6 Miles

# INTRODUCTION

## (1)

ANYONE trying to construct a biography of Wordsworth faces a problem: the poet spent a lifetime sifting, selecting, and ordering much of the material for it himself.

Officially he was opposed to biography. It was clear, of course, to both admirers and detractors that autobiography was the well-spring of his creative powers. His, as Keats said, was the poetry of the 'egotistical sublime'.[1] Wordsworth wrote about real places and events, about the River Wye, Grasmere, London, Bruges, the Yarrow, about tours of Scotland and Italy. He memorialized his own experiences and recollections, his family, people met with in chance encounters, and old friends. The Preface to *The Excursion* (1814), the notes appended to particular lyrics, and the tantalizingly brief but revealing personal words in the 1842 volume *Poems, Chiefly of Early and Late Years* even encouraged interest in the poet by sketching in a biographical context for the work. But further biographical probing was always thwarted. 'In truth my life has been unusually barren of events', he told Anne Taylor in 1801, formulating a useful untruth which he repeated thirty-six years later when parrying another probe with the remark that his life was 'bare of entertainment and interest'.[2] He forbade Barron Field, an intelligent disciple, to publish his *Memoirs of Wordsworth* and was so appalled by the unauthorized use made of letters and recollections after Coleridge's death that he declared he hoped not a scrap of his own correspondence would survive.

Even as he deflected biographical enquiry, however, Wordsworth was writing autobiography, not in the published poems, but in documents which remained unpublished until after his death, known only to his family and closest friends. There was the celebration of life with his sister Dorothy called *Home at Grasmere*. There were the notes on the whole canon of his poetry dictated in 1843, an impressively comprehensive attempt by an old man to bring together the work of a lifetime in one unifying review, and the autobiographical notes dictated to his nephew in 1847. Above all there was *The Prelude*.

The first version of this autobiographical poem, in two books, was completed but not published in 1799. A greatly expanded version in thirteen books was completed but not published in 1805. Wordsworth could not fix on a title for it, but he often referred to it, as in a letter to Sir George Beaumont of 25 December 1804, as his poem on 'the growth of my own mind'. He revised the poem at intervals throughout his later life, but by 1839 it had assumed its final form in fourteen books. Immediately after Wordsworth's death the poem was published, in 1850, under the title determined by his widow and executors: *The Prelude: Growth of a Poet's Mind*.

Critics disagree about the relative merits of the thirteen- and fourteen-book versions, but none would dispute that *The Prelude* is Wordsworth's greatest poem. It encompasses and unifies many genres. Satire and narrative, description and meditation, the visionary and the deliberately banal—all are exploited in Wordsworth's most sustained use of the flexible blank verse he made his characteristic instrument. As a poem it is a wonderful achievement. For the biographer, however, it is a problem. As an autobiography it is open to question, partly because like all autobiographies it is selective, but more importantly because unlike most others it was written not only to present a self-image to posterity but to assist the writer to understand his own life, so that the rest of it might be lived more purposefully and in accordance with truths perceived in the act of writing the poem. Since I have attempted to resist the shaping so persuasively offered by Wordsworth in his own self-representation in *The Prelude*, it is important to spell out what my attitude is to the poem as a biographical source. Readers who are not familiar with the poem may wonder what all the fuss is about, while those who know it well will find the following brief account unsatisfactory. Both, I hope, will prefer to have the issue discussed here rather than be irritated by cautions and explanations interjected throughout the early chapters.

### (2)

A comparison with other autobiographies might help identify the particular oddity of *The Prelude*. Whatever their beliefs about the relationship between the man who suffers and the mind that creates, many nineteenth- and twentieth-century writers have in practice been anxious to determine the image of themselves presented to contemporaries and to posterity. Dickens supplied his biographer with such a compelling account of that part of his life most open to misconstruction that Forster printed it at length and thus allowed his subject a privileged place as autobiographer within a biography. Trollope wrote his own life but retained it for posthumous publication, ensuring that during his lifetime at least the public image of the forthright, energetic, and purposeful English gentleman was not affected by the revelation of the misery and aimlessness of his early years. In *Praeterita* Ruskin movingly evoked his childhood and youthful relationship with his parents, but, in a book described by his most recent biographer as 'pledged to avoid painful memories', he evaded altogether the catastrophe of his sexual life as an adult.[3] Hardy wrote the greater part of his own biography, drawing on sources which he then burnt, but arranged for it to appear after his death, as if written by his second wife. Needless to say this autobiography masquerading as biography is reticent about his marriages and much else which recent biographers have rightly judged to be of great interest to anyone wanting to understand Hardy's imagination.

In the various ways with which they dealt with the often discomfiting memories of their own lives, each of these writers indicates the degree of importance they think should be attached to certain private experiences of someone whose life has its real significance and its public dimension in published work. But they all have one thing in common. Dickens, Trollope, Ruskin, and Hardy wrote their autobiographies when they were already famous, generally towards the end of their lives. It was from the security of rich achievement that they looked back to discern the forces that had shaped the creation of *Oliver Twist* and *David Copperfield*, *Modern Painters* and *The Stones of Venice*, *The Chronicles of Barsetshire*, and *The Wessex Novels*. The patterns discerned might appear suspect or self-servingly partial when considered against other evidence, the autobiographies themselves might take on a rather different significance from the one intended when subjected to the kind of literary analysis applied to their subjects' avowedly imaginative work—none the less these are books written by people who have demonstrated their power and earned the right to present themselves as they think fit to a public whose regard they have already won.

Wordsworth's position when he began his autobiographical writing in 1798–9 was the opposite of theirs. Britain had been at war with France since 1793 and as Napoleon had just crowned his Italian campaign by seizing power as First Consul of the French it was clear that the war would drag on for many years yet. At home stability had been achieved after nearly a decade of unrest, but only at the cost of silencing by force rather than argument dissident opinion that would erupt again as soon as the conflict ended. Bread riots, mutiny, and the ever-present threat of the fermenting Irish were enough to justify anyone fearing for the social order.

Throughout this period Wordsworth had wanted somehow to be involved in shaping the destiny of his ideologically riven country, but how he might do so had never been clear and now, at the end of the decade, his personal position was on any rational assessment lamentable. At 28 years of age he had neither a settled income nor the professional qualifications needed to secure one. He had no home, a recent visit to Germany being only the latest in a series of rather fortuitous brief settlements. In an impetuous love affair in France he had fathered an illegitimate daughter, from whom he was separated and whom he could not support. Involvement in radical politics had inspired an eloquent pamphlet and some protest poems, but as none of them had been published Wordsworth could hardly claim, as

Southey and Coleridge plausibly could, that he was a public figure in political-literary life. A share, even the major share, in an anonymously issued slim volume of *Lyrical Ballads*, and two old-fashioned loco-descriptive poems that did not sell, were not much to show for the years since he had left Cambridge.

Such a judgement was certainly the one his relatives had arrived at and Wordsworth was sensible enough to realize that by the standards of a successful Penrith draper or an attorney it was reasonable. But he was convinced that it was wrong, not just unsympathetic, or narrow, but profoundly wrong. It ignored what really mattered—that immersion in radical politics had forced him to assess and then reassess his beliefs about Man, God, and the nature of Social Justice, as an enlightened man should; that for a would-be writer experiments in verse forms and different genres are of value, whether published or not. Above all it ignored the fact that during the most satisfying and creative year of his life so far, 1797–8, he had become convinced that he had a vocation, literally that he was called to be a major poet. In March 1798 he was contemplating a poem on 'Nature, Man, and Society' so ambitious that he could declare, 'I know not any thing which will not come within the scope of my plan'.[4]

The disparity between Wordsworth's exulting confidence in himself and what he had actually achieved, between his Miltonic grandeur of conception and the fact that he had published little of any significance, was something he recognized. From his struggle to confront it and to explore its implications emerged his first *apologia pro vita sua*, the *1799 Prelude*.

The climax to the poem keys together the whole structure in a counterpoint of public and private worlds:

>                                   if in these times of fear,
> This melancholy waste of hopes o'erthrown,
> If, 'mid indifference and apathy
> And wicked exultation . . .
>                                        . . . if, in this time
> Of dereliction and dismay, I yet
> Despair not of our nature, but retain
> A more than Roman confidence, a faith
> That fails not, in all sorrow my support,
> The blessing of my life, the gift is yours,
> Ye mountains, thine, O Nature.

Everything has been shaped to support this contention. Memories of intense moments of joy or fear in childhood, speculations about the evolution of individual consciousness, a rhapsodic evocation of the coming of religious awareness—everything serves the dominant aim of demonstrating how this poet learned to recognize the strength of the individual mind and to acknowledge the responsibility of gifts bestowed on him.

Like the reminiscences of formative years offered by Dickens or Trollope or Ruskin or Hardy the *1799 Prelude* selects and emphasizes its material to elucidate the significant pattern the writer perceives, but Wordsworth's autobiographical account differs in one very important respect. Although it reaches right back to 'the infant Babe' and celebrates 'unfading recollections' of childhood pursuits, the real importance of the poem lies not in what it says about the past but in what it promises about the future. The great Victorians looked back to childhood and youth knowing that it had led to a lifetime of literary achievement. Theirs is a genuine retrospect. Wordsworth on the other hand looks back as a young man, one with the future before him but little other than faith to support him in the belief that he will be worthy of the task to which he perceives he has been called. When Wordsworth settled in the Lake District in 1799 he could not have been certain that he was going to remain there for the rest of his life, but in simultaneously returning to his origins and completing the analysis of the evolution of his own poetic powers he was announcing that his youth was over, that he had made his choice of life, and that from now on he was going to live obedient to his calling. The *1799 Prelude* is a justification of this choice.

In the following years Wordsworth began to establish himself as a writer. Editions of *Lyrical Ballads* in 1800, 1802, and 1805 carried his name on the title-page and offered the public such characteristic works of his genius as *Michael* and *The Brothers*. He wrote many of his most famous poems, such as *Resolution and Independence*, sonnets and lyrics such as 'Earth has not anything to shew more fair' and 'I wandered lonely as a cloud'. The pugnacious, self-justifying Preface to *Lyrical Ballads* attracted the attention of reviewers, so that the literary world became aware of Mr Wordsworth as one of a rather dangerous group of young poets, the 'Lake School'. And throughout this period Wordsworth continued to struggle with poetry that was intended for the great work announced in 1798.

When Wordsworth returned in 1803 to the poem on the growth of his own mind, therefore, he did so from a completely different position from the one at which he had stood in 1798–9. Now he had real achievement to show for his choice of life. In 1798–9 he hoped, with confidence, that it was right. Now he knew it was. True, the great poem, *The Recluse*, was not yet written, but it was in process and much else had been completed. He could feel with reason that he had been right to acknowledge his vocation and to return to his native mountains 'with the hope of being enabled to construct a literary Work that might live'.[5]

This new assessment of his own maturity is what shapes the *1805 Prelude*. As he looks back on his life as an undergraduate, on his experiences in

France, on his involvement in radical politics and his subsequent withdrawal, Wordsworth shapes his memories so as to affirm through sheer weight of evidence three convictions. The first is that whatever wrong paths he might have explored and whatever errors he might have committed, at some profound level he had been working out his destiny. Beneath the adventitious circumstances of wandering and confused years Wordsworth's 'true self' had survived, not just unviolated but strengthened by all that had threatened it. The second is that the retired life of the imagination is the truly creative life, not the secular world of academic competition or of revolutionary activism. It is thus vital to Wordsworth to demonstrate how early in his life he became aware of this truth and how unignorable were the proofs offered him. The third conviction is that Wordsworth's experiences and his education under Nature's tutelage had formed him to be the celebrant of Man, to 'think', as Keats put it, 'into the human heart'.[6] Again and again he places experiences in an evolutionary sequence in which love of Nature is said to lead to love of Man. Such a conviction was the impulse behind Wordsworth's definition of his poetic intent in March 1798 and is what determines the declaration with which the *1805 Prelude* ends. Once again he looks back to the summer of 1798 and reaffirms the noble purpose to which he and Coleridge had then dedicated themselves:

> though too weak to tread the ways of truth,
> This age fall back to old idolatry,
> Though men return to servitude as fast
> As the tide ebbs, to ignominy and shame
> By nations sink together, we shall still
> Find solace in the knowledge which we have,
> Blessed with true happiness if we may be
> United helpers forward of a day
> Of firmer trust, joint labourers in the work—
> Should Providence such grace to us vouchsafe—
> Of their redemption, surely yet to come.
> Prophets of Nature, we to them will speak
> A lasting inspiration, sanctified
> By reason and by truth; what we have loved
> Others will love, and we may teach them how:
> Instruct them how the mind of man becomes
> A thousand times more beautiful than the earth
> On which he dwells, above this frame of things
> (Which, 'mid all revolutions in the hopes
> And fears of men, doth still remain unchanged)
> In beauty exalted, as it is itself
> Of substance and of fabric more divine.

Everything in the *1805 Prelude* is designed to show that this is a worthy task, that it is what Providence has called him to perform, and that he is equal to his 'High calling'.

In the *1805 Prelude* Wordsworth thus presents a teleological account of the formative years of his life. With his interpretative key everything can be seen as contributing to his growth into what he was already destined to be, a great poet of a particular kind. But we must resist the proffered key. The magnitude and grandeur of Wordsworth's own attempt to shape the understanding of his life will only be recognized for what it is when it is acknowledged that it is not the only way of shaping or understanding it.

## (3)

*The Prelude* also faces the biographer with another problem. Between 1803 and 1805 Wordsworth wrestled with drafts of his autobiographical poem, revising, cutting, reinstating, until he arrived at a structure in thirteen books. As studies of the manuscripts have revealed, he was ready to try out radical alterations to the organization of his material, but eventually he was satisfied—for a time at least. The poem that resulted from Wordsworth's most arduous labour of composition is both coherent in its overall scheme and wonderfully dense in local detail. It is the detail that causes problems.

The first is that on occasions *The Prelude*, both 1799 and 1805 versions, is our main, if not only, source for evidence that certain events took place. Did Wordsworth really steal a boat on Ullswater and sense the mountain terrifyingly pursue him? Did he get lost on Penrith Beacon while still an infant? Did he really meet a Discharged Soldier? The questions seem ludicrous. These are some of the best-known incidents in Wordsworth's young life and are embodied in poetry of such power that they are certainly amongst the most memorable. None the less the following cautions have to be registered: that the only evidence we have is poetic evidence; that Wordsworth did not scruple elsewhere to tamper with 'the facts' if they spoiled an imaginative conception; that he was steeped in traditions of literary, dramatic, and iconographic representation.

One example can serve to focus this aspect of the problem. In Book IV of the *1805 Prelude* Wordsworth recalls his 'dedication walk'. He is coming home after a night of dancing:

>                    Magnificent
> The morning was, a memorable pomp,
> More glorious than I ever had beheld.
> The Sea was laughing at a distance; all
> The solid Mountains were as bright as clouds,

Grain-tinctured, drenched in empyrean light;
And in the meadows and the lower grounds
Was all the sweetness of a common dawn,
Dews, vapours, and the melody of birds,
And Labourers going forth into the fields.
. . . I made no vows, but vows
Were then made for me: bond unknown to me
Was given, that I should be—else sinning greatly—
A dedicated spirit. On I walked
In blessedness, which even yet remains.

We might ask why no room was found in the *1799 Prelude* for such a momentous experience, but the more obvious question is when and where did this walk take place? Book IV covers Wordsworth's long vacation in 1788 and T. W. Thompson, the historian of his Hawkshead days, accepts that date and tries to prove that Wordsworth was walking back to Colthouse over Claife Heights, having been a guest at Belle Grange. Robert Woof, however, cautions against such certainty, pointing out that the poet may have been conflating a Hawkshead experience with one four years earlier, on the evidence of his recollection that his first voluntary verses 'were written after walking six miles to attend a dance at Egremont'. Noticing the sea 'laughing at a distance' more easily fits an Egremont memory than one of walking over Claife Heights. The truth is that, as Woof says, the 'historical facts about the "dedication walk" are still elusive'.[7]

In this example our grasp on the facts is uncertain, but the uncertainty need provoke no scepticism about the claim Wordsworth makes that it was on such a dawn, wherever he may have been, that he felt an access of blessedness. In the case of a much more important moment in the *1805 Prelude*, however, this relation between the facts and Wordsworth's gloss on them is reversed. At the climax of the poem stands the account of the climbing of Snowdon. The passage opens, 'In one of these excursions', which would seem to date the ascent in 1793, given that the immediately preceding event to which 'these' seems to refer is firmly datable in that year. There is hard evidence that Wordsworth climbed Snowdon in 1791 and so we can ignore the chronological implications of the opening line. After Wordsworth has described the ascent and his visionary experiences in the mist, he continues:

A meditation rose in me that night
Upon the lonely mountain, when the scene
Had passed away, and it appeared to me
The perfect image of a mighty mind
Of one that feeds upon infinity, . . .

and as Jonathan Wordsworth crisply put it, 'there can be no doubt at all that the statement is untrue'.[8] The meditation on the Creative Imagination focuses ideas that Wordsworth had been exploring in poetry and prose since 1798, but there is no evidence from letters or poems that in 1791 he was thinking about the topic or that had he done so he would have formulated his ideas in these terms. This is the language of Wordsworth's maturity, expressing ideas which have taken shape during his actual poetic practice. To graft them on to an account of an incident in 1791 is to falsify the facts in the service of the poem's grand strategy of demonstrating how all of Wordsworth's experiences served to make him a poet.

Working with the facts and Wordsworth's interpretative glosses would be easier were they to remain static. But they do not. Some experiences are described in each of the versions of *The Prelude* but are changed with each rewriting. Changes of factual detail are rarely very important or troubling. The *1805 Prelude* account of the stolen boat episode adds to the 1799 version the information that the lake was Ullswater and that Wordsworth had gone there during his school holidays. The reader who knows the geography of the Lake District may puzzle over what he was doing in Patterdale when, according to an unused line written for the *1799 Prelude*, he was on his way to the family home at Cockermouth, and may conclude that eventually Wordsworth could not remember himself, since he cut out any detail that might locate the scene when he revised the passage for the final version of the poem. But whether the lake was Ullswater or not is of absolutely no importance to understanding what happens in the description of the child's exploit and in all versions the gloss placed upon the experience remains essentially the same.

With another very important episode, however, the gloss itself, and thus the meaning of the event, is subject to revision. There is no doubt that during his first days at Hawkshead School Wordsworth watched the recovery of a man drowned at Esthwaite. His name is known and the date on which he died. In the *1799 Prelude* the event is placed together with other such 'tragic facts / Of rural history' which, Wordsworth asserts, impressed his mind with images which accrued significance with the passing of time.[9] In the *1805 Prelude* the episode is removed from the narrative dealing with school-days to Book V, where it functions within the context of a lengthy diatribe against modern modes of education. Now Wordsworth declares that, as he watched the corpse rise out of the lake, 'no vulgar fear, / Young as I was, a child not nine years old / Possessed [him]', because he had encountered such sights before 'among the shining streams / Of fairyland, the forests of romance' and thus saw the grisly sight hallowed 'With decoration and ideal grace'.[10] In the *1799 Prelude* the incident, combining with the other 'spots of time', functions as one element in the model

Wordsworth is proposing for understanding the operation of memory in the evolution of the creative mind. In the *1805 Prelude* it is an exemplary illustration in a discussion of the place of Fancy in education. The context as well as the gloss provide such different fields for interpretation that, as has been pointed out by the scholar who has studied all of the details of revision most carefully, it is as if Wordsworth were unsure 'about the incident's dense core of import'.[11] The biographer must conclude that, for all Wordsworth's attempts to tell us, we cannot know what the boy felt on 19 June 1779.

A specific date introduces the second problem with detail in *The Prelude*. Wordsworth is known as the poet of childhood and it is easy to see why. The descriptions of childhood pursuits and childish feelings in *The Prelude* are some of his most powerful poetry, capable of evoking in readers a recollection of their own 'eagerness of infantine desire'. But to see Wordsworth as essentially the poet of childhood—a perception encouraged by Victorian illustrated editions of his work—is to misunderstand him completely. Throughout his greatest period of creativity Wordsworth was interested in the development of the adult mind, the adult moral sense, and sought to demonstrate its evolution in one exemplary specimen—himself. Habitually, in *Tintern Abbey*, in the *Ode: Intimations of Immortality*, in *The Prelude*, he describes a development in which absorption in Nature leads onwards to an awareness of the 'still sad music of humanity'.

In all of these poems there is an implied chronology and in *Tintern Abbey* and *The Prelude* the broad pattern is tied into ascertainable dates. The difficulty is that the dates do not tally. In *Tintern Abbey* Wordsworth describes himself in 1793 as utterly intoxicated by Nature:

> The sounding cataract
> Haunted me like a passion: the tall rock,
> The mountain, and the deep and gloomy wood,
> Their colours and their forms, were then to me
> An appetite: a feeling and a love,
> That had no need of a remoter charm,
> By thought supplied, or any interest
> Unborrowed from the eye.

In *The Prelude*, on the other hand, 1793 is presented as a time when 'thought' was leading Wordsworth to a deeper understanding of the worth of common man and to the hope that he might celebrate in verse 'men as they are men within themselves'.[12] Overall the model of human development proposed in both poems is the same, but it has to be explicated solely in terms of the poetic strategy of each work. Any attempt to make each congruent with the other, or either congruent with the actual datable events of Wordsworth's life, leads only to confusion.

# PART I

Oh mystery of man, from what a depth
Proceed thy honours!

(*1805 Prelude*, XII. 328–9.)

# 1770–1787

WORDSWORTH was not only the first person to attempt his biography but also the first to point out that any interpretative analysis of the growth of his mind was doomed to incompleteness. Just as he is about to make a particularly subtle discrimination between one stage and the next in his response to natural beauty he exclaims in the *1799 Prelude*:

> But who shall parcel out
> His intellect by geometric rules,
> Split like a province into round and square?
> Who knows the individual hour in which
> His habits were first sown even as a seed?
> Who that shall point as with a wand, and say
> 'This portion of the river of my mind
> Came from yon fountain'?[1]

That Wordsworth knew no certainty could be achieved did not stop him searching, and the *1799 Prelude* began the most sustained self-examination in English poetry. The river, Wordsworth knew, had its origin somewhere.

Genealogical unravellings are always a forbidding entrance to any biography. With Wordsworth, however, it is more than usually important to establish the kind of family into which he was born, for his life from birth to the writing of the *1799 Prelude* is a pattern of severances and ruptures counterpointed with periods of continuity and calm, which began in a childhood that seemed to give a solid start to life and to promise a secure future but denied both in his most formative years.

William Wordsworth was born on 7 April 1770, the second child of John and Ann Wordsworth of Cockermouth, a little town on the northern edge of the Lake District. His parents were young, but well connected, and his father held a responsible position that offered much to someone zealous and energetic. Ann (b. 1747) was the daughter of William Cookson, a successful linen draper in Penrith, and of Dorothy, sister and heiress of James Crackanthorpe of Newbiggin Hall. Her husband John, whom she married in 1766, was born in 1741 to Richard Wordsworth of Sockbridge, near Penrith, and Mary, daughter of John Robinson of Appleby. Richard Wordsworth was Clerk of the Peace and Receiver General of Westmorland and his sons followed him into the administration of local affairs, Richard (1733–94) becoming Collector of Customs at Whitehaven and John law-agent to the most powerful man in the district, Sir James Lowther.

The house in which Wordsworth was born is still the most imposing dwelling in the main street of Cockermouth. It is now visited as the birthplace of a great poet, but in 1770 its significance was very different. Built in the middle of the century, it is, with its front nine windows wide, as Pevsner says, 'quite a swagger house for such a town',[2] and that was what it was meant to be, for it symbolized the wealth and dominance of one man who himself and through his family was to influence Wordsworth for the whole of his life.

Visiting Cockermouth in 1779 the young William Wilberforce noted that 'The Borough is absolutely Sir James Lowther's'.[3] It was, and so was much else, including Wordsworth's father. Sir James, fifth Baronet of Lowther, created first Earl of Lonsdale in 1794, was an extraordinarily powerful man, but also, in the judgement of one contemporary, 'truly a Madman, tho' too Rich to be confin'd'.[4] His influence came partly from inherited wealth, in particular the enormous coal and trading interests of the Whitehaven branch of the family, partly through marriage to the daughter of the third Earl of Bute, and it was directed single-mindedly by Sir James towards acquisition of political control of the whole of the North-west. Described by one scholar who has studied his electoral manœuvrings as 'megalomaniac . . . tyrannical, ruthless, without tact, and given over to fits of suspicion, jealousy and indecision',[5] Lowther took on other major landowners in election after election and by 1774 was puppet-master of nine members of the House of Commons.

As his law-agent John Wordsworth became Bailiff and Recorder of Cockermouth, a borough Sir James had gained control of at great expense in 1756, and Coroner of the Seigniory of Millom, a tract of land between the Duddon sands in the south and Whitehaven in the north-west. Living rent free in his fine house, John Wordsworth administered Sir James's affairs, settling bills such as £24,000 expended on election 'expenses' between 1767 and 1769, dealing with grievances, and keeping loyalties in good repair.[6]

That their father was the arm of a man hated as much as he was feared would hardly have troubled the infant children of John and Ann Wordsworth (Richard, b. 1768; Dorothy, b. 1771; John, b. 1772; Christopher, b. 1774), although the connection was later to afflict them all. On the contrary, Wordsworth's earliest memories dwell on the 'giddy bliss' offered to a child by a house whose garden was bordered by the 'alder shades and rocky falls' of the River Derwent, where he

> a four years' child,
> A naked boy, among thy silent pools
> Made one long bathing of a summer's day,
> Basked in the sun, or plunged into thy streams,
> Alternate, all a summer's day, or coursed
> Over the sandy fields, and dashed the flowers
> Of yellow grunsel; or, when crag and hill,
> The woods, and distant Skiddaw's lofty height
> Were bronzed with a deep radiance, stood alone
> A naked savage in the thunder shower.[7]

The bottom of the garden, where the privet hedge sheltered a sparrow's nest, and the more forbidding playground of the ruins of Cockermouth Castle, with its dungeons beneath flower-topped walls, remained magical terrains in the memory of the poet as late as his seventy-third year.[8]

It is significant, however, that in the opening of *The Prelude*'s account of boyish pleasures Wordsworth moves from the passage quoted straight to school-days at Hawkshead, thus eliding some five years of his childhood which were unsettled and far from uniformly happy. It may be that fostering his career at a critical stage took John Wordsworth away from home a great deal or that his wife found the demands of her family overwhelming, but for whatever reason William and Dorothy were packed off to the Cookson grandparents at Penrith for periods of time that from a child's perspective must have seemed endless. There is evidence that Wordsworth was staying in Penrith when only 3 years old and that long visits took place from 1775 to 1776 and over the winter of 1776/7.[9]

Staying with relatives need not be an ordeal, even for a home-loving, sensitive child. Remembering his first visit to Uncle Richard brought to the aged poet's mind a vision of beauty: 'I remember being struck for the first time by the town and port of Whitehaven, and the white waves breaking against its quays and piers, as the whole came into view.'[10] His memories of the Penrith household, however, which bulk inordinately large in the sparse autobiographical notes Wordsworth dictated to his nephew in 1847, are in a different register:

I was of a stiff, moody and violent temper; so much so that I remember going once into the attics of my grandfather's house at Penrith, upon some indignity having been put upon me, with an intention of destroying myself with one of the foils which I knew was kept there. I took the foil in hand, but my heart failed. Upon another occasion, while I was at my grandfather's house in Penrith, along with my eldest brother, Richard, we were whipping tops together in the large drawing-room, on which the carpet was only laid down upon particular occasions. The walls were hung round with family pictures, and I said to my brother, 'Dare you strike your whip through that old lady's petticoat?' He replied, 'No, I won't'. 'Then,' said I, 'here goes;' and I struck my lash through her hooped petticoat, for which no doubt, though I have forgotten it, I was properly punished. But possibly, from some want of judgment in punishments inflicted, I had become perverse and obstinate in defying chastisement, and rather proud of it than otherwise.[11]

Many years later William and Dorothy were to bring up another little boy separated from his parent and then, Dorothy explained, their 'grand study' was 'to make him happy'.[12] Little Basil Montagu was clearly not to suffer as they had—suffering the poet still protested against at the end of his life.

One other memory of Penrith remained vivid to Wordsworth and he ensured it should remain so by 'enshrining' it at a key moment in all versions of *The Prelude*.[13] What the poetry records is the transformation of an ordinary mischance into an epiphany. Out riding towards Penrith Beacon, 'While I was yet an urchin, one who scarce / Could hold a bridle', Wordsworth became separated from the servant James, his 'encourager and guide'. Frightened, the boy dismounted and stumbled down into Cowraik Quarry, only to realize that he was on the spot where, as he believed, a wife-murderer had hung in chains. He struggled up again and noticed a pool, the Beacon, and a girl with a pitcher on her head, making her way against the wind. For the child these must have been minutes of rising panic, but what Wordsworth over twenty years later remembered most clearly of all, or, to be more cautious, what struck him as his memory yielded up the scene, was how all of the elements seemed harmonized into one composition:

> It was in truth
> An ordinary sight but I should need
> Colours and words that are unknown to man
> To paint the visionary dreariness
> Which, while I looked all round for my lost guide,
> Did at that time invest the naked pool,
> The beacon on the lonely eminence,
> The woman and her garments vexed and tossed
> By the strong wind.[14]

Shuttled between Cockermouth and Penrith Wordsworth received little formal education. In Penrith he attended Ann Birkett's school, where his future wife Mary Hutchinson was also an infant pupil, and in Cockermouth received instruction at the Reverend Mr Gilbanks's grammar school. In neither academy can the quality of education have been high. At Hawkshead School one of the ushers taught Wordsworth 'more of Latin in a fortnight than I had learnt during two preceding years at the school of Cockermouth', he was later to recall, but his memories of dame-school were more positive, to judge from a later comment in which Wordsworth possibly looks back through a favourite poem, Shenstone's *The School Mistress*, to his own teacher: 'The old dame did not affect to make theologians or logicians; but she taught to read; and she practised the memory, often, no doubt, by rote; but still the faculty was improved'.[15]

Knowledge of vital kinds, however, was being absorbed. According to his first biographer, his nephew Christopher, 'the poet's father set him very early to learn portions of the works of the best English poets by heart, so that at an early age he could repeat large portions of Shakespeare, Milton and Spenser'.[16] It was a faculty he was to keep in repair for the whole of his life. There is abundant evidence that the poet who was later to exclaim, 'Oh wondrous power of words, how sweet they are', and to exploit that power so prodigally, never forgot poetry, however slight, which had moved him.* Nor was he ever to forget or underestimate the other kind of knowledge gained at this time, the awareness that the external world takes on meaning when mediated through human love. In the poem *The Sparrow's Nest*, which has already been alluded to, Wordsworth describes approaching the nest with the timorous Dorothy and then celebrates her in this lovely tribute:

> The Blessing of my later years
> Was with me when a boy:
> She gave me eyes, she gave me ears;
> And humble cares, and delicate fears;
> A heart, the fountain of sweet tears;
> And love, and thought, and joy.

We do not need to attribute to the child Wordsworth an unnatural consciousness. This is clearly the adult recalling Dorothy's gifts to him over many years. But nor need we doubt that in locating Dorothy's blessings so far back Wordsworth was essentially right or that their mutual affection was the one absolute good he remembered from his Cockermouth years.

---

* *1805 Prelude*, VII. 121. The importance of memory to all aspects of W's creativity is such that it is worth emphasizing how amazing was his recall of verse in one particularly striking example. In 1787 or 1788 one of W's school-friends, Charles Farish, introduced him to exercises in versification in the manner of Spenser and Shakespeare composed by his brother John Bernard. At least 10 years later W incorporated a line from Farish's *The Heath* in his own description of a heath with a gibbet mast for *Adventures on Salisbury Plain*. Some 46 years later, when preparing the poem for publication as *Guilt and Sorrow*, he altered the stanza in which the line appears, remembered its source, and acknowledged it in a note. W had first read the not very distinguished verses about 56 years earlier. See *Salisbury Plain Poems*, 126 and 231.

It was an affection that was tested very early on. In 1778 Ann Wordsworth contracted pneumonia, as a consequence, Wordsworth believed, 'of being put, at a friend's house in London, in what used to be called a "best bedroom" ', and died around 8 March. The children were at Penrith and Wordsworth later recalled that his last glimpse of his mother was as 'she was reclining in her easy chair' in her parents' house.[17] The effect of her death upon the family was immediate and destructive. In *The Prelude* Wordsworth said of his mother that 'she left us destitute, and as we might / Trooping together',[18] an astonishing comment which testifies to how keenly he still felt in adulthood that his mother's death was a vicious blow. But 'Trooping together' is not quite right. At such a crisis another family might have drawn closer together. This one split apart.

On 13 June Dorothy left Penrith in the company of Elizabeth Threlkeld, her mother's cousin, and Elizabeth's brother William, destined to spend the rest of her childhood in their home at Halifax. She did not see her brother William again for nine years. That their love for one another was extraordinarily strong in adult life is a fact that will demand consideration later. What needs to be emphasized here is that for Dorothy the death of her mother and separation from her brothers were fused into one unforgettably painful severance. Years later she wrote to Lady Beaumont: 'Oh! my dear friend, you measure my heart truly when you judge that I have at all times a deep sympathy with those who know what fraternal affection is. It has been the building up of my being, the light of my path. Our Mother, blessed be her Memory! was taken from us when I was only six years old.'[19] The association of her thoughts, from brother's love to mother's death, reveals how closely loss of both remained in Dorothy's mind as inseparable.

A little under a year after Dorothy's departure William too entered a new world. On about 15 May 1779 he and Richard left Penrith and, once the entrance fee had been paid, joined the grammar school at Hawkshead.

## (2)

'Beloved Hawkshead'—so Wordsworth remembered in 1799 the place which retained a permanent hold on his affections. Wishfully appropriating it he calls it his 'native vale', later 'my darling vale', and lovingly dwells on the intense delight he felt on returning from Cambridge to what had been for eight years his real home. It is not difficult to see why the place kindled 'unfading recollections',[20] for memories of Hawkshead and the vale of Esthwaite intertwined all that mattered most to him: natural beauty, people, pleasure in simple things, and the stirring of the imagination to embody them in poetic forms.

Hawkshead is in Furness at the northernmost reach of Lancashire into the Lake District. To the east is Windermere and to the south-west

Coniston. Now it is ringed by car parks and a bypass, but in Wordsworth's time it was little visited, as there were no proper roads and the grandeurs of the Lake District are elsewhere. The opening up of the Lakes had already begun, but those who wanted to experience the sublime or thrill to the echoes of cannon fired across water beneath overhanging mountains sought out Borrowdale and Langdale, Ullswater and Windermere.* It is true that the most celebrated viewing station on Windermere, marked out in West's enormously influential *Guide to the Lakes* (1778) as offering a 'magnificent scene', was situated just to the south-east of Hawkshead on the heights above the ferry on the lake, but tourists with West in hand will not have been encouraged to explore the area by his account of Hawkshead's own lake, Esthwaite, which is perfunctory.[21]

The small village was a working community. Its prosperity had rested on wool, but even when Kendal took over as the major centre for the trade there was still activity in the many industries whose remains—ruins, or converted buildings, or just place-names on the map—remind us that the Lake District was once alive with a greater variety of occupations than it is today. The ironworks to the south demanded charcoal from the abundant woodlands and the services of freight carriers on Windermere. There were mines and quarries on the Tilberthwaite and Coniston Fells.[22] Farmers required joiners, blacksmiths, saddlers, and factors in goods and livestock. Nor was Hawkshead really cut off. The ferry on Windermere, easily reached through Near and Far Sawrey to the east of Esthwaite, gave access to the road to the north and to the growing town of Kendal to the south.

Hawkshead's prosperity in Wordsworth's time was indicated by a fine church which, freshly roughcast and whitewashed in 1785, seemed to sit 'like a throned lady, sending out / A gracious look all over its domain', by the handsome vicarage, and above all by the renown of its grammar school.[23] Founded in 1585 by Edwin Sandys, Archbishop of York, the school stands just below the church and Wordsworth remembered them as often linked by village activity when he wrote in a draft for his own Lake District guide:

---

* William Hutchinson describes this tourist's delight on Ullswater in his *An Excursion to the Lakes: In Westmoreland and Cumberland, August 1773* (London, 1774), 68–70: 'The vessel was provided with six brass cannon, mounted on swivels;—on the discharge of one of these pieces, the report was echoed from the opposite rocks, where by reverberation it seemed to roll from cliff to cliff, and return through every cave and valley; till the decreasing tumult died away upon the ear . . . At intervals we were relieved from this entertainment, which consisted of a kind of wondrous tumult and grandeur of confusion, by the music of two French horns, whose harmony was repeated from every recess which echo haunted on the borders of the Lake . . . As we finished our repast, from a general discharge of the guns we were roused to new astonishment; for altho' we had heard with great surprise the former echoes, this exceeded them so much that it seemed incredible: for on every hand the sounds were reverberated and returned from side to side, so as to give us the semblance of that confusion and horrid uproar, which the falling of these stupendous rocks would occasion, if by some internal combustion they were rent to pieces, and hurled into the Lake'.

Along the eastern end of the Church runs a stone seat, a place of resort for the old
people of the Town . . . a few years back they were amused by the gambols &
exercises of more than 100 Schoolboys some playing soberly on the hill top near
them while others were intent upon more boisterous diversions in the fields
beneath.[24]

The number of pupils seems surprisingly large if one tries to imagine
lessons in the small two-storey building, but it is a testimony to the
reputation of an institution that attracted pupils from a wide area and sent
many of them on to Cambridge better prepared than most of their peers.
Some of the boys lodged in the headmaster's house, but many were boarded
out with local families, and it was Wordsworth's good fortune to be placed
with someone who gave him not a lodging but a real home.

*The Prelude* is rich in tributes of love but none is more touching than this
to Wordsworth's 'old dame':

> The thoughts of gratitude shall fall like dew
> Upon thy grave, good creature: while my heart
> Can beat I never will forget thy name.
> Heaven's blessing be upon thee where thou liest
> After thy innocent and busy stir
> In narrow cares, thy little daily growth
> Of calm enjoyments, after eighty years,
> And more than eighty, of untroubled life—
> Childless, yet by the strangers to thy blood
> Honoured with little less than filial love.[25]

The woman who attracted this affection was Ann Tyson, who, after being
in domestic service with the Knotts of Rydal, married Hugh Tyson in 1749.
Her husband was a master joiner, supplying furniture, windows and
shutters, wheels, and other farm equipment, but his business seems to have
declined from the 1750s and Ann began herself to supplement their income.
In a small way she dealt in grocery—tea, sugar, spices, and dried fruit—and
in drapery, including shirts and gowns which she made to order. From 1779
she also took in boarders from the school, usually three or four, although her
accounts show that in the autumn half of 1786 she was being mother to no
fewer than eight boys.[26] Living at first in Hawkshead itself, where
Wordsworth joined them at Whitsuntide in 1779, Hugh and Ann Tyson
moved in 1783 to Colthouse, a tiny hamlet about half a mile east of the
village proper, and here Wordsworth lived during school terms until he left
for Cambridge in 1787.[27]

For Wordsworth Ann Tyson's cottage was clearly home. With Richard,
and eventually his brothers Christopher and John and their cousin Richard,
he found a secure centre to his life, watched over by a woman he always

regarded with a tenderness which is caught so beautifully in his loving recollection of her nodding over her Bible in front of the fire.[28] But Wordsworth's memories of these eight years give a sense that he regarded the whole region as home, as a little Paradise, enclosed to the west by Coniston and the mountains, to the east by Windermere, and to the south by the sea. This sense of Hawkshead as Wordsworth's 'happy valley', of course, serves the overall purpose of the opening books of *The Prelude*, which is to demonstrate that 'old Grandame Earth', with the 'playthings which her love designed for him', fostered the young child with a loving discipline particularly fitted for the nourishment of a poetic mind, and must be recognized for the selective and didactic account it is. The magnificent poetry of childhood recollection, however, cannot be disregarded, for it is the indispensable record, and the only one we have, of what Wordsworth meant when he referred in *Tintern Abbey* to the 'coarser pleasures of my boyish days / And their glad animal movements'.

School hours were long, but Wordsworth's recollections in *The Prelude* filter out restrictions to convey the common adult sense that as a child he had all the time in the world.[29] They demonstrate, too, that all of the variety of the district was exploited in the search for pleasure. 'The woods of autumn, and their hidden bowers / With milk-white clusters hung' tempted the boys, clad in old clothes hoarded by Ann Tyson for just this purpose, to penetrate the woods. As the elderly Wordsworth fondly remembered: 'Like most of my school-fellows I was an impassioned Nutter. For this pleasure the Vale of Esthwaite, abounding in coppice wood, furnished a very wide range.'[30] On the lower slopes of the hills woodcocks could be snared, while on the higher crags ravens' nests challenged the boys to find the courage to reach and destroy the eggs of this vermin. Wordsworth's evocation captures the delight in physical exertion:

> Oh, when I have hung
> Above the raven's nest, by knots of grass
> Or half-inch fissures in the slipp'ry rock
> But ill sustained, and almost, as it seemed,
> Suspended by the blast which blew amain,
> Shouldering the naked crag, oh, at that time,
> While on the perilous ridge I hung alone,
> With what strange utterance did the loud dry wind
> Blow through my ears; the sky seemed not a sky
> Of earth, and with what motion moved the clouds![31]

The 'perilous ridge', however, hardly conveys the real danger of this activity, which wrecked the one nesting expedition for which independent witness survives. Early in 1783 Wordsworth joined John Benson, William and Fletcher Raincock, Edward Birkett, Tom Usher, and Will Tyson on an expedition to Yewdale Crags. As he neared the nest John Benson became 'crag fast', stuck, with his nerve gone. A local waller—a builder of drystone walls—and his son eventually hauled the terrified lad to safety, but all of the group must have shuddered at how close their friend had come to joining others commemorated in the oral tradition of the neighbourhood, 'the tragedies of former time, / Or hazards and escapes'.[32]

That many such hazards did not have so fortunate an outcome had been impressed on Wordsworth as soon as he arrived in Hawkshead. As if anticipating the accusation that he showed a Panglossian disregard for Nature's darker side he remarks in the 1799 *Prelude*:

> I might advert
> To numerous accidents in flood or field,
> Quarry or moor, or 'mid the winter snows,
> Distresses and disasters, tragic facts
> Of rural history[33]

but the one he singles out is not an industrial or farming accident but the unexplained drowning of James Jackson, schoolmaster at nearby Sawrey, seemingly while bathing in Esthwaite on 18 June 1779. How Wordsworth later interpreted the significance of the episode—its place in the development of his mind—is open to question, but there is no reason to doubt that he is remembering the facts when he describes finding the pile of clothes by the shore and watching the next day when

> There came a company, and in their boat
> Sounded with iron hooks and with long poles.
> At length the dead man, 'mid that beauteous scene
> Of trees and hills and water, bolt upright
> Rose with his ghastly face.[34]

The hills also offered another pleasure not unmixed with danger. In *The Prelude* one beautiful line—'on rainy days / When I have angled up the lonely brooks'[35]—captures the young boy exercising the skill he had learnt on the banks of the Derwent. But the 'small streams in the neighbourhood of Hawkshead' did not satisfy, he later recalled:

and I fell into the common delusion, that the further from home the better sport would be had. Accordingly one day I attached myself to a person living in the neighbourhood of Hawkshead, who was going to try his fortune, as an angler, near the source of the Duddon. We fished a great part of the day with very sorry success, the rain pouring torrents; and long before we got home, I was worn out with fatigue;

and if the good man had not carried me on his back, I must have lain down under the best shelter I could find.[36]

It is noticeable that in his accounts in *The Prelude* of birds-nesting, snaring, and angling, Wordsworth makes himself a solitary adventurer, whereas in all of the descriptions of lake sports he celebrates pleasures taken in the company of his friends. Rowing on Windermere led them on exploration of the little islands or across the lake to the White Lion at Bowness on the eastern shore. Such outings, Wordsworth suggests, were the regular 'pastime of our afternoons' in summer, but one in particular remained in his memory on account of its tranquil and beautiful close:

> But ere the fall
> Of night, when in our pinnace we returned
> Over the dusky lake, and to the beach
> Of some small island steered our course, with one
> The minstrel of our troop, and left him there,
> And rowed off gently, while he blew his flute
> Alone upon the rock, oh, then the calm
> And dead still water lay upon my mind
> Even with a weight of pleasure, and the sky,
> Never before so beautiful, sank down
> Into my heart and held me like a dream.[37]

On Coniston, too, the boys made their own pleasures, rowing beneath a line of ancient trees which cast, 'With its long boughs above the water stretched, / A gloom through which a boat might sail along / As in a cloister',[38] or broiling fish on the shore with utensils borrowed from Coniston Hall. And in winter the smaller lake nearby, Esthwaite, could be the source of pleasure Wordsworth long enjoyed. In 1830 Dorothy Wordsworth proudly reported of her brother: 'He is still the crack skater on Rydal Lake'.[39] As he executed his curves the 60-year-old no doubt remembered the 'games confederate', when he and his friends 'all shod with steel', paying no heed to the darkness and the cold, 'hissed along the polished ice', and made the mountains ring with their shouts and laughter.[40]

Exploring from Hawkshead, Wordsworth found in Coniston and Windermere, Yewdale, Tilberthwaite, and the area now known as Tarn Hows a richly varied domain, on whose northerly flank, from the top of Loughrigg Fell, it seems likely that he now first caught a glimpse of the place in which he was to make his own first real 'abiding place', Grasmere.[41] Just occasionally wanderlust carried him beyond it, to the romantic ruin of Furness Abbey and to the sea,[42] but such expeditions cost money for horse-hire and were, as the deliberately heightened language of knight-errantry in *The Prelude* suggests, rare adventures. For the most part the vale of Esthwaite and its environs sufficed for the boy who was later to declare that, whereas books were the 'passion' of his friend Southey, his 'passion' was wandering.[43] Recollection of nocturnal rambles—'"twas my joy / To wander half the night among the cliffs / And the smooth hollows'—is balanced by memories of walks around Esthwaite 'before the hours of school' and of even earlier excursions, as he slipped out to sit 'Alone upon some jutting eminence / At the first hour of morning, when the vale / Lay quiet in an utter solitude'.[44]

Wordsworth's account in *The Prelude* leaves out much that one would like to know more about. T. W. Thompson has recovered an anecdote about the schoolboys lining up along a lane to taunt in silent insolence one William Rigge, a Quaker slate-merchant they disliked, as he passed on horseback: 'Thinking he would end this, he one day stopped and greeted them, but instead of replying verbally they sprang to attention and saluted him. That was more than he could bear . . .'[45] Wordsworth, we are assured, took no part in the incident, but there must have been many such pranks in which he did. *The Prelude* says nothing about the awakening of sexual awareness, although the number of bastard children in the area mentioned by Thompson suggests what must have been one stimulus to adolescent curiosity. Nor does the poem give any sense of the variety of the people Wordsworth encountered in this small community. Fortunately other evidence does, for Wordsworth drew upon local characters for other poems, or mentioned them in his notes, and this material, fleshed out by Thompson's detective scholarship, can give us some idea of the people whose idiosyncrasies were lodged in Wordsworth's mind during these formative years.

Writing to a young admirer of his poems in 1802 Wordsworth declared that 'People in our rank of life are perpetually falling into one sad mistake, namely, that of supposing that human nature and the persons they associate with are one and the same thing'.[46] That Wordsworth was at least aware how sad this mistake was must be attributed to the richness and variety of what would have seemed to many a crampingly small world. Most of its inhabitants, of course, were ordinary people—shepherds and farm labourers, blacksmiths, saddlers, cobblers and carpenters, the quarrymen and the more mysterious charcoal-burners, shopkeepers and merchants, innkeepers and the Windermere ferryman—and it was these people, each having an important function in a working community, who always seemed to Wordsworth to possess a stability and worth against which the sophisticated world could be tested. Later experiences in France and life in Grasmere only confirmed the set of mind unconsciously established now which was to determine *Lyrical Ballads* and the 1800 Preface, to shape *The Prelude* and *The Excursion*, to find expression at the very end of his life in the poem 'I know an aged man', and then to influence another generation through the George Eliot of *Adam Bede* and *Silas Marner* and other novelists who are Wordsworth's true heirs in the Victorian period.[47]

Hawkshead figures, however, also gave glimpses of the vagaries of human nature or of other worlds beyond the vale of Esthwaite. From the village itself Wordsworth remembered 'a youngster about my own age, an Irish boy, who was a servant to an itinerant conjuror', whom he led to his favourite spot, the station above the ferry-house peninsula on Windermere, 'to witness the pleasure I expected the boy would receive from the prospect of the islands below, and the intermingling water. I was not disappointed.'[48] His poem *The Two Thieves*, which records the innocent depredations of the senile shoemaker Daniel Mackreth and his grandson Dan, was, he says, 'described from the life, as I was in the habit of observing when a boy at Hawkshead School . . . No book could have so early taught me to think of the changes to which human life is subject . . .'[49] The elegiac 'Matthew' poems compose from 'a solid foundation in fact and reality' the image of a loving and much-loved man, who embodies in his sadness, masked by wit and gaiety, much that Wordsworth remembered, Thompson suggests, of John Harrison, village schoolmaster, Thomas Cowperthwaite, ironmonger, and John Gibson, attorney.[50]

One group of characters influenced Wordsworth more profoundly. In 1797–8 he developed a recent poem *The Ruined Cottage* into a complex narrative in which the bare story of Margaret is told by a Pedlar who interprets its significance for the poet. In subsequent revision it was this figure who engrossed Wordsworth. As he establishes his character, filling in details about his early life and education and the growth of his imaginative powers, it is clear that once again the poet is assessing his own development, a supposition confirmed by the appearance in *The Prelude* of lines written to describe the Pedlar. None of the early versions of the poem was published, but in *The Excursion* (1814) it is the Pedlar, now called the Wanderer, who opens the poem with Margaret's story and determines the rest of its movement.

In the imagined figure of the Pedlar Wordsworth tried over many years to explore ways of expressing what he had learnt about life and it is obvious that we must not attempt an over-literal identification of the figure whose name even changes through versions of the poem. None the less, in 1843 Wordsworth acknowledged that 'much of what he says and does had an external existence, that fell under my own youthful and subsequent observation'. In particular he refers to a Hawkshead packman 'with whom I had frequent conversations upon what had befallen him, and what he had observed during his wandering life', a Scot called James Patrick.[51]

If this man, who had seen much 'of men / Their manners, their enjoyments and pursuits / Their passions and their feelings',[52] extended the boy's knowledge and imagination with tales of other people and places, so did Ann Tyson. During her years in domestic service she had moved with the family of George Knott to an iron foundry at Bonaw in Argyllshire. It was, says Dorothy Wordsworth in her journal of the Scottish tour of 1803, 'a place of which the old woman with whom William lodged ten years at Hawkshead used to tell tales half as long as an ancient romance'.[53] It is probable that Wordsworth's lifelong fascination with the Border Country and Lowland Scotland, and in particular with the culture and the places recorded in the ballads, starts here. But on winter evenings, gathered 'by the warm peat fire', Ann Tyson's young charges would also have heard stories about their own locality—about a Whig and a Jacobite who sought to hide from the ruin of their fortunes in the obscurity of Hawkshead, about two men called Weston thought to be highwaymen,[54] about a shepherd whose son first brought joy but subsequently misery to his old age, about a local girl called Mary Rigge, who died broken-hearted at age 21, leaving her son, sadly named Benoni, 'the child of sorrow', as testimony to her seduction—and in the mind of at least one of the attentive boys these human-centred stories lodged 'Until maturer seasons called them forth'.[55]

Many years later Wordsworth tried to define truly poetic and creative minds. One of their characteristics, he said, was watchfulness: 'they build up greatest things / From least suggestions',[56] and this was certainly one of his own virtues. He was a poet who kept his eyes open and one who wanted to hear what people had to tell. He was, in Robert Woof's fine phrase, 'a poet who listened'.[57] At Ann Tyson's fireside Wordsworth listened, and what he learned at that impressionable age was that common life furnished endless materials for the imagination and, perhaps more important, that narrative was a means of transmitting the past live into the present, a focus for binding and preserving.[58] In due course, Wordsworth was to respond profoundly to Burke's vision of the organic union of past and present and his declaration in one of the most magnificent passages of the *Reflections on the Revolution in France* that 'People will not look forward to posterity, who never look backward to their ancestors'.[59] In predisposing Wordsworth to assent to this assertion Ann Tyson must claim an earlier place than Burke in the history of the 'Growth of a Poet's Mind', for in her Wordsworth found an interpreter and the human centre to a world which was always to remain an ideal, powerfully shaping his conceptions of the possibilities of human community.[60]

(3)

To place Hawkshead and boyish pursuits first in an account of Words-worth's school-days is to succumb to the sequence the poet himself provided in *The Prelude*. It is difficult to resist. In a flow of memories ordered in verse of a quality he was never again to sustain at such length, Wordsworth irresistibly conveys the vigorous delight of childhood and 'the eagerness of infantine desire'. And the emphasis is just. Arming ourselves with scepticism against the palpable design of his autobiographical account, we still have no reason to doubt that Wordsworth did intensely enjoy his education in the eye of Nature or that he was right to see his childhood pleasures as determining both his own make-up and his lifelong convictions about education.[61] But although a superficial reading of *The Prelude* could suggest that Wordsworth thought Nature alone had made him a poet, he knew it was not so. The poet of the *1799 Prelude* might linger on the image of himself as a naked savage, but he wrote as he did then because of study, instruction, example, and in finding these at the right time and in the right place Wordsworth was as fortunate as possibly any other English poet has been. To put it more directly, Hawkshead Grammar School was not just situated in a place that offered everything for the energies of a growing boy, it was a very good school.

During his time there Hawkshead School, staffed by four or possibly five teachers including the headmaster, was presided over by James Peake to the end of the first half of 1781, Edward Christian to July 1782, William Taylor till his death in June 1786, and Thomas Bowman, who had already been 'usher' or assistant master at the school for $2\frac{1}{2}$ years and was still in office when Wordsworth left for Cambridge in 1787.[62] There is no reason to believe that Wordsworth was any more responsive than most little boys to the teaching he received when very young, but Taylor and Bowman, who were able men, overlapped with Wordsworth's adolescence and were clearly formative influences on him.

As a 'grammar' school Hawkshead gave a good grounding in the Classics. Here, however, unlike in many other schools, a good grounding did not mean wearisome rote learning and exercises in verse composition in Latin and Greek. Wordsworth was taught in a humane way, to judge from this recollection: 'Before I read Virgil I was so strongly attached to Ovid, whose *Metamorphoses* I read at school, that I was quite in a passion whenever I found him, in books of criticism, placed below Virgil. As to Homer I was never weary of travelling over the scenes through which he led me. Classical literature affected me by its own beauty.'[63] Wordsworth continued to educate himself in the Classics after school, but that he was able to delight in the poetry as something more than an academic chore, to feel in the 1790s the contemporaneity of Juvenal, and to profit from the ideas of Cicero and Seneca must be attributed to early teaching of rare quality.[64]

Comparable in importance—at least potentially so for a future Cambridge undergraduate—was the teaching of mathematics and science or

Natural Philosophy. As the key to success in Cambridge was mastery of both, Hawkshead's close connection with the University ensured that emphasis in teaching of the abler boys was determined by what the University wanted. Here again instruction by men who had first-hand acquaintance with Newton's *Principia* and *Opticks* and with Euclidean mathematics seems to have carried Wordsworth over the threshold of uncomprehending competence which is often the limit of a more literary sensibility, into an imaginative response both to the beauty revealed by Newtonian physics and to the permanence of geometry's 'independent world / Created out of pure intelligence'.[65] That this was unusual is suggested by the survival through Bowman's son of the story that his father, the headmaster, left Wordsworth 'in his study once for what he thought would only be a minute or two, telling him to be looking for another book in place of the one he had brought back. As it happens he was kept half an hour or more by one of the school tenants. When he got back, there was Wordsworth poring over a book, so absorbed in it he did not notice my father's return. And "what do you think it was" my father would say, or "you'll never guess what it was". It was Newton's "Optics". And that was the book Wordsworth was for borrowing next.'[66]

English grammar and composition were taught, of course, but Wordsworth's wry remark that 'One of my Schoolmasters, whom I most respected and loved, was, unfortunately for me, a passionate admirer of Dr Johnson's prose' suggests that he did not think this an unqualified good. French and the indispensable social art of dancing were also available at extra cost from a Mr Mingay and the Wordsworth boys benefited from both.[67]

The importance of any school, however, lies not so much in the formal curriculum or even in the quality of the teaching as in the encouragement it offers to a pupil's own interests and the possibilities it opens up. For Wordsworth Hawkshead offered two benefits in particular. The first was that it made books available. Wordsworth had grown up in a household that valued books and from what he called his father's 'golden store' he read during his earliest days at school 'all Fielding's works, *Don Quixote*, *Gil Blas*, and any part of Swift that I liked; *Gulliver's Travels*, and the *Tale of the Tub*, being much to my taste'.[68] The school offered more, both from the Boys' Book Club library of modern works to which Richard and William became subscribers in 1781 and from the school library proper, where from amongst the many volumes which reflected the school's ecclesiastical founder Wordsworth picked out books of travel, history, and biography and tasted the addictive power of the written word. 'He was', said Bowman's son, 'one of the very few boys, who used to read the old books in the School Library.'[69]

The second benefit was the activity of two headmasters who valued English literature, especially poetry, unusually highly as a part of a liberal education and attempted to ensure that the vigour of recent work was felt in their remote domain. Of William Taylor, Wordsworth only says that 'He loved the poets',[70] but in the inscription to a copy of Chatterton's *Miscellanies* (1778) presented to Taylor, Edmund Irton more specifically thanks him for his 'luminous and pertinent reflections on the poets of our time, and especially the unhappy boy whose genius is evident in many of the pieces contained in this slender volume'.[71] Taylor's love of literature was shared by his successor Bowman, who, according to his son's reminiscences already quoted, 'believed that he did more for William Wordsworth by lending him books than by his teaching . . . I remember him telling how he lent Wordsworth Cowper's "Task" when it first came out, and Burns' "Poems".'[72] Wordsworth himself acknowledged larger debts, recalling that it was through Bowman that he became acquainted with Langhorne, Beattie, Percy's *Reliques*, Crabbe, Charlotte Smith, and Joseph and Thomas Warton.[73]

Bowman clearly cared passionately about making his pupils aware of contemporary writing, considering it of 'infinite importance' to young people 'to have opportunities of access to a variety of useful Books'. He 'used to get the latest books from Kendal every month' and lent them out, and in 1789 founded a New Library, inviting the boys to subscribe for new purchases and to give on leaving the school 'a present of such Volume or Volumes . . . as he may think proper . . . to be preserved with particular Care as a Memorial of the Donor'.

As a result of the enthusiasm of both men Hawkshead School library was unusually well stocked with contemporary literature.[74] Much has been written about the 'burden of the past' on young poets of the Romantic period, their sense of being oppressed by the weight of past poetic achievement, but despite the evidence of abundant reading there is no trace of this oppression in Wordsworth's early work. Responding to the accent of recent poetry with all the passion of an awakened adolescent, alive to the beauty of language, he found confirmation that the poets of the day were in a continuum with the Classics prescribed for study and a stimulus to emulation. As Wordsworth and his friend John Fleming 'strolled along / By the still borders of the misty lake / Repeating favourite verses with one voice',[75] they had cause to be grateful to masters who valued the literature of their own tongue and who were young enough themselves, perhaps, still to feel some of the enthusiasm they fostered in their pupils. But Wordsworth had more particular cause to be grateful to them, for under their system he was encouraged not just to read but to write.

(4)

In August 1794 a very much changed Wordsworth gazed at the gravestone
of William Taylor and reading over the lines from Gray's *Elegy* inscribed on
it remembered

> the kind hope
> Which he had formed when I at his command
> Began to spin, at first, my toilsome songs.[76]

In composing for *The Prelude* words supposedly said to himself on that
occasion Wordsworth was giving formal shape to what he recollected feeling
as he visited the grave of the teacher who had not lived to see his pupil's
promise fulfilled, and we have once more to be cautious about poetry written
in 1804 on an incident of 1794 in which the poet claims to have thought
about events of a decade earlier still. There is plenty of other evidence,
however, that Wordsworth did consistently locate in 1783-4 the beginnings
of his poetry and the coming into consciousness of his own aesthetic sense,
and for a moment of such importance it ought to be assembled.

In *The Prelude* Wordsworth declares that he was about 13 years old

> when first
> My ears began to open to the charm
> Of words in tuneful order, found them sweet
> For *their own sakes*—a passion and a power—
> And phrases pleased me, chosen for delight,
> For pomp, or love.[77]

In his fourteenth summer he recalls having been so moved by the last
radiance of the setting sun that he extemporized an address to such 'Fair
scenes', although he adds that this was as 'a momentary trance / That far
outran the habit of my mind'.[78] In *The Idiot Boy*, written in 1798, the
narrator speaks of an apprenticeship of fourteen years bound to the Muses
and in old age Wordsworth was just as specific about the time at which he
entered into his 'strong indentures'.[79] In the 1843 note to *An Evening Walk*
he quotes a particular image and observes:

I recollect distinctly the very spot where this first struck me. It was in the way
between Hawkshead and Ambleside, and gave me extreme pleasure. The moment
was important in my poetical history; for I date from it my consciousness of the
infinite variety of natural appearances which had been unnoticed by the poets of any
age or country, so far as I was acquainted with them: and I made a resolution to
supply in some degree the deficiency. I could not have been at that time above 14
years of age.[80]

For once Wordsworth is quite consistent. He was about 14 years old when his adolescent sensibility, constantly stimulated by the natural beauty of his environment and finding expression in language for its own sake, was given direction by William Taylor's demand that his boys should learn to respect the craftsmanship of the poets they read by trying verse composition themselves.

Between the second half of 1784 when Wordsworth tackled Taylor's assignment, verses on 'The Summer Vacation', and 1787, when he left Cambridge, composition clearly became an important part of Wordsworth's life.[81] Verses entered into a very handsome manuscript notebook were no doubt proudly discussed with fellow poet Charles Farish, whose surviving compositions suggest how engaged they were with experiments in versification and poetic structures.[82] The *Gentleman's Magazine*, it seems, did not favour a contribution sent in by Wordsworth and Robert Greenwood, but the *European Magazine* did, and in March 1787 the schoolboy poet had the thrill for the first time of seeing his own words in print.[83] If, as the story goes, an older boy did ask Wordsworth, 'How is it, Bill, thee doest write such good verses? Doest thee invoke Muses?' one hopes that he made a suitably oracular reply.[84]

The two 'public' poems of this period give no indication of what was really promising in Wordsworth's schoolboy writing. His lines on the second centenary of Hawkshead School are a strong imitation of the formal couplets of Pope and Johnson, but imitation is what they are, and the published sonnet *On Seeing Miss Helen Maria Williams Weep at a Tale of Distress* is as empty a confection as any poem could be. At the end of his school-days, however, Wordsworth was in the toils of a long poem called *The Vale of Esthwaite* which is an altogether more interesting prelude to his mature work. Fragmentary though they are, surviving manuscripts show that Wordsworth shared Keats's conviction that a young poet had to try a long poem as 'a test of Invention . . . the Polar Star of Poetry' and that he was struggling with the architectural problems inherent in any long work.[85] The merging of Gothic play of Fancy with quieter rendering of personal experience is not successful, but the scale of the attempt shows ambition and there is much that does succeed. Many lines suggest, too, that the claim that Wordsworth wanted to celebrate 'the infinite variety of natural appearances' was not just an old man's boast. The description of the mist rising above the lake and the vale (3–18), or this image:

> While in the west the robe of day
> Fades, slowly fades, from gold to gray,
> The oak its boughs and foliage twines
> Mark'd to the view in stronger lines,
> Appears with foliage marked to view,

> In lines of stronger browner hue,
> While, every darkening leaf between,
> The sky distinct and clear is seen

or this:

> The ploughboy by his gingling wain
> Whistles along the ringing lane,
> And, as he strikes with sportive lash
> The leaves of thick o'erhanging ash,
> Wavering they fall; while at the sound
> The blinking bats flit round and round[86]

for all their clumsiness do convey an attempt to render vividly and precisely what has really been observed as well as anything in Cowper's *The Task*. Most important of all, in *The Vale of Esthwaite* Wordsworth draws on what are to be the richest sources of all of his poetry: first, the strength of his attachment to a particular place and his yearning for some localized home for his imaginative activity; second, his conviction that his own feelings, his experiences of friendship, loss, or desire, demanded exploration in poetry. There is nothing in *The Vale of Esthwaite* to match *The Prelude*, but that poem, Wordsworth's greatest, and one of the key works of European Romanticism, begins in the unfinished memorial to his schoolboy years.

(5)

Whether the *1799 Prelude* is a record of an exceptional responsiveness or of an ordinary responsiveness exceptionally remembered, it undoubtedly moves readers by the power with which it evokes those childhood moments of sensory apprehension when we are most aware of the reach of our own mind, of our relation to the world beyond ourselves. What Wordsworth was later to hymn as 'High instincts',

> those obstinate questionings
> Of sense and outward things,
> Fallings from us, vanishings;
> Blank misgivings of a Creature
> Moving about in worlds not realized

is embodied dramatically when the boy steals a boat on Ullswater at night and senses the terrifying admonition of the mountain which seems to pursue him across the lake.[87] His sense of the shifting boundaries of self and the outer world is beautifully expressed in memories of solitary dawns when

such a holy calm
Did overspread my soul that I forgot.
The agency of sight, and what I saw
Appeared like something in myself, a dream,
A prospect in my mind.*

The abundant emotions of youth searching for a worthy focus, the sense of awe and reverence for natural beauty, the reaching out for some high purpose—all of these are celebrated in the climax to the *1799 Prelude*, in which Wordsworth describes his rapture in his seventeenth year at feeling 'the sentiment of being spread / O'er all that moves, and all that seemeth still' and his 'bliss' at existing in a world where 'blessings spread around me like a sea'.[88]

Such magnificent poetry offers a testimony to Wordsworth's state of mind which it would be ridiculous to disregard for lack of corroborative evidence. That it is highly partial, however, becomes obvious once we look at the organization of the *1799 Prelude* as an autobiographical record. Wordsworth's memories of childhood focus briefly on infancy before the death of his mother and then almost entirely on his days actually at school. Hawkshead is 'the home / And centre of these joys' and school-friends and Ann Tyson people his world. From the *1799 Prelude* one could think that Wordsworth had no other life than his term-time existence, no other acquaintance than the one enjoyed then. And there can be no doubt that such a shaping of his memories, such a wholesale exclusion, registers feelings of alienation and bitterness which affected him quite as profoundly as the more benign influences he was prepared to acknowledge.

Shortly before Christmas 1783 William, Richard, and Christopher Wordsworth returned home to Cockermouth only to find their father very ill as a result of spending the night in the open after losing his way on the journey back from his duties as Coroner of the Millom area. Although only 42 years old John Wordsworth was not robust enough to rally and he died on 30 December.[89]

What the 13-year-old boy felt at this second bereavement it is impossible to say, but, although father and son can hardly have been close, it was clearly a profound shock. Memories surface in the *Vale of Esthwaite* and inspire

---

* *1799 Prelude*, II. 397–401. Joseph Farington recorded that W told Constable in 1806 'that while He was a Boy going to Hawkeshead School, His mind was often so possessed with images so lost in extraordinary conceptions, that He has held by a wall not knowing but He was part of it'. *Farington*, VIII. 3164. Entry for 12 Dec. 1807. In old age W repeated the statement in the IF note to the *Ode: Intimations of Immortality*: '. . . I was often unable to think of external things as having external existence, and I communed with all that I saw as something not apart from, but inherent, in my own immaterial nature. Many times while going to school have I grasped at a wall or tree to recall myself from this abyss of idealism to the reality.' *Grosart*, III. 194.

some of the finest writing in the *1799 Prelude*. What is striking, however, is that in both poems what Wordsworth recalls is not the actual death of his father but the intensity of his own longing to be home. As he waited for the horses sent to fetch them, 'feverish, tired, and restless', Wordsworth sheltered from a stormy day in the lee of a drystone wall, a sheep on his right hand and a whistling hawthorn on his left, and it was these elements rather than his father's death-bed that remained imprinted on his mind, to be recovered as he remembered 'that dreary time'.[90]

For the adult Wordsworth composing in 1799 his most searching analysis yet of the growth of his own mind and the evolution of his poetic powers, the nature of these memories, and the fact of their survival, take their place in the dominant interpretative schema of *The Prelude* in which all loss is converted into gain. By 1799 the waiting for the horses has become one of those 'spots of time' sanctified by their mysterious power to nourish and repair the mind and the 'wind and sleety rain / And all the business of the elements' are transformed into a 'fountain', a spring ever flowing to refresh the poet who returned to them. But such a schema—and appreciating it is a key to understanding all of Wordsworth's poetry of memory—is extrapolated from the complexities of life by a poet who has become convinced that joy and fear, loss and gain, work together, 'all gratulant if rightly understood'.[91] For the schoolboy, however, the immediate effects of his father's death were felt very differently.

The Wordsworth children, now homeless, passed officially into the care of their uncles, Richard Wordsworth of Whitehaven and Christopher Crackanthorpe Cookson.[92] They became dependants. From now on all of the money for their daily living was administered by their guardians—Ann Tyson's account, bills for horse-hire, for books, for extras such as the French and dancing lessons, for clothing and pocket money, all had to be settled.[93]

They had to be settled, moreover, by guardians who had good reason to be concerned about the future financing of their charges. At John Wordsworth's death the disadvantages of being in the service of Sir James Lowther were revealed. It was not just that, as Dorothy Wordsworth reported, they discovered that 'amongst all those who visited at my father's house he had not one real friend',[94] but also that their father, it became clear, had used more than $4\frac{1}{2}$ thousand pounds of his own money in pursuing Sir James's affairs. The sale of John Wordsworth's assets brought in a small amount,[95] but the bulk of the Wordsworths' inheritance was still to be recovered, and presumably it was expected it would be when, after $2\frac{1}{2}$ years of gathering evidence, the claim on the recently ennobled Lord Lonsdale was delivered to Lowther Hall on 30 August 1786. His lordship declined to acknowledge it, leaving the Wordsworths with no option but to join battle with the man their father had served, the most powerful figure in the North-west of England.

The effect of this noble contumacy on Wordsworth was long lasting. In the future, when the claim was finally settled in 1804 after the death of Sir James, Wordsworth was to become at first the acquaintance and eventually the intimate friend of the next Lord Lonsdale and to serve the family cause as zealously as his father had done, but it was on a footing of social intercourse to which his father could never have aspired. One can only speculate on how conscious Wordsworth was of satisfaction in re-establishing the place of the Wordsworth family in the affairs of the Lonsdales. In the short term, however, the rejection of their claim only intensified the bitterness of children feeling their isolation as orphans and dependants and in Wordsworth the bitterness was sustained in the years to come by a conviction that such tyranny was not an isolated case but a symptom of the essential relationship between governors and the governed in an unjust society. The newly radicalized voice that spoke in 1793 in *A Letter to the Bishop of Llandaff* of 'the baleful influence of aristocracy and nobility upon human happiness and virtue' was drawing on experience.[96]

The worst effect of their father's death, and again it was a lifelong shaping influence on Wordsworth, was that it deprived them of a home. From 1784 onwards Wordsworth had no base. The roof that was unquestionably his, the home that would welcome him with love and security, was in Hawkshead, and that he had to leave at the end of each term for either Whitehaven or Penrith.[97] Wordsworth's sympathy for vagrants, the feeling informing the line 'And homeless near a thousand homes I stood',[98] above all the strength of his later reverence for the values of rootedness, continuity, and sustained love, all originate now.

Wordsworth's guardians behaved responsibly, but it was not likely that Whitehaven or Penrith could ever have become, emotionally, his home. He was clearly a strong-minded youth resenting his enforced dependency, while his Penrith relatives, for their part, seem to have come to resent the obligation laid upon them. For whatever reason animosities grew and flared into the open at the very end of Wordsworth's school-days.

The early summer of 1787 ought to have been a very happy time. So, *The Prelude* suggests, it was. Dorothy had returned from Halifax after nine years away and appeared to her brother 'a gift then first bestowed'. At their separation Dorothy had been only a child, but now she was a young woman of nearly 16 and as they got to know each other again Wordsworth felt 'blest . . . with a joy / Above all joys, that seemed another morn / Risen on mid-noon'.[99] In rambles around Penrith, up on to the Beacon with its commanding view towards Scotland, or along the River Eamont to Brougham Castle, William and Dorothy were joined by Mary Hutchinson, and looking back, after two years of marriage, to that summer seventeen years before Wordsworth remembered it tenderly as 'the blessed time of early love'.[100]

In _The Prelude_'s account of this moment of reunion, however, Wordsworth acknowledges 'a strong / Confusion' as he struggles with a memory which insists on placing alongside Dorothy, and Mary his future wife, the figure of Coleridge, whom none of them had yet met. It is a significant confusion. Thinking back to 1787 Wordsworth wants to draw together all of the people he most deeply loved in defence against different memories of anger and alienation. For the contemporary evidence of Dorothy Wordsworth's account of that vacation gives a very different picture from _The Prelude_. In a letter to her lifelong friend Jane Pollard, written after two months in the Cookson house, Dorothy laments bitterly the way she and her brothers are being treated. Their grandparents scold them; the servants are insolent, rightly judging how they may treat dependants who ought to be grateful, not proud. At the beginning of the holidays Uncle Christopher had demonstrated his power over them by feigning not to realize that the boys would need horses to fetch them from Hawkshead and William had to teach him his duty by hiring a horse himself and riding to Penrith to remonstrate, with the unsurprising result that 'my Uncle Kit . . . has taken a dislike to my Br Wm.'. It is a long and sad letter, which rises to a poignant climax: 'We always finish our conversations which genenally take a melancholy turn, with wishing we had a father and a home'.[101]

For Dorothy the end of the holidays intensified her misery and sense of isolation as she contemplated remaining in Penrith, where she was certain she was not wanted. For her brothers, however, it must have been a relief, even though it meant further splitting up. Richard, the eldest, had been settled since 1786 under articles with his cousin Richard Wordsworth of Branthwaite; John and Christopher returned to school at Hawkshead in early August; in October William left the Lake District for the first time in his life, for another place that was to provide a lodging but not a home: Cambridge.*

---

* It is an indication of the atmosphere in Penrith not only that W returned to Hawkshead with his brothers to fill the gap until he should leave for Cambridge, but also that DW clearly thought this arrangement a result of malice, to judge from her comments to Jane Pollard, 6 and 7 Aug. 1787: 'When I wrote to you last I had some faint hopes that [W] might have been permitted to stay with me till October. You may guess how much I was mortified and vexed at his being obliged to go away. I absolutely dislike my Uncle Kit who never speaks a pleasant word to one, and behaves to my Br Wm in a particularly ungenerous manner.' _EY_, 7–8.

# 1787–1792

(1)

IN his very popular poem *The Minstrel* James Beattie upbraids those spirits vouchsafed 'a portion of celestial fire':

> Wilt thou debase the heart which God refin'd?
> No; let thy heaven-taught soul to heaven aspire,
> To fancy, freedom, harmony, resign'd;
> Ambition's groveling crew for ever left behind

and in the story of Edwin, the minstrel, he illustrates the sentiment.[1] To the indulgent eye of Dorothy the fact that 'the whole character of Edwin resembles much what William was when first I knew him after my leaving Halifax' just gave her brother added charm.[2] To his guardians, however, the identification, had they recognized it, could only have given cause for further anxiety. This was not the time for high-souled rejection of the world of men, but for diligent attention in Cambridge to whatever was necessary to secure a career and independence. Happily there was no real reason to doubt that Wordsworth would be successful in worldly terms. Hawkshead was a good school which had prepared him as well as any of its numerous pupils already welcomed in the University. He had, in addition, connections who could ease the way to academic and Church preferment. But within five years it was clear that Wordsworth had thrown away every advantage. After an excellent start he had abandoned serious academic competition, taking only a pass degree. He had alienated relatives and seemed determined not to accept the proffered opening of a career in the Church. He had marked his coming of age by fathering a child on a Frenchwoman without the means to support the child or marry the mother. Just as important for his future prospects, he had been infected by the virulent contagion of radicalism, becoming one of 'that odious class of men called democrats'[3] just at the time when authority was not discriminating too subtly between shades of political principle but dividing up citizens into simple categories, the 'loyal' and the 'seditious'.

Not all foreign travels, emotional entanglements, or political awakenings are lastingly significant, especially when experienced by someone still young. It is clear, however, that the five years 1787–92 were of the greatest importance to Wordsworth. They were the determining prelude to the most crucial years of his life, 1793–9; they profoundly affected his relations with relatives and with his immediate family, especially Dorothy; they haunted him and demanded reassessment until well into his middle age; they left in the persons of his child and her mother a testimony, which could not be revised as youthful poems could, about the effects of powerful emotion unguided by considered or tested principle.

They were not years Wordsworth could forget, but they were, not surprisingly, ones he found difficult to deal with when he attempted in *The Prelude* to elucidate the design of his whole life. In the poem certain events are omitted, others played down, and the temporal order is so disrupted that without the help of footnotes a reader would find it hard to work out the chronology of Wordsworth's activities at this time.[4] What must have been the most traumatic experience, the relationship with Annette Vallon and the birth of their child, is pushed to the margins, replaced by deeply affecting imaginative experiences amongst the Alps or on Snowdon. And the problem for the biographer is that evidence other than the poem is so scanty. The context of Wordsworth's life can be assembled in a detailed collage—the people he knew, the political and social mood of the time, the public events of which he must have been aware—but the figure of Wordsworth himself remains indistinct and what he actually felt, thought, and even did knowable only in part.

(2)

In 1831 his former Cambridge tutor James Wood, by then Master of St John's College, invited Wordsworth to sit for a portrait from an 'eminent artist' of his own choosing, as 'A numerous body of our Fellows have expressed to me an earnest wish that the College should possess a lasting Memorial of a quondam Member of the Society whose literary character stands as high as yours'.[5] If the Fellows had been able to read the unpublished *Prelude* they might not have been so enthusiastic. There Cambridge figures as a place of Error, significant in the poet's development only by its failure to fulfil the proper function of a place of learning. 'I could shape / The image of a place', says Wordsworth,

> Which with its aspect should have bent me down
> To instantaneous service, should at once
> Have made me pay to science and to arts

And written lore, acknowledged my liege lord,
A homage frankly offered up like that
Which I had paid to Nature.[6]

But Cambridge was not it. In fact throughout Wordsworth's recollections in *The Prelude* he seems to have difficulty in focusing on what Cambridge actually was. He writes as if he is certain of his final assessment—'I was not for that hour / Nor for that place'—but is unable to fix on anything that might convey a sense of the 'house / Of letters' in which he knew himself to be 'a lodger . . . and no more'.[7] There are, of course, memorable images— the freshman 'rich in monies and attired / In splendid clothes'; getting drunk on toasts to the memory of Milton; running back to college for compulsory chapel—but overall Wordsworth's account of his student years is eloquently unspecific.[8]

That Cambridge life as a whole disappointed him is not very surprising. What usually troubles a new student—loneliness, lack of money, a sense of class-consciousness—did not distress him unduly. Although only a sizar, not a nobleman or gentleman-commoner, Wordsworth had a robust sense of his own worth, enough money to deck himself in 'gentleman's array', and a circle of acquaintances which included his most intimate friends from school.[9] The disappointment stemmed rather from the fact that like any other schoolboy he had created his own image of the place that had fostered Spenser, Milton, and Newton, and it inevitably 'melted fast away' in face of the reality.[10] But even here, and with Wordsworth's words to assure us that it was so, we have to be cautious, for we simply do not know what the reality, for Wordsworth, was. Henry Gunning's *Reminiscences* can be drawn on for evidence of aristocratic profligacy and academic servility, of idleness on a spectacular scale, of rivalries and feuding, and his anecdotes, such as the one about the horsemen who 'had betted they would ride round the courts in a certain number of colleges, between the hours of seven and nine', and did, are more memorable than anything Wordsworth offers about Cambridge *mores*.[11] But we do not know what Wordsworth, a student enjoying his own round of 'invitations, suppers, wine, and fruit',[12] felt at the time about activities which he had neither the inclination nor the money to indulge in. All we know for certain is that when he looked back in *The Prelude* he saw in Cambridge all the follies of the wider world personified:

> here was Labour, his own Bond-slave; Hope
> That never set the pains against the prize;
> Idleness, halting with his weary clog;
> And poor misguided Shame, and witless Fear,
> And Simple Pleasure, foraging for Death;
> Honour misplaced, and Dignity astray . . .[13]

If Wordsworth is unspecific about what disappointed him in Cambridge at large, he does focus more sharply on how Cambridge failed him as an academic institution and how he failed it. Twice he refers to his dislike of competitive examinations, 'when the man was weighed / As in the balance', giving as his reason his perception that the feelings engendered, the 'Small jealousies and triumphs good or bad', the 'passions . . . low and mean', damaged the contestants and only made for 'spurious fame and short-lived praise'.[14] It was a system Wordsworth decided to ignore. In his examination in December 1787 he was placed in the first class, but the following June dwindled to a second and, after deciding not to read for Honours, Wordsworth left Cambridge with a degree that made him no different from any other man who had been 'up' and satisfied the University's not very arduous minimum requirements.[15]

In his account of *Wordsworth's Cambridge Education* Ben Ross Schneider has uncovered enough evidence of tension and breakdown amongst those who did compete to give plausibility to Wordsworth's declared reason for recoiling from the system.[16] But although a principled opposition to an anti-intellectual and certainly unimaginative academic system may have determined Wordsworth's behaviour, it seems more likely that its motive force was a resistance to having his life shaped for him by those he did not like and in ways he could not approve.

Wordsworth had been well trained at Hawkshead, especially in mathematics, excellence in which would be a prerequisite for advancement at the University. He went up to a college with strong connections from his school, in the expectation that he would in due course fill the Fellowship at St John's currently held by his Uncle William Cookson. His uncle was a friend of William Wilberforce and interest gained in that quarter could hardly fail to help in the quest for preferment. Having his father's cousin John Robinson as MP for Harwich might add weight at some future time, as might the friendship of a former master of Hawkshead School, Edward Christian, now a lecturer and soon to be a Professor of Law.[17] In short, Wordsworth entered Cambridge both dependent on the goodwill of his guardians who were putting up the money and only too well aware that he was expected to exploit both his native intellect and the advantages which connections might provide to prepare for himself a future in the Church or just possibly the law.

Neither career can have seemed very appealing. The law was the chosen field of his stolid elder brother Richard, and who wants to follow in a brother's footsteps? The Church visible, embodied in such a Cambridge figure as Richard Watson, the Bishop of Llandaff, who preferred planting trees on his Windermere estate to pastoral duties in his diocese where he never resided,[18] would not have beckoned to a youth who, even if untouched personally by the local evidence of Dissent,[19] had wit enought to realize that the Anglican Church did not have a monopoly of intellect or goodness of life. Both careers, moreover, were approved of by his guardians and that was enough to turn him against them.

In failing to exert himself Wordsworth was, as he later admitted, expressing 'proud rebellion and unkind'.[20] As soon as he has made that admission in *The Prelude*, however, he immediately recants it, or rather overwhelms it by speculating on what virtues—originality, intuitive truths, love of Nature—may have been fostered by his independence, and in this strategy of concession and withdrawal the lines are typical of Wordsworth's whole treatment of his time at St John's. On the one hand he admits that he was anxious 'About my future worldly maintenance', but on the other celebrates his birthright as a 'chosen son' of Nature so rhapsodically that such fears seem trivial.[21] He deplores the fact that,

> Rotted as by a charm, my life became
> A floating island, an amphibious thing,
> Unsound, of spungy texture

yet immediately expounds his vision of an ideal academic community at such length and with such power that self-blame is effaced.[22]

Whatever Wordsworth thought about his waywardness at the time he can hardly have been justifying it as the pre-ordained behaviour of a great poet. It seems certain, moreover, that *The Prelude* and the elderly poet's few remarks recorded in the *Memoirs* underplay how much reading he did do in the prescribed texts.[23] He may have abandoned the course for Honours, but Wordsworth read in moral philosophy, in Euclid, and Newton, and kept fresh the enjoyment of the Classics as living literature, which had been awakened at Hawkshead, by translation and free imitation poetic exercises of his own.[24] What *The Prelude*'s retrospective vision does register, of course, is Wordsworth's memory that what mattered most to him was his exploration of poetry. Italian lessons with Agostino Isola directed him to the pleasures of Tasso and Ariosto and stimulated a lifelong interest in Italian literature and history, evidenced later in translations and the record in poetry of his tour.[25] But undoubtedly most of his reading was in English poetry, more particularly in recent work. It is impossible to distinguish between poets first read now and those Hawkshead favourites reassessed with a more adult discernment, but the list of those who are living presences for the poet of *An Evening Walk* is impressive: Spenser, Milton, Shakespeare, Drayton, and Thomson among the older writers, Burns, Greenwood, Beattie, Young, Gray, Collins, Goldsmith, Darwin, Moses Browne, and Charlotte Smith among the more recent.[26] In his own poetry Wordsworth was to move away from the highly allusive mode then fashionable and even to repudiate some of his enthusiasms, but he was always a very literary poet, one who deepened his knowledge throughout his most creative years and who, even when experimenting most daringly in his own verse, sought inspiration from the masters of the English tradition. He never read passively, nor was he doing so now. He was looking for support in a substantial work of his own.

(3)

*An Evening Walk*, begun most probably in autumn 1788 and essentially completed before Wordsworth left Cambridge, is a poem which still has not received its critical due. Had Wordsworth died at the same age as Keats— that is, before *Lyrical Ballads* and *Poems, in Two Volumes*—he would not be known as one of our greatest writers, but would certainly appear in any literary history of the period as the author of one of the best examples of the loco-descriptive poem.[27] It is a work of self-conscious artifice, allusive, highly wrought, perhaps a little precious in its dramatic transitions and modulations of mood. It is an exercise in poetry-making.

The poem reveals its motivating drives at the outset:

> Far from my dearest friend, 'tis mine to rove
> Thro' bare grey dell, high wood, and pastoral cove;
> His wizard course where hoary Derwent takes
> Thro' craggs, and forest glooms, and opening lakes,
> Staying his silent waves, to hear the roar
> That stuns the tremulous cliffs of high Lodore:
> Where silver rocks the savage prospect chear
> Of giant yews that frown on Rydale's mere.[28]

The whole of *An Evening Walk* unfolds like this, bringing into the compass of one imagined walk a survey of Lake District life, its occupations, its variety of wood and vegetation, its dangers as well as its delights. And it is all seen by an observer whose intense feeling for the place is made all the stronger for his awareness that time and circumstance threaten to divide him from what he most identifies with.

The keenest loss is announced in the opening line: the loss of Dorothy, now living in the vicarage at Forncett in Norfolk with William Cookson and his new wife, but in the fiction of the poem removed to some distant place where all the poet can do is offer the tribute of a poem to be heard, he knows, 'with soft affection's ear'.[29]

Melancholy reflection on past and present, the lament for past joys, the mind accordant to the promptings of Nature, the address to an absent loved one—these are such common tropes of later eighteenth-century poetry that one suspects Wordsworth conceived of the poem's dominant tone just by turning the leaves of his favourite authors. But one has to recognize, too, that no matter how much was poetical stock-in-trade, the poem does bring into focus what were currently the most painful and inchoate aspects of Wordsworth's life.

In the first place, University life once again obstructed the flow of familial feeling that had meant so much to them all when Dorothy returned from Halifax in 1787. Then they had discovered that the only thing that could lessen the misery of 'wishing we had a father and a home' was their bond with one another and all the evidence suggests that that bond now began to carry more weight, not less. In 1788 Dorothy travelled south with Uncle William Cookson and paid a one-day visit to Cambridge on the way to Forncett. No doubt she found her brother as 'exceedingly becoming' as the other undergraduates with their 'smart powdered heads with black caps like helmets . . . and gowns something like those that clergymen wear',[30] for her references to him in letters now become fonder and fonder. The following summer vacation, despite having incurred his uncle's displeasure by refusing to produce verses on the death of the Master of his college,[31] Wordsworth went to Forncett and stayed for some weeks. One can only conjecture at the nature of their conversation and the depth of their absorption in one another from the astonishing intensity of Dorothy's later description of her brother's 'sort of violence of Affection if I may so Term it which demonstrates itself every moment of the Day when the Objects of his affection are present with him', and by the candour with which over the coming years she confesses to her most intimate friend, Jane Pollard, her hopes for that moment when her 'Brother fired with the idea of leading his sister to such a retreat as Fancy ever ready at our call hastens to assist us in painting' will take her to a home of their own.[32]

*An Evening Walk* is shaped with Dorothy in mind as its ideal reader, a presence deeply missed. There can be no doubt that in its yearning for the sights and sounds of the Lakes the poem reflects what Wordsworth was also keenly feeling, namely, that he really belonged among the mountains. He is recalled by an undergraduate contemporary as 'speaking very highly in praise of the beauties of the North; with a warmth indeed which, at that time, appeared to me hardly short of enthusiasm',[33] and in his poem he creates, as he was always to do, both an act of homage to the visible world and a work of art which would be a 'power like one of Nature's', offering its own sources to which his imagination could 'repair, and thence . . . drink / As at a fountain'.[34]

More important than the beauty of 'craggs, and forest glooms, and opening lakes', however, was the appeal of the Lakes as a place where he would be welcomed as nowhere else. 'Glad greetings' from Ann Tyson, 'and some tears perhaps', met him when he went straight to Hawkshead in June 1788 and attracted him to stay again with his 'old dame, so motherly and good' from late July till the beginning of the academic year in Cambridge and throughout August and September the following year.[35]

The significance of these two vacations is clear. On the one hand Wordsworth wanted to be with his brother Christopher and with Ann, his surrogate mother. On the other hand his willingness to treat his relatives with consideration was diminishing by the year. The atmosphere in Penrith had been cool before Wordsworth left for Cambridge. In 1788 he seems to have passed as much time as possible at Hawkshead. Most of the summer of 1789 he spent avoiding Penrith, conveying when he did call in an unmistakable air of duty unwillingly done, to judge from Christopher Cookson's remarks to his nephew Richard: 'Your Bro^r. W^m. called here on Friday last in his road to Cambridge . . . I should have been happy if he had favoured me with more of his Company, but I'm afraid I'm out of his good graces'.[36] In the long vacation of 1790, however, Wordsworth turned a hint of disdain into an overt snubbing act of rebellion. Despite his Uncle Christopher's conviction that he was extravagant and the admonition of his MP relative that he should work hard and 'stick close to College for the first two or three years',[37] Wordsworth set off clandestinely on a foreign tour. Not even Dorothy knew that his plan was to walk across a country convulsed by revolution.[38]

(4)

After two months of travelling Wordsworth was gleefully anticipating the discomfiture of those Cambridge friends who had condemned the whole scheme as 'mad and impracticable' and had 'threatened us with such an accumulation of difficulties as must undoubtedly render it impossible for us to perform the tour'.[39] His self-congratulation is understandable, for Wordsworth's European tour really was a remarkable achievement, a demonstration of courage, physical and mental stamina, resourcefulness, and frugality of which he was rightly proud. Between early July and late September 1790 Wordsworth and his undergraduate friend Robert Jones travelled nearly three thousand miles, walking at least two thousand of them, many over mountainous terrain, at a rate of more than twenty, sometimes more than thirty, miles a day.[40] It must have been a severe test of recent acquaintance, but they returned to England with such a strengthened regard for each other that twenty-five years later Jones could declare to Wordsworth, 'I can assure you that a Day seldom passes that I do not think of you with feelings of inexpressible affection.'[41] They lived economically—in September Wordsworth boasted of having spent not more than twelve pounds from a budget of twenty—and travelled light, 'bearing our bundles . . . upon our heads, with each an oak stick in our hands'.[42] Thirty years later Jones, now a portly bachelor clergyman, recalled that 'We were early risers in 1790 and generally walked 12 or 15 miles before breakfast and after feasting on the morning Landscape how we afterwards feasted on our Dejeuner of whatever the house might afford'.[43] What kind of boots did they wear? Were they shaved from time to time by a village barber, or did they grow beards? How did schoolboy French stand up and how much of his pocket copy of Ariosto did Wordsworth find time to read?[44] There is so much that one would like to know, but it is not difficult to imagine why two such travellers would excite, as Wordsworth reported, 'general curiosity'.[45]

Wordsworth and Jones crossed from Dover to Calais on 13 July at a significant moment in the history of France, the 'very eve / Of that great federal day' on which, celebrating the anniversary of the fall of the Bastille, Louis XVI pledged allegiance to the new constitution at an altar erected in the Champ de Mars. But although they were caught up in the festivities of a 'whole nation . . . mad with joy',[46] and fell in on their journey south with delegates returning home from Paris, their route through France was determined not by a wish to be present at a turning-point in European history but by eagerness to experience for themselves what they had only read about, the sublimity of the Alps. Thomas Gray had described the approach to the Grande Chartreuse as 'one of the most solemn, the most romantic, and the most astonishing scenes'.[47] William Coxe had written equally rapturously of the mountains and glaciers, concluding, moreover, of Switzerland that 'there is no country in which happiness and content more universally prevail among the people',* and so it was southwards that Jones and Wordsworth hastened.

Having arrived in Lyon, partly on foot, partly by boat along the Saône, they visited the monastery of the Grande Chartreuse 4–5 August, and then proceeded first to Lake Geneva and then to the 'wondrous Vale of Chamouny . . . With its dumb cataracts and streams of ice'.[48] Eastwards next, they crossed the Alps at the Simplon Pass and descended through the

---

* It is not clear which edition of Coxe W knew in 1790. The book appeared as William Coxe, *Sketches of the Natural, Civil, and Political State of Swisserland: In a series of letters to William Melmoth, Esq.* (London, 1779; 2nd edn. 1780). It was translated as *Lettres de M. William Coxe à M. W. Melmoth, sur l'état politique, Civil et naturel de la Suisse: Traduites de l'anglois, et augmentées des observations faites dans le même pays, par le traducteur* [Ramond de Carbonnières] (2 vols., Paris, 1781; 2nd edn. 1782). A further English version appeared as *Travels in Switzerland: In a Series of Letters to William Melmoth, Esq.* (3 vols., London, 1789). A copy of this last book was given to Hawkshead School by William and Christopher Raincock in 1792. W certainly knew the French edition by 1792, as he acknowledges his indebtedness to it in *Descriptive Sketches*, and by then he would have been fluent enough in French to read it with ease. It seems likely, however, that on his 1790 tour he was guided by the first and simplest English version.

Ravine of Gondo to Lake Maggiore by 19 August. Continuing to follow Coxe in reverse they then made their way along the Lake of Lugano and Lake Como, before going circuitously via Lucerne to Lake Constance. The Rhine Falls at Schaffhausen, celebrated by Coxe, were visited on 8 September,[49] before they returned to Lucerne and thence eventually to Basle. Here they bought a boat which they used to make more rapid progress down the Rhine, before selling it in Cologne. From Cologne they travelled to Aix-la-Chapelle (now Aachen) and landed in England, almost certainly via Ostend, about 11 October.

Such a journey, whose extent and physically testing nature cannot possibly be conveyed in such a bald statement of the itinerary, was bound to have its 'little disasters'. One such was the miserable night spent 'deafened and stunned / By noise of waters' at the Spittal of Gondo.[50] Another was the occasion when the two travellers misinterpreted the chiming of an Italian clock and got up thinking morning was near, when in fact it was still the dead of night.[51] The frightening immensity of the woods, the insect stings, the louring presence of the mountains, rustles in the undergrowth suggesting who knows what to tired and bewildered minds—all are detailed in *The Prelude*'s splendidly evocative account of a traveller's nightmare.[52] The thunderstorm that was so intense that Wordsworth and Jones lost contact and actually spent the night of 22 August in different villages must have been another severe test of their personal resources.

Such mishaps, however, were more than counterbalanced by impressions which Wordsworth had confidently declared 'will never be effaced'.[53] Of the 'awful solitude' of the Grande Chartreuse Dorothy later wrote: 'I do not think that any one spot which he visited during his youthful travels with Robert Jones made so great an impression on his mind . . . in my young days, he used to talk so much of it to me'.[54] Lake Como seems to have moved Wordsworth as a place of especial beauty and peace, where 'a thousand dreams of happiness . . . might be enjoyed upon its banks, if heightened by conversation and the exercise of the social affections'.[55] The glaciers of Chamonix thrilled him, as they were later to thrill Shelley, as the visible embodiments of awe-inspiring power.* Above all there was the sublimity of the Alps.

For any reader of Wordsworth 'the Alps' must bring to mind Book VI of *The Prelude* and the intense, commanding poetry in which Wordsworth

* On his visit of 1816 Shelley was moved by the mountains to 'a sentiment of extatic wonder, not unallied to madness', but also appalled by the glaciers which 'flow perpetually into the valley ravaging in their slow but irresistible progress the pastures and the forests which surround them, and performing a work of desolation in ages which a river of lava might accomplish in an hour, but far more irretrievably . . .' His letter to Peacock of 22–7 July 1816 is a fascinating counterpart to W's letter of 6 and 16 September 1790 and *1805 Prelude*, VI. See *The Letters of Percy Bysshe Shelley*, ed. Frederick L. Jones (2 vols., Oxford, 1964), I. 495–502.

describes the events of 17 August 1790. On that day he and Jones set off with others from Brig to cross the Alps at the Simplon Pass. They ate at midday at the Old Stockalper Spittal,[56] but lingered at the table longer than the main party, which set off again without them. When they did continue Wordsworth and Jones thought to catch up with the group as they followed a track which led, as they expected, still higher, but they did not do so. Questioning a peasant they learned that they had mistaken their way. Back they must go to where they had branched off up the mountain track and thence downwards, following the current of a stream. Jones and Wordsworth were still keyed up for an ultimate experience of the sublime, but what the peasant was trying to tell them, through the barriers of language and their reluctance to believe, was that they had, in fact, already crossed the Alps. The next few hours were evoked fifteen years later in some of Wordsworth's finest poetry:

> The dull and heavy slackening that ensued
> Upon those tidings by the Peasant given
> Was soon dislodged; downwards we hurried fast,
> And entered with the road which we had missed
> Into a narrow chasm. The brook and road
> Were fellow-travellers in this gloomy Pass,
> And with them did we journey several hours
> At a slow step. The immeasurable height
> Of woods decaying, never to be decayed,
> The stationary blasts of water-falls,
> And everywhere along the hollow rent
> Winds thwarting winds, bewildered and forlorn,
> The torrents shooting from the clear blue sky,
> The rocks that muttered close upon our ears,
> Black drizzling crags that spake by the way-side
> As if a voice were in them, the sick sight
> And giddy prospect of the raving stream,
> The unfettered clouds and region of the heavens,
> Tumult and peace, the darkness and the light
> Were all like workings of one mind, the features
> Of the same face, blossoms upon one tree,
> Characters of the great Apocalypse,
> The types and symbols of Eternity,
> Of first and last, and midst, and without end.[57]

This is the language of Wordsworth's maturity, fully adequate to convey a sense of the awesome grandeur of the scene. It is not the language of 1790. Then, at 20 years old, Wordsworth could only find second-hand ways of saying how overwhelmed he was. In his letter to Dorothy from Lake

Constance he avoids describing the glaciers of Chamonix by saying, 'You have undoubtedly heard of these celebrated scenes, but if you have not read of them any description which I have here room to give you must be altogether inadequate', and his declaration that 'Among the more awful scenes of the Alps, I had not a thought of man, or a single created being; my whole soul was turned to him who produced the terrible majesty before me', although no doubt heartfelt, is no more than a reworking of Gray's, 'Not a precipice, not a torrent, not a cliff, but is pregnant with religion and poetry. There are certain scenes that would awe an atheist into belief without the help of other argument.'[58]

It is entirely characteristic that Wordsworth should make fine poetry from an event years after it happened, but this example of the difference between contemporary and recollected experience and utterance is particularly interesting. As usual the lines cannot be taken as a factual description, since Wordsworth is certainly conflating details observed in various places, but that is a trivial point. *The Prelude* is not a *Baedeker* in verse. More important things are revealed by the difference between 1790 and 1804–5. The first is that although Wordsworth had been brought up amongst mountains, his experience of them in 1790 was indivisible from his reading in the literature of the picturesque and the sublime. He knew Gray and Coxe. His visit to Dovedale during his second long vacation was probably prompted by an account of the area in Hutchinson's *An Excursion to the Lakes*.[59] It is not surprising that now, in 1790, he should use the familiar language of such books to express his own feelings. The second is that the Crossing of the Alps passage in *The Prelude* is such immensely confident poetry not only because by 1804–5 Wordsworth had developed poetic resources at his command, but also because his imagination had come to dwell on the event which, out of all the other abundant but inchoate impressions, made the Alps a personal experience and the Ravine of Gondo a place to which unique, private sensations were attached, which had no parallel in the literature of the sublime.

If Wordsworth outgrew some of the formulations of his 1790 letter, however, one passage in it was prophetic. 'Ten thousand times in the course of this tour', he wrote, 'have I regretted the inability of my memory to retain a more strong impression of the beautiful forms before me, and again and again in quitting a fortunate station have I returned to it with the most eager avidity, with the hope of bearing away a more lively picture. At this moment when many of these landscapes are floating before my mind, I feel a high [enjoyment] in reflecting that perhaps scarce a day of my life will pass [in] which I shall not derive some happiness from these images.'[60] The declaration anticipates the lines from *Tintern Abbey*:

> here I stand, not only with the sense
> Of present pleasure, but with pleasing thoughts
> That in this moment there is life and food
> For future years[61]

and just as that poem's confidence was justified by the flowering of the poetry after 1798, so the youthful confidence of the 1790 letter was validated in the years to come by the use Wordsworth made of the Alpine images he was so anxious to hoard. They are the basis for his next long poem, *Descriptive Sketches*, which was dedicated to Jones, for the marvellous poetry of Book VI of *The Prelude*, for a sonnet as late as 1822,[62] and for much else throughout his work. Recollection of them, moreover, sharpened in Wordsworth a hunger to re-experience what had already been used and reused in art, and so in 1820, in a family group and with much fussing about overcharging by insolent innkeepers, he set off again to repeat the tour and test against the reality the impressions which he had optimistically claimed in 1790 'will never be effaced'. *Memorials of a Tour on the Continent, 1820* and Dorothy's *Journal of a Tour on the Continent (1820)* record that journey, the most poignant of all of Wordsworth's many revisitings.[63]

Poetry, fame, and the self-esteem that spurs one to haggle with innkeepers, however, were all in the future when Wordsworth landed at Dover in October 1790. His duty for the present was to finish reading for his degree. He had been missing Dorothy—'I have thought of you perpetually', he told her in his September letter—and hoped to spend time with her at Forncett. That he went straight to Cambridge instead suggests that he had discovered he was wrong in hoping that his Uncle William Cookson 'as he was acquainted with my having given up all thoughts of a fellowship . . . may perhaps not be so much displeased at this journey'.[64]

### (5)

Writing to his Cambridge friend William Mathews in the following year, Wordsworth commented on his recent months spent in London: 'my time passed in a strange manner; sometimes whirled about by the vortex of its *strenua inertia*, and sometimes thrown by the eddy into a corner of the stream'.[65] The image of directionless motion aptly characterizes the whole of the year from November 1790 to November 1791, one of the most unsettled and unfocused periods of Wordsworth's life.

In early December 1790 he at last visited Dorothy in Forncett and lived again with her every moment of his Continental tour. 'At that time', Dorothy told Jane Pollard, 'the weather was uncommonly mild; we used to walk every morning about two hours, and every evening we went into the garden at four or half past four and used to pace backwards and forwards 'till six.'[66] Dorothy had not seen her brother for over a year and this visit was decisive in shaping her fancy of the perfect future—a life of daily intimacy with him. After a further separation of $2\frac{1}{2}$ years she was still dwelling on the 'Remembrance of those long, long conversations . . . supported by my Brother's arm' and eulogizing 'William my earliest and my dearest male Friend': 'he was never tired of comforting his sister, he never left her in anger, always met her with joy, he preferred her society to every other pleasure, or rather when we were so happy as to be within each other's reach he had no pleasure when we were compelled to be divided'.[67]

Whether or not Wordsworth shared his sister's dream, he was powerless at the moment to make it a reality. After six weeks he returned to Cambridge to complete his studies. If his nephew's account is to be believed, he spent the week before his examinations reading Richardson's *Clarissa*,[68] but none the less he managed to close his undistinguished University career with a BA on 21 January 1791.

Wordsworth went next to London, where he stayed until late May. He lived alone, presumably in lodgings, but where is not known. Nor is much known for certain about what he actually did during these months, for the account of life in the capital given in Book VII of *The Prelude* is not only unspecific about detail, but clearly draws for its imagery of the baffling and multitudinous city on later impressions gained on visits in 1793, 1795, and 1802.

From London Wordsworth went to Wales, to stay with Robert Jones in his family home at Plas-yn-Llan in Denbighshire, where he enjoyed both the welcome of his Alpine companion and, as Dorothy archly reported, 'the company of three young ladies . . . without a rival'.[69] Eager to repeat the pleasure of the previous summer, the two young men explored North Wales, visited the noted travel writer Thomas Pennant, and, possibly spurred by an account of just such an expedition in his *A Tour in Wales*, climbed Snowdon at night to see the sun rise. In dedicating *Descriptive Sketches* to Jones Wordsworth yoked together his pleasure in the Alps and in Wales, but expressed his fear that he might never write about Jones's 'native mountains'. In fact an account of their ascent of Snowdon became the climax to *The Prelude*, a structural counterpart to the Crossing of the Alps passage and fully its equal in poetic power.*

---

* The account of the climbing of Snowdon in *1805 Prelude*, XIII. 1–65 is a striking example of W's characteristic process of composition, in which recollections of both an actual event and literary sources combine to produce poetry of great immediacy. To sources in Beattie's *The Minstrel* and James Clarke's *Survey of the Lakes*, this passage might be added for what it contributes to the imagery of the passage W wrote in 1804 describing his experience in 1791: 'A vast mist enveloped the whole circuit of the mountain. The prospect down was horrible. It gave an idea of numbers of abysses, concealed by a thick

In early September Wordsworth left Wales for London and then went on to Cambridge. A month later he was back in London, determined on yet another change of place. By 22 November Wordsworth had arrived in Brighton, where he introduced himself to the poet and novelist Charlotte Smith, who was distantly connected with his family, and five days later he was once again in France.[70]

The following period was so momentous that it would be easy to regard this unsettled year of 1791 as insignificant, a marking time, merely a prelude to Wordsworth's second visit to France and so, in a sense, it was. But as a prelude the whole period is not without significance. We may surmise, in fact, although the evidence is scanty, that this period of aimlessness stirred aspects of Wordsworth's being into consciousness in a way that profoundly affected both the coming months in France and the whole course of his adult life.

Two interrelated features of 1791 stand out. The first is that during this time Wordsworth began to take stock of himself. He was not in a strong position. Cambridge friends were shaping their lives in the expected ways, Greenwood towards a University life with a Fellowship, Jones and Terrot towards the Church, Fletcher Raincock towards the law, and even Mathews, uncertain as to his eventual career, had a position in a school. Two of his brothers had happily taken the opportunities which family connections offered. After being articled to Richard Wordsworth of Branthwaite, his brother Richard was moving up in the law by transferring to an office in Gray's Inn. John, now in the service of the East India Company, had sailed to the Orient in the *Earl of Abergavenny*, a merchantman part owned by John Robinson and commanded by his cousin Captain John Wordsworth. But he, who had had more advantages than either of his brothers, had left Cambridge without a Fellowship or an alternative career. He was still dependent on his relatives for money, nor did that situation seem likely to change in the near future. The Lonsdale claim had been lodged in 1786. In February 1791 the latest of Lord Lonsdale's delaying manœuvres had been defeated and the way prepared for a full hearing at the Carlisle assizes. But the family victory in the court in August was an empty one, as the final settlement of the amount to be paid was referred to an arbitrator and further delay ensued.[71] Wordsworth knew that he was to inherit a small independence, but how small and when were still uncertain, and in the mean time the humiliating requests for money had to continue.

smoke, furiously circulating around us. Very often a gust of wind formed an opening in the clouds, which gave a fine and distinct visto of lake and valley. Sometimes they opened only in one place; at others, in many at once, exhibiting a most strange and perplexing sight of water, fields, rocks, or chasms, in fifty different places . . .' Thomas Pennant, *A Tour in Wales* (2 vols., London, 1784), II. 164. For Beattie and Clarke see Jonathan Wordsworth, *William Wordsworth: The Borders of Vision* (Oxford, 1982), 310–12.

To the family Wordsworth's proper course seemed clear—he should in due time take holy orders. John Robinson, the MP for Harwich, was prepared to use his interest to get Wordsworth a curacy at once, although he could not be ordained until he was 23, and Uncle William Cookson advised a course of study in Oriental languages at Cambridge. But guardedly, and with much temporizing, Wordsworth resisted these attempts to plot his life for him. He did not know what he was going to do and the jaunty tone he adopts to Mathews does not disguise concern and perhaps self-disgust. He could declare that 'my gaiety increases with my ignorance, as a spendthrift grows more extravagant, the nearer he approximates to a final dissipation of his property', and in another letter, 'I am doomed to be an idler throughout my whole life. I have read nothing this age; nor indeed did I ever', but Wordsworth knew that he had to grasp at something. Mathews himself, however, miserably grinding away at schoolteaching, was an example to him of what a toll of health and spirits an uncongenial occupation could take, and although he played the sage, attempting to check his friend's dissatisfaction from 'overshadowing and destroying . . . every neighbouring image of chearfulness and comfort', the idea that he might himself end up 'vegetating on a paltry curacy' was intolerable.[72] Some half-agreement was perhaps reached with John Robinson, when Wordsworth called on him in September 'to inform him that I was not of age'[73] to take orders, but the return to Cambridge for study was clearly a feint. By 7 November Richard was soliciting Uncle Richard for money to finance his brother's trip to France,[74] and by the twenty-third Wordsworth was writing from Brighton with the relief of someone smelling freedom in the sea air. Now, it seems, the promise to study Oriental languages, which privately he tells Mathews is a ridiculous scheme, was made only to 'oblige' his uncle. Anyway, it could be shelved until he returned from France.[75]

Why France? Even allowing for English ignorance of the real state of affairs there, Richard's excuse for his brother that 'some retired Place in France' would be more 'improving' for someone 'passing the Time previous to his Taking Orders' was far-fetched.[76] A society which had nationalized the property of the Church, promulgated a Civil Constitution for its clergy, and released into Europe the virus of rationalism and sceptical free thought was hardly the place for a potentially anti-clerical waverer. In *The Prelude* Wordsworth says that he went to France 'Led thither chiefly by a personal wish / To speak the language more familiarly',[77] and it is likely that it was in his mind that fluency in the language could only widen the choice of career open to him. More significant impulses, however, were at work impelling Wordsworth back to France, and their origins are to be looked for in his experiences in London.

Wordsworth stayed in London at a more than usually exciting time. In 1789 the revolutionary events in France had been generally welcomed, guardedly by some but rhapsodically by others who echoed Anna Seward's delight: 'So France has dipt her lilies in the living streams of American freedom, and bids her sons be slaves no longer . . . few English hearts . . . there are, that do not wish victory may sit upon the swords that freedom has unsheathed'.[78] But the cautious welcome given by those who sensed that 'Superficially the Revolution was an embodiment of acceptable Enlightement ideas'[79] turned to alarm when it became clear that the English Channel could not guarantee that revolutionary ferment remained a strictly French affair. British constitutional reform movements stirred with renewed vigour. Dissenters felt heightened expectations that long-standing grievances might be settled as authority responded to the flow of more libertarian ideas. There seemed grounds for believing, in short, that the French infection threatened to destabilize the established social order. To a vocal minority the vision of the Dissenting minister Richard Price—'now, methinks, I see the ardour for liberty catching and spreading; a general amendment beginning in human affairs; the dominion of kings changed for the dominion of laws, and the dominion of priests given way to the dominion of reason and conscience'[80]—was a glimpse of a glorious future, but to others it was the credulous folly of the disaffected, of those incapable of recognizing the real nature of human society and the meaning of the past.

In November 1790 Edmund Burke magnificently but provocatively put the conservative response to this quickening of reformist ardour in his *Reflections on the Revolution in France* and immediately sparked off a war of the press.[81] Die-hards such as Edward Tatham, Rector of Lincoln College, Oxford, hastened to congratulate Burke on his opposition to 'that slow poison which has been so industriously administered and insinuated with such consummate art in the veins of our countrymen',[82] but many others, such as Thomas Paine in *Rights of Man*, James Mackintosh in *Vindiciae Gallicae*, Mary Wollstonecraft, Joseph Priestley, Capel Lofft, sought to answer Burke point by point, and in doing so revealed in their passion, their exercise of reasoned argument, and above all in their vision of the true relation between past and future just how deeply the French contagion had taken.[83] Nor was the ideological conflict confined to the press.

Throughout 1790 the alliance of Burke and Fox in Parliament had been under strain and now it shattered in spectacular fashion. A debate on 15 April in which Fox had declared the new French constitution 'the most stupendous and glorious edifice of liberty, which had been erected on the foundation of human integrity in any time or country',[84] was only the prelude to one of 6 May in which Burke, exclaiming 'Fly from the French constitution', declared to Fox and to the House, 'Our friendship is at an end'. According to the *Parliamentary History* Fox rose but could not speak at once, for 'Tears trickled down his cheeks and he strove in vain to give utterance to feelings that dignified and exalted his nature'.[85]

Throughout this period, from late January to late May 1791, Wordsworth was living in London. He read 'eagerly / Sometimes, the master pamphlets of the day',[86] among which were certainly Burke and Paine. He attended debates in the Commons and, even if not present at any of the clashes between Fox and Burke, he could not have remained ignorant of such a widely reported and talked-of rupture. Most important of all, however, is the evidence that at this time Wordsworth got to know men for whom the pamphlets and the parliamentary debates were matters of intense personal concern and through them learned just how ideological issues were embodied in the lives of ordinary people.

In old age Wordsworth recalled how during his stays in London he had heard the famous Dissenter Joseph Fawcett preaching in the meeting-house at the Old Jewry:

It happened to me several times to be one of his congregation through my connection with Mr. Nicholson of Cateaton Street, Strand, who at a time, when I had not many acquaintances in London, used often to invite me to dine with him on Sundays; and I took the opportunity (Mr. N. being a Dissenter) of going to hear Fawcett, who was an able and eloquent man.[87]

This note alone is enough to suggest something of what Wordsworth was referring to when he admitted that during his time in London 'False preconceptions were corrected'. By mixing with Unitarian Dissenters he would have learned at first hand the grievances of people excluded by the Test and Corporation Acts from full civic and political participation.[88] He would no doubt have heard accounts of how attempts to remedy the exclusion had been blocked repeatedly by Parliament and of how the most recent moves in 1790 had been defeated, partly because Fox, the Dissenters' champion, had been unwise enough to invoke the example of reforms in France.[89] Something of this, of course, Wordsworth already knew, but now Dissent was given a human face by men whose qualities of mind showed just how ungenerous was Burke's ridicule of them as 'Wholly unacquainted with the world in which they are so fond of meddling, and inexperienced in all it's affairs'.[90] Conversations with the Unitarian Nicholson must also have prompted Wordsworth to consider in a new light how far the established Church, towards which he was supposed to be looking for a career, was the repository of Truth and a force for social good.

Wordsworth's note on Fawcett, however, contains a further level of significance which has been unrecognized until recently. Nicholas Roe has established that Samuel Nicholson was a member of the Society for Constitutional Information, a pressure group for political reform, now active again in the wake of the Revolution in France.[91] The Society's membership included many who were to play a prominent and often hazardous part in radical agitation in the early 1790s, such as the Cambridge exile John Jebb, the lawyer John Frost, John Horne Tooke, tried for his life in 1794, and Joseph Johnson, friend and publisher of such writers as Joseph Priestley, Mary Wollstonecraft, Tom Paine, and William Godwin, who was to publish Wordsworth's poems in 1793 and to welcome him at the bookshop in St Paul's Churchyard, a meeting-place for radicals of all persuasions.[92] There is no evidence that Wordsworth met any of these people now, although it is possible that he did. But Nicholson would have made no secret of his membership of the Society and one may be sure that, at the very least, Wordsworth would have been made aware of the views and aspirations of men who saw in the revolution in French society a hopeful portent for reform in their own. Historians may debate just how important these and other reformers were in the 1790s, but the fact that the Dissenters were divided in their response to the French Revolution or that in fact radical agitation only briefly ruffled the surface of public life is unimportant.[93] What has to be registered is that for the first time in his life Wordsworth was becoming politically aware, by associating with men who cared passionately about certain ideas and causes and who were hostile, from varying standpoints, to the present order of society.

In *The Prelude* Wordsworth depicts himself in London as absorbed in exploration of all that the city has to offer—crowded streets, theatres, exhibitions, the famous sights such as the Tower and Guildhall—and there is no reason to doubt that much of his time was passed in this way. But he also read, listened to 'talk / And public news',[94] and, though he was as yet only a spectator of the ideological lightning that presaged the storm of the years that followed, he cannot have been indifferent to it. As he awakened to radical causes and the new current of ideas, 'vegetating on a paltry curacy' must have seemed like a culpable retreat. He was enabled to read the signs of the times, so that the significance of the Birmingham riots in July, when the house and laboratory of Joseph Priestley were sacked by a Church and King mob, must have been clearer to him than it would have been only a few months before.[95] He was made aware, moreover, that in France in 1790 he had no more than glimpsed a new society, whose nature and significance were now the subject of wholly contradictory interpretations. Was the fall of the Bastille 'the greatest event . . . that ever happened in the world! And how much the best!', as Fox averred, or was it, as Burke would have it, the beginning of an unnatural course, a 'fond election of evil', which could only engender 'treasons, robberies, rapes, assassinations, slaughters and burning throughout [the] harrassed land'?[96] In deciding to return to France Wordsworth may have been temporizing to escape the pressure from his relatives, but he was also going back to judge for himself.

(6)

As he approaches 'Residence in France' in *The Prelude* Wordsworth predicts that his theme

> will be found
> Ere we shall far advance, ungenial, hard
> To treat of, and forbidding in itself.[97]

The biographer can only echo his words. The year 1792, in which Wordsworth became a father and an awakened supporter of the French cause, was one of the most important in his life, but it is impossible to be certain of the significance of almost everything about it. Contemporary evidence is very thin and Wordsworth's recollections in old age are tantalizingly incomplete. *The Prelude* is rich in suggestion, but as biographical evidence it has to be treated even more circumspectly than usual, for when Wordsworth looked back in 1804 over his years of revolutionary zeal he did so with something more than the conventional hindsight of a happily married man reviewing youthful impetuosities. In 1792 and the immediately following years Wordsworth's own life underwent a revolution and from that convulsion and the profound questioning it precipitated issued all of his greatest poetry between 1797 and 1804. Wordsworth assured Coleridge in *The Prelude* that some day he would expound 'What then I learned—or think I learned—of truth',[98] but in fact his major poems ever since 1797, in all their variety of subject-matter and genre, had been just such an exposition, whether they overtly drew on his French experiences or not. The principles which underlie everything he wrote, what it is that constitutes what Leslie Stephen was to call 'Wordsworth's Ethics', were established in the troubled years after 1792 and embodied, dramatized, and explored in the poems of Wordsworth's maturity.[99] But the poems and prose were never final statments of 'Truth', but stages in a continuing process of analysis which made discoveries with each return upon the meaning of past experience. Nor was *The Prelude* of 1804–5 a final statement either—the difficulty Wordsworth found in treating a theme 'forbidding in itself' drove him to further exploration of it in *The Excursion* (1814)—but it is the most sophisticated, and what it deploys is precisely the analytical depth and conceptual range not commanded by the uncertain, discomfited, naïve youth of 1792, whose thoughts and feelings one would like to recover.

Scanty though the contemporary evidence is, there is enough to reveal how disingenuous was Wordsworth's remark in 1801 that 'in truth my life has been unusually barren of events',[100] and a simple presentation of it is a necessary foundation for any speculation about its significance.

On 26 November 1791 Wordsworth crossed the Channel to Dieppe. His destination was Orléans, where he had already arranged accommodation at the city's best hotel, but Paris had to be seen first. Arriving there on 30 November, after two days delay in Rouen, he stayed until 5 December, absorbing the atmosphere of the city through visits to the now famous places such as the Champ de Mars, the Pantheon, and the ruins of the Bastille. Charlotte Smith had given him letters of introduction and it was perhaps through one of these, possibly addressed to no less a person than Brissot, that Wordsworth was enabled to attend the Legislative Assembly.[101] Throughout his stay a furious debate was in progress on the revolt of the Negroes in Saint-Domingue, but what it would have meant to Wordsworth can be judged from his admission to his brother, 'I am not yet able to speak french with decent accuracy.'[102]

Once in Orléans, where he arrived on 6 December, Wordsworth found himself lodgings with a hosier and hatter which, although 'a very handsome apartment on the first floor', were, he assured Richard, really very cheap.[103] Helen Maria Williams, whose sensibility had been the subject of his first published poem, had just left the city and so he was unable to make use of another of Charlotte Smith's letters of introduction,[104] but he did present himself to Thomas Foxlow, a successful Lancashire cotton manufacturer now in business in Orléans, and through him hoped to be 'introduced to the best society this place affords'.[105] In his lodgings he had the company of 'a young gentleman of Paris' and 'two or three officers of the Cavalry' but he also spent some of his evenings with a 'very agreeable' family and here it seems probable that he met Annette Vallon.[106]

Evidence that he did so is lacking, but Annette and her brother Paul were certainly close to the family of André-Augustin Dufour, a magistrate's clerk in Orléans.[107] What is certain is that by 3 February Wordsworth had moved on yet again, abandoning his comfortable apartment to go to Blois, and that he must have done so to be with Annette in her home town, for within a month or two at most she was pregnant.

While in Blois Wordsworth became the intimate friend of an older man, the 37-year-old Michel Beaupuy, a captain in the 32nd, Bassigny, regiment, and through him entered as something more than an uncomprehending spectator the political life of the town. But conjecture about the course of his relationship with Annette during this time is without firm foundation. Had he known of his friend's love affair William Mathews would have understood Wordsworth's excuse that he had not written earlier because,

'Since my arrival day after day and week after week has stole insensibly over my head with inconceivable rapidity', but from the letter itself he could have gleaned nothing.[108] Wordsworth continues to advise Mathews on his future, touches on mutual friends, comments on French politics, and indicates when he expects to return home. Annette is not mentioned at all. Nor does she appear directly in a letter to Richard of 3 September, although it is clear that the anxieties about money and his own future expressed in it reflect Wordsworth's increasingly urgent sense of his own position.[109]

Although when writing to his brother Wordsworth clearly expected to remain at Blois, waiting for the money Richard was asked to send, he did not do so. Sometime in September he returned to Orléans, following Annette, who had gone back to the Dufours. There he made arrangements for Dufour to represent him at the baptism of the expected child and by about 29 October he was in Paris, *en route* for England. Anne-Caroline Wordsworth was born on 15 December 1792 and by the end of the month her father was back in London.

The evidence so barely outlined here is sufficient to indicate why his personal experiences in 1792 must have shaken and changed Wordsworth, but it cannot suggest how they did so, or to what extent. On so many questions one can only speculate. But there is speculation and speculation. Why, for example, did Wordsworth linger in Paris for over six weeks when he should either have been supporting Annette as her confinement approached or getting back to England with all possible speed to raise money and make plans for their future? Mary Moorman declares that 'Paris so enthralled him that in the end it was only the cutting off of funds from home that induced him to return' and Hunter Davies follows suit, claiming that November 1792 was such a dramatic moment in French affairs that 'No student of the human race would want to have missed it'. F. M. Todd, on the other hand, suggests that what delayed him was dilatoriness in issuing passports and that Wordsworth 'spent most of his weeks in Paris waiting for permission to leave'.[110] Both speculations seem plausible, the first carrying more weight for being the reason Wordsworth himself offers in *The Prelude*,[111] but, as neither can be settled on until further evidence is discovered, both can be allowed currency.

More far-reaching conjectures, however, about Wordsworth's experiences, his motivation, and his state of mind have, of course, been offered about this period, and because they tend to slide from conjecture into statement of fact, gathering coherence as later interpretation confirms the initial conjecture, they are dangerous. To declare, as Mary Moorman does, that Wordsworth felt for Annette 'all the worship of a great first love, even if it is admitted that probably the attraction was felt at first more on her side than on his', or, as Todd does, that 'had he never met Annette, there is no reason to believe that his political or poetic development would have been materially different',[112] is to erect foundations for the interpretation of the next, crucial, years of Wordsworth's life on sand. If what follows seems timid, the reason is that caution seems best when we know so little.

When Wordsworth gave an account of this period—twelve years later it should be noted—in *The Prelude*, he dealt with the major stages of his political awakening fairly directly. In Books X to XII, which cover the years after his return to England, dislocations of chronology, massive lacunae, recapitulations that do little to clarify obscurities, crucial vaguenesses of definition, all signal the effort involved in subduing biographical information to the overall poetic design. In Book IX, however, the political narrative proceeds without apparent strain and one can flesh it out by reference to contemporary events and speculate on what Wordsworth might or might not have seen, done, and thought, without (at least on present evidence) departing from the shape provided in the poem. In doing so, one can approach the big question: what did Wordsworth make of the political and social situation in France?

In 1790 Jones and Wordsworth had crossed the Channel

> when Europe was rejoiced,
> France standing on the top of golden hours,
> And human nature seeming born again.[113]

On Wordsworth's return in 1791 the atmosphere in France was very different. Hopes that progress towards needed constitutional, fiscal, and social reform would be peaceful were dimming, as groups struggled for power in the vacuum created by royal vacillation. Danton in the Cordeliers, Barnave, Duport, and Lameth of the Feuillants, Robespierre, Brissot, Desmoulins of the Jacobin Club were emerging as powerful figures, whose personalities and constantly shifting strategies were to dominate and ultimately subvert the Legislative Assembly in the coming year.[114] In June fears that the king was relying on counter-revolutionary support from émigrés had been fuelled by his abortive flight to Varennes and in August by the Declaration of Pillnitz, which threatened armed intervention by Austria and Prussia at any further outrage against Louis and the Royal Family. On 17 July blood had flowed on the Champ de Mars, the site of the Fête de la Fédération, as the National Guard fired on a crowd demanding the abdication of the king. At the end of 1791 France was, in the words of one historian, 'deeply divided and quite ungoverned'.[115]

It is impossible to be sure what impact the mood of Paris made on Wordsworth in December 1791, but the account in *The Prelude* can almost certainly be trusted. He had

                                                    abruptly passed
                        Into a theatre of which the stage
                        Was busy with an action far advanced[116]

and although he knew enough about recent events to identify the places to
visit, it is doubtful whether a five-day stay, even one that included an
introduction to the Assembly and the Jacobin Club, can have made him
inward with the ramifications of the power struggles in progress. Nor does
his letter to Richard of 19 December from Orléans suggest any recent
sophistication of his political awareness. The observation, 'I find almost all
the people of any opulence are aristocrates and all the others democrates', is
crude.[117] His landlord M. Gellet-Duvivier was implacably hostile to the
Revolution[118] and the Royalist officers on the brink of leaving to join the
émigré forces, whose fevered state is so memorably described in *The
Prelude*, were not likely to be subtle in their attempt 'to bring me over to
their cause'.[119] What Wordsworth needed was an intelligent guide. In
Blois, for a few decisive weeks, he found one: Michel Beaupuy.

    Michel Beaupuy (1755–96) had joined the army in 1771 and reached the
rank of captain by the time he was stationed at Blois.[120] A well-educated
man, familiar with the major writers of the French Enlightenment and
schooled by twenty years' experience in the army, Beaupuy clearly
impressed Wordsworth first of all simply by the charismatic force of his
personality. Its qualities stand out in the fullest tribute paid to anyone in
*The Prelude*:

                                                       A meeker man
                 Than this lived never, or a more benign—
                 Meek, though enthusiastic to the height
                 Of highest expectation. Injuries
                 Made *him* more gracious, and his nature then
                 Did breathe its sweetness out most sensibly,
                 As aromatic flowers in Alpine turf
                 When foot hath crushed them. He through the events
                 Of that great change wandered in perfect faith,
                 As through a book, an old romance, or tale
                 Of Fairy, or some dream of actions wrought
                 Behind the summer clouds. By birth he ranked
                 With the most noble, but unto the poor
                 Among mankind he was in service bound
                 As by some tie invisible, oaths professed
                 To a religious order. Man he loved
                 As man, and to the mean and the obscure,
                 And all the homely in their homely works,
                 Transferred a courtesy which had no air

Of condescension, but did rather seem
A passion and a gallantry, like that
Which he, a soldier, in his idler day
Had payed to woman. Somewhat vain he was,
Or seemed so—yet it was not vanity,
But fondness, and a kind of radiant joy
That covered him about when he was bent
On works of love or freedom, or revolved
Complacently the progress of a cause
Whereof he was a part—yet this was meek
And placid, and took nothing from the man
That was delightful.[121]

'Man he loved / As man'—here is the key. In Orléans Wordsworth had associated with men blinkered by self-concern, who saw in the Revolution only a threat to their own security and privilege. Now he had encountered a wider view, a more selfless concern, a vision of something finer in the possibilities of human society, all captured in the following dramatic passage:

And when we chanced
One day to meet a hunger-bitten girl
Who crept along fitting her languid self
Unto a heifer's motion—by a cord
Tied to her arm, and picking thus from the lane
Its sustenance, while the girl with her two hands
Was busy knitting in a heartless mood
Of solitude—and at the sight my friend
In agitation said, ''Tis against that
Which we are fighting', I with him believed
Devoutly that a spirit was abroad
Which could not be withstood, that poverty,
At least like this, would in a little time
Be found no more . . .[122]

No doubt Beaupuy's image remained so vividly in Wordsworth's mind because he was conscious that what he owed most to him had been a personal example. But Beaupuy must also have assisted him in another way, by supporting him and interpreting events as he, a young foreign visitor, participated in the political life of Blois. In the club Les Amis de la Constitution Wordsworth would have sensed the pace at which affairs were moving and the goal towards which they were inexorably tending, by hearing of, if not actually meeting, Grégoire, newly elected Constitutional Bishop of Blois, who, after service in the Assembly until its dissolution in

September 1791, had recently headed a demand that Louis should be dethroned.[123]

Beaupuy's regiment left Blois on 27 July 1792, as France slipped deeper into crisis. On 20 April war had been declared on Austria, but in an early engagement French troops broke and in retreat murdered their general, Dillon. In June the Tuileries were invaded and hundreds of the insurgents and the defending Swiss Guard were killed. In August the king was suspended amidst plotting and accusations amongst factional leaders and growing disorder amongst the populace, both in Paris and in the provinces. Wordsworth may well have witnessed one example in the food riots in Orléans in September.[124] In September, too, in Paris, prisoners were slaughtered by mobs convinced that counter-revolutionaries were biding their time in prison, awaiting deliverance from outside and the overthrow of the Revolution.

On 19 May Wordsworth had told Mathews that 'in London you have perhaps a better opportunity of being informed of the general concerns of france, than in a petty provincial town in the heart of the kingdom itself', but the fact that he immediately relates the murder of General Dillon rather belies this observation.[125] Nor is there reason to doubt that he was generally informed about the deepening turmoil or that he was aware of how far the nation had moved from the 'golden hours' of 1790. Few names are mentioned in Book IX of *The Prelude*, but two who are recalled as 'powers', J. L. Carra and A. J. Gorsas, are, significantly, journalists. In his *Annales patriotiques* Carra was pressing throughout 1792 for initiative in the war against the foreign enemy, while Gorsas in his *Courrier* steadily maintained a radical position, even becoming 'one of the principal apologists for the September massacres'.[126]

Through conversation with Beaupuy and the members of Les Amis de la Constitution, through reading the newspapers, above all, perhaps, simply by observing how ordinary people responded to the news from Paris passed on by word of mouth, Wordsworth must have been increasingly aware that he had become deeply involved with Annette at a time when the future of every citizen was insecure and even the survival of the state in its present form uncertain. What his stay in Paris would have done is bring into focus both the events of the past year and the nature of the volatile situation in the capital, only glimpsed from Orléans and Blois.

When Wordsworth returned to Paris at the very end of October 1792 a decisive stage of the Revolution had been reached. Throughout the summer, with the threat of foreign invasion ever present, the possibility of any limited constitutional reform had been swept away by the violence of the attack on the Tuileries on 10 August, by the deposition and imprisonment of the king, and by the September Massacres. The defeat of the Austrians and

Prussians at Valmy on 20 September, however, and the Declaration of the Republic immediately afterwards provided a respite in which the newly constituted National Convention could debate the future of the Revolution, which, for the moment, meant essentially the future of the king.

That debate dominated the Convention from 13 November 1792 until 17 January 1793. It was shaped by struggles for power, of whose existence Wordsworth was made aware the moment he reached the city. On 29 October Jean-Baptiste Louvet denounced Robespierre in the Convention and published his indictment, the final words of which could not be more clear: 'Je t'accuse d'avoir évidemment marché au suprême pouvoir'.[127] On 5 November Robespierre replied, regained the initiative, and signalled the ascendancy of his group. In the history of this turbulent period it was not the single decisive moment which *The Prelude* suggests it was, only yet another crisis, but one may surmise that it remained memorable to Wordsworth, a bewildered spectator, because it was one moment in which the powers at work were visible in human actors in a comprehensible drama.

It is doubtful whether Wordsworth could have understood much of the situation in Paris. In *The Prelude* he emphasizes his sense of exclusion, as he looked

> as doth a man
> Upon a volume whose contents he knows
> Are memorable but from him locked up,
> Being written in a tongue he cannot read[128]

and quotes from *Macbeth*, as if only Shakespeare's dramatic embodiment of power preying upon the very foundation of its own security were adequate to convey his own sense of uncomprehending dread. It is not surprising that he should do so. The events of 1792 and the shifting allegiances and groupings of the principal actors defied, and still defy, reduction into analytical patterns, or into the kind of arresting but misleading tableaux in which good confronts evil that Wordsworth creates out of Louvet and Robespierre.* He would certainly have needed help to make any sense out of

* Confusion has been caused by the tendency of commentators to interpret the proceedings of the Assembly and the Convention on party-political models. Mary Moorman speaks of the Girondins as 'sentimentalists among the revolutionaries' and of 'Brissot, Roland, and the Girondins' as 'genuine revolutionaries' (I. 172 and 204–5). Louvet is described by the editors of the *Norton Prelude* as 'moderate' (X. 103 n. 4). As W is thought to have associated with Brissot and clearly admired Louvet's vain stand against Robespierre, he is thus identified with a moderate party called the Girondins, seen as opposed to what is by implication the immoderate party, the Jacobins. But as M. J. Sydenham, *The French Revolution* (1965), 161, points out, this is to create 'an imaginary party'. It also falsifies, as W does in *The Prelude*, what the Brissotins were. During the first months of W's stay in France, Brissot, a member of the Jacobin Club, was pressing for war against Prussia and Austria and for severe measures against the king. In the power struggle with Robespierre he was out-manœuvred and labelled a 'moderate', i.e. a counter-revolutionary. But in no sense was he moderate, as that term might be used of nineteenth- or twentieth-century British political figures of the left. What marks Brissot, Louvet, and

what he observed. It is tempting to think that he may have renewed his acquaintance with Brissot, then locked in struggle with Robespierre and the Jacobin Club from which he had recently been expelled. Of Gorsas Wordsworth later declared, 'I knew this man', and it seems possible that he met him now.[129] There were Englishmen in Paris, too, such as James Watt, and James Losh, who afterwards became a firm friend.[130] Thomas Paine, the infamous author of *The Rights of Man*, who had been introduced into the National Convention by Grégoire on 21 September, was toasted on 18 November at a banquet in White's Hotel, and it is possible that Wordsworth was among those radicals who raised their glasses and offered their 'fraternal homage' to the Republic on that occasion.[131]

Whoever and whatever Wordsworth saw, there can be no doubt that these weeks in Paris accelerated his political education, for its progress through the year can be traced quite clearly. By 19 May he had seen enough to be convinced that the changes in society brought about by the Revolution were irreversible, but his perception that the future of France would really be decided in battle between the patriot army and foreign invaders is simplistic, no more than could be expected of a foreigner reading the newspapers in a provincial town.[132] Nor can much be made of Wordsworth's political utterance in poetry at this time. In September or October 1792 he concluded *Descriptive Sketches* with a call for earth's renovation:

> Oh give, great God, to Freedom's waves to ride
> Sublime o'er Conquest, Avarice, and Pride,
> To break, the vales where Death with Famine scow'rs
> And dark Oppression builds her thick-ribb'd tow'rs:
> Where Machination her fell soul resigns,
> Fled panting to the centre of her mines;
> Where Persecution decks with ghastly smiles
> Her bed, his mountains mad Ambition piles;
> Where Discord stalks dilating, every hour,
> And crouching fearful at the feet of Pow'r,
> Like Lightnings eager for th'almightly word,
> Look up for sign of havoc, Fire, and Sword;
> —Give them, beneath their breast while Gladness springs,
> To brood the nations o'er with Nile-like wings;
> And grant that every sceptered child of clay,
> Who cries, presumptuous, 'here their tides shall stay',
> Swept in their anger from th'affrighted shore,
> With all his creatures sink—to rise no more.[133]

Madame Roland, in fact, is their lack of political sense. If W's dangerous fantasies of the time, recollected in *The Prelude*, X. 176–95, were encouraged by association with such people, one can only be glad that he was removed from their influence when he returned to England, otherwise he too might have perished, 'A poor mistaken and bewildered offering' (*1805 Prelude*, X. 196).

As commentators have observed, the whole poem is the most passionate verse Wordsworth had yet written, and this climax certainly reveals its author to be fiercely anti-monarchist,[134] but the passage operates at such a level of generality as to make it applicable to all political situations, or to none. No monarch or statesman ever felt threatened by posturing like this. Within three months of his return to England, however, Wordsworth had written *A Letter to the Bishop of Llandaff*, and this, although not a work of great polemical sophistication, does command attention, in a way that the verse of *Descriptive Sketches* does not, because it displays personal familiarity with recent events and the nature of the real issues in France. The writer who chides the Bishop for not having 'attended to the history of the French revolution as minutely as its importance demands'[135] is consciously exploiting the superiority that only his stay in Paris can have given him.

During 1792 Wordsworth's political awareness was intensified and, as was suggested earlier, it is possible to speculate about the process with some confidence on the basis of *The Prelude*'s account. Conjecture about what he witnessed, or what he might have thought, could be wrong in detail, but there is sufficient congruity between the poem and contemporary evidence to indicate along what lines conjecture might safely be made. With Wordsworth's more personal, emotional life, however, the case is altogether different. During 1792 he fathered a child on a French Catholic woman four years older than himself. Marie Anne, known as Annette (1766–1841), was the sixth child of Jean Vallon, surgeon. On his death, sometime before 1788, her mother Françoise had remarried, again to a surgeon, and her two brothers had taken their father's place at the charitable hospital Hôtel Dieu at Blois. Her brother Paul was a lawyer's clerk in Orléans. Wordsworth did not marry Annette when he could have done and, although she clearly expected that he would marry her in due course, the idea of doing so does not seem to have determined his behaviour for very long. And this is all that can be said with any confidence about Wordsworth and Annette in 1792.

The temptation to imagine the nature of their relationship is, of course, very strong. To discover sexual passion and the responsibility it entails in so short a time must deeply affect anyone who is not callously self-centred, and Dorothy's account of Wordsworth's 'sort of violence of Affection . . . which demonstrates itself every moment of the Day when the Objects of his affection are present with him' suggests he was not that.[136] But there is simply no evidence on which to conjecture either that Wordsworth was deeply in love with Annette or, conversely, that his union with her was a short-lived passion which he was forced to take seriously only because she became pregnant. Annette's surviving letters certainly show how much she longed for Wordsworth's return.

Come, my love, my husband [she wrote on 20 March 1793], and receive the tender embraces of your wife, of your daughter. . . . She grows more like you every day. I seem to be holding you in my arms. Her little heart often beats against my own; I seem to feel her father's: but why, Caroline, are you so insensible? Why does not your heart stir when your mother's is beating so? O my beloved, soon it will be stirred when I shall say to her: 'Caroline, in a month, in a fortnight, in a week, you are going to see the most beloved of men, the most tender of men.' Then my Caroline's heart will be moved, she will feel her first emotion and it will be of love of her father.

To Dorothy she confessed: 'His image follows me everywhere; often when I am alone in my room with his letters I think he has entered . . . emerging from my mistake as from a dream I see him not, the father of my child; he is very far from me. This scene is often repeated and throws me into extreme melancholy'. But are they, as Mary Moorman asserts, 'letters . . . of a girl who not only loves but knows herself beloved'?[137] They could as easily be read as the cries of a woman who is beginning to fear that she has been abandoned.

The evidence of *The Prelude* likewise seems to point in two directions. At the end of Book IX Wordsworth tells the story of the lovers Vaudracour and Julia, whose passion for each other crosses the boundaries of class, disrupts family loyalties, and ends in the death of mother and child and the insanity of Vaudracour. The story seems to have been based on fact and when Wordsworth told a fellow Cumbrian, Joshua Wilkinson, in 1793 that he was going to put it into fiction, it may be that what attracted him was the possibility of treating the repressive behaviour of Vaudracour's father and his exploitation of the law as an analogue for what Wordsworth had learned about the situation in pre-revolutionary France.[138] When he included the story in *The Prelude*, however, he was clearly attempting to record obliquely something of what his relationship with Annette had meant to him during his year in France twelve years ago.

The very existence of the episode in *The Prelude*, though, invites contradictory interpretations. On the one hand, the fact that in a poem which usually employs the confessional mode Wordsworth should have substituted the third-person narrative of Vaudracour and Julia for an account of his affair with Annette, not mentioned anywhere else in the poem, might suggest that he did not regard the relationship as a personal crisis or as having contributed in any significant way to his development as a poet. Such an interpretation would, of course, say something about Wordsworth in 1804 and about the compulsion to rewrite his life history which determines *The Prelude*, but nothing about 1792. On the other hand, one might be astonished that the story of Vaudracour and Julia appears at all. In 1804 Wordsworth was a married man. His family knew all about

Annette and Caroline and in 1802 Dorothy had even accompanied Wordsworth to France to meet them and make financial arrangements. But even so, tact might have dictated silence if truth were not to insist on a direct treatment of the subject. That Wordsworth—twelve years later—could not quite ignore his youthful passion might suggest that, however coherent were the interpretative patterns he was constructing in *The Prelude*, he knew that without some gesture towards it they would be incomplete. Whatever interpretation is put upon Book IX, the fact is that we do not know how Wordsworth felt about Annette at the end of 1792 nor what his state of mind was when he returned to England in December.

# 1793–1795

(1)

On 21 January 1793 Louis XVI was guillotined in Paris. Eight days later two poems were published in London, *An Evening Walk* and *Descriptive Sketches*, 'By W. Wordsworth, B.A. of St. John's, Cambridge'. To bring these two events together may seem factitious, but it will serve to underline what was most important in Wordsworth's life at that time. For him, George Eliot's observation that 'there is no private life which has not been determined by a wider public life' was a fact of bitter experience.[1] At every point he was under pressure from events which were beyond his control, grand happenings on the world stage which made his own anxieties seem both insignificant by contrast and yet also more intense.

When Wordsworth returned to England in late December 1792 his position was bad and it rapidly became desperate. Faced with Annette's pregnancy earlier in the year he had reluctantly decided to take up William Cookson's offer of a curacy, though, as he told Mathews, 'Had it been in my power I certainly should have wished to defer the moment'.[2] He was being optimistic. By July 1793 Dorothy was lamenting to Jane Pollard that 'my Uncle has not invited Wm to Forncett, but he is no favorite with him alas! alas', but even to such an intimate friend she draws back from explaining the 'foundation of the prejudices of my two Uncles against my dear William', declaring 'the subject . . . an unpleasant one for a letter'.[3] When and how the rupture occurred is not known, but clearly Cookson found Wordsworth's behaviour in France unpardonable, withdrew the offer of assistance, and refused to welcome him at his house. The road to what Dorothy recognized would 'in the End be a certain Provision'[4] was closed. At the beginning of 1793 Wordsworth was 22 years old, the father of an illegitimate child, and without an income.

What little he could do he did in haste. In May 1792 he had stiffened Mathews's resolution by asserting, 'The field of Letters is very extensive, and it is astonishing if we cannot find some little corner, which with a little tillage will produce us enough for the necessaries, nay even the comforts of life',[5] and now he acted on his belief by publishing with Joseph Johnson the poem he had written at Cambridge, *An Evening Walk*, and his new work of the last summer, *Descriptive Sketches*. 'As I had done nothing by which to distinguish myself at the university', Wordsworth later told Mathews, 'I thought these little things might shew that I could do something.'[6] No doubt they did. Neither poem is a 'little thing', and they caught the notice of the discerning, amongst them Coleridge, at once, but though their publication in handsome quartos strengthened Wordsworth's self-esteem, they did not contribute to the solution of his problems. Johnson did nothing to push them; the reviews were indifferent; and although, according to Christopher Wordsworth, they were eagerly discussed in literary groups in Cambridge, Exeter, and Derby, they did not sell.[7] For the moment Wordsworth had used up what literary stock he had and was no further forward.

During his months of lodging with Richard in Staple Inn, Wordsworth, so De Quincey records, began to exhibit such signs of strain that his companions were forced to play cards with him every night 'as the best mode of beguiling his sense of distress, what ever it might be'.[8] It is not difficult to imagine why. Uppermost in his mind were worries about Annette and his future, but these personal problems which he could not immediately resolve merged with a more generalized anxiety generated by affairs quite outside his control and, it may be conjectured, by the collision of expectation and reality.

Throughout 1792 in France Wordsworth had been increasingly moved by the energies of a nation seeking to realize a vision of freedom from the tyrannies of power, ignorance, and want, and to defend the gains it had made against threats from without. 'My heart was all / Given to the people, and my love was theirs', Wordsworth remembers in *The Prelude*, catching the note of generalized and idealized fervour which is projected in *Descriptive Sketches*, where the political vision owes much to reading and little to experience.[9] In France, precluded from intimate knowledge of the politics of the Revolution and cut off from reliable news of events at home, Wordsworth may well have believed 'Devoutly that a spirit was abroad / Which could not be withstood', or, reading the British Addresses presented to the National Convention in November, have returned home in the expectation that a new idealism and reforming energy would be as apparent everywhere as it was in France.[10]

The reality was quite otherwise. Reformist groups such as the London Society for Constitutional Information, the London Corresponding Society, and their provincial affiliates were active, but in their strictly constitutional demands for universal suffrage and annual parliaments they manifested a very different radicalism from that which Wordsworth had seen in France. Joel Barlow might assure the French National Convention, on behalf of the Society for Constitutional Information, that 'After the example given by France revolutions will become easy; reason will make rapid progress, and it would not be surprising if in a shorter time than we should venture to predict, there were to arrive from the continent addresses of congratulation to a National Convention in England',[11] but he was certainly not expressing the views of more than a handful of extremists. Samuel Nicholson, Joseph Johnson, and others of their circle with whom Wordsworth was now mixing stopped well short of wanting the French experience repeated in England. That English constitutional reform was so rapidly associated with French Revolution had been its handicap since 1790.[12] The execution of Louis was a disaster.

Limited though their aims were, the reforming societies, especially the vigorous London Corresponding Society, were seen as a threat to the state. While Wordsworth had been in France the Royal Proclamation against Seditious Writings of 21 May 1792 had begun a campaign which was intensifying as he returned. On 18 December Paine was convicted, in his absence, of having published a seditious libel in the second part of *The Rights of Man*, and in the coming months a number of printers and newspaper proprietors were given heavy sentences for uttering sedition, which often meant no more than issuing *The Rights of Man*.[13] The English people had not risen as the French had done, and when war between England and France was declared on 1 February there was, despite the activities of radical groups, not the slightest likelihood that they would do so.

Placed in such a context the source of Wordsworth's 'sense of distress' becomes clearer. Only months before in a letter to Mathews he had lauded England as 'a free country, where every road is open, where talents and industry are more liberally rewarded than amongst any other nation of the Universe'.[14] Now it was clear that the government of this 'free country' was determined to suppress dissent at home and to join with other powers to crush the freely chosen liberty of another nation. That its action would separate him from Annette and their child only intensified Wordsworth's broadly based sense that he was now an alien in his own country. As he remembered in *The Prelude*:

> I felt
> The ravage of this most unnatural strife
> In my own heart; there lay it like a weight
> At enmity with all the tenderest springs
> Of my enjoyments. I, who with the breeze
> Had played, a green leaf on the blessed tree
> Of my beloved Country—nor had wished
> For happier fortune than to wither there—

Now from my pleasant station was cut off,
And tossed about in whirlwinds. I rejoiced,
Yea, afterwards, truth painful to record!
Exulted in the triumph of my soul
When Englishmen by thousands were o'erthrown,
Left without glory on the Field, or driven,
Brave hearts, to shameful flight. It was a grief,
Grief call it not, 'twas anything but that,
A conflict of sensations without name,
Of which he only who may love the sight
Of a Village Steeple as I do can judge,
When in the Congregation, bending all
To their great Father, prayers were offered up
Or praises for our Country's Victories,
And 'mid the simple worshippers, perchance,
I only, like an uninvited Guest
Whom no one owned, sate silent, shall I add,
Fed on the day of vengeance yet to come![15]

When he wrote this passage in 1804 Wordsworth perhaps needed no stimulus to remember the bitterness of impotent outrage it so memorably records. Had he wanted one, he need only to have turned to what he wrote at the time, *A Letter to the Bishop of Llandaff*.

At the outset of the Revolution Richard Watson, Bishop of Llandaff, had given 'hearty approbation' to the determination of the French 'to free themselves and their posterity from arbitrary power'. The sanguinary progress of events, however, had disgusted him and on 30 January 1793 he denounced the Revolution in an Appendix to a sermon first published in 1785.[16] The French, he claimed, now 'exhibit to the eye of contemplation an humiliating picture of human nature, when its passions are not regulated by religion or controlled by law'. Asserting that there were Englishmen who would emulate the crimes of France in pursuit of liberty and equality, he proceeded to argue that both already existed under the law in Great Britain and that the constitution, although not perfect, was built on the sure foundation of experience. Demanding, 'look round the globe, and see if you can discover a single nation on all its surface so powerful, so rich, so beneficial, so free and happy as our own', he concluded by rejoicing at the vigilance of the government, through which the 'hopes of bad men have been disappointed, and the understandings of mistaken men . . . enlightened by the general and unequivocal judgment of a whole nation'.

Watson's pamphlet is not very remarkable. Watered-down Burke, it argues the usual conservative case, but notably without the appeal to Christian quietism that characterizes William Paley's *Reasons for Contentment*, also published in 1793. To the reviewers, who noticed it generously, it seemed a valuable word in season rather than an original contribution to the philosophy of human rights. Something about it, however, touched Wordsworth more deeply. Perhaps it was disappointment that Watson, previously respected as a champion of the Dissenters, should have welcomed the suppression of free enquiry, 'the eyes of the human race'.[17] Perhaps it was the complacency of Watson's remark that the 'provision which is made for the poor in this kingdom is so liberal, as, in the opinion of some, to discourage industry' (particularly galling in a man notorious for landing positions for which he was not qualified), or the scorn he levels at 'peasants and mechanics' who presume to amend the constitution of their country. Perhaps it was above all simply that an idealistic and hopeful young man was blighted by Watson's defensive and insular caution. For whatever reason, Wordsworth replied at once, not in the bishop's measured tone but with root and branch denunciation.

Declaring at the outset that he writes in 'a republican spirit', Wordsworth defends the execution of Louis XVI, asserts the right of the French people to choose their mode of government, considers the problems inherent in all systems of electoral representation, with emphasis on the wisdom of the people governed, attacks the mutually sustaining powers of the monarchy, aristocracy, and law which control English so-called liberty, and scorns Watson's complacency over the lot of the poor. In conclusion, he defiantly proclaims that 'The Friends of Liberty congratulate themselves upon the odium under which they are at present labouring' and, 'Conscious that an enemy lurking in our ranks is ten times more formidable than when drawn out against us', thanks the bishop for his 'desertion'.

Many aspects of the *Letter* might be dwelt on—for example, that it is weakest where Wordsworth tackles the general topics of the division of legislative and executive powers and strongest in his attack on the 'thorny labyrinth of litigation', where personal experience of the Lonsdale suit fuelled his condemnation of 'the consuming expense of our never-ending process, the verbosity of unintelligible statutes, and the perpetual contrariety in our judicial decisions'—but two in particular are worth especial notice. The first is that this is a very radical document indeed. Wordsworth alludes to the objects of the English 'Friends of Liberty', universal suffrage and annual parliaments, but the tenor of his polemic goes far beyond anything that all but a few Painite extremists among them would have endorsed. Wordsworth not only defends the execution of the king but argues that aristocracy, without which 'monarchy cannot exist', must be swept away too, as a system of 'fictitious superiority' which spawns the idle, the corrupt, the profligate, and the tyrannical. Taking up a position sadly familiar to the twentieth century, he declares that the 'sweet emotions of compassion' are 'evidently dangerous where traitors are to be punished' and that inhumanity must be condoned in a period of revolution, for 'Alas! the obstinacy & perversion of men is such that [Liberty] is too often obliged to borrow the very arms of despotism to overthrow him and in order to reign in peace must establish herself by violence'. What is to Burke in the *Reflections* the wisdom of traditional deference, by which high and low exist in a mutually supportive system of hierarchical relations, is to Wordsworth the tyranny of custom under which the mass of men labour in chains, unresisting because 'we are taught from infancy that we were born in a state of inferiority to our oppressors, that they were sent into the world to scourge and we to be scourged'. It is the duty of the 'philosopher', Wordsworth implies, to awaken men to this truth: 'Slavery is a bitter and poisonous draught; we have but one consolation under it—that a nation may dash the cup to the ground when she pleases'.

At any time since 1789 writing of this kind would have been seditious. After the declaration of war, had the *Letter* been published, it would have been close to treason. But it was not published, and this is the second important point about it. Joseph Johnson had an honourable record as a publisher of radical literature and was to go to prison in 1799 for issuing a reply by Gilbert Wakefield to another exhortation to the nation from Bishop Watson, but even he had thought it prudent by extricate himself from the publishing of Paine's *The Rights of Man, Part First* in 1791 and it may be that he declined Wordsworth's polemic as just too dangerous. It may be, on the other hand, that Wordsworth himself decided not to publish it. Whatever the reason *A Letter to the Bishop of Llandaff* remained hidden until after Wordsworth's death, as did all of his other radical writings before *Lyrical Ballads* of 1798. Unlike Coleridge and Southey, unlike Horne Tooke and Thelwall and many other writers and orators, the radical Wordsworth—whose seriousness and sincerity are not in question—never acquired a public identity.

### (2)

It must give pleasure to every reflecting mind who has any regard to the happiness of his country, or his own as undivided, to see members of the legislature contributing their exertions to defend our happy Constitution from the inroads of evil-minded persons, who find an interest in overturning the fundamental principals of order and society.[18]

Such was the opinion of one commentator in 1793 and Wordsworth can have had no doubt as the war fever mounted that he was speaking for many. Oppressed by such unthinking conservatism, as well as intensely worried about his personal position, Wordsworth must have felt trapped and impotent during his time in London. An early summer tour of the West Country promised relief, or at least a change. In the event it rather exacerbated Wordsworth's mood and stimulated him to a second polemic.

Early in July, with five guineas in his pocket advanced by Richard, Wordsworth left London to begin his tour. His companion was William Calvert, a friend from Hawkshead days who had inherited money from his father,[19] and their destination was the Isle of Wight. This lovely place, however, only reminded Wordsworth of present realities, for daily he watched the fleet gathering in the Solent and each evening he heard the cannon at sunset, with

> a spirit overcast, a deep
> Imagination, thought of woes to come,
> And sorrow for mankind, and pain of heart.[20]

After a month's stay, about which nothing is known, they set off on the mainland, only to come to an inglorious halt when Calvert's horse 'not much accustomed to draw in a whiskey (the carriage in which they travelled) . . . began to caper one day in a most terrible manner, dragged them and their vehicle into a Ditch and broke it to shivers'. Dorothy's account continues with the essentials of what is known: 'Mr C mounted his Horse and rode into the North and William's firm Friends, a pair of stout legs, supported him from Salisbury, through South into North Wales'.[21]

It is strange that the two friends went on separately. Perhaps an introverted and anxious Wordsworth was proving a difficult companion, or perhaps Calvert did not share Wordsworth's love of walking and could not face the long haul to Robert Jones at Plas-yn-Llan. For whatever reason Wordsworth was alone as trudged across Salisbury Plain and thus receptive to 'imaginative impressions, the force of which', he declared in his seventy-third year, 'I have felt to this day'.[22] In 1838 he told John Kenyon that 'overcome with heat and fatigue I took my siesta among the Pillars of Stonehenge; but was not visited by the muse in my Slumbers',[23] but *The Prelude* paints a darker picture. Wordsworth was alone in the immense waste. A storm of extraordinary intensity lashed southern England with hailstones as big as six inches round.[24] Before him were the incomprehensible 'monuments and traces of antiquity with which that region abounds'[25] and there, he remembers in *The Prelude*:

> While through those vestiges of ancient times
> I ranged, and by the solitude o'ercome,
> I had a reverie and saw the past,
> Saw multitudes of men, and here and there,
> A single Briton in his wolf-skin vest
> With shield and stone-axe, stride across the Wold;

The voice of spears was heard, the rattling spear
Shaken by arms of mighty bone, in strength
Long mouldered of barbaric majesty.
I called upon the darkness; and it took,
A midnight darkness seemed to come and take
All objects from my sight; and lo! again
The desert visible by dismal flames!
It is the sacrificial Altar, fed
With living men; how deep the groans; the voice
Of those in the gigantic wicker thrills
Throughout the region far and near, pervades
The monumental hillocks; and the pomp
Is for both worlds, the living and the dead.[26]

For once *The Prelude* can be trusted as a biographical record, for in it Wordsworth draws on the poem brought into being at the time by the intensity of whatever these experiences were. He may not have been 'visited by the muse in my slumbers', but he was soon afterwards, and *Salisbury Plain*, or, as Wordsworth alternatively called it, *A Night on Salisbury Plain*, was the result. Of course this strange and over-wrought poem did not issue entirely from immediate experience. Almost no poem of Wordsworth ever does. Memories of a traveller's death on Stainmore in Yorkshire and of the dying woman in *An Evening Walk* merge with recollection of passages in sources as diverse as Rousseau, Chatterton, Spenser, and the antiquarian writers on Stonehenge.[27] There can be no doubt, however, that what fused them was Wordsworth's experience on Salisbury Plain, which quickened his imagination 'to compare what we know or guess of those remote times, with certain aspects of modern society, particularly in what concerns the afflictions & calamities to which the poor are subject'.[28]

The comparison is made at once and then forcefully urged through every aspect of the poem. Echoing Rousseau's *Discours sur l'origine de l'inégalité parmi les hommes* Wordsworth opens with the proposition that life was actually better for the savage 'naked and unhoused / And wasted by the long day's fruitless pains' than it is for modern man, since his 'hard lot' was shared with others who 'Repose in the same fear, to the same toil awake', whereas ours is made more painful by the sight of those 'who on the couch of Affluence rest / By laughing Fortune's sparkling cup elate'.[29] It is an astonishing view that could not be sustained for long in the hortatory tones of the opening stanzas. In the stories of the two travellers on Salisbury Plain Wordsworth gives it human form. A solitary and desperate man, looking for a 'hovel from the storm to shield his head', encounters an equally desperate and terrified woman. They comfort each other and she relates her history. Driven out of her home, robbed by war of her husband and children, she now wanders aimlessly with 'no earthly friend' and 'no house in prospect but the tomb'. Morning dawns brightly and as the pair wander down into a more welcoming valley the poet bids them adieu and closes the poem, as it had begun, with a direct address to the reader. Once again the comparison is insisted on. It may be that human sacrifice in Druidical rite is no longer practised, but is modern warfare, blessed by Superstition's priests, essentially different? Private life is 'Unblessed by Justice' and the poor 'crushed by their own fetters helpless sink'. Repeating the last points of *A Letter to the Bishop of Llandaff*, Wordsworth proclaims the folly of those legislators who believe that 'Exile, Terror, Bonds, and Force' may stand 'at Wisdom's porch' and in a final exhortation cries:

> Heroes of Truth pursue your march, uptear
> Th'Oppressor's dungeon from its deepest base;
> High o'er the towers of Pride undaunted rear
> Resistless in your might the herculean mace
> Of Reason; let foul Error's monster race
> Dragged from their dens start at the light with pain
> And die; pursue your toils, till not a trace
> Be left on earth of Superstition's reign,
> Save that eternal pile which frowns on Sarum's plain.

Although the use of the Spenserian stanza and frequent personification give a highly literary gloss to *Salisbury Plain*, for Wordsworth the abstractions, Want, Oppression, Law, and so on, embodied realities he knew. The story of the woman's father driven out by the territorial ambition of a powerful neighbour was drawn from an incident at Calgarth on Windermere with which he had long been familiar,[30] and was impassioned by his first-hand acquaintance with exploitation of the law in the Lonsdale suit. 'All that relates to her sufferings as a Soldier's wife in America & her condition of mind during her voyage home', he notes, 'were faithfully taken from the report made to me of her own case by a friend who had been subject to the same trials & affected in the same way.'[31] By the time the poem was completed in 1794, moreover, the reference in the denunciation of 'Exile, Terror, Bonds and Force' and the 'gory hand' of Justice would have been unmistakable. In May 1793 John Frost, who had been in Paris on behalf of the Society for Constitutional Information in November 1792 when Wordsworth was there, was sentenced to six months in Newgate and an hour in the pillory for uttering sedition.[32] In May also William Frend was tried before a University court and expelled from Cambridge for issuing an anti-war pamphlet, *Peace and Union Recommended*.[33] In August the Scottish radical Thomas Muir was sentenced to fourteen years transportation for sedition. In September Thomas Fysshe Palmer received a sentence of seven years' exile. The following January Maurice Margarot and William Skirving were each transported for fourteen years.[34] The millennial vision of the concluding stanza may have been out of touch with the political realities of 1793-94, but the poem's denunciation of contemporary government was not. All of these men were members of properly constituted societies pursuing non-violent reform. That their sentences were so savage, foregone conclusions to trials that were travesties, demonstrated one way in which authority intended 'to defend our happy Constitution from the inroads of evil-minded persons, who find an interest in overturning the fundamental principles of order and society'. But like *A Letter to the Bishop of Llandaff*, *Salisbury Plain* was only a private utterance of outrage and alienation. Remaining unpublished, it contributed nothing to the cause of the 'Friends of Liberty'.

(3)

After crossing Salisbury Plain Wordsworth went via Bath to Bristol and thence up the Severn to the Wye before continuing on foot into Wales. His journey was rich in experiences on which he later drew—his visit to Tintern Abbey, the encounter near Builth with the tinker forerunner of Peter Bell, and at Goodrich Castle with the little girl recalled in *We are Seven*—but he must have been glad to reach the welcome of Robert Jones's house at last, from where he could send Dorothy an account of his wanderings.

How long he stayed at Plas-yn-Llan, and where he went next, are uncertain. Late in life Wordsworth told Carlyle that he had witnessed the execution of the journalist Gorsas.[35] Proscribed with other Girondins at the beginning of the Terror, Gorsas had returned from Normandy to Paris, where he was recognized and guillotined on 7 October 1793. Can Wordsworth really have been there? In the absence of any other corroborative evidence from Wordsworth himself or any member of his circle, it is not surprising that scholars have had difficulty in accepting Carlyle's record. There is so much against the possibility that Wordsworth went to France now. How would he have made the crossing? How could he have paid for it? Why go to Paris at the height of the Terror, risking certain imprisonment if not death, if the object of the visit was to see Annette at Blois? But the evidence that he did is very strong. Carlyle, the historian of the French Revolution, was not likely to mistake the name of Gorsas any more than Wordsworth was to invent such an experience as watching the execution of a man he knew. What can reasonably be conjectured about Wordsworth's state of mind also supports the case. Throughout 1793 he had been in a highly wrought condition. It was now ten months since he had seen Annette and he had never seen his own daughter. Possibly he had heard nothing from Annette either, at a time when the news from France was heavy with accounts of the execution of those suspected of counter-revolutionary sympathies. If any letter had got through, Wordsworth could have learned of the execution of his former landlord, M. Gellet-Duvivier, on 13 July, and of the outlawing of Annette's own brother Paul in June.[36] Common sense would have told Wordsworth that to return to France was folly, but common sense had not deterred him from a 'mad and impracticable' expedition in 1790 and it is not difficult to believe that a courageous but desperate 23-year-old might have disregarded its advice again.

If Wordsworth did see Gorsas die it must have been a traumatic event. But even if he did not, the news reaching England of the rise of the Terror and the execution of the Brissotins, added to daily evidence at home of repressive measures against radical activists, was quite enough to account for Wordsworth's recollection in *The Prelude* that he felt himself implicated in some obscure way and that for months or even years

> I scarcely had one night of quiet sleep
> Such ghastly visions had I of despair
> And tyranny, and implements of death,
> And long orations which in dreams I pleaded
> Before unjust Tribunals, with a voice
> Labouring, a brain confounded, and a sense,
> Of treachery and desertion in the place
> The holiest that I knew of, my own soul.[37]

To make conjecture about Wordsworth's state of mind on the evidence of a visit to France that may not have taken place, and on the recollection of *The Prelude* written eleven years later, is clearly unsatisfactory—unsatisfactory but irresistible, for one would so much like to know how Wordsworth thought of himself and the evolving shape of his life at this time. Lacking all humanizing detail as it does, what evidence there is simply indicates that Wordsworth had become a gentleman vagrant and that when in February 1794 he admitted to Mathews, 'I have been doing nothing and still continue to be doing nothing', he was summing up with unsparing accuracy.[38] During the previous year he had lived briefly in London, the Isle of Wight, and Wales, and had slept under many roofs between Salisbury and Plas-yn-Llan. By the close of the year he had moved north again. He spent Christmas at Whitehaven, where he obtained a further advance of £20, and then passed on to the Calverts at Keswick and to Armathwaite, the home on Bassenthwaite of John Spedding, a friend from Hawkshead School.[39] It is possible that he visited Penrith, but by 17 February he was certainly in Halifax, reunited with Dorothy at the home of Elizabeth and William

Rawson.[40] One would gladly exchange any number of the many anecdotes recorded from Wordsworth's later years for just one that might convey some idea of what he was like now or what his relatives and friends made of him, but nothing seems to have survived. All that can be said for certain is that by February 1794, although his wandering was far from over, its most unsettled period had come to a close.

(4)

Throughout 1793 Dorothy had been longing to escape from the domestic round at Forncett, with an eagerness that became painfully intense as the months passed without a date being fixed for a visit to Halifax. In August she wrote to Jane Pollard, 'Oh count, count the Days, my Love till Christmas how slowly does each day move! and yet three months and Christmas will not be here. Three months!—long, long months, I measure them with a Lover's scale',[41] and this is only one of many such moments in which Dorothy reveals how miserable she now was. Admitting 'I am often sad, very, very often', she was feeding on the expectation that soon she would recapture the pleasures of childhood and enjoy 'all the sweets of female friendship': 'Oh Jane with what Transport shall I embrace you: My dear Friend we shall live over again those Days.'[42] Dorothy's keenest delight, however, was the promise that somehow or other William would join her in Halifax. Jane Pollard was enjoined to keep this a secret, for Dorothy was anxious that William Cookson should not know 'beforehand or even afterwards, that the scheme was a *premeditated* one'.[43] Her letters make it clear, however, that at whatever risk she was determined to meet him again.

Since the end of 1788 Dorothy's life had consisted of duties in a small country parish, domestic matters, and looking after babies. It was natural that she should look forward to William's company and to experiencing vicariously the fuller life of someone who had travelled abroad, lived in London, and known the excitement of sexual passion and physical hardship. There is, none the less, something so obsessive about Dorothy's praises of her brother in her letters to Jane Pollard and such unrestrained fantasy in her image of him 'fired with the idea of leading his sister to such a retreat as Fancy ever ready at our call hastens to assist us in painting', that one would be bound to wonder how far Wordsworth would welcome such a burden of expectation, were it not for the evidence that he felt as intensely as she did. In a letter now lost, but quoted by Dorothy, he assured her: 'How much do I wish that each emotion of pleasure and pain that visits your heart should excite a similar pleasure or a similar pain within me, by that sympathy which will almost identify us when we have stolen to our little cottage!'[44] Dorothy's life was becoming stultified; Wordsworth's was in chaos. In their desire to be together was fused their urge to restore the family bond, whose sundering Dorothy felt especially strongly, to be assured of love, and to find a resting place in which to take stock of the present and, if possible, plan the future.

Having met at last in Halifax in January 1794, Wordsworth and Dorothy seized the opportunity of prolonging their time together when in early April William Calvert generously offered them Windy Brow, his farmhouse on the slopes above Keswick. They travelled by coach to Kendal and then on foot made what is still a breathtaking entrance to the Lakes along the eastern shore of Windermere to Low Wood, where the Langdale Pikes first come fully into view, and then over White Moss to Grasmere. The next day they walked the thirteen miles to Keswick through a landscape which becomes more and more majestic until the moment when above the town the full grandeur of Skiddaw and Blencathra appears.

Dorothy's letters from Windy Brow make it plain what this time meant to her. She was thrilled with everything—with her 'wonderful prowess in the walking way', with the local people, 'the most honest cleanly sensible people I ever saw in their rank of life', with the view from the house over what Gray had called the 'Vale of Elysium',[45] where Bassenthwaite leads the eye to the mass of Skiddaw and Derwentwater to the mountains at the jaws of Borrowdale, a prospect so splendid that 'it is impossible to describe its grandeur'. Above all there was 'the opportunity I have of enjoying my brother's company', the pleasure of frugal housekeeping with him—'our breakfast and supper are of milk and our dinner chiefly of potatoes . . . we drink no tea'—and of learning from him. It is with the pride of one who feels that she has improved the hour that Dorothy declares to her aunt Mrs Christopher Crackanthorpe, who had questioned the propriety of her being at Windy Brow 'rambling about the country on foot': 'I have regained all the knowledge I had of the French language some years ago, and have added considerably to it, and I have now begun reading Italian, of which I expect to have soon gained sufficient knowledge to receive much entertainment and advantage from it'.[46]

For Dorothy this time of freedom and delight was of the greatest importance. It marked the end of one period of her life. She did not return to the domestic bondage of Forncett and only a year or so after leaving Windy Brow in mid-May 1794 she was once again living with her brother, as she was then to do uninterruptedly to the end of his life. For Wordsworth it was a time of equal importance. Drinking in pleasure from the landscape and resting in the stability of his relationship with Dorothy, he seems to have begun the attempt to establish what really mattered to him and to take more command of his own life.

The evidence for this rather grand assertion is to be found in the poetic manuscripts which date from Windy Brow. One is a small home-made notebook into which Wordsworth and Dorothy entered fair copies of some of Wordsworth's schoolboy poems and *Salisbury Plain*, his first sustained composition since *Descriptive Sketches*.[47] Although in May 1794 he described the poem as 'written last summer',[48] it may reasonably be assumed that, as usual with Wordsworth, copying out and fresh composition went on simultaneously, and that the poem's concluding call for the onward march of Reason seemed as urgent to him now as it had done when first conceived on Salisbury Plain. The other is a copy of the published *An Evening Walk* into which are entered revisions which, together with revisions also copied out in the *Salisbury Plain* notebook, transform the poem into a fascinating new work.[49]

In revising *An Evening Walk* Wordsworth was behaving as he was to behave throughout his creative life. He was, firstly, responding productively to criticism. Wordsworth did not like criticism any more than anyone else. He could be very touchy, as Charles Lamb was to discover when he ventured one or two observations about *Lyrical Ballads*,[50] and his later warfare with Francis Jeffrey of the *Edinburgh Review* has given currency to an image of him as a poet quite unable to tolerate anything less than praise. But the truth is very different. Wordsworth was always angered by criticism that revealed sloppy reading of what he had written with such pains, and he had little time for the professional reviewer.[51] Criticism from other creative writers, however, no matter how minor, or from people whose intelligence Wordsworth respected, was always taken seriously and frequently acted upon. At Forncett Dorothy and his brother Christopher had 'amused [themselves] by analysing every line and prepared a very bulky Criticism . . . to transmit to William'.[52] Criticism from such a source could be welcomed and used.

Secondly, and more importantly, in revising Wordsworth was bringing his past work into conformity with his present thinking. To Wordsworth poems were not discrete objects, to be published and then later classified as 'early', 'middle period', 'later poems', and so on, but emanations of a mind which needed to register its evolution not only in new work but in continued contact with old. His continual rewriting stems from a determination to treat his poems as living presences and to change or discard whatever no longer seems adequate. The revisions to *An Evening Walk* are the earliest examples of this compulsion. Written in youth and only 'huddled up' for publication in 1793, the poem demanded reconsideration.

Although they nearly double the length of the original, the revisions do not quite amount to a finished and publishable work and Wordsworth seems to have abandoned them to be pillaged for attractive lines for *The Ruined*

*Cottage* later on.[53] They are, none the less, of considerable significance, two elements in particular being worth comment. The first is that one passage seems to carry the strident hostility to 'Superstition' found in *Salisbury Plain* even further. There the 'Heroes of Truth' are urged to wield the 'herculean mace / Of Reason' against 'Superstition's Reign', but in the following passage of the revisions to *An Evening Walk* Wordsworth seems to envisage the displacement of Godhead itself in the triumph of Truth:

> the sun sinks down above,
> Sinks slowly to a curve and lessens still,
> Gives one bright glance, and drops behind the hill.
> Spirit, who guidst the orb and view'st from high
> Thrones, towers, and fanes in blended ruin lie;
> Roll to Peruvian vales thy gorgeous way;
> See thine own temples mouldering in decay;
> Roll on, till, hurled from thy bright throne sublime,
> Thyself confess the mighty arm of Time;
> Thy star must perish, but triumphant Truth
> Shall tend a brightening lamp in endless youth.[54]

The second is that Wordsworth treats the essential subject-matter of *An Evening Walk* in a much more thoughtful way. In the 1793 poem he had presented the interaction of the sights and sounds of Nature with the mind that registered them in a simple manner:

> No purple prospects now the mind employ
> Glowing in golden sunset tints of joy,
> But o'er the sooth'd accordant heart we feel
> A sympathetic twilight slowly steal,
> And ever, as we fondly muse, we find
> The soft gloom deep'ning on the tranquil mind.[55]

Such commonplace formulae had satisfied the undergraduate steeped in Gray and Collins, but now they seemed to open fascinating questions that demanded exploration, about how the mind responds to Nature, what the value is of such activity of intellect and emotion, and what is the place of Divinity, of the supreme mind, in creation. Drawing heavily on Akenside's *The Pleasures of Imagination*, Wordsworth proposes a more dynamic model of Man and Nature, which emphasizes the power of the imaginative mind to reach through the material world to truth, through the penetration of

> A heart that vibrates evermore, awake
> To feeling for all forms that Life can take;
> That wider still its sympathy extends,
> And sees not any line where being ends;

Sees sense, through Nature's rudest forms betrayed,
Tremble obscure in fountain, rock, and shade;
And while a secret power those forms endears
Their social accents never vainly hears.

Such 'favoured souls'

taught
By active Fancy or by patient thought
See common forms prolong the endless chain
Of joy and grief, of pleasure and of pain.[56]

As Paul Sheats has said in an excellent discussion of the revisions, Wordsworth is struggling to convey his sense that 'the visible world . . . testifies to the moral harmony of a benign nature and a virtuous man'.[57] To embody this perception in dramatic and narrative form, to formulate a poetic language that would carry it into a reader's imagination, to explore its implications for man as a social being, and encounter its limits—this was to be the work of Wordsworth's greatest poetry. But many of these questions, which were to preoccupy Wordsworth for the whole of his creative life, took shape now, as he reworked *An Evening Walk*.

## (5)

The confidence engendered in Wordsworth at Windy Brow by creative work, stability, and shared affection was to determine his life in the months to come. It did so, most dramatically, by convincing someone other than Dorothy that he had gifts that ought not to be allowed to wither. Sometime in May, Raisley, younger brother of William Calvert, offered to share his income with Wordsworth, solely, Wordsworth was convinced, 'from a confidence on his part that I had powers and attainments which might be of use to mankind'.[58] Calvert was due to come into full control of his inheritance on coming of age in September 1794, but as he was already seriously ill with tuberculosis, he took steps to secure his intentions by making a will in which Wordsworth was promised £600, later raised to £900, subject only to assurances, which Richard Wordsworth provided, that the legacy would not be claimed immediately against money already advanced for Wordsworth's education.[59] In October Wordsworth offered to accompany the worsening invalid to Lisbon, but their journey was abandoned when even the first stage to Penrith proved too taxing. In the coming months Calvert declined rapidly—in November Wordsworth reported that he could not even bear being read to, on 7 January he was 'barely alive'—and he died on 9 or 10 January 1795, Wordsworth being with him to the end.

In *The Prelude* Wordsworth pays tribute to Raisley Calvert, 'Himself no poet / Far less a common spirit of the world', as one who with Dorothy and Coleridge had enabled him to realize his destiny.[60] In 1805, as he concluded the great poem on the development of his own mind, Wordsworth was certain that his destiny had always been that he should become a major poet. In 1794 his eventual goal was unclear. But he was right to remember Calvert in this way. Even before Windy Brow he had come to a firm decision that 'all professions . . . are attended with great inconveniences, but that of the priesthood with the most', but the question, 'what is to become of me' would not have been resolved by such negatives, and in early 1794, to judge from his letter to Mathews of 23 May, Wordsworth was desperate for money.[61] Calvert's generosity did not transform the financial situation—the money was released only fitfully and in small amounts[62]—but it greatly affected Wordsworth's sense of possibilities. In putting such trust in him Calvert reinforced his image of himself when it most needed reinforcement and placed on him an obligation, which Wordsworth readily and optimistically received, to use his particular gifts of intellect and imagination for the betterment of mankind.

In 1794, with Britain at war with France and 'Exile, Terror, Bonds, and Force' suppressing the Friends of Liberty at home, Wordsworth was in no doubt as to what this obligation entailed. On 11 May William Mathews had written from London to suggest that they and another unknown young man should found a monthly miscellany. Although many such journals already existed, most of them were pro-government, written, it seemed to Wordsworth, 'to maintain the existence of prejudice and to disseminate error', and he seized the idea of countering them with 'a vehicle of sound and exalted morality' with fervour.[63] In replying to Mathews on 23 May he spelt out his principles as if already drafting an editorial address: 'I solemnly affirm that in no writings of mine will I ever admit of any sentiment which can have the least tendency to induce my readers to suppose that the doctrines which are now enforced by banishment, imprisonment, etc. etc., are other than pregnant with every species of misery. You know perhaps already that I am of that odious class of men called democrats, and of that class I shall for ever continue.' On 8 June Wordsworth suggested a title, *The Philanthropist a Monthly Miscellany*, and responded to Mathews's 'explicit avowal of [his] political sentiments' with a still more outspoken declaration of his own:

I disapprove of monarchical and aristocratical governments, however modified. Hereditary distinctions and privileged orders of every species I think must necessarily counteract the progress of human improvement: hence it follows I am not amongst the admirers of the British constitution.

It is no wonder that Richard felt constrained to counsel, 'I hope you will be cautious in writing or expressing your political opinions. By the suspension of the Habeas Corpus Acts the Ministers have great powers.'[64]

In believing that to publish a journal dedicated to free enquiry would be to act for the common good and in conceiving of it in the way he did, Wordsworth was registering the new influence on his life, the writings of the foremost radical intellectual of the age, William Godwin. Godwin's *Enquiry Concerning Political Justice and its Influence on Morals and Happiness* had been published in February 1793. When Wordsworth first read it is not known, but, as Nicholas Roe has pointed out, Wordsworth's letter to Mathews of 17 February 1794 clearly indicates that he was thinking about it, and later letters planning the *Philanthropist* reveal that by then he had absorbed its essential message.[65]

Forbidding though it is in bulk, Godwin's relentless application of reasoned enquiry to all aspects of social life is written with a directness that advertises the charm of Reason and leaves no doubt as to meaning, and much of it would have attracted Wordsworth immediately:

A numerous class of mankind are held down in a state of abject penury, and are continually prompted by disappointment and distress to commit violence upon their more fortunate neighbours. The only mode which is employed to repress this violence, and to maintain the order and peace of society is punishment. Whips, axes and gibbets, dungeons, chains and racks are the most approved and established methods of persuading men to obedience, and impressing upon their minds the lessons of reason.

It is perhaps impossible to shew that a single war ever did or could have taken place in the history of mankind, that did not in some way originate with those two great political monopolies, monarchy and aristocracy.

Hereditary wealth is in reality a premium paid to idleness, an immense annuity expended to retain mankind in brutality and ignorance.[66]

The writer of *A Letter to the Bishop of Llandaff* and *Salisbury Plain* did not need to be persuaded by such observations. What clearly did influence, and exhilarate, Wordsworth, however, was Godwin's belief in the power of Truth. Despite the sorry evidence of human history, Godwin stresses repeatedly that 'There is not . . . the smallest room for scepticism respecting the omnipotence of truth':

Truth is the pebble in the lake; and however slowly in the present case the circles succeed each other, they will infallibly go on till they overspread the surface. No order of mankind will for ever remain ignorant of the principles of justice, equality and public good. No sooner will they understand them, than they will perceive the coincidence of virtue and public good and private interest: nor will any erroneous establishment be able to support itself against general opinion. In this contest sophistry will vanish and mischievous institutions sink quietly into neglect. Truth will bring down all her forces, mankind will be her army, and oppression, injustice, monarchy and vice will tumble into common ruin.[67]

In this faith it was the warrior duty of the good man to think, for 'No man can be eminently virtuous, who is not accustomed to an extensive range of reflection', and to diffuse thought, for 'The revolutions of states, which a philanthropist would desire to witness, or in which he would willingly co-operate, consist principally in a change of sentiments and dispositions in the members of those states. The true instruments for changing the opinions of men are argument and persuasion.'[68]

In the summer of 1794 Godwin's was the voice Wordsworth most needed to hear. Firstly, it convinced him that by writing, by using his imagination and powers of language, he would be *actively* campaigning, not just for universal suffrage or annual parliaments, but for the wider reign of Truth. Wordsworth now recognized that the duty of 'every enlightened friend of mankind' was to 'let slip no opportunity of explaining and enforcing those general principles of the social order which are applicable to all times and all places; he should diffuse by every method a knowledge of those rules of political justice, from which the farther any government deviates the more effectually must it defeat the object for which government was ordained'.[69] Mankind walked in darkness, but Wordsworth declares, 'I would put into each man's hand a lantern to guide him'.[70] The *Philanthropist* was to be such a lantern.

Secondly, Godwin's overall conception of the progress of Truth eased Wordsworth's perplexities and assisted him to formulate his own interpretation of recent events. In *A Letter to the Bishop of Llandaff* Wordsworth had defended the French Revolution as necessary and implied that a convulsion of the same magnitude would be needed to reform British society. Now, with the Terror fresh in his mind, Wordsworth argues to Mathews that revolutionary violence is the enemy of Truth and that as the 'infatuation, profligacy and extravagance of men in power' seem to be hastening the country towards conflagration, it is more than ever urgent to demonstrate that there is no necessary link 'between justice and the sword'. Wordsworth's declaration, 'I recoil from the bare idea of a revolution', is not, in this context, a retreat, but the first steps of an advance from one who has realized where the real battleground lies.[71]

The scheme for the *Philanthropist* came to nothing.[72] Although Wordsworth hoped to make some money from the journal, he stressed that he could not put any into establishing it and in the letter on 8 June warned

Mathews that he would be unable to go to London to assist in launching the venture. By 1 October, when he offered to accompany Raisley Calvert to Lisbon, he was clearly pulling out altogether and in early November was neither 'much surprized nor mortified' when Mathews told him that he too had withdrawn to take a post as a parliamentary reporter. Planning the journal, however, and formulating his ideas had been of the greatest value. Not only had it enabled him to identify the life of the mind with the cause of good and so recognize a field of endeavour in which he could be of use, it had also led him to a faith which even in current events could discern the irresistible progress of Truth.

Confirmation of this progress came first from France. The execution of the Brissotins on 31 October 1793 had marked the onset of the Terror and the ascendancy of the Robespierrists. A decree of 4 December had concentrated power in the Committee of Public Safety. Counter-revolutionaries, however defined, were executed in large numbers. As Wordsworth put it in *The Prelude*, 'the goaded land waxed mad'. But when Robespierre attacked his enemies on 26 July 1794, demanding yet another purge against subverters of the state, he was already on the defensive. He was proscribed on 27 July and executed the following day.

When the news reached England in August Wordsworth was visiting Dorothy, who was staying with cousins at Rampside, a tiny village at the southernmost tip of Furness. In *The Prelude* Wordsworth relates how finding the grave of William Taylor of Hawkshead School had set him musing on past and present. Perhaps he wondered what his teacher would have thought of his pupil, now a shaken but unrepentant republican. The news that Robespierre was dead, tossed to him by a traveller, transformed his mood:

> Great was my glee of spirit, great my joy
> In vengeance, and eternal justice, thus
> Made manifest: 'Come now, ye golden times',
> Said I, forth-breathing on those open sands
> A hymn of triumph, 'as the morning comes
> Out of the bosom of the night, come ye.
> Thus far our trust is verified: behold,
> They who with clumsy desperation brought
> Rivers of blood, and preached that nothing else
> Could cleanse the Augean stable, by the might
> Of their own helper have been swept away.
> Their madness is declared and visible;
> Elsewhere will safety now be sought, and earth
> March firmly towards righteousness and peace'.

It was the joy not of an English patriot exulting in the tribulations of the enemy, but of an adherent of the French cause, able now to look with 'unabated confidence' towards the future and the progressive liberation of mankind.[73]

Cause for similar rejoicing over events at home occurred later in the year. Throughout 1794 the Pitt government had been moving against radical leaders. On 23 May—the same day that Wordsworth had declared himself one 'of that odious class of men called democrats'—a bill to suspend Habeas Corpus received Royal Assent. In May Thomas Hardy, founder and secretary of the London Corresponding Society, John Thelwall, Horne Tooke, and others were arrested. Thomas Holcroft gave himself up on 7 October and joined the other defendants against whom the Grand Jury of Middlesex had found a true bill on a charge of high treason the previous day.

At the Old Bailey the accused were defended by Thomas Erskine, principally, and the account of how his restrained eloquence and tactical skill saved first Hardy, then Tooke and Thelwall, from the gallows and led to the abandonment of the proceedings against the other nine defendants is still enthralling. But they were defended outside the court no less ably by Godwin. In his *Cursory Strictures* against the charge to the jury delivered by the Lord Chief Justice, Sir James Eyre, Godwin demonstrated in impassioned but always lucid argument that nothing in the indictment could be construed as treason and that, in truth, at 'the most important crisis in the history of English liberty' men were being tried for their lives on 'hypothesis, presumption, prejudication and conjecture'.[74]

To Wordsworth the acquittals between 5 November and 5 December were 'in every point of view . . . interesting to humanity',[75] exemplary proof of Godwin's affirmation at the end of *Political Justice* that 'truth is irresistible'.[76] In a letter to Mathews he continued:

The late occurrences . . . will abate the insolence and presumption of the aristocracy by shewing it that neither the violence, nor the art, of power can crush even an unfriended individual, though engaged in the propagation of doctrines confessedly unpalatable to privilege: and they will force upon the most prejudiced this conclusion that there is some reason in the language of reformers. Furthermore, they will convince bigotted enemies to our present constitution that it contains parts upon which too high a value cannot be set. To every class of men occupied in the correction of abuses it must be an animating reflection that their exertions, so long as they are temperate will be countenanced and protected by the good sense of the country.[77]

Wordsworth was wrong, as government action in the next two years was to prove. For the moment, however, he seemed justified in believing that a great victory for liberty had been won and it was inevitable that he should want to be nearer the centre of political affairs as the tide of progress flowed on.

It is possible that Wordsworth's admission, 'I begin to wish much to be in town',[78] was also connected with continuing anxiety about his own situation. In January 1795 he confessed to Mathews, 'I have lately felt much uneasiness of mind'.[79] As he wrote those words Raisley Calvert was very near to death and that alone was sufficient reason for the uneasiness. But perhaps there was more to it. Viewing recent political events Wordsworth saw cause for optimisim, but looking at his own recent life he saw little for self-satisfaction. Since publishing *An Evening Walk* and *Descriptive Sketches* he had declared himself a friend of liberty, had written *A Letter to the Bishop of Llandaff* and *Salisbury Plain*, and had planned in a radical journal to 'give every additional energy in my power' to foster 'the changes of opinion respecting matters of Government which within these few years have rapidly taken place in the minds of speculative men'.[80] But not a word had been published. While Hardy, Thelwall, Tooke, and Holcroft were on trial for their lives as a result of their public commitment to the cause, he had contributed nothing. Nor had he yet secured by his own efforts the means to be of use. In a recent letter his brother Richard had remarked:

There is one Circumstance which I will mention to you at this time. I might have retired into the Country and I had almost said enjoyed the sweets of retirement and Domestick life if I had only considered my own Interest. However as I have entered the Busy scenes of a Town life I shall I hope pursue them with comfort and credit. I am happy to inform you that my Business encreases daily and altho' our affairs have been peculiarly distressing I hope that from the Industry of ourselves at one time we will enjoy more ease and independence than we have yet experienced.[81]

This is a savage digression in a business letter. Pompous it might be, but the implied rebuke was justified and Wordsworth would have been very thick-skinned not to wince. Annette and Caroline were unprovided for. He still had no employment. Even the unlooked-for boon of Raisley Calvert's bequest could not have been secured without the credit-worthiness of his industrious brother. There was much to cause him 'uneasiness of mind' and to make him aware of the disparity between his optimistic view of the progress of public affairs and what he felt when he considered his own.

Since leaving Cambridge Wordsworth had repeatedly hoped that he would find a way ahead in London. He did so again. Mathews, now reporting for the *Telegraph*, might be able to find him newspaper work and at least there would be the stimulation of being at the centre of politics at a time when, he was convinced, 'things are beginning to turn with respect to the war'.[82] A little over a month after Raisley Calvert's funeral on 12 January 1795 Wordsworth was back in London.

Within weeks of arriving in the capital Wordsworth was at the centre of non-parliamentary political life. On 27 February 1795, he took tea at the home of William Frend in a group that included Thomas Holcroft, John Tweddell, James Losh, William Godwin, and George Dyer, amongst others. How he came to be invited is not known, but it was possibly through Losh, or more probably through Mathews, who had made Godwin's acquaintance the previous December.

Every one of these men was a radical. Holcroft had been one of the accused in the Treason Trials and though released without trial on 1 December 1794 was now a marked man. Losh was, like Holcroft, a member of the Society for Constitutional Information, and had known Godwin since early 1794. Tweddell had welcomed the French Revolution at its outset in a speech in Trinity College chapel, Cambridge, and now 'took every opportunity of speaking his sentiments most freely, and, to those who watched the signs of the times, most indiscreetly'.[83] Dyer, formerly of Emmanuel College, was author of *Complaints of the Poor People of England* and the friend who had introduced Coleridge to Godwin in December 1794. Their host, William Frend, deprived of his Fellowship and banished from Cambridge, was now an active member of the London Corresponding Society.[84]

The most famous of the group, and intellectually the most formidable, was Godwin. In *Political Justice* he had, in Hazlitt's words, 'carried with him all of the most sanguine and fearless understandings of the time'.[85] His novel, *Things as They Are; or, The Adventures of Caleb Williams*, had caught the imagination of many readers by the relentlessness of its 'general review of the modes of domestic and unrecorded despotism, by which man becomes the destroyer of man'.[86] It was the *Cursory Strictures*, however, that had made him the hero of the hour. When Horne Tooke kissed Godwin's hand, 'vowing that he could do no less by the hand that had given existence to that production',[87] he was acknowledging publicly what all radicals believed, that Godwin had done almost as much as Erskine to save the Treason Trial defendants from death.

Although he had associated with radicals ever since 1789, Godwin was an independent, somewhat lonely figure, who was later to complain that he had been misunderstood and abandoned.[88] Unitarians such as Frend, Dyer, and Coleridge baulked at his atheism and Thelwall quarrelled bitterly with him in November 1795 over his principled opposition to pressure groups such as the London Corresponding Society and to political lecturing.[89] For the moment, though, Godwin was the focus of admiring attention, and, after meeting him at Frend's house, Wordsworth eagerly sought to know him better. He called on him the next morning and in March and April, when he was actually living in the same street as Godwin, he paid him five further visits.[90]

In public Godwin was notoriously 'the most diffuse and tiresome of speakers' and he hated to speak to an unwilling listener, but he had a passion for what he called 'colloquial discussion' and Wordsworth was not an unwilling listener.[91] What they talked about is not known, but one may conjecture. Godwin was working on the second edition of *Political Justice* and may have tested ideas on his visitor. A second edition of *Caleb Williams* was also in preparation and they may have discussed how far the novel succeeded in its aim 'to expose the evils which arise out of the present system of civilised society'.[92] In the aftermath of the Treason Trials the London Corresponding Society was in crisis and Godwin may have impressed on Wordsworth his conviction that organizations and mass meetings such as the one planned for 29 June were alien to the pursuit of Truth: 'Human beings should meet together, not to enforce, but to enquire'.[93]

Godwin undoubtedly influenced Wordsworth's thought—his next poem, *Adventures on Salisbury Plain*, is his most Godwinian work—but it is also possible that, very indirectly, he had a further influence on Wordsworth's life by introducing him to Basil Montagu. Montagu, whom Godwin had met in 1794, was the illegitimate son of the fourth Earl of Sandwich. He had married to his father's displeasure in 1791, but his wife had died in 1793, leaving him with a son, also called Basil, to bring up as best he could in his chambers in Lincoln's Inn. Wordsworth lived with Montagu at some point during this time in London and what they had in common—a Cambridge past, mutual friends, uncertain futures—cemented a friendship so precious to Montagu that he declared later, 'I consider having met William Wordsworth the most fortunate event of my life'.[94]

Through Montagu Wordsworth also made a further lifelong friend, Francis Wrangham, another liberal-minded Cambridge man who was now curate at Cobham in Surrey. Much later in life Wordsworth despaired of Wrangham's verses and is recorded as having been much amused when a friend at Rydal Mount extemporized a song:

> And the Muses in Chorus
> Sing, Wrangham don't bore us,
> Wrangham don't bore us.[95]

But on a visit to him in July 1795 he recognized a serious poet and had soon made plans with him—never fulfilled—for the joint composition of a topical satire.

In this widening circle of friends, all of radical persuasion, Wordsworth certainly found the intellectual stimulation he was looking for. But fundamentally his position since coming to London had not altered. He still had no home; without employment he was using up what money he had; Dorothy was once again reduced to travelling from one family of friends to another; literary composition was at a standstill. It is not surprising that he closed without hesitation on an offer that seemed to resolve most of these difficulties.

Through Montagu and Wrangham Wordsworth had met John Frederick and Azariah Pinney, sons of a very wealthy Bristol merchant and sugar plantation owner, John Pretor Pinney. John Frederick, the elder brother, was studying at Lincoln's Inn; Azariah had been a pupil of Wrangham's at Cobham, but was now also in London. Wordsworth's impact on them must have been considerable and immediate, for his needs evoked the same quality of generosity that both Calverts had shown the year before. By late July it had been agreed that Wordsworth should become tenant of Racedown Lodge, a house that John Pinney senior owned in North Dorset, and that he should occupy it rent free, on the understanding that he would accommodate the Pinneys and their friends on occasional visits. Their offer was also designed to help Montagu. He later recalled that seeing him 'perplexed and misled by passions wild and strong', Wordsworth had 'endeavoured to eradicate my faults and to encourage my good disposi-tions'.[96] Whatever this means, it is clear that Montagu thought Words-worth a humane influence and so it was also agreed that Dorothy should be summoned from the North and that together, for £50 a year, the Wordsworths would look after little Basil. From all points of view the scheme looked promising. Montagu would be relieved of a burden; the child would benefit from being out of the city; Dorothy would be '*doing some-thing*', freed at last from the 'painful idea that one's existence is of very little use'; and Wordsworth would have, Dorothy forecast, 'such opportunities of studying as . . . will be not only advantageous to his mind but his purse'.[97]

Had he known that his sons had assured the prospective tenant of Racedown that he need not pay any rent John Pinney senior might have been less cordial, but as it was he invited Wordsworth to wait for Dorothy at his house in Bristol. It was a generous offer, which gave Wordsworth after his arrival about 21 August an introduction to the circles of commerce and property which had made Bristol the second most flourishing city in the country. Not surprisingly, however, he also used the time to seek out some of the figures who were prominent in the city's no less vigorous intellectual life. He met the bookseller and publisher Joseph Cottle, who, priding himself on his eye for literary promise, offered Wordsworth ten guineas for a current work, almost certainly the Juvenalian satire projected with Wrangham.[98] He met Robert Southey, who, shying away as Wordsworth had done from 'starving in creditable celibacy upon 40 pounds a year'[99] in holy orders, had already at age 21 passed through his period of radical poetry and politics, ardent adherence to Godwin, and a fantastic scheme for the foundation of an ideal community in America, and was now floundering, looking for prospects of a more secure way of life. Mulling over Wordsworth's attempts to start the satire, Southey, never lacking in fluency or invention, contributed what Wordsworth later admitted were the two best lines in it.[100] More important, sometime between late August and late September 1795—it is impossible to be more precise—he met Samuel Taylor Coleridge.

How this meeting took place is not clear. Very late in life Wordsworth recalled that he had met both Coleridge and Southey 'in a lodging in Bristol', whereas Lady Beaumont in 1810 said that it was 'at a Political Debating Society where on one occasion Wordsworth spoke with so much force & eloquence that Coleridge sought to know him'.[101] Either, in fact, might have sought out the other. Early in 1795 Coleridge, then aged 22, had delivered three political lectures in Bristol in spite of the attempts of what he called 'uncouth and unbrained Automata' to gag him.[102] News of the stir he had caused had reached his friend George Dyer in February and through him the rest of the London circle. Possibly Wordsworth had actually read *A Moral and Political Lecture*, whose eloquent analysis of the current scene and denunciation of 'Those two massy Pillars of Oppression's Temple, Monarchy and Aristocracy',[103] would only have made him the more anxious to meet such an active friend of liberty.

Coleridge, on the other hand, had reasons for wanting to meet Wordsworth unconnected with any skill he might have displayed at a political debate. As a poet he had straightaway recognized the genuine merit of *An Evening Walk* and had quoted from it in his own poetry.[104] Whenever and wherever their first meeting took place, the new acquaintance pleased them both. On one occasion Wordsworth read his *Salisbury Plain* with such an impact that Coleridge could claim in 1817, 'while memory lasts I shall hardly forget the sudden effect produced on my mind'.[105] Wordsworth's contemporary verdict was given on the man—'his talent appears to me very great'.[106] But when Wordsworth left Bristol for Racedown with Dorothy on 26 September what neither he nor Coleridge can have foreseen was that a friendship had begun which was profoundly to affect their lives as private individuals and to determine their destinies as poets.

# 1795–1797

PLACE-NAMES are used in an interesting way in most accounts of Wordsworth's poetic development. Writers on, say, Dickens or Yeats, when identifying moments of artistic growth, refer to books—to the transitional form, for example, of *Martin Chuzzlewit*, or to the self-conscious maturity of *Responsibilities*. Lovers of Wordsworth might do likewise, pointing to *An Evening Walk*, or *Lyrical Ballads*, or *The Prelude*, as key writings, but they are at least as likely to mark out the poet's spiritual odyssey by referring to 'Windy Brow', 'Racedown', 'Alfoxden', 'Dove Cottage', 'Rydal Mount'. These were places, it is understood, in which self-discovery or achievement or consolidation occurred, whose particular nature, which may or may not be in evidence in specific poems, can be evoked by naming that one special place.

In using this topographical currency readers are, of course, following Wordsworth's lead. *The Prelude* substantiates its account of the poet's spiritual journey, its record of awakening, crisis, recovery, and maturity in the innermost world of the mind and heart, by locating it on the map. That Hawkshead, Cambridge, London, Paris, function within traditional poetic usage in which city and country, crowds and solitudes, carry well-understood literary meanings does not alter the fact that these places of the mind were real places as well.

Racedown has functioned almost too perfectly as a real and emblematic place. The house where Wordsworth and Dorothy lived from late September 1795 stands beside the road from Crewkerne to Lyme Regis in Dorset. It was and is an isolated spot. Alfoxden, where they moved to in July 1797, is folded in amongst little Somerset hills, in a more friendly landscape where no one is very far from a neighbour or an inn. The two houses, and the move to one and then the other, seem to demand figurative interpretation. At Racedown, so *The Prelude* suggests, Wordsworth retired from the activity and bewildering stimulation of the London and Bristol circles into the lonely abysses of his own mind, whence he was slowly drawn back into the world by the influence of Nature and the loving ministrations of

Dorothy. This is the pattern offered by Books X and XI of the *1805 Prelude* and accepted by Mary Moorman when she sums up Dorothy's role: 'To bring him back again to his "first love" was both her prayer and her task; she felt that the life he had been leading in London was not his true life; if once his communion with Nature could be restored, he would once more follow his true vocation. And this was what happened at Racedown.'[1] But this is too neat. Wordsworth's 'crisis' was not unique; it was not resolved by abandoning a 'false' life for a 'true' one; its relation to his discovery of his 'true vocation' is unclear; other agencies as well as Dorothy and Nature were at work.

## (2)

When Wordsworth had settled at Windy Brow in the spring of 1794 he had found himself compelled to order the fragments of his recent experience by working on *Salisbury Plain* and the revision of *An Evening Walk*. At Racedown the pattern at first was repeated. After only one month there he was able to tell Wrangham that he had made to *Salisbury Plain* 'alterations and additions so material as that it may be looked on almost as another work'.[2] But this description must not be misconstrued. Considerable changes to the structure of the poem do make *Adventures on Salisbury Plain* a more sophisticated work than *Salisbury Plain*, but it is not a break with it or with the main current of Wordsworth's recent thought, but rather an embodiment of what reading, intellectual contact, and personal observation had given him since his return from France.

It would be surprising had it been otherwise. Political events had demonstrated that Wordsworth's rejoicing over the outcome of the 1794 Treason Trials had been premature. Things had not begun 'to turn with respect to the war', nor had the Pitt government been forced to the 'conclusion that there is some reason in the language of reformers'. On the contrary, the suspension of Habeas Corpus had not been lifted and during his first months at Racedown what Wordsworth had called the 'violence [and] the art of power' demonstrated in the negation of this symbol of human rights had strengthened its hold on those 'engaged in the propagation of doctrines confessedly unpalatable to privilege'.[3]

On 26 October a huge crowd in Copenhagen House Fields in Islington had been addressed by John Thelwall and other leading figures of the London Corresponding Society. It was a political act, deliberately organized just before the beginning of a new session of Parliament to voice popular demands being ignored at Westminster. On 29 October the king's coach in procession to the state opening was surrounded by a crowd shouting 'No Pitt, No War, Bread, Bread', and a missile shattered one of the windows. A connection between these two events was readily made. Although a culprit, one Kyd Wake, was arrested for the actual assault, the government seized the outrage as a pretext for action against the disaffected more generally. By early November a Royal Proclamation had outlined the Treasonable Practices Bill, which extended the definition of treason, and the Seditious Meetings Bill, which, with much parade of distinction between legal and illegal meetings, effectively subjected all debating clubs, lectures, and one-off protest meetings to the discretion of local magistrates.[4] Liberals of every hue united in furious protest and Wordsworth, though isolated in Racedown, was well aware of this new phase in the onslaught against liberty and of the dangerously exposed role played in the resistance to it by his new friend Coleridge. On 26 November 1795 Azariah Pinney sent him a letter in which he cut short an account of his brother's love affair to report on 'that fearful cloud, ominous of destruction that hangs over the Political Horizon'. Two meetings at Bristol Guildhall are described in which Coleridge was eloquent in demands for a petition to be carried to Westminster. If such remonstrances are not attended to, says Pinney, 'I dread the consequences—the murmurs of the people will for a time be suppressed by the military forces, but whenever circumstances shall favour resistance, their complaints will burst forth with the whirlwind's fury'.[5] The petitions were disregarded and on 18 December the 'gagging acts' became law.

In his letter Pinney asked Wordsworth to 'let me know what you think', but added at once, 'I can almost anticipate your sentiments'. It is a revealing remark. Clearly in Pinney's eyes Wordsworth was a committed radical, one of the London group who, whatever their intellectual divergencies and personal antipathies, would be certain to react as one to this further evidence of the contumely of those in power. But Wordsworth's radicalism was sustained quite as much by what he saw in his rural seclusion as by events in London. It did not need an enquiry concerning political justice to convince anyone that the hardships to be endured in a long war pressed more severely on the poor and weak than on the rich and powerful. The winter of 1794–5 had been exceptionally hard. Throughout the following year prices had risen and food riots had broken out.[6] In his 'On the Present War' Coleridge had inveighed against seeing 'Over a recruiting place . . . pieces of Beef hung up to attract the half-famished Mechanic'.[7] Now at Racedown Wordsworth saw for himself. He lamented that the 'country people are wretchedly poor; ignorant and overwhelmed with every vice that usually attends ignorance in that class, viz—lying and picking and stealing &c. &c.'.[8]

This conjunction of national political events and his own local observation intensified Wordsworth's sense of outrage and moved him once again to poetry. In the *Imitation of Juvenal* the corruptions of power and wealth are attacked in savage couplets which expose both the degradation of the urban élite—its gaming, sexual profligacy, stupidity—and the system of tyrannical power needed to preserve its existence.[9] But although the poem is worth much more attention than it has yet received, and Wordsworth was pleased enough with it to hope that it would soon be published, it was not completed and one may surmise that it faltered precisely because its intensity depends so much on the narrowness of its focus on people whom, essentially, Wordsworth did not care enough about even to denounce. *Adventures on Salisbury Plain*, on the other hand, makes the connection between peasants living in hovels 'not at all beyond what might be expected in savage life'[10] and society as a whole, in a way that reveals the genuineness of Wordsworth's humanitarian concern and the intensity of his anger.

(3)

Returning to the fair copy of *Salisbury Plain*, made when he and Dorothy were last living together at Windy Brow, Wordsworth began to draft new lines.[11] At first he tinkered with the poem, but as he worked on the relationship between the traveller and the woman, and especially on a passage which offers words of comfort, Wordsworth realized that here was the potential for a much more complex and rewarding structure. *Salisbury Plain* had sandwiched an illustrative episode between opening and closing declamations that pointed up its significance. *Adventures on Salisbury Plain* works entirely through interlocking human stories. It begins with the traveller, now a sailor, meeting a decrepit soldier who is struggling across Salisbury Plain to reach his poverty-stricken daughter. After helping him the sailor presses on and his solitary state is now accounted for. He is an outlaw. After war service he had returned home only to be press-ganged into a further tour of duty. Denied any bounty, and so penniless, he had murdered and robbed, hoping to provide for his family, but had fled from their sight. He meets the terrified woman sheltering from the storm and listens to her history of how she lost her husband and children in the war. Morning comes and, moving on, they stumble on a terrible scene, in which a man has just struck his infant son to the ground. The sailor again gives comfort and they descend into a valley. Encountering a sick woman, who has been driven from parish to parish by uncaring overseers, the sailor now discovers the double significance of his crime. Not only has he shed innocent blood, but he has also ruined his family, for the woman is his wife, hounded out of her home by suspicion that her husband was the guilty man. The sailor breaks down, begs forgiveness, and gives himself up to the law. At the close of the poem his body is hanging on a gibbet.

A synopsis like this mangles any poem, but it is necessary if the characteristics of *Adventures on Salisbury Plain* are to be brought out. It indicates, firstly, the relentlessness of the poem's onslaught on the 'calamities of war as they affect individuals', which, Wordsworth told Wrangham, was one of its objects.[12] The soldier is sick and in pain, his feet half bare and his clothes ragged. The sailor was press-ganged and denied reward. The woman he meets is a soldier's widow, a homeless, penniless vagrant, haunted by the memory of how

> in one remorseless year,
> Husband and children! one by one, by sword
> And ravenous plague, all perished . . .[13]

The synopsis suggests, too, how tightly Wordsworth deploys incidents, to given an alternating movement, in which extreme suffering caused by man's inhumanity to man is countered by the comfort given by these particular individuals to one another.

Such a synopsis of the 'plot' cannot indicate the two aspects of the poem which are really of most interest. The first is Wordsworth's use of landscape. In *Salisbury Plain* Wordsworth had insisted on the emblematic significance of the huge waste by reference to savage man, Druids, and spectral visitants. But in revision these are mostly abandoned and images of the plain work unobtrusively to sustain the changing moods of the narrative sequence. No suggestion emerges, however, that the landscape itself has any meaning or value. In a later poem, *The Ruined Cottage*, the Pedlar directs the poet to draw on the 'natural comfort' available to those who can read the landscape with tutored eye.[14] In *Adventures on Salisbury Plain* the similar phrase 'natural sympathy' refers only to the human bond created between the sailor and the woman.

The second interesting feature is the resourcefulness with which Wordsworth develops what are stock elements of contemporary protest literature. Socially conscious poetry was commonplace. Magazines regularly stirred the sympathies with laments for or by widows, prostitutes, and the poor.[15] Wordsworth knew and admired John Langhorne's *The Country Justice*, in which the brutality of Poor Law officers is contrasted with the instinctive compassion of a man who is a robber.[16] Southey's *Botany Bay Eclogues* paralleled Wordsworth's attempt to 'expose the vices of the penal law', [17] and Joseph Fawcett's widely and favourably reviewed poem *The Art of War* had impressed him.[18] Even Joseph Cottle had pointed out in the Preface to his *Poems* (1795) that, by flashing on the imagination a specific scene, poetry could make an effective protest against the horror of war.[19] What makes Wordsworth's poem special is that disparate elements of protest are fused by one controlling vision.

It is a very dark one. At an early stage of composition Wordsworth tried to draft a stanza in which the sailor would comfort the woman with talk 'Of social orders all-protecting plan / Delusion fond . . . / And of the general care man pays to man'.[20] This 'Delusion fond' is torn apart in the poem. The 'slaves of Office' spurn the sailor's just claim for reward; the aged soldier is an outcast in the country he has served; the soldier's widow is penniless; the sailor's wife is denied parish relief. In *Political Justice* Godwin had asked in his chapter 'Of the Application of Coercion', 'Who is it that in his sober reason will pretend to assign the motives that influenced me in any article of my conduct, and upon them found a grave, perhaps a capital penalty against me?'[21] *Adventures on Salisbury Plain* demonstrates what this means in the individual case. In the 'violated name' of Justice the law condemns and hangs the sailor, for the law can take no account of the fact that his is essentially 'a heart to life's best ends inclined',[22] or that in committing the murder he was driven by intolerable need, or that what was then his crime had earlier been honoured as his military duty.

In such a society human beings can do nothing more than foster kindliness to one another when they can. Faced with the poor family on the heath, the trembling mother, the bleeding child, and the blaspheming father, the sailor declares the truth for all of them:

> 'Tis a bad world, and hard is the world's law;
> Each prowls to strip his brother of his fleece;
> Much need have ye that time more closely draw
> The bond of nature, all unkindness cease,
> And that among so few there still be peace:
> Else can ye hope but with such num'rous foes
> Your pains shall ever with your years increase.[23]

But even as he is disclosing 'these homely truths' his wife is dying because of what he has done, and the discovery of this is too much for him. The sailor welcomes death and the poem closes:

> They left him hung on high in iron case,
> And dissolute men, unthinking and untaught,
> Planted their festive booths beneath his face;
> And to that spot, which idle thousands sought,
> Women and children were by fathers brought . . .[24]

When he published a revised version of the poem in 1842, *Guilt and Sorrow: or, Incidents upon Salisbury Plain*, the elderly Wordsworth blenched from the horror of the last stanza and changed it.[25] But in 1795 the body turning in the wind seemed an appropriate image with which to end a poem in which occurrences in common life in contemporary society match the darkest imaginings of Gothic fiction.

(4)

Wordsworth had decided to publish *Adventures on Salisbury Plain* if he 'could get anything for it',[26] and clearly the most likely source of money was the ebullient Cottle. When Cottle made him a present of Southey's *Joan of Arc* Wordsworth replied in January 1796 with a promise of his own poem 'in a few days', although it is not clear whether this was a bait or in accordance with some agreement reached when they had first met in Bristol. On 6 March Azariah Pinney, who had joined his brother already staying in Racedown, carried the manuscript to Bristol, and reported on the twenty-fifth:

I delivered it on my arrival here to Cottle and requested that Coleridge would inspect it, which he appears to have done with considerable attention, for I understand he has interleaved it with white paper to mark down whatever may strike him as worthy your notice . . . You may expect to hear from him soon, but lest this should come to your hand before any communication from him; I have the pleasure to inform you that he feels so lively an interest to bring forward so valuable a Poem (as he terms it) that he assures me his Bookseller will assist him in such manner in the publication that he can secure you from every Expence without risque to himself, and you will receive the profits that may arise after the expenses are paid.[27]

Not for the last time Coleridge was too sanguine about publishers and money. Although Pinney promised James Tobin on 12 April that he would see the poem in print 'within the duration of a few Weeks', in reality nothing was happening. Cottle had already lost money on Coleridge's periodical *The Watchman*, and as for Coleridge, he was so stretched keeping that doomed project going that he can have had no time to promote even a poem in which he had expressed such interest. He sent the manuscript to Lamb, who read it 'not without delight' and promised to return it to Wordsworth when he was next in London.[28] By June the manuscript was back in its author's hands— unpublished.

Wordsworth's reaction to this missed opportunity is not known, but there are a number of reasons for surmising that he may have become indifferent to the poem's fate almost as soon as he sent it off with Pinney. He does not express annoyance in any of his surviving letters, nor does anyone else suggest that he was put out. Relations with Cottle remained cordial, while friendship with Coleridge and Lamb deepened. Most important of all, other evidence indicates that in every way, both intellectual and personal, Wordsworth was moving on so rapidly that *Adventures on Salisbury Plain* could not but seem a memorial to a time gone by rather than a vital concern of the present.

The primary evidence can be stated easily enough. After completing *Adventures on Salisbury Plain* Wordsworth worked only fitfully on the

*Imitation of Juvenal* and on 21 March declared to Mathews, 'As to writing it is out of the question'.[29] One lyric, *Address to the Ocean*, was published in the local *Weekly Entertainer* for November 1796, probably in emulation of Coleridge and Southey, whose work had recently featured there, but it is a poor piece, hardly above the level of other verse in this dreary magazine.[30] Experiments in versification, in which the same narrative is told in blank verse and in Spenserian stanzas, and a fragmentary *Gothic Tale* seem to be a poet's five-finger exercises on ideas suggested by *Adventures on Salisbury Plain*.[31] But when Wordsworth did end this barren spell he did so spectacularly. In October 1796 he was, Dorothy said, 'ardent in the composition of a tragedy',[32] and by the spring of the following year he had completed a five-act blank verse drama which demonstrated in its successfully realized formal ambition, and in the profundity of its themes, that Wordsworth's recent months had been anything but barren. By comparison with *The Borderers*, *Adventures on Salisbury Plain* seems very limited. The poem closes a movement in Wordsworth's intellectual life. The play begins the exploration of themes which are to absorb him till his death.

How did such a breakthrough occur? That is what is not clear. As Wordsworth looked back in *The Prelude* over this period of his life he was certain that then had been his trial and deliverance. From the high ground of a further eight or nine years of artistic achievement and personal happiness, he could see that his months at Racedown had been crucial in his development towards becoming the poet of *Lyrical Ballads*, *The Prelude*, and *The Recluse*. Accordingly, in the retrospective narrative all local detail and peripheral matters are stripped away to dramatize what he thought essentially had happened. In Book X Wordsworth presents himself as torn by conflicting emotions as the French Revolution pursued its uncertain course, increasingly betraying its origin in ideals, and as at home political repression revealed the intellectual and moral bankruptcy of those in power. Feeling that nothing was certain, that no ideal or faith or traditional order could be accepted without enquiry, he took, he says 'the knife in hand' and

> Endeavoured with my best of skill to probe
> The living body of society
> Even to the heart

What followed this dissection of the living body is described in such marvellous verse, in which the tortuous syntax and play of rhythms seem cumulatively to enact the poet's self-destructive tumult, that it deserves to be quoted in full:

> Thus I fared,
> Dragging all passions, notions, shapes of faith,

> Like culprits to the bar, suspiciously
> Calling the mind to establish in plain day
> Her titles and her honours, now believing,
> Now disbelieving, endlessly perplexed
> With impulse, motive, right and wrong, the ground
> Of moral obligation—what the rule
> And what the sanction—till, demanding proof,
> And seeking it in everything, I lost
> All feeling of conviction, and in fine,
> Sick, wearied out with contrarieties,
> Yielded up moral questions in despair,
> And for my future studies, as the sole
> Employment of the inquiring faculty,
> Turned towards mathematics, and their clear
> And solid evidence.[33]

From this hopeless quest for Truth—hopeless because mistaken in its object and false in its method—he was, Wordsworth says, rescued by Dorothy, who 'in the midst of all, preserved me still / A poet', and by 'Nature's self', who

>                                through the weary labyrinth
> Conducted me again to open day,
> Revived the feelings of my earlier life,
> Gave me that strength and knowledge full of peace,
> Enlarged, and never more to be disturbed.[34]

In the context of *The Prelude* this account seems absolutely convincing (setting aside the persuasive power of blank verse as subtle as Shakespeare's or Milton's), because it clinches the exposition of the poem's dominant message—that Nature had chosen Wordsworth to be her prophet, that he had *always* been potentially the great poet he had become, and that bewilderment and crisis had only temporarily obscured him 'as a clouded not a waning moon'.[35] To readers of Carlyle's *Sartor Resartus*, John Stuart Mill's *Autobiography*, Tennyson's *In Memoriam*, or Mark Rutherford's *Autobiography* and *Deliverance*, Wordsworth's narrative of his descent into and recovery from the abyss describes a familiar progress, and translation into twentieth-century terms has made it more familiar with talk of Wordsworth's 'nervous breakdown'. But as an account of the Racedown period it is too stark, too confident in its elisions and retrospective patterning. Faced with Wordsworth's spiritual autobiography in *The Prelude*, of course, one can hardly claim access to an alternative 'truth' about this time. What one can say is that in 1796 the movement of Wordsworth's life was not clearly defined and that from the many forces operating on him it was impossible then to distinguish the long-lasting from the transitory. But the essential proposition of *The Prelude* cannot be gainsaid. During his time at Racedown Wordsworth did change, or mature, or develop, or whatever inadequate word can be used to describe the moment in which someone seems to become more completely self-assured. By the late spring of 1797 he was, according to Dorothy, as 'cheerful as any body can be . . . the life of the whole house'.[36] He was, moreover, a man who was drawing others to him. No longer an acolyte to another man's system or an aspirant for a place in the metropolitan world, Wordsworth was beginning to exploit his own intellectual resources and to mark out his own field of action.

(5)

A month after settling in at Racedown Wordsworth begged Mathews to order him 'immediately six pairs of shoes 4 of the very strongest kind double soles and upper leathers and 2 common London street shoes'.[37] In assessing the various factors in Wordsworth's life at this time it would be easy to underestimate the significance of these shoes. At last Wordsworth and Dorothy were back together in the country, and so although Joseph Gill the caretaker did his share in the garden and Peggy Marsh, who joined them as a servant, assisted them in washing, cooking, and all household tasks, they had to rely on their own energies for work and pleasure. Crewkerne, the postal town, was seven miles away. Lyme Regis, to which Wordsworth walked in late October 1795 to look up Nicholas Leader, a member of the Mathews, Godwin, Montagu circle, was, as he pointed out with self-congratulation to the city-bound Mathews, 'at least eight miles and a half from Racedown'.[38] Nearby hills Pilsdon Pen and Lewesdon Hill were explored, the latter probably with particular pleasure after they had read William Crowe's poem *Lewesdon Hill*, which Azariah Pinney sent them on 20 November.[39] Wordsworth had to work in the garden 'hewing wood and rooting up hedges', while Dorothy indoors was occupied with washing, cooking, shirt-making, and prolonging the life of old clothes.[40] The Pinney brothers stayed as paying guests on and off between 2 January and 6 March 1796, and after riding, hunting, and coursing with them, Azariah Pinney reports, Wordsworth's 'usual appetite shewed itself at the dining Table'.[41]

Throughout this period Wordsworth and Dorothy were, moreover, learning what it means to be parents. In months little Basil Montagu, who had been 'extremely petted from indulgence and weakness of body; and perpetually disposed to cry', was transformed into 'a lusty, blooming, fearless boy', judged by Dorothy to be 'the most contented child I ever saw'.[42] It was done, she told Jane Marshall, now a mother herself, by a system 'so simple that in this age of systems you will hardly be likely to follow it':

We teach him nothing at present but what he learns from the evidence of his senses. He has an insatiable curiosity which we are always careful to satisfy to the best of our ability. It is directed to everything he sees, the sky, the fields, trees, shrubs, corn, the making of tools, carts, &c &c &c. He knows his letters, but we have not attempted any further step in the path of *book learning*. Our grand study has been to make him *happy* . . .[43]

Above all other influences of this kind in importance, perhaps, is the fact that for twelve months Wordsworth shared every part of his life with Dorothy, who was happier than she had ever been in what she later, significantly, called 'the first home I had',[44] and from November 1796 to June 1797 with Mary Hutchinson as well. Mary, whom Dorothy had last seen in April the previous year at her brother Tom's farm at Sockburn, had been nursing her sister Peggy, who was dying of consumption, and she needed to recover from the strain. She entered completely into the household—'we are', Dorothy exulted, 'as happy as human beings can be'.[45] It was an extraordinary prefiguring of the future, as Wordsworth sat round the table with the sister who was never to live apart from him again and the woman he was to marry in 1802. Together with shared memories of the North and childhood experiences, they re-established a sense of continuity, which was strong enough to incorporate the knowledge of Annette. One letter, from half a dozen sent, did get through to remind Wordsworth of responsibilities, but it was a reminder of the past, no longer a real factor in the present.[46]

(6)

Wordsworth did not spend the whole of 1796 at Racedown. From 1 June to 9 July he was in London. Here he met Charles Lamb and recovered the manuscript of *Adventures on Salisbury Plain* and once more mixed with the Godwin circle. On 7 June he and one of the Pinney brothers called on the philosopher and later had supper with him at Montagu's. On the eighteenth Montagu, a devout Godwinian, was again host to a larger group— Wordsworth, Godwin, James or John Tobin, and John Stoddart, described by Lamb as a 'cold hearted well bred conceited disciple of Godwin'.[47] The following day Wordsworth, Stoddart, and Godwin again took supper at Lincoln's Inn. A week later on 25 June Wordsworth, James or John Tobin, Godwin, and Robert Allen, a friend of Lamb, Coleridge, and Southey and currently very close to Stoddart (which Lamb asserted 'does him no good'),[48] met again over supper at Stoddart's.

There was much to talk about—the abortive overtures for peace made to the French early in 1796 and the subsequent reaffirmation of the government's determination to prosecute the war; the effect at home of the 'gagging acts'; the fortunes of the radical cause, now being promoted most visibly in the lecturing and journalism of John Thelwall. But there can be little doubt that amongst these friends Godwin himself and his views would have been the focus of conversation. He had brought out a second edition of *Caleb Williams*, including the preface prudently suppressed in the first,[49] but the changes to the novel were slight compared to those made for the new edition of *Political Justice*, in which Godwin demonstrated that his work was not a statement of the Truth but a genuine *Enquiry*. Early positions on the importance of pleasure and the place of feeling in virtuous action, on the relation between self-love and general benevolence, on the essential doctrine of perfectability, had all been subjected to Godwin's own critique.[50] The group might have discussed how the changes affected the strictures levelled against *Political Justice* in the new liberal *Monthly Magazine*, where 'The Enquirer' (William Enfield) had recently asked, 'Is Private Affection inconsistent with Universal Benevolence?'[51] Godwin's current thinking on the pursuit of Truth must also have been a talking point, not least because it was more easily grasped than philosophical distinctions. In the second edition of *Political Justice* Godwin had declared that 'Truth dwells with contemplation. We can seldom make much progress in the business of disentangling error and delusion, but in sequestered privacy, or in the tranquil interchange of sentiments that takes place between two persons.'[52] In reality Godwin had always believed this, but to Thelwall at least, who quarrelled bitterly with him, it looked like a retreat into political quietism.[53]

Eighteen months before, discussions like this had fired Wordsworth with a passion that had still been ablaze as he composed *Adventures on Salisbury Plain* in November 1795. But what had then answered his needs clearly did so no longer. Wordsworth's response to the second edition of *Political Justice*, sent by Montagu, had been: 'I expect to find the work much improved. I cannot say that I have been encouraged in this hope by the perusal of the second preface, which is all I have yet looked into. Such a piece of barbarous writing I have not often seen. It contains scarce one sentence decently written.'[54] This is quite extraordinary. Godwin's Preface, which is perfectly well written, is simply an explanation of why he thought revision necessary and in what sections it is most obvious. Perhaps Wordsworth reacted to its egotism, as he certainly did to the outrageous self-regard of Southey's preface to *Joan of Arc*, which made him declare its author 'a coxcomb'.[55] Perhaps Godwin's breakdown of topics such as 'Of Personal Virtue and Duty', 'Of Rights', 'Of Obedience', and his formidable 'Summary of Principles' suddenly seemed wearisome to one who had been exposed to pamphlet warfare on similar topics ever since undergraduate days. Maybe Godwin's conversation no longer impressed him. Every time you make an assertion, said Lamb, 'Professor Godwin' wants 'explanations, translations, limitations'.[56] Possibly Wordsworth even ploughed through the revised *Political Justice* and found it rebarbative. Whatever the reason, it is clear that Wordsworth's response to Godwin and his work now converged with the current of his own reading and speculations. In *The Borderers* at the end of 1796 Godwinian thought is not the shaping model, as it had been for *Adventures on Salisbury Plain*, but the catalyst for a critique of the tendency of all abstract reasoning.

(7)

Wordsworth may not have got beyond the Preface to the second edition of *Political Justice*, but throughout his stay at Racedown he was reading a great deal else. The London friends who prophesied that he would turn into a cabbage from too much anxiety about cultivating them could not have been more mistaken.[57] The library at Racedown Lodge was astonishingly large for a tenanted house—over 300 titles of history, biography, poetry, philosophy, and theology—and the Wordsworths revelled in it.[58] Even during the visit of the Pinney brothers early in 1796 reading was not abandoned, though 'we have not got on', Dorothy wrote, 'with our usual regularity'.[59] In the letter to Mathews already quoted, in which Wordsworth declared writing out of the question, it is striking that the alternative he mentions to writing is not an outdoor pursuit, but reading. With the Pinneys' departure, 'I have *returned*', Wordsworth said, 'to my books'.[60] He borrowed books from Azariah Pinney, solicited them from Mathews, received them solicited or not from Cottle and Losh, and made efforts to recover his own collection left in Montagu's chambers. He begged for a London newspaper. It is as if Wordsworth were anxious not to be cut off and determined to gather to himself a rich intellectual resource.

What Wordsworth read is uncertain. He did not keep a commonplace book and so, tantalized by the surviving catalogue of the Racedown library, one can only wonder whether he now read Clarendon's *History of the Rebellion*, or the treatise that so profoundly influenced Coleridge, Cudworth's *True Intellectual System of the Universe*, or Ray's *Wisdom of God in the Works of Creation*, or whether he turned more often to Cicero, Pliny, Ovid, Seneca, Virgil, or Bacon, Beaumont and Fletcher, Cowley, Denham, Dryden, Oldham, Prior, and Waller. With only 'winter occupations books, solitude and the fire-side . . . we are never dull',[61] wrote Dorothy, and surely the Racedown copies of *Gulliver's Travels* and *Joseph Andrews* contributed to this contentment. Wordsworth made a point of mentioning to Mathews the Italian authors represented in the library, including Machiavelli and Boccaccio, and later told him that under his tutelage Dorothy had started on Ariosto. In *The Prelude* Wordsworth recalls how important geometry was to him at this time—Euclid's *Elements* was on the fourth shelf of one of the large bookcases on each side of the fire in what Dorothy described as the 'prettiest little room that can be'.[62]

Nor can we know how much Wordsworth may have read which he had no cause to mention in his letters. All of his friends were enthusiasts for literature (Dorothy noted that the Pinneys 'are fond of reading'[63]) and shared their current excitements with one another. In a letter of 3 August 1796 to Azariah Pinney, for example, John Tobin mentions Wrangham's poems and Stoddart's translations of Schiller's *Fiesco* and recommends 'You must read *The Monk* a novel & Lenora a translation from the German—which is to be found in the Monthly Magazine the best work by the bye of that sort which has been publish'd for some time'. The *Monthly Magazine* was in the parcel of books Losh sent Wordsworth on 20 March 1797, but one wonders whether he had seen a copy earlier when the Pinneys visited in September, or whether Azariah Pinney had then passed on a copy of Lewis's *The Monk*.

All of this is conjecture. For some of Wordsworth's reading, however, harder evidence does exist and it enables us to sense if not the direction of his thought then at least its field of activity.

Throughout this period Wordsworth was preoccupied by France, the conduct of the war, and questions raised by the course of the Revolution. In July 1793 he had watched the fleet gathering in the Solent with the anguish of a patriot cut off from the mood of his own countrymen. Now, in November 1795, he caught a glimpse from a hill near Racedown of another fleet bound for the West Indies, but how different his feelings must have been.[64] In 1793 he had been convinced that 'the struggle which was beginning, and which many thought would be brought to a speedy close by the irresistible arms of Great Britain being added to those of the allies . . . would be of long continuance, and productive of distress and misery beyond all possible calculation',[65] and everything that had happened since had confirmed his fears. Suppression of political liberties, marauding press-gangs, the stealthy work of government spies, rising prices and distress among the poor, maimed soldiers and penniless widows—all could be traced to the war. But whereas in 1793 it had been clear to Wordsworth that the war was an attempt by one tyrannical state to throttle another which had just thrown off its tyrants, now such a simplistic attitude was out of the question. Robespierre and the Terror had darkened the bright promise of the Revolution, but his fall had not restored it. Wordsworth still trusted in the ideas of the early Republicans and shared the conviction of all radicals that the war could have been avoided. But with the expansionist aims of the French becoming more and more apparent, especially after the rejection in 1796 of British peace feelers and the triumphs of Napoleon's Italian campaign, it was no longer possible to believe that the war was being prosecuted solely from the malevolence of the Pitt government or even to have faith that somewhere amidst the turmoil in France the ideals of the Revolution remained intact.

That not a word of these matters appears in Wordsworth's surviving letters of the period should cause no surprise. As a fervent radical in 1794 Wordsworth had wanted to spell out his beliefs to Mathews, partly to declare them and partly to have the pleasure of hearing them echoed by another believer. But now in 1796 Wordsworth had no clear-cut creed to announce, not even the counter-creed of the one-time zealot who had lost his faith. He was searching and pondering and there can be no doubt that much of what he read on French affairs only added to his perplexity. On the one hand there were the books supplied in late November 1795 and January 1796 by Azariah Pinney—Louvet's *Narrative of the Dangers to which I have been Exposed, since the 31st of May 1793*, Madame Roland's *An Appeal to Impartial Posterity*, and Helen Maria Williams's *Letters: Containing a Sketch of the Politics of France . . . and of the Scenes which have Passed in the Prisons of Paris.*[66] Every newspaper and magazine carried reports on the progress of the war and sketches of French politics, but these memoirs, all published in 1795, gave eye-witness testimony to what had happened when the destruction of 'habit, custom, law' had left an open space for the passions of men to work in.[67] With continuity broken, trust inoperative, and friendships severed by suspicion masked in ideology, society disintegrated, and the terrible procession of those going to the guillotine, which Helen Maria Williams describes, was the result. To Wordsworth, who was the only one of the London circle to have been near the carnage, these accounts gave human form to the fears he remembered as pressing upon him in Paris and were certainly recalled as he described his French experiences in *The Prelude.*[68]

On the other hand there was Burke. Early in 1796 the 'oglings and glances of tenderness' with which the British government coquetted with the French over proposals for peace moved the aged and sick Burke to a last philippic against the Revolution—his *Letters on a Regicide Peace.*[69] Wordsworth received a copy in Losh's parcel of 20 March 1797, but it seems certain that he would have known them, at least in part, in the year of publication, as long extracts were published in the *Weekly Entertainer.*[70]

They are a passionate and eloquent appeal, full of scornful imagery and personal loathing, and anything but balanced. Burke even sees the acquittal in the 1794 Treason Trials as a national disgrace: 'Public prosecutions are become a little better than schools for treason; of no use but to improve the dexterity of criminals in the mystery of evasion'.[71] They are none the less extremely impressive and even moving. In the parcel from Losh Wordsworth also received Thomas Erskine's *A View of the Causes and Consequences of the Present War with France*, which argued the opposite case.[72] To Erskine, entering the war was a grave political error which must be remedied as soon as possible by a negotiated peace. But whereas Erskine's is a balanced and sensible plea, it seems puny compared to Burke's *Letters*, because it speaks only in terms of temporary politics, whose dynamics were being changed by Napoleon even as he wrote. Burke, on the other hand, even on his death-bed (as he projects himself), is possessed by the larger and nobler vision so magnificently set out in the *Reflections on the Revolution in France*. France must be resisted because the Revolutionaries had struck at the concept of nationhood embodied in English society. 'Nation is a moral essence', Burke declares, and it is on this conviction that all of the frantic accumulation of argument and evidence in the *Letters* rests.[73] Nation is a moral essence because a true nation—the English—embodies justice and respect for law, reverence for the past, awareness of man's nature as a creature of feelings, prejudices, domestic loyalties, and in its totality reflects man's acknowledgement of his status before God. It is because he expresses this vision that Burke was so important to Wordsworth. His unfairness and prejudice could be disregarded. What mattered was his conviction that politics were trivial, mere local expediency, unless they realized in social form the real needs and the true nature of man.

## (8)

In the *Weekly Entertainer* for 21 November 1796 Wordsworth published *Address to the Ocean*, noting that the first line, 'How long will ye be round me roaring', was taken 'From Mr. Coleridge'.[74] Coleridge had himself quoted from *An Evening Walk* in his *Lines Written at Shurton Bars* and pointed out his debt.[75] Both poets were playing the civilized eighteenth-century game of open literary allusion, but Wordsworth's borrowing and note are of more than usual significance. At a time when he was particularly receptive to stimulus and intellectual nourishment, a new influence had entered his life, one which was soon to matter more than anything else he did or read in this transition year.

Coleridge was himself in an unsettled state, as he was to be through much of his adult life. Throughout 1795 he had watched the plan for an ideal community in America dwindle; in October had somewhat unwillingly married Sara Fricker; in November had denounced Southey as a turncoat in what is surely one of the most terrible letters ever sent from one friend to another, and by the end of the year was desperately looking round for a livelihood. But although he dreaded pressure—'Anxieties that stimulate others, infuse an additional narcotic into my mind'—the amount of work he produced is amazing.[76] In December 1795 he published a revised verion of his February lectures as *Conciones ad Populum* and his lectures on the Two Bills as *The Plot Discovered*.[77] Next came *The Watchman*, a weekly subscription enquiry into political and moral issues, which he planned, marketed, and wrote single-handedly until May 1796.[78] During this time he was also writing poetry and in April *Poems on Various Subjects* appeared.[79]

Over the winter 1795–6 Wordsworth only heard at second hand of Coleridge's doings—of the quarrel with Southey, of his public attack on the 'gagging acts', and of his tour of the Midlands to beat up subscribers for *The Watchman*. But by the spring closer contact was made. On 25 March Azariah Pinney offered to send Wordsworth *The Watchman*. By May he had read Coleridge's poems and had had sufficient correspondence with him for Coleridge to refer to him as 'A very dear friend of mine'.[80] Correspondence must have continued—Coleridge always fostered friendships by letter— and by the turn of the year Coleridge was talking of soliciting Wordsworth's help in revision for the second edition of his *Poems*.[81] Losh's parcel of books of 20 March 1797 included, presumably at Wordsworth's request, Coleridge's *Conciones ad Populum* and *Ode on the Departing Year*. The intimacy which was formed so rapidly when the two men met early in 1797 had a solid foundation of knowledge and intellectual respect.

What was it that appealed to Wordsworth so strongly? Initially, perhaps, the attraction of power. Coleridge was always thinking and what he called 'the *Tug* of Brain' in him was intense.[82] His letters, notebooks, and the reports of his conversation all record his ceaseless attempt to analyse his own experience and to ensure that what he gained as a 'library-cormorant'[83] was at his command. Coleridge wrote with power. The 1795 lectures and *The Watchman* survey, analyse, argue, and denounce with a confidence that is astonishing in a 23-year-old. Politically, too, Wordsworth and Coleridge were broadly in sympathy. Coleridge's denunciations of the Pitt govern- ment and the barbarity of the war may have been commonplaces of radical rhetoric, but no one else known personally to Wordsworth had either analysed so cogently the corruption of government and the established Church or written so humanely about ignorance and want. On every page of *The Watchman* and *Conciones ad Populum* Wordsworth would have found sentiments that echoed his own. 'And if in the bitter cravings of Hunger the dark Tide of Passions should swell, and the poor Wretch rush from despair into guilt, then the GOVERNMENT indeed assumes the right of Punishment though it had neglected the duty of Instruction, and hangs the victim for crimes, to which its own most sinful omissions had supplied the cause and the temptation.'[84] What is this, from 'On the Present War', but a text for *Adventures on Salisbury Plain?*

Wordsworth will have been struck, however, not just by power, but by power in service of ideas, unfamiliar ideas that offered fascinating possibilities of exploration. Late in life Wordsworth said that Coleridge was 'one of the two beings to whom my intellect is most indebted',[85] and although it was compounded when the two were in almost daily contact after June 1797, there can be no doubt that the debt began to accumulate now. Firstly, it was striking that Coleridge had seen through Godwin. 'I do consider Mr. Godwin's Principles as vicious; and his book as a Pandar to Sensuality', he declared in *The Watchman*, adding, 'Once I thought otherwise . . .',[86] as proof that his rejection of Godwin was the result of study and thought, not of prejudice. The examination of *Political Justice* which Coleridge promised, moreover, was certain to deploy speculations far more adventurous than Wordsworth's own and to be grounded in a faith which was, for him, at best merely inoperative.[87]

His first meeting with Coleridge must have shaken Wordsworth, for here was a committed radical whose politics were saturated in religion, not the religion of the established Church, that unholy union of property, power, and the spirit, but the essential religion of Christ. In conversation with this passionate man, who had been delivering lectures on revealed religion in Bristol throughout May and June 1795, Wordsworth must have seemed, as Coleridge declared, 'at least a *Semi*-atheist',[88] since Coleridge did not just refer everything to the judgement of faith, he lived and breathed in the conviction that 'We see our God everywhere—the Universe in the most literal Sense is his written language'.[89] But even if they had not mentioned religion at their first meeting—which is to suppose the impossible—the range of Coleridge's religious thought was evident to Wordsworth as soon as he began to read *Poems on Various Subjects* in 1796. To say that it was clear would be wrong. Coleridge's speculative poems are so dense that commentators are still unravelling their meaning, but their ambition must have been clear enough. In *Effusion XXXV* (later called *The Eolian Harp*) Coleridge's thoughts swell into the question,

> what if all of animated nature
> Be but organic Harps diversly fram'd,
> That tremble into thought, as o'er them sweeps
> Plastic and vast, one intellectual Breeze,
> At once the soul of each, and God of all?[90]

*Religious Musings*, the most substantial poem in the volume and the one on which Coleridge said 'I rest for all my poetical credit', speaks of the upward progression of the spirit,

> Till by exclusive consciousness of GOD
> All self-annihilated, it shall make
> God its identity: God all in all!
> We and our Father ONE![91]

This was not the Christianity of Bishop Watson's *Apology for the Bible* or of Paley's *Evidences*. Here was a religious faith which encompassed a vision of the future of the whole species without ever losing sight of the individual human being. It recognized man as he is, yet believed in man as he might become, not through a regenerated social order but through the perfection of the self in God. It offered a great deal to someone searching for a way forward from Godwinian rationalism.

(9)

It would be ridiculous to imply that *The Borderers* was the inevitable climax to 1796, or that its genesis has somehow been accounted for in this brief survey of Wordsworth's reading and activities during the year. But it is certain that he could not have written it earlier, for it draws not only on his experiences in France and his appalled reaction later to the Terror but also on reflection on those events which was by no means at an end. Since composition—the working out of possibilities of the germ of his story—was part of that process of reflection, not a concluding report, drama was the ideal form. The long prose exposition of the main character's psychology, which he wrote in the spring or summer of 1797, suggests that the idea of the play preceded its shaping, that Wordsworth was working from the abstract to the concrete. But the manuscripts show that it was not so. Wordsworth was gripped ('ardent' was Dorothy's word[92]) by a story which only unfolded its multivalent possibilities as he subjected it to drama's overriding demand—that ideas be given life in people and action. *The Borderers* is always categorized as a philosophical or metaphysical play. It is, but only in the sense that *King Lear*, *Macbeth*, and *Othello*, its great models, are. In Wordsworth's tragedy, as in Shakespeare's, there is no one philosophy or metaphysic, but an embodiment of many conflicting attitudes to life. Its purpose is not to encapsulate thought but to awaken it, or, as Wordsworth implied when he quoted Horace as an epigraph, 'to stir up, to soothe, to fill with false fears'.[93]

The action takes place in 1265 in the northern border country. Rivers persuades Mortimer, the leader of a band of outlaws, that an old man claiming to be Baron Herbert is an impostor who intends to betray Matilda into the clutches of a voluptuary. Mortimer comes to believe that it is his duty to kill Herbert, but he cannot strike the blow, preferring to leave the blind old man to take his chance with Providence and the elements on a bare heath. When he believes that the murder is done, Rivers reveals that Herbert is innocent and that his intention has been to get Mortimer to cut himself off from the constraints of petty morality. In fact Herbert does die and Mortimer goes off, a Cain figure, seeking his own death.

That the play is indebted to *King Lear* and *Othello* is obvious even from this synopsis, and scholars have noted that Wordsworth is drawing too on Schiller's *The Robbers*, Godwin's *Caleb Williams*, and even on Ann Radcliffe's *Romance of the Forest*.[94] But *The Borderers* is not a pastiche. Wordsworth exploits echoes of Shakespeare skilfully, deepening his vision of a contemporary horror by allying it with the timeless one embodied in *King Lear* and *Macbeth*, and other borrowings are simply absorbed.

The nature of the play's concern with contemporary moral issues, despite its historical setting, is evidenced in the conception of the agent of all of the action, Rivers. Once Mortimer is in his power he explains his own motivation and in a different play this could seem clumsily undramatic. But here his speeches—and he has all the best lines—are compelling precisely because they are uttered by a man whose claim to greatness is that he knows himself all round. He sees things as they are, unafraid of the mysteries and terrors that have overawed man since time began. Rivers is the hero in a drama of his own conceiving, in which he has triumphed to become a new kind of man.

Rivers explains how a crisis in his own life forced him to examine 'words and things'.[95] He realized the potential might of the enfranchized human mind and in his speculations became an adventurer,

> a being who had passed alone
> Beyond the visible barriers of the world
> And travelled into things to come.[96]

His conclusion is that in a world which has no meaning, where suffering alone is permanent, only weaklings consent to be governed by the 'opinions and the uses of the world'.[97] Freedom and power come to those who throw off

> a tyranny
> That lives but by the torpid acquiescence
> Of our emasculated souls, the tyranny
> Of moralists and saints and lawgivers

and obey

> the only law that wisdom
> Can ever recognize: the immediate law
> Flashed from the light of circumstance
> Upon an independent intellect.[98]

When *The Borderers* was published in 1842 Wordsworth added a note explaining that the play had its origin during his time in France when he was eye-witness to the truth that as 'sin and crime are apt to start from their very opposite qualities, so are there no limits to the hardening of the heart, and the perversion of the understanding to which they may carry their slaves'.[99] But this was written by an old man for a new generation to whom Robespierre and the French Revolution were just history. His profounder comment on the origins of the play had been made much earlier, in *The Prelude*. Here, in Book X, Wordsworth quotes Rivers's 'independent intellect' speech when explaining how it was that, at a time when the ideals of the Revolution were being betrayed and war welcomed,

> the philosophy
> That promised to abstract the hopes of man
> Out of his feelings, to be fixed thenceforth
> For ever in a purer element,
> Found ready welcome.[100]

This is important. In *The Prelude*, nearly ten years after the period to which it refers, Wordsworth is completely sure of his argument. He and other 'young ingenuous' idealists longed, he says, for man to 'start / Out of the worm-like state in which he is'[101] and so were attracted by any philosophy—and he seems to refer principally to Godwin, though grossly simplifying him—which could analyse man as he is and yet offer rational grounds for believing in his possible renovation.[102] But the pursuit of Truth through speculation and theory, 'demanding proof / And seeking it in everything', led only to despair, from which he was rescued by Dorothy and Nature.[103] The experience is completed, its meaning understood. In *The Borderers*, however, the experience is presented more fully and in a more rough-edged way, as Wordsworth dramatizes a conflict whose urgency he still felt and whose significance he had not yet mastered.

For *The Borderers* is a play which ends but which does not have a resolution. Within a year or so of hearing Wordsworth read it Charles Lamb seized on the phrase 'independent intellect' for his anguished poem *Living without God in the World*. Here he inveighs against those who preach 'energies omnipotent in man, / And man of his own fate artificer'.[104] Rivers is certainly such a man. In *Religious Musings* Coleridge hymns scientists and thinkers, Milton, Newton, Hartley, Priestley, the elect, 'whoe'er from earliest time / With conscious zeal had urged Love's wondrous plan, / Coadjutors with God'.[105] Perverting this vision, Rivers declares himself leader of the new elect, self-bounded, self-knowing, free. But it is striking that in the play, although Rivers condemns himself, no other structure of values emerges at all strongly. Herbert trusts in 'him who feeds | The pelican and ostrich of the Desert',[106] but dies none the less. The sight of a twinkling star halts Mortimer's first murderous attempt, but does not stop him from killing Herbert in the end. Matilda's love for her father is an absolute good, but in this play the joyous reunion of Lear and Cordelia is not re-enacted. Mortimer constantly feels the tension between his reason and his instinctive feelings of humanity, prompted by memory and compassion, but he is readily subverted by one who seems to offer 'proof' that the 'world is poisoned at the heart'.[107] His ultimate knowledge, moreover, does not bind him more closely to the rest of suffering humanity. The play ends as he pronounces his self-chosen doom:

> I will go forth a wanderer on the earth,
> A shadowy thing, and as I wander on
> No human ear shall ever hear my voice,
> No human dwelling ever give me food
> Or sleep or rest, and all the uncertain way
> Shall be as darkness to me, as a waste
> Unnamed by man! and I will wander on
> Living by mere intensity of thought,
> A thing by pain and thought compelled to live,
> Yet loathing life, till heaven in mercy strike me
> With blank forgetfulness—that I may die.[108]

(10)

When Wordsworth completed the first full version of *The Borderers* by June 1797 he must have exulted in what he had achieved. It was his most substantial and original work and he had proved equal to the task of composing on a large scale and over quite a long period of time. With hindsight one can see that the play is something more than an artistic challenge successfully overcome, for it marks the beginning of the exploration of human suffering and of the nature of Nature in its widest sense which is to motivate his finest work in the near future. But intellectual history depends on this kind of hindsight. Its satisfying patterns (with attendant falsifications) only emerge after the event. In early 1797 Wordsworth may have been pleased with the consciousness that his powers were expanding, but it is certain that what pressed on him most urgently were anxieties about his future in which the poet could not be separated from the man.

Primarily he was worried about money. Wordsworth ought to have been comfortably off. Although Lord Lonsdale's machinations had blocked his inheritance, Raisley Calvert had tried to ease his future with the legacy which began to be paid over in the late summer of 1795. But in October Wordsworth had lent £300 to Montagu and the following January another £200 to a friend of Montagu, Charles Douglas. He was to receive ten per cent interest and Montagu and Douglas signed a promissory note to that effect when he was in London in July 1796. In August Montagu signed a more formal annuity bond and agreed to pay the premiums on an insurance on his life.

At the time these transactions no doubt seemed both generous and prudent. But Montagu was in no position to repay interest regularly and money became increasingly tight. In her first surviving letter from Racedown Dorothy took a pride in detailing to her old friend Jane Marshall just how cheaply they were going to be able to live.* By March 1796, however, she was complaining about the cost of coal and a year later there was an air of desperation about Wordsworth's admission to Wrangham that unless postage were pre-paid on any parcel sent, 'ten to one I shall not be able to release [it] from the post office' and his description of himself as 'living upon air and the essence of carrots cabbages turnips and other esculent vegetables, not excluding parsley the produce of my garden'.[109]

Throughout 1795 and 1796 Richard Wordsworth was paying bills and advancing money, small sums for the most part, but all noted down as an accumulating debt. In London on 2 July Wordsworth had had to borrow two guineas more. In November Joseph Gill lent a guinea.[110] In March Azariah Pinney had written in some embarrassment:

We were obliged to let my Father into the knowledge of the whole transaction relative to the deficiency of the Cash I rec'd for him at Race-down, as circumstances rendered it impracticable to conceal it effectually from him. We did it as gradually as was possible, but all our precaution did not disappoint his Anger—for some time he was so hurt that he determined to write to Mr Perkins to desire he would call on you for the Money, but at our earnest request he relinquished his intention. I assure you the change was not produced suddenly but required time and much solicitation . . . I can only add that I am sorry it ever happened for it has caused us much uneasiness and my father still more.[111]

Pinney senior had been sufficiently angry about something to think of setting his lawyer on to Wordsworth. Possibly it is just that he had only now found out that the Wordsworths were living rent free, but the phrase

* DW to Jane Marshall [7 Mar. 1796]. *EY*, 166: '. . . . Coals are so expensive. You would be surprized to see what a small cart full we get for three or four and twenty shillings, but we have such a habit of attention and frugality with respect to the management of our coals that they last much longer than I could have supposed possible.'

'deficiency in the Cash' and Pinney's regret that 'it ever happened' suggest rather that Wordsworth had actually borrowed, or been given, money not properly belonging to Azariah and John Pinney during their stay at Racedown at the beginning of the year.

A constant niggle about money became acute anxiety in 1797. In May Wordsworth wrote his brother a very miserable letter indeed.[112] He was suffering from 'a terrible cold' and Basil and Dorothy too were ill, but these personal causes for gloom are mentioned only in a sentence at the end. The rest of the long letter is about money and it must have appalled the orderly lawyer Richard. Outlining the history of his transactions with Montagu and Douglas, Wordsworth revealed just how insecure was his grasp on his financial affairs, how guilty he felt about the money owed to Richard, and how desperate he was about the latest blow. His cousin Robinson Wordsworth, soon to be married, had asked somewhat brusquely for £250 in part payment 'of what is now owing by you to our family'.[113] Wordsworth could hardly deny the reasonableness of the request—money had after all been spent in expectation of settlement of the Lonsdale claim— but he could only appeal to Richard to try to take care of the problem and suggest that, by reading out the relevant part of the letter, Richard put pressure on Montagu. 'Pestered with letters' on the matter from Richard Wordsworth of Branthwaite and John Robinson, MP for Harwich, and aware of the family gossip that 'he had used his Uncle's children very ill',[114] Wordsworth became more and more anxious. By June 1797 he was talking of the need to find some cash to 'pacify' his own relatives.[115] Although the urgency lapsed—the claim was not finally settled until 1812—Robinson Wordsworth's request was a sharp reminder to Wordsworth of just how precarious his position was.[116]

Wordsworth's worries about money were acute. They are also well documented. They must have merged, however, with a more generalized concern, giving shape to a question which had been in abeyance during his months of reading, reflection, and writing at Racedown.

Put bluntly the question was, 'What am I?' On the title-page to the Prospectus announcing the forthcoming *Watchman* Coleridge is identified as 'Author of Addresses to the People, A Plot Discovered, &c. &c.'.[117] The two '&c. &c.' may be a little hyperbolic, but the description is true and important. It declares that this periodical, bearing the motto

> That All may know the TRUTH;
> And that the TRUTH may make us FREE!!

is to be conducted by a radical activist, whose credentials can be inspected in recently published work. What could Wordsworth have announced about himself? He was a radical who had—for whatever reason—remained silent.

Firm declarations of political principles in private letters contributed nothing to the cause. In July 1798 the crusadingly Tory *Anti-Jacobin* published a cartoon by Gillray and underneath it verses by Canning which list subversives and connect them—ludicrously and promiscuously—with French atheism. One section reads:

> And ye five other wandering Bards that move
> In sweet accord of harmony and love,
> C—dge, and S–th–y, Ll—d and L—be and Co.
> Tune all your mystic harps to praise Lepaux!

What is significant in this is the name it omits. Canning was taking his cue from George Dyer's *The Poet's Fate* (1797), in which he encouraged young poets to 'Join Pantisocracy's harmonious train' and in a footnote named Southey, Coleridge, Wordsworth, Lloyd, and Lamb.[118] Canning omits Wordsworth. Of course, he needed a rhyme for Lepaux, but even so it indicates that he knew that to the readers of the *Anti-Jacobin* Wordsworth's name would be unknown, or at least not identified with the mystical lunatics of radicalism. Publicly Wordsworth had no existence.

Put so bluntly the question, 'what am I?', may seem ludicrous. The answer was what it always had been, that Wordsworth was a poet. This was certainly Wordsworth's view when he wrote *The Prelude* and it determines Mary Moorman's account of this period. But if Wordsworth had declared himself 'Poet' on some hypothetical census form in early 1797, considerations about the meaning of the title would still have remained. For Wordsworth had become a poet who did not publish poems. He had last published work of any significance in 1793. Since then he had written two long Spenserian poems, a number of shorter lyrics, and the Juvenal imitation—and nothing had been made public. Amongst his own acquaintance, Robert Lovell, Southey, Lamb, Wrangham, Coleridge, and Dyer all wrote poetry and either had recently published or were soon to publish their work. Even John Stoddart was in print with his translation of Schiller's *Fiesco*.[119]

It is difficult to believe that Wordsworth had not thought about this, or that he did not do so more urgently when anxieties about money grew pressing in early 1797. But it was not simply a question of money. Wordsworth never earned much from his writing and after the hostile reception of his *Poems, in Two Volumes* in 1807 he published little for many years. But by then both the meagre reward and the opprobrium could be borne, because he was buttressed not only by a tested faith in his own vocation but by the certainty that in the eyes of the world he was a writer. In 1797 Wordsworth had neither the money nor the public identity.

At this moment the example of Coleridge was enormously important.

After the failure of *The Watchman* Coleridge, now a father, was more than ever in thrall to those 'two giants yclept BREAD & CHEESE' and almost any scheme that promised to fulfil their 'most imperious commands'[120] was entertained—opening a school in Derby, writing for the *Morning Chronicle* in London, becoming a Unitarian minister. At his most desperate Coleridge gratefully received a grant from the recently established Royal Literary Fund (a significant recognition that he was an acknowledged writer) and help from a number of friends.[121] But the critical success of *Poems on Various Subjects*, which was sold out in the year of publication 1796, and his pleasure at being recognized by the Reviews inclined Coleridge more and more to think of himself as a poet.[122] He put great effort into revision for a second edition of his poems, showing particular concern for the make-up and coherence of the volume, and the news that Sheridan wanted him to write a tragedy 'on some popular subject' only strengthened his determination to succeed.[123] When Coleridge and Wordsworth met again in March 1797 they were both in the same situation relative to bread and cheese, but Coleridge was actually a successful poet who had explained and justified his aesthetic principles in the Preface to his *Poems* and was now daring to claim the title of Poet, boldly.[124]

Coleridge's example was important, moreover, because he seemed to have gained some certitude about what Johnson in *Rasselas* calls the 'choice of life'. Throughout 1796 Coleridge had grasped at anything, causing Lamb to tell him more than once, 'I grieve from my very soul to observe you in your plans of life, veering about from this hope to the other & settling no where'.[125] But almost as Lamb was writing these words, Coleridge was declaring, 'I have . . . snapped my squeaking baby-trumpet of sedition and have hung up its fragments in the chamber of Penitences' and announcing his determination to seek a place of retirement, where he could bring up his children in circumstances favourable to virtue and the Christian life.[126] He settled finally on Nether Stowey, a tiny village in north-west Somerset, and moved in at the end of 1796, not, as he later told his brother, to vegetate, but to 'muse on fundamental & general causes—the "causae causarum" . . .'.[127] When Wordsworth visited Coleridge at Nether Stowey in March 1797 he was faced with a man of considerable public achievement who had withdrawn from active politics, convinced that in retirement he could, through study, reflection, and writing, be of more use to mankind.

## (11)

The meeting in March was brief but fateful. Wordsworth was on his way back home from Bristol, where he had spent ten days with Montagu at the close of his short visit to Racedown to see his son. There he had made the social round, renewing his acquaintance with James Losh, now moved from London because of ill health, and meeting John Wedgwood and his family. Naturally he called on Cottle and possibly it was his account of Coleridge's new life that prompted Wordsworth to call in at Nether Stowey.

He found him, however, not in a state of rustic contentment but in the grip of a 'depression too dreadful to be described'.[128] Literary conversation was the cure. They discussed Southey's *Poems* and, finding themselves in agreement that he 'writes *too much at his ease*', may have gone on to ruminate on the requirements of true poetry. Certainly Coleridge's extraordinary and only half-facetious declaration to Cottle immediately after Wordsworth had left, 'I should not think of devoting less than 20 years to an Epic Poem', suggests that he had been fired by lofty talk.[129] Possibly they discussed Coleridge's comments on *The Monk* in the February issue of the *Critical Review*. 'Figures that shock the imagination, and narratives that mangle the feelings, rarely discover *genius*, and always betray a low and vulgar *taste*', he had asserted, originating one of the aesthetic issues which he and Wordsworth were to thrash out often in the coming year.[130] Above all they must have discussed their current work and have discovered with delight that they were both writing tragedies. The *Monthly Magazine* had observed in its first number that the 'grand, the sublime, the Shakespearian, and the Miltonic, seem beyond the grasp of modern bards . . . the Tragic Muse has been in a deep lethargy for many years.'[131] *Religious Musings* had disproved the first part of this lament. With Sheridan encouraging him to write for the stage, Coleridge must have roused Wordsworth to the hope that together they could disprove the second.

Within a short time they were comparing progress, but on this occasion it was Coleridge who sought out Wordsworth. He arrived at Racedown between 4 and 7 June and to the end of their lives the Wordsworths recalled the eagerness of his coming: 'We both have a distinct remembrance of his arrival. He did not keep to the high road, but leaped over a gate and bounded down a pathless field by which he cut off an angle.'[132] For Coleridge their welcome remained a touchstone by which to judge the warmth of all others. Pleased by the reception Sir George and Lady Beaumont gave him in 1804 Coleridge wrote to Wordsworth, 'I was welcomed *almost* as you welcomed me at Racedown'.[133]

The two poets were eager to show what they had been doing. 'The first thing that was read after he came', Dorothy wrote, 'was William's new poem *The Ruined Cottage* with which he was much delighted; and after tea he repeated to us two acts and a half of his tragedy *Osorio*. The next morning William read his tragedy *The Borderers*.'[134] Although Wordsworth was 'a strict & almost severe critic', he thought '*very* highly' of *Osorio*, Coleridge wrote, adding that he had hopes of finishing the play during his stay of 'a few days'.[135] But it was more than poetry that kept Coleridge away from his wife and baby until 28 June. The group at Racedown were clearly delighting in each others' company. 'He is a wonderful man', Dorothy reported, 'His conversation teems with soul, mind, and spirit . . . At first I thought him very plain, that is, for about three minutes: he is pale and thin, has a wide mouth, thick lips and not very good teeth, longish loose-growing half-curling rough black hair. But if you hear him speak for five minutes you think no more of them.'[136] Coleridge's judgement was simple: 'Wordsworth is a great man'.[137]

On 28 June Coleridge returned home, no doubt to warn his wife that they had got to find room in their tiny cottage for guests, for almost at once he returned to Racedown to carry off Wordsworth and Dorothy to Nether Stowey. They did not know it, but they were leaving Racedown for good.

# 1797–1798

## (1)

In 1805 Wordsworth recalled 'in clearer view / Than any sweetest sight of yesterday', the year when 'on Quantocks grassy hills / Far ranging and among the sylvan coombs' he and Coleridge had 'wantoned in wild Poesy'.[1] This was a beautifully judged memory with which to close the 'Poem addressed to Coleridge', as it was amidst the Quantock Hills that Wordsworth acknowledged the poetic vocation which the closing lines of *The Prelude* reaffirm, and Coleridge who fired him to Miltonic ardour for the labour it entailed. Above all, 'wantoned in wild poesy' is exactly right. Later portraits of both poets, Haydon's *Wordsworth on Helvellyn*, for example, or Washington Allston's 1814 painting of Coleridge, depict them as solitary beings, dwelling calmly in the immensity of their own thoughts.[2] But in 1797–8 they were increasingly in love with one another, and daily contact, endless talk, madcap walking expeditions, and, most important of all, writing and planning poems made them, simply, very happy. Irritants and problems, ranging from smoky chimneys to government spies, overshadowed them, but in their despite they laughed a lot. When he first met Wordsworth in May 1798, Hazlitt noticed 'a convulsive inclination to laughter about the mouth'.[3] Wordsworth said of *The Idiot Boy*, 'composed in the groves of Alfoxden', that he 'never wrote anything with so much glee', and remembered how the opening line of *We are Seven* had amused them all as an in-joke.[4] In this joyfulness Coleridge wrote nearly all of his greatest poems, *This Lime-tree Bower my Prison*, *The Ancient Mariner*, *Kubla Khan*, *Frost at Midnight*, while Wordsworth revelled in discovering his power across a range of styles and forms, in narrative, in meditative verse, and in his lyrical ballads. It is always called the *annus mirabilis* and so it was. But it was also a time when expectations were raised which were to trouble Wordsworth for most of his life, embedding in him a sense that, for all of his achievement, he had failed in his highest ambition, and when a relationship was established between the two poets in which the seeds of great future pain were planted from the start.

(2)

When William and Dorothy arrived at Nether Stowey on 2 July 1797 it was presumably their intention to stay only for a while before returning to Racedown. They were made very welcome by Coleridge and Sara, but the tiny cottage in Lime Street must have been uncomfortable, even though the infant Hartley behaved, according to his doting father, like 'a very seraph in Clouts',[5] and it became more cramped still when Charles Lamb joined them five days later. As much time as possible was spent out of doors. Thomas Poole, the wealthy tanner who had helped the Coleridges settle in Nether Stowey, had given them access to his garden and arbour, and it was probably in its shade that Wordsworth read out his new poem, *Lines Left upon a Seat in a Yew-tree.* Lamb was deeply moved. Still in a state of shock after the killing of their mother by his sister Mary in a fit of insanity, Lamb felt himself unfitted for society and on this visit, by his own admission, did not talk much. In walks over the hills and in the conversation at Poole's, however, he found some restoration and on his return to London begged for a copy of the *Yew-tree Lines,* as if they might succour him in his lonely life. He told Coleridge, 'I have no topic to talk of. I see nobody, and sit and read or walk alone, and hear nothing.'[6]

But Wordsworth and Dorothy also explored the neighbourhood on their own. On 4 July they discovered, about four miles from Stowey, 'a sequestered waterfall in a dell formed by steep hills covered with full-grown timber trees' and, further into the park, the mansion Alfoxden House. They must have mentioned to Coleridge their 'passing wishes' that some cottage might be found in such a lovely area, for it was quickly established that the big house itself was to let.[7] By 7 July Wordsworth had entered into an agreement with the agent for Alfoxden's owner Langley St Albyn, who was still a minor, that he should have the house for £23 a year, and on 16 July they moved in.

That the lease was witnessed by Tom Poole explains how the business arrangements were settled so quickly. Although Poole was a man of strong radical sympathies—'I wish he would cease to torment us with his democratick sentiments', his cousin Charlotte wrote after one tea-time altercation—his influence in the community was considerable, partly because of his evident integrity and concern for the welfare of local people, partly because of his intelligence and culture, and not least because his devotion to his tannery and farming interests had made him wealthy. Poole's probity was sufficient guarantee for Mr Bartholomew, and it soon became a touchstone for Wordsworth of all that was genuine. Over the year he came to admire Poole enormously, especially for 'his conduct to his Labourers and poor neighbours', and when he told him in 1801 that he had had him in mind while writing *Michael*, Wordsworth testified to what he had learned from Poole's example of the virtue of steadfast commitment to a principled life in one intensely loved place.[8]

Why the business matters were settled so quickly, however, and why the Wordsworths moved in without even returning to Racedown, can only be attributed to their delight in finding a house that offered so much.[9] It was set amidst the kind of natural beauty that they always responded to—woods, streams, hills, and hidden dells, all raised to the sublime by open prospects to the sea. Dorothy tried to evoke its attractions for Mary Hutchinson and her description cannot be bettered:

The house is a large mansion, with furniture enough for a dozen families like ours. There is a very excellent garden, well stocked with vegetables and fruit. The garden is at the end of the house, and our favourite parlour, as at Racedown, looks that way. In front is a little court, with grass plot, gravel walk, and shrubs . . . The front of the house is to the south, but it is screened from the sun by a high hill which rises immediately from it. The hill is beautiful, scattered irregularly and abundantly with trees, and topped with fern, which spreads a considerable way down it. The deer dwell here, and sheep, so that we have a living prospect. From the end of the house we have a view of the sea, over a woody meadow-country . . .[10]

Much that thrilled Dorothy would still strike a visitor today. Set back a little from the lane that winds up from the road to Holford, Alfoxden offers seclusion, guaranteed by the trees and the sheltering hill, yet promises grandeur and expansiveness through glimpses of the sea. If the Wordsworths went back down the lane they could drop through the trees to a spot which captivated William, for whom it was an unfading recollection forty-five years later:

The brook fell down a sloping rock so as to make a waterfall considerable for that country, and across the pool had fallen a tree, an ash, if I rightly remember, from which rose perpendicularly boughs in search of the light intercepted by the deep shade above. The boughs bore leaves of green that for want of sunshine had faded into almost lily-white; and from the underside of this natural sylvan bridge depended long and beautiful tresses of ivy which waved gently in the breeze that might poetically speaking be called the breath of the waterfall. This motion varied of course in proportion to the power of water in the brook.[11]

If, on the other hand, they walked on up from the house, they had access to the hills which in one direction offered views across the Bristol Channel to the Welsh mountains and in the other miles of easy walking.

With its nine bedrooms and three parlours Alfoxden was, as Dorothy said, a mansion, and they were pleased at the thought that they could easily accommodate any friends such as the Pinneys, or Montagu, or others who might arrive. A week after moving in they gave a house-warming dinner for fourteen people and must have delighted in being hosts in such a fine setting and on such a grand scale. But the main attraction of Alfoxden was simply that it was near Nether Stowey. Throughout their stay at Racedown both Wordsworths had felt the lack of stimulating company, which was not eased by entertaining their neighbours who had, Dorothy reported, 'not much conversation'.[12] Now they were within reach of a man whose genius revealed itself unceasingly, and most characteristically, in talk. 'In digressing, in passing from subject to subject', wrote Hazlitt, 'he appeared to me to float in air, to slide on ice.'*

On this occasion in 1798 Coleridge had talked *at* Hazlitt, as he tended to do when he thought he had an impressionable listener, but he clearly talked *with* Wordsworth and 'his exquisite Sister'[13] and the three rapidly became inseparable. They were apart for brief periods in August and September, for two or three weeks in December 1797, and for a month in early 1798, but otherwise they spent as much time together as possible. Early in November they explored the coast to Lynton and the astonishing Valley of Rocks. Barely had Coleridge returned to his family than they set off again, once more out to the coast to Watchet, striking inland as far as Dulverton before swinging back home. They were clearly undaunted by weather—November is not an obvious month for a walking tour that takes in Exmoor, nor is four o'clock a sensible time to set off—and the short days of winter made no difference to the contact between them. 'Walked a great part of the way to Stowey with Coleridge . . .'; 'Walked to Stowey with Coleridge . . .'; 'Walked to Stowey over the hills . . . the roads in some parts frozen hard . . .'; 'Walked with Coleridge near to Stowey . . .'; 'Walked alone to Stowey. Returned in the evening with Coleridge . . .'; 'A deep snow upon the ground. Wm and Coleridge walked . . . to Stowey.' So Dorothy records twelve days in February 1798 in her journal.[14] Friendship with Sara Coleridge was maintained, but barely. On 7 March Dorothy notes, 'William and I drank tea at Coleridge's', and on 13 April, 'In the evening went to Stowey. I staid with Mrs Coleridge. Wm went to Poole's. Supped with Mrs Coleridge', but the entries more often recorded Coleridge visiting them, and sometimes staying overnight. At the end of the twelve months at Alfoxden Dorothy valued 'Coleridge's society' as 'an advantage which I prize the more, the more I know him'.[15] Threatened by possible separation from Wordsworth in 1798 Coleridge declared, 'Poole and I cannot endure to think of losing him'. 'Tho' we were three persons', he later said, 'it was but one God.'[16]

---

* *Howe*, XVII. 113. There are many accounts of Coleridge's conversation. Keats's description in his letter of 14 Feb.–3 May 1819 is one of the finest and best known. In C's letter of 20 Mar. 1796, however, the reader will find an excellent contemporary example of how his mind worked. In one dense paragraph C begins by announcing his wife's miscarriage and proceeds by connected, imaginative progression until he ends with questions about the nature of God.

(3)

In his *Lines Written at Bridgewater ... 27th of July, 1797*, John Thelwall pictured for Coleridge an ideal of domestic rural retirement:

>                              by our sides
>           Thy Sara, and my Susan, and, perchance,
>           Allfoxden's musing tenant, and the maid
>           Of ardent eye, who, with fraternal love,
>           Sweetens his solitude.[17]

Such retirement, with time for 'suspending oft the arm / And half-driven spade' to muse in tranquillity, was what Thelwall desperately needed. Throughout late 1795 and 1796 he had once more been harried by the authorities. In April 1796 his paper the *Tribune* had been suppressed. In August a gang of sailors, acting under orders, had broken up his lectures at Yarmouth and he was again silenced by mob violence in Norwich in May 1797. Dogged by spies and informers wherever he spoke, eventually he gave way under the pressure.[18] When he arrived at Nether Stowey on 17 July 1797 he was a broken man, looking for a retreat for himself and his family, and it is not surprising that he should have grasped at Coleridge in his cottage and Wordsworth at Alfoxden as models of what a quiet life might be. As they sat by the stream in the glen at Alfoxden, Coleridge later recalled, he had said to Thelwall, ' "Citizen John, this is a fine place to talk treason in!" "Nay! Citizen Samuel," replied he, "it is rather a place to make a man forget that there is any necessity for treason". '[19]

If one were to rely solely on Dorothy's journal record it would be easy to share Thelwall's image of the seclusion at Alfoxden. She was intensely responsive to natural stimuli—'her eye watchful in minutest observation of nature', Coleridge noticed[20]—and in the lavish but subtle beauties of the Quantocks and Alfoxden she found constant delight. In journal entries such as this one for 27 January she seems to strain, as Hopkins does in his, to catch the essence of a scene or of a natural phenomenon:

Upon the whole an uninteresting evening. Only once while we were in the wood the moon burst through the invisible veil which enveloped her, the shadows of the oaks blackened, and their lines became more strongly marked. The withered leaves were coloured with a deeper yellow, a brighter gloss spotted the hollies; again her form became dimmer; the sky flat, unmarked by distances, a white thin cloud.

After leaving Alfoxden she wrote to Mrs Rawson:

I am writing in a front room, in one of the most busy streets of Bristol. You can scarcely conceive how the jarring contrast between the sounds which are now for ever ringing in my ears and the sweet sounds of Allfoxden makes me long for the country again. After three years residence in retirement a city in feeling, sound, and prospect is hateful.[21]

This sums up what above all Alfoxden had meant to her.

Clearly Wordsworth joined her in this kind of delight. At Alfoxden they shared their pleasure, alerting one another to nature's particularities as if bestowing gifts—'William called me into the garden to observe a singular appearance about the moon'[22]—and the clarity with which Wordsworth recalled this or that favourite spot in the references to Alfoxden in the Fenwick notes suggest how deeply indebted he felt as a poet to its tranquillity and harmony. But evidence other than Dorothy's journal makes it equally clear that for the two poets retirement was a complex, not a simple, state. It is time to ask just what kind of retirement it was.

The question has an academic ring, but in fact it was being asked by powerful figures at the time. On 8 and 11 August 1797 Dr Daniel Lysons of Bath alerted the Home Office to the suspicious behaviour of the tenants at Alfoxden. Repeating what his cook had told him of gossip she had heard from one Charles Mogg, a former servant at Alfoxden, Lysons identified the Wordsworths as 'an emigrant family' who had 'contrived' to get hold of the house. Their relationship to one another was dubious—'the master of the House has no wife with him, but only a woman who passes for his Sister'— and their behaviour even more so. They go, said Lyons, on nocturnal or diurnal expeditions, taking notes on their observations of the terrain. 'They have been heard to say they should be rewarded for them & were very attentive to the River near them.'[23]

Almost all of this information, of course, was correct. But what interpretation was to be put on it? Alarm bells sounded in Whitehall. James Walsh, an experienced government agent, was immediately dispatched. An interview with Mogg at Hungerford confirmed the details—Walsh's report of 11 August speaks of the Alfoxden tenants as definitely 'French people' who rambled most part of the night. By 15 August the spy was at the Globe Inn, Stowey, with £20 in his pocket for loosening local tongues. The picture became much clearer as soon as he heard that Thelwall had been at Alfoxden, for Walsh had been playing cat and mouse with this democrat ever since 1792. He at once reported back that 'this will turn out no French Affair but a mischiefous gang of disaffected Englishmen' and in a final report confirmed his hunch, from further details he had learned locally, by saying that Wordsworth and Coleridge, under the protection of Poole, 'a most Violent Member of the Corresponding Society', seemed to be involved in publishing from 'a Press in the House', that they entertained visitors from London and Bristol, and that the notorious Thelwall was one of their friends.

Walsh had no difficulty in getting information. Suspicion of strangers, envy of the people in the great house who seemed not to need to do honest work, mistrust of Poole, who, it was believed, had tried to introduce Paine's sedition into Stowey—all fuelled the gossip. 'To what are we coming', exclaimed Charlotte Poole, when she heard that 'Mr Thelwall has spent some time at Stowey this week with Mr Coleridge, and consequently with Tom Poole'.[24] The landlord of the Globe Inn and his customers were shaking their heads no doubt over the same question.

The speed with which the Home Office acted, however, was prompted by understandable alarm and by wider views than those of Charles Mogg. The country was at war. In February 1797 1,200 French troops landed near Fishguard, having abandoned their first priority which was to destroy Bristol. The invasion collapsed in two days, but it caused a run on the banks and contributed to the government crisis which deepened with the mutinies at the Nore and Spithead in April and May.[25] By demonstrating that the French could evade naval defences, the landing highlighted Britain's vulnerability and strengthened fears that the French would strike from the west, aided by the rebellious Irish and their friends in the radical societies. 'Emigrants' who entertained the likes of Thelwall and who spent much of their time either looking out to sea or studying the lie of the land were a legitimate target for the intelligence service. Their retirement was most likely far from innocent.

The Home Office probably kept the Alfoxden 'gang' under observation— in January 1798 Coleridge complained that one of his letters had been intercepted[26]—but no action was taken on Walsh's reports. Local fears, however, were not assuaged. Wordsworth's lease of Alfoxden was an open one, that is, it allowed for the possibility of renewal, but by September 1797 he had been told that the tenancy would lapse at the end of the year and even Poole's testimony to Mrs St Albyn that Wordsworth was 'in every respect a gentleman', who was 'of all men alive . . . the last who will give one cause to complain of his opinions, his conduct, or his disturbing the peace', was to no avail.[27] Hardly had the Wordsworths settled in at Alfoxden before they knew that within months they would once more be on the move.

That Wordsworth was ejected from Alfoxden because of his association with seditionists such as Coleridge and Thelwall is sadly ironic, for in 1797 and 1798 all three were clearly no longer, either in act or in spirit, part of the radical campaigning world to which it was assumed they belonged. Thelwall—who, it must be remembered, had endured being on trial for his life—was in retreat, beaten. Wordsworth had only ever given tacit support to the radical activists. Not a word of his political opinions had been published and in this year no word was even uttered that compares with his *Letter to the Bishop of Llandaff*, or with his 1794 letters to Mathews, or with the Juvenal imitation. In 1821 he told his old radical friend James Losh that the French invasion of Switzerland in 1798 had decisively altered his sympathies, but there is no mention of it in his letters at the time.[28] Coleridge was more overtly in retreat. His dispirited 'I am out of heart with the French' of 1796 became indignant and public repudiation in *The Recantation: An Ode* in April 1798. 'I am wearied with politics, even to soreness', he wrote in July 1797 and in March 1798 assured his brother that although 'A man's character follows him long after he has ceased to deserve it . . . I have snapped my squeaking baby-trumpet of Sedition & the fragments lie scattered in the lumber-room of Penitence'.[29]

In seceding from political action, or even from a belief that radical politics, as currently practised, could promote the general good, Wordsworth and Coleridge were not unique. In his *Thoughts: Occasioned by the Perusal of Dr Parr's Spital Sermon . . . April 15, 1800*, Godwin identified the spring of 1797 as the moment when adherents of the revolutionary cause fell off. Unwilling any longer to be isolated from the community of general feeling, disheartened and subject to the law that 'Zeal, though it be as hot as Nebuchadnezzar's furnace, without a continual supply of fuel will speedily cool', then it was, he says, that one by one radicals became apostates and signalled their conversion by attacks on the philosopher they had once revered.[30] Godwin's *Thoughts* dwell on Mackintosh, Parr, and Malthus, but his bitter analysis appears to fit exactly the case of Wordsworth and Coleridge.

In one all-important respect, however, they elude Godwin's censure. For both poets the year 1797–8 was not one of quietist withdrawal, but a period of great mental activity, in which they sought to define what would be for them the most appropriate field of endeavour. Although they did not know it, both in fact were already laying the foundations of very different lives, and their differing impulses will be examined separately in the pages that follow. But they were united in their conviction that each could learn from the other and that together they were dedicated to influencing (to quote from the title of Godwin's great work) 'General Virtue and Happiness'.

## (4)

Wordsworth's Alfoxden year began with the *Yew-tree Lines* and ended with *Tintern Abbey*. The first is a memorial to a man whose life was lived in fragments. A 'youth, by genius nursed, / And big with lofty views', he was checked by disappointments in the real world, and so retired to indulge his melancholy and pride in solitude. Gazing on the beauty of Nature only intensified his sense of isolation, which deepened till he died. The second is, as it were, Wordsworth's hymn of thanksgiving for the opposite life. As the poet looks back even as far as childhood, he celebrates the energies in the natural order that make for unity, which enable man to know himself part of the great whole of the active universe. In the *Yew-tree Lines* Nature is the 'stone-chat, or the glancing sand-piper'. In *Tintern Abbey* Nature offers access to

> a sense sublime
> Of something far more deeply interfused,
> Whose dwelling is the light of setting suns.

It is a power in which the poet is well pleased to find

> The guide, the guardian of my heart, and soul
> Of all my moral being.

This astonishing declaration is made in all seriousness. The intense intellectual and poetic activity during the Alfoxden year that gave Wordsworth the confidence to make it is recorded in poems which explore positions and open up problems, testifying sometimes in their incompleteness to the struggles of a mind at full stretch.

The period, in fact, divides into three stages, each of which transmitted such intellectual and creative energies into the next that the whole seems to develop inevitably to the major achievement with which the year ends. Even the first stage from July to December 1797, which consisted (speaking of Wordsworth's intellectual life) of three non-events, was only apparently unproductive. From two of these negatives Wordsworth learned a great deal. From one he did not, at the time, learn enough.

The first non-event was Tom Wedgwood's attempt to involve Wordsworth in his endeavour to 'anticipate a century or two upon the large-paced progress of human improvement'.[31] Wedgwood, son of the famous Josiah and independently wealthy at age 26, was a highly intelligent and genuinely philanthropic man, whose thinking had been moulded by a variety of Enlightenment writers, but especially by Godwin. Appalled by what he saw as the randomness of the process by which each human being develops— 'what a chaos of perceptions! If one were ignorant of the resulting produce, idiocy would certainly suggest itself as the only possible one. How many opposing tendencies which have negatived each other!'—he logically concluded that the only way to eliminate randomness would be to control the input of perceptions so as to eliminate waste and maximize human potential. Obviously control could not begin too early. He therefore outlined to Godwin his plan for an establishment, superintended by such 'philosophers' as Godwin, Beddoes, Holcroft, and Horne Tooke, in which a child could be reared under laboratory conditions. The infant's sensory responses would be developed in a 'nursery [with] plain grey walls with one or two vivid objects for sight & touch' and all contact with the overwhelming stimulus of the external world would be forbidden: 'The gradual explication of Nature would be attended with great difficulty; the child must never go out of doors or leave his own apartment'. To run this academy for genius Wedgwood knew, he said, of only two people 'at all likely for this purpose'— Wordsworth and Coleridge. Wordsworth, he believed, 'has only to be convinced that this is the most promising mode of benefitting society to engage him to come forward with alacrity'.

Wedgwood visited Alfoxden in September 1797 and it cannot have taken him long to realize how mistaken he was. A man who thought time well spent observing the fallen ash tree in the stream and who was bringing up little Basil with 'no other companions, than the flowers, the grass, the cattle, the sheep that scamper away from him when he makes a vain unexpecting chase after them', would hardly answer his purpose.[32]

Wedgwood's impact on Wordsworth, none the less, was considerable. He made him ponder. For the scheme—which was no sillier than the Victorian educational theories satirized in *Hard Times*—was a logical extension of eighteenth-century theories of mind, all deriving from Locke, which were certainly the basis of Wordsworth's own conception of how the mind functioned. But he knew, by instinct and from his own experience, that Wedgwood's plan to systematize human development was ludicrously and dangerously wrong-headed. The question was, given that its foundations could be traced to sound philosophy, how could it be shown to be so wrong? In the coming months Wordsworth wrote a powerful attack on distorted education, which was eventually incorporated in Book V of *The Prelude*,[33] but in much else that he wrote now, not so obviously directed at Wedgwood's scheme, one can see that the poet's mind is returning again and again to the questions it had raised.

A second non-event was the attempt at collaboration with Coleridge. Throughout the Alfoxden year the two poets were engaged in such a subtle dialogue that poems such as *Frost at Midnight* and *Tintern Abbey* seem almost the creation not of two minds but one.[34] Attempts at real collaboration, however, failed completely. On the first of their walking tours in November 1797 Coleridge suggested that they jointly compose a poem in three cantos on the death of Abel. Wordsworth was to write the first canto, Coleridge the second, and whoever finished first was to set about the third. Thirty years later Coleridge recalled:

Methinks I see his grand and noble countenance as at the moment when having despatched my own portion of the task at full finger-speed, I hastened to him with my manuscript—that look of humourous despondency fixed on his almost blank sheet of paper, and then its silent mock-piteous admission of failure struggling with the sense of the exceeding ridiculousness of the whole scheme—which broke up in a laugh . . .[35]

The failure was repeated on their second tour only days later. On the way to Watchet Wordsworth and Coleridge planned out *The Ancient Mariner*, with the hope that they might defray the expenses of the trip by selling the ballad to the *Monthly Magazine*. Wordsworth suggested many of the elements of the poem—the killing of the albatross, the spectral persecution of the mariner, the navigation of the ship by the dead sailors—but when it came to actually writing it he could manage only two or three lines. 'As we endeavoured to proceed conjointly', he remembered years later, 'our respective manners proved so widely different that it would have been quite presumptuous in me to do anything but separate from an undertaking upon which I could only have been a clog.'[36] Fired though he was by Coleridge's conversation and by his creative fertility, Wordsworth had proved incapable of writing to order or to another man's plan. That he allowed himself later in the year to suppress the significance of these failures was to cause him immense anxiety in the future.

The third non-event which in reality was highly important was the attempt to get *The Borderers* staged. The tragedy had been revised and completed during the summer and autumn of 1797 and by 20 November had been dispatched to Covent Garden. 'We have not the faintest expectation that it will be accepted',[37] Dorothy told Mary Hutchinson, but her comment can be taken as the usual disclaimer one makes while hoping very much that a wish will come true, for a little over a week later she and Wordsworth were in London, she for a change of scenery and visits to Covent Garden and Drury Lane, he to make alterations to the play 'at the suggestion of one of the principal Actors of Covent Garden', Thomas Knight. Thomas Harris, the theatre's manager, was unimpressed and by 13 December had 'pronounced it impossible that the play should succeed in the representation'.[38]

Wordsworth's response to this rebuff is very revealing. He was hurt and with some arrogance, understandable but amazing in a 27-year-old who had published almost nothing, he seems to have blamed the rejection on 'the deprav'd State of the Stage at present' and to have declared himself undecided whether to wait for reform or to publish at once.[39] But his failure evidently made him think about the kind of literary achievement he did value, or thought was within his power. On 23 January 1798 Coleridge wrote to him about 'Monk' Lewis's extremely successful and profitable play *Castle Spectre*, clearly in response to a letter from Wordsworth in which he had most probably picked up the argument about gross effects in literature advanced by Coleridge in his review of *The Monk* earlier in the year:

This play proves how accurately you conjectured concerning *theatric* merit. The merit of the Castle Spectre consists wholly in it's *situations*. These are all borrowed, and all absolutely *pantomimical*; but they are admirably managed for stage effect. There is not much bustle; but *situations* for ever.[40]

The discussion of the relation between incident and literary value must have continued once Wordsworth and Coleridge were again in daily contact, for it surfaces in repeated statements in the work of 1798—in *The Ruined Cottage*, *The Idiot Boy*, *Simon Lee*, and *Peter Bell*—that in these poems 'the feeling therein developed gives importance to the action and situation, and not the action and situation to the feeling'.[41] The rejection of *The Borderers* forced Wordsworth to define one tenet of his poetic belief. A less beneficial effect was that it predisposed him to think, even before he had begun to publish in earnest, that work of any lasting merit was bound to be opposed to current taste.

## (5)

On Coleridge's arrival at Racedown in June 1797 Wordsworth had read to him his new poem *The Ruined Cottage* and *The Borderers*. Once the tragedy had failed, he concentrated on his narrative poem. The second phase of his Alfoxden year consists of his struggle with it.

Significantly, it was a struggle marked by pauses rather than completion. Although unquestionably, as Coleridge said, 'one of the most beautiful poems in the language', no version of *The Ruined Cottage* entirely satisfied Wordsworth. He revised it repeatedly before eventually publishing it as Book I of *The Excursion* in 1814.[42] But even that poem ends inconclusively, anticipating the full elucidation of its meaning in the greater (but never to be-written) whole of *The Recluse*. Unlike, say, *Tintern Abbey*, versions of *The Ruined Cottage* are always provisional, as if throughout its composition Wordsworth found that his material raised questions and presented difficulties which resisted resolution into a satisfying final form.

In 1797 the poem was a simple narrative in which the Pedlar, dwelling on the difference between the ruined cottage as it now is and as he once had known it, recounts the sufferings of Margaret. Unable to support his family as war blights the rural economy, Robert deserts Margaret and enlists, pathetically leaving his bounty money to buy for his children the bread he can no longer provide by his own labour. Slowly the family disintegrates and eventually Margaret dies, clinging to the last to the 'torturing hope' that Robert will return. Margaret is clearly linked to the Female Vagrant of *Adventures on Salisbury Plain* and to the soldier's widow in Southey's *Joan of Arc*, as well as to other abandoned victims in contemporary poems of sentiment or anti-war protest, but she originated in Wordsworth's first-hand observation of the impact of national politics on the helpless poor.[43]

Wordsworth was not, however, recapitulating on his social protest poetry of 1793 to 1795. He focuses now on Margaret's suffering for quite different ends. In January and February 1798 he revised the poem, developing the Pedlar into a wise and experienced figure who controls the responses of the innocent poet-listener to the tragic story, which still remains the core of the poem. Though 'untaught, / In the dead lore of schools undisciplined', the Pedlar is a 'chosen son', who perceives the 'moral life' in all the phenomena of the universe:

> In all shapes
> He found a secret and mysterious soul,
> A fragrance and a spirit of strange meaning.

At the end of the first part of his narrative the Pedlar pauses and asks,

> At this still season of repose and peace,
> This hour when all things which are not at rest
> Are chearful, while this multitude of flies
> Fills all the air with happy melody,
> Why should a tear be in an old Man's eye?
> Why should we thus with an untoward mind
> And in the weakness of humanity
> From natural wisdom turn our hearts away,
> To natural comfort shut our eyes and ears,
> And feeding on disquiet thus disturb
> [The calm] of Nature with our restless thoughts?

It is an odd and disturbing question, to which the obvious answer seems to be a forthright, 'Why not?' The Pedlar has already told of Margaret's death and he ends his story with the bleakest possible epitaph:

> here, my friend,
> In sickness she remained, and here she died,
> Last human tenant of these ruined walls.[44]

A tear may be the 'weakness of humanity', but it seems the instinctive response of anyone not aware of whatever the 'natural wisdom' is, to which the Pedlar refers. The poet-listener (or reader) might also want to know how the Pedlar has acquired the authority to speak as he does.

Wordsworth immediately attempted to answer these questions. In a long addition the Pedlar's ability to perceive the moral life of the universe is traced to the visionary experiences of his childhood and the meaning of his words on 'natural wisdom' and 'natural comfort' is expounded in the difficult passage of philosophical verse printed as the Appendix to this book.

Wordsworth never wrote more important lines than these. Both passages were for him, as Keats said of certain key lines in *Endymion*, 'a regular stepping of the Imagination towards a Truth'.[45] In the first addition Wordsworth depicts experiences of the Pedlar's childhood and youth as an education through the senses and the imagination, which is entirely unlike the education Tom Wedgwood proposed. It fitted him

> By his intense conceptions to receive
> Deeply the lesson deep of love which he
> Whom Nature, by whatever means, has taught
> To feel intensely, cannot but receive.[46]

In the second addition (see Appendix) the Pedlar provides the metaphysical underpinning to this conviction, spelling out the argument, not as an intuition but as a demonstrable truth, that love of Nature, which demands intense participation in the life of 'this majestic imagery, the cloud, / The ocean, and the firmament of heaven', must lead both to a perception of the harmony of all things and to acceptance 'of human suffering or of human joy'. The Pedlar's exhortation to the poet, 'no longer read / The forms of things with an unworthy eye', and his concluding words of reconciling wisdom do not diminish Margaret's tragedy. By absorbing it into a larger whole the Pedlar enables the poet to pass beyond impotent grief and thus justifies the telling of her story.

Both passages are too long and rich for explication here, but a number of observations must be made about writings which were so important in Wordsworth's development.

The first is that they demonstrate the creativity of the relationship between Wordsworth and Coleridge in the Alfoxden year. Many passages in his working notebook reveal that Wordsworth was trying to evoke states of mind in which one registers most fully 'The exceeding beauty of this earth and . . . The loveliness of Nature', and to link this to an outgoing, humane activity of the whole being, the opposite of the solipsistic absorption of the recluse in the *Yew-tree Lines*.[47] Coleridge enabled Wordsworth to make the link. As Jonathan Wordsworth has finely put it, Coleridge 'made available to Wordsworth the materials of much of his greatest poetry'.[48] Without *Religious Musings* and *This Lime-tree Bower my Prison*, and without Coleridge's exposition in conversation of Hartley, Priestley, Berkeley, and others, Wordsworth would not have written either additional passage as he did.

Coleridge lived and breathed his religious faith so intensely that inevitably he and Wordsworth found they disagreed on some things. 'On one subject we are habitually silent', Coleridge told his friend John Estlin, 'we found our data dissimilar, & never renewed the subject . . . he loves & venerates Christ & Christianity—I wish, he did more.'[49] What the one subject is, is not known—and it is impossible to believe Coleridge remained habitually silent on any topic—but it is clear that whatever reservations he may have had about tenets of belief, Wordsworth drew largely on the superabundant store of Coleridge's reading and thought. Even after their personal intimacy had gone, Wordsworth continued to recognize Coleridge as one of the two beings 'to whom my intellect is most indebted'.[50]

What Coleridge absorbed from Cudworth, Hartley, Berkeley, demands books for explication, not a thumb-nail sketch. What he conveyed to Wordsworth, however, can at least be suggested more briefly from lines he wrote as Wordsworth was revising *The Ruined Cottage*. In *Frost at Midnight* Coleridge expresses his hopes for his own son Hartley (named after that 'great master of *Christian* philosophy'[51]):

> *thou*, my babe! shalt wander like a breeze
> By lakes and sandy shores, beneath the crags
> Of ancient mountain, and beneath the clouds,
> Which image in their bulk both lakes and shores
> And mountain crags: so shalt thou see and hear
> The lovely shapes and sounds intelligible
> Of that eternal language, which thy God
> Utters, who from eternity doth teach
> Himself in all, and all things in himself.
> Great universal Teacher! he shall mould
> Thy spirit, and by giving make it ask.

Here is Coleridge's most profound conviction. The phenomena of the natural world signify, even as they are most wonderfully themselves, the transcendental reality. The language of the heavens is the language of God. In 'this faith *all things* counterfeit infinity', and, as Coleridge said in *This Lime-tree Bower*:

> No plot so narrow, be but Nature there,
> No waste so vacant, but may well employ
> Each faculty of sense, and keep the heart
> Awake to Love and Beauty![53]

In the lines on the Pedlar Wordsworth describes him drinking in the beauty of the sunrise and says:

> Ah! *then* how beautiful, how bright, appeared
> The written promise. He had only learned
> To reverence the volume which displays

> The mystery, the life which cannot die,
> But in the mountains did he FEEL his faith,
> There did he see the writing. All things there
> Breathed immortality, revolving life,
> And greatness still revolving, infinite;
> There littleness was not, the least of things
> Seemed infinite, and there his spirit shaped
> Her prospects—nor did he *believe*; he saw.[53]

Through his contact with the principle of things, with Godhead, which is evoked so rapturously in the verse, and through his wide experience of men, especially of those in lowly stations in life, the Pedlar can place the sufferings of Margaret within the harmony of creation.

The second point to be made about Wordsworth's revisions to *The Ruined Cottage* is that in glossing his vivid depiction of childhood and adolescent experiences through the medium of eighteenth-century theories of mind, Wordsworth showed that he was prepared to take whatever philosophical formulations seemed to help. Unlike Coleridge he was not a philosopher, nor did he feel the compulsion to eradicate uncertainties which drove Coleridge to a lifetime's philosophical enquiry. Trying to identify a single 'philosophy' in Wordsworth's poetry by tracing its language to an original philosophic source is fruitless.

The third is that the second additional passage must have revealed to Wordsworth that he had simultaneously made a breakthrough and arrived at an impasse. Assisted by Coleridge, Wordsworth had found a language in which to explore his convictions about God, Nature, and the unignorable fact of suffering in the world. But he was too sensible to believe that in a matter of months he had found *answers*, and too humane and serious to feel that a personal conviction was of any worth unless it were translated into moral action, that is, somehow transmitted for the benefit of others. But Wordsworth was also too astute to think that the passage 'Not useless do I deem . . .' pointed his way ahead. For the lines, notwithstanding their considerable verbal and rhythmic dexterity, have only a limited effect. They convey thought more effectively than anything in Akenside or Cowper, but by remaining only on the level of abstraction they cannot fuse in the reader's imagination with the story of Margaret they are meant to encompass. To translate his private convictions into public and actively beneficial discourse, Wordsworth had to find other means than purely philosophical blank verse.

## (6)

In the third stage of the Alfoxden year Wordsworth did just that. Working on *The Ruined Cottage* seems to have generated energies and confidence. In

March Dorothy brought Mary Hutchinson up to date on Wordsworth's poetry, reporting that 'His faculties seem to expand every day, he composes with much more facility than he did, as to the *mechanism* of poetry, and his ideas flow faster than he can express them'.[54] When Hazlitt visited in May he was in no doubt that he was in the company of genius. At 20 years old he was ready to be enchanted—and he was. 'Wordsworth, looking out of the low latticed window, said, "How beautifully the sun sets on that yellow bank!". I thought within myself, "With what eyes these poets see nature!".'[55] In his essay twenty-five years on from which this quotation comes, *My First Acquaintance with Poets*, Hazlitt recalled a great deal— Wordsworth 'in a brown fustian jacket and striped pantaloons', looking like the rover in *Peter Bell*, his talking 'very naturally and freely, with a mixture of clear, gushing accents in his voice, a deep guttural intonation, and a strong tincture of the northern *burr*, like the crust on wine', his appetite as he 'began to make havoc of the half of a Cheshire cheese on the table'. Most important of all, he remembered that, as Wordsworth's recent lyrical poems were read out, 'the sense of a new style and a new spirit in poetry came over me. It had to me something of the effect that arises from the turning up of the fresh soil, or of the first welcome breath of Spring . . .'.

March to June 1798 was Wordsworth's first great period of lyric creation. In poem after poem he tried lyrical, dramatic, and narrative forms of embodying or articulating ideas which had been preoccupying him in the last year and which had emerged into one kind of clarity during his work on *The Ruined Cottage*. The Pedlar had asked,

> was it ever meant
> That this majestic imagery, the clouds,
> The ocean, and the firmament of heaven,
> Should be a barren picture on the mind?[56]

In *Lines* ('It is the first mild day of March'), *Lines Written in Early Spring*, 'A whirl-blast from behind the hill', the poet gave his answer in rapturous celebration of 'the blessed power that rolls / About, below, above', discerned in the sun, the clouds, in birds, and flowers:

> The birds around me hopped and played:
> Their thoughts I cannot measure,
> But the least motion which they made,
> It seemed a thrill of pleasure.[57]

Much of the revision to *The Ruined Cottage* had been concerned with the Pedlar's education, in which the mountain tops had taken the place of Tom Wedgwood's grey-walled nursery. *We are Seven* and *Anecdote for Fathers* are further fruits of Wordsworth's musing on that pernicious scheme. In both poems the 'wisdom' of the adult dwindles before the superior wisdom of children dwelling in their own world of instinct and imagination.

Two poems, *Expostulation and Reply* and *The Tables Turned*, fuse Wordsworth's thinking about Nature and education. They arose, he said, 'out of conversation with a friend who was somewhat unreasonably attached to modern books of moral philosophy', and as Hazlitt records that he 'got into a metaphysical argument with Wordsworth . . . in which we neither of us succeeded in making ourselves perfectly clear and intelligible', it seems possible that it was Hazlitt he had in mind.[58] Young though he was, Hazlitt was no tyro in metaphysical speculation. He had gained his independence from the Dissenting world of his father by the vigour of his own research into Hume and Hartley, Berkeley and Godwin, and he expected to argue with Coleridge and Wordsworth as an equal on the great questions about the relation of the mind to the phenomenal world. Wordsworth's poems beautifully capture the spirit of the Alfoxden encounter, in which the fleeting substances of metaphysics were pursued on walks over the hills or over an onslaught on a Cheshire cheese. Simultaneously light-hearted, yet seriously meant, as all the best of his didactic lyrics are, these two poems express Wordsworth's conviction that Nature

> has a world of ready wealth,
> Our minds and hearts to bless—
> Spontaneous wisdom breathed by health,
> Truth breathed by chearfulness.
>
> One impulse from a vernal wood
> May teach you more of man;
> Of moral evil and of good,
> Than all the sages can.
>
> Sweet is the lore which nature brings;
> Our meddling intellect
> Mis-shapes the beauteous forms of things;
> —We murder to dissect.
>
> Enough of science and of art;
> Close up these barren leaves;
> Come forth, and bring with you a heart
> That watches and receives.[59]

The charge of this conviction must not be defused. Coleridge observed that 'Wordsworth's words always *mean* the whole of their possible Meaning',[60] and Wordsworth unquestionably intends these lines to be taken seriously. But both poems have to be read in the context of others, for poems such as *Simon Lee, Old Man Travelling, The Last of the Flock*, and the lines on the Discharged Soldier make it clear that Wordsworth is expressing no simple

Panglossian optimism. The heart that watches and receives finds testimony everywhere that suffering is the permanent condition of human life.

These poems on suffering demonstrate that the passion of Wordsworth's radical years survived. The old man travelling could be one of the figures toiling across Salisbury Plain, as could the soldier, discharged into poverty after honourable service to his country. The Mad Mother, Simon Lee, Goody Blake, and Harry Gill all cling to life as wretchedly as the Female Vagrant. Throughout 1797 debate had been carried on in Parliament, in books and pamphlets, and in the correspondence columns of the magazines on how best to cope with the growing mass of the absolutely impoverished.* *The Old Cumberland Beggar* and *The Last of the Flock* are Wordsworth's contribution to the controversy. When Dr Burney commented on *Goody Blake and Harry Gill*, 'if all the poor are to help themselves, and supply their wants from the possessions of their neighbours, what imaginary wants and real anarchy would it not create?', he was rightly registering with alarm that these are political poems on contemporary themes.[61]

None of these poems, however, is at all like *Salisbury Plain* and *Adventures on Salisbury Plain* and the difference between them marks the distinctive character of Wordsworth's radical utterance. Both of those poems work from the generalized to the particular. The figures and incidents serve abstractions which are identified either in the poem, 'Truth', 'Justice', 'Freedom', or in Wordsworth's comments elsewhere, 'the vices of the penal law'. These new poems, on the contrary, originate in a particular observation of a figure or in an incident and they concentrate on it intensely, as if depicting it in all its particularity will unveil its significance. Wordsworth anticipated that readers who had thrilled to fast-moving incident, machinery, and colour in translations of Bürger's ballads or in Gothic fiction such as Lewis's *The Monk* would be puzzled, and so in the 'Advertisement' to *Lyrical Ballads* (1798) he explained that against the 'gaudiness and inane phraseology of many modern writers' he offers only the 'language of conversation' and 'a natural delineation of human passions, human characters, and human incidents'. The repetition of 'human' deliberately directs the reader away from incident. In *The Idiot Boy* the poet comically pretends that the Muses have deserted him, so that he cannot relate one half of Johnny's adventures. *Peter Bell* opens with a mock-serious

---

* The war and the poor harvests of 1794–5 made the plight of the poor more severe and brought to a focus current concern about the cost, inefficiency, and perhaps inhumanity of the Poor Laws. In 1797 a 'Bill for the better Support and Maintenance of the Poor' caused widespread reaction, ranging from considered treatises to choleric letters to the magazines. In *The Old Cumberland Beggar* W (somewhat indiscriminately) addresses the 'Statesmen' who are eager 'To rid the world of nuisances', but he could as well have been addressing the writer of a letter to the *Monthly Magazine*, 2 (Dec. 1796), 858–9, whose views 'On the Impropriety of relieving Beggars' represent those who maintained that while indigenous poor deserved support the vagrant must be discouraged.

search for a subject, in which the poet rejects the 'land of Fairy' for the doings of 'This little earth of ours'.

Much has been written about the style of these lyrical ballads and about the ways in which Wordsworth diverged, radically and originally, both from the magazine poetry of the day, which he rightly deplored, and from the mainstream eighteenth-century poets to whom he owed so much.[62] What needs to be stressed, however, is that Wordsworth's literary experimentation was serving political ends. Addressing himself to the poetry-reading public—that is, to the legislating, voting, rate-paying, opinion-forming middle class—Wordsworth wanted to defamiliarize poetry and the subject-matter of poetry, to remove 'the film of familiarity and selfish solicitude'[63] which dulls the eye and hardens the heart. And what the reader's awakened sensibility was asked to comprehend was the pathos, tragedy, or dignity inherent in the burbling of an idiot boy, in the gratitude of an enfeebled old man, or even in the shuffling gait of an old Cumberland beggar. Later in life Coleridge analysed Wordsworth thus:

having by the conjoint operation of his own experiences, feelings, and reason *himself* convinced *himself* of Truths, which the generality of persons have either taken for granted from their Infancy, or at least adopted in early life, he has attached all their own depth and weight to doctrines and words, which come almost as Truisms or Common-place to others.[64]

This is brilliantly, absolutely right. The foundation of the radical humanism of the lyrical ballads can sound platitudinous. Elizabeth Gaskell could quote without awkwardness the passage from *The Old Cumberland Beggar* which ends with, 'we have all of us one human heart', but not many others can.[65] But our discomfiture is a measure of the success of a poet who wanted above all in these lyrical poems to challenge the assumption of all poetry readers— 'Gentlemen, persons of fortune, professional men, ladies, persons who can afford to buy or can easily procure books'—that 'human nature and the persons they associate with are one and the same thing'.*

## (7)

*Lyrical Ballads* 1798 was a joint production by Wordsworth and Coleridge, testimony to a year in which each had given love and intellectual companionship unstintingly to the other. Wordsworth's claim at the end of the two-part *Prelude* addressed to Coleridge in 1799, however, that they

---

* W to John Wilson, 7 June 1802. *EY*, 355. Appreciation of these poems always seemed to W a touchstone of a reader's sympathies. Referring to a selection of his work aimed at young people, W wrote to Edward Moxon, 13 June [1831]: 'Mr Quillinan talks of omitting the Idiot Boy—it was precisely for his perception of the merit of this Class of Poems that I allowed Mr Hine to make the Selection'. *LY*, II. 401.

both 'by different roads at length have gained / The self-same bourne', is far from being an accurate or comprehensive summing-up of their relationship during the Alfoxden year.

In *Reflections on Entering into Active Life* Coleridge had affirmed his determination in 1795 to sally forth 'to fight the bloodless fight / Of Science, Freedom, and the Truth in Christ',[66] but what the poem reveals more strongly is the hold that the idea of retirement had on his imagination. After the failure of *The Watchman* his yearning intensified. He rebutted the suggestion that retirement smacked of monasticism. 'Can he be deemed monastic who is married, and employed in rearing his children?—who *personally* preaches the truth to his friends and neighbours, and who endeavours to instruct tho' Absent by the Press? In what line of Life could I be more *actively* employed?' More whimsically he declared to Poole his intention of working '*very hard*—as Cook, Butler, Scullion, Shoe-cleaner, occasional Nurse, Gardener, Hind, Pig-Protector, Chaplain, Secretary, Poet, Reviewer, and omnium-botherum shilling-scavenger . . .'.[67] With Poole's help the dream was realized at Nether Stowey. Despite the generous aid of friends, however, Coleridge could not support his family and by the end of 1797 he was on the brink of taking up the offer of a living from the Unitarian congregation in Shrewsbury. Once again he was rescued by friends. On 17 January 1798 he accepted from Tom and Josiah Wedgwood an annuity of £150 for life.

Although, compounding their generosity, the Wedgwoods annexed 'no condition whatever' to their gift,[68] Coleridge recognized that it conferred immense obligations. 'Disembarrassed from all pecuniary anxieties yet unshackled by any regular profession, with powerful motives & no less powerful propensities to honourable effort',[69] Coleridge now saw himself as a dedicated spirit, freed not for a life of selfish ease, but for exertion in the cause of Truth. While still at Shrewsbury he wrote to Poole, 'I long to be at home with you, & to settle & persevere in, some mode of repaying the Wedgwoods thro' the medium of Mankind'.[70] He used a similar phrase on 7 March, declaring his (and Poole's) conviction that Wordsworth's recent blank verse was more likely to 'benefit mankind' than anything else he had written, and three days later maintained the elevated tone in the claim to his brother: 'I have for some time past withdrawn myself almost totally from consideration of immediate causes, which are infinitely complex & uncertain, to muse on fundamental & general causes—the "causae causarum"'.[71]

Coleridge's need to justify his life meshed in with the other compulsion that dominated him, his need to find an intellectual equal he could love. In November 1795 he had quarrelled bitterly with Southey, acknowledging 'You have left a large Void in my Heart—I know no man big enough to fill it'.[72] For a while Lamb filled Southey's place, but in 1798 that friendship too disintegrated in mutual recrimination. Coleridge was very close to Tom Poole—'consolidated' was his word[73]—but Poole could not match Coleridge's fervour for poetry as Southey and Lamb had done. It was Wordsworth who filled the void. 'Wordsworth is a great man', Coleridge told Estlin from Racedown in June 1797. A week later he enthused—not without malice—to Southey: 'Wordsworth is a very great man—the only man, to whom *at all times* & in *all modes of excellence* I feel myself inferior'. 'The Giant Wordsworth—God love him!', he exclaimed to Cottle in March 1798. In May he wrote to Estlin, 'I have now known him a year & some months, and my admiration, I might say, my awe of his intellectual powers has increased even to this hour—& (what is of more importance) he is a tried good man'.[74]

In one letter Coleridge does not praise Wordsworth directly, but he pays him the highest possible compliment. On 10 March 1798 he wrote a very long self-justification to his brother, from which some passages have already been quoted. He abjures politics, declaring, 'I wish to be a good man & a Christian—but I am no Whig, no Reformist, no Republican', explains the reason for his retirement, 'to muse on fundamental & general causes', and then says: 'I love fields & woods & mountains with almost a visionary fondness—and because I have found benevolence & quietness growing within me as that fondness [has] increased, therefore I should wish to be the means of implanting it in others—& to destroy the bad passions not by combating them, but by keeping them in inaction'.[75] The ideas are not new to Coleridge—he had said almost as much as this to Dyer in March 1795. What is significant is that he explains the associationist psychology which underlies his remarks by quoting at length to his brother Wordsworth's passage of philosophic blank verse 'Not useless do I deem'. The creative interaction at work here is fascinating. Coleridge's reading and thought has enabled Wordsworth to formulate complex ideas in poetry. Wordsworth's poetry is so powerful that Coleridge seizes on it as a means of conveying to his non-philosophic brother what he himself believes.

Given the intensity of Coleridge's need to further the benefit of mankind and the awe in which he held Wordsworth as a man and as a philosophic poet, what happened seems inevitable. Ever since 1796 Coleridge had been pondering a large-scale critique of Godwin, but his reading and thought were expanding so rapidly that writing was certain to be long delayed. He knew that he had to study German if he were to benefit from the most advanced theology and philosophy, and once the Wedgwood money made possible the visit to Germany he had longed for as early as May 1796, chances that he would complete any work of his own receded still further. Wordsworth, on the other hand, was writing with such power that,

Coleridge told Hazlitt, 'his soul seemed to inhabit the universe like a palace, and to discover truth by intuition, rather than by deduction'.[76] On 6 March Wordsworth announced to James Tobin: 'I have written 1300 lines of a poem in which I contrive to convey most of the knowledge of which I am possessed. My object is to give pictures of Nature, Man, and Society. Indeed I know not anything which will not come within the scope of my plan.' Five days later he told Losh the title of the projected poem—*The Recluse: or, Views of Nature, Man, and Society*. The excitement, the grandeur of the conception, the confidence hardly warranted by actual achievement so far, all reveal how completely Wordsworth had entered into Coleridge's vision. At 28 years of age Wordsworth assumed the title Coleridge was determined to confer upon him—philosopher-poet.[77]

(8)

Wordsworth's statement to Tobin and Losh was momentous. The philosophical-poetical ambition so unguardedly disclosed affected Wordsworth's sense of his identity as an artist. It weighed on him throughout his most creative years and it became a critical factor in his relationship with Coleridge. But from the start, though the ambition was real enough, the poetic form in which it might be realized was uncertain, and as references to it can only bewilder a reader unfamiliar with Wordsworthian scholarship, some outline account of the problem needs to be given here.[78]

Only two things are certain. The philosophical poem conceived in 1798 was to be entitled *The Recluse*. It was never completed, nor did Wordsworth ever publish a poem called *The Recluse*.

He wrote a good deal towards it. In the summer of 1798 he clearly thought that most of his recent blank verse would form part of *The Recluse*. In 1800 an autobiographical blank verse poem called *Home at Grasmere* (to be discussed in Chapter 7) was written as a first book for *The Recluse*, but though Wordsworth revised it in 1806, it was not published and no further books were composed in this autobiographical, reflective vein. In 1814 Wordsworth published *The Excursion*, a blank verse, quasi-dramatic poem in nine books, of which a version of *The Ruined Cottage* forms Book I, and it was with this volume that he made the project of *The Recluse* public. A long prose Preface announced that *The Excursion* was only a portion of a planned three-part whole called *The Recluse*. The Preface concluded with lines taken from the conclusion to *Home at Grasmere*, which Wordsworth invited the reader to regard 'as a kind of *Prospectus* of the design and scope of the whole poem'. These lines are always referred to as the 'Prospectus' to *The Recluse*. At various times Wordsworth composed a little poetry which he liked to think of as part of the grand scheme (which will be discussed in the appropriate chapters), but in reality *The Recluse* was dead after 1815.

It will be clear from this account that the only part of *The Recluse* to be *published* in Wordsworth's lifetime was *The Excursion*. During the years in which he might have been writing the rest of the poem, he poured out his views on 'Nature, Man, and Society' in *The Prelude*, but as Wordsworth was clear that publication of such a nakedly personal poem could not be justified until the philosophical master-work to which it was a prelude were complete and published, it remained in manuscript to the end of his life.

Into old age Wordsworth was oppressed by a sense of failure. *The Excursion* was unquestionably a substantial achievement, which eventually established his fame as moral-philosophical poet, but the project announced privately in 1798 and publicly in 1814 had not been accomplished and, while readers waited for the rest of *The Recluse* promised in the Preface to *The Excursion*, Wordsworth knew it never would be. Why? Subsequent chapters will consider some of the reasons in the narrative of Wordsworth's repeated attempts to work on the poem, but two factors can properly be discussed here as they have a bearing on Wordsworth and Coleridge in 1798.

The first is that it seems certain that Wordsworth floundered with *The Recluse* because the project was so undefined. 'My object is to give pictures of Nature, Man, and Society' announces an ambition, not a poem. Something must have been sketched out by Wordsworth and Coleridge in 1798, but what is not known. There is some much later evidence. After the publication of *The Excursion* in 1814 Coleridge sent Wordsworth an account of what he had thought *The Recluse* was supposed to consist of (a letter which will be discussed in Chapter 10),[79] and much later still he is recorded as giving in conversation an outline of what the project agreed in 1798 was. Both sweep across human history and limitless fields of knowledge and are so much at variance with what Wordsworth had done by 1798, or was ever likely to do, that one might conclude that Coleridge's vision of *The Recluse* had expanded, or, equally plausibly, that in 1798 he and Wordsworth had been content to leave the details of the execution of the philosophical poem vague.

The second is that whatever Wordsworth and Coleridge thought they were agreeing on in 1798, the scheme for a philosophical poem, at least according to Coleridge's likely definition, was conceived with the wrong poet in mind. Coleridge expected Wordsworth, he later recalled, 'to assume the station of a man in mental repose, one whose principles were made up, and so prepared to deliver upon authority a system of philosophy'.[80] But this statement crucially mistakes the nature of Wordsworth's genius. He did not have, ever, a 'system of philosophy' to deliver, and he spent a lifetime searching for 'authority' in poetry which is essentially exploratory of what he does know and can trust. In many poems Wordsworth wrote with authority, but never 'upon authority'. His is a poetry of questioning, of gleams, flashes, intimations, visionary moments. Wordsworth was not, and could not become, the poet of Coleridge's imaginings.*

(9)

The scheme for *The Recluse* was born of the joy the poets felt in each other's company, of their pride in each other's intellect, and of their shared faith in poetry. Everything seemed possible in this, the happiest of their years together. But even during the *annus mirabilis* there were portents of how and why their relationship in the future would come under strain.

Coleridge said that his 'vice' was a 'precipitance in praise'. If it was a vice, it was more life-giving than Southey's 'perpendicular Virtue' and its benefit for Wordsworth was considerable.[81] Poole, however, worried that Coleridge was too absorbed in this one relationship. When the two poets split up in Germany, later in the year, Poole was relieved, commenting to Coleridge, 'so there is an end of our fears about amalgamation, etc.'.[82] What fears? Poole insisted that to learn German Coleridge had to live amongst Germans, and perhaps his words meant only that he had feared the company of the Wordsworths would slow his progress. But perhaps he alluded to deeper fears. In May 1799 Coleridge was assuring Poole that he was *not* allowing Wordsworth to dictate his choice of where to live and declaring so fulsomely, 'I told him plainly that *you* had been the man in whom *first* and in whom alone I had felt an *anchor!*', that one suspects Poole must have mentioned again his anxiety that Coleridge was losing his independence.[83] Poole's accusation that Coleridge was in 'prostration' before Wordsworth, however, was too much and stung him in March 1800 to justify his reverence for the man he prophesied would prove to be 'a greater poet than any since Milton'.[84] But a decade later a rift had opened between them and Coleridge had come to think that Poole had been right. By that sad time his joyful acknowledgement in 1798 of Wordsworth's genius had come to seem 'voluntary self-humiliation'.[85]

The fault lines of this future rift were marked out by three events during the Alfoxden year. In itself the first did not affect Wordsworth very much, but it is worth mentioning briefly because it prefigured the tangle of

---

* Hazlitt mentions that even in 1798 at Alfoxden C had had reservations about W as a lyric poet: 'He lamented that Wordsworth was not prone enough to believe in the traditional superstitions of the place, and that there was a something corporeal, a *matter-of-fact-ness*, a clinging to the palpable, or often to the petty, in his poetry, in consequence . . . He said, however (if I remember right), that this objection must be confined to his descriptive pieces, that his philosophic poetry had a grand and comprehensive spirit in it . . .' *Howe*, XVII. 117.

bitterness, accusation, and self-justification in which Coleridge and Wordsworth were to thrash about during 1810–12.

In November 1797 Coleridge, as 'Nehemiah Higginbottom', published three mock sonnets in the *Monthly Magazine*, in ridicule of the 'affectation of unaffectedness, of jumping & misplaced accent on common-place epithets . . . puny pathos &c &c', which disfigured the poetry of Charles Lloyd, Lamb, and, as he confessed, Coleridge himself.[86] It was a very odd thing to do. True, Lloyd was only a recent acquaintance, who had come to study with him as a pupil-boarder, and he was an undistinguished poet, but none the less Coleridge had flatteringly incorporated Lloyd's work in the 1797 second edition of his own *Poems*. Lamb, whose much better work also appeared in the 1797 volume, had been a friend since school-days and had reason to believe that he counted in Coleridge's affections. Both were wounded. Southey rightly thought that he was ridiculed too, and so the bile began to flow. Lloyd fomented trouble, even attempting to win over Dorothy Wordsworth to his view that Coleridge was a villain. Much worse, he rapidly completed a novel, *Edmund Oliver*, whose 'hero' was clearly drawn from anecdotes about Coleridge's wayward early life which only Southey can have supplied. When it appeared in April 1798 it was Coleridge's turn to be deeply hurt. Hoping that he might bring him back to Stowey for some sort of reconciliation, Wordsworth went in search of Lloyd in May, but he travelled to Bristol in vain. Lloyd had already left and the wound between him and his one-time mentor continued to fester.

Three aspects of Coleridge's personality which were to bear painfully on Wordsworth in the future are revealed in this affair. The first is that Coleridge was seemingly unaware of his own power-play and unthinking about the emotional situation of the others involved. 'I think they [the sonnets] may do good to our young Bards', he told Cottle, referring to one friend, Lloyd, who had already shown signs of mental instability and another, of long-standing, Lamb, whose creative work was about all that stood between him and black depression in this time of his great calamity.[87] The second is that faced with a valued friendship on the point of disintegration Coleridge remained stiff-necked. His letter of early May 1798 to Lamb was nothing like the denunciation of Southey in 1795, but it was no more likely to heal a breach. The third is that when he was in distress and searching for understanding and self-justification, Coleridge drew comfort from what was undoubtedly the truth, namely, that he was cleverer and more learned than all of his friends. In 1795 he had reminded Southey that in their joint enterprises, the tug of brain had been all his, which was accurate but more wounding than Coleridge can possibly have realized. Now he seemed to Lamb to be playing the sage, the lofty philosopher-theologian, a posture Lamb strongly resented and sent up in a savagely witty letter, which begins, 'Learned Sir, my Friend', and ends, so very sadly, 'I remain, Your friend and docile Pupil to instruct, Charles Lamb'.[88] Twelve years later Coleridge was to torment himself, and so exacerbate the quarrel with Wordsworth, by dwelling on the fact that he had sacrificed his own originating and creative genius to the career of another man. And as he did so, in the dreadful, self-lacerating notebook entry for 3 November 1810, he released again into his system the poison of the quarrel with Lloyd.

The distress caused by the Lloyd–Lamb–Coleridge rupture was felt by them all, especially since Lamb was such a sympathetic and evidently genuine person, and partisan for Coleridge though he was, Wordsworth must have puzzled over his friend's part in it all. To the significance of two other events, however, it is likely that he hardly gave any thought. But they were pregnant with meaning which he certainly would dwell on in due course.

At the end of 1797 Coleridge was desperate to find ways of supplementing his income. In early December he agreed with Daniel Stuart that for a guinea a week he would undertake to supply poetry regularly for the *Morning Post*. But Coleridge was the last poet who could have stomached the obligation to write to order. Stuart, as owner and publisher of the paper, was soon pressing for copy and Coleridge turned to Wordsworth for help. In the *Morning Post* for 14 December 1797 appeared *The Convict*, the first of seven poems from Wordsworth's notebooks which Coleridge continued to draw on in the spring of 1798.[89]

Wordsworth and Coleridge were not niggardly. Coleridge was giving him so much that Wordsworth was unquestionably happy to offer him material to appropriate and revise. But the episode (which did not end in 1798) introduced a new element into their relationship. For the first, but not the last time, Wordsworth was bailing Coleridge out, demonstrating that he was the more prolific poet and, perhaps, the more reliable man.

Similar dynamics operated in the publication of *Lyrical Ballads*. Almost since moving into Alfoxden the Wordsworths had known that they would be obliged to leave at midsummer 1798. Coleridge longed to get to Germany and they wanted not to lose his company. As early as March it was settled— all of them, Sara Coleridge included, would go to Germany, 'where we purpose to pass the two ensuing years in order to acquire the German language, and to furnish ourselves with a tolerable stock of information in natural science. Our plan is to settle if possible in a village near a university, in a pleasant, and, if we can a mountainous country.'[90] The delights of Stowey and Alfoxden were to be replicated and their deficiencies made up abroad.

It was a bold, not to say foolhardy, scheme, given that Europe was at war and that none of them knew anything at first hand about conditions in

Germany.[91] But all that seemed to threaten its execution was lack of money. Although a little more of the Calvert bequest had come in and Montagu had paid interest on his loan, the Wordsworths were in difficulties throughout the Alfoxden year, being forced to borrow small sums from Poole, Cottle, and Tobin. In June Dorothy even had to write to Richard for cash to pay the last of the rent so that they could leave Alfoxden. Money had to be earned.

Once more they turned to Cottle. For some time Coleridge had been negotiating with him about a third edition of his poems, but in March 1798 he put to him Wordsworth's suggestion that Cottle might publish *Osorio* and *The Borderers* as one volume and versions of *Salisbury Plain* and *The Ruined Cottage* as another.[92] This clearly interested Cottle and on 12 April Wordsworth was tempting him to visit Alfoxden: 'I have gone on very rapidly adding to my stock of poetry. Do come and let me read it to you, under the old trees in the park.'[93] Dorothy's confident assertion at the end of the month that he was 'about to publish some poems. He is to have twenty guineas for one volume, and he expects more than twice as much for another which is nearly ready for publishing' was premature, intended to reassure Richard that they had worked out how to finance the German trip, but it does indicate what Wordsworth's expectations were.[94] Early in May he insisted that Cottle visit them, declaring, 'I say nothing of the Salisbury plain 'till I see you, I am determined to finish it, and equally so that You shall publish I have lately been busy about another plan which I do not wish to mention till I see you; let this be *very*, *very*, soon'.[95]

At last, about the twenty-second of the month, Cottle did come. He stayed a week, during which Wordsworth and Coleridge took him on their favourite expedition to Lynton and the Valley of Rocks and negotiated about publication. When he left he almost certainly carried with him the manuscripts of poems eventually included in *Lyrical Ballads*. But even now the matter was not settled. In later life both poets spoke of *Lyrical Ballads* as if it were the outcome of a considered aesthetic programme, dating from the time of their attempted collaboration on *The Ancient Mariner* in 1797.[96] In fact, as a letter of Coleridge makes clear, the existence of *Lyrical Ballads*, as opposed to some other volume(s), was still a matter of contention as late as June 1798. Coleridge addressed Cottle with a note of exasperation and then declared:

Wordsworth & I have *maturely weigh'd* your proposal, & this is our answer—W. would not object to the publishing of Peter Bell *or* the Salisbury Plain, singly; but to the publishing of *his poems* in two volumes he is decisively repugnant & oppugnant—He deems that they would want variety &c &c—if this apply in his case, it applies with tenfold force to mine.—We deem that the volumes offered to you are to a certain degree *one-work*, in *kind tho' not in degree*, as an Ode is one work—& that our different poems are as stanzas, good relatively rather than absolutely:—Mark you, I say *in kind* tho' not in degree.—[97]

The vigour and severity of the tone are very revealing. Coleridge was struggling, rather anxiously, for a place in the plans for publication. Cottle had clearly been struck, as Hazlitt had at the same time, by the originality and verve of Wordsworth's lyrics and narratives and he seems to have made an offer to publish Wordsworth's poems in some form alone. Coleridge was being edged out, and it is not difficult to see why. In his earlier overtures to Cottle Wordsworth had clearly indicated that he would like to see some of his poems appear separately. A third edition of Coleridge's poems was still a possibility. With Wordsworth, however, Cottle had a new name. As he later admitted he was thrilled by the prospect of 'becoming the publisher of the first volumes of three such Poets as Southey, Coleridge, and Wordsworth; a distinction that might never again occur to a Provincial bookseller'.[98] He would have been aware, moreover, that Wordsworth had a number of new poems to hand, whereas Coleridge, who had composed little since November 1797, did not.

The poets got their way. *Lyrical Ballads* was published in one volume. The opportunity of presenting substantial works such as *Peter Bell* or *Salisbury Plain* was lost, with the result that the very slim volume that did appear had to be padded out with a few poems that pre-date the lyric experiments of 1798. Cottle also acquiesced in anonymous publication. 'Wordsworth's name is nothing—to a large number of persons mine *stinks*', Coleridge declared, smarting from the lash of the *Anti-Jacobin*, and Cottle gave way.[99]

Although it conforms to the joint wishes Coleridge had put so forcefully to Cottle, however, *Lyrical Ballads*, as finally issued after much delay on 4 October 1798, demonstrates how strongly the balance of forces in the relationship of Wordsworth and Coleridge had shifted towards Wordsworth. Nineteen of the twenty-four poems were his. His finest contribution, *Tintern Abbey*, was added when the volume was already in the press. Bibliographical evidence suggests that the 'Advertisement' which prefaces the volume was also added late, and almost certainly on Wordsworth's initiative. When Cottle began to dither about whether he should actually publish the volume, it was Wordsworth who attempted to ensure its appearance by negotiating with his former publisher Joseph Johnson.[100] In acknowledgement of all that he had gained from Coleridge during the *annus mirabilis*—intellectual stimulus, support, love—Wordsworth subjugated himself in *Lyrical Ballads*. But there can be little doubt that at one level he regretted doing so. In March Wordsworth had told Tobin, 'There is little need to advise me against publishing; it is a thing which I dread as much as death itself'.[101] Once he began to publish in earnest, however, he became determinedly professional and zealous to promote his own work. When a second edition was called for he made sure that the world knew that essentially *Lyrical Ballads* was his.

(10)

At the end of the Alfoxden year the Wordsworths were in a limbo of expectation. They knew that soon they would be *en route* for Germany, but exactly when was uncertain. On 3 July Dorothy thought it improbable that it would be in under two months, 'as I have no doubt that many things will delay the Coleridges which they have no idea of at present'.[102] *Lyrical Ballads* was said to be 'in the Bristol press' at the end of May, but there was no telling how long Cottle would actually take to issue the volume.[103] They had to find somewhere to live and some way of passing the time—cheaply. That Wordsworth was ready to sell his two volumes of Gilpin's *Observations*, which he had been so anxious to retrieve from London in March 1796, indicates how pressed they were for ready money.[104]

In June Wordsworth went to Bristol, as Dorothy rather grandly put it, 'to superintend the printing' of *Lyrical Ballads*.[105] On his return they prepared to leave, arranging to store most of their possessions at the Coleridges' cottage. On 25 June they left Alfoxden and, via Nether Stowey, made their way to Bristol. Their base for the summer was Shirehampton, just outside the city, where James Losh, suffering from ill-health, had taken a cottage. Some part of what could have been a tedious interval under yet another strange roof was passed in the way the Wordsworths liked best, exploring. On 10 July William and Dorothy crossed the Severn and walked to Tintern, setting a pattern of daily walks of about twenty miles. The next day they went on to Goodrich and on the following returned to Tintern, where they passed the night. On the thirteenth they arrived back in Bristol. Three weeks later they were off again, touring the Usk and once more the Wye valleys for at least the first week in August.[106] It was, according to Wordsworth, 'quite an unpremeditated scheme. Mr Coleridge proposed it to us one evening and we departed the next morning at six o'clock.'[107] On this tour they visited Thelwall, now living at Llyswen Farm near Brecon. The sight of this brave man, a hero of the first phase of the radical activism of the 1790s and a casualty of the second, now trying to rebuild his life, must have reminded Wordsworth and Coleridge how relatively easy had been their own passage through the reefs of politics. Sometime after 10 August the Wordsworths travelled by way of Oxford to London, where they parted sadly from little Basil, who was going to stay with an aunt. Coleridge, but not after all Sara, joined them early in September and on the fourteenth they left London for Yarmouth and Germany.

Such is the factual account of the close of the Alfoxden year and it has been given in brief deliberately. For details of where Wordsworth slept or whom he met seem more than usually unimportant compared with the literary fact that he marked the end of the *annus mirabilis* by writing his first completely assured and unquestionably great poem: *Lines Written a Few Miles above Tintern Abbey, on Revisiting the Banks of the Wye during a Tour, July 13, 1798.*

Composed during the first Wye tour and written down, as the date in the title indicates, at its close, *Tintern Abbey* was printed as the last poem in *Lyrical Ballads.* Whether or not this placing was intentional, it is entirely appropriate, for the poem is both the climax to Wordsworth's first great creative period and a prefiguring of the future poems which seem most quintessentially 'Wordsworthian'. It is magnificently sonorous—'I have not ventured to call this Poem an Ode', Wordsworth remarked, 'but it was written with a hope that in the transitions, and in the impassioned music of the versification would be found the principal requisites of that species of composition'.[108] It harmonizes the elegiac and the triumphant, so that the coloration of both moods mingles but does not dissolve. It is shaped by the activity of a mind determined to generate from the past energy for the present and future. As all of Wordsworth's greatest autobiographical poems do, *Tintern Abbey* seizes imperiously on the 'facts', to forge a poetic fiction with which to convey essential truth. Characteristically too, and this is why its impassioned music is magnificent and not magniloquent, the poem discloses questions and doubts which challenge its confidence and beckon to the future—to *The Prelude, Ode to Duty, Ode: Intimations of Immortality, Elegiac Stanzas . . . Peele Castle,* and *Ode: Composed upon an Evening of Extraordinary Splendor and Beauty.*

*Tintern Abbey* creates its complete and persuasive fiction in two fascinatingly high-handed ways. The first is the way of exclusion. Despite the topographical specificity of the title, which promises to locate it in an established tradition of landscape poems, *Tintern Abbey* strikingly avoids localizing detail. It opens with the evocation of a particular place—'These waters', 'these steep and lofty cliffs', 'These plots of cottage-ground'—but for all its apparent specificity the scene remains generalized. Wordsworth passes over everything that gave the area its actual day-to-day character—the commercial traffic on the river, the charcoal-burners serving the iron furnaces along its banks, whose smoke, Gilpin noted in his *Observations on the River Wye* (1782), 'issuing from the sides of the hills; and spreading its thin veil over a part of them, beautifully breaks their lines, and unites them with the sky', the beggars at Tintern Abbey itself, whose wretched hovels defeated even Gilpin's capacity for harmonizing everything into the picturesque.[109] What counts, it soon becomes clear, is not the sequence of verbs in the opening section which register the scene, 'hear', 'behold', 'view', 'see', but the pronoun 'I', four times repeated. The poet is concerned not with what is seen in itself, but with the eye that sees. Neither Tintern Abbey nor the River Wye is the subject of the poem. The poet himself is.

The figure is presented by the way of history-making. For the first time in his poetry Wordsworth presents his whole life as a series of distinct phases, characterized by different responses to Nature. Boyish days, with their 'glad animal movements', give way to a time when

> The sounding cataract
> Haunted me like a passion: the tall rock,
> The mountain, and the deep and gloomy wood,
> Their colours and their forms, were then to me
> An appetite: a feeling and a love,
> That had no need of a remoter charm,
> By thought supplied, or any interest
> Unborrowed from the eye.[110]

This period in turn yields to maturity, when the man looks on Nature 'not as in the hour / Of thoughtless youth'. Chronological pointers are given in the title, 1798, the five years retrospect to 1793, and before that to 'boyish days', but the chronological movement is of less importance than the line of moral development on which each phase is placed. The 'aching joys' and 'dizzy raptures' of 1793, the poet declares, have continued in memory to feed, restore, and influence him, so that now they act in conjunction with the power of experience which has taught him

> To look on nature, not as in the hour
> Of thoughtless youth, but hearing oftentimes
> The still sad music of humanity.

The past and the present will combine, moreover, against all the adversities the future might bring, to sustain the poet's 'chearful faith that all which we behold / Is full of blessings'.

Two points need to be made about this self-representation. The first is that factually it is not true. It is not surprising that Wordsworth should have erased what he was in 1793—tormented by his impotent hostility to his own country's policies, by his responsibility to Annette and their child, by lack of direction and of financial independence. But it is surprising that he should present 1793 as the time when Nature was 'all in all' and 1798 as the moment when he felt most at one with the cause of humanity, for in 1793 Wordsworth had been a radical patriot, his heart given to the people and to the French cause, whereas in 1798 he was hymning Nature's power to 'feed this mind of ours, / In a wise passiveness'.[111]

The second is that Wordsworth introduces here a conviction which is repeated in various forms in all of his later autobiographical poems, namely, that his development obeys a providential economy of loss and gain. Wordsworth evokes the 'aching joys' of youth only to declare:

> Not for this
> Faint I, nor mourn nor murmur: other gifts
> Have followed, for such loss, I would believe,
> Abundant recompence.

Change is the inevitable condition of life, but in *Tintern Abbey* Wordsworth affirms not only that through memory nothing is really lost, but also that change yields 'abundant recompence'.

In presenting his own life in these terms Wordsworth created the poetic fiction which was to be the foundation of all his work. No matter how often revised and reshaped, its essential form remained intact. But never again was he to express with such assurance the faith on which everything—his poetry, his sense of self, his awareness of vocation—was now grounded. The quotation is long, but too vital to be cut short:

> I have felt
> A presence that disturbs me with the joy
> Of elevated thoughts; a sense sublime
> Of something far more deeply interfused,
> Whose dwelling is the light of setting suns,
> And the round ocean, and the living air,
> And the blue sky, and in the mind of man,
> A motion and a spirit, that impels
> All thinking things, all objects of all thought,
> And rolls through all things. Therefore am I still
> A lover of the meadows and the woods,
> And mountains; and of all that we behold
> From this green earth; of all the mighty world
> Of eye and ear, both what they half-create,
> And what perceive; well pleased to recognize
> In nature and the language of the sense,
> The anchor of my purest thoughts, the nurse,
> The guide, the guardian of my heart, and soul
> Of all my moral being.

'Therefore' is the pivotal word in this declaration. Wordsworth offers not mysticism, but an argument. His participation in Godhead validates his love of and trust in Nature: through love of Nature he participates in the Divine.

By the summer of 1798 Wordsworth was possessed by a profoundly religious vision. *Tintern Abbey* is his impassioned ode to joy.

It is this awed, reverent, above all confident vision that determines the structure of the poem. Here Wordsworth began the task, which *The Prelude* completed, of tracing in his own former life the providential power which had shaped him through years of uncertainty to what he now was. But even the joyful affirmations of *Tintern Abbey* cannot obscure the presence of questions which were to drive Wordsworth to repeated and perplexed poetic exploration. His conviction was that love of nature led to love of man. In the Pedlar's additional lines, 'Not useless do I deem . . .', he had attempted to prove it as a coherent philosophical-psychological argument. In *Tintern Abbey* he proclaims it as *knowledge*, gained from his own experience. But neither *The Ruined Cottage* nor *Tintern Abbey* explains *how* this process takes place nor establishes what the relation may be between one poet's personal sense of joy and his awareness of the brute fact of suffering in the world. That the questions are unanswerable did not deter Wordsworth from tackling them. In July 1798 he thought he was about to do so in *The Recluse*. In the event, the questions preoccupied him throughout his creative life.

# 1798–1799

(1)

AT 11 a.m. on 16 September 1798 the German packet slipped out of Yarmouth to the open sea. At once the passengers began to turn frog-coloured—'Wordsworth shockingly ill', Coleridge reported, 'his Sister worst of all—vomiting, & groaning, unspeakably!'[1] They were delayed by fog at the mouth of the Elbe and when they reached Hamburg on the nineteenth had difficulty in finding accommodation in a dirty, stinking city, where children defecated in the streets and shopkeepers (they were convinced) gloated over their skill at cheating foreigners.* It was not an auspicious start to a tour which, as a tour, turned out for the Wordsworths a complete failure.

Coleridge was fascinated by everything. Whereas Dorothy's Hamburg journal is a lifeless, uncomprehending account of sights, prices, and menus, Coleridge's letters home vividly register his excitement at the strangeness of it all—the immense hats of the women, the incessant pipe-smoking, the strange bells and door-knockers, the street of prostitutes.[2] He was determined to enjoy himself and at once used his credit note at Remnant, the English bookseller, and the letters of introduction supplied by the Wedgwoods. Through Coleridge's contacts they met Friedrich Klopstock, and on three occasions Wordsworth conversed in French with the venerable father of German poetry. Respect was due to the 74-year-old author of the massive epic *Der Messias*, even though Wordsworth was disappointed not to discover in his countenance 'the marks either of sublimity or enthusiasm', but since Klopstock knew little about English poetry, preferred Glover to Milton, had not heard of Cowper, thought Schiller extravagant, and

---

* In view of the spy episode one wonders whether W and C were aware, as they journeyed to Hamburg, that they were going to a city which was under constant government scrutiny as a place which 'has long been the receptacle of those disaffected persons who have fled from Great Britain or Ireland, either from apprehension of the consequences of the treasonable practices in which they have been engaged, or for the purpose of assisting the conspiracies carried on against their respective countries'. *Annual Register*, 41 (1799), 224–5, noting the 'Report of the Committee of Secrecy of the British House of Commons, printed the 15th of March 1799'.

Wieland superior to Goethe, their conversation seems to have consisted largely of rather formal declarations of opinion, made genial by expressions of kindly regard.[3]

Becalmed in 'an ugly City that stinks in every corner', which offered neither culture—they walked out of the theatre in the second act of an unintelligible piece—nor company, the party had to decide what to do next.[4] At once the real problem became clear. Coleridge knew why he was there. He wanted to learn German—'a noble Language—a very noble Language'—and, once equipped, to meet scientists, theologians, and moral philosophers.[5] He refused, moreover, to be worried about money. Having left Sara at home (her place being taken by John Chester, a Stowey disciple and friend), Coleridge trusted that his annuity, and the support of the Wedgwoods through their bankers, the Von Axens, would see him through. The Wordsworths, on the other hand, had no very clear purpose, beyond a lukewarm desire to learn the language, and had been fretting about money from the moment they landed. And so they separated. Although his reconnaissance of fashionable Ratzeburg had indicated that it would be an expensive place, Coleridge moved there with Chester on 30 September. Three days later, lonely and thinking wistfully of Alfoxden, the Wordsworths set off across appalling roads on the three-day journey to Goslar.

Although he was often intensely homesick, Coleridge prospered. Soon he was reporting that he had 'now dined at all the Gentlemen's & Noblemen's Houses within two or three miles of Ratzeburgh' and boasting that as he worked at German from morning to night, 'my progress is more rapid than I could myself have believed'.[6] Early in February he moved to Göttingen, then at its zenith as an intellectual centre, where he matriculated at the University to gain access to Blumenbach's lectures on physiology and natural history and to the library, which he delared 'without doubt . . . the very first in the World'.[7] He met other English students and, in this home of biblical higher criticism, planned out a study of 'the most formidable Infidel', Lessing.[8] Much about Germany and the Germans disgusted Coleridge—the cheating, drunkenness, sexual laxity—but in Göttingen he was, as a recent scholar has put it, 'at the fine point of consciousness of his age'.[9] When he returned home in July, followed by his box of metaphysical books, Coleridge had recognized that his life's work now had a European horizon.

The Wordsworths' experience was completely different. 'Once the residence of Emperors . . . now the residence of Grocers and Linen-drapers', Goslar, they discovered, had little to recommend it, save that it was cheap.[10] They found lodgings with Frau Deppermann, a draper's widow, but as the sort of *en pension* arrangement Wordsworth had enjoyed in France seemed unknown, they lived and ate alone, dependent for occasional company on their landlady, a French *émigré* priest, and a deaf neighbour with bad teeth. As Wordsworth ruefully told Josiah Wedgwood, 'with bad German, bad English, bad French, bad hearing, and bad utterance you will imagine we have had very pretty dialogues'.[11] They could not entertain and were not invited out, perhaps, as Coleridge surmised, because Dorothy was taken for Wordsworth's mistress. All hopes of learning German 'with reference to literary emolument' were dashed and the onset of a particularly cold winter made them prisoners, yearning for the release of spring.[12] They left as soon as they could. Early in February Dorothy sketched out plans for a two month tour, taking in Erfurt, Eisnach, and possibly Weimar, but this was an ambitious itinerary for a country in which they often found themselves walking 'above the ankles in water, and sometimes as high in clay'.[13] At the end of the month they walked to Nordhausen, suffering some indignity from officious soldiers on the way, which only intensified feelings of alienation already heightened by the stares of the country people, and eventually they joined Coleridge at Göttingen on about 20 April 1799.[14] It was an emotional reunion, but not even his company could keep them long, burning as they were 'with such impatience to return to their native Country'.[15] They struck north as rapidly as the roads and transport would allow and on 1 May landed once again at Yarmouth.


(2)

'We have had a pleasant residence at Goslar', Wordsworth told Josiah Wedgwood as their stay was ending.[16] In fact the evidence, even the details given in this letter, suggest that it had been a trying time, particularly for Dorothy. At Racedown and Alfoxden she had been running a household, with Peggy to talk to as they washed, cooked, and looked after little Basil. With Mary Hutchinson's long visit to Racedown and the constant company of Coleridge, Sara, Poole, and other visitors at Alfoxden, though isolated and dependent, she had never been lonely or without a proper place. In Germany, however, she had no role and, abroad for the first time, experienced in addition the overwhelming sense of disorientation which a foreign language and the unintelligible signals of another culture can impose. Rambling about, as they had in the West Country, was impossible, both because she was a woman and because of the intense cold. An hour a day together, muffled up in heavy furs, was what they aimed for. To a degree never experienced before, Dorothy was totally dependent on her brother. One letter vividly catches her situation. On 14 or 21 December 1798 she transcribed for Coleridge Wordsworth's recent lyrics and long passages of blank verse, crowding the page in what must have been hours of copying. Towards the end she writes—almost as if Coleridge were in the next room—'William's foot is on the stairs. He has been walking by moonlight in his fur gown and a black fur cap in which he looks like any grand Signior.'[17] As she was to do for much of her adult life, Dorothy was working for William and waiting for his return.

To Coleridge this relationship already seemed potentially damaging. In December he had exclaimed in a letter:

> William, my head and my heart! dear William & dear Dorothea!
> You have all in each other; but I am lonely, and want you!

'I need not say', Wordsworth replied, 'how much the sentiment affected me.'[18] Privately to Sara, however, Coleridge expressed his reservation:

[Wordsworth] seems to have employed more time in writing English than in studying German—No wonder!—for he might as well have been in England as at Goslar, in the situation which he chose & with his *unseeking* manners— . . . His taking his Sister with him was a wrong step—it is next to impossible for any but married women or in the suit of married women to be introduced to any company in Germany. Sister [here] is considered as only a name for Mistress.—Still however *male* acquaintance he might have had—& had I been at Goslar, I *would* have had them—but W., God love him! seems to have lost his spirits & almost his inclination for it.[19]

His response to the intensity of the brother-sister relationship is revealed too in an extraordinary comment to Poole. Quoting 'A Slumber did my spirit seal', which Wordsworth had sent him in December, Coleridge said of this 'most sublime Epitaph': 'whether it had any reality, I cannot say.—Most probably, in some gloomier moment he had fancied the moment in which his Sister might die.'[20] In a letter all about his own grief at the death of his infant son Berkeley, Coleridge recognizes that a comparable grief for Wordsworth could only centre on the loss of the one being he loved above all others.

(3)

In the absence of any evidence such as her later Grasmere journal provides, it is futile to speculate about what Dorothy's feelings were. Manuscript evidence does survive, however, to reveal how Wordsworth coped with the isolation and silence of that Goslar winter. He turned in, intensely, upon himself.

As I have had no books [he reported to Coleridge], I have been obliged to write in self-defence. I should have written five times as much as I have done but that I am prevented by an uneasiness at my stomach and side, with a dull pain about my heart.

I have used the word pain, but uneasiness and heat are words which more accurately express my feeling. At all events it renders writing unpleasant. Reading is now become a kind of luxury to me. When I do not read I am absolutely consumed by thinking and feeling and bodily exertions of voice or limbs, the consequence of those feelings.

A little later Dorothy confirmed, 'William is very industrious: his mind is always active; indeed, too much so; he overwearies himself, and suffers from pain and weakness in the side'.[21]

Throughout his life Wordsworth complained of physical symptoms whenever struggling with embryonic ideas or revising work whose particular form no longer satisfied him. In Goslar he was profoundly engaged in a creative process which involved both of these struggles. At Alfoxden Wordsworth had broken through to a kind of lyrical poetry which was entirely his own and much that he wrote now suggests that he was continuing to reflect upon it. He drafted a fragmentary *Essay on Morals*, in which he argued that any systematic treatise on conduct is bound to be impotent because it could not be 'written with sufficient power to melt into our affections, to incorporate itself with the blood & vital juices of our minds'.[22] Possibly Wordsworth had in mind Burke's denunciation of moral theorists: 'This sort of people are so taken up with their theories about the rights of man, that they have totally forgot his nature. Without opening one new avenue to the understanding, they have succeeded in stopping up those that lead to the heart.'[23] He was certainly weighing the value of such poems as the *Lyrical Ballads* and pondering the justification for poetry as a means of conveying truth to the heart by passion which he was to set out in the Preface to *Lyrical Ballads* of 1800. Comments on language in a letter to Josiah Wedgwood also anticipate later speculation about the relation between words and the feelings they excite and the special power of poetry to resist linguistic decay and inertia.[24] In a very important letter about Bürger's poems (which Wordsworth had bought in Hamburg), he returned to his earlier discussion with Coleridge about the place of incident in poetry and declared in a passage which both indicates what he had hoped to achieve in the Alfoxden lyrics and anticipates the fuller argument of the 1800 *Preface*: 'I do not so ardently desire character in poems like Burger's, as manners, not transitory manners reflecting the wearisome unintelligible obliquities of city-life, but manners connected with the permanent objects of nature and partaking of the simplicity of those objects. Such pictures must interest when the original shall cease to exist.'[25] Some of the lyrics Wordsworth wrote at Goslar refine aspects of the ballads of the Alfoxden period. In those Wordsworth had dwelt upon suffering and loss, but usually within a stated or implied social context, which revealed Simon Lee or the shepherd of *The Last of the Flock* as victims of particular circumstances.

Now, in the exquisitely restrained 'Lucy' and 'Mathew' poems, Wordsworth presented loss as the constant of human existence, as if he were searching to express what every heart has felt in irreducible spareness of form.[26]

At Alfoxden, however, Wordsworth had also written *The Ruined Cottage* and *Tintern Abbey* and accepted the call of *The Recluse*, and it is the reverberations of this work, both achieved and promised, which form the epicentre of the creative surge that possessed him now.

In the notebook which contains Dorothy's Hamburg journal and the *Essay on Morals*, Wordsworth began to work up blank verse about his own childhood. It is one of the most exciting of all the manuscripts now in the Wordsworth Library at Grasmere, for as Wordsworth proceeds in a zig-zag fashion, sometimes in ink, sometimes in pencil, copying out or just drafting, the beginnings of his greatest poem, *The Prelude*, take shape.[27] Starting with the image of himself as a four years' child, bathing in the Derwent at Cockermouth or standing alone, 'A naked savage in the thunder shower', Wordsworth releases memories of birds-nesting among the perilous crags, of snaring woodcocks in the moonlight, of hooting to the owls across Windermere, and of stealing a rowing-boat on Ullswater. The tone of the verse is awed, reverent, above all grateful for the process by which a 10-year-old could hold

> unconscious intercourse
> With the eternal beauty drinking in
> A pure organic pleasure from the lines
> Of curling mist or from the smooth expanse
> Of waters coloured by the cloudless moon.

In one draft passage in which the tempest of creation is called 'a storm not terrible but strong', Wordsworth refers to

> trances of thought
> And mountings of the mind compared to which
> The wind that drives along th'autumnal [?leaf]
> Is meekness

which suggests the turbulent impulses which drove him to compose so rapidly what Dorothy called a 'mass' of verse. To these memories Wordsworth added others, notably the two 'spots of time' and passages of reflection, so that by the time he left Goslar a coherent 400-line poem on his early years had come into being.

Its shape was determined by the fact that the creative energy which so disturbed Wordsworth now was generated by linked, but in some ways conflicting, impulses. In the Pedlar lines for *The Ruined Cottage* (some of

which were soon incorporated into this new autobiographical poem) and in
*Tintern Abbey* Wordsworth had already begun to give an account of his own
life, which took as its starting-point a profound gratitude that somehow,
despite all loss, pain, and discontinuity, he had survived, not just as a whole
and joyful man, but as a creative being. Now Wordsworth returned to the
brief and schematic accounts he had already attempted, and deepened them
by sensuous evocations of the pleasures and pleasing terrors of childhood
and by meditation on memory's power both to retain an image of the self as
one evolving whole and to draw nourishment from the past for the
sustenance of the present and the future:

> There are in our existence spots of time
> Which with distinct pre-eminence retain
> A fructifying virtue, whence, depressed
> By trivial occupations and the round
> Of ordinary intercourse, our minds
> (Especially the imaginative power)
> Are nourished, and invisibly repaired.[28]

From this conviction and the immense gratitude it engenders issues all the
most beautiful poetry of this sustained exercise of memory.

But the verse also voices questions about its own nature and existence.
From the earliest drafts the question 'Was it for this' demands an answer:

> Was it for this
> That one, the fairest of all rivers, loved
> To blend his murmurs with my nurse's song,
> And from his alder shades, and rocky falls
> And from his fords and shallows sent a voice
> To intertwine my dreams, for this didst thou
> O Derwent . . .

The antecedent of 'this' is implied in the very act of writing the poem and
the answer is a jubilant yes. Repeatedly Wordsworth affirms in apostrophes
to the 'Gentle powers' of nature that

> not in vain ye spirits of the springs
> And ye that have your voices in the clouds
> And ye that are familiars of the lakes
> And standing pools, ah not for trivial ends
> Through snow & sunshine & the sparkling plains
> Of moonlight frost and through the stormy [?day]
> Did ye with such assiduous love pursue
> Your favourite and your joy.

The conviction of the Pedlar lines and *Tintern Abbey* is repeated—the poet's life has been shaped by a generous, providential power.

Unlike the earlier poems, however, this new (as yet incomplete) verse acknowledges that 'this', the creative power of the present moment, entails an obligation for the future. In a very striking passage at the end of his Goslar drafting Wordsworth addresses Coleridge directly, explaining that

> my hope has been that I might fetch
> Reproaches from my former years, whose power
> May spur me on, in manhood now mature,
> To honourable toil. Yet, should it be
> That this is but an impotent desire,
> That I by such enquiry am not taught
> To understand myself, nor thou to know
> With better knowledge how the heart was framed
> Of him thou lovest, need I dread from thee
> Harsh judgements if I am so loth to quit
> Those recollected hours that have the charm
> Of visionary things, and lovely forms
> And sweet sensations that throw back our life
> And make our infancy a visible scene
> On which the sun is shining?[29]

The lines reveal how urgently Wordsworth responded to the creative impulse he now felt. In recollections of childhood experience and in the attempt to order and interpret them he was discovering abundant materials for poetry of a quite new kind and quality. In the spring and summer of 1798 Wordsworth had recognized his vocation and the creative flow of Goslar had amply confirmed that the magnitude of the task he envisaged had not paralysed his imaginative power. But it was not *The Recluse*. That 'honourable toil' still had to be attempted.

### (4)

Wordsworth's writing had been the one positive in a period which had been otherwise just a marking time. Earlier in the year Mrs William Rawson had lamented privately that he was 'spending his Youth in so unprofitable a way', and even if no such comment ever reached him, Wordsworth's own self-reproaches were active enough to picture the censure of some of his family and acquaintance.* As soon as he got back to England he acted

---

* Quoted *E Y*, 254 n. 2. On 22 Nov. Margaret Spedding wrote to her brother William about W and C, who had visited on the 9th, and commented: 'I do not think Wordsworth seems to be making much out in the way of literature—there was a volume of poems, called "Lyrical Ballads" published the other day by him & . . . Coleridge—by way of making forty pounds for their tour to the Continent—but they are really such queer odd sort of things, that if everybody was of my mind, profits would not answer for a journey'. *WL*.

vigorously to dispel them by attempting to put his affairs in order. On 13 May he wrote to Richard asking for an immediate statement of where he stood and was dismayed at what he learnt. Nothing had been paid to the Wedgwoods on account of the £110 Wordsworth had drawn through their bankers, so an apologetic letter had to go to Josiah Wedgwood on the twenty-third. Worse still, Montagu and Douglas had both defaulted, and an angry Richard, finally losing patience with Montagu's dishonoured promissory notes, was now threatening him with 'steps which will be extremely distressing to myself and unpleasant to you'.[30]

Richard had also been involved in the confusion over *Lyrical Ballads*, which now had to be sorted out. Before leaving England Wordsworth had asked Cottle to relinquish his rights in the volume in favour of Joseph Johnson, solely, he now insisted, 'on account of its being likely to be very advantageous to me'.[31] Cottle had been instructed to apply to Richard for compensation. But Wordsworth now discovered that in October 1798 Cottle had not unreasonably objected to Wordsworth's proposal, claiming to believe that he was worrying unnecessarily about his (Cottle's) welfare and insisting that he had undertaken to publish the volume and still wanted to do so. 'This Business', Richard told his brother sternly, 'also requires your immediate attention.'[32] Cottle explained that he had, in fact, disposed of the edition to the firm of J. and A. Arch, intending to quit the business of publishing, and Wordsworth's letter of 2 June indicates that he, Wordsworth, was mollified. It also indicates, none the less, that he was determined to impose his own will on the situation. He chided Cottle for damaging his chance of making a profitable connection with a major publisher, Johnson, calculated what he thought Cottle owed him, and twice demanded to know what was to happen to the copyright of *Lyrical Ballads*.

Wordsworth's firmness had to do with more than just the money outstanding on the poems. He was clearly attempting to recover control over his own publishing. The issuing of the 1798 *Lyrical Ballads* had been a haphazard affair, but despite Wordsworth's regular declarations such as, 'My aversion from publication increases every day', he was never to publish haphazardly again.[33] What one historian of the rise of the profession of literature has defined as the 'whole concept of authorship, implying intellectual property, copyright and contractual obligations',[34] became very important to Wordsworth and his letters suggest that he was beginning now to conceive of himself more professionally as a poet. He was thinking about publishing, making money, establishing a reputation, marketing, and accumulating material for future volumes.

He seems, for example, to have been reflecting on the missed opportunity of the summer of 1798. In February he told Coleridge that he had been 'hewing down' *Peter Bell* and revising *Adventures on Salisbury Plain*. He was very concerned about the safety of the manuscript of *The Borderers* and by the end of the year had had a new fair-copy manuscript made.[35] Both of these poems Cottle had been prepared to publish in 1798 and even the play had been a subject for negotiation. That Wordsworth returned to them now suggests that he was taking stock of what he had ready apart from *The Ruined Cottage* (which Cottle had also wanted to publish), which had merged inextricably with plans for *The Recluse*.

On the other hand there is the evidence of Wordsworth's proprietary concern over what had been published, *Lyrical Ballads*. His reference to them in October 1798 as 'my poems' may have been unguarded, but by 1799 he had certainly come to think of the volume as his.[36] He enquired anxiously of Cottle, 'Can you tell me whether the poems are likely to sell', and was not satisfied with the vague reply he received: 'You tell me the poems have not sold ill. If it is possible, I should wish to know *what number* have been sold.'[37] Despite what was to become a habitual disclaimer that 'I care little for the praise of any . . . professional critic, but as it may help me to pudding', he was attentive to reviews and furious that Southey had noticed the volume unfavourably in the *Critical Review*. Astonishingly he declared, 'He knew that money was of importance to me. If he could not conscientiously have spoken differently of the volume, he ought to have declined the task of reviewing it.'[38] Ominously, and sadly, too, Wordsworth suppressed his pain at criticism of his own contributions by fostering a conviction that 'The Ancyent Mariner has upon the whole been an injury to the volume'. Unilaterally he decided that, should a second edition be called for, he would scrap Coleridge's poem and 'put in its place some little things which would be more likely to suit the common taste'.[39] At the end of 1799, full of happiness at being settled at last in the Lake District, Wordsworth wrote to Coleridge in a gush of affection, 'take no pains to contradict the story that the L.B. are entirely yours. Such a rumour is the best thing that can befall them'.[40] His behaviour a year later, when a second edition of *Lyrical Ballads* was being prepared, was to demonstrate that his earlier comment on *The Ancient Mariner* reflected more accurately his real attitude to the 1798 volume.

(5)

Wordsworth could do little more than attempt to re-establish a grip on his financial and professional affairs. But one uncertainty could be settled—where he and Dorothy were to live. In the 'long & affectionate letters' which passed between the Wordsworths and Coleridge in Germany this had clearly been an issue from the beginning of the year.[41] On 4 January Coleridge told Poole that: 'Wordsworth is divided in his mind, unquietly divided, between the neighbourhood of Stowey & the N. of England. He cannot think of settling at a distance from *me*, & I have told him that I *cannot* leave the vicinity of Stowey', but Dorothy's hope, already expressed the previous month, that she and Wordsworth might 'decoy' Coleridge to the North of England indicates that they were already feeling a very strong pull towards their birthplace.[42] By the time they met Coleridge at Göttingen they had already decided and though Coleridge reported them as 'affected to tears at the thought of not being near me', they were not to be deflected.[43] On landing in England, the Wordsworths went at once to the Hutchinson family farm at Sockburn-on-Tees, where they stayed until late December with Thomas and George and their sisters Mary, Sara, and Joanna.

As they settled in with this very close family group, the Wordsworths were apparently in some confusion. Starved of books at Goslar and aware that the philosophic poem *The Recluse* would call for serious reading, Wordsworth had told Coleridge that 'he deemed the vicinity of a Library absolutely *necessary* to his health, nay to his existence' and had suggested that that of Sir Frederick Vane, the MP for Carlisle, might serve.[44] But this was a flimsy excuse for moving north, intended to give Coleridge a reason he could appreciate for their desire to go home, and although in July Dorothy suggested to Poole that they might move back to the Stowey neighbourhood if a suitable house were available, what they really wanted was that Coleridge should join them.[45]

Their hesitant but inexorable movement back to the Lake District was completed late in the year—and Coleridge was won over at the same time. Late in October Cottle came north at Wordsworth's urging and Coleridge, in an abrupt change of plan which left his wife not even knowing where he was, joined him. On 27 October, the day after their arrival, Wordsworth, Coleridge, and Cottle set off westwards. Troubled by rheumatism and no doubt daunted by Wordsworth's expectation of what a walking tour could encompass, Cottle dropped out at Greta Bridge, leaving the two poets to press on together over the forbidding waste of Stainmore. At Temple Sowerby, just east of Penrith, they heard by chance that John Wordsworth was staying nearby at Newbiggin, having attended the funeral of their Uncle Kit on 17 October.[46] They contacted him and together entered the Lakes through Kentmere and along secluded roads, possibly through Troutbeck, to Windermere.

Crossing the ferry at Bowness, they walked to Hawkshead and then on to Rydal and Grasmere, which they reached on 3 November. The idyllic vale did not fail to have the effect it had had when Wordsworth was still a schoolboy. 'Coleridge enchanted with Grasmere and Rydal', he reported to Dorothy.[47] On the fifth they said farewell to John at Grisedale Hause, where the path from Grasmere crosses over the mountains to Patterdale, 'on a day when light & darkness coexisted in contiguous masses, & the earth & sky were but *one!*[48] and on the eighth they left Robert Newton's inn by Grasmere Church for Keswick. Striking westwards they reached Buttermere, Wordsworth almost certainly making a detour via Cockermouth, and then they began a thrilling sweep into the heart of the mountains via Ennerdale to Wastwater and over the pass into Borrowdale. Touching on Keswick once again they went down the western shore of Ullswater and back up the eastern to Thomas Clarkson's house at Eusemere. 'C[oleridge] was in high Spirits & talked a great deal', Catherine Clarkson wrote. 'W[ordsworth] was more reserved but there was neither hauteur nor moroseness in his Reserve. He has a fine commanding figure is rather handsome & looks as if he were born to be a great Prince or a great General. He seems very fond of C. laughing at all his jokes & taking all opportunities of shewing him off.'[49] Around 17 November Coleridge set off back to Sockburn and thence to London, leaving Wordsworth alone for a further week. He returned to the Hutchinsons and Dorothy on 26 November.

Coleridge was awed by what he had seen. Wordsworth had bombarded him with sensation in a perfectly designed route which led from the domestic and agricultural at Hawkshead and Grasmere to the sublime on Helvellyn to the still more magnificent in Wasdale and Borrowdale before a conclusion of supreme beauty on Ullswater. He had beheld, he said, 'a vision of a fair Country'.[50]

For Wordsworth, however, the tour had been something more. It was one of the key experiences of his life. As he had drafted his recent autobiographical poetry, memories of his childhood in the Lakes had surfaced from their deepest recesses. Now by returning to the scenes of their origin he was consciously putting them to the proof, testing them as a basis for a life that might be lived. Much, inevitably, distressed him. Since he had been at school Claife Heights above the western shore of Windermere had been enclosed and new whitewashed villas dotted the shore of the lake. He was 'much disgusted with the New Erections and objects about Windermere', he told Dorothy, referring perhaps in particular to the Reverend William Braithwaite's pleasure house which disfigured his favourite 'station' above the ferry-house peninsula.[51] Ann Tyson had died in 1796 and even Hawkshead itself had changed. The market square was not as Wordsworth remembered it but now boasted

> A smart assembly-room that perked and flared
> With wash and rough-cast, elbowing the ground
> Which had been ours.[52]

But this kind of disappointment was as nothing compared with his exhilaration among the mountains or the sense of intimacy and belonging he felt as he guided Coleridge into Rydal park to see the hidden beauty of the upper fall. 'We are right glad to find ourselves in England, for we have learnt to know its value', Wordsworth had told Cottle in the month of their return.[53] Now he knew for certain in which part of England he wanted to live.

Even the few days spent with his brother served to strengthen the pull on Wordsworth to return home. John Wordsworth had gone to sea in 1788 and was now working his way up in the service of the East India Company.[54] In the last eleven years he had only spent a few months all told in England and had last met his brother over four years ago, but before beginning his voyaging he had been at school in Hawkshead and had found in Ann Tyson's affection a substitute for the home and parental love the Wordsworths had lost. As they walked along Esthwaite past Colthouse and into Hawkshead, watching the church on the mound and the grammar school below it come into view, John must have been moved quite as strongly as his brother by memories of when they were last really together, for within a day or two he had offered Wordsworth £40 to buy some land at Grasmere on which they could build a home.[55]

That scheme came to nothing, but John's generous and instinctive support for the idea that they should have a home in the Lakes was possibly the decisive prompting Wordsworth needed. In a letter to Dorothy of 8 November he mentioned that 'There is a small house at Grasmere empty which perhaps we may take',[56] and although evidence is lacking it seems certain that, once Coleridge had left him alone on the eighteenth, Wordsworth went back to Grasmere in a state of high excitement to negotiate for the house. As he walked he composed a hymn of thanksgiving, which was later used as the 'glad preamble' to the 1805 *Prelude*. Exulting like the Israelites freed from the 'house / Of bondage', Wordsworth welcomed the providential power that vouchsafed him a glimpse of the Promised Land and matched the promise with an energy now felt within,

> A corresponding mild creative breeze,
> A vital breeze which travelled gently on
> O'er things which it had made, and is become
> A tempest, a redundant energy,
> Vexing its own creation.[57]

When he returned to Sockburn it was to finalize arrangements and to fetch Dorothy to Dove Cottage.

On 17 December they set off on a journey across the Pennines of which even Wordsworth, strong walker though he was, felt proud. They went on horseback with George Hutchinson as far as Leyburn, and then on foot proceeded up Wensleydale along half-frozen roads to Askrigg. Keyed up rather than disheartened by intermittent snow-showers, they covered twenty-one miles the next day, but even anxiety about the distance and the shortness of the daylight could not prevent them from spending an hour clambering around the ice at Hardraw Force. 'Will you believe me', Wordsworth boasted to Coleridge, 'when I tell you that we walked the next ten miles, by the watch over a high mountain road, thanks to the wind that drove behind us and the good road, in two hours and a quarter, a marvellous feat of which D. will long tell.'[58] A further seven miles covered in an hour and thirty-five minutes brought them to Sedbergh. On the nineteenth they reached Kendal, where they bought furniture, and on the twentieth they made the last stage of the journey to Grasmere in a post-chaise. The house was very cold and the chimney in one of the upstairs rooms 'smoked like a furnace', but no matter. For £8 a year they had at last a permanent home.[59]

## (6)

Wordsworth's increasing decisiveness since returning from Germany stemmed in large part from his confidence that he had completed a long and original poem. He had probably started on the second part of his autobiographical work in May, but substantial progress was not made until September. He worked up drafts into a connected sequence before the November visit to the Lakes and returned to it once he was back at Sockburn. Before the Wordsworths set off for Grasmere Mary Hutchinson and Dorothy had transcribed two fair copies of both parts of a poem that just fell short of 1,000 lines of Wordsworth's most characteristic blank verse.[60] Coleridge was so impressed by the description of the boy hooting to the owls across Windermere that he exclaimed, 'had I met these lines running in the deserts of Arabia, I should have instantly screamed out "Wordsworth!"'[61] Most readers will understand why. The descriptions of the Winander boy, of the stealing of the boat, of the visit to Furness Abbey, and of the boy minstrel playing his flute alone upon a rock as the twilight gathers over Coniston water would have to appear in anyone's anthology of quintessential Wordsworth. The *1799 Prelude* is a major achievement.

As it opens the second part of the poem resembles the first in offering accounts of boyhood pleasures shared with school-friends which linger with especial sweetness in the poet's memory. The descriptive verse is direct and assured. But once Wordsworth begins to categorize the kinds of effect Nature had upon the growing boy its character changes and the assurance gives way to admissions that the subject no longer allows for directness or clarity. Exploiting the traditional rhetorical devices for confessing incapacity, while actually introducing further complexity—a manœuvre in which he was always to display considerable skill—Wordsworth drives backwards in time right to the 'Babe who sleeps / Upon his Mother's breast', to ground his speculation about how one apprehends the physical world and becomes conscious of an independent self.[62] This passage, which anticipates much Victorian autobiography and twentieth-century child psychology, is one of the most perceptive in the whole corpus of English Romantic poetry. Wordsworth is seeking to demonstrate that creative power is a fundamental human attribute, that its origins and development cannot be parcelled out by 'geometric rules', and that its survival depends on the constant struggle of the 'first creative sensibility' against the 'regular action of the world'.[63]

In this very complex passage—which is too long to quote, but impossible to paraphrase adequately—it seems likely that Wordsworth was drawing on conversation with Coleridge in Göttingen and possibly on letters that are now lost, for Coleridge had been driven to speculations of a similar kind. In letters of 6 April 1799 to Poole and 8 April to his wife he had written in deep distress and perplexity after learning of the death of his son Berkeley. From a conviction that 'My Baby has not lived in vain—this life has been to him what it is to all of us, education & development', Coleridge had groped towards consolation in ideas about vital force and the imperishability of '*Life, Power, Being!*' and to Sara, more tenderly, had said:

To look back on the life of my Baby, how short it seems!—but consider it referently to non-existence, and what a manifold and majestic Thing does it not become?— What a multitude of admirable actions, what a multitude of *habits* of actions it learnt even before it saw the light? and who shall count or conceive the infinity of its thoughts and feelings, it's hopes and fears, & joys, and pains, & desires, & presentiments, from the moment of it's birth to the moment when the Glass through which we saw him darkly was broken . . .[64]

Given the intensity with which Coleridge always pursued his current preoccupations and the immediate sympathy for ideas which both poets showed to one another, it seems likely that Coleridge's anguished 'curious fancies' did lodge and germinate in Wordsworth's mind. But even if this suggested connection might be mistaken, there can be no doubt that, as he concluded his poem, and as he shaped the whole, Wordsworth was responding to Coleridge.

On the face of it the *1799 Prelude* is a direct love-offering to Coleridge. The poem, which opens and closes with graceful allusion to *Frost at Midnight*, presents him as the more penetrating thinker, one more skilled in the kind of enquiry of which this poem is but a hesitant essay:

> Thou, my Friend, art one
> More deeply read in thy own thoughts, no slave
> Of that false secondary power by which
> In weakness we create distinctions, then

Believe our puny boundaries are things
Which we perceive and not which we have made.
To thee, unblinded by these outward shews,
The unity of all has been revealed . . .[65]

But the poem also reveals Wordsworth asserting himself against Coleridge in two ways which were to be of great significance for their future relationship and for Wordsworth's developing sense of his own poetic identity.

At some point in the late summer of 1799 Coleridge must have learnt about Wordsworth's recent composition, for on 12 October he wrote:

I long to see what you have been doing. O let it be the tail-piece of 'The Recluse!' for of nothing but 'The Recluse' can I hear patiently. That it is to be addressed to me makes me more desirous that it should not be a poem of itself. To be addressed, as a beloved man, by a thinker, at the close of such a poem as 'The Recluse,' a poem *non unius populi*, is the only event, I believe, capable of inciting in me an hour's vanity— vanity, nay, it is too good a feeling to be so called; it would indeed be a self-elevation produced *ab extra*.[66]

This letter and Wordsworth's reaction set a pattern for future years. After a lapse of time Wordsworth surfaces with something demonstrably achieved. Coleridge, who in the same time has completed nothing, seems to welcome it, but actually disparages the work by wishing it were something else. In immediate response Wordsworth is checked, but then he reasserts more vigorously the validity of what he has been doing. So it was now. After getting Coleridge's letter Wordsworth faltered, but when he returned to Part II, fresh from the excitement of the tour of the Lakes, it was to enlarge the scope and aggrandize the tone of the poem.[67] Incorporating material he had written about the Pedlar in 1798, Wordsworth brought the *1799 Prelude* to a climax with a rhapsodic hymn to the 'one life':

                              I was only then
        Contented when with bliss ineffable
        I felt the sentiment of being spread
        O'er all that moves, and all that seemeth still,
        O'er all that, lost beyond the reach of thought
        And human knowledge, to the human eye
        Invisible, yet liveth to the heart,
        O'er all that leaps, and runs, and shouts and sings
        Or beats the gladsome air, o'er all that glides
        Beneath the wave, yea, in the wave itself

And mighty depth of waters: wonder not
If such my transports were, for in all things
I saw one life and felt that it was joy.[68]

This passage confirms the whole poem as an exalted utterance of religious faith and joy, profounder in perception and richer in imagery, rhythm, and harmony of composition than any English poetry of its kind since Milton. 'Nature, Man, and Society' was the planned scope of *The Recluse*, to which Coleridge insisted this poem ought only to be the tail-piece.[69] In concluding in such an affirmative and elevated fashion, it is as if Wordsworth were demonstrating in his offering to Coleridge that this was at least one way in which he knew he could write, and write well, about the first two of those dauntingly vague and massive topics.

The last great passage of the *1799 Prelude* also registers Wordsworth's sympathetic resistance to Coleridge. Between February and June 1799 James Mackintosh had delivered *Lectures on the Law of Nature and Nations*.[70] Converted from his ardent support for the French by Burke, the author of *Vindiciae Gallicae* held up to scorn the views of philosophers and visionaries on the prospects for human progress. Godwin in particular was ridiculed and Mackintosh did not bother with fine discrimination. 'Nothing', Hazlitt recalled, 'could withstand his envenomed tooth . . . As to our visionary sceptics and Utopian philosophers, they stood no chance . . . he did not "carve them as a dish fit for the Gods, but hewed as a carcase fit for hounds".'[71] Coleridge was appalled, possibly because he sensed that to the man in the street the difference between Mackintosh's retraction and that of the author of *The Recantation: An Ode* would seem small. But there was a distinction, he believed, between the crude reversal of view in which Mackintosh seemed to glory and the thoughtful reappraisal in which he and Wordsworth were engaged and it was vital that it be spelt out. In the summer he wrote to Wordsworth:

I am anxiously eager to have you steadily employed on 'The Recluse.' . . . My dear friend, I do entreat you go on with 'The Recluse'; and I wish you would write a poem, in blank verse, addressed to those, who, in consequence of the complete failure of the French Revolution, have thrown up all hopes of the amelioration of mankind, and are sinking into an almost epicurean selfishness, disguising the same under the soft titles of domestic attachment and contempt for visionary *philosophes*. It would do great good, and might form a part of 'The Recluse', for in my present mood I am wholly against the publication of any small poems.[72]

Wordsworth's response was intelligently self-protective. Once again Coleridge was laying a charge on him and once again there was a crucial vagueness both about how the task might actually be realized and about the audience to be addressed. Those who had 'thrown up all hopes of the amelioration of mankind' were numerous perhaps, but they hardly constituted a distinct subset in the poetry-reading public. Wordsworth's strategy was to appropriate the subject by paraphrasing Coleridge's letter, while resisting its wider claim on him. Coleridge was looking for a generalizing utterance on behalf of the saving remnant of those who still believed human progress possible. All that Wordsworth was prepared to assert was that *he* was still optimistic and that he knew why:

>                if in these times of fear,
> This melancholy waste of hopes o'erthrown,
> If, 'mid indifference and apathy
> And wicked exultation, when good men
> On every side fall off we know not how
> To selfishness disguised in gentle names
> Of peace, and quiet, and domestic love,
> Yet mingled, not unwillingly, with sneers
> On visionary minds, if in this time
> Of dereliction and dismay, I yet
> Despair not of our nature, but retain
> A more than Roman confidence, a faith
> That fails not, in all sorrow my support,
> The blessing of my life, the gift is yours,
> Ye Mountains! thine, O Nature! thou hast fed
> My lofty speculations, and in thee
> For this uneasy heart of ours I find
> A never-failing principle of joy
> And purest passion.[13]

These lines relate directly to the decision to retire to Grasmere. In 1798 Wordsworth had confronted his destiny in *The Recluse* and acknowledged that it was to be his life's work. But questions about the nature of the task and his own claim to the authority necessary to carry it out had surfaced during his struggles with *The Ruined Cottage* and the Pedlar material. The *1799 Prelude* had taken shape as he had reflected on them. With the confident myth-making of *Tintern Abbey* providing a model, Wordsworth presented his own life as guided by a providential power, which had fostered his creativity, heaping on him privileges which demanded in return dedication to a great task. What had been obvious so far was the apparent disjunction between the random course of Wordsworth's life and the design he now saw as having shaped it from his earliest days. In December 1799 Wordsworth acted to make his life as man and as poet coherent in all its parts. He had chosen his vocation. His 'more than Roman confidence' was to be the ground of _The Recluse_ and a lifetime's poetry. Deliberately distancing himself from the political centre, from publishers, and the whole professional world of literature, he had chosen his home, not as a negative retreat from the 'real world' but as a positive commitment to an austere and dedicated life amidst the elemental forms of nature. His model was not Cowper, the stricken deer retiring from the herd, but Milton, seeking the quiet of Horton to equip himself through reflection and study for a life dedicated to high endeavour.[74]

The decision to return to the Lakes was a momentous one. Wordsworth's life so far had strikingly lacked direction or success, in either the mundane world or the world of art and intellect. From now on it had to validate the confidence of the close of the _1799 Prelude_. He entered 1800 with everything at stake, needing to demonstrate to his family, to Coleridge, to Calvert and the Pinneys, above all to himself, that he was a chosen son and that he had mistaken neither his gifts nor the importance of his calling.

He was, moreover, fully aware of the significance of what he was doing. Shortly after moving to Grasmere Wordsworth welcomed the task ahead of him in lines which fourteen years later he was still proud to offer 'as a kind of _Prospectus_ of the design and scope of the whole Poem' (The Recluse) and as a testimony to the exalted mood in which it was conceived.[75] With great literary tact but extraordinary daring Wordsworth invokes Milton in order to present his own as yet unwritten work as comparable to _Paradise Lost_. Jehovah, hell, chaos, night, death—none of these, Wordsworth declares,

> can breed such fear and awe
> As fall upon me often when I look
> Into my soul, into the soul of man,
> My haunt, and the main region of my song.

Milton's theme was Paradise lost. Wordsworth's is to be Paradise reclaimed:

> Paradise & groves
> Elysian, blessed island in the deep
> Of choice seclusion—wherefore need they be
> A history, or but a dream, when minds
> Once wedded to this outward frame of things
> In love, find these the growth of common day?

But the 'Prospectus' ends in a tone that is movingly different from the majesty of what has gone before:

O great God,
To less than thee I cannot make this prayer:
Innocent mighty spirit, let my life
Express the image of a better time;
Desires more wise, & simpler manners, nurse
My heart in genuine freedom; all pure thoughts
Be with me, & uphold me to the end.

As he took up life at Grasmere Wordsworth sensed that he was about to conduct an experiment in living in which life and art should exist in reciprocal and mutually strengthening relation. His vocation to his art had determined his choice of life: his way of life would, he hoped, attest the genuineness of the values to be conveyed through his poetry.

# PART II

I ask what is meant by the word Poet?
What is a Poet?
(Preface to *Lyrical Ballads*, 1802.)

# 1800–1802

(1)

GRASMERE, William Wilberforce remarked, 'gives one the idea of Rasselas's happy Valley'. He was not thinking hard about the implications of Johnson's fable, just echoing Gray's earlier comment that this was a 'little unsuspected paradise'.[1] It is easy to see why. Grasmere is surrounded in three quarters by hills—Dunmail Raise, Stone Arthur, and the Fairfield mass to the north and east, Helm Crag and Silver How to the west, and from any one of them, but especially from Silver How and Red Bank at the southerly end of the lake, the water and the village marked out by the church tower seem grouped expressly for picturesque composition. Even on the more open south approach, the road leads over the little hill of White Moss Common and seems to harmonize the scene by leading the eye from the grandeur of the views to the north and west down to the little group of houses at Town End.[2] From their cottage the Wordsworths looked over a meadow to the lake and all that is needed is De Quincey's account of their main room 'very prettily wainscotted from the floor to the ceiling with dark polished oak', dimly lit by 'a perfect and unpretending cottage window, with little diamond panes, embowered at almost every season of the year, with roses', for one to imagine that the Wordsworths moved into a ready-made rural idyll.[3] But it was not so. They arrived in a period of severe frost—Wordsworth was soon skating on nearby Rydal—at a six-roomed cottage which would have fitted into any one floor at Racedown and Alfoxden. It was damp, gloomy, and almost unfurnished. Their first task was to make it a home.

Although they both caught colds and Dorothy was 'racked with the tooth-ache', they painted and furnished the house they were determined to be pleased with. Dorothy at once dreamed of 'a seat with a summer shed on the highest platform of this our little domestic mountain', which they later built, and Wordsworth decided to enclose a few yards at the front of the house, partly, he said 'for the sake of a few flowers and because it will make it more our own'. They learned where and how to get provisions by talking to their immediate neighbours, whom they 'uniformly found kind-hearted frank

and manly, prompt to serve without servility'. Molly Fisher, who lived with
her married brother just across the road at Sykeside, was happy to come in
for a few hours work each day in return for two shillings a week and meals on
Saturdays.[4]

Making themselves at home, however, involved more than just sewing
bed-curtains or cleaning out the well. Within days of arrival Wordsworth
told Coleridge of his plans to make a front garden, giving the reasons already
quoted. But they are not his only ones. He went on: 'Besides, am I fanciful
when I would extend the obligation of gratitude to insensate things? May
not a man have a salutary pleasure in doing something gratuitously for the
sake of his house, as for an individual to which he owes so much.' It is a very
revealing fancy. 'Wedded to this outward frame of things / In love',
Wordsworth is drawing even the stone walls and slate roof of his cottage into
affectionate relationship with its inhabitants.[5] He continued to do so
throughout the years at Grasmere, but never more strongly than in 1800 as
he tried to incorporate the region into his imagination, to claim it, and so
make himself truly at home.

*Home at Grasmere* is the title of the poem which occupied Wordsworth
early in 1800.[6] Eventually conceived of as an introductory first book of *The
Recluse*, it clearly originated in Wordsworth's desire to celebrate the good
fortune that had led him to this place and to take hold of its features by
touching them with his imagination. Return to Grasmere has been the
fulfilment of a schoolboy dream, a resumption of continuity with an earlier
self, and as Wordsworth gestures to 'That Ridge', 'Yonder grey stone', 'Yon
Cottage', he uses the language of religious exultation—'bliss', 'joy', 'boon',
'surpassing grace'. The suggestion that this life is an election to salvation is
enhanced by the fancy that the valley has tested them by putting 'the temper
of our minds to proof' through two months of severe storm, and that they
have been found worthy of its love. And what is the blessing they are now fit
to enjoy?

> 'tis the sense
> Of majesty and beauty and repose,
> A blended holiness of earth and sky,
> Something that makes this individual Spot,
> This small abiding-place of many men,
> A termination and a last retreat,
> A Centre, come from whereso'er you will,
> A Whole without dependence or defect,
> Made for itself and happy in itself,
> Perfect Contentment, Unity entire.

The impulse to embrace Grasmere and its region, to draw it into an active
relationship with its new inhabitants, underlies a series of poems also

written now, *Poems on the Naming of Places*. Most of them relate some new pleasure found locally, such as this:

> Up the brook
> I roamed in the confusion of my heart,
> Alive to all things and forgetting all.
> At length I to a sudden turning came
> In this continuous glen, where down a rock
> The stream, so ardent in its course before,
> Sent forth such sallies of glad sound, that all
> Which I till then had heard, appeared the voice
> Of common pleasure: beast and bird, the lamb,
> The Shepherd's dog, the linnet and the thrush
> Vied with this waterfall, and made a song
> Which, while I listened, seemed like the wild growth
> Or like some natural produce of the air
> That could not cease to be.[7]

'A narrow girdle of rough stones and crags', by contrast, tells of an incident which shocked the poet out of his complacent self-congratulation that he could now read the signs of his new dwelling-place. But what is special to all of these poems is that each records a moment when on to the names of mountains and streams used since time immemorial are grafted the poet's own name and the names of those he loves—Dorothy, Mary Hutchinson, and her sister Joanna.

The climax of *To Joanna* is an incantatory roll-call of the mountains which echo Joanna's laugh: Helm Crag, Hammar Scar, Silver How, Loughrigg, Fairfield, Helvellyn, Skiddaw, Glaramara. All of these can be found on the map, but when the poem was published in *Lyrical Ballads* 1800 many readers must have been puzzled by such a determined gazetteer of very specific provincial place-names and quite bewildered by the line about 'That ancient Woman seated on Helm-crag', until they came to Wordsworth's note explaining that it refers not to a human being but a configuration of rocks. *Michael*, the finest of the Grasmere poems, begins as uncompromisingly:

> If from the public way you turn your steps
> Up the tumultuous brook of Green-head Gill . . .

and goes on in the published text to use the local place-names, Dunmail Raise and Easedale and, in unpublished drafts, Helvellyn, Thirlmere, Fairfield, Dove Crag, Grisedale Tarn, and more.[8] The names make Wordsworth's intention clear. In *Home at Grasmere* he had recognized the lure of the Arcadian myth and dismissed it, dwelling on stories of the inhabitants of Grasmere which reveal that they of course share the human lot of pain. At one point he exclaims:

>                                  Is there not
>      An art, a music and a stream of words
>      That shall be life, the acknowledged voice of life?
>      Shall speak of what is done among the fields,
>      Done truly there, or felt, of solid good
>      And real evil, yet be sweet withal,
>      More grateful, more harmonious than the breath,
>      The idle breath of sweetest pipe attuned
>      To pastoral fancies?[9]

*Michael* is Wordsworth's answer to 'pastoral fancies'. This is an English pastoral. Every schoolboy knew where sheep grazed in Theocritus and Virgil. Now Wordsworth re-sites the pastoral on the Lake District hills. Pope had written about Daphnis, Strephon, and Damon, adhering to the genre's dictate: 'We must use some illusion to render a Pastoral delightful; and this consists in exposing the best side only of a shepherd's life, and in concealing its miseries'.[10] Wordsworth writes about Michael, Isabel, Luke, whose life consists of steady labour, by day and night, just to hang on to all they have, their little tract of land. In the end their efforts are obliterated and nothing is left but the oak

>      That grew beside their Door; and the remains
>      Of the unfinished Sheep-fold . . .
>      Beside the boisterous brook of Green-head Gill.

But memories of them do survive and in the poem have found permanent form. *Michael* is the greatest of the poems in which Wordsworth drew Grasmere to himself. It is also his finest celebration of the values of fortitude, constancy, and love he believed he found there.

What confirmed Grasmere most strongly as Wordsworth's true 'abiding place' was the fact that those he loved shared his pleasure in it. Dorothy had long been incorporated into his life, but now Wordsworth seems to have felt more intensely than ever before just how much his survival, his happiness, and his vocation owed to her—not just to her support, hard work, and uncomplaining self-effacement, but to the fineness of her whole being. The most beautiful lines in *Home at Grasmere* record his gratitude:

>          Where'er my footsteps turned,
>      Her voice was like a hidden Bird that sang;
>      The thought of her was like a flash of light
>      Or an unseen companionship, a breath
>      Of fragrance independent of the wind.[11]

It was especially pleasing that John too was so thrilled with their new life. This 'never-resting Pilgrim of the Sea' arrived between voyages towards the end of January and seems to have entered fully into life at Town End, sharing the sense that it was an adventure that knitted together fragmented lives. Dorothy recalled how he had 'paced over this floor in pride . . . exulting within his noble heart that his Father's Children had once again a home together'.[12] He planted, made little conveniences for the cottage, walked, fished, and explored. When Mary Hutchinson arrived in late February to stay until early April, it was John, she remembered, who first 'led me to everything that I love in this neighbourhood'.[13] One spot in particular he made his own. A retiring man—Wordsworth claimed that their father 'used to call him Ibex, the shyest of all the beasts'—John often sought the quiet of the fir-grove above Town End.[14] When Wordsworth discovered the path his brother had trodden out between the trees he recorded his delight in a lovely and little-known tribute to John, 'When first I journeyed hither'. In this poem Wordsworth calls his brother 'A silent Poet', because of his 'watchful heart . . . inevitable ear / And an eye practised like a blind man's touch'. After his death these were the qualities Dorothy remembered most clearly, 'so fine an eye that no distinction was unnoticed by him, and so tender a feeling that he never noticed anything in vain', and it was these qualities that disposed John not only to 'a perfect sympathy with all our pleasures', but to a supportive understanding of Wordsworth's hopes for himself as a poet who might 'do something for the world'.[15] He left them on 29 September, soon to become captain of the *Earl of Abergavenny*. When they said goodbye to him at Grisedale Tarn, John had become an integral member of the domestic group—Wordsworths, Hutchinsons, Coleridges—emotionally centred on the cottage at Town End. They did not know that he would never return.

'I would to God, I could get Wordsworth to re-take Alfoxden', Coleridge declared to Poole in March 1800, 'the Society of so great a Being is of priceless Value—but he will never quit the North of England.'[16] This realistic assessment left Coleridge with no alternative. He arrived on 6 April and, by the time he left on 4 May, had arranged a house for his family in Keswick. On 29 June Coleridge, Sara, and Hartley squeezed into the cottage at Town End and for nearly a month, despite an illness which confined Coleridge to bed for part of the time, enjoyed a life of walking, fishing, talking, and exploring, which seemed to promise that the unity of Alfoxden days could be re-established. One letter of Coleridge's records an evening of particular delight:

We drank tea the night before I left Grasmere on the Island in that lovely lake, our kettle swung over the fire hanging from the branch of a Fir Tree, and I lay & saw the woods, & mountains, & lake all trembling, & as it were *idealized* thro' the subtle smoke which rose up from the clear red embers of the fir-apples which we had collected. Afterwards, we made a glorious Bonfire on the Margin, by some alder bushes, whose twigs heaved & sobbed in the uprushing column of smoke.[17]

Towards the end of July the Coleridges moved into Greta Hall, a house so beautifully situated that Coleridge was soon boasting to Godwin, 'I question if there be a room in England which commands a view of Mountains & Lakes & Woods & Vales superior to that in which I am now sitting'. The house was only half a mile from the town, which pleased Sara; Hartley, 'a Spirit dancing on an aspen Leaf', was happy, as ever;[18] the landlord, William Jackson, was a cultivated, self-educated man, whose books were at Coleridge's disposal; access to the library of Sir Wilfrid Lawson was promised. There was no reason to doubt that Coleridge was entering a new period of stability in which he could pursue his journalism and grander literary projects, fortified by the knowledge that conversation with Wordsworth was only half a day's walk away.

Other friends played their part in rooting the Wordsworths in Grasmere. Throughout the summer of 1800 they saw a lot of the Sympson family, who lived at High Broadrain on the Keswick road out of Grasmere. James Losh and his wife called in September, the first of a series of visitors—Thomas and Catherine Clarkson from Eusemere; John Marshall, husband of Dorothy's old friend Jane Pollard; Robert Jones, Wordsworth's Alpine companion; Thomas Myers, their cousin, and his father; Charles Lloyd, a less welcome visitor, now living with his wife at Old Brathay near Ambleside; John Stoddart, who stayed for nearly a week; and Sara Hutchinson, whose gaiety and intellectual sharpness enlivened the long evenings of November and December. Wherever they had lived before—at Windy Brow, in London, at Racedown, and Alfoxden—the Wordsworths had been adjuncts of other people's circle of acquaintance. Now, for the first time in their lives, they were really settled and drawing people to them.

(2)

Wordsworth had settled on Grasmere decisively. Retirement there was 'a choice of the whole heart', not a weak indulgence but 'an act / Of reason that exultingly aspires'.[19] He now acted with the same determination to forward his literary career.

By April 1800 sales of *Lyrical Ballads* encouraged Wordsworth to issue a further edition. Although the two volumes that eventually appeared on 25 January 1801 were, strictly speaking, a second revised edition of volume I and a first edition of volume II, Wordsworth had so completely taken control that *Lyrical Ballads* 1800 bears only residual marks of the collaborative effort of 1798. The title-page to both volumes announces them as by 'W. Wordsworth', whose identity is further promoted by the substantial Preface and the notes. Even the layout and typography represent his decisions. In August Wordsworth gave instructions about the title-pages, the layout, and the order of the poems and about the prefatory motto. In October he ordered changes to the title-page, 'even if it is already struck off', changes which would have eliminated reference to *Lyrical Ballads* altogether, and only a few days later sent further instructions about order and the need for separate title-pages for some poems. The printers at Biggs and Cottle must have come to dread these imperious letters, but still they came. On 18 December Wordsworth was worrying about the shape of the volumes—*Michael* must end volume II, he insisted—and about the effect of the title-page. He insisted, too, on how *Michael* should be printed, that is, on the actual appearance of the type at certain points. In another letter of the same date Wordsworth rehearsed for Longman and Rees, the publishers, what he understood to be the terms, 'To avoid any mistakes', carefully established the position over copyright, and astonishingly dictated his 'particular request that no Books be advertized at the end of the volumes. If you have given any directions to Mr Biggs that such advertisements should be printed pray let such orders be countermanded . . .' The tone of this instruction conveys Wordsworth's grasp on all aspects of publication. He was thinking about *Lyrical Ballads* as a commercial product to be marketed, suggesting to Longman that it would be a good idea to send 'a few copies to the amount of half a dozen or so to persons of eminence either in Letters or in the state'. But he was also worrying about the poems down to the smallest detail. As late as 19 December he was still being a printer's nightmare:

In the Poem of Michael about the middle of the first part you will find this line—

  '*The Clipping Tree*, a name which still it bears'

Take a pen and alter the word '*still*' into the word 'yet' let the line be printed—

  '*The Clipping Tree*, a name which yet it bears'.

A few lines from the End of the first part of the same poem you will find this line—

  'But when the Lad, now ten years old, could stand' &c

alter the manuscript with a pen and let it be printed thus

  'But soon as Luke, now ten years old, could stand.'

When the volumes were issued *Michael* lacked a whole passage. A 'shameful negligence', Wordsworth called it, but it is tempting to think it the revenge of a printer goaded for more than six months by intermittent, imperfect copy and contradictory commands.[20]

Wordsworth was working under intense pressure. Preparing and checking copy at a worrying distance from the printing house would have been burden enough without the need to compose new poems and the Preface. Not surprisingly he became ill. Coleridge recognized the psychosomatic symptoms—'He is well, unless when he uses any effort of mind—then he feels a pain in his left side, which threatens to interdict all species of composition to him'—but he recognized too how serious Wordsworth's condition was, reporting in September that 'Wordsworth's health declines constantly'.[21] Not surprisingly, also, Wordsworth seems to have become completely self-absorbed.

The assistance of others was essential. Humphry Davy in Bristol was asked to oversee proof—not a silly idea as Davy, although pre-eminent as a scientist, had considerable experience of publishing—and Dorothy and Sara copied out poems in sheets for the printer. Most of all Wordsworth relied on Coleridge, to negotiate initially with Longman, to deal with Biggs and Cottle, and even to copy out manuscripts and write letters on his behalf. He seems to have done so, however, with scant regard for the feelings of his former collaborator. Nursing his conviction that the strangeness of *The Ancient Mariner* had damaged the 1798 volume (despite the fact that the edition had sold out), Wordsworth encouraged Coleridge to revise its diction. He decided too that it should no longer be allowed to stand first in volume I. Not satisfied, Wordsworth also added this highly subversive note:

I cannot refuse myself the gratification of informing such Readers as may have been pleased with this Poem, or with any part of it, that they owe their pleasure in some sort to me; as the Author was himself very desirous that it should be suppressed. This wish had arisen from a consciousness of the defects of the Poem, and from a knowledge that many persons had been much displeased with it. The Poem of my Friend has indeed great defects; first, that the principal person has no distinct character, either in his profession of Mariner, or as a human being who having been long under the control of supernatural impressions might be supposed himself to partake of something supernatural: secondly, that he does not act, but is continually acted upon: thirdly, that the events having no necessary connection do not produce each other; and lastly, that the imagery is somewhat too laboriously accumulated. Yet the Poem contains many delicate touches of passion, and indeed the passion is everywhere true to nature; a great number of the stanzas present beautiful images, and are expressed with unusual felicity of language; and the versification, though the metre itself is unfit for long poems, is harmonious and artfully varied, exhibiting the utmost powers of that metre, and every variety of which it is capable . . .[22]

The coolness of this assessment was in contrast to the much longer note which preceded it, appended to his own *The Thorn*, in which Wordsworth defended very warmly what readers have generally found one of the most uncomfortable of all the lyrical ballads.[23]

As the editor of Coleridge's letters notes, there are reasons for doubting that 'he saw Wordsworth's ungracious note before it appeared in print',[24] but there was other evidence of Wordsworth's reluctance to allow Coleridge any real part in the new volumes. Coleridge's poem *Love*, which was to replace Wordsworth's *The Convict*, was a trifle, but *Christabel* was not. Completing it drained Coleridge, who was under constant pressure from his obligation to write political articles for Stuart. None the less, Wordsworth excised it, declaring: 'It is my wish and determination that (whatever the expence may be, which I hereby take upon myself) such Pages of the Poem of Christabel as have been printed . . . be cancelled—I mean to have other poems substituted'.[25] Wordsworth's explanation that the 'Style of this Poem was so discordant from my own that it could not be printed along with my poems with any propriety' was reasonable enough for Coleridge to repeat it, but the decision unquestionably marked a severance.[26] The first edition of *Lyrical Ballads* had been the climax to the Alfoxden year, but the second belonged to Grasmere and Wordsworth was clearly not prepared to admit anything that seemed out of keeping with his conception of the new volume. It is not surprising that Coleridge failed to contribute to the *Poems on the Naming of Places*, as had been planned, nor that at the end of the year he should have summed up his status so bleakly: Wordsworth 'is a great, a true Poet—I am only a kind of a Metaphysician'.[27]

Wordsworth's treatment of Coleridge over *Lyrical Ballads* 1800 was certainly unfeeling. It was due in part to the fact that Coleridge was maddening. 'You spawn plans like a herring', Southey told him, 'I only wish as many of the seed were to vivify in proportion.' Wordsworth had heard enough already about the planned Life of Lessing and the Letters from Germany to feel a like irritation, especially as Coleridge was once again using his, Wordsworth's, poetry to fulfil his obligations to Stuart.[28] Partly it was due, also, to unrecognized resistance to Coleridge's constant urging that he get on with 'his great Work'. It was due most of all, however, to Wordsworth's overmastering determination to speak to the public in his own voice, with a volume of poems which should exhibit a coherent identity and unignorable seriousness of purpose.

What that purpose was, was spelt out in the essay prefixed to volume I. In later life Wordsworth declared in exasperation: 'I never cared a straw about the theory—& the Preface was written at the request of Coleridge out of sheer good nature', but this is not to be taken at face value.[29] Coleridge's fertile theorizing brain certainly contributed—in September 1800 he claimed that 'The Preface contains our joint opinions on Poetry'—but Wordsworth cared more than a straw about theory.[30] Although he revised the Preface in 1802, he did so by enlarging rather than repudiating it and in 1815, when he issued his first Collected Works, he not only wrote a completely new theoretical treatise and a supplementary essay but reprinted the Preface to *Lyrical Ballads* as well.

Lamb was uneasy about the theorizing and told Wordsworth that he 'wished that The Critical preface had appeared in a separate treatise.—All its dogmas are true and just and most of them new, *as* criticism.—But they associate a *diminishing* idea with the Poems which follow, as having been written for Experiments on the public taste, more than having sprung (as they must have done) from living and daily circumstances.'[31] But Lamb completely mistook Wordsworth's purpose. He was not writing critical theory in the abstract but summing up his own achievement in the Alfoxden and Grasmere poems, establishing his reasons for believing that these two small volumes contained poetry 'well adapted to interest mankind permanently, and not unimportant in the multiplicity and in the quality of its moral relations'.[32]

Since no one except the professional student of literature is likely to read the Preface to *Lyrical Ballads* 1800, it would be easy to pass over it. But it is a key document in Wordsworth's career and in the history of English Romantic poetry. Its importance does not lie in the power of its exposition. Nor is it important as an original contribution to aesthetics. Wordsworth draws on familiar ideas from eighteenth-century debate on primitivism, the nature of pleasure, and the relation of poetry to prose, without refining anything to a new level of subtlety or certainty. Some of its propositions are not even new to Wordsworth—the account of the Pedlar's wanderings among lowly men, the Pedlar's own justification for telling Margaret's story, and Wordsworth's letter to Coleridge about Bürger's poems all anticipate points in the Preface and the psychological model which underlies the discussion of how poets compose and how readers read is the Hartleian one shaping the lines 'Not useless do I deem . . .'. Nor does the prose offer the excitement one can always find in any of Coleridge's letters or in *Biographia Literaria*. After such a parade of negatives what is left? The radical emphasis of what is being said and the fact that Wordsworth is saying it now.

The radical thrust of Wordsworth's main propositions is unmistakable. In the key paragraph he announces that he has taken subjects from 'Low and rustic life' for his attempt to trace 'the primary laws of our nature', and then proffers no fewer than fifteen reasons (disregarding parentheses and ramification of main-clause points) for believing that in such subjects the poet will come close not only to essential human nature but to the source of a truly 'philosophical language'. Clause piled on clause batters home an argument that tries to cover far too much, but whose direction is clear. For fundamental human concerns, the 'great and simple affections of our nature', and for a permanently valid language, men must turn not to the polite world of refined manners and educated speech but to the world of *Simon Lee*, *The Brothers*, and *Michael*. And by redefining the pastoral in these poems Wordsworth was not engaged in a purely literary act. As a poet he recognized the appropriate methods and the proper sphere of art and knew that a poem's primary task was 'producing immediate pleasure'. But it is equally true that Wordsworth could never have spoken of a 'purely literary act'. For him poetry was a moral agent or it was nothing. By loosening the hold of expectation as to what was appropriate subject-matter and treatment for this particular genre (and in the future for others), Wordsworth hoped to arouse readers' imaginations and thus release into the world one grain more of intellectual and spiritual activity. The ambition behind the *Lyrical Ballads* pastorals was quite as large as that which had conceived *The Recluse*.

In certain particulars this argument allied Wordsworth more closely than he might have cared to admit to Paine and other fighters in the cause of democratic discourse and confirmed for readers in 1801 that Wordsworth's was, as Hazlitt put it, 'a levelling Muse'.[33] But Wordsworth also justifies his poetry with a quite different kind of argument. His work will be found unlike the poetry of the day, he declares, in language, in subject-matter, but above all in its tendency to disclose the quiet, the simple, the unregarded aspects of human nature. It is a poetry of discrimination, in which 'the feeling therein developed gives importance to the action and situation and not the action and situation to the feeling'. And such poetry is, he asserts, more than ever necessary:

For the human mind is capable of excitement without the application of gross and violent stimulants; and he must have a very faint perception of its beauty and dignity who does not know this, and who does not further know that one being is elevated above another in proportion as he possesses this capability. It has therefore appeared to me that to endeavour to produce or enlarge this capability is one of the best services in which, at any period, a Writer can be engaged; but this service, excellent at all times, is especially so at the present day. For a multitude of causes unknown to former times are now acting with a combined force to blunt the discriminating powers of the mind, and unfitting it for all voluntary exertion to reduce it to a state of almost savage torpor. The most effective of these causes are the great national events which are daily taking place, and the encreasing accumulation of men in cities, where the uniformity of their occupations produces a craving for extraordinary incident which the rapid communication of intelligence [news] hourly gratifies.

This unexpectedly intense denunciation is an important moment in the history of English nineteenth- and early twentieth-century literature. Wordsworth offers no evidence that the rise of city populations and the spread of newspapers and magazines makes for barbarism rather than civilization or that 'causes unknown to former times' were really in operation. What he does do is assert that there is a tendency in the culture of the time which it is the duty of poetry to counteract and which possibly only poetry can counteract. Here the adversarial stance of the true writer—adopted by such diverse figures as Shelley, Carlyle, Arnold, Morris, D. H. Lawrence, and many others—was established.

It was also a moment of the greatest importance to Wordsworth. The lofty idea of *The Recluse* had inspired him in his retirement to Grasmere. In the 'Prospectus' he had reaffirmed his theme and measured himself against the greatest didactic poet, Milton. This grand poem, however, was Coleridge's dream and Wordsworth's secret, known only to a few and unannounced to the public until 1814. But Wordsworth had no intention of remaining unknown or silent until *The Recluse* should be completed. In *Lyrical Ballads* he declared himself, not just as an original poet but as a censor of the age, who, through apparently unassuming poems, was intent on moral and thus social reform. Publishing these two volumes was a decisive act. It established Wordsworth's name; it declared his pretensions; and contrary to Coleridge's hopes, it determined that Wordsworth would be known as a lyrical and narrative poet.

The importance of the *Lyrical Ballads* to Wordsworth is evident from his anxiety that they should be noticed and not misread. Rightly judging that statesmen are not given to considering lyrical poetry as of any political significance whatsoever, Wordsworth accompanied the presentation copy sent to Charles James Fox with an eloquent letter which implies that though both poet and politician were working to similar ends, Fox might need to have pointed out the purpose behind *The Brothers* and *Michael* and the social implications of poems written 'with a view to shew that men who do not wear fine cloaths can feel deeply'.[34] Wordsworth expected Lamb, however, to recognize the importance of *Lyrical Ballads* without being told and he reacted to a letter of discriminating comment from him intemperately. According to Lamb's report 'A long letter of four sweating pages' was immediately dispatched, reinforced by 'four long pages, equally sweaty, and more tedious' from Coleridge, to bludgeon him into due appreciation.[35] Wordsworth's clumsiness reveals real worry: if Lamb failed to see the significance of *Lyrical Ballads*, what hope was there of the public at large?

(3)

By June 1801 Wordsworth knew that *Lyrical Ballads* 1800 was a success, when, with only 130 copies left, Longman invited him to prepare a new

edition. For this and the previous one Wordsworth was paid only £80—
'little better than swindling' in John Wordsworth's judgement—but now he
sensed that his bargaining position was strengthening and told Richard: 'As
soon as this next shall be disposed of, the copyright will revert to me, and I
shall take care to know precisely upon what terms a Bookseller can afford to
take it, and he shall not have it a farthing under'.[36] Montagu was only just
beginning to make his way in the law and could not be relied on yet to
honour his debt, and in June 1801 Wordsworth had generously made over
£30 of his Longman payment to Coleridge, so his ever-present anxiety
about money was real. But these were boom years for publishing poetry and
Wordsworth was determined that, even with poems 'written upon a theory
professedly new, and on principles which many persons will be unwilling to
admit', he would win a share of the market.[37]

It was not commercial considerations, however, which impelled Wordsworth to revise *Lyrical Ballads* 1800 for a new edition. The two volumes
could simply have been reissued, with all of the printer's blunders corrected,
but this was never Wordsworth's way. To republish a poem without first
subjecting it to scrutiny would be to concede that it had reached a final form.
But Wordsworth could not bear the idea of finality. His manuscripts show
just how hard he struggled throughout his life to bring poems into being.
Draft lines are brought together in a fair copy, which is then often so
disfigured with interlining, crossing out, and marginalia that another fair
copy has to be made in a process that could continue even while the printers
were running off early sheets, harassed by an author who was relentlessly
inconsiderate of their needs. First publication was a pause—the poem
attained a discrete identity—but further publication always renewed the
process, stimulating the creation of new work and revision of the old in a
continuous flow. In April 1801 Wordsworth sent Anne Taylor a list of
revisions for *The Female Vagrant* because that poem, he said, did not
conform to the principle he had laid down in the Preface that he had 'at all
times endeavoured to look steadily at my subject'.[38] Here his practice is
revealed. *The Female Vagrant*, an early poem, is to be revised into supposed
conformity with a principle Wordsworth had not articulated when he
originally wrote it. And this was his usual practice. He revised his work for
every new edition and even aged 70 was still tinkering with some of the
Alfoxden ballads. When he published his early work in the 1842 *Poems,
Chiefly of Early and Late Years*, he seemed to be offering faithful readers
glimpses of his past. They could not know that *Guilt and Sorrow* and *The
Borderers* had been thoroughly updated. Nor was revision confined to
published poems. *The Prelude*, for example, remained in manuscript until
Wordsworth's death, but it was thoroughly revised at intervals after its
apparent completion in 1805.[39]

Wordsworth's revision was compulsive and it always brought him illness, fatigue, and sleepless nights. For the 1802 edition of *Lyrical Ballads* he changed single words, phrases, and occasionally whole lines in most of the poems in volume II. Stanzas were omitted in *The Female Vagrant* and *Poor Susan*, and the stanza order changed in *Simon Lee*. *Ruth* was substantially altered. *Lines Written near Richmond* was moved to the second volume and retitled *Remembrance of Collins, Written upon the Thames, near Richmond*. The 1800 note on *The Ancient Mariner* was dropped, as were *The Dungeon* and *A Character*. Recording such changes will seem pedantry to some readers, as, even cumulatively, the revisions do not add up to much. What is important is that Wordsworth, recognizing no scale of priorities or relative degrees of importance, thought all revision important, and that it cost him great labour.

Revision of *Lyrical Ballads* 1800 was Wordsworth's one achievement in a year that was not conducive to sustained original composition. Throughout 1801 if the Wordsworths were not away visiting they were entertaining guests at Town End. From late January to late February they were first at the Clarksons at Eusemere and then with the Coleridges at Keswick. A further visit to Keswick took a week in April and at the end of the year they once again stayed with the Clarksons for nearly a month. For three weeks in September Wordsworth was in Scotland, for Basil Montagu's wedding. At Town End they repeatedly welcomed Coleridge for short visits and were joined by Sara Hutchinson in March and November and by Mary, her sister, in October. Over the summer and autumn they were sought out by Christopher Wordsworth, ardent in pursuit of Charles Lloyd's sister Priscilla; by Samuel Rogers, the first of many eminent literary visitors over the years; by Halifax friends Samuel and Martha Ferguson and Elizabeth Threlkeld; by Thomas Hutchinson and by Thomas and Catherine Clarkson, who were fast becoming real friends. Tea and supper with the Lloyds at Old Brathay and fishing, walking, and eating with the Sympsons of High Broadrain continued to make up the ordinary social round.

All of these visitors were welcome (the Lloyds less so than the others) and the Wordsworths delighted in revealing the beauties of Grasmere and, with Thomas Hutchinson, exploring the Langdales and Windermere. Sara and Mary Hutchinson were more than welcome. Their visits were longed for. But the cottage at Town End was small and every sound carried through its thin walls and wooden floors. However welcome, each fresh arrival was an intrusion. Wordsworth regularly composed out of doors, fortified by food which Dorothy would carry to him,[40] but it is not surprising that with such an unsettled life, and with anxieties about money and his own and Coleridge's health pressing on him, Wordsworth did nothing towards *The Recluse*.

Over the turn of the year Wordsworth began to compose again. What he did, however, was make a series of false starts. Two are unimportant. In December, inspired by reading Chaucer in Robert Anderson's *The Works of the British Poets*, Wordsworth worked on free translations of *The Manciple's Tale*, *The Prioress's Tale*, *Troilus and Cressida*, and the wrongly attributed *The Cuckoo and the Nightingale*.[41] The gusto of the verse suggests that he enjoyed the challenge, but the poetry had no connection with *The Recluse* and was leading nowhere. Then in February 1802 Wordsworth returned to *Peter Bell*. Unlike the Chaucer this was serious work. *Peter Bell* was a substantial narrative which, though connected in treatment and theme to the essential lyrical ballads, was still unpublished. But feeling his way back into the poem seems not to have restored any of the ebullience in which it had originated at Alfoxden. Wordsworth only tinkered with revisions and had another fair copy prepared.[42]

Two other returns to earlier work, on the other hand, were highly significant. On 26–7 December 1801 Wordsworth composed lines for a further book of his autobiographical poem, almost certainly the opening of what became Book III of the *1805 Prelude*.[43] This was a momentous step. The *1799 Prelude* had been a selective account of the poet's development, designed not to present a chronology of his life but to reveal the shaping forces which had fitted him to become a philosophic poet. What the conclusion of the poem pointed to was the greater work yet to come, *The Recluse*. But the chronological framework allowed for almost limitless expansion, should the poet decide that other experiences had been significant enough to warrant inclusion. By returning to the *1799 Prelude* Wordsworth was certainly approaching *The Recluse* as he had done before, through the poem on his own life. By describing his entry into Cambridge, however, he was acknowledging that the selective shaping of the *1799 Prelude* had been inadequate. For the moment he did little, but within two years the desire to give a more comprehensive, historically organized account of his own life would become irresistible.

Returning to the *1799 Prelude* seems to have produced the effect Wordsworth had hoped for in the original poem—it spurred him on 'To honourable toil' on *The Recluse*. But once again Wordsworth delayed original composition by returning to Alfoxden work, *The Ruined Cottage* and *The Pedlar*. Possibly he hoped to recapture from what had been achieved then his original impulses towards *The Recluse*. More likely, he knew that progress was impossible as long as the major poem of that period remained in troublingly unsettled form. Once *The Ruined Cottage* material was clarified, *The Recluse* could proceed.

In 1798 the story of Margaret had been told by the Pedlar, whose own education and experience had been related by the poet-listener himself.

Recognizing that the account of the philosophic Pedlar threatened to dominate the poem, Wordsworth had restructured it to foreground Margaret's story. The Pedlar material had been entered separately in the manuscript and plundered for the *1799 Prelude*. Now, early in 1802, Wordsworth returned to what still engrossed him, the account of the formation of the Pedlar and, through intricate splicing and cross-referencing in the manuscript, attempted to develop the earlier lines into a coherent poem, *The Pedlar*. Drawing on Sara Hutchinson's memories of James Patrick, the 'intellectual Pedlar' of Kendal with whom she had passed some of her childhood, Wordsworth gave his character a new identity as 'Patrick Drummond' and attempted to fuse his earlier verse about the youth's profoundly religious experience of Nature with a more mundane narrative of his employment, wanderings, and habits.[44] It was uncongenial work, a mixture of fresh composition and revision, and it badly strained him. 'Wm wrote out part of his poem and endeavoured to alter it, and so made himself ill'; 'Wm worked at the Pedlar all the morning. He kept the dinner waiting till 4 o'clock—he was much tired'; 'William wished to break off composition, and was unable, and so did himself harm'; 'William sadly tired and working still at the Pedlar'—so Dorothy records Wordsworth's travail.[45] He knew, moreover, that he was struggling. On 7 February 1802 Dorothy notes: 'We sate by the fire and did not walk, but read the pedlar thinking it done but lo, though Wm could find fault with no one part of it— it was uninteresting and must be altered'. Wordsworth's self-criticism is severe but accurate. *The Pedlar* 1802 is uninteresting. Divorced from the story of Margaret and padded out with additional scraps of narrative, the poem seems on the verge of becoming either another pastoral like *Michael* or another autobiographical retrospect akin to the *1799 Prelude*. But it is neither, and although Wordsworth talked in March of publishing *Peter Bell* and *The Pedlar*, the poem was once again shelved.

Even as Wordsworth laboured on *The Pedlar*, however, a very different impulse towards composition began to possess him, which transformed this barren winter into a spring and summer matching in creativity those of 1798. Between March and June 1802 he wrote more than thirty lyrics. Some, such as *The Sailor's Mother*, *Alice Fell*, and *Beggars*, are similar to those 1798 lyrical ballads which dramatize an encounter between the poet and another human being. But the most striking of the new poems dramatize the poet encountering, so to speak, his own joy, welling up at the sight of a flower, or a bird, or a butterfly. They transpose into the lyric register the sense of wonder and reverent humbleness which Wordsworth had expressed in a loftier vein in *Home at Grasmere* and the 'Prospectus' to *The Recluse*:

> Prophet of delight and mirth,
> Scorned and slighted upon earth!
> Herald of a mighty band,
> Of a joyous train ensuing,
> Singing at my heart's command,
> In the lanes my thoughts pursuing,
> I will sing, as doth behove,
> Hymns in praise of what I love![46]

Some of the poems are lyrical in the simplest meaning of the word—that is, they are as near to extempore utterance as the written word can be. On 16 April Wordsworth and Dorothy parted for a while at Brothers Water, Wordsworth sitting on the bridge while Dorothy explored the path into the wood. 'When I returned', she recorded, 'I found William writing a poem descriptive of the sights and sounds we saw and heard.' It could not be more direct:

> The cock is crowing,
> The stream is flowing,
> The small birds twitter,
> The lake doth glitter,
> The green field sleeps in the sun;
> The oldest and youngest
> Are at work with the strongest;
> The cattle are grazing,
> Their heads never raising;
> There are forty feeding like one![47]

'Among all lovely things my Love had been' was likewise written out of doors, but in very different conditions. Riding back from visiting Mary Hutchinson at Bishop Middleham in Durham, 'Just when William came to a well or a Trough which there is in Lord Darlington's Park', Dorothy noted, 'he began to write that poem of the glow-worm. Not being able to write upon the long Trot. Interrupted in going through the Town of Staindrop. Finished it about 2 miles and a half beyond Staindrop. He did not feel the jogging of the horse while he was writing but when he had done he felt the effect of it and his fingers were cold with his gloves.'[48] Other poems have a relationship with the language of Dorothy's journal and some, as her entries make clear, were revised and altered. But what they all have in common is an apparent spontaneity, an air of joyous freedom.

It is achieved, of course, through delicate art. Reading in Jonson, Cowley, Spenser, had temporarily released Wordsworth from the thrall of Milton and eighteenth-century Miltonic blank verse, even from the thrall of his

ncited him to emulation of the metrical virtuosity of the
d Jacobean poets.[49] Each poem draws attention to its own
g the reader's eye and ear by the unexpected, as if insisting on
tence as *poetic* art over a considerable range of tones, from the
i *The Tinker* to the impassioned sublimity of the *Ode*:
'Poetry is passion', Wordsworth had declared in 1800. But
metre, n̶e̶ w insisted, supremely determined the success with which poetic
passion is conveyed. Most people 'greatly under-rate the power of metre in
itself'.[50]

Meeting resistance to the metrical quiddity of his own poems, Gerard
Manley Hopkins conceded that 'it is the virtue of design, pattern, or inscape
to be distinctive and it is the vice of distinctiveness to become queer'.[51]
Wordsworth's lyrics of 1802, and others which followed up to the
publication of *Poems, in Two Volumes* in 1807, are certainly distinctive—and
queer. Teetering on the facile, they are easily parodied or, worse, overlooked
in favour of the more evidently weighty verse. But they were of the greatest
importance to Wordsworth and the pride he took in them undoubtedly
underpinned the affirmation he now made. In the spring of 1802 he
prepared new copy for the Preface to the *Lyrical Ballads*, third edition,
changing the 1800 one so substantially that the two Prefaces ought always to
be treated as separate.[52] He wrote at length on metre and put in an
Appendix a defence of his assertions about 'what is usually called poetic
diction'. More remarkable than either of these additions, however, is the
answer Wordsworth gives to his own question: 'what is meant by the word
Poet? What is a Poet?'

He is a man speaking to men: a man, it is true, endued with more lively sensibility,
more enthusiasm and tenderness, who has a greater knowledge of human nature,
and a more comprehensive soul than are supposed to be common among mankind; a
man pleased with his own passions and volitions, and who rejoices more than other
men in the spirit of life that is in him; delighting to contemplate similar volitions and
passions as manifested in the goings-on of the Universe, and habitually impelled to
create them where he does not find them . . .

Unlike the biographer or the historian, the poet need acknowledge only one
overriding imperative—that he should give pleasure. But 'this necessity of
producing immediate pleasure' is not 'a degradation of the Poet's art':

It is far otherwise. It is an acknowledgement of the beauty of the universe, an
acknowledgement the more sincere, because it is not formal, but indirect; it is a task
light and easy to him who looks at the world in the spirit of love: further, it is a
homage paid to the native and naked dignity of man, to the grand elementary
principle of pleasure, by which he knows, and feels, and lives, and moves.

Finally, with a grandeur matched only by Shelley in his *Defence of Poetry*, Wordsworth defines his 'sublime notion' of Poetry as the 'breath and finer spirit of all knowledge' and of the Poet as:

the rock of defence of human nature; an upholder and preserver, carrying every where with him relationship and love. In spite of difference of soil and climate, of language and manners, of laws and customs, in spite of things silently gone out of mind and things violently destroyed, the Poet binds together by passion and knowledge the vast empire of human society, as it is spread over the whole earth, and over all time. The objects of the Poet's thoughts are everywhere; though the eyes and senses of man are, it is true, his favourite guides, yet he will follow wheresoever he can find an atmosphere of sensation in which to move his wings. Poetry is the first and last of all knowledge—it is as immortal as the heart of man.

This is a glorious affirmation, but an astonishing one to make at the close of the Enlightenment and of the first phase of the Industrial Revolution. Scientists and engineers, philosophers and political thinkers, philanthropists and social activists had transformed every aspect of life from cups and saucers to concepts of Deity, and yet it is poetry which Wordsworth declares 'the most philosophic of all writing'. This is more than a declaration of the importance of humane learning, more than an assertion of the imagination against the pressure of a sceptical, scientific, or utilitarian ethos. Wordsworth confers upon the poet the roles of chronicler and preserver, of comforter and moral guide, of prophet and mediator. His reference to the 'divine spirit' of the poet is not a lazy one. To the author of *The Dunciad* such exalted affirmations would have seemed ravings. Johnson, who defined the poet as 'An inventor; an author of fiction; a writer of poems; one who writes in measure', would have thought them nonsense, probably blasphemous nonsense. Even readers accustomed to place poetry as the highest of the literary arts and familiar with the many eighteenth-century disquisitions on the theory of poetry could not have been prepared for the sublime and comprehensive credo Wordsworth published in June 1802.

That it was *published* is the important point. Wordsworth had written like this before. To Tobin in March 1798 he had declared that he could not conceive of anything that would not come within the scope of his planned philosophic poem. In the *1799 Prelude* he had claimed the status of a chosen son, strong to withstand dereliction and dismay, fitted by Nature for honourable toil. The 'Prospectus' to *The Recluse* had envisioned his poetry as 'a light hung up in heaven to chear / Mankind in times to come!' He also repeated his aspirations in this spring of 1802. At the end of May he received his first serious letter of homage, from an unknown Glasgow student, John Wilson.[53] Wordsworth was touched, not least because the 17-year-old Wilson relied so heavily on the Preface for the terms in which he praised the philosophy and morality of the *Lyrical Ballads*. But Wordsworth's reply was long and passionate not because Wilson praised him, but because in criticizing the conception of *The Idiot Boy* he had revealed that he was still far from appreciating the radical character of the poems and from sharing Wordsworth's vision of the poet's role. Once again Wordsworth reveals how grand it is:

You have given me praise for having reflected faithfully in my poems the feelings of human nature. I would fain hope that I have done so. But a great Poet ought to do more than this he ought to a certain degree to rectify men's feelings, to give them new compositions of feeling, to render their feelings more sane pure and permanent, in short more consonant to nature, that is, to eternal nature, and the great moving spirit of things. He ought to travel before men occasionally as well as at their sides.[54]

But none of these claims or aspirations had been published. Now, in this third edition of *Lyrical Ballads*, Wordsworth had declared himself. That there was an incongruity between the unassuming nature of the poems in the volumes and the Preface which introduced them could not escape notice. By presenting himself as both theorist and practitioner Wordsworth had made himself particularly vulnerable to attack.

(4)

In the preceding sections Wordsworth's poetic career from 1800 to 1802 has been outlined through a summary account of his writing. Deliberately so, for attempts to locate the genesis of a particular poem in details of daily life are generally crass and reductive. There can be little doubt, however, that the shape of Wordsworth's movement from the achievement of *Lyrical Ballads* 1800 into barrenness, then struggle, and finally to the distinctive achievement of 1802 was in a general way moulded by events at Grasmere and, in the spring of 1802, even specifically determined by them. The curve of his development plots also a development in his relationship with Coleridge.

The picnic on the island at Grasmere in late July 1800 seemed to promise that the community of Alfoxden was about to be re-established in the Lakes. Keswick was thirteen miles from Grasmere, but regular intercourse between the two households was still possible, as it had been in 1798. The poets were working together again on *Lyrical Ballads* and *The Recluse* remained their joint aspiration. But when Wordsworth, Dorothy, and Mary Hutchinson sat round the fire on Christmas Eve 1801 and, as Dorothy records, thought about the last year as they read her journal, they sensed that the spirit of Alfoxden had gone forever.

Throughout 1801 Coleridge was in torment. He was frequently very ill with stomach and bowel ailments, gouty swellings to joints and testicles, and sweats and fevers consequent on the opium which he took increasingly to relieve his pain. Subjugation to the drug produced 'Disgust, Despondency, & utter Prostration of Strength', which were only exacerbated by contemplation of his circumstances, from which he dreamt of escaping to St Nevis or the Azores.[55] He was desperate for money, but though as active as ever in reading, thinking, and making plans—witness the extraordinary letters of February to Davy and Josiah Wedgwood—incapable of writing solely for cash.[56] Increasingly unhappy at home, he took refuge in self-justifying analyses of his wife's lack of intellect, sensibility, and self-command and in a growingly obsessive fantasy that in Sara Hutchinson he had met the woman he could love. What had started in November 1799 as a flirtation on an evening of 'Conundrums & Puns & Stories & Laughter'[57] at Sockburn rapidly became a one-sided passion which drove Coleridge to seek Sara out at her brothers' farms at Bishop Middleham and Gallow Hill, reckless of the effect on his wife. Self-absorption made him misjudge his relationship even with Tom Poole. It is not surprising that this generous friend was wounded by being told, 'It is impossible that you should feel with regard to pecuniary affairs as Wordsworth or as I feel', but it is amazing that their friendship survived Coleridge's replies to his remonstrances, which not only repeat the offence but analyse other faults of Poole's as well.[58]

In judging Coleridge's domestic misery the Wordsworths were wholly partisan. 'Mrs Coleridge is the most extraordinary character—she is the lightest weakest silliest woman!',[59] Dorothy said, in one of two comments about Sara which are quite uncharacteristically vicious. Wordsworth tried to help financially by lending Coleridge £30. To his other troubles they were also tenderly sympathetic. Coleridge left for London in November to write regularly for Stuart and after they had parted from him Dorothy 'eased [her] heart by weeping'.[60] Bluffly, Wordsworth chided for her 'nervous blubbering', but in fact he was no more immune than she was to the effect of the wretchedness Coleridge now poured out in his letters. Dorothy records their response again and again: 'Coleridge's were very melancholy letters ... We were made very unhappy'; 'We had a melancholy letter from C ... We walked home almost without speaking'; his letter made us uneasy about him. I was glad I was not by myself when I received it'; 'A heart-rending letter from Coleridge—we were as sad as we could be'; 'two very affecting letters from Coleridge'. When Coleridge arrived back at Grasmere on 19 March 1802 'he seemed half stupefied' and after he had gone to bed, Wordsworth and Dorothy sat up talking till four the next morning, deeply agitated by his condition.[61]

Sympathetic though he was to Coleridge—and the word hardly suggests the degree of emotional involvement he felt—it is clear that by the spring of 1802 Wordsworth was responding strongly against him in two ways that have an important bearing on Wordsworth's own poetry and on his sense of himself as a poet.

On 25 March 1801 Coleridge told Godwin, 'The Poet is dead in me'. This was only one of a number of such declarations and the fact that the announcement to Godwin is made in strikingly imaginative prose could not disguise the apparent accuracy of Coleridge's self-assessment. Although his capacity for theorizing and arguing about poetry was undiminished, the power to write it seemed to have yielded against the onslaughts of money worries, ill health, and personal unhappiness. This was bad enough. Put simply, Coleridge's experience demonstrated how difficult it was to survive by literature alone and how vulnerable were the personal resources—health, calmness, confidence—on which the poet had to rely. What was worse was that Coleridge seemed to be colluding in his own disintegration by rationalizing it through analysis and explanation. But though the Wordsworths were obviously aware of this process—they seem, for example, to have accepted at face value Coleridge's account of how discord at home numbed his creative powers—its full extent did not become apparent until the spring of 1802.

On 21 April Coleridge read to Wordsworth and Dorothy his verse *Letter to Sara Hutchinson*. 'I was affected', Dorothy wrote, 'and was on the whole, not being well, in miserable spirits.'[62] It is easy to see why. Though formally addressed to Sara, the poem was directed at Wordsworth and more especially at the Wordsworth who had recently questioned in the *Ode: Intimations* the loss of earth's 'celestial light' and 'visionary gleam'. Coleridge's response to Wordsworth's open questions was devastatingly coherent and comprehensive. Analysing his own case, he explains the causes which have suspended his 'shaping Spirit of Imagination'—a sense of isolation from loved ones, domestic misery, the habit of abstract thought. On these particulars, however, and with direct allusion to the *Ode*, Coleridge builds the more general case. The sources of power which he and Wordsworth had hymned in *Tintern Abbey* and *Frost at Midnight* were, in a sense, illusory. There is no power outside the self:

> It were a vain Endeavor,
>    Tho' I should gaze for ever
> On that Green Light that lingers in the West!
> I may not hope from outward Forms to win
> The Passion & the Life whose Fountains are within!
>
> O Sara! we receive but what we give,
> And in *our* Life alone does Nature live . . .

Initially Wordsworth must have been as affected as Dorothy by this revelation of how completely Coleridge was absorbed in creating self-exculpatory strategies from his own distress. Very quickly, though, his resistance to Coleridge's downward pressure exerted itself in a strongly positive response. Between 3 and 9 May he composed *The Leech Gatherer* (later called *Resolution and Independence*) and, in response to criticism from Sara and Mary Hutchinson, substantially revised it between 14 June and 4 July.[63] The second version is the finer and critics have rightly dwelt on the importance of Wordsworth's revisions, but in both versions the significance of the poem as an indicator of Wordsworth's response to Coleridge is much the same. Wordsworth confronts the introverted defeatism of the *Letter* directly. Plunged into dejection by self-generating fears about his future as he recalls the fate of burnt-out geniuses such as Chatterton and Burns, the poet encounters the aged leech gatherer and is admonished to a firmer mind, not so much by what the old man says as by the witness of his uncomplaining fortitude and perseverance to the resources of the human spirit.

*The Leech Gatherer*, however, was important to Wordsworth in a way that this brief account of its homiletic narrative does not reveal. Wordsworth, Dorothy, and John Wordsworth had met the actual leech gatherer two years earlier, and on 3 October 1800 Dorothy had noted details about his appearance and his life-story in her journal. Now Wordsworth returned to the encounter, drew on his memory and on the written account, and transformed the information by his own imagination, compelling it to serve his needs. In itself, in whatever version, *The Leech Gatherer* testifies to Wordsworth's capacity to seize on something outside himself, however trivial the material, and to find in memory and written evidence, in facts and in fiction, the challenge to imaginative creation. In the *Letter* Coleridge had highlighted the relation between outer and inner, which always troubled him as an area of philosophic, theological, and poetic perplexity. In *The Leech Gatherer* Wordsworth evades—as he was always to do—a binary opposition he could not resolve philosophically and which he never really understood. For the poet, the poem demonstrates, the source of power lies neither in inner or outer but in 'blended might', in 'an ennobling interchange / Of action from within and from without'.[64]

Possibly the most important aspect of *The Leech Gatherer* as a document of 1802 is that it is a lyric. Faced with the complexities of the *Letter* in 1798 Wordsworth might have engaged with Coleridge's ideas in philosophic blank verse, such as the 'Not useless do I deem' lines. In 1802 he wrote a lyric and this in itself was a further act of self-assertion. Coleridge had not wavered in the hostility he admitted in 1799 to 'the publication of any small poems'.[65] Then he had been anxious that nothing should deflect Wordsworth from *The Recluse*, and now that anxiety was keener than ever. But Coleridge was beginning to suspect that Wordsworth's concern for his lyrics and his fresh burst of writing in 1802 stemmed from 'a radical

Difference in our theoretical opinions respecting Poetry'.[66] A year later he went further. Writing 'small Poems' was 'hurtful'. A 'Great Work' was Wordsworth's 'natural Element—the having been out of it has been his Disease—to return into it is the specific Remedy, both Remedy & Health'.[67] But Coleridge was quite wrong. Lyrical utterance was for Wordsworth a natural mode. Throughout his life he embodied his conviction that the 'objects of the Poet's thoughts are everywhere', recorded his travels, mourned the loss of those he loved, charted his own development, and exhorted his countrymen, in lyric poems. Twentieth-century preoccupation with what he did not publish—with *The Prelude*, *The Ruined Cottage*, and, more recently, *Home at Grasmere*—has obscured the fact that Wordsworth established his reputation on *Lyrical Ballads* and the entirely lyrical *Poems, in Two Volumes* of 1807, in which most of the 1802 lyrics appeared for the first time. Wordsworth believed that one day he would offer the world a great philosophic poem in blank verse and this remained his 'last and favorite aspiration'.[68] What he was actually doing between 1798 and 1807 was identifying himself publicly with the lyric, and ennobling it in the hierarchy of genres by the claims made in the Prefaces of 1800 and 1802.

### (5)

On 11 February 1802 Dorothy read Jonson's *To Penshurst* to her brother. 'We were much delighted.' A month later 'William was reading in Ben Jonson—he read me a beautiful poem on Love'. This was almost certainly the *Epode* to *The Forest* and one can see why Jonson gave them pleasure, for both poems celebrate values embodied in daily life in the cottage at Town End.[69]

'True love', Jonson declares in the *Epode*, is a divine essence which 'in a calm and god-like unity / Preserves community'. It is the 'elixir of all joys' and 'more fresh than are the Eden bowers'. In *Home at Grasmere* Wordsworth had likewise celebrated love as the power that combines, preserves, and gives meaning, and had located his experience of such love in the mutual dependence of himself and Dorothy:

> Long is it since we met to part no more,
> Since I and Emma heard each other's call
> And were Companions once again . . .[70]

Their love for each other was very strong—it had to be to survive frequent changes of roof, lack of money, the ordeal of Germany, and physical hardship. It was domestic. Brother and sister clearly took pleasure in being together all of the time—reading, walking, digging, building, and planting.

One characteristic entry in Dorothy's journal (8 May 1802) begins: 'We sowed the Scarlet Beans in the orchard, I read Henry 5th there. William lay on his back on the seat.' It was also, unquestionably, profoundly sexual. Another journal entry reads in part: 'I went and sate with W. and walked backwards and forwards in the orchard till dinner time—he read me his poem. I broiled Beefsteaks. After dinner we made a pillow of my shoulder, I read to him and my Beloved slept—I afterwards got him the pillows and he was laying with his head on the table when Miss Simpson came in. She stayed tea. I went with her to Rydale. No letter!'[71] This is not an exceptional entry. In others Dorothy calls Wordsworth 'my darling' and quite unselfconsciously records how she soothed him by touching, or sat close to him in silent communion. Work in the garden, composition of a poem, cooking, and reading—all these various aspects of their daily life are harmonized within the atmosphere created by an acknowledged and expressed love.

It is, however, as important to note that Miss Simpson stayed to tea and that Dorothy was dashed by not finding letters at Rydale, as that Wordsworth slept on her shoulder, for these facts point to the most significant aspect of the Wordsworths' love for one another. Exceptionally intense though it was, it was not exclusive. They were hospitable as a matter of course and always ready to put visitors up, despite the smallness of the cottage, but their deepest pleasure was in absorbing others into their intimate life. First there was John, then Mary Hutchinson soon after they had settled in at Town End, and then Sara for a month at the end of 1800 and a much longer stay from November the following year. Although both sisters had homes and responsibilities elsewhere—Sara was living with George Hutchinson at Bishop Middleham near Durham and Mary with Thomas at Gallow Hill near Scarborough—Town End increasingly drew them. When they were there they were not visiting, they were at home. When they were away, the Wordsworths entreated them to return: 'My dearest dear Mary I look forward with joy to seeing you again . . . God bless you. I wish that you were here that you were both here to talk with us, you and dearest Sara.'[72]

The existence of this community of loved and loving people—what Thomas McFarland in a brilliant discussion has called 'The Significant Group'—was of fundamental importance to Wordsworth.[73] He loved with tenacity, as if to ground himself in the being of others, and feared the psychic disintegration that threatened in even the idea of a mass or a crowd in a city street. Even the notorious *Leech Gatherer* affair demonstrates the importance of such a community to Wordsworth as poet. Mary and Sara criticized the first version of the poem, Sara judging the latter part 'tedious'. Wordsworth was staggered and on 14 June wrote mildly to Mary but very censoriously to Sara. The tone of his quite inadequate self-defence is unpleasant, but very revealing in its severity. Sara was one of the significant group on whose judgement he relied totally. His immediate response was to hector. Then he completely revised the poem.

At the end of *To Penshurst* Jonson identifies real living:

> Now, Penshurst, they that will proportion thee
>     With other edifices, when they see
> Those proud, ambitious heaps, and nothing else,
>     May say, their lords have built, but thy lord dwells.

The little cottage at Town End was not Penshurst, but in these lines Jonson touches on its essential value. At last Wordsworth and Dorothy were dwelling. Coleridge's optimism that Wordsworth would uproot himself again to accompany him to the Azores or St Nevis was sheer fantasy. Wordsworth and Dorothy even became reluctant to go to Greta Hall. At a midway point between Grasmere and Keswick they all carved their initials—W.W. M.H. D.W. S.T.C. J.W. S.H.—on 'Sara's Rock' (see Pl. 6), but warmth, generosity, ease were identified with Town End and not Greta Hall. There, Dorothy wrote, 'we are never comfortable after the first 2 or 3 days'.[74] Increasingly Coleridge sought refuge at Town End or called in there on his way to Keswick, as if drawing strength to face the discord at what he could no longer feel was home.

What this one 'dear perpetual place' meant to Wordsworth is made clear by the way he marked the end of the first phase of life there.[75] It is not clear when Wordsworth decided that he wanted to marry Mary Hutchinson, but on 29 April 1801 he wrote:

How we wished for our dear dear friends you and Sara. You will recollect that there is a gate just across the road, directly opposite the firgrove, this gate was always a favorite station of ours; we love it far more now on Saras account. You know that it commands a beautiful prospect: Sara carved her cypher upon one of its bars and we call it her gate. We will find out another place for your cypher, but you must come and fix upon the place yourself. How we long to see you my dear Mary.

It is a curious but unmistakable love letter. Mary must come and claim some part of their favourite place as her own. On 14 February 1802 Wordsworth saw her at Penrith and ten days later Coleridge said that he expected Wordsworth to marry soon. Another meeting took place at Middleham in early April.

At this meeting Wordsworth must have told Mary that he was determined to see Annette before their marriage, for it was only in the month before that such a reunion had become possible. On 1 October peace preliminaries between France and Britain had been concluded, which enabled letters to pass regularly between Town End and Blois, but the formal Treaty of Amiens was not signed until 27 March 1802. Nobody believed the peace would last long, not even the signatories, and Wordsworth was eager to see Annette while travel to France was still possible, and to meet his daughter. By introducing Annette and Caroline to Dorothy, moreover, he would at last be able to include her in one part of his life she had not shared.

On 25 April Wordsworth and Dorothy read Spenser's *Prothalamion* and as the time approached for them to set off from Grasmere, ultimately for Gallow Hill, Wordsworth worked on his own 'song to celebrate a forthcoming wedding' (OED). His 'poem on Going for Mary' as Dorothy called it, is very striking.[76] On the one hand it consciously marks their departure from Grasmere as *Home at Grasmere* had marked their arrival. Wordsworth dwells on the cottage, on the garden they have created, on the poems he has written, and the joy they have known, memorializing a way of life that can never be the same again. On the other hand, the poem insists that such is the capacity of this 'Dear Spot' to reciprocate love, that Mary will 'wed' it as she has wed her husband, will 'love the blessed life which we lead here' as she loves him. Rootedness and continuity will be strengthened, not weakened, by her arrival and by the extension of the Town End group.

It is a poignant poem. Wordsworth never relinquished anything that had really mattered to him—the memory of a place, a few lines of poetry, a friendship. He went on believing his relationship with Coleridge was unaltered, for example, long after it had begun to change. So now he enshrined the spirit of his last two years at Grasmere in a form that could not fade. Dorothy knew better. She had no fears about the marriage. 'Mary Hutchinson', she told Richard, 'is a most excellent woman—I have known her long, and I know her thoroughly; she has been a dear friend of mine, is deeply attached to William, and is disposed to feel kindly to all his family.' But she was anxious to secure some income from her brothers so that although, without question, she would continue to live at Town End, she could 'consider myself as boarding through my whole life with an indifferent person'.[77] For so long in everyone's eyes it had been 'Wordsworth & his exquisite Sister'. But on 2 September Coleridge wrote: 'It is absolutely necessary, that I should have one spare Room always ready for Wordsworth & his Wife / and tho' Dorothy would, of course, always accompany them . . .'.[78] Dorothy was realistic enough to know that this would be the order of precedence from now on.

'Wordsworth & his Wife'—Coleridge must have written those words uneasily, for he too was registering the impact of Wordsworth's marriage. On 19 November 1801 he told Godwin that in Grasmere, 'tho' we were three persons, it was but one God'. By April 1802, however, he was aware that this trinity had expanded and was dwelling on his gnawing conviction, which was not unfounded, that he was no longer an integral member of the larger group. In the *Letter to Sara Hutchinson* he had written as an insider now outside:

> Oh! it weighs down the Heart!
> To *visit* those I love, as I love thee,
> Mary, & William, & dear Dorothy,
> It is but a temptation to repine—
> The transientness is Poison in the Wine,
> Eats out the pith of Joy, makes all Joy hollow,
> All Pleasure a dim Dream of Pain to follow!
> My own peculiar Lot, my house-hold Life
> It is, & will remain, Indifference or Strife—
> While *ye* are *well & happy*, 'twould but wrong you
> If I should fondly yearn to be among you—
> Wherefore, O wherefore! should I wish to be
> A wither'd branch upon a blossoming Tree?

'What is Life', Coleridge had exclaimed, 'gangrened, as it is with me, in its very vitals—domestic Tranquility.'[79] As he wrote this to Southey, he must have recalled that he had been strong-armed into marrying Sara Fricker by this fellow Pantisocrat and have been conscious of how differently Wordsworth was proceeding towards an extension of the domestic tranquillity he already enjoyed.[80] There is evidence, too, that Coleridge was disturbed by the visit to Annette. Writing to Sara Hutchinson on 10 August 1802 he confessed, 'I seem, I know not why, to be beating off all Reference to Dorothy & William, & their Letters . . . '. On Wordsworth's wedding day (which was also the anniversary of his own), Coleridge published in the *Morning Post* a revised version of the *Letter*, now addressed to Wordsworth as 'Edmund' and titled *Dejection: An Ode*. Yet a week later, in an extraordinary reversal of mood, he published a vicious squib called *Spots in the Sun*, which names a certain 'Annette' and can only be read as convicting Wordsworth of sanctimoniousness and hypocrisy.[81] It is impossible to reconcile the compliment and the attack, except by the supposition that Coleridge was goaded by the contrast between himself, suffering from his one great error of the heart, and Wordsworth, who was, as it were, settling his account before starting a new phase of life in which passionate inclination and moral obligation would be one.

(6)

Senior members of Mary's family disapproved of her intention to marry a man without a profession, no better than 'a Vagabond'.[82] In fact, however, in 1802 Wordsworth's financial position unexpectedly improved. On 24 May Sir James Lowther, Earl of Lonsdale, died and shortly afterwards his heir, his cousin Sir William Lowther, indicated that all just claims on the estate would be met. When finally presented on 8 October the Wordsworths' claim amounted to £10,388. 6s. 8d.[83] There was a fairy-tale appropriateness about Sir James's timing and Dorothy records how she and Wordsworth walked up and down in the garden at Town End, talking 'sweetly together about the disposal of our riches'.[84] But Wordsworth was extremely anxious that the claim should be pursued tactfully, so as to secure a good result quickly. He insisted that they should not haggle over interest and was so suspicious of all lawyers' wiles that he made it offensively clear to Richard that he would be watching his every move. Some delay was to be expected, but when Wordsworth and Dorothy left Grasmere on 9 July they were confident that the long injustice to their father and to his children was about to be rectified.

Travelling via Keswick and Eusemere they reached Gallow Hill on 16 July and ten days later set off for London and Dover. By 1 August Wordsworth was once again in France.

When one would most value Dorothy's perceptive observation and comment the journal fails. They stayed for a month in Calais, but Dorothy, who has chronicled recent events day by day, skims over the period in one entry, clearly written later, which mentions where they lodged, that Wordsworth bathed, that the sea was very striking, and nothing at all that one wants to know. How did she feel as she met the woman her brother had loved? What was Annette's reaction to the man who had caused her so much pain? And Caroline? She, Dorothy says, was delighted, as she walked with them, to see the shooting lights on the water. But did she, now 9 years old, immediately warm to a 32-year-old foreigner, an enemy of her country who spoke rusty French, whom she had been taken to meet as her father? It seems unlikely.

Nor is it easy to interpret the known facts about the visit. After the Treaty of Amiens the English flocked to Paris, some to see what a post-revolutionary state would be like, others to look at the art treasures Napoleon had looted, others to get a glimpse of the First Consul himself. Wordsworth's scorn for this rush 'to bend the knee / In France, before the new-born Majesty', is loftily expressed in his sonnet *Calais, August, 1802*, but it is at least as likely that he and Annette avoided Paris because she, as a known Royalist, wanted to keep out of the capital, and because they both realized that the tourist invasion would force up the price of accommodation. But even so, Calais seems a symbolic choice. It is as if Wordsworth were prepared to go to France, but only just. On the other hand, they stayed a month. This is a long time to spend in lodgings in a drab seaside town and argues a real commitment to re-establishing contact with Annette and to getting to know Caroline. To judge from the sonnet 'It is a beauteous Evening . . .', Wordsworth felt fondly towards his daughter and future relations with Annette suggest that generally the visit was a success. Wordsworth had no doubt already discerned what the stability of his marriage would prove, that Mary was strong enough to cope with the knowledge that her husband had responsibilities to a child who was not hers.

One longs for more evidence on which to speculate about Wordsworth's feelings about Annette and their daughter, if only to counterbalance the records Wordsworth did leave. A series of sonnets on political themes is no substitute for more intimate revelation. If only Wordsworth had written nakedly revealing letters such as Coleridge's or a poem to Annette comparable to the *Letter to Sara Hutchinson*. He did not. But it would be quite wrong to argue from the absence of one kind of evidence and the existence of another that Wordsworth felt little, or that he transferred emotion for Annette into a public register. A man as possessed as Wordsworth was by the past and by memory, who valued as he did the primary affections of our nature, and who was so moved by images of the permanent surviving against time's erosion, must have been deeply stirred. But we do not know. The sonnets, on the other hand, reveal that Wordsworth's visit to France did arouse strong feelings, but in a way that one might not have expected.

Wordsworth and Dorothy had not gone far. From Calais they were convinced they could see lights on the English coast. None the less Wordsworth was overwhelmed by yearnings for England, expressed in *Composed by the Sea-side, near Calais* and in *Composed in the Valley, near Dover*, where he dwells lovingly on common sights with the very characteristically English sense that they are somehow qualitatively different on this side of the Channel:

> Dear fellow Traveller! here we are once more.
> The Cock that crows, the Smoke that curls, that sound
> Of Bells, those Boys that in yon meadow-ground
> In white sleeved shirts are playing by the score,
> And even this little River's gentle roar,
> All, all are English . . .

Wordsworth never forgot those boys and eighteen years later their sons playing cricket on the same spot were to remind him of how joyful he had felt in 1802 at being home.[85]

Wordsworth's feelings for 'my dear Country', however, were very different from the unmixed longings of Browning's *Home Thoughts from*

*Abroad* or Rupert Brooke's *Grantchester*. Everyone knows 'We must be free or die, who speak the tongue / That Shakespeare spake', 'Great Men have been among us', 'Milton! thou should'st be living at this hour', but these lines (like the Harfleur and Agincourt speeches from *Henry V* which Wordsworth and Dorothy had been reading in May) are too often quoted out of their context, which reveals how complex Wordsworth's patriotic stirrings were. They were aroused by strong and dismaying negative pressure. Wordsworth remained true to the republican ideal that had fired him a decade before, but the evidence was overwhelming that France was diverging further and further from it. When he and Jones had paced along in 1790 'A homeless sound of joy was in the Sky', but now Wordsworth only caught in the greeting 'Good morrow, Citizen!' a hollow echo of that hopeful time.[86] Again in *Calais: August 15, 1802*, he contrasts the seeming indifference of the ordinary citizen to the proclamation of Bonaparte as First Consul of the Republic for life to the earlier time when rejoicing was shared nationwide. In another sonnet, *To Toussaint L'Ouverture*, he lamented the tyranny that had imprisoned the Haitian leader for resisting Napoleon's edict re-establishing slavery. Wordsworth was forced to register afresh that 'France' and 'Liberty' had long since stopped being synonymous. England, on the other hand, could only be hailed as the friend of liberty for want of a better, as the strikingly disenchanted sonnet 'England! the time is come . . .' makes clear. Wordsworth deplores his country's 'trespasses', recognizes its selfish territorial and commercial designs, and concludes, 'Oh grief! that Earth's best hopes rest all with Thee!'

The strategy by which Wordsworth ordered these conflicting impulses is implicit in the poetic form he was now using. On 21 May 1802 Dorothy had read him some of Milton's sonnets and Wordsworth acknowledged 'These manly and dignified compositions . . . crowding into narrow room more of the combined effect of rhyme and blank verse than can be done by any other kind' as the model for his own.[87] Milton emerges, however, not just as a model for style but as the voice of a nobler age, whose 'manners, virtue, freedom, power' must be restored if military victory is to be of any worth. Milton, Sidney, Marvell, Harrington, Vane—these 'Moralists' testify to the true spirit of English liberty, now choked by luxury, greed, and selfish aims. As all effective moral censors do, Wordsworth was simplifying the past in order to alert the present to its degeneration and to provide a positive image of the better way. He was also, once again, declaring himself Milton's heir. The 'Prospectus' to *The Recluse*, with its challenge to *Paradise Lost*, remained unpublished. But when Stuart printed five of the sonnets in the *Morning Post* he made sure that readers would take notice, by announcing them as 'written by one of the first Poets of the age [and] among his best productions'.[88]

(7)

On 31 August Wordsworth and Dorothy arrived back in London, to stay in Montagu's rooms in the Inner Temple. Charles and Mary Lamb were near neighbours in Mitre Court Buildings and after dinner on 7 September Lamb offered to show them round Bartholomew Fair in West Smithfield. Neither Lamb nor Wordsworth were merely disinterested sightseers. Wordsworth could be moved by London—witness *Composed upon Westminster Bridge* ('Earth has not anything to shew more fair') and the later *St Paul's*—but what always affected him was the city's potential for beauty brought out by the dawn light or a transfiguring snowstorm. Lamb, by contrast, was passionately in love with the actual. In his letter about *Lyrical Ballads* he had told Wordsworth:

Separate from the pleasure of your company I don't much care if I never see a mountain in my life.—I have passed all my days in London, until I have formed as many and intense local attachments, as any of you **Mountaineers** can have done with dead nature. The Lighted shops of the Strand and Fleet Street, the innumerable trades, tradesmen and customers, coaches, waggons, play houses, all the bustle and wickedness round about Covent Garden, the very women of the Town, the Watchmen, drunken scenes, rattles; . . . coffee houses, steams of soups from kitchens, the pantomimes, London itself, a pantomime and a masquerade, . . . The wonder of these sights impells me into night-walks about her crowded streets, and I often shed tears in the motley Strand from fullness of joy at so much Life—.[89]

A visit to the Lakes earlier in August, however, had unsettled him. After climbing Helvellyn and Skiddaw and wading up the bed of the Lodore Falls Lamb conceded 'that there is such a thing as that, which tourists call *romantic*', but he knew, none the less, that 'Fleet Street & the Strand are better places to live in for good & all than among Skiddaw'.[90] Lamb now understood Wordsworth's great passion a little better. As he guided him past the jugglers, tumblers, musicians, ventriloquists, hucksters, and catch-penny freaks such as 'The horse of knowledge, and the learned pig', Lamb no doubt hoped that Wordsworth would appreciate his.[91]

The Wordsworths were lingering in the city for a family conference. The *Earl of Abergavenny* had just returned and about 11 September John joined Richard, Dorothy, and William to discuss their affairs. His news was bad. Dorothy and William had invested around £350 in John, assured that the customary private trading engaged in by all East India Company captains would show a good return. But hit by delays on voyage and fluctuations in the market, John had returned in money difficulties, although how severe was not yet clear.[92] Only months earlier this loss would have been a disaster. Now it was compensated for by the expectation of the Lowther settlement.

When they left London on 22 September Wordsworth and Dorothy were satisfied that Richard was doing everything possible to further their claim.

They reached Gallow Hill on the twenty-fourth and almost at once Dorothy fell ill. For almost two months she had been adjusting herself to the emotional demand of meeting other people—first Annette and Caroline, then the Lambs and Richard and John, then, in a brief visit to Windsor, William Cookson and his family—and all had been in preparation for an event she knew she dreaded. As she confessed to her old friend Jane Pollard: 'I have long loved Mary Hutchinson as a Sister, and she is equally attached to me this being so, you will guess that I look forward with perfect happiness to this Connection between us, but happy as I am, I half dread that concentration of all tender feelings, past, present, and future which will come upon me on the wedding morning'.[93] The night before the wedding she slept wearing the wedding ring (though not on her second finger) and when she gave it to Wordsworth on the morning of 4 October he slipped it back on again and 'blessed [her] fervently'.[94] Perhaps in this little private ritual Wordsworth had meant to comfort Dorothy and reassure her of her continuing place in his life, but it was such a potent gesture that it is hardly surprising that Dorothy succumbed completely to hysteria. She did not go down to Brompton Church but lay on her bed, 'neither hearing or seeing anything', until the cry that the married couple were coming up the avenue drove her in one movement out of her room and into Wordsworth's arms. All of them must have been very glad it was over.

In later life Wordsworth often retraced his steps, with variations, over significant journeys he had made. His married life with Mary began with such a one. After the wedding-breakfast—and it was properly a breakfast for the ceremony had taken place a little after 8 a.m.—Mary, William, and Dorothy began the journey back to Grasmere along the roads brother and sister had paced with such eagerness two years before.

# 1803–1805

FIVE quotations say all that needs to be said at this stage about the marriage of William and Mary Wordsworth. The first is Coleridge's observation on 15 January 1804: 'It does a man's heart good, I will not say, to know such a Family, but even—to know, that there *is* such a Family . . . [Wordsworth's] is the happiest Family, I ever saw'.[1] The second is from the conclusion of Wordsworth's poem on his wife, 'She was a Phantom of delight', where he speaks of Mary's qualities:

> The reason firm, the temperate will,
> Endurance, foresight, strength and skill:
> A perfect Woman; nobly planned,
> To warn, to comfort, and command;
> And yet a Spirit still, and bright
> With something of an angel light.

The third is Dorothy's account to Catherine Clarkson of her walk back to Grasmere after a visit to Eusemere in June 1803: 'the whole vale of Brothers Water . . . indeed it seemed as beautiful a place as there need be in a beautiful world. I met William at the top of the Hill above our own house, he was on the look-out for me. Mary was at home Dear Creature! She was overjoyed to see me.'[2] The fourth is Dorothy again, now Aunt Dorothy, rhapsodizing over the baby, John, born 18 June 1803: 'He has blue eyes, a fair complexion . . . a body as fat as a little pig, arms that are thickening and dimpling and bracelets at his wrists, a very prominent nose, which *will be* like his Father's, and a head shaped upon the very same model. I send you a lock of his hair sewed to this letter.'[3]

Only Mary's voice is missing. That is best heard from some years later. In 1810 husband and wife were separated for some time, so that Wordsworth had cause to do what was never needed in the ordinary routine of their shared life—*write* to Mary about his feelings for her. Her reply, after nearly eight years of married life and the bearing of five children, begins:

O My William!

it is not in my power to tell thee how I have been affected by this dearest of all letters—it was so unexpected—so new a thing to see the breathing of thy inmost heart upon paper that I was quite overpowered, & now that I sit down to answer thee in the loneliness & depth of that love which unites us & which cannot be felt but by ourselves, I am so agitated & my eyes so bedimmed that I scarcely know how to proceed.[4]

By the spring of 1803 it was clear that the prophetic hope Wordsworth had uttered in 'Farewell, thou little Nook of mountain ground' had been fulfilled. Mary had come to Town End and 'the blessed life which we lead here' had been shaped into a new and even stronger configuration. The slow-maturing love of Wordsworth and Mary now found sexual expression; their lifelong commitment to each other evidently had an intensely passionate base. Mary loved Dorothy quite simply—she was, Mary told her children in 1851, 'henceforth my chosen companion thro' life'.[5] To her roles as amanuensis, companion, and home-maker, which were not diminished, Dorothy added a new one as what Mary called a 'second Mother' to the children.[6]

Such domestic stability over many years was both a spontaneous growth and the result of much care, self-effacement, and discipline—the 'Cottage in Grasmere Vale', Coleridge said, 'would be a proud sight for Philosophy'—and it was of incalculable benefit to Wordsworth.[7] In late life he declared, 'It was poor dear Coleridge's constant infelicity that prevented him from being the poet that Nature had given him the power to be',[8] gratefully aware of how much his own productivity had owed to the unwavering support of his wife. In 1805 all of the Wordsworths were to rely on each other in the first great grief of their adult lives. Two years after that Wordsworth was to discover how lavishly he could draw on Mary for strength and encouragement when he had to face the fact that he appeared to be failing in his poetic mission.

The effect of the happiness at Grasmere and of their new financial solidity was apparent at once. Wordsworth was no longer a wanderer of uncertain occupation, but a settled, married man, with two editions of *Lyrical Ballads* to his name. A new firmness of tone entered his letters to his still unmarried elder brother Richard and Dorothy followed suit. Early in 1803 Richard had succeeded in negotiating an advance of £3,000 of the Lonsdale money, which John requested should be made over to him so that he could invest for his next voyage. Wordsworth and Dorothy hesitated over security for Dorothy's share of the money, Richard grew cross, and John became more insistent. On 22 April Dorothy stated her position firmly to Richard and followed it up on 30 April and 1 May with a letter to Richard and John which must have shocked them both by its grasp of detail, its worldly prudence, and most of all by the severity of its tone.[9] This little skirmish was significant. Dorothy was clearly determined to look after herself. Wordsworth was no longer prepared to defer to his successful lawyer brother. The centre of gravity in the Wordsworth family had shifted to Grasmere.

(2)

One result of this new self-confidence was a decision which was unquestionably selfish. In the summer of 1803 Wordsworth and Dorothy made plans for a tour of Scotland with Coleridge. They justified it to themselves on grounds of health—they could afford to travel, they told Richard firmly, and it would do them good.[10] But the truth was that the spirit that had impelled Wordsworth to walk across France to the Alps, across Salisbury Plain into Wales, around Lower Saxony, and into the most westerly reaches of the Lake District was at work again, spurring him to an activity which was more than self-reward or prophylaxis against winter ailments. By this time Wordsworth knew himself well enough to recognize that when he had exclaimed amongst the Alps in 1790, 'perhaps scarce a day of my life will pass [in] which I shall not derive some happiness from these images',[11] he had touched on the source of his poetic creativity. After nearly three years of settlement in Grasmere and two editions through the press, he was looking for change, stimulus, and sensation, the raw material of poetry.

Joanna Hutchinson was to stay with Mary who, Dorothy was assured, 'does not look forward to being left alone with one gloomy thought'.[12] This may be doubted. Two years later Dorothy told Lady Beaumont that she would not be prepared to go on a second tour without Mary, which suggests she had come to realize what being cooped up with a baby had meant, and in 1810 Mary revealed some soreness, when she told Wordsworth of her longing to make a tour of Wales or Scotland alone with him.[13] But in 1803 she was wise enough to sense that the Alfoxden trio wanted to be together again and that for her husband it was a timely, if not vital, act of poetic recuperation.

Cautiously learning how to drive their 'outlandish Hibernian vehicle', an Irish jaunting-car, Wordsworth and Dorothy set off from Keswick with Coleridge on 15 August 1803.[14] A fortnight later they split up, Coleridge having decided to press on alone, and the two Wordsworths reached home again on 25 September.

Dorothy's *Recollections of a Tour Made in Scotland A.D. 1803* records a journey which was not shaped according to a predetermined scheme yet which took on a satisfying symmetry. In began with Burns, whose home and grave they visited on 18 August, and ended with Walter Scott, in whose company they spent the week 17–23 September exploring the eastern border region. In between they learned just how different from their own was the culture on which these, the two great shapers of modern Scottish literature, drew. As they went north—Blair Atholl was the farthest point—they encountered poverty worse even than that amongst the peasantry at Racedown in 1795. English, they found, did not come readily to many, but whereas in France Wordsworth could speak French, Cambridge had not taught him Gaelic. Money, it was a lesson to discover, was of little attraction to people living in a subsistence economy. Distance determined the lives of men and women struggling against an unyielding landscape and a harsh climate, whose rigour, even in September, Wordsworth and Dorothy experienced at first hand, as they sat huddled up but still soaked through on their open car. At Glencoe and the supposed site of Rob Roy's grave they learned something of the importance of history—and the idea of the past—to people whose national and regional identity had been forged largely in defeat.

There was nothing romantic about their tour—they slept in wet sheets, went hungry on occasions, had a bad accident with the jaunting-car, got cold and tired and wet. But these privations seem not to have dulled their sense of the romantic or their gratitude for the kindliness of people who generously made them welcome with the little they had to give. Wordsworth never forgot the beauty of the Highland girl at the ferry-house on Loch Lomond or the strange excitement he and Dorothy felt when, with the sun setting over Loch Katrine, a woman exclaimed, 'What! you are stepping westward'. One moment can stand for the many such experiences Dorothy describes—28 August on the road to Tarbet:

While we were walking forward, the road leading us over the top of a brow, we stopped suddenly at the sound of a half-articulate Gaelic hooting from the field close to us; it came from a little boy, who we could see on the hill between us and the lake, wrapped in a grey plaid; he was probably calling home the cattle for the night. His appearance was in the highest degree moving to the imagination: mists were on the hillsides, darkness shutting in upon the huge avenue of mountains, torrents roaring, no house in sight to which the child might belong; his dress, cry, and appearance all different from anything we had been accustomed to. It was a text, as Wm. has since observed to me, containing in itself the whole history of the Highlander's life—his melancholy, his simplicity, his poverty, his superstition, and above all, that visionariness which results from a communion with the unwordliness of nature.[15]

Throughout their tour both travellers attempted to 'read' the scenes before them and their experiences and, as Dorothy's last sentence suggests, they continued to think about them after their return. Her sustained work of ordering and reflection, the *Recollections*, occupied her, in distinct phases, until the end of May 1805. As usual Wordsworth dealt with his experiences in a different way. Episodes and images were allowed to seep through to the deep strata of his imagination. Some poetry was written shortly after returning, notably *Yarrow Unvisited* and *To a Highland Girl*, but he did not, in his own fine phrase, 'interrogate his memory' about much that had moved him most deeply until 1805.[16] Then, at a period of intense grief, images of joy and human strength welled up from the Scottish tour, confirming once again Wordsworth's trust that in present experience he was storing up 'life and food / For future years'.

(3)

1803 saw the foundation of two friendships. Such a natural event would not need stressing were it not that for a number of reasons Wordsworth is thought of as a solitary, unapproachable being. Much of his most striking poetry conveys the exhilaration of lonely places and the 'self-sufficing power of solitude', and Hazlitt's perception that 'It is as if there were nothing but himself and the universe. He lives in the busy solitude of his own heart' has seemed to many an accurate assessment.[17] In his middle years Wordsworth undoubtedly became defensively prickly and the anecdotal testimony of how often the 'egotistical sublime' was manifested in hauteur has remained current.

It is true that Wordsworth did not think friendship easy. In response to an ardent letter from the 17-year-old Thomas De Quincey, he wrote in July 1803: 'My friendship it is not in my power to give: this is a gift which no man can make, it is not in our power: a sound and healthy friendship is the growth of time and circumstance, it will spring up and thrive like a wildflower when these favour, and when they do not, it is in vain to look for it'. More memorably, he said to Coleridge, 'I am naturally slow to love and to cease loving'.[18] But what these comments, and all of his personal dealings, reveal, is that Wordsworth was a man who held the idea of friendship in awe and who clung to his friends tenaciously, valuing the bond in proportion as time and vicissitude tested it.

The first new friend was Scott. On their September visit Wordsworth and Dorothy had warmed to the generous manner in which Scott had shared with them his hospitality, time, and local knowledge. They were struck by the affection he inspired—'in almost every house', Dorothy noted, 'he can find a home and a hearty welcome'.[19] But what drew Wordsworth more particularly was his feeling of kinship with a man in the grip of a passion which was increasingly becoming the central drive of his life.

Just one year younger than Wordsworth, Scott was by profession a lawyer and had been Sheriff of Selkirkshire for three years. At Jedburgh assizes they had watched him 'in his cocked hat and sword, marching in the Judge's procession to the sound of one cracked trumpet' and had discovered the respect in which he was held when the innkeeper at Melrose refused even to show Dorothy available beds 'till she was assured from the Sheriff himself that he had no objection to sleep in the same room with Wm.'.[20] But his passion was the Border Country, its landscape, history, and culture. 'His local attachments', Dorothy declared, 'are more strong than those of any person I ever saw', and it is notable that she does not add 'except for William's'.[21]

The *Mintrelsy of the Scottish Border* (1802) was Scott's first celebration of these local attachments and even if he had written nothing else this labour of love would be enough to reveal why Wordsworth knew he had met a kindred spirit.[22] In this collection of border ballads Scott comes through in the very long historical introduction and in the voluminous detailed notes as a genuinely learned historian convinced that in the ballad lore of popular culture is a kind of history which must survive. As Wordsworth had done in the 1800 *Lyrical Ballads* Preface, Scott presents his collection as an alternative tradition of true poetry, which would be a challenge to prevailing taste:

the reader must not expect to find, in the border ballads, refined sentiment, and, far less, elegant expression; although the stile of such compositions has, in modern hands, been found highly susceptible of both. But passages might be pointed out, in which the rude minstrel has melted in natural pathos, or risen into rude energy.[23]

Something of this 'natural pathos' and 'rude energy' Scott was trying to capture in his own *The Lay of the Last Minstrel*, the first four cantos of which he recited to Wordsworth and Dorothy in their lodgings at Jedburgh.

Scott's sense that the poet could both preserve the past and transmit it, and his imaginative engagement with the voices of the long dead still heard in the ballads, were shared by Wordsworth, who knew that he could learn a great deal from Scott's knowledge of Scottish history and poetry. Acting on his belief that 'There can be no valuable friendship where the parties are not mutually capable of instructing and delighting each other', Wordsworth hastened to bind Scott to him.[24] Shortly after returning from Scotland he wrote a letter full of gratitude and graceful allusion to Scott, his poetry, and the Borders, in which he urged him to visit Grasmere soon. He signed himself, 'Your sincere Friend, for such I will call myself, though slow to use a word of such solemn meaning to any one'.[25]

In this letter Wordsworth sent his sonnet *Composed at* [Neidpath] *Castle*, which Lockhart claims Scott learned by heart, and on 16 January 1805 he sent *Yarrow Unvisited*, saying that he had written it 'not without a view of pleasing you' and inviting Scott to emend place-names in the text to make it more genuinely a poem of the Border Country.[26] At first it seemed likely that this, the making of poetry, would be the enduring bond between them, but increasingly they both became aware how irreconcilable were their attitudes to their art. At their first meeting Wordsworth had been staggered by Scott's breezy observation that 'he was sure he could, if he chose, get more money than he should ever wish to have from the booksellers',[27] and when the sales of *The Lay of the Last Minstrel* (1805) and *Marmion* (1808) proved his confidence was not misplaced, Wordsworth fortified himself against his own lack of financial success by asserting that Scott had written down to his audience and demeaned his own genius. For his part Scott could never understand Wordsworth's unwillingness to consider public taste, believing that he showed poor 'judgement in chusing such subjects as the popular mind cannot sympathise in. It is unwise and unjust to himself.'[28]

As a friend, however, Scott kept and strengthened his hold on Wordsworth's affections. He was unfailingly generous and hospitable. Wordsworth always admired his dedication to the region he loved and eventually had to admit that Scott had 'diffused more innocent pleasure than ever fell to the lot of any human being to do in his own lifetime'.[29] Most important of all, as Scott struggled to honour his debts in later life, battling against illness, he came to seem a noble image of the writer broken in the service of his art. Some of Wordsworth's last really fine poems were to be tributes to this 'great and amiable man'.[30]

Wordsworth's second important new friendship lasted almost as long and was untouched by any element of competitiveness or envy. In the summer of 1803 Wordsworth met the man whom Scott declared 'By far the most sensible and pleasing man I ever knew'—Sir George Beaumont.[31]

What brought them together was Beaumont's deep attachment to the Lakes and his reverence for art. After a first visit in 1777, he had spent his honeymoon with his wife Margaret in Keswick the following year and exhibited *A View from Keswick* as his first Academy showing in 1779. At least five further visits before the end of the century confirmed his passion and now in 1803 he had returned to Keswick, renting part of Greta Hall.

Had he known who occupied the rest of the house he might have hesitated, for Beaumont had met Coleridge earlier in the year at William Sotheby's in London and had disliked him. He was soon captivated, however, by Coleridge's conversation and in particular touched by his selfless advocacy of Wordsworth's powers. The pleasure he had already received from *Lyrical Ballads* was enhanced by meeting the poet, so much so that before he left Keswick Beaumont arranged that Coleridge should present Wordsworth with the deeds of a parcel of land at Applethwaite, under Skiddaw.

This extraordinary generosity seems to have stunned Wordsworth. He already knew that Beaumont admired him. The gift of two of Beaumont's drawings had indicated as much. But this gift was of a different magnitude—it was clearly an act of patronage. Calvert had similarly surprised him, but then the two men had known each other and had been of the same generation and class. Beaumont was scarcely known to him, was seventeen years older, and, as a substantial landowner with properties in Essex and Leicestershire as well as a house in London, was well outside his social sphere. Eight weeks elapsed before he acknowledged the offer and when he did his anxiety to explain why he had found the letter almost insurmountably difficult to write indicated how nervously he entered into a relationship which, whatever disclaimers were uttered on both sides, could not be, at least at the beginning, between equals.[32] He asked to be allowed to consider himself as 'Steward of the land', free to make improvements with an eye to building or to return it if that proved impracticable.

Beaumont's reply demonstrated what Wordsworth called his 'extreme delicacy of . . . mind', as all his dealings with the Grasmere circle were to do until his death in 1827.[33] He suggested that he had been moved to act by his desire to please Coleridge—'I soon found there was no means of doing this so effectually as by accommodating his friend'—and by his conviction that by increasing the 'enjoyment you [Wordsworth and Coleridge] would receive from the beauties of nature by being able to communicate more frequently your sensations to each other' he would thus contribute 'to the pleasure & improvement of the world by stimulating you both to poetical exertions'. His final appeal could not have been resisted by the most wary of beneficiaries: 'plant it delve it—& build upon it or not, as it suits your convenience, but let me live & die with the idea the sweet place with its rocks, its banks, & mountain stream are in the possession of such a mind as yours'.[34]

This splendid letter cleared the way for one of the most important friendships of Wordsworth's life. Its ground was personal regard—Wordsworth confessed he felt 'irresistible drawings' towards the Beaumonts—but it grew because each respected and admired the other and wished to learn.[35] Beaumont was an enthusiastic collector and advocate of a national gallery of paintings. He was also himself an artist, gifted enough to win the respect of Lawrence, West, Constable, Haydon, Wilkie, Farington, and others who, enjoying hospitality at Coleorton in Leicestershire or Grosvenor Square in London, formed something of a Beaumont circle into whose company Wordsworth was eventually introduced. After their first exchange of letters, Wordsworth was soon discussing Sir Joshua Reynolds's *Discourses*, which Beaumont had given him, and expressing the hope that in due course Beaumont would use his own collection to instruct him in 'some

of those finer and peculiar beauties of Painting which I am afraid I shall
never have occasions of becoming sufficiently familiar with pictures to
discover of myself'.[36] Beaumont for his part was convinced of Wordsworth's genius and, as an unknown eye-witness recalled many years later,
had to endure the scorn of many of his London friends because of his
advocacy of his merits.* According to Farington, as early as March 1804
Beaumont was telling friends that 'He was infinitely indebted to Wordsworth for the good he had recd. from his poetry which had benefitted Him
more, had more purified His mind, than any Sermons had done'.[37]

An old acquaintance was also renewed at this time. After an extended stay
in Portugal Southey had returned to England and was now looking to settle.
'Would to Heaven, you were at Keswick', Coleridge wrote on 12 March
1803, adding his judgement that Wordsworth and Southey 'would agree far
better now, than you might perhaps have done 4 or 5 years ago'.[38] Southey
prospected in Keswick in May and in September moved into Greta Hall.
Coleridge's prophecy proved correct. On 16 October Wordsworth told
Scott that 'Southey whom I never saw much of before I liked much better
than I expected; he is very pleasant in his manners and a man of great
reading'.[39] There could be no immediate friendship. Southey had come to
the Lakes very anxious about Coleridge's behaviour towards his wife
(Southey's own wife's sister) and suspected that he spent too much time
finding solace with the Wordsworths when he should have been in Keswick
with his family. In 1807, as Coleridge's determination to separate from Sara
became fixed, Southey's anger was directed at the whole self-absorbed
Alfoxden–Grasmere set. In one letter, from the specific accusation that the
Wordsworths 'have always humoured him [Coleridge] in all his follies,
listened to his complaints of his wife, and when he has complained of his
itch, helped him to scratch, instead of covering him with brimstone
ointment, and shutting him up by himself', he passed to a diatribe about
Wordsworth's own vanity and egotism.[40]

None the less over the years a bond was established of a kind best glossed
by Keats's shrewd words about friendship: 'The sure way . . . is first to know
a Man's faults, and then be passive, if after that he insensibly draws you
towards him then you have no Power to break the link'.[41] Wordsworth
could not esteem Southey as a poet—though 'highly pleased' with *Madoc*
(1805), he felt that 'The Poem fails in the highest gifts of the poet's mind
Imagination in the true sense of the word, and knowledge of human Nature
and the human heart'—but he came to admire his industry and professional
commitment to literature.[42] Southey's rectitude verged on the priggish, but

---

* Writing to Anne Hayman, 2 Oct. [1842], an unknown correspondent recalls: 'I remember Sir Geo.
& Ly Beaumont's bringing him to Grosvenor St a thousand years ago,—when their admiration was
laughed at & his Poetry held very cheap . . .'. MS, Beinecke Library, Yale University.

the way he gave support to Coleridge's family was admirable. As all friends did, Wordsworth regretted Southey's withdrawal later in life into his library, but he never forgot that, when he was grieving for the death of his brother and later for two of his children, the sympathy of this bookish man had been so spontaneous and warm.

## (4)

The friend above all friends was still Coleridge. Between August 1803 and January 1804, however, his relationship with the family at Town End deteriorated rapidly, but in a peculiarly poignant way. All of the Alfoxden friends had loved each other so deeply, and had drawn so much on what Wordsworth was later to call 'this consecrated Fount / Of murmuring, sparkling, living love', that they evaded their growing sense of rupture.[43] The Wordsworths loved Coleridge as much as ever, but it was increasingly difficult to esteem one who seemed so reckless of his responsibilities to his family and, as breadwinner for it, to his own health. Coleridge, for his part, loved and admired them all, as individuals and as a family, but envy and bitterness gnawed away at him, compounded by self-disgust, whose reproaches he confided only to his notebooks. Even as it was disintegrating, they all tried to keep the structure of their relationship intact and they succeeded for some years to come. But the struggle had a profound effect on Wordsworth as poet.

Tension first became unignorable on the Scottish tour. 'I never yet commenced a Journey with such inauspicious Heaviness of Heart before', Coleridge told Southey, referring primarily to his fears that the weather would exacerbate his disease, of whose diagnosis 'there now remains no Shade of Doubt: it is a compleat & almost heartless Case of Atonic Gout'.[44] But Coleridge no doubt had other fears. Understandably he felt excluded by the closeness of brother and sister and admitted, in a very sad notebook entry, to feeling envy and 'little ugly Touchlets of Pain & little Shrinkings Back at the Heart' on hearing that Wordsworth had written a new poem.[45] They grew irritable with each other and came close to quarrelling, as weary tourists will, over trivia, such as the dimensions of the Bowder Stone in Borrowdale. Each man indicted the other of hypochondriasis and only their separation prevented these private thoughts from bursting out into open accusation.

After their return tension became worse. On 14 October 1803 Coleridge wrote to Poole about Wordsworth's 'Self-involution' and although he claimed to feel only 'friendly Regret & disinterested Apprehension', his bitterness is apparent: 'I saw him more & more benetted in hypochondriacal Fancies, living wholly among *Devotees*—having every the minutest Thing, almost his very Eating & Drinking, done for him by Sister, or Wife—& I trembled, lest a Film should rise, and thicken on his moral Eye'.[46] Twelve days later what was ostensibly a philosophical discussion provided the occasion for an open quarrel. Hazlitt was in Keswick working on portraits of Coleridge, his son Hartley, and Wordsworth. Although now set on a career as a painter, Hazlitt had lost none of his zest for philosophical-theological discussion. Whereas in 1798, however, he had thrilled to Wordsworth's poetry and Coleridge's eloquence, marvelling, 'With what eyes these poets see nature', he now found himself allied with Wordsworth against Coleridge in an argument on just how Nature was to be seen. Coleridge's notebook record of this 'most unpleasant Dispute', in which his assailants 'spoke so irreverently so malignantly of the Divine Wisdom', dismisses Hazlitt, but dwells with evident pain on Wordsworth's faults and concludes, 'O dearest William! Would Ray, or Durham, have spoken of God as you spoke of Nature?'[47]

The crisis and a temporary release of tension came over the turn of the year. In the last months of 1803 Coleridge was near to complete mental and physical breakdown. He never wavered in his sense of duty to his wife and children, but he knew he was incapable of performing it—and so despised himself. His letters and notebooks testify to his extraordinary intellectual activity, but nothing had been achieved to justify the Wedgwood bounty. He hoped in due course, he told Poole, to 'render a good Account of what may have appeared to you & others a distracting Manifoldness in my Objects & Attainments', but for that hope to be fulfilled he needed health.[48] Denying to himself how much his genuine ailments were intensified by his drug-taking and by his struggle against addiction, Coleridge became fixated on the idea that a warm dry climate would save him. The word is not too strong. His letters at this time dwell obsessionally on this one point. On 20 December 1803 he arrived at Town End, to take leave of the Wordsworths on the first stage of a journey to the Mediterranean.

Here he broke down totally. He stayed in Grasmere for over three weeks and for much of that time he was in bed, sick and, as Dorothy put it, 'haunted by ugly dreams' that made him wake up screaming, afraid of sleep itself.[49] 'Continually wanting coffee, broth or something or other', Coleridge was selfishly fretful, but none the less Mary and Dorothy nursed him 'with more than Mother's love' and sat by his bed to comfort him in his nightmares.[50] Coleridge's response says so much about the state of their relationship now. He was, on the one hand, deeply grateful. The day after he left Grasmere he wrote to Richard Sharp about the Wordsworth family— 'the happiest Family I ever saw'—about the sources of that happiness, and about his undimmed conviction that Wordsworth 'will hereafter be admitted as the first & greatest philosophic Poet'.[51] On the other hand, he noted privately soon after 'the Hardheartedness of healthy People', contrasting his own exquisite sensitivity to damp with Wordsworth's 'Hypochondriasis'.[52] Not until escape was imminent could Coleridge's feelings flow towards Grasmere in the unmixed way they had once done. On 4 April 1804 he wrote a farewell letter from Portsmouth to 'dearest & most revered William' and to 'my beloved Dorothy'—'O dear dear Friends! I love you, even to anguish love you.'[53] Five days later the *Speedwell* at last set sail with Coleridge on board, bound for Sicily and Malta. They did not see him again for over two years.

## (5)

The near crisis with Coleridge agitated all of the Grasmere household. Even his loving farewell letter was dreadful. The mercurial, inspiring man they had once known now confessed to 'sinkings and misgivings, alienation from the Spirit of Hope, obscure withdrawings out of Life . . . a wish to retire into stoniness & to stir not, or to be diffused upon the winds & have no individual Existence'.[54] From now on, it had to be admitted, Coleridge was the focus of 'many melancholy, fearful, and unhappy feelings'.[55] Wordsworth was affected, however, in a more specific way, for his sense of his own poetic identity was so bound up with memories of Coleridge at Alfoxden and their joint aspirations for *The Recluse.*

By late 1803 it was clear that Coleridge was hostile to all that Wordsworth had been doing recently. On 14 October he announced to Poole that Wordsworth had at last yielded to 'urgent & repeated—almost unremitting—requests & remonstrances' and had 'made a Beginning to his Recluse', 'A Great Work, in which he will sail; on an open Ocean, & a steady wind; unfretted by short tacks, reefing, & hawling & disentangling the ropes—great work necessarily comprehending his attention & Feelings within the circle of great objects & elevated Conceptions—this is his natural Element—the having been out of it his Disease—to return into it is the specific Remedy, both Remedy & Health'. Coleridge went further—and at this point begged Poole to destroy the letter—declaring his 'hostility towards the plan of several of the Poems in the L. Ballads', whose composition had tempted Wordsworth to desert his 'former mountain Track to wander in Lanes & allies'.[56]

Coleridge was convinced that writing short poems was actually harmful to Wordsworth and his hostility was not just to *Lyrical Ballads.* Musing on the dispute with Hazlitt and Wordsworth, Coleridge privately addressed Wordsworth in his notebook: 'surely always to look at the superficies of Objects for the purpose of taking Delight in their Beauty, & sympathy with their real or imagined Life, is as deleterious to the Health & manhood of

Intellect, as always to be peering & unravelling Contrivances may be to the simplicity of the affections, the grandeur & unity of the Imagination'.[57] Looking and taking delight is just what Wordsworth had done in the 1802 lyrics. Poems on glow-worms, lesser celandines, and cattle feeding at the foot of Brothers Water were, to Coleridge, more than trivia. They were actually damaging to Wordsworth's proper genius.

It is one thing to suspect a radical difference of opinions respecting poetry, quite another to insist, in unremitting remonstrances, that what is being written is deleterious. Wordsworth must have been troubled by Coleridge's views. In the two editions of *Lyrical Ballads* 1800 and 1802 he had appeared before the public as a writer of original and challenging lyric and narrative poems. He took pleasure in the lyrics of 1802 and in the mastery of a new form in the sonnet. However, in the minds of his immediate circle and of his friends and acquaintances such as Tobin, Losh, the Wedgwoods, Poole, the Beaumonts, Southey, and others, above all in Coleridge's mind, Wordsworth's poetic identity was vested in the much-announced *Recluse*. A disturbing split was opening up between public and private perception of him as a poet.

How he was perceived publicly—or at least in some circles—had been clear to Wordsworth for some time. Reviewing *Lyrical Ballads* 1800 in June 1801 the *Monthly Mirror* had identified the new school of poetry with a new and repugnant school of philosophy, but had not wished to 'withhold our warm eulogium' from 'Mr Wordsworth, who may be regarded as the senior professor in this Parnassian college'.[58] Francis Jeffrey in the newly founded *Edinburgh Review* had been more specific and less generous. Ostensibly discussing Southey's *Thalaba* in October 1802, he had attacked the new '*sect* of poets' as '*dissenters* from the established systems in poetry and criticism', who 'constitute, at present, the most formidable conspiracy that has lately been formed against sound judgment in matters poetical'. Jeffrey's assault on Wordsworth, whom he mentions directly, and on the *Lyrical Ballads* Preface as a 'kind of manifesto', is motivated by political disagreement and at least does Wordsworth the honour of taking him seriously. His linguistic radicalism, Jeffrey claims, subverts social order, as does the general drift of these new poets, who are distinguished by a 'splenetic and idle discontent with the existing institutions of society'.[59]

While professing—not for the last time unconvincingly—that he knew nothing of magazine reviews, Wordsworth recognized that the 'Review of Thalaba is throughout under that disguise an attack upon me' and the earnestness with which he encouraged Thelwall to smash Jeffrey in his own pamphlet war on the *Edinburgh Review* indicates how angry he was.[60] Wordsworth claimed not to understand references 'to the School about which so much noise (I am told) has been made', but he could not ignore the evidence that for some it had a real and offensive existence. In 1803 an unknown Peter Bayley published a volume of poems which part parodied and part plagiarized Wordsworth, mocked the writing of Prefaces, and mentioned him by name in a scornful footnote.[61] Wordsworth and Coleridge blew this up out of all proportion. Attacking Bayley became 'the cause', which Coleridge thought to take up, but which in the end Southey prosecuted. 'Enough of this nonsense', Wordsworth blustered to Scott in October 1803, but the 'nonsense' still rankled enough to spur him to a spluttering paragraph of self-defence against this 'wretched creature of the name of Peter Bailey' six months later.[62]

Both Wordsworth and Coleridge were alarmed. In 1798 Coleridge, victim of the *Anti-Jacobin*, had told Cottle that his name stank while Wordsworth's was unknown.[63] Now he found that his former reputation as a radical coterie poet survived to class him with a new school of which Wordsworth was the acknowledged chief, just as he was becoming more and more aware of real differences between them. Wordsworth, for his part, had to recognize that, having escaped notice during the danger years of the 1790s, he now had a reputation which was, as Coleridge pointed out, '*sectarian*'.[64] Jeffrey's critique, moreover, had been just—not sympathetic, perhaps not accurate, but just. *Lyrical Ballads* was in opposition to prevailing taste; the Preface was a manifesto; the poems were unmistakably radical. And Wordsworth had published nothing since that might serve to modify perception of the poems and Preface or to expound the philosophical and political thinking they embodied. 'Hereafter', as Coleridge averred, Wordsworth might be 'admitted as the first & greatest philosophical Poet'.[65] For the moment he was known and judged as the author of *Lyrical Ballads*.

(6)

Wordsworth's anxieties must have been focused at one particularly poignant moment. On 4 January 1804, just before his departure south, Coleridge noted, 'in the highest & outermost of Grasmere Wordsworth read to me the second Part of his divine Self-biography'.[66] At the end of that poem Wordsworth had spoken of his more than Roman confidence in human nature, hymned the power of Nature in which he found 'A never-failing principle of joy / And purest passion', and bidden farewell to his brother-poet:

> Fare thee well:
> Health and the quiet of a healthful mind

Attend thee, seeking oft the haunts of men—
But yet more often living with thyself,
And for thyself—so haply shall thy days
Be many, and a blessing to mankind.[67]

Now Wordsworth was pledging them anew to goals which are invoked in the closing of the *1799 Prelude* but which had so far eluded them both. Coleridge had found neither health nor a quiet mind and had written no great work as 'a blessing to mankind'. Wordsworth had made his home among the mountains and done a great deal, but the 'honourable toil' which the poem had hailed was still to come.[68]

This symbolic moment, which was very like that in *Michael*, where a covenant is enacted between Michael and Luke, even to its setting in the mountains above Grasmere, inaugurated an astonishingly productive phase of Wordsworth's life. And everything of any importance that he wrote stems from this renewal of their covenant. The poems embody a profound and continuing reassessment of his own life as a poet; they are marked by a new *gravitas* of tone; they are all related, with varying levels of closeness, to Coleridge, the *annus mirabilis* of Alfoxden, and *The Recluse*.

On 21 November 1803 Dorothy had reported slightly anxiously that her brother was not yet 'seriously employed',[69] but once he did begin, most probably shortly after this reading took place, Wordsworth acted decisively. A satisfactory form for *The Ruined Cottage* and *The Pedlar* had escaped him ever since 1798. Now he reunited the philosophical history of the Pedlar with the story of Margaret in a poem of 883 lines, elaborating both the Pedlar as a realized character and the dramatic interplay between poet-listener and Pedlar-narrator.[70] It is impossible to say whether he returned to a structure which had formerly seemed questionable because he saw how it might work within a larger whole, or whether the larger whole suggested itself as he pondered the implications of the poem he had now created. What is clear is that in MS E of 1804 the poem essentially took the shape it was to retain until it appeared as Book I of *The Excursion* in 1814 and that by 6 March 1804 Wordsworth was at last announcing with confidence that he had completed 'one Book' of the 'moral and Philosophical Poem' to which he intended to 'devote the Prime of [his] life and the chief force of [his] mind'.[71]

By early March Wordsworth had also written two meditative lyrics, *Ode to Duty* and *Ode: Intimations of Immortality*.[72] The former is no one's favourite poem. Dealing largely in abstractions, it was quoted by the sterner Victorians, but by hardly anyone else, since it lacks what usually makes Wordsworth's poetry so memorable—the mnemonic power of rhythm, cadence, and phrasing, and vividly realized images. The *Ode: Intimations*, by contrast, rich in phrases that have entered the language and provided titles for other people's books, is Wordsworth's greatest achievement in rhythm and cadence. Together with *Tintern Abbey* it has always commanded attention as Wordsworth's strongest meditative poem and Wordsworth indicated his assessment of it by ensuring through the layout and printing of his volumes that the *Ode* stood apart.[73] None the less, both odes are complementary and both reflect Wordsworth's thinking about his life's work in 1804.

On 8 February 1804 Coleridge fantasized briefly about what he and Wordsworth might achieve could they only be together in an agreeable climate such as Sicily's, but stopped short with the reflection: 'But Mortal Life seems destined for no continuous Happiness save that which results from the exact performance of Duty—and blessed are you, dear William! whose Path of Duty lies thro' vine-trellised Elm-groves, thro' Love and Joy & Grandeur'.[74] This was no casual *sententia*. Towards the end of 1803 Coleridge had been immersed in Kant's *Foundations of the Metaphysics of Morals*. He entered passages in his notebook and as always reflected on them profoundly and with urgency. As a philosophical enquirer Coleridge found much that he agreed with in Kant's discussion of authority and law, but as an erring human being he was acutely aware of the gap between the abstract truths and life as it is lived. On 6 December he declared 'Kant and all of his School . . . bad analysts of aught but Notions', and around the same time, knowing that he did *not* feel that in him Reason and Will were synonymous, Coleridge judged Kant 'a wretched Psychologist'.[75]

Wordsworth's *Ode to Duty* reflects conversations with Coleridge on this topic, which was not of merely abstract concern to either of them. As in all of his retrospective poems, Wordsworth invokes one state of being only to welcome another which is its proper, natural, and better successor. Relying on the 'genial sense of Youth', Wordsworth suggests, he has lived as if love and joy were all-sufficient. But now he looks for other strength, to integrate his individual self with the natural law. It is a quiet and considered recognition of mature need:

> From no disturbance of my soul,
> Or strong compunction in me wrought,
> I supplicate for thy controul:
> But in the quietness of thought:
> Me this perpetual freedom tires;
> I feel the weight of chance desires:
> My hopes no more must change their name,
> I wish for a repose that ever is the same.

The power evoked is that of the 'Stern Lawgiver! [that] dost wear / The Godhead's most benignant grace' and it is to this power that Wordsworth commends his life:

> I myself commend
> Unto thy guidance from this hour;
> Oh! let my weakness have an end!
> Give unto me, made lowly wise,
> The spirit of self-sacrifice;
> The confidence of reason give;
> And in the light of truth thy Bondman let me live!

Far from being a retreat or a betrayal of earlier faith the *Ode to Duty*, as a recent scholar has argued, 'rededicates the poet to a life of disciplined mental conduct'.[76]

The *Ode to Duty* was a transitional poem. Wordsworth was not satisfied with it in 1804. At each recension he introduced revisions and Coleridge contributed to its final form as the manuscript was prepared for the press at the end of 1806. In theme and tone it looks to later poems, *The Happy Warrior, Elegiac Stanzas . . . Peele Castle*, and, obliquely, even to *The White Doe of Rylstone*. The *Ode: Intimations*, on the other hand, was a strongly affirmative conclusion to earlier work. In March 1802 Wordsworth had written the first four stanzas. His lament for the fading 'visionary gleam' had been counterpointed and in a sense answered by Coleridge's *Dejection: An Ode*. Now Wordsworth returned to his own disturbing and challenging stanzas, but instead of writing a new or different poem to embody his current thought, he developed a meditative structure from the existing stanzas, so that the questions of the opening seem to create the terms by which they are met in what follows.

In stanzas I–IV Wordsworth had asked, 'Where is it now, the glory and the dream?' Stanzas V–VII play with the paradox that 'growing up' is also a 'growing away' from the joyous elemental strengths of childhood. In *The Prelude* childhood is described as a 'long probation', a 'time of trial ere we learn to live / In reconcilement with our stinted powers', but in the *Ode* the figure of the growing child dramatizes more vividly the painful truth that all infants long to pass this trial, eager to grow up, heedless that in the 'light of common day' 'clouds of glory' are blotted out. Loss is presented as the condition of life. But even as stanza VIII closes on an image of custom, numbing as deeply as frost, a final movement of affirmation begins. The poet admits loss, but it is not the sole condition of life. In *Tintern Abbey* Wordsworth had opposed to 'such loss' the 'Abundant recompence' of mature life and he does so again now in an affirmation which is all the stronger for including knowledge of pain and suffering. Stanzas IX–XI celebrate the power of memory that sustains continuity with the earlier self and declares the continuing blessedness of life lived in full consciousness:

> What though the radiance which was once so bright
> Be now for ever taken from my sight,

Though nothing can bring back the hour
Of splendour in the grass, of glory in the flower;
    We will grieve not, rather find
    Strength in what remains behind,
    In the primal sympathy
    Which having been must ever be,
    In the soothing thoughts that spring
    Out of human suffering,
    In the faith that looks through death
In years that bring the philosophic mind.

And oh ye Fountains, Meadows, Hills, and Groves,
Think not of any severing of our loves!
Yet in my heart of hearts I feel your might;
I only have relinquish'd one delight
To live beneath your more habitual sway.
I love the Brooks which down their channels fret,
Even more than when I tripp'd lightly as they;
The innocent brightness of a new-born Day
    Is lovely yet;
The Clouds that gather round the setting sun
Do take a sober colouring from an eye
That hath kept watch o'er man's mortality;
Another race hath been, and other palms are won.
Thanks to the human heart by which we live,
Thanks to its tenderness, its joys, and fears,
To me the meanest flower that blows can give
Thoughts that do often lie too deep for tears.

All of Wordsworth's major poetry affirms gain even as it evokes most poignantly the shared human sense of loss. But none, not even *The Prelude*, does so more eloquently than this.

## (7)

Both of these odes were considerable achievements after the relative barrenness of 1803, but they are only a part of what Wordsworth now wrote during this, the most steadily fruitful period of his whole career. On 20 July 1804 he declared to Sir George Beaumont, 'It is such an animating sight to see a man of Genius, regardless of temporary gains whether of money or praise, fixing his attention solely upon what is intrinsically interesting and permanent, and finding his happiness in an entire devotion of himself to such pursuits as shall most ennoble human nature'.[77] Ostensibly the subject of this reflection was Sir Joshua Reynolds, but as Wordsworth dwelt on how the grandeur of his aims were matched by his 'deep conviction of the necessity of unwearied labour and diligence', he was clearly thinking of himself. Forgivably so, for during the previous six months Wordsworth had regained his 'former mountain Track' and had composed thousands of lines of his most complex poetry.

What Wordsworth was doing is not in dispute—abundant manuscript evidence survives—but the significance of what he was doing is.[78] Although now engaged in major work, he was not writing *The Recluse* as such, but the poem on the growth of his own mind, *The Prelude*. No part of *The Recluse* proper was touched until 1806. In late 1803, however, Coleridge had rejoiced that Wordsworth was once again turning to his great work and *The Pedlar* indicates that this was not a wholly mistaken view of his direction. What had happened?

One reading of the evidence would conclude that the pattern of 1798–9 was repeating itself. Unable to make progress with a poem conceived in grand but inhibitingly vague terms and separated from the stimulus of Coleridge's philosophical discourse, Wordsworth turned in on himself to write, not about 'Nature, Man, and Society', but about his own mind.[79] His letters to Coleridge support this view. On 6 March 1804 he told him, 'I am very anxious to have your notes for the Recluse' and at the end of the month, on hearing that Coleridge had been severely ill, he begged that the promised letter on *The Recluse* should be written and dispatched: 'I cannot say what a load it would be to me, should I survive you and you die without this memorial left behind'.[80] Once again, it can be argued, Wordsworth evaded the task he could not face. Whatever his later justifications of it might be, composing *The Prelude* was a substitute for getting on with *The Recluse*. That it was Wordsworth's finest poem is one of the great ironies, and that he never felt justified in publishing it one of the most puzzling phenomena, of literary history.

The evidence, however, can bear a more positive interpretation. On 4 January 1804 Wordsworth had read to Coleridge the second part of the *1799 Prelude*. The confident assertion of those closing lines spurred him on to complete *The Pedlar*, as one book of *The Recluse*, but they also stimulated thought about what he had and had not achieved, about who he now was and what kind of great work he might now consider appropriate both to his genius and to the needs of the age.

Wordsworth's liberating breakthrough came as he realized that dealing with these contending thoughts was a necessity, the pre-condition of any further composition towards *The Recluse*, but that dealing with them might itself be the substance of a poem which would have an integral relation to the major philosophical whole. Anxieties about *The Recluse*, his self-doubts, his perplexities and fears about the recesses of his own psyche, Wordsworth recognized, need not be evaded or repressed, but could be confronted, articulated, and shaped in poetry, and the recognition released the energy for composition. Early in 1804 he wrote an opening to the poem in which, significantly evoking Milton's Samson and the Christ of *Paradise Regained* as well as Adam and Eve walking into the fallen world, he dramatized himself facing the great test of his life. The contrast between the joyful confidence he had once felt and his present drooping fearfulness introduces the poem. In May 1805 he concluded it with a return to joy as he re-dedicated himself and Coleridge to their joint task. What Wordsworth had discovered in between was how to exploit the hesitant, probing, personal voice so that apparent perplexity could become the generative principle for a complex structure.

The more positive interpretation of Wordsworth's activity in 1804–5 being suggested here is supported, moreover, by the evidence that he grew more confident about the value of his work as it progressed. The *1799 Prelude* had been a limitedly private autobiography, a therapeutic act designed to convert 'Reproaches' into 'power' for 'honourable toil', and Wordsworth confessed to Beaumont that he had begun the 1804 composition 'because I was unprepared to treat any more arduous subject, and diffident of my own powers'.[81] As the larger work took shape, however, Wordsworth began to insist that although secondary to *The Recluse* as a whole his new poem was definitely part of it. To De Quincey he called it a 'tributary' to the 'larger and more important work', but to Beaumont he described it as 'a sort of portico' to *The Recluse* and it was this architectural metaphor he was to elaborate on when introducing *The Recluse* project in the Preface to *The Excursion* in 1814.* Both images indicate the same attitude to the poem. Wordsworth's sense of literary decorum prohibited him from thinking that the publication of such an avowed autobiography could be justified before the appearance of the main philosophical work which would enable the public to judge the pretension of the poet, but in 1804 he looked forward hopefully to the day when publication would be justified.

(8)

Over the late winter and spring of 1804 Town End became a poetry factory. On 8 February, before leaving England, Coleridge begged for a volume of all of Wordsworth's manuscript poems—'Think what they will be to me in

---

* W to Thomas De Quincey, 6 Mar. [1804]. *EY*, 454. W to SGB, 3 June 1805. *EY*, 594. In 1814 W claimed in the Preface to *The Excursion* that [*The Prelude* and *The Recluse*] 'have the same kind of relation to each other . . . as the Anti-chapel has to the body of a gothic Church. Continuing this allusion, he may be permitted to add, that his minor Pieces, which have been long before the Public, when they shall be properly arranged, will be found by the attentive Reader to have such connection with the main Work as may give them claim to be likened to the little Cells, Oratories, and sepulchral Recesses, ordinarily included in those edifices.'

Sicily!'[82] Despite all of their household tasks, made more trying by winter weather, and Mary's discomfort from the early effects of pregnancy, Dorothy and Mary at once began to race against time to provide a copy for Coleridge before he sailed. The beauty of the manuscript volume which survives in the Wordsworth Library belies the effort it cost. Wordsworth's poems, Dorothy said, were 'scattered about here and there in this book and that, one Stanza on one leaf, another on another which makes the transcribing more than twice the trouble' and 'were in such wretched condition and so tedious to copy from' that the poet's 'almost constant superintendence' was required.[83] When he was not at their side interpreting his scrawl, Wordsworth was out of doors under his umbrella, walking up and down in the toils of composition. 'And though the length of his walk be sometimes a quarter or half of a mile', Dorothy reported, 'he is as fast bound within the chosen limits as if by prison walls.'[84]

At first Wordsworth conceived of 'a Poem on my own earlier life which will take five parts or books to complete' and manuscript evidence suggests that he came close to shaping it.[85] Books I–III of the *1805 Prelude* would have led into a fourth Book compressing much of the present Books IV–V and then to a climax in the last book with the ascent of Snowdon and the 'spots of time' sequence from the *1799 Prelude*.

As Wordsworth paced up and down, however, other ideas began to attract him, intimations of altogether richer possibilities in a more ambitious structure, and by the end of the first week of March he seems to have changed his plan dramatically. He now constructed a narrative of his 1790 walking tour and of his residence in France in 1791–2, consisting largely of *1805 Prelude*, Books VI, IX, and part of X.

At the opening of Book VII Wordsworth admits that

> slowly doth this work advance.
> Through the whole summer have I been at rest,
> Partly through voluntary holiday
> And part through outward hindrance.

This is clearly a poetic device—a particularly significant one in the history of Romantic poetry. In a daring contrast to those moments where Milton invokes Divine aid for his lofty song, Wordsworth invites the reader to meet the poet in his own poem and to consider the personal considerations that weigh in the creation of a sustained composition. But the lines are also simply a statement of fact. The summer weather encouraged visits to friends. At the end of September Wordsworth and Dorothy took the jaunting-car for a tour into Ennerdale, Wasdale, and the Duddon valley. Visitors sought them out. On 16 August Mary gave birth to a daughter, Dorothy, who came to be known as Dora.

As the autumn came to a close, however, Wordsworth began to work again—Dorothy noted that 'starlight walks and winter winds are his delight—his mind I think is often more fertile in this season than in any other'.[86] He now composed, though not in a straightforward progress, Books VII, VIII, and the rest of X. All work on *The Prelude* stopped in February 1805 when the death of John stunned the Grasmere household, but by late April Wordsworth had resumed and on 3 June 1805 he was able to tell Beaumont with relief, 'I finished my Poem about a fortnight ago'.[87]

In many ways the thirteen-book *Prelude* reveals its origins in the two-part poem of 1799. Both are addressed, very tenderly in places, to Coleridge, not as the only possible, but as the ideal, reader. Both are autobiographies in which strict matters of fact are subordinated to an overall design, intended to reveal how the writer became, and then survived as, a particular kind of poet. But the *1805 Prelude* is not simply an expanded version of the *1799 Prelude*, a voicing of what the poet had earlier chosen to leave unexpressed. It is a poem of 1804–5, shaped by what were now Wordsworth's most insistent concerns.

An unexpected scrap of news passed on from Dorothy to Catherine Clarkson introduces the first of these. On 3 October 1803 Wordsworth went to Ambleside 'to volunteer his services with the greatest part of the Men of Grasmere'.[88] In 1793 he had sat in church in turmoil, unable to join in prayers for his country's victory. Now, ten years later, he was responding to the call to arms, ready to play his part in repelling the invasion by the French expected ever since the Peace of Amiens had formally ended on 18 May. Seen from the point of view of a French general Wordsworth's military commitment was comical. As Dorothy was shrewd enough to realize, if the French reached any part of the country where her brother's services might be needed, the invasion would already have triumphed. From Wordsworth's point of view, however, his willingness to exercise two or three times a week with the Volunteers was very significant. It was an indication of the political reassessment in which he was now engaged, which took its simple, visible form in his 'military apparel' and its complex one in the *1805 Prelude*.[89]

Though never in uniform, Coleridge had carried the standard—and the similarities and differences between the two men are very revealing. In a series of articles in the *Morning Post* in October and November 1802 he had scorned the dishonest peace, attacked Bonaparte as the predictable monster growth of the French Revolution, looked to the restoration of the French Monarchy, characterized his own kind of anti-Jacobinism, and, in two sensational letters which Stuart hesitated to print unamended, had pilloried Fox as one committed to peace at any price, whatever the threat to his own country. 'In all of these essays', their modern editor declares, 'there is a lapse of precise memory about earlier hopes and avowals . . .'.[90] A harsher judgement still might be made on Coleridge's letter to Sir George Beaumont a year later.[91] Here, in a very long and contorted apologia, Coleridge utterly disavowed his earlier self. The Bristol lectures, *The Watchman*, and all of the radical sympathies which had brought the spy to Nether Stowey were repudiated, not as opinions and attitudes which had been reconsidered, but as rubbish which had always been nothing more than the 'Drivel of a Babe'. The conviction that had enabled Coleridge to face down hostile crowds in Bristol was dismissed as the vanity of an orator who rejoiced in 'an ebullient Fancy, a flowing Utterance, a light & dancing Heart, & a disposition to catch fire by the very rapidity of my own motion'. Detaching himself from all of his radical associates, Coleridge declared that he and Southey had been insulated from all organizations and movements whatsoever, those 'Ascarides in the Bowels of the State'. Wrenching himself free of his own history, Coleridge here began the re-writing of it which was to culminate in *Biographia Literaria*.

Wordsworth's reassessment of his past took a different form. He had, of course, published nothing subversive between 1793 and 1798, so a radical past could not publicly reproach him as it did Coleridge and was to do to Southey in 1817, when his violently seditious *Wat Tyler* was resurrected.[92] Even so, it is doubtful whether Wordsworth could ever have written as Coleridge did to Beaumont, for his strongest instinct was to search for the continuity between past and present selves, to demonstrate an essential wholeness of being. 'It is not in my Nature to neglect old Friends', he assured Wrangham early in 1804, 'I live too much in the past for anything of that kind.'[93] It is a striking remark from someone only 33 years old. Wordsworth was not prepared to relinquish anything of value, especially not his own past.

Figures from earlier years reappeared now to remind him of the progress of others during the turbulent decade. One was John Thelwall, who dined with them at Town End on 26 November 1803. Memories must have flooded back of their time together at Alfoxden in 1798, when 'the agitator' had been in flight, beaten at last by the power of the state which had only narrowly failed to claim his life in the 1794 Treason Trials. Another was William Frend, who, driven out of Cambridge into the world of London radicalism because of his religious unorthodoxy and anti-war views, had stood out in the 1790s as an early martyr in the cause of liberty of thought and speech. Now Frend sent Wordsworth a copy of his *Patriotism: or, The Love of our Country*, which is such a vehemently pro-English utterance that it is impossible to imagine that its author had ever suffered persecution from Church and State. 'Dedicated to the Volunteers of The United Kingdom', the essay searches scripture and ancient and modern history for evidence that patriotism has 'its origin in nature' and concludes that 'Christianity does not prohibit the claims of nature nor disavow the rights of patriotism'.[94]

Frend's emphasis on the Englishness of English patriotism, exemplified in such as Alfred ('The character of Alfred is one of the finest on record'), would have appealed to Wordsworth, since his own recent sonnets *To the Men of Kent*, *Anticipation*, *Lines on the Expected Invasion*, and the four entitled *October 1803* continue the vein of those of 1802.[95] Though debauched and full of guile, England, recalled to the spiritual purity and unity of purpose that had determined past glories, is still the world's best hope. Faced with the threat to the nation's identity, Wordsworth was a staunch patriot and the fact that in 1802 he urged John to read Spenser's *A View of the Present State of Ireland* indicates that he shared the common (and traditional) view of who the enemies were.[96] But in 1791 Wordsworth had also been 'a patriot', when the word carried a different value as one sympathetic to the French cause.[97] As he wrote *The Prelude* in 1804–5 Wordsworth sought to understand himself as he had been then, from the vantage-point of what he knew he was now, convinced, unlike Coleridge, that as a patriot in both senses of the word he was still essentially the same person.

Wordsworth employs three strategies, which all work to give a similar impression. Far from needing to disavow earlier beliefs, the poem suggests, the mature man can recognize in them much that was good in itself and conducive to moral growth. First, he dwells on the glad dawn of the Revolution, on the joy he and Jones saw in every face as they tramped through the villages of France, and on the idealism that fuelled it. It is a highly charged and very significant moment when Beaupuy, meeting the

> hunger-bitten girl
> Who crept along fitting her languid self
> Unto a heifer's motion,

exclaims,

> 'Tis against that
> Which we are fighting.

Wordsworth recalls that this was his moment of commitment. He too believed

> Devoutly that a spirit was abroad
> Which could not be withstood, that poverty,
> At least like this, would in a little time
> Be found no more, that we should see the earth

Unthwarted in her wish to recompense
The industrious, and the lowly child of toil.[98]

In his *Edinburgh Review* article Jeffrey had affirmed his conviction of the
essential distinction between the classes: 'The love, or grief, or indignation
of an enlightened and refined character, is . . . in itself a different emotion
from the love, or grief, or anger, of a clown [a peasant], a tradesman, or a
market-wench'.[99] Wordsworth had responded to the hungry girl from
exactly the opposite conviction and Jeffrey had not been mistaken in
discerning it in *Lyrical Ballads*: 'we have all of us one human heart'.[100]
What happened after that hopeful time—the ascendancy of Robespierre,
the Terror, the rise of Bonaparte, and now, the final degradation, his
coronation as emperor—all demonstrate how little the youth knew about
human nature, or the lure of power, and how naïve was his understanding of
how societies function. But nothing in the poem subverts the attraction of
that instinctive humanitarian generosity of spirit which had survived to be
embodied in *The Ruined Cottage* and *Lyrical Ballads*.

Wordsworth further suggests that the writer of the *Letter to the Bishop of
Llandaff* and the 1794 letters to Mathews, who had planned to fight for
liberty of thought in the *Philanthropist*, had been reacting intelligently to
events. As the 1804 patriot Volunteer looks back to the outbreak of war in
1793 and the years of government repression which followed, his anger once
again wells up as he recalls that

Our shepherds (this say merely) at that time
Thirsted to make the guardian crook of law
A tool of murder. They who ruled the state,
Though with such awful proof before their eyes
That he who would sow death, reaps death, or worse,
And can reap nothing better, childlike longed
To imitate—not wise enough to avoid—
Giants in their impiety alone,
But in their weapons and their warfare base
As vermin working out of reach, they leagued
Their strength perfidiously to undermine
Justice, and make an end of liberty.[101]

In 1805 Southey by chance met the man, one Lord Somerville, who claimed
he had been instrumental in setting the spy on to the democrats of
Alfoxden.[102] He was unrepentant. 'Once a Jacobin, always a Jacobin', was
his view. Had he been able to read this passage he would surely have claimed
it as proof that he was right.

The third strategy determines the presentation of the most difficult part
of the poem, the account of Wordsworth's mental turmoil after returning

from France. In retrospect Wordsworth could see that 1793 to 1796–7 —from *Salisbury Plain* and *Llandaff* to *The Borderers* and *The Ruined Cottage*—had been the period in which his direction had been most uncertain. From it, none the less, he had emerged sure enough of his powers as a poet to embrace soon after the challenge of *The Recluse*. In *The Prelude*, X–XI, he dramatizes this as a test whose duration is unclear but of whose intensity the magnificent verse at X. 863–904 leaves no doubt. He was, he claims, led further and further into error

> by reasonings false
> From the beginning, inasmuch as drawn
> Out of a heart which had been turned aside
> From Nature by external accidents,
> And which was thus confounded more and more,
> Misguiding and misguided.[103]

What needs to be noticed, however, is that even here the mature poet stresses that, though his method and premises were faulty, the youth's aim was noble. He was possessed by a vision, a hope

> that man should start
> Out of the worm-like state in which he is,
> And spread abroad the wings of Liberty,
> Lord of himself, in undisturbed delight.
> A noble aspiration!—yet I feel
> The aspiration –but with other thoughts
> And happier· for I was perplexed and sought
> To accomplish the transition by such means
> As did not lie in nature . . .[104]

At the close of this passage Wordsworth admits he was constructing a work of 'false imagination, placed beyond / The limits of experience and truth'. *The Prelude* is both a record of and, in its imaginative power, a testimony to what Wordsworth had discovered of the meaning of those words.

'Imagination', 'experience', 'truth'—the connection between these concepts was the other major concern of the 1804–5 work on *The Prelude*. In the 1800 note to *The Thorn* Wordsworth used the word 'imagination', but felt that a gloss was called for. What he offered was straightforward: 'imagination, by which word I mean the faculty which produces impressive effects out of simple elements'.[105] When he judged that *Madoc* 'fails in the highest gifts of the poet's mind Imagination in the true sense of the word', however, there is a deeper resonance to the term.[106] Southey's poem 'abounds in beautiful pictures and description', it is animated, the situation of one of the characters is 'highly interesting', and his speech on occasion 'particularly interesting', and yet the poem lacks the ultimate power, true Imagination—whatever that is. A definition of 1815, as direct as that of 1800 but loftier and more capacious, leaves no doubt: 'Fancy is given to quicken and beguile the temporal part of our nature, Imagination to incite and to support the eternal'.[107]

The distance between the first and last definitions marks out the whole range of eighteenth-century uses of this most protean of terms. In the first, Imagination is a creative faculty associated with the making of works of art. In the last it is a function of man's spiritual being. And there is no doubt that in travelling this distance Wordsworth's poetry does reflect changes in his own thought. The philosophical poetry of 1798 and 1799 and the Preface to *Lyrical Ballads* of 1800 had subscribed, broadly speaking, to the associationist model of the mind formulated, refined, and disseminated by such thinkers as Locke, Hartley, and Priestley. That of 1804–5 emphasizes the mind's creative power and its vital function in all acts of perception. For analogues to this model one looks to Tetens, Kant, and Schelling and, for its source in Wordsworth's thinking, to Coleridge.[108]

What needs to be stressed, however, is that although Wordsworth's understanding of the term 'Imagination' had grown in sophistication since 1798, so that now he conceived of the mind's operations in a different way, he was preoccupied by the same questions now as then, was pursuing the same goals. The lines 'Not useless do I deem', concerned with the play between the receptive mind and the external world, had attempted to answer the question of how personal sensory experience ministered to the development of moral awareness, to love, and to social good. *The Prelude* throughout is concerned with the same issues. Its most important sequences—the crossing of the Alps in Book VI and the ascent of Snowdon in Book XIII—use language and concepts unavailable to Wordsworth in 1798, but their underlying anxiety is the same as it had always been. With the insistence of the practical moralist who wanted his poetry to be of *use*, Wordsworth is searching for ways of explaining the value of Imagination, to affirm its moral function and thus the validity of his poetic vocation as he conceived it.

Such terms make *The Prelude* sound forbiddingly abstract, and it is not. Quite unlike Akenside's *The Pleasures of the Imagination*, for example, whose verse denies the title, *The Prelude* interests because all of its 'philosophy' arises from one man's life-story, and it grips the reader because of the specificity with which experience of many kinds is rendered. Understanding the poem's overall structure, however, must lead eventually to abstractions because at its heart are Imagination, Love, Truth, and because these concepts are grounded in faith in the ultimate abstraction,

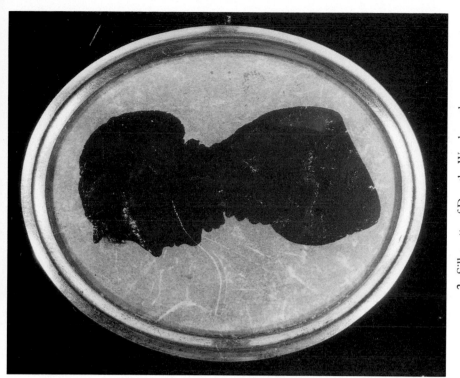

2. Silhouette of Dorothy Wordsworth.
The only known likeness of her as a young woman.

1. Robert Hancock (1730–1817).
Pencil and chalk portrait of Wordsworth aged 28 (1798).

3. Amos Green (1735–1807). Sepia-wash drawing c.1806, the earliest known picture of the Wordsworths' cottage at Town End, Grasmere, later known as Dove Cottage.

4. Francis Towne (1740–1816). Pen, ink, and watercolour, *Grasmere From the Rydal Road* (*c.*1807).

5. The 'Rock of Names', bearing the initials carved in 1801–2 of William, Dorothy, and John Wordsworth, Mary and Sara Hutchinson, and Samuel Taylor Coleridge.

6. George Dance (1741–1825). Pencil drawing of Samuel Taylor Coleridge aged 33 (21 March 1804).

7. Richard Carruthers (1792–1876). Oil painting of Wordsworth aged 47 (1817).

8.  Benjamin Robert Haydon (1786–1846). Pencil and chalk portrait of Wordsworth aged 48 (1818). Known in the Wordsworth family as the 'Brigand'.

9. Edward William Wyon (1811–85). Wax medallion of Wordsworth aged 65 (1835).

10. Benjamin Robert Haydon (1786–1846). *Wordsworth on Helvellyn*. Oil portrait of Wordsworth aged 72 (1842).

the one
Surpassing life, which—out of space and time,
Nor touched by welterings of passion—is,
And hath the name of God.[109]

Because, in short, *The Prelude* is a religious poem. Imagination is presented as the power that enables Man to convert into knowledge that which he perceives, to shape his world. In alliance with Love it binds him to his fellow beings. Through Imagination man lives, an inmate of an active universe,

By sensible impressions not enthralled,
But quickened, rouzed, and made thereby more fit
To hold communion with the invisible world.[110]

And this is his 'paramount endowment'—that in the exercise of its highest powers Imagination gives man a glimpse of the Divine which encompasses all:

Such minds are truly from the Deity,
For they are powers; and hence the highest bliss
That can be known is theirs—the consciousness
Of whom they are, habitually infused
Through every image, and through every thought,
And all impressions; hence religion, faith,
And endless occupation for the soul,
Whether discursive or intuitive;
Hence sovereignty within and peace at will,
Emotion which best foresight need not fear,
Most worthy then of trust when most intense;
Hence chearfulness in every act of life;
Hence truth in moral judgements; and delight
That fails not, in the external universe.[111]

## (9)

'The faith that looks through death' was soon tested. John Wordsworth returned from his second voyage to China in August 1804 and at once set about raising the money for investment in a third. As he set sail on 1 February 1805 he was optimistic that 'a very good voyage . . . if not a *very great* one' was in prospect.[112] In the late afternoon of 5 February, however, the *Earl of Abergavenny* struck the Shambles off Portland Bill. Some passengers were taken off; others, as the ship broke up, were carried to safety on spars and driftwood; others clung to the rigging, fighting the cold until they were rescued. 155 of the 387 passengers and crew survived, but John was not amongst them. He stayed at his command and was last seen shortly before midnight by Thomas Gilpin, the fourth mate, clinging to a rope, insensible with cold, before the sea swept him away.

The news reached Grasmere in a letter from Richard on 11 February and for two days Mary, Dorothy, and Wordsworth wept inconsolably. 'Grief will . . . and must, have its course', Wordsworth wrote to Southey, 'there is no reason in attempting to check it under the circumstances which we are all of us in here.'[113] With the death of John, with whom they associated only 'comfort and expectation and pleasure', Wordsworth felt keenly that 'the set is now broken', and his exclamation 'God keep the rest of us together' reveals his sense that everything he most valued, the stable family in one loved place, was under threat.[114]

'Do not think our grief unreasonable', Wordsworth urged Beaumont. 'Of all human beings whom I ever knew [John], was the man of the most rational desires, the most sedate habits, and the most perfect self-command.'[115] This note is sustained throughout all that he now wrote about his brother. Even though it provoked fresh tears, dwelling on John as the perfect man seems to have given comfort. 'Our Brother was the pride and delight of our hearts', Wordsworth declared simply to Scott, 'as gentle, as meek, as brave, as resolute, as noble a spirit as ever breathed.'[116] More fulsomely he told Beaumont,

my departed Brother . . . walked all his life pure among the impure. Except a little hastiness of temper when any thing was done in a clumsy or bungling way, or when improperly contradicted upon occasions of not much importance, he had not one vice of his profession. I never heard an oath or even an indelicate expression or allusion from him in my life, his modesty was equal to that of the purest Women. In prudence, in meekness, in self-denial, in fortitude, in just desires, and elegant and refined enjoyments, with an entire simplicity of manners, life and habit, he was all that could be wished-for in man . . .[117]

To Losh Wordsworth emphasized that, contrary to some rumours in circulation, John had died at his post, blameless of the wreck, dying as he had lived, 'steady to his duty in all situations'.[118]

John's death was the first of many great griefs Wordsworth was to suffer in his adult life—the deaths of two young children, the mental collapse of Dorothy, and finally the death of Dora—and in his letters he made no attempt to suggest that it was other than it was: 'I feel that there is something cut out of my life which cannot be restored'.[119] Once the initial anguish had given way to a steady state of pain and sadness, however, Wordsworth seems to have faced his loss, consciously and thoughtfully, as a test of maturity. Two days after reading Richard's letter he wrote to Christopher, 'at present I weep with them [Dorothy and Mary] and attempt little more. Hereafter I hope we shall all shew a proper fortitude', and this is the word, 'fortitude', to which he repeatedly returns.[120] The traditional Christian answer to the tormenting question 'Why was he taken away?' was accepted. Human reasoning cannot advance on the 'monstrous' conclusion that 'upon the supposition of the thinking principle being destroyed by death, however inferior we may be to the great Cause and ruler of things, we have *more of love* in our Nature than he has', except 'upon the supposition of *another* and a *better world*'.[121] But the absence of any further theological speculation in any of Wordsworth's letters at this time suggests that while this supposition was acknowledged as providing a base for the struggle against grief, it was not the spur to personal endeavour he needed. Fortitude, on the other hand, made demands. Quoting Aristotle's views he wrote to Sir George Beaumont: 'It is . . . the property of fortitude not to be easily terrified by the dread of things pertaining to death . . . it is the property of fortitude to labour and endure, and to make valorous exertion an object of choice'.[122]

When he quoted this passage Wordsworth was actually evoking John's qualities, but there can be no doubt that he was drawn to it because Aristotle's definition spoke to his own condition. Fortitude—for which Wordsworth said he trusted in God—could carry him through this crisis and in making valorous exertion an object of choice he knew that he would be keeping faith with John. To both Beaumont and Losh he explained how. John, Wordsworth said,

encouraged me to persist, and to keep my eye steady on its object. He would work for me (that was his language), for me, and his Sister; and I was to endeavour to do something for the world . . . This is the end of his part of the agreement, of his efforts for my welfare! God grant me life and strength to fulfill mine! I shall never forget him, never lose sight of him, there is a bond between us yet, the same as if he were living, nay far more sacred, calling upon me to do my utmost, as he to the last did his utmost to live in honour and worthiness.[123]

In 1798 Wordsworth had embraced the idea of *The Recluse* with a kind of joyous gravity. Since then the project had become freighted with all that he owed to Coleridge. But Wordsworth's enduring seriousness about the poem, and his belief that he was working towards it long after it was clear that it would never be finished, can only be understood if one remembers that in 1805 completing *The Recluse* became a trust, made sacred by his brother's death.

(10)

Sometime in March or April Wordsworth yielded to what he described as 'a strong impulse to write a poem that should record my Brother's virtues and be worthy of his memory,' but, 'overpowered' by his subject, he faltered in extempore composition and did not dare ask Mary or Dorothy to write it down for fear of upsetting them afresh.[124] Finishing *The Prelude*, however, and moving on to *The Recluse* was an obligation for which he could draw strength from the knowledge that John would have honoured his poet-brother's return to his duty. In April he began to reassess the manuscript material that already existed for the later body of the poem and to shape it towards a conclusion. Much of Book XI and the whole of XII and XIII were rapidly composed to complete the poem in late May.

This last section is the keystone to *The Prelude's* ambitiously elaborate structure. Having celebrated the survival of his own imaginative powers and the continuing, mysterious strength of the resources made available through memory, Wordsworth moves first to a meditation on the nature and function of Imagination in the Ascent of Snowdon passage and then to a hymn to Love. But it is also a very moving personal document. Love is praised as the ultimate power:

> From love, for here
> Do we begin and end, all grandeur comes,
> All truth and beauty—from pervading love—
> That gone we are as dust . . .[125]

As the poem moves to its close, however, the abstraction Love is humanized by images of those to whose love the poet owes his being. Lines 211–46 of Book XIII are a beautiful tribute to Dorothy's gentle influence and they are counterpointed by the immediately following passage which honours Coleridge's lavishly shared powers. It is this image of Coleridge that inspires the poem's triumphant conclusion. Wordsworth anticipates their joy at Coleridge's return,

> Restored to us in renovated health,
> When, after the first mingling of our tears,
> 'Mong other consolations, we may find
> Some pleasure from this offering of my love.[126]

And as he recollects how at Alfoxden they 'Together wantoned in wild Poesy' and formed the grand conception of *The Recluse*, Wordsworth is strengthened to reassert, despite all doubt whether he will be granted life and power, that as 'Prophets of Nature' he and Coleridge are still united under a sacred obligation to instruct mankind

> how the mind of man becomes
> A thousand times more beautiful than the earth
> On which he dwells, above this frame of things
> (Which, 'mid all revolutions in the hopes

And fears of men, doth still remain unchanged)
In beauty exalted, as it is itself
Of substance and of fabric more divine.[127]

When he had finished *The Prelude* Wordsworth was weighed down by a dejection which was, he told Beaumont, of a kind quite new to him. The thought that John would have taken pleasure in his achievement, but could not, hung upon him; even the poem itself 'seemed to have a dead weight about it, the reality so far short of the expectation'.[128] It was, moreover, though a long and substantial work, one which could not be published until a longer and more substantial still had been written. That Longman issued another edition of *Lyrical Ballads* in October served only to underline the fact that Wordsworth was being judged by the critics and the poetry-reading public on two volumes essentially unchanged since 1800.

Completing *The Prelude* was, none the less, a significant and very positive moment. In the retrospective narrative Wordsworth had taken possession of his own past, ordered his memories, and celebrated the powers which had shaped him to be a poet, not, as an old man might, to round off his life, but to declare the rightness of his judgement that he was a great poet, to justify his decision to settle in Grasmere to write, and to reaffirm the vocation which gave meaning to both his life and his writing.

Two resumed activities indicate the mood of confidence that now strengthened him. After John's death the much-loved garden at Town End had been neglected. 'Alas! our Garden is not what it used to be!', Dorothy wrote, 'it has neither been cleaned nor dug—and the shrubs are run wild. We could not turn our eyes to it but with pain.'[129] The severance between dweller and place which Wordsworth had dramatized so powerfully in *The Ruined Cottage* was being re-enacted. But in May they 'turned to the melancholy garden, and put it into order', finishing the orchard-hut, where they could sit to read or write, and tackling the maintenance of the cottage itself.[130]

Similarly facing what he had been unable to face, Wordsworth returned to a spot made sacred by John's death. On 29 September 1800 he and Dorothy had parted from their brother just beyond Grisedale Tarn, where the path drops down into Patterdale, and had 'stood till [they] could see him no longer, watching him as he *hurried* down the stony mountain'. At age 73 Wordsworth could still pin-point the place to within two or three yards.[131] On 8 June 1805 he returned there with a neighbour to fish, but overwhelmed by memories of John he left his companion and extemporized, in floods of tears, a poem memorializing John and the place where they had said farewell. Two days later he went back again with his fishing-rod and parted very cheerfully from Mary and Dorothy at the same spot, on his way to stay in Patterdale. 'You will judge', Dorothy observed to Lady Beaumont, 'that a happy change has been wrought in his mind when he chuses John's employments, and one of John's haunts (for he delighted in the neighbourhood of Patterdale) for such a purpose.'[132]

Letting his tears flow as he composed in the solitude beneath Fairfield and Helvellyn released Wordsworth to write about his grief for John. Earlier he had confessed to Beaumont that the subject had been too painful for him, but now, in three very personal and touching poems, he faced out deliberately all that upset him most.[133] In the Grisedale Tarn poem, 'I only looked for pain and grief', he dwelt on the fact that when John had hurried down the mountain side he was leaving Grasmere for the last time. On 2 April 1801 John had written about his pleasure in the flowers on the Isle of Wight—'the daisy's after sunset are like little *white* stars upon the dark green fields'—and in *To the Daisy*, thinking of this and of the flower on John's grave, the poet finds a pleasure which heals the pain of knowing that his body was in the sea for six weeks before being recovered for burial at the other end of the country.[134] Finally, in 'Distressful gift! this Book receives', Wordsworth writes in John's own notebook some poetry which he knows his brother will never read. 'I never wrote a line without a thought of its giving him pleasure', he told Losh.[135] Now he wrote in full consciousness that this bond could only be sustained as a consoling private fiction:

> And so I write what neither Thou
> Must look upon, nor others now.
> Their tears would flow too fast;
> Some solace thus I strive to gain,
> Making a kind of secret chain,
> If so I may, betwixt us twain
> In memory of the past.

These three poems are not epitaphs—Wordsworth thought of them as entirely private—but they embody the essence of what he considered an epitaph should be, 'truth hallowed by love—the joint offspring of the worth of the dead and the affections of the living!'[136] and honouring John in this way helped him combat the slide into dejection that threatened after he had completed *The Prelude*.

Friendship and summer activities helped as well. At the beginning of August Southey stayed at Town End for a few days and on the eleventh Wordsworth made his way via Park House, where Dorothy was visiting Sara and Tom Hutchinson, back to Southey at Keswick.[137] The Greta Hall house-party included Walter Scott and as they walked the following day to Watendlath they must have discussed poetry—but from what different positions. Southey was on tenterhooks about the reception of his newly published *Madoc*, gloomily forecasting that he would 'get no solid pudding by it'.[138] Scott, by contrast, was basking in the immediate and astonishing sales of his *The Lay of the Last Minstrel*, published in January, which demonstrated that there was a public eager to pay to be pleased—if the pleasing did not demand too much intellectually.[139] And Wordsworth—he had published no new volume since 1800, yet had the reputation of being the leader of a conspiracy against poetic order. But their differing levels of worldly success—and Scott did not realize how different they were until he saw the simplicity of the cottage at Grasmere—made no difference to their pleasure in being together.[140] On 14 August Wordsworth, Humphry Davy, and Scott climbed Helvellyn out of Patterdale, where they had spent the previous night, and as late as 1843 Wordsworth still had a fond memory of Scott scrambling along Striding Edge, beguiling his companions with 'many stories and amusing anecdotes, as was his custom'.[141]

What helped Wordsworth most of all over the summer of 1805, however, was the writing of lyrics which he soon began to think might form part of a publishable collection.[142] During the spring Dorothy had been completing her *Recollections of a Tour Made in Scotland A.D. 1803* and her questions about places and distances, dates and times, must have stirred memories. First came the memorial to Ossian, *Glen-Almain*, and then, on 3 June, *Stepping Westward*, composed, according to a note which Dorothy made in her fair-copy manuscript, while they and 'little Dorothy were walking in the green field, where we are used to walk, by the Rothay'.[143] Other Scottish poems followed during and over the turn of the year—*Rob Roy's Grave*, *The Solitary Reaper*, and *To the Sons of Burns*.

The finest of them all, *The Solitary Reaper* is a poem of particular interest. Had Wordsworth not seen isolated figures set against the immensity of the Highland landscape the poem would not have been written. What actually brought it into being, however, was not a remembered scene but this sentence from his friend Thomas Wilkinson's manuscript *Tours to the British Mountains*: 'Passed a female who was reaping alone: she sung in Erse as she bended over her sickle; the sweetest human voice I ever heard: her strains were tenderly melancholy, and felt delicious, long after they were heard no more'.[144] In lines written only months before Wordsworth had tried to describe the powers of higher, creative, and imaginative minds:

> They build up greatest things
> From least suggestions, ever on the watch,
> Willing to work and to be wrought upon.
> They need not extraordinary calls
> To rouze them—in a world of life they live . . .[145]

Together with *Resolution and Independence*, *The Solitary Reaper* is the best example in Wordsworth's lyric poetry of this power at work. A few words, touching Wordsworth by their own beauty, awaken memories of forms, colours, and physical sensations, which finally issue as a specific image, rendered as dramatically as if Wordsworth were composing extempore, gesturing to the girl at her task before him. And it is striking that what particularly moves him is the image of someone with few material comforts, toiling arduously, but joyously self-sufficient in her own power of song.

# 1806–1810

## (1)

ON Christmas Day 1805 Dorothy wrote a long letter to Catherine Clarkson. Present realities distracted her—Johnny roaring outside, soaked through, little Dorothy fretful with a cold, two plum-puddings bubbling, and a sirloin of beef threatening to burn in front of the fire—but her mind was on the past. Molly Fisher downstairs in the kitchen reminded her of their arrival at Town End six Christmasses ago and that memory led her to think of the years since and inevitably of John. All in all, she concluded, 'though the freshness of life was passed away even when we came hither, I think these years have been the happiest of my life,—at least, they seem as if they would bear looking back upon better than any other, though my heart flutters and aches striving to call to my mind more perfectly the remembrance of some of the more thoughtless pleasures of former years'.[1] Was Dorothy conscious that she was quoting from *Tintern Abbey* and more directly from *The Prelude*? Perhaps not, but the echo in 'thoughtless pleasures of former years'[2] indicates how immersed she was in her current winter task of copying out *The Prelude* and suggests that her brother's retrospective poem to Coleridge reinforced her own inclination to look back.

Dorothy's mood, in which a sense of loss mingled with contented celebration, was shared by Wordsworth. As they waited anxiously for news of Coleridge he was, at least so Dorothy assured the Beaumonts, 'reading for the nourishment of his mind, preparatory to beginning' on *The Recluse*.[3] In fact he was responding to a quite different impulse. Between January and March 1806 Wordsworth wrote *Benjamin the Waggoner*, a long but deftly controlled dramatic narrative about how the waggoner who plied between Keswick and Kendal finally lost his job through a generosity of heart that was unfortunately allied to a weakness for strong drink. The tragicomic tale was composed, Wordsworth later said, 'con amore', and the love is evident in the way he celebrates Benjamin—his concern for his horses, his instinctive feel for his terrain, his compassion, and his jollity.[4] The spirit of the verse recalls both the dramatic ballads of 1798 and the lyrics of 1802. Its local piety, the description of the journey through Grasmere and along by

Thirlmere, allies *Benjamin* with *Michael*, the *Poems on the Naming of Places*, and all the other poems that celebrate Grasmere life. It might almost seem a poem that Wordsworth could have written at any time since December 1799.

At one point, however, the significance of the poem for Wordsworth now, in 1806, becomes apparent. Describing Benjamin travelling north towards Keswick, Wordsworth dissolves the boundaries of poetic fiction and fact by breaking into the narrative to address the rock of names on which the Grasmere circle had in reality inscribed their initials as they passed by the same road:

> Ah! dearest Spot! dear Rock of Names
> From which our Pair thus slaked their flames!
> Ah! deem not this light strain unjust
> To thee and to thy precious trust,
> That file which gentle, brave, and good,
> The [?de]ar in friendship and in blood,
> The hands of those I love the best
> Committed to thy faithful breast!
> No, long as I've a genial feeling
> Or one that stands in need of healing
> I will preserve thy rightful power
> Inviolate till life's final hour.

Mid-way between Greta Hall and Town End the stone remained, as poignant a reminder of unfulfilled hopes as the ruins of Michael's sheep-fold. When they had gouged out the lettering in the stone, John had looked set to make a fortune and Coleridge and Wordsworth had been committed to each other and to *The Recluse*. The closing lines of *The Prelude* reaffirmed that commitment, but the elegiac wistfulness that suffuses *Benjamin the Waggoner* suggests that Wordsworth knew that with John's death and Coleridge's decline the creative unity rooted in the chosen life at Grasmere and memorialized in the Rock of Names had splintered.

As Wordsworth was completing his new poem fears for and about Coleridge possessed him and Dorothy. The previous October he had admitted to Sir George that the 'expectation of Coleridge not a little unhinges me', but now they were tormented by the possibility that he had been taken by the French or lost at sea. 'How powerless do we feel!', Dorothy exclaimed to Lady Beaumont in January, 'wishing, wishing ever wishing'.[5] By 2 March 1806, however, they had news at last that he was definitely safe, having reached Naples *en route* for home. When Wordsworth left for London on 29 March he more than half-hoped that Coleridge would arrive while he was there.

Wordsworth's primary motive for going south was self-preservation. With Mary well on in pregnancy he might have been expected to stay at home. But his absence was probably welcome. Dorothy, Mary, and Sara, as well as Wordsworth, were 'crammed' in the cottage, as Dorothy put it in March 1806, 'edge-full', together with the children John and Dorothy and a young nurse Hannah Lewthwaite, so that 'Every bed lodges two persons at present'. Colds were passed from one to the other, Wordsworth was 'tormented with the piles', and they were all tense with foreboding about Coleridge.[6] 'I am chiefly come', Wordsworth told Catherine Clarkson once he had reached London, 'to crowd as much people and sight seeing as I can into one month with an odd sort of hope that it may be some use both to my health of body and mind: I am not quite so well as I was . . . last summer.'[7]

It was an important visit, marking Wordsworth's entry into polite London life. He already had old friends there, of course, and he sought them out—Godwin, Montagu, and Lamb, whom he delighted with a reading of *Benjamin the Waggoner*. But now he mingled with many others—Joseph Farington, Henry Edridge, David Wilkie, James Northcote, and, under the patronage of Sir George Beaumont, endorsed by his Grosvenor Square address, Wordsworth even attended a rout given by the Marchioness of Stafford and, at a ball given by Mrs Charles James Fox, was introduced by Rogers to Fox himself.

Later in life Wordsworth was sneered at for enjoying London society, but he would have been less than human had he not enjoyed it now. He was particularly pleased with himself over the meeting with Fox and many years later was still regaling company with a dramatic account of how Fox, rising from a card-table, had said, 'I am glad to see Mr Wordsworth, though we differ as much in our views of politics as we do in our views of poetry', to which Wordsworth had replied, 'But in poetry you must admit that I am the Whig and you the Tory'.[8] By far the most important thing that happened during this London visit, however, was something that touched him more deeply than parties and spirited conversation.

At the Royal Academy Exhibition for 1806 Beaumont presented three pictures. One would have given Wordsworth unmixed pleasure, since its subject was suggested by his own poem *The Thorn*,[9] but one of the others, *A Storm: Peele Castle* affected him at a much deeper level. Piel Castle (as it is correctly spelt) stands on an island off the southern tip of Furness, opposite the tiny village of Rampside where Wordsworth had stayed in the late summer of 1794. In Beaumont's painting its ruin towers against a sky split by lightning, while a ship labours in an angry sea. Troubled that a scene of threatened shipwreck would remind Wordsworth of the circumstances of John's death, Beaumont tried not to draw his attention to the canvas, but (as he later admitted) he need not have feared.[10] Wordsworth was no longer caught unawares by grief as he had been a year ago. He absorbed Beaumont's picture in a profound meditation which brought together image (the one before him and the one he, Wordsworth, would have painted in 1794) and reality (the tranquil sea and the sea in which John drowned), past and present, the innocent and the chastened mind, in what is one of his richest poems, and certainly the finest poem for John, *Elegiac Stanzas, Suggested by a Picture of Peele Castle, in a Storm, Painted by Sir George Beaumont*.

Throughout his visit, Wordsworth boasted to Wrangham, he had been 'so much engaged that [he] did not read five minutes all the time [he] was there'.[11] As soon as he got back to Grasmere, however, he took up his usual pursuits as wholeheartedly as ever. 'Since I reached home', he told Lady Beaumont, 'I have passed the chief part of my time out of doors, much of it in a wood by the Lake-side . . . the Muses without any wooing on my part came to me there one morning . . .'[12] He wrote three poems about incidents that had caught his imagination in London, *Stray Pleasures*, *Star-gazers*, and *The Power of Music*, and *Elegiac Stanzas*. Much more significantly he returned to *The Recluse* and by 1 August could tell Sir George that he had 'written 700 additional lines'.[13]

This was a momentous statement. From their first meeting Beaumont had understood that Wordsworth was engaged on a great philosophical work. *The Prelude* had apparently been its harbinger and since the completion of that poem Wordsworth had been declaring for a year that he was anxious to take up his life's work. Now at last he did. Possibly *Elegiac Stanzas* and thoughts of John prompted him. The imminence of Coleridge's home-coming was certainly a spur. Returning to the 1800 poem *Home at Grasmere*, with its affectionate tributes to both of them, Wordsworth added new material and revised and shaped the whole into a coherent introductory book which concluded with the confident announcement of a universal theme: 'On Man, on Nature, and on human Life'.[14]

Other words in the letter to Beaumont, however, were equally significant—and worrying. 'I . . . have written 700 additional lines. Should Coleridge return, so that I might have some conversation with him upon the subject, I should go on swimmingly.' Wordsworth had written an introductory book, but to what? *Home at Grasmere* is a moving and thought-provoking work, but it contains no hints as to what further poem might follow. The concluding passage appears to do so, but while it is possible to see how its promise of exploration of the recesses of the Mind of Man might be said to be fulfilled in the whole of Wordsworth's valuable output, it is difficult to imagine how a poet might use such lofty lines as the way into actually plotting out an original structure for an as yet unwritten poem. In

August 1806 Wordsworth trusted contact with Coleridge would restore him as it had in 1798 and 1800. He would keep faith with their joint mission; Coleridge would outline and assist into being what was at the moment little more than an article of faith.

The unreality of this expectation was exposed when they were at last reunited in October. For months the Wordsworths had longed for this event. Once the news of Coleridge's landing was confirmed Dorothy was so over-wrought that she could not bring herself even to write to Catherine Clarkson until she was able to report that she had seen him. But when their reunion did take place it was, paradoxically, ill-timed, a hole-and-corner affair of meetings in hotel rooms, marred by suppressed shock, anger, and alarm—a sad prefiguring of the next few years.

On 15 June 1806 Mary gave birth to a son, Thomas. His arrival, and Mary's ill health following her most painful labour yet, made life at Town End even more uncomfortable. During the summer months the lack of space and privacy could be tolerated, but in the winter, Dorothy now believed, the cottage would actually be unhealthy. In the long term they had to move. In the short term they needed somewhere more spacious to pass the winter. Sir George Beaumont was building a new house at Coleorton in Leicestershire and had some time since urged the Words-worths to take over the adjacent Hall Farm, while he and Lady Beaumont were in London. They now gratefully accepted and on 26 October set off for Kendal on the first leg of their slow and uncomfortable chaise journey south.

As they did so they were all disappointed that they had not yet seen Coleridge, and not a little irritated, since they had already delayed their departure so long that they would only see the Beaumonts briefly before they left for London. But Coleridge seemed unable to bring himself to face them or, and this the Wordsworths recognized was the real cause of his aversion to the North, his wife. 'He dare not go home', was Wordsworth's opinion, 'he recoils so much from the thought of domesticating with Mrs Coleridge . . . What a deplorable thing!'[15] Coleridge had landed on 17 August and since then had been largely in London, procrastinating about seeing his wife, whom he did not even write to for a month. Eventually he set off northwards, arriving in Penrith, where he hoped to contact Sara Hutchinson, half an hour after she had left for Kendal to join the Wordsworths *en route* for Coleorton. Coleridge wrote that he could not come to Kendal just for a brief meeting; the Wordsworths sent a special messenger to insist that he should; Coleridge changed his mind and forestalled the envoy by arriving himself at a different inn in Kendal and sending his messenger across.

Dorothy's account of the reunion suggests how painful it was for them all.

He is utterly changed [she told Catherine Clarkson] and yet sometimes, when he was animated in conversation concerning things removed from him, I saw something of his former self. But never when we were alone with him. He then scarcely ever spoke of anything that concerned him, or us, or our common friends nearly, except we forced him to it; and immediately he changed the conversation to Malta, Sir Alexander Ball, the corruptions of government, anything but what we were yearning after.[16]

That Coleridge evaded discussion of his personal affairs is not surprising. A month before, Wordsworth had told him sharply in a letter that he was treating his wife intolerably and 'in a less degree . . . [his] friends and acquaintances'.[17] Although they recognized that Coleridge and Sara were quite incompatible—'Coleridge is as little fitted for her as she for him, and I am truly sorry for her', was Dorothy's judgement—they hoped none the less that reflecting upon his duties and the needs of his children, Coleridge 'might have returned home with comfort, ready to partake of the blessings of friendship . . . and to devote himself to his studies and his children'.[18] The pre-condition of such re-entry into tolerable domestic life was, of course, that he should suppress altogether his feelings for Sara Hutchinson and, so the Wordsworths thought, abandon his plan to give lectures in London over the winter. Since Coleridge had made it clear, at least to the Lambs, that he wanted to separate from his wife, since he was proud that Davy was pressing him to lecture at the Royal Institution, and since his love for Sara Hutchinson was, he believed, the one pure element in his make-up, the mismatch in Kendal could hardly have been more complete. What did remain was the strength of the affection that had once bound them so tightly and Wordsworth's conviction that Coleridge had to be helped: 'I believe if anything good is to be done for him, it must be done by me'.[19] By 7 November he had accepted Coleridge's current determination to leave his wife and was offering him refuge at Coleorton, hopeful that there he might settle down to work.

(2)

The Wordsworth family arrived at Coleorton in a sorry state. Three days on the road had exhausted the children, especially Thomas, who seemed to have whooping cough. Mary was low, Sara suffered from recurrent tooth trouble, and Wordsworth added to the nuisance of continuing piles what he described as 'a violent cold, the worst far I ever had in my life'.[20] But their new surroundings soon compensated for the pain of the journey. The environment was excitingly unfamiliar. Sunsets produced grand effects over the flat landscape; light from the coal-pits hinted at wildness and the picturesque as they shone in the gathering dark. Domestically, apart from a smoky chimney and some discord over laundry arrangements, everything seemed made to please. There were rooms to spare, an ever-burning fire and hot kitchen stove (fuelled from coal mined on the estate), produce from the farm and dairy—even Sir George's wine cellar which they had been told to raid at will.

The Beaumonts were exceedingly generous—the Wordsworths stayed at Coleorton till June 1807—but their generosity caused no discomfiture and this mattered, for Wordsworth had recently learned what it was to feel an uncomfortable gratitude. In November the previous year, when he was already somewhat anxious about how he would house his family in the future, Wordsworth had been attracted by a small farm in Patterdale called Broad How. His friend Thomas Wilkinson was empowered to negotiate the purchase at no more than £800, to be raised partly in cash and partly by mortgage. On the intervention of another prospective buyer, the Rector of Patterdale, and a consequent jump in the asking price to £1,000, however, Wilkinson approached Lord Lowther. He pledged himself for the difference of £200, but asked that Wordsworth be kept in ignorance of his contribution. This, of course, Wilkinson could not agree to and he told Wordsworth everything, when he explained that Broad How was now his. Wordsworth was bemused. 'Strange it is', he commented to Sir George, 'that W could not perceive, that if I was unwilling to pay an exorbitant price out of my own money, I should be still more unwilling to pay it out of another's . . .'.[21] He was also embarrassed. He had received a considerable act of patronage—however delicately executed—from some one he did not know, who had demonstrated his rank and its power in this gift quite as unmistakably as the mad, bad earl had done in his malice more than twenty years before. Wordsworth's letter of thanks was constrained and brief.[22] Its tone acknowledges that all that he can offer the greatest landowner and most powerful figure in the North-West is thanks and a well-phrased compliment.

With Sir George and Lady Beaumont Wordsworth had never felt such constraint. The gift of Applethwaite had dazed him, but he never doubted that Beaumont did value his poetry and was thus giving appropriately where he had received. Exchange of further gifts—pictures, money on occasions, even game sent up by the carrier, on the one hand, and poems on the other—maintained the delicate balance of reciprocity and strengthened the affection. As the Beaumonts began their winter in London, Sir George told Wordsworth: 'Were I to express to you how much our interest and if possible our regard is encreased by a personal knowledge of your family of love, it might appear like affectation', to which he replied simply: 'My dear Sir George, / I was moved even to weakness by your Letter; it is indeed a great happiness to me to be beloved by you, and to think upon what foundation that love rests'.[23] But Wordsworth was always delighted to be able to increase his contribution, so to speak, to the friendship and so when Sir George shrewdly offered him the possibility of doing so at Coleorton, he accepted it with an enthusiasm that surprised his family, the Beaumonts—possibly even Wordsworth himself.

What Sir George suggested was that Wordsworth should take charge of creating a winter garden for the new house. He had good reason for thinking that the challenge would appeal to him. At Grasmere the Wordsworths had nurtured their little plot of steeply rising ground into a very beautiful cottage garden, combining plants taken from the mountain sides with shrubs which gave the whole an appropriate identity, and in one of the most eloquent letters he ever wrote Wordsworth had shown that their success was due not to chance but to consideration of the principles involved in planting and shaping. Revealing how thoughtfully he had looked at the landscaping of great houses he and Dorothy had visited on their Scottish tour, Wordsworth had declared that 'Laying out grounds . . . may be considered as a liberal art, in some sort like Poetry and Painting; and its object like that of all the liberal arts is, or ought to be, to move the affections under the controul of good sense . . . speaking with more precision . . . to assist Nature in moving the affections . . .'.[24] But no one had reason to suppose that he had the interest or command of detail displayed in the plan sent to Lady Beaumont. This astonishing document—around $3\frac{1}{2}$ thousand words long—offers specific recommendations about plants, colours, sizes, and shapes, determined throughout by attention to 'the presiding Image'. This one passage typifies the whole:

Proceeding with the Path, we cross the end of a long Alley of which I shall speak afterwards, we then are brought to a small Glade or open space, belted round with evergreens, quite unvaried and secluded. In this little glade should be a bason of Water inhabited by two gold or silver fish, if they will live in this climate all the year in the open air; if not, any others of the most radiant colours that are more hardy: these little creatures to be the 'Genii' of the Pool and of the place. This spot should be as monotonous in the colour of the trees as possible, the enclosure of evergreens, the sky above, the green grass floor, and the two mute Inhabitants, the only images it should present unless here and there a solitary wild Flower.

Wordsworth won over Mr Craig, the head gardener, and over the winter and spring the project was realized.[25]

This was an important moment for Wordsworth. It was possible to be fully conversant with theories of the picturesque and to have a working vocabulary drawn from Gilpin without having any first-hand experience of Nature at different seasons and in diverse forms. Wordsworth knew mountains, lakes, cloud-formations, trees, and colours, not as static images viewed in a Claude glass or in the illustrations of a book, but as ever-changing, dynamic powers. But before the October 1805 letter to Beaumont and the planning of the winter garden, he had not *formulated* his ideas 'upon the subject of taste in natural beauty'.[26] His success in both writing about it and embodying it gave him authority. When he met the Beaumonts' friend Uvedale Price, whose *Essays on the Picturesque* (1794) marked a new phase of landscape theory, he did so as an equal.[27] In the future his advice, especially on tree-planting, was to be sought by others. Most important of all, his success encouraged him in due course to write at length on landscape and to become, in prose as well as in poetry, the chief interpreter of the Lake District. This Wordsworth, as a recent scholar has put it, is 'fundamental to the whole post-pictorial culture of landscape in England'.[28]

## (3)

Wordsworth was busy, but he like the others was waiting with anxious expectancy. On 21 December Coleridge at last arrived with Hartley and all relaxed as once again Coleridge was folded into their domestic embrace. 'I think I never was more happy in my life', Dorothy told Lady Beaumont two days later, 'than when we had him an hour by the fireside; for his looks were much more like his own old self, and, though we only talked of common things, and of our Friends, we perceived that he was contented in his mind and had settled his affairs at home to his satisfaction.'[29]

Shortly after Coleridge's arrival that same fireside was the setting for one of the most poignant scenes in English literary history. On successive evenings Wordsworth read out *The Prelude*, fulfilling the hope he had expressed so touchingly at the end of Book XIII that once Coleridge was 'Restored to us in renovated health' they would both find 'Some pleasure from this offering of my love'. He had reason to be proud. Since Coleridge's departure for the Mediterranean in 1804, he had written a further eight books of his poem and had even discarded some hundreds of lines of substantial merit. As he brought his reading to a close with the eloquent lines which re-dedicate the two poets to their task as 'Prophets of Nature', Wordsworth could justifiably feel that he had achieved a great deal and that, with Coleridge returned, *The Recluse* could be faced boldly.

By January 1807 Coleridge had addressed Wordsworth in turn in the blank verse effusion *To William Wordsworth: Lines Composed, for the Greater Part on the Night on which he Finished the Recitation of his Poem . . . Concerning the Growth and History of his Own Mind* and his poem lays bare the latent tensions and ambivalences of the situation. Gathered round the fire were 'All, whom I deepliest love, in one room all!', their attention focused on the one whom Coleridge addresses as 'O Friend! O Teacher! God's great gift to me!'[30] Wordsworth's delivery of 'A Tale divine of high

and passionate Thoughts / To their own music chaunted' has confirmed that
he now stands 'in the Choir / Of ever-enduring Men'. But inevitably the
recollections in Book XIII of *The Prelude* of

> That summer when on Quantock's grassy hills
> Far ranging, and among the sylvan Coombs,
> Thou in delicious words, with happy heart,
> Didst speak the Vision of that Ancient Man,
> The bright-eyed Mariner

were a spur to self-reproach. Then, Coleridge says, he had a 'nobler mind',
but now he is vexed by

> Fears self-willed, that shunned the eye of Hope;
> And Hope that scarce would know itself from Fear;
> Sense of past Youth, and Manhood come in vain,
> And genius given, and Knowledge won in vain;
> And all which I had culled in wood-walks wild,
> And all which patient toil had reared, and all
> Commune with thee had opened out—but flowers
> Strewed on my corse, and borne upon my bier,
> In the same coffin, for the self-same grave!

And absorption in what Wordsworth had achieved—and admiration and
love—could only check, not remove, the goad driven in by the contrast
between Wordsworth's fertility and his own barrenness and the 'Poisons of
Self-harm' stimulated in one who knew himself an unworthy partner in
their joint labour.

For a poem ostensibly strewing 'triumphal wreaths' before Wordsworth's
advancing, *To William Wordsworth* is astonishingly self-revealing. But
privately Coleridge was recording a deeper anguish still. On 28 November
1806 he coined a new name for Sara Hutchinson, 'Elpizomene'—the hoped-
for-one—and affirmed in his notebook that his feelings for her were
unchanged: 'My beloved! I love you / indeed I love you . . .'. But now at
Coleorton Coleridge began to torture himself not only with the well-
founded suspicion that Sara preferred Wordsworth to himself, but with the
fear that the two had actually become lovers in the Queen's Head at
Stringston, half a mile from Coleorton Church, at 10.50 a.m. on 27
December. Scourged by his own belief that he lacked 'so much that must be
lovely in the Heart of Woman, Strength, Manliness, & Manly Beauty',
Coleridge later in the year voiced his agony at 'the vision of that Saturday
Morning—of the Bed' and wretchedly protested: 'W. is greater, better,
manlier, more dear by nature, to Woman, than I—I—miserable I!—but

does he—O No! no! no! no! he does not—he does not pretend, he does not
wish, to love you as I love you Sara!'[31]

Coleridge's notebook entries make painful reading, but not more so than
the poem in which Wordsworth uttered his feelings of pain and loss. *A
Complaint* places emotion in a literary tradition—this is a lover's lament—
but at Coleorton in early 1807 these lines can hardly have been thought of as
having a purely literary genesis:

> There is a change—and I am poor;
> Your Love hath been, nor long ago,
> A Fountain at my fond Heart's door,
> Whose only business was to flow;
> And flow it did; not taking heed
> Of its own bounty, or my need.
>
> What happy moments did I count!
> Blessed was I then all bliss above!
> Now, for this consecrated Fount
> Of murmuring, sparkling, living love,
> What have I? Shall I dare to tell?
> A comfortless, and hidden WELL.
>
> A Well of love—it may be deep—
> I trust it is, and never dry:
> What matter? if the Waters sleep
> In silence and obscurity.
> —Such change, and at the very door
> Of my fond Heart, hath made me poor.

Coleridge must have identified himself in this poem[32] and with his
honourable recognition that Wordsworth was the more productive poet
metamorphosed in his nightmares into the ugly and ineradicable conviction
that Wordsworth was the more beloved because he was a more manly man,
it is not difficult to imagine what self-restraint and checks on the unguarded
remark must have been necessary for daily life to carry on at Coleorton over
the late winter and spring of 1807. But they all managed to persuade
themselves that a *modus vivendi* was possible. Before Coleridge's arrival
Dorothy had been worried lest they could not regulate his brandy drinking
and by 24 January she admitted to Lady Beaumont that she feared he would
never leave off 'strong stimulants' entirely. But in February that 'Coleridge
has determined to make his home with us' was reported as a fact which
would necessitate the Wordsworths finding a new and larger house and in
May a lonely and homeless Coleridge told Stuart that being part of
Wordsworth's family circle was 'almost all-the-world' to him.[33]

Harmony was maintained in part by the fact that the household was busy
working to further Wordsworth's reputation. More than a year earlier he

had thought of publishing some smaller poems, but then, as Dorothy had explained to Lady Beaumont, he backed off, feeling 'that having been so long silent to the world he ought to come forward with a work of greater labour'.[34] As the 'silent poet' had just issued a fourth edition of *Lyrical Ballads* the first part of her explanation makes little sense. But the second is clearly right. Wordsworth thought that he must present either something substantial or at least something new. By early November 1806 he had decided on the latter. At first the plan was for one volume but soon Longman had agreed to two. Dorothy, Mary, and Sara transcribed from two earlier manuscript collections and Coleridge assisted in overseeing the printer's copy and, in a collaborative effort with the poet himself, contributed to the final version of the much-revised *Ode to Duty*. Once again the busyness and togetherness of Grasmere in 1800 was restored. As they had then for the preparation of *Lyrical Ballads*, the Wordsworth circle delighted in the labour and unity of purpose. The last copy was sent off in early April and on 28 April 1807 *Poems, in Two Volumes* appeared.[35]

The labour may have brought Wordsworth and Coleridge together, but the publication was none the less charged with such significance for both of them that tremors from it over the years were to be felt in the furthest reaches of their relationship.

In a prefatory 'Advertisement' Wordsworth had planned to inform his readers that having been 'for some time . . . engaged' on 'a work of length and labour' whose completion date could not even be guessed at, he had had to overcome a reluctance to publish more short poems.[36] At the last moment these personal words were dropped. The reason why is unclear—and printing costs certainly come into it—but all the other evidence suggests that had the 'Advertisement' been printed it would have been false to the spirit in which this publication was conceived and being energetically pushed forward. For Wordsworth clearly regarded *Poems, in Two Volumes* very seriously. When Longman at first offered derisory terms, Wordsworth planned to issue the volume at his own expense. He took care over the arrangement of the poems, grouping them under such headings as 'Poems Written during a Tour in Scotland', 'Moods of my Own Mind', and 'Sonnets Dedicated to Liberty', aiming, as their recent editor observes, 'to create a richer and more dramatic context for the reader's experience than an undivided format could allow'.[37] He watched carefully over the preparation of copy and printing and even instructed the printer precisely about format: 'These two Volumes are to be printed uniform with the Lyrical Ballads, in a stanza of four lines, four stanzas in a page; the first page of each Poem only printing 2 or 3 stanzas according to the length of the Title . . . NB This will imply that the stanzas must never be broken into different Pages . . . And I will thank you to be as speedy with the work as possible . . .'.[38]

Poems, in Two Volumes was important to Wordsworth because these two unpretentious octavos, unbuttressed by prefatory theorizing, were, in fact, a decisive statement of poetical independence, both to the world and to Coleridge. Viewed from one perspective the scheme originating at Alfoxden could be seen as going, rather fitfully, to plan. *The Prelude* had been completed and delivered up to Coleridge's judgement. Its final lines hail the great task of *The Recluse* which could now be confronted. Viewed from another perspective, however, Wordsworth's position in 1807 as he published *Poems, in Two Volumes* looks very different. It might seem that, whatever became of *The Recluse*, Wordsworth was determined to shape a career and to present his own poetical identity to the public. *Lyrical Ballads* had gone out in three editions under his name, but in origin that collection, including the self-defensive theorizing which prefaced it, was inextricably linked to Coleridge and to his part in Wordsworth's entry to his first great period. But now Wordsworth was putting forward poems that belonged entirely to the years after he had made his decision to return to the Lake District, poems, moreover, which were the most challenging he had ever published. Although many were entirely subjective, some even having overt autobiographical reference, and although some exhibited what Coleridge had flinched at, 'a daring Humbleness of Language & Versification, and a strict adherence to matter of fact even to prolixity',[39] the poems were to appear without any preface to orientate the reader's response. The whole collection was proof that Wordsworth had moved on since *Lyrical Ballads*, evidence to himself and his circle that failure to make progress with *The Recluse* was matched by prolific and original composition in other forms, and, finally, a weighty demonstration that Coleridge had been completely wrong in condemning 'the habit of writing such a multitude of small Poems' as 'hurtful to him'.[40] Ultimately, maybe, *The Recluse* would establish Wordsworth as a philosophic poet. But *Poems, in Two Volumes* presented his claim to be the most original, copious, and various lyric poet since the seventeenth century.

Once *Poems, in Two Volumes* was off their hands and better weather and longer days in mid-April made travelling more tolerable, the whole group, save for Dorothy who remained to look after the children, went to London for a holiday. The Wordsworths stayed with Basil Montagu and at Lambeth with their brother Christopher, who was now domestic chaplain to the Archbishop of Canterbury. They met old friends, including Godwin, and enjoyed some sightseeing, especially a visit to the Tower in the company of Scott. As much time as possible was spent with the Beaumonts, of course, and in Sir George's company they met Farington at the Royal Academy exhibition and possibly also Constable. Poet and painter had been introduced in October 1806, when Constable was staying with the Hardens at Brathay Hall on the northern tip of Windermere. They ought to have got on, as Constable was encountering the Lake District for the first time, but no friendship was formed. Wordsworth's conversation about how he apprehended the world as a child struck Constable only as egotism.[41] About 5 May Sara left to visit Catherine Clarkson in Bury and a day later the Wordsworths and Scott travelled to Coleorton, leaving Coleridge in London. Scott soon pushed on, but, unwilling to lose him, Wordsworth and Dorothy accompanied him as far as Lichfield. On 3 June the Beaumonts arrived and in a little ceremony that celebrated Wordsworth's work on the winter garden he and Sir George planted a cedar. A week later their long stay at Coleorton ended. Planning a leisurely return home, the party travelled via Nottingham and Sheffield to Halifax, where they visited their oldest friends, Mrs Threlkeld, the Rawsons, and the Marshalls. Mary, Sara, and the children went on ahead about 6 July, leaving Dorothy and Wordsworth once more to walk and explore. They rambled along the River Wharf to the ruins of Bolton Abbey, over the moors to Gordale and Malham Cove, and then to Settle. At Kendal the family were reunited before arriving home on 10 July.

They had been away more than eight months and were saddened to find on their return that the place they knew so intimately had changed. Death had taken friends and acquaintances, from old Mr Sympson, the curate of Wythburn, to a little girl who had been in the grip of whooping cough as they had left the previous year. 'All the trees in Bainriggs are cut down', Dorothy reported, 'and even worse, the giant sycamore near the parsonage house, and all the finest firtrees that overtopped the steeple tower.'[42] And even though they were glad to be home—the children especially were delighted—anxiety about the future pressed on them. Agreement had been reached that they should leave their cottage for Allan Bank, a much larger house in Grasmere, but no date had been fixed for their tenancy and it looked as if another cramped winter might have to be endured.

As long as the freedom of summer lasted, however, the Wordsworths were determined to enjoy it. In July the Beaumonts came north again to Keswick and Wordsworth at once went to visit them, followed by Dorothy, who stayed twelve days. Thomas Clarkson, who was now completing his great *History ... of the Abolition of the African Slave-trade*, called for a day in Grasmere. During August Wordsworth accompanied the Beaumonts to Lowther and there, for the first time, met the figure who was going to be so important in his future, Sir William Lowther, recently created Earl of Lonsdale. Set on rebuilding Lowther Castle, Lord Lonsdale had employed George Dance, the architect of Beaumont's new house at Coleorton, but the elderly Dance had handed the commission over to his brilliant pupil Robert Smirke.[43] Work had begun the previous year and Wordsworth and

Lonsdale were able to ignore any awkwardness they may have felt over the past relations of their two families, or the earl's generosity over Broad How, by finding common ground in discussion of possible landscape designs. In late August a further indication that Wordsworth was welcome in polite society was given by an invitation to dine at the Low Wood Hotel on Windermere with Lord and Lady Holland.[44] The Beaumonts returned south around 13 September and the summer concluded with Wordsworth and Mary making a brief tour of the northern and western Lake District, which included a nostalgic visit to the house at Cockermouth 'with the privet hedge still full of roses as it used to be 30 years ago'.[45]

## (4)

In Book VII of *The Prelude* Wordsworth notes how autumnal premonitions of winter spurred him towards composition. They did so now. For *Poems, in Two Volumes* he had written *Song, at the Feast of Brougham Castle* in which, welcoming the restoration of Lord Clifford to his estates after the Wars of the Roses, the Minstrel celebrates the legends and history of the country to the east of the Lake District—the rivers Eamont and Eden, the towns of Skipton and Brough, Brougham Castle itself. This stirring of the historical imagination, enlivened by love for local places and names, had been quickened in the summer by their visit to the ruins of Bolton Abbey. What Wordsworth had read of the Rising in the North in 1569, in the ballad of that name in Percy's *Reliques* and in *The History and Antiquities of the Counties of Westmorland and Cumberland* by Nicolson and Burn, was now given a poetic focus by a legend recounted in Whitaker's *The History and Antiquities of the Deanery of Craven* and in October he began a long historical narrative, *The White Doe of Rylstone*.[46]

Wordsworth was gripped by his work and in later life he defended the poem in loftiest terms,[47] but there was an ambivalence about the project from the start, which perhaps explains why the poem was not published in 1808, why it failed when it was published in 1815, and why it has never been loved even by readers who enjoy the whole range of Wordsworth's poetry. On the one hand it looked like a possible money-spinner. Scott's *The Lay of the Last Minstrel* had sold spectacularly—in 1806 Wordsworth reported to Scott, 'I heard of you and your Last Minstrel every where in London'—and Wordsworth was writing in a similar vein.[48] *The White Doe* tells the story of the part played by the Norton family in the doomed Rising of the North in skilfully varied octosyllabics which push the story on briskly. The narrative itself, the speeches of the characters, and the build-up of the plot are much better than is usually supposed—certainly as vigorous as anything in Scott.

It is not to be imagined that Wordsworth began to write simply for the market, but he was worried about money—Longman had offered only 100 guineas for *Poems, in Two Volumes*—and in choosing a historical subject for treatment in this manner, at this moment, he was certainly not unaware of the readership which Scott had proved to exist.[49]

But Wordsworth was not Scott and *The White Doe of Rylstone* would not gratify the expectations of readers of *The Lay of the Last Minstrel*. In May 1807 Wordsworth had assured Lady Beaumont that he looked only to the future for the success of his poetry: 'It is impossible that any expectations can be lower than mine concerning the immediate effect of [*Poems, in Two Volumes*] upon what is called the Public'. 'It is an awful truth', he declared, 'that there neither is, nor can be, any genuine enjoyment of Poetry among nineteen out of twenty of those persons who live, or wish to live, in the broad light of the world', and went on to remind her of Coleridge's dictum 'that every great and original writer, in proportion as he is great or original, must himself create the taste by which he is to be relished . . . and if this be possible, it must be a work *of time*'.[50] *The White Doe* is written as if to ensure that this defensive prophecy should be fulfilled. Its focus moves from the 'gross and visible action', the failed rebellion, to the 'victories in the world of spirit', won by Emily as she obeys her brother's command to suffer and endure.[51] All of the 'Romantic' possibilities in the story of the white doe herself are translated into a higher register, through a poetic treatment which culminates, as Wordsworth explained later, in 'nothing less than the Apotheosis of the Animal'.[52] As Scott had shown and Byron was triumphantly to show a decade later, readers were eager for romantic tales in verse, full of colour, action, and changes of mood. But all that *The White Doe of Rylstone* had in common with *The Lay of the Last Minstrel* or *The Corsair* was that it was a tale in verse.

With a version of the poem completed, Wordsworth went to London in late February 1808. He made the long journey then, in spite of the winter, because Coleridge seemed to need help. They had heard that 'Coleridge himself thinks that he *cannot* live many months'[53] and though the Wordsworths were somewhat sceptical, the news that Coleridge was likely to abandon his lectures at the Royal Institution did seem to indicate that his situation was serious. But Wordsworth was ready to be in London on his own account. Determined to ask 100 guineas for a thousand copies of *The White Doe*, he expected to be able to arrange for publication while there as well as to profit from Coleridge's appraisal of the new work. What happened, however, was neither a satisfactory business negotiation nor a useful critical engagement, but a mess. Both men were depressed about their individual circumstances—Wordsworth primarily about bad reviews and their impact on his ability to care for his dependants, Coleridge about his lectures, his health, and above all the chaos of his emotional life—and both were prickly with each other. They were continuing to offer mutual comfort and support as they had first done ten years before, but their relationship was now only a simulacrum of what it had been. Each was privately so critical of the other that any flow of feeling between them was readily distorted by tension, with the result that in the spring of 1808 each took a further big step towards the final rupture.

Wordsworth offered *The White Doe* to Longman, but although the poor reviews of *Poems, in Two Volumes* put him in a weak position, he made it weaker still by an extraordinary refusal to let the publisher inspect the poem. Not surprisingly, no deal was struck. On 3 April he quit London, summoned home by alarming news about Sara Hutchinson's health, leaving Coleridge with the understanding that he was now Wordsworth's plenipotentiary. Though harassed by his own commitments, Coleridge once again busied himself for Wordsworth, so successfully that Longman agreed to the terms, on Coleridge's undertaking that he would see the volume through the press.

Working on Wordsworth's behalf, however, stirred the sediment of Coleridge's feelings and around 12 May all his rancour, hurt, and self-pity spilled out in a letter and a horrible notebook memorandum about the conduct of all of the Wordsworths to him, Wordsworth's 'High Self-opinion' pampered by Dorothy and Mary, the cruelty of Poole, the Wedgwoods, Southey, his brothers, and above all the hardness of heart which Wordsworth's happy marriage had engendered in him.[54] The letter itself does not survive, but it is clear from Wordsworth's response that it opened up other wounds old and new—Wordsworth's attitude to the Lloyd affair in 1798, his dealings with Stoddart, most painful of all, his alleged attempt to monitor Coleridge's correspondence with Sara Hutchinson and to poison her mind against him. More than half-convinced that the author of such a letter must be 'in a lamentably insane state of mind', Wordsworth drafted a majestically calm reply, answering Coleridge's points specifically, but with reference to general principles of conduct.[55] It is almost certain that he, wisely, thought better of sending it. What he did do, however, caused more pain than a direct rebuke might have done. Overwrought and torn between his own instincts and family pressures, Wordsworth decided at last to please himself over *The White Doe*. He wrote directly to Longman, cancelling all plans for publication, and gave a clear impression that Coleridge had been wrong to interfere.

Bitterly angry, Coleridge wrote a letter to Wordsworth on 21 May which reveals layer on layer of hurt. He first extricates himself from any suggestion that he had shared the Lambs' distaste for the poem, but in so doing makes telling criticisms of the poem as it then was. The convolutions of an almost unintelligible passage about the relationship between the manuscript *Christabel*, *The Lay of the Last Minstrel*, and *The White Doe* suggest that Coleridge was more chagrined than he could admit that Wordsworth had once again finished a poem which was deeply indebted to one which he, Coleridge, still could not complete. Finally, and very directly, Coleridge asserts that he 'assuredly was commissioned . . . to retalk the matter with the Longmans' and reveals his anger that Wordsworth should have gone over his head to the publishers with the damaging suggestion that he 'had proceeded without authority'.[56] Two days later Coleridge wrote to Francis Jeffrey, scourge of 'the Lakers' in the *Edinburgh Review*, beginning an exchange of views in which he sought to convince the most influential critic of the day that he was no longer justified in classing him with Wordsworth and Southey.[57]

Coleridge's anger added pain to an already bleak period. Wordsworth's stay in London had been miserable and unproductive, but as he was leaving 'in a very thoughtful and melancholy state of mind', he had caught a vision of the city under snow, with the 'huge and majestic form of St Pauls, solemnised by a thin veil of falling snow'. In *Resolution and Independence* Wordsworth had felt 'admonished' by the old leech gatherer on the lonely moor. Now 'this unthought-of sight, in such a place' affected him similarly, as he told Sir George: 'My sorrow was controlled, and my uneasiness of mind not quieted and relieved altogether, seemed at once to receive the gift of an anchor of security'.[58] But at home there was no calm or security. When he arrived Sara Hutchinson seemed to be getting stronger, but she had coughed up blood, a symptom, it seemed, of incipient consumption, and he was gloomy that 'there is in the present state of her constitution much ground for serious alarm'.[59] Worse still, his son John went down on 6 April with what looked like meningitis, suffering terribly himself and throwing the whole household into panic. 'We resigned ourselves to our loss, and contemplated the poor Innocent's sufferings with awful dread', Dorothy wrote about 18 April, exhausted, but relieved that by now she could see that the nursing of the three women had brought him through severe influenza.[60] They were all afflicted as well by a Grasmere tragedy. On the night of 19 March George and Sarah Green, two very poor cottagers, died on the snow-covered fells between Langdale and their home in Easedale. Eight children under 16 had to be cared for, one, Sally, already being in service with the Wordsworths. Mary was active with other local ladies in finding boarding for them. Wordsworth very successfully solicited money from personal friends and public figures and arranged for its invest-ment to provide funds for subsistence, clothing, and schooling until the children were grown up. In May, at Wordsworth's urging, Dorothy wrote a moving account of the events, intending it for publication not immediately but 'Thirty or forty years hence', when it would serve, like *Michael* or *The Brothers*, as a memorial to a pastoral tragedy and communal compassion.[61]

To add to Wordsworth's anxieties, he was at loggerheads with Dorothy. Increasingly worried about money, she had lamented to Catherine Clarkson the previous July, 'alas! poetry is a bad trade; and William's works sell slowly'. But she was optimistic about *The White Doe*. It could never be popular like *The Lay of the Last Minstrel*, she knew, but she thought that 'the story will help out those parts which are above the common level of taste and knowledge, and that it will have a better sale than his former works, and perhaps help them off'.[62] At the news that Wordsworth was setting off from London without a contract for publication she snapped and reproached him fiercely:

We are exceedingly concerned to hear that you, William! have given up all thoughts of publishing your Poem. As to the Outcry against you, I would defy it—what matter, if you get your 100 guineas into your pocket? Besides it is like as if they had run you down, when it is known you have a poem ready for publishing, and keep it back. It is our belief, and that of all who have heard it read, that the *Tale* would bear it up—and without money what *can* we do? New House! new furniture! such a large family! two servants and little Sally! we *cannot* go on so another half-year; and as Sally will not be fit for another place, we must take her back again into the old one, and dismiss one of the Servants, and work the flesh *off our poor bones*. Do, dearest William! do pluck up your Courage—overcome your disgust to publishing—It is but a *little trouble*, and all will be over, and we shall be wealthy, and at our ease for one year, at least.[63]

It is the cry of a woman who is wearing out. Coleridge might lament her 'exceeding anxiety about pecuniary matters' as evidence of 'a decaying of genial Hope & former light-heartedness', but Dorothy had a different perspective.[64] For thirteen years she had lived hand to mouth, but she was no longer young and Alfoxden's gaiety could not be sustained with three small children to be cared for, with a fourth child expected at the end of the summer, and with Sara Hutchinson now a permanent member of the family and her sister Joanna likely to become one. They needed more room and more money. The space was gained at last in May, when they moved across the village to Allan Bank. Wordsworth had once declared Mr Crump's recently built mansion a 'temple of abomination', but now it was taken eagerly as the solution to one problem.[65] But the concern about the family income grew stronger once Wordsworth had decided to ignore the entreaties of Dorothy and Mary that he should publish *The White Doe*.

(5)

Wordsworth's odd and clumsy behaviour over *The White Doe* marked the beginning in 1807–8 of a dark phase in his life. The generosity and gaiety, the 'convulsive inclination to laughter about the mouth' which Hazlitt had found so winning in 1798, were frequently overshadowed by spiky self-centredness.\* Early in 1808 Southey claimed that 'entire & intense selfishness' was 'so pure & unmixed a passion in him that Ben Jonson would have had him in a play had he been his contemporary' and Henry Crabb Robinson, an admirer who was later to become an intimate friend, noted on meeting him in London that 'He is not attentive to others . . . He does not spare those he opposes'.[66] It is significant, however, that both comments locate Wordsworth's egotism in his zeal for 'his own productions' and his 'sense of his own worth'. As a husband, father, brother, and provider Wordsworth was rarely selfish, but whatever impinged on his integrity as poet roused him—and that was now being subjected to its severest challenge.

The reviews of *Poems, in Two Volumes* were devastating. In July 1807 Byron set the pattern by praising some of the sonnets and the *Song . . . Brougham Castle*, but dismissing the rest of the poems as 'common-place ideas' clothed 'in language not simple, but puerile . . . namby-pamby'. The *Critical Review* in August lamented Wordsworth's drivelling vanity and entreated him 'to spend more time in his library and less in company with the "moods of his own mind"'. In November the *Satirist* recommended that the volumes, which consisted mostly of 'miserable trash', should be bound uniformly with 'Mother Goose's melodies'. In December Francis Jeffrey in the *Edinburgh Review* exhibited specific poems one by one as 'evidence' for the 'verdict against this publication': *Beggars*, 'a very paradigm of silliness and affectation'; *Alice Fell*, 'such trash'; *Yarrow Unvisited*, 'a very tedious and affected performance'; *Foresight*, 'quintessence of unmeaningness'; *Ode*, 'beyond all doubt the most illegible and unintelligible part of the publication'. James Montgomery in the *Eclectic Review* for January 1808 thought the poems a disaster compared with *Lyrical Ballads* and declared the *Ode* 'a wilderness of sublimity, tenderness, bombast and absurdity'. The *Cabinet* in April relied on such terms as 'contemptible effusions', 'trash', 'conceit', 'puerile affectation', 'bombast'.[67]

Wordsworth was being judged. That Jeffrey made plain by emphasizing how important *Poems, in Two Volumes* was, in that it reaffirmed poetic

---

\* 'My First Acquaintance with Poets', *Howe*, XVII. 118. Lamb's dismay at W's manner is revealed in a splendidly waspish comment to Manning, 26 Feb. 1808: 'Wordsworth the great poet is coming to town. He is to have apartments in the Mansion House. He says he does not see much difficulty in writing like Shakespeare, if he had a mind to try it. It is clear then nothing is wanting but the mind. Even Coleridge a little checked at this hardihood of assertion.' *Marrs*, II. 274–5.

intentions which he had earlier censured and thus 'brought the matter to a test'. But Wordsworth was also being mocked. In 1808 *The Simpliciad: A Satirico-didactic Poem* offered *Hints for the Scholars of the New School.*[68] This able satire laments the current degradation of true simplicity and in a spoof scholastic commentary quotes many specimens of the ludicrous as authority for its judgements. Though addressed to Wordsworth, Southey, and Coleridge, its target is Wordsworth. Lines from his poems are quoted with derision in over half the volume and, of course, out of context they do, especially cumulatively, often look silly. The satire's dedication is vicious— these false poets must be extirpated because their work subverts rationality, respect for authority (the ancients and the laws of poetry), and common sense—and its conclusion menacing:

> . . . 'tis as well to kill
> As strive to cure a madman 'gainst his will.

In the *Examiner*, 28 August 1808, Leigh Hunt added his pennyworth, pillorying Wordsworth as one of 'The Ancient and Redoubtable Institution of Quacks'. The *British Critic* in March the following year reminded readers of *The Simpliciad*, finding its strictures on *Poems, in Two Volumes* entirely justified: 'such flimsy, puerile thoughts, expressed in such feeble and halting verse, we have seldom seen'.[69]

Wordsworth was realistic enough to know what the effect of such notices would be. Beseeching Wrangham to use his influence in the *Critical Review*, he remarked that 'the immediate sale of books is more under the influence of reviews than is generally supposed, and the sale of this work is of some consequence to me'. Or, as Southey neatly put it, reviewers 'cannot *blast* our *laurels*, but they may *mildew* our *corn*'.[70] *Poems, in Two Volumes* sold badly. However fervently Lady Beaumont might proselytize—and she was very fervent—a coterie following could not compensate for hostile reviews and seven years later 230 of the 1,000 copies printed still awaited buyers.*

While Richard was prospering and Christopher rising in the Church, it began to look as if Wordsworth would be unable to support his family. But the effect on sales was not the most worrying aspect of this critical onslaught. Abuse—the reiteration of 'namby-pamby', 'childish', 'puerile', and so on— could be endured. The accusation that the recluse of the Lakes had cut himself off from civilization and intellectual nourishment was so ignorant that while it might affect sales it could not unsettle the poet. Even Jeffrey's attack on Wordsworth's 'system', with its portrait of crazed poets suffering

---

* Lady Beaumont was imperious. She converted Uvedale Price, but failed with Farington when she insisted on him studying the Preface to *Lyrical Ballads*: 'Sir George was more moderate. He told me & warned me of the danger of not approving it, adding "That Lady B. was as intolerant in Her opinion as Bishop Bonnor on religious matters".' *Farington*, IX. 3425–6, entry for 28 Mar. 1809.

'much pains to keep *down* to the standard which they have proposed to themselves', perhaps cut less deeply than he imagined. The linguistic theory of the 1800 and 1802 Prefaces was confused and Wordsworth had made no subsequent effort to defend it *as theory*. But on one all-important topic what the reviewers were saying could not be evaded. Jeffrey was the most articulate, but in most the argument was the same: Wordsworth obstinately goes on 'connecting his most lofty, tender, or impassioned conceptions, with objects and incidents which the greater part of his readers will probably persist in thinking low, silly, or uninteresting'.

Wordsworth conceded at once that in this one sentence Jeffrey had struck home. Such comments told him that he had failed in what he valued most. It was not surprising that reviewers liked the sonnets or the *Song*. They understood their genre. But scorn of the other lyrics, especially of 'Moods of my Own Mind', meant that Wordsworth had made no headway in awakening an imaginative response to the familiar, the homely, and the unregarded. Crabbe, Jeffrey declared in April 1808, always did so, because he 'shows us something which we have all seen, or may see, in real life; and draws from it such feelings and such reflections as every human being must acknowledge that it is calculated to excite'.[71] On the contrary, 'Crabbe's pictures', Wordsworth declared a few months latter, 'are mere matters of fact, with which the Muses have just about as much to do as they have with a Collection of medical reports, or of Law cases'.[72] And in these two judgements about the nature of the poetic imagination is the essence of the conflict between reviewer and poet which was to continue for another ten years.[73]

Wordsworth had armed himself against attack. 'London wits and witlings' would never feel for poetry, he had told Lady Beaumont—an awful truth, 'because to be incapable of a feeling of Poetry in my sense of the word is to be without love of human nature and reverence for God'. Even 'grave, kindly-natured, worthy persons, who would be pleased if they could', he feared, would miss the significance of his poems, for 'their imagination has slept; and the voice which is the voice of my Poetry without Imagination cannot be heard'.[74] His trust, Wordsworth declared, was in posterity. But even such lofty sentiments had not proofed him against the severity of the attack or the overtness of Jeffrey's intention to rob him of readers altogether by convicting him of 'an insult on the public taste'.

Wordsworth registered the impact of this critical offensive in two ways. One, while entirely understandable, was damaging to himself. He withdrew *The White Doe* and published no new volume of poems until 1814. That in itself was less important than the fact that the decision not to publish reinforced a growing tendency to see himself as embattled in righteousness against an uncomprehending world. He had always been touchy about criticism, but now he became extremely defensive. Lamb's response to *The White Doe*, for example, provoked a long critique of the poem's strengths in a letter to Coleridge, which concluded with a diatribe: 'Let Lamb learn to be ashamed of himself in not taking some pleasure in the contemplation of this picture . . . of one thing be assured, that Lamb has not a reasoning mind, therefore cannot have a comprehensive mind, and, least of all, has he an imaginative one'.[75] Over the next decade Wordsworth's friends were often to be dismayed by emanations of the same spirit.

More insidious was the effect of the defensiveness on Wordsworth's image of the relationship between poet and audience. In *Home at Grasmere* he had invoked Milton's 'Fit audience find though few', but in the 1802 Preface to *Lyrical Ballads* had stressed the universality of poetry and the value of the poet who, though a specially endowed being, was 'a man speaking to men'. Assuring Lady Beaumont in May 1807 of his unconcern for the 'immediate effect' of his poems 'upon what is called the Public', however, Wordsworth seems to disdain the majority of his possible audience and, more ominously still, in his letter to Southey about Jeffrey's review he even speaks of unresponsive readers as 'in a state of degradation'.[76] Five months later Dorothy reports him at his bleakest: 'He has no pleasure in publishing—he even detests it—and if it were not that he is *not* over wealthy, he would leave all his works to be published after his Death'.[77] Scorn of the bourgeois audience as irredeemably degraded, or at least as just stupid, was to become a favoured Romantic consolation for poets and novelists in the nineteenth and early twentieth centuries, but it was a damaging attitude for the poet of *The Ruined Cottage* or *Michael* to take comfort in. His poetry was grounded in 'the great and simple affections of our nature' and in 1800 Wordsworth had been sure that its power to enlarge imaginative capability was needed, 'especially so at the present day'.[78]

Wordsworth's sense of his vocation—'I wish either to be considered as a Teacher, or as nothing', he told Beaumont in February 1808—was what supported him and fostered his other, productive, response to the reviews.[79] Jeffrey's censure was galling, not only because it was wrong but because Wordsworth knew that he was not the poet of the *Edinburgh*'s imaginings. Much more 'evidence' was available, at least to the poet. Lying unpublished were *The Ruined Cottage* and *The Pedlar*, *Home at Grasmere* and *The Prelude*, very substantial poems in the kind of blank verse on which his reputation largely rested (*Tintern Abbey* was often invoked favourably in the reviews). In his own self-image he was not just the poet of 'Moods of my Own Mind', but a philosophic poet, Milton's heir, the poet of *The Recluse*. But as Jeffrey pointed out when Coleridge plaintively avowed that he had moved on since the 1790s, the world could only judge what the world was allowed to see.* Private convictions, unpublished formulations, could not be summoned in defence. In this Jeffrey was right. And when eventually Wordsworth broke his silence—as a publishing poet—he did so with a flourish of defiance. In 1814 *The Excursion*, a blank verse philosophical poem in nine books, announced itself as only part of *The Recluse*, a massive project, long meditated by the poet who revealed himself in an autobiographical preface as shaping his whole writing life to its fulfilment. The following year Wordsworth collected his lyric *Poems*, introduced them with a new theoretical essay, and reissued the offending Preface to *Lyrical Ballads*. Jeffrey had spoken of a test. Here was his answer. In 1808, however, Wordsworth knew that he had to get on with *The Recluse*.

Over the late spring and summer he wrote three blank verse meditations as part of the project. Each originated in personal observation. The first, *St Paul's*, records the vision of the cathedral through a veil of falling snow which he had described to Beaumont. *To the Clouds* was suggested, the poet said later, as he watched the clouds 'driving over the top of Nab Scar across the vale' between Rydal and Grasmere. The last and longest, *The Tuft of Primroses*, starts as a lament for the changes that had ravaged Grasmere during the Wordsworths' absence at Coleorton.[80] But although each of these poems is accomplished—*St Paul's* is particularly striking—and Wordsworth felt confident enough to tell Samuel Rogers in September that he had completed 'about 500 lines of my long Poem',[81] this work was abandoned half-way through a line and marked, in fact, the end of sustained composition of this kind of poetry for *The Recluse*.

The poems themselves suggest one possible cause for Wordsworth's failure to proceed. Each is a reprise of earlier work, but in a more muted tone. *St Paul's* enshrines a 'spot of time' like those in *The Prelude*, a gift of experience which renewed the poet, but the verse lacks the joyous assurance of earlier visionary moments that here is contained the power of 'future restoration'. *To the Clouds* begins as a hymn to movement, energy, light, and colour, but the meditation on poetic creativity to which it rises seems impoverished when compared with the Snowdon passage in *The Prelude*. *The Tuft of Primroses* picks up *Home at Grasmere*. Both poems dwell on man's need of a sanctuary. The earlier poem's affirmation, however, that the holy place of Grasmere would be a source of joy and creative achievement is countered in *The Tuft of Primroses* by an elegiac tentativeness and by questions about time and loss which the poem is only beginning to

---

* On 27 May 1808 Jeffrey quite justifiably emphasized that a writer's reputation must rest on his published work: 'when I class Mr Coleridge with Mr Wordsworth and Mr Southey I *must* be understood to speak of the Mr Coleridge who wrote visions for the Maid of Arc and sonnets to its author—These performances are all that the public knew of him—they live still'. WL.

adumbrate as it breaks off. All three poems seem to be a coda rather than the overture to a new phase of creation.

The more immediate cause of Wordsworth's blockage was that the meditations have no place in any existing or planned structure, nor do they look as if they are about to create one. Wordsworth could tell Rogers that they were part of his 'long Poem', but what long poem? For ten years *The Recluse* had existed as a concept, but although *The Ruined Cottage* and *Home at Grasmere* indicated the different kinds of poetry which the completed work might contain, neither in itself signalled how a larger structure might develop. Wordsworth did not know what genre he was working in, nor what audience he might be addressing. Luckily for his self-confidence—and thus ultimately for that part of *The Recluse* which was completed, *The Excursion*—he was soon engrossed in a different project in which he was able to express his views on 'Nature, Man, and Society', confident of both his genre and intended readership. Fifteen years after the *Letter to the Bishop of Llandaff* Wordsworth returned to writing in prose about politics.

(6)

Allan Bank is a large, though not handsome, house, standing in rising ground a little to the west of Grasmere village. It seemed to offer all that the family wanted. The adults could have rooms of their own at last; there was space enough for friends to stay; the children had a little paradise to explore with the slopes of Silver How in one direction and the lake in the other. They kept a cow and two pigs. And yet by December 1808 Dorothy was declaring the house 'literally not habitable', acknowledging what they all felt, that once a suitable alternative were found, probably not, alas, in Grasmere, they would move again.[82] Allan Bank never became a home.

The main obstacle to their comfort was smoke. Before they had occupied it, Dorothy had noted that the house was exposed 'to the full force of the East wind, and of every other except the North, from which it is very imperfectly screened', but then she had been worried about cold.[83] What they discovered once the winter set in was that scarcely a chimney would draw. 'There was one stormy day', she told Jane Marshall, 'in which we could have no fire but in my Brother's Study—and that chimney smoked so much that we were obliged to go to bed with the Baby in the middle of the day to keep it warm, and I, with a candle in my hand, stumbled over a chair, unable to see it.'[84] Everything was filthy—'Dishes are washed, and no sooner set into the pantry than they are covered with smoke'—but smarting eyes and sore throats had to be accepted, for without fires the damp of the big, draughty house would have been unendurable. Chimney experts were sent by Mr Crump, but the problem was only alleviated, never solved.

Other considerations made Allan Bank seem only a temporary resting place. One was that in the longer term they would want to be near a grammar school, such as Hawkshead. Another, more immediately pressing, was money. The cost of furnishing the new house, however sparsely, had been considerable and it was expensive to run. Now continuously worried about how they would manage, Dorothy had to pester the dilatory Richard for a statement of their financial situation, beg him to pay outstanding bills, and even ask for a little cash as a gift for herself. The cost of coal and the scope for little economies on housekeeping preoccupied her, as she, Mary, Sara, and the servants struggled with the washing, baking, cooking, and the endless task of keeping things clean. By May 1809 Dorothy confessed that unless Wordsworth acted upon his 'resolution to write upon publick affairs in the *Courier*, or some other newspaper, for the sake of getting money . . . I know not how we can go on'.[85]

Expenses at Allan Bank were related to the size of the domestic circle there at any one time, and though that fluctuated, it was never small. Despite all the recent acrimony, Coleridge joined the family at the beginning of September 1808, as had been planned when the tenancy had first been taken up. Hartley and Derwent, now at school in Ambleside, joined their father at weekends during term. His daughter Sara stayed for a month after her father's arrival, until she was collected by Mrs Coleridge, who remained a week—astonishingly, for she was under the same roof as her estranged husband, the woman he loved, and the family she blamed in part for the breakdown of her marriage. Not counting short-stay visitors such as Tom or George Hutchinson, or the boys at the weekend, it was not uncommon for there to be as many as a dozen at table.

In November another figure added a welcome gaiety and all the interest of novelty to their lives—Thomas De Quincey. Exactly a year before, in 1807, the 22-year-old De Quincey at last met his idol, Wordsworth, after four years of intermittent correspondence and hesitant approaches.[86] An admirer of Coleridge—he had given him £300 anonymously—he had become a fast friend of Sara Coleridge and her children and now he quickly bound himself to all the Wordsworths. He was impressed by their plain living and unconventionality and thrilled to have been accepted into the household of the poet of whom he had formed so exalted an image. For their part the Wordsworths, especially the women, valued him simply because he was 'loving, gentle, and happy'. In 1807 De Quincey had gone back to Oxford, where he was still an undergraduate, but now he came to live in Allan Bank, accepted, as Dorothy said, 'as if he were one of the Family'.[87] He loved the children and they returned his love. When they were apart, Dorothy never failed to report their prattle to him, and it always included, 'when will he come?' Fully in earnest in his desire to share the Grasmere way of life, De Quincey took over the tenancy of the cottage at Town End in February 1809 and, plundering his modest fortune, began to fit it out to receive his enormous library. He celebrated the next New Year by entertaining the family in their own old home and by delighting all the children in the vale with a fireworks display.

De Quincey's presence indicates once again the power of attraction exerted by the Wordsworths as a domestic group, but now the principals in it were attempting to maintain harmony in a situation where the potential for discord and tension was much higher than ever before. From the start Dorothy doubted the propriety of their sheltering Coleridge and his children so close to his abandoned home, nor was she sanguine that he would master the self-destructive habits which made him so difficult to live with. Coleridge was lonely and, feeling unloved, reacted to any perceived slight, as a sad record left by his daughter Sara reveals. Speaking of the Allan Bank period she recalled:

I think my dear father was anxious that I should learn to love him and the Wordsworths and their children, and not cling so exclusively to my mother, and all around me at home. He was therefore much annoyed when, on my mother's coming to Allan Bank, I flew to her, and wished not to be separated from her any more. I remember his shewing displeasure to me, and accusing me of want of affection. I could not understand why. The young Wordsworths came in and caressed him. I sate benumbed; for truly nothing does so freeze affection as the breath of jealousy. The sense that you have done very wrong, or at least given great offence, you know not how or why—that you are dunned for some payment of love or feeling which you know not how to produce or to demonstrate on a sudden, chills the heart, and fills it with perplexity and bitterness. My father reproached me, and contrasted my coldness with the childish caresses of the Wordsworths. I slunk away, and hid myself in the wood behind the house, and there my friend John, whom at that time I called my future husband, came to seek me.[88]

Coleridge could not fail to see, moreover, that De Quincey was winning the affection and trust which at Alfoxden had been exclusively his.

As before at Coleorton, tension was absorbed in fervent intellectual activity in which domestic affairs were subordinated to gathering information, transcribing manuscripts or taking dictation, sending letters, and dealing with printers—all the birth-pangs of new publication. Little Sara Coleridge watched her father, De Quincey, Southey, and Wordsworth pace up and down in talk at Allan Bank and, though what she most vividly remembered was how much she wanted to pull out the handkerchief that dangled from one of their pockets, she sensed the earnestness with which they used 'to discuss the affairs of the nation, as if it all came home to their business and bosoms, as if it were their private concern!'[89] Her memory of the mood of the household can be trusted. Coleridge was planning a periodical which would redeem the failure of *The Watchman* and reveal how far he had travelled since those Jacobinical days. Wordsworth, too, was eager to make a public statement. Ever since 1802 he had glanced at politics in his sonnets, especially those in *Poems, in Two Volumes* which, he told Lady Beaumont, 'collectively make a Poem on the subject of civil Liberty and national independence',[90] but the wider scope of his convictions, and the weight of his despondency at the tone of political life, had so far been confined to private letters or to dinner-table conversation of the kind that had so shocked De Quincey when he first heard Wordsworth 'giving utterance to sentiments which seemed absolutely disloyal'.[91] In 1808 a topical issue focused his ideas and incited him to speak out, with the confidence, which he had not enjoyed since the early 1790s, that he might be a voice for a considerable body of opposition opinion.

In May 1808 a general revolt took place in Spain against French invasions and the proposed imposition of Joseph Bonaparte as King of Spain. British aid was promised and in August forces under Wellesley landed on the Portuguese coast for an advance to Lisbon. A French army commanded by Junot was defeated, but the victory was not pursued and by the terms of a convention, sued for by the French and agreed to in late August, the routed army was allowed, in the words of Article II, to 'evacuate Portugal with their arms and baggage; they shall not be considered as prisoners of war; and, on their arrival in France, they shall be at liberty to serve'.[92] The news broke in the English press on 16 September and was at once construed by many as a national humiliation. A defeated army had been allowed to dictate the terms of its own withdrawal, intact and with honour. A Board of Inquiry was instigated in November, but throughout October Wordsworth, Southey, and others made efforts to rouse opinion locally with the intention of framing a County Address to the king about this 'grievous national disgrace'.[93] When it was made clear that Lord Lonsdale would not allow such activity to go unchallenged, Wordsworth defiantly reached out to a wider audience through newspaper and pamphlet.

He became totally engrossed in *The Convention of Cintra*—obsessed would be a better word. The topic, Dorothy wrote in December, 'has interested him more than words can express. His first and his last thoughts are of Spain and Portugal', and since Coleridge reports on one occasion that he and Wordsworth were still at work at 3 a.m. there must often have been little time between last and first thoughts.[94] Stuart's *Courier* carried sections on 27 December 1808 and 13 January 1809, but thereafter all efforts were concentrated on preparing the whole essay for issue as a substantial pamphlet. Ever eager to help, De Quincey went to London in late February to supervise the printing. Had he ever experienced Wordsworth in the throes of publication he might have hesitated. As always in dealings with printers, Wordsworth was imperious, self-centred, and thoughtless. De Quincey struggled to respond to a stream of commands, often only partially intelligible, and to order what Coleridge called 'Wordsworth's own Sybill's Leaves blown about by the changeful winds of an anxious Author's Second-thoughts',[95] only to find himself blamed for delays. When an important note he had written on the siege of Saragossa was countermanded, even he ventured 'to complain a little of the very great injustice which he [Wordsworth] has done me . . .'. In reply Wordsworth made only a minimal apology before giving him further instructions.[96] At a very late stage fears that he would end up in Newgate for libel gripped the author, to the amusement of Sara Hutchinson who declared, 'We Females . . . have not the least fear of Newgate—if there was but a Garden to walk in we think we should do very nicely',[97] but it was the harassed De Quincey who had to check the text for dangerous passages and negotiate cancellations with the printer. Contrary to Wordsworth's suspicions, he had worked as expeditiously as possible and it was not his fault that the pamphlet did not appear until 27 May 1809.

*The Convention of Cintra* cost Wordsworth more toil than any other of his prose works. Though on 26 November 1808 Southey had expected any day to hear that it was finished, it took Wordsworth much longer than expected—eventually to the barely disguised irritation of his family. Why did he become so involved? A number of reasons suggest themselves. When writing *The White Doe of Rylstone* Wordsworth had scorned historical information offered by Scott, preferring to rest on what he called 'traditionary and common historic records'.[98] Quite properly he had used only what suited him as a poet. But now he was presenting an argument that had to deploy accurate and verifiable information if it was to be effective. For Spanish and Portuguese geography and cultural history he could call on Southey's assistance, but other details had to be gleaned from diverse sources and marshalled with caution. It is clear, too, that Wordsworth was anxious to make an impact. His name, especially if linked to *Lyrical Ballads* or *Poems, in Two Volumes*, would, he suspected, raise hackles in enemies ready to 'call forth the old yell of Jacobinism'.[99] The essay needed to be constructed with time-consuming care. The most important reason, however, was touched on by Coleridge when he remarked that 'a considerable part [of the pamphlet] is almost a self-robbery from some great philosophical poem, of which it would form an appropriate part, & be fitlier attuned to the high dogmatic Eloquence, the oracular [tone] of impassioned Blank Verse'.[100] Coleridge had in mind, of course *The Recluse*—and he was right. Wordsworth laboured so long over *The Convention of Cintra* because subjecting political events to the test of general principles released a torrent of ideas, feelings, and convictions which he had had no occasion before to formulate in prose. He was, obliquely, writing as if for *The Recluse*.

Wordsworth's argument is straightforward. The Convention of Cintra is a catastrophe, militarily, because it betrays allies and forfeits the opportunity to inflict considerable, and symbolically significant, damage on Napoleon, the 'fallen Spirit', who, operating like Satan beyond morality, deserves no quarter. But it is a national disgrace because of what it reveals about the state of Britain. It could only have been perpetrated and subsequently condoned by leaders who lack not courage nor talent but 'widely-ranging intellect' and imagination. Britain's rulers had failed to see that nothing could resist the spirit of liberty which inspired the Americans to win their freedom. They had failed to see the majesty of spirit at work at the dawn of the French Revolution. And now, displaying 'the same presumptuous irreverence to the principles of justice, and blank insensibility to the affections of human nature', they had failed to perceive that in the Spanish uprising was a manifestation of *spiritual* power which alone can guarantee 'the ultimate salvation of a people'. This is the indictment—not that Britain's leaders are venal and corrupt (though they are), but that their exercise 'of prudence, of sagacity, and of all those qualities which are the darling virtues of the worldly-wise' has made them incapable of understanding their own country's history, insensible to what motivates common men to heroic exertion, and purblind to the truth that ultimately what count are not guns but the 'moral virtues and qualities of passion which belong to a people'.

The contention about military policy is urged through discussion of tactics, the articles of the Convention, and of other supporting documents. But the real power of *The Convention of Cintra* lies in the energy of the prose and the inventiveness of its baroque ornamentation. If Wordsworth has a model it is Milton rather than Burke, but again and again in images and manner of address the *Reflections* are evoked and *Cintra* is not damaged by the comparison. Both writers were possessed by a vision—Burke of the organic unity of past and present, Wordsworth of spiritual power—and in both it is a vision rather than an argument which is projected by rhythm, cadence, imagery, and all the freedom of English syntax. *The Convention of Cintra* is one of the masterworks of English Romantic prose.[101]

It is not difficult, however, to understand why it did not sell, or why Lord Lonsdale found it distasteful. According to Farington, he thought it 'written in a very bad taste, not with plainness & simplicity such [as] is proper to a political subject, but in a style inflated & ill suited to it'.[102] In short, the earl found it difficult to follow. Understandably, for some sentences soar page-long. But it may be, also, that he was shrewd enough to recognize *Cintra* for what it was—a Tract for the Times with a distinctly radical orientation. Wordsworth laments the course of French policy, but he both recalls with pleasure the origins of the Revolution and condemns afresh the wickedness of the British government in 1793 in pursuing a war against liberty. In one passionate outburst beginning 'O sorrow! O misery for England', he imagines his country reproached by 'her Alfred, her Sidneys, and her Milton'. But the essential radicalism of *Cintra* is not here, but in the constant reference to human nature, common passions, the human heart. Statesmen and courtiers, he asserts, cocooned in their 'exclusive and artificial' situation, lack vital knowledge—'a knowledge of human kind'.

On 7 June 1809 Farington noted a dinner-table conversation: 'Lady Beaumont spoke of Wordsworth's pamphlet on the "Cintra convention", in very high terms, as above the political writings of Burke & others.— . . . Sir George said, drily, That Lady Beaumont spoke of the Book as if she was *employed to sell it.*—She sd. she Had caused the sale of some of them.'[103] But even Lady Beaumont's advocacy could not carry off the small edition and two years later 178 of the 500 copies were sold as waste paper. *Cintra's* impact on policy or on the tone of national life was nil. Its importance for Wordsworth, however, was enormous. Ever since the late 1790s he had been exploring his radical years, reassessing, piecing together ideas and reflections—in *The Borderers*, in his political sonnets, in *The Prelude*. *Cintra* had both brought a great deal into focus and charged him with energy for further exploration. Within twelve months Wordsworth was once again making himself ill by the intensity of his effort on new poetic composition.

(7)

Wordsworth promised to bring the Convention of Cintra 'to the test of those Principles, by which alone the Independence and Freedom of Nations can be Preserved or Recovered'.[104] While he was struggling to bring his pamphlet into being, Coleridge too was hard at work on a project whose object was 'to refer men to PRINCIPLES in all things; in Literature, in the Fine Arts, in Morals, in Legislation, in Religion'—his weekly paper, *The Friend*.[105]

Every aspect of this project was Coleridgean. Coleridge had aspired to such a paper for many years and when he set about realizing it in the autumn of 1808 he did so with zeal. But the promise of publication in January 1809 had been far too hasty, for when the New Year came he still had neither printer nor publisher. Calling on extraordinary resources of energy and recuperative powers that continually surprised his friends, Coleridge found a printer in Penrith, arranged delivery of paper, set up a network of subscribers, and organized distribution, all the time planning the contents of the weekly essays to be written entirely by himself. Since these demanded not only knowledge, ideas, and eloquence, which he had, but also, being weekly, unremitting self-discipline, which he did not, it seemed as if Coleridge were undertaking exactly the kind of work in which he would be most likely to fail. The Wordsworths were not sanguine. In March Wordsworth told Poole that he had 'not much hope' and when two months later the first *Friend* still had not appeared, he declared it better that 'it should never commence. It is in fact *impossible* utterly impossible—that he should carry it on . . .'.[106] Nor surprisingly he urged Poole to burn the letter. But when number 1 was issued on 1 June 1809 both Wordsworth and Dorothy had to admit that Coleridge's resolution was impressive and that the auguries for *The Friend* were good.[107]

It was, however, far too demanding a task for any one person. From the fourth issue Sara Hutchinson became Coleridge's amanuensis and both toiled to exhaustion, but by number 11, 26 October, Coleridge was overstretched. He began to draw on old stock of his own and on whatever appropriate material Wordsworth could provide.

That stand-by of harassed editors, the planted letter, elicited Wordsworth's first prose contribution. In 1802 John Wilson had written warmly and intelligently to Wordsworth. Recently, being independently wealthy, Wilson had moved to Windermere and over the previous year this 'very amiable young man' had conquered his neighbours in Grasmere.[108] There was an agreeable reciprocity. Wordsworth allowed his young admirer to become privy to his manuscript poetry and helped him in his own composition. For his part Wilson, whose vitality and love of sport and fun became legendary, offered generous hospitality to all of the Allan Bank family and even carried Wordsworth off for a week's fishing in June 1809.[109] At the end of the year he decided to assist Coleridge. Signing himself 'Mathetes', the learner, he wrote a long letter to *The Friend*, enquiring how a young idealist might best be guided in his encounters with the world.[110] What is needed, 'Mathetes' suggests, is a Teacher 'conspicuous above the multitude in superior power, and yet more in the proclamation of disregarded Truth'—such a man, indeed, as Wordsworth.

'Mathetes's letter was woolly, hypothetical, and repetitive and the encomium on Wordsworth absurdly unrestrained, but it served its purpose. A reply was called for. What Wordsworth provided is very interesting, not because of its wisdom or the quality of its educational insight (although claims could be made for both), but because it shows how confidently Wordsworth now possessed his own experience. Assessing youth's possibilities, Wordsworth once more defends his own choice of life. A man will be tempted, he argues, by the World and by Intellectual Prowess. The one promises 'the huzzas of the multitude', the other 'solitary and unremitting labour, a life of entire neglect perhaps, or assuredly a life exposed to scorn, insult, persecution, and hatred; but cheered by encouragement from a grateful few, by applauding Conscience, and by a prophetic anticipation, perhaps, of lasting fame—a late though lasting consequence'.[111] Beautifully recapturing the tone of the early *Prelude*, Wordsworth speaks of Nature's way of teaching, of the ascent to Reason and to the discovery of knowledge in books, but insists that a 'Teacher' cannot be a substitute for experience. The young must make their own mistakes, for 'there is nothing whereupon the Mind reposes with a confidence equal to that with which it rests on those conclusions, by which truths have been established the direct opposite of errours once rapturously cherished . . .'.[112]

The *Reply to 'Mathetes'* was an occasional essay, but it both drew together all of Wordsworth's previous utterances on education in his poetry and letters, and propelled him further, as *Cintra* had, towards his next major phase of poetic composition. His second prose contribution to *The Friend* is of similar importance and interest. Late in 1809 Wordsworth had made available six translations of Epitaphs by the Italian poet Chiabrera and when Coleridge found himself 'utterly unprovided' for *The Friend* due out on 22 February 1810 he gave him the first section of a three-part meditation on epitaphs prompted by his recent work.[113] These *Essays upon Epitaphs* drew on his past thought, implicitly justified his present practice, and prepared the way for his eventual comprehensive reassertion in 1814 and 1815 of his pretensions as moralist, poet, and aesthetic theorist. In each one a conviction, or a preoccupation, or a particular strength of Wordsworth's mind comes through in writing of exceptional verve and clarity.[114]

The first essay, which dwells on the motives that compel men to memorialize the dead, is notable chiefly for the urgency with which Wordsworth asserts his own conviction that unless 'an intimation or assurance within us, that some part of our nature is imperishable' counterbalance our knowledge of death, 'such a hollowness would pervade the whole system of things, such a want of correspondence and consistency, a disproportion so astounding betwixt means and ends, that there could be no response, no joy'. *We are Seven*, *Tintern Abbey*, Books I, II, VI, and XIII of *The Prelude*, the *Ode* (significantly subtitled 'Intimations of Immortality' when next printed) will all flood in on the reader who turns to this eloquent passage. *The Brothers* is recalled, too, by Wordsworth's emphasis on both the practical and the symbolic significance of 'a parish-church, in the stillness of the country' as 'a visible centre of a community of the living and the dead; a point to which are habitually referred the nearest concerns of both'.[115] Wordsworth's reverence for the Church as the outward and visible embodiment of what is assured by faith, fed on school-day memories of the function of Hawkshead's 'throned lady' in the community, on his own feeling for whatever powers can best bind men together in 'relationship and love',[116] and, perhaps most deeply now, on the yearning expressed in *Elegiac Stanzas . . . Peele Castle* towards whatever can remain steadfast in the face of shock or time's erosion.

In a generously humanitarian spirit that recalls *Lyrical Ballads* the second essay ponders the relationship between the virtues inscribed on humble gravestones and actual lives. It is closer, Wordsworth maintains, than one might think. Vice obtrudes itself upon our notice, but 'how few know anything of the trials to which Men in a lowly condition are subject, or of the steady and triumphant manner in which those trials are often sustained . . .'. The discussion then passes easily to the language of specific epitaphs. It is clear after only a page or two that here, and in the third essay, Wordsworth is refining much that he has already mulled over in the 1802 *Lyrical Ballads* Appendix on Poetic Diction and his declaration that 'the taste, intellectual Power, and morals of a Country are linked in mutual dependence' only repeats the justification advanced in the Preface to *Lyrical Ballads* for the poems themselves. But something is new—the acuteness and the trenchancy of Wordsworth's critical demonstration through close reading. Phrases, lines, images are examined with passionate clarity in analysis which seems anything but an academic exercise. Wordsworth studies text as if awed by his recognition, as poet and critic, that 'Words are too awful an instrument for good and evil to be trifled with: they hold above all other external powers a dominion over thoughts'.

The second and third essays were not published in *The Friend*: it stopped without warning at number 27, 15 March 1810. Throughout the previous fifteen issues Wordsworth and Coleridge had been interacting once more, but the time was past when joint endeavour could transmute, or even suppress, personal friction. There had undoubtedly been some mutual benefit. Without Wordsworth's assistance the paper would have collapsed earlier. On the other hand, *The Friend* had served Wordsworth well. Coleridge had defended 'My heart leaps up' against Jeffrey, puffed *Cintra* lavishly, and by reprinting some of the sonnets and excerpting two long passages from *The Prelude* had kept his name and works before the subscribers.[117] The sad irony is, however, that, even as Coleridge was publicly lauding 'my honoured Friend William Wordsworth', the strain of creating a periodical, with this name of all possible names, precipitated the long-impending crisis and destroyed what remained of the Alfoxden friendship.

Before publication had even begun Wordsworth gave Poole his 'deliberate opinion' that

Coleridge neither will nor can execute any thing of important benefit either to himself his family or mankind. Neither his talents nor his genius mighty as they are nor his vast information will avail him anything; they are all frustrated by a derangement in his intellectual and moral constitution—In fact he has no voluntary power of mind whatsoever, nor is he capable of acting under *constraint* of duty or moral obligation.[118]

The cessation of *The Friend* confirmed the first part of this judgement and Coleridge's personal conduct, in the eyes of the Wordsworths, confirmed the rest. They came to think that he was exploiting Sara, and as she became thinner and evidently ill Dorothy exploded to Catherine Clarkson, 'do not think that it is his love for Sara which has stopped him in his work—do not believe it: his love for her is no more than a fanciful dream—otherwise he would prove it by a desire to make her happy. No! He likes to have her about him as his own, as one devoted to him, but when she stood in the way of other gratifications it was all over.'[119] In this bitter letter, which contrasts so appallingly with the anxious but caring entries of her 1802 journal, Dorothy leaves no doubt about her meaning: Coleridge is a 'slave of stimulants', a habitual self-deceiver and deceiver of others, and wholly self-absorbed. 'We have no hope of him', she wrote in April 1810. By November she had written him off: 'I am hopeless of him, and I dismiss him as much as possible from my thoughts'.[120]

(8)

It is sadly ironic that even as the disintegration of his relationship with Coleridge was nearing its critical moment, Wordsworth was at work once more on the project that had first cemented their friendship—*The Recluse*. He was spurred back to it by a number of impulses. From the start Coleridge's hopes for the poem had been based on what it could say to their particular generation. 'I wish you would write a poem', he had told Wordsworth in 1799, 'addressed to those, who, in consequence of the complete failure of the French Revolution, have thrown up all hopes of the amelioration of mankind . . . It would do great good . . .'.[121] Wordsworth had never stopped thinking on these matters and *The Convention of Cintra* had disclosed how much he had to say about politics, ideals, faith, and the necessity for a hope which is not ignorant optimism but the testimony of experience to the potential of human nature. But, as the fervour of many passages in *Cintra* had also revealed, thinking about politics now was not an exercise in abstract speculation. Wordsworth still recalled what he had felt at the dawn of the French Revolution and at the outbreak of the war and in meditating on the progress of speculative minds since then he was subjecting himself (and inevitably Coleridge too) to scrutiny. And in thinking about his own life, Wordsworth could not but confront the accusation implicit in most criticism of *Poems, in Two Volumes*, that by deliberate choice he had withdrawn from the mainstream flow of contemporary life and thought to a backwater where he had succumbed to his own fantasies.

*The Recluse* was always to justify Wordsworth's return to his native mountains, and it was now more than ever necessary that it should appear, as a massive refutation of Jeffrey and his ilk. But the poem had foundered. *Home at Grasmere* lay in manuscript, a magnificent introduction to nothing. The *Tuft of Primroses* and *To the Clouds* had petered out, revealing Wordsworth's deepest concerns, but yielding no way forward. Real thought—profound, considered, and fully articulated thought—was finding occasional form in *Cintra*, the *Essays upon Epitaphs*, even in the *Reply to 'Mathetes'*, but not in the impassioned music of blank verse. Wordsworth was blocked. His strategy for release was to return to the origins of *The Recluse* and to the poem of 1798 which had continued to vex him as a possibility not yet fully explored—*The Ruined Cottage*.

In its most recent revision the poem had been shaped to a satisfying completeness. But the quasi-dramatic form of the dialogue, in which the Pedlar, established as a full character, tutors the poet-listener in ways of understanding human suffering, offered possibilities for further extension and these Wordsworth now exploited in a simple but extraordinarily bold manœuvre. Margaret, whose suffering is the core of *The Ruined Cottage*, is dead before the poem's action begins. She lives only in the Pedlar's memory and in his narration of her story. Now Wordsworth imagines the Pedlar (renamed the Wanderer) and the poet encountering a living sufferer, who, like the poet, needs the benefit of the Wanderer's wisdom, but who, unlike him, is far from ready to accept it.[122] In other words, the dramatic potential of the form is enlarged to admit genuine challenge and question, not from a novice but from one whose view of life is grounded in bitter experience.

In this new character, the Solitary, Wordsworth embodies the dark potentialities of his own life. Disappointed in the revolutionary hopes for human regeneration, baffled in his search for truth, and betrayed by his trust in the unaided intellect, an egotist without a role, the Solitary has retired to a remote spot among the mountains, there to feed on his own despondency. He yearns for repose and speaks eloquently about his understanding of monks and hermits who sought peace

> Not as a refuge from distress or pain,
> A breathing-time, vacation, or a truce,
> But for its absolute self; a life of peace,
> Stability without regret or fear;
> That hath been, is, and shall be evermore![123]

But the Solitary's yearning is a deadly one, the obverse of what Wordsworth had celebrated in *Home at Grasmere*. He reads the surface of the earth but is open to nothing but confirmation of his own settled convictions.

He is, however, still capable of rapture, in spite of himself. When the three first meet, the Solitary tells of a visionary moment when through the mist the clouds had disclosed an imperial city:

> Clouds, mists, streams, watery rocks and emerald turf,
> Clouds of all tincture, rocks and sapphire sky,
> Confused, commingled, mutually inflamed,
> Molten together, and composing thus,
> Each lost in each, that marvellous array
> Of temple, palace, citadel, and huge
> Fantastic pomp of structure without name,
> In fleecy folds voluminous, enwrapp'd.[124]

And it is this imaginative potential that gives the Wanderer his opening. He treats the despondent recluse as one who has yielded to the atrophy of the very power that would give him renewal. There is, the Wanderer insists, 'one adequate support / For the calamities of mortal life' and one only, 'Faith absolute in God', but this faith is not to be taken from authority but won through the unceasing exercise of an awakened imagination, which, reading the signs of the natural world, breaks through to intimations of the imperishable beyond.[125]

Much of this verse is superb, but it is impossible to give any idea of its quality in brief quotation. Dense argument is expounded with astonishing syntactical resourcefulness over long and finely orchestrated periods, whose harmonies can only work on a reader totally involved in holding on to the sense over the long span. None of it was published until it became Books II to IV of *The Excursion* in 1814, nor is it clear that as he wrote it Wordsworth had a plan of the whole poem in mind. But its importance to him now cannot be overestimated. Much of the blank verse is as good as most of *The Prelude*—different in many ways, but as powerful. After a confused and rather barren period Wordsworth was writing at the top of his bent. He was, moreover, writing with confidence and command. The dialogues of the Wanderer and the Solitary repeatedly allude to his own earlier poetry—to *Ode to Duty*, the *Ode: Intimations of Immortality*, *Elegiac Stanzas . . . Peele Castle*, and to *The Prelude*. Verse from 1798, notably 'Not useless do I deem . . .', at last takes its place in a fully organized section of *The Recluse*.[126] And this retrospective reach is not in the least accidental. Wordsworth was articulating afresh his faith in the imagination and its powers, examining how far and in what ways he was still prepared to assert, in the words of *Tintern Abbey*, 1798:

> Therefore am I still
> A lover of the meadows and the woods,
> And mountains; and of all that we behold
> From this green earth; of all the mighty world
> Of eye and ear, both what they half-create,
> And what perceive; well pleased to recognize
> In nature and the language of the sense,
> The anchor of my purest thoughts, the nurse,
> The guide, the guardian of my heart, and soul
> Of all my moral being.

Keats later declared *The Excursion* one of the 'three things to rejoice at in this Age',[127] and it was to become eventually the poem which most often accompanied Victorian Lake District devotees who revered Wordsworth as sage and moral teacher. A pleasing symmetry can be perceived with hindsight in the fact that as he was writing these books, much the finest poetry of the whole, he was also engaged in the first version of what was to become the other volume of his most often packed in knapsacks, the *Guide to the Lakes*.

This important work came into being very uncertainly. In 1807 Wordsworth had thought of writing a guide, but in 1808 had emphatically told the Reverend J. Pering that in his one attempt 'an insuperable dullness' had overwhelmed him. Having passed his life among the lakes and mountains, he declared, 'I should be utterly at a loss were I about to set myself to a formal delineation of them . . . where to begin, and where to end'.[128] In June 1809, however, Joseph Wilkinson, Rector of East and West Wretham in Norfolk, asked Coleridge if he or Wordsworth would introduce a volume of his Lake District views. Wilkinson, who had lived not far from Greta Hall at Ormathwaite before moving to Norfolk, had much to recommend him. He was not a fashionable artist 'doing' the Lakes, but a talented amateur who drew from both love and real knowledge of the landscape in which he had lived. He was, moreover, an old acquaintance. Wordsworth hesitated, none the less. Tourists crowded the inns in summer, 'off-comers' were building houses, and metropolitan artistic interest in the area had quickened, but he clearly did not yet trust the market and feared that the projected *Select Views in Cumberland, Westmoreland, and Lancashire* would damage the livelihood of the Ambleside artist, his friend William Green.[129] Assured by Wilkinson that their work was quite unlike, and almost certainly attracted by a fee, Wordsworth eventually agreed and over the next year produced the letterpress to the forty-eight engravings.[130] It appeared anonymously—for what reason or on whose decision is not clear.

What is clear is that once he had started to write Wordsworth felt anything but 'an insuperable dullness'. He seized on the project as something of his own, paying almost no attention to the engravings or to what might have been expected by way of introduction to an elegant publication. This was, in fact, a book that had been waiting to be written and its time had come. Wordsworth had alluded in general terms to life among the mountains in the Preface to *Lyrical Ballads* and given glimpses of the customs, language, and hidden delights of the region in footnotes to his poems which (unknown to him) had been tantalizing enough to tempt at least one traveller towards the Duddon valley.[131] He had celebrated the landscape and its inhabitants in his poetry. Most important of all, he had read enough of the most influential topographical literature to know what he did not want to do. What he had to say was founded on intimate knowledge, on walking by day and night in all seasons and in all weathers throughout the Lakes. He was writing not as a connoisseur, but as a dweller. *Select Views* is a very rare book, but the reader should search for Wordsworth's contribution in its later independent form, called the *Guide to the Lakes*.[132] It is by far Wordsworth's most attractive and accessible prose and were it not for the utilitarian connotations of 'guide' it would be recognized more freely for what it is, a gem of Romantic writing.

In a very late poem Wordsworth affirmed a lifelong conviction:

> Vain is the glory of the sky,
> The beauty vain of field and grove,
> Unless, while with admiring eye
> We gaze, we also learn to love.[133]

That Wordsworth loves what he describes in *Select Views* is obvious in every word    he even manages to claim at one point that the rain in the Lake District, though heavy, is not like rain elsewhere. It does not dampen the spirits, but lifts them, as with the clouds and mists it continually transforms the landscape into new combinations of forms. He is particularly attentive to gradations of colour, especially those of autumn, and to the variety of natural formation. Both the distant and the near are relished—the mountain, 'a spirit incumbent upon the imagination', and the ripples along the lake shore. But *Select Views* is not just an evocation of natural delights. As Wordsworth accounts for the characteristic features of Lake District settlements, of the cottages and farms and walls and roads, he unfolds a vision of harmonious natural, economic, and human development, whose continuation, he claims, is now threatened by forces from without. Referring constantly to his own birth-date, 1770, as if it really marked the end of an era, Wordsworth laments the economic factors he is powerless to influence but fiercely decries the insensitive building and planting everywhere evident, which could be checked. The very people most likely to buy Wilkinson's engravings were subjected to a polemic against the insensitivity and greed of their kind.

In promoting this Burkean vision of an organic community, whose history is written in the dry-stone walls, whose spiritual centre is the parish church, the meeting-place of the living and the dead, Wordsworth was drawing together all of the convictions imaged in other ways in *Home at Grasmere*, *Michael*, *The Brothers*, *The Prelude*, and in his more recent work, *Cintra*, *Essays upon Epitaphs*, and the poetry towards *The Excursion*. That he did so now is significant in one further respect. Wordsworth had been labelled a 'Laker' by critics who signalled by this opprobrious term their scorn for his provincial fanaticism, with its attendant social, political, and poetical subversion. In *Select Views* Wordsworth reaffirmed his identity as a 'Laker', claiming the title as a blazon of honour.

(9)

Throughout the period in which Wordsworth was composing *Select Views* and the poetry towards *The Excursion* the whole family was hard pressed. Dorothy was as worried as ever about money, justifiably. They intended 'to give over drinking tea', she told Richard, 'and if possible, to take a house where coals are cheaper'. Coleridge's presence weighed on them. Dorothy complained that he lay in bed till midday, only came out of his room for meals, and then 'Sometimes . . . does not speak a word'.[134] In April 1810 Wordsworth's second daughter Catherine (born 1808) had a convulsive fit which left her temporarily paralysed on the right side. Mary was pregnant again and gave birth to her last child, named after his father, on 12 May. They all needed a change.

Their movements turned on Mary's confinement. At the beginning of May Coleridge left, to everyone's relief, for a lengthy stay once more at Greta Hall. The infant William was baptized on 24 June, with De Quincey and John Wilson standing as godfathers, and a week later Dorothy and Wordsworth departed for a visit to Coleorton. Mary had no change of scene, but being free of Coleridge and the others for a while must have been some relief. From Coleorton Wordsworth travelled to Hindwell in Radnorshire, where John Monkhouse and Tom Hutchinson were now farming, and there was reunited with Sara Hutchinson, who had been staying with her brother and cousin since March. Dorothy went in the other direction, first to Cambridge, where she made a pilgrimage to her brother's old college, and then on to Bury and much-loved Catherine Clarkson. Wordsworth returned to Allan Bank at the beginning of September, Dorothy a month later.

The summer ended with a poignant reminder of Alfoxden and a very different past. At the end of September 1810 Basil Montagu arrived, with his third wife, to sample the pleasures of the region which so evidently nourished his revered friend. Naturally they made contact with Coleridge, and sensing both the impermanence of the situation at Greta Hall and the inevitably of further decline if Coleridge remained cut off from the stimulus of London and purposeful activity, Montagu saw an opportunity to repay some of the kindnesses earlier shown to him by offering Coleridge a home. When Montagu set off for London on 18 October, Coleridge was with him.

For Wordsworth the years between Coleridge's return to England in 1806 and his final departure from the Lake District in 1810 had been Janus-faced. Professionally he had taken a check. The reception of *Poems, in Two Volumes* had been a blow, the withdrawal of *The White Doe of Rylstone* a defeat. But he had won through and could now foresee a day when critics would be confounded by the appearance of both a substantial part of *The Recluse* and a collection of his other poems organized on fresh principles. Poetically Wordsworth was silent, but not silenced. Domestically it had been a trying period. The foundation of Wordsworth's being, his marriage and family life, was absolutely steady. But the pressures upon it were considerable—money worries with five small children, the forced move from the cottage to smoky Allan Bank, the terrifying illnesses of John and Catherine, Dorothy's weariness and Sara's worrying symptoms, the erosion of his relationship with Coleridge. A severe attack of eye-disease—his second—raised the spectre of future blindness.[135] When the family waved Coleridge and the Montagus off, however, they had no premonition that the most pain-laden period of their lives so far was about to begin.

# 1810–1815

## (1)

'WE find that C is offended with William', Dorothy reported to Catherine Clarkson in May 1811. She would have chosen a stronger word than 'offended' if she had known that for months Coleridge had been frenzied by the certainty that Wordsworth had betrayed him, that his dearest friend had become his 'bitterest Calumniator'.[1]

Troubled that Montagu had no idea what he was taking on, Wordsworth had told him before he left Grasmere what living with Coleridge meant. In itself this was not disloyal. A man, Southey observed, ought to be free to speak to another about a mutual friend. But, as he also shrewdly observed, normal proprieties just did not apply to Coleridge and Montagu, when 'of the one almost every part of his conduct is matter of grief and shame, and the other is a cracked pitcher, spoiled in the making, and treacherous because of the flaw'.[2] On reaching London the cracked pitcher spilled out to Coleridge that he had been 'commissioned' by Wordsworth to say that he had no hope of him and that as a 'rotten drunkard', always running up bills at neighbouring pot-houses, he had been an 'absolute nuisance' at Allan Bank.[3]

Coleridge broke immediately with Montagu, but the 'never-closing, festering Wound of Wordsworth & his Family' tormented him.[4] That Wordsworth could have housed him while concealing the feelings he revealed to such a man as Montagu indicated to Coleridge that he must have been mistaken for years. Suppressed resentments and forgotten hurts surfaced as he reviewed his life, over lonely hours in a Covent Garden hotel. Everything began to coalesce—the Wordsworths' part in the quarrel with Lloyd and Lamb in 1798, their determination to shield Sara Hutchinson from the vexation of his love, Wordsworth's unfeeling behaviour over *The White Doe*, Dorothy's idolatry of her brother and his increasingly unattractive prudence, the damage still being done to his own poetic reputation because he was identified with the subversive theory and practice of *Lyrical Ballads*—and what emerged was the unbearable conviction that he had been 'Not *Loved* but one whose Love is what has given pleasure'.[5]

Writing in his notebook on 3 November 1810, at great length as if struggling to master intolerable pain before it drove him mad, Coleridge fixed his interpretation of the last fourteen years:

what many circumstances ought to have let me see long ago, the events of the last year, and emphatically of the last month, have now forced me to perceive.—No one on earth has ever LOVED me. Doubtless, the fault must have been partly, perhaps chiefly, in myself. The want of reliability in little things, the infliction of little pains, the trifling with hope, in short, all that render the idea of any person recall more pains than pleasures—these would account for the loss of Friendship—But that I never possessed in reality, but only that Semblance of Friendship, the being pleased with *my* Admiration & attachment—this I believe owing in part to my voluntary self-humiliation / My habitual abasement of myself & talents in comparison with the merits of my Friend.[6]

During his most desperate months in London the Allan Bank family knew nothing about Coleridge's suffering. When news of it reached them through his wife, however, his behaviour seemed as inexplicable to them as theirs did to him. To take Montagu's word without confronting Wordsworth and to write and gossip about the affair to others—could this really be Coleridge? Confident that they 'deserved no blame', Dorothy at first trusted that Coleridge's 'fancies will die away of themselves', but as the months passed without direct word from London she became increasingly bitter. She was no more proof against poisonous memories than Coleridge was and his stay at Coleorton and Allan Bank furnished her with many. By the following year she declared harshly that, to her at least, Coleridge's conduct 'proves what we have long been sure of that he is glad of a pretext to break with us, and to furnish himself with a ready excuse for all his failures in duty to himself and others'.[7] Dorothy was angry and partisan and made sure that their friends, especially Catherine Clarkson, were too. Wordsworth remained immovable. He would not justify himself to Coleridge until the grounds of his complaint were stated at first, not second, hand.

(2)

The quarrel pierced Coleridge 'with the suddenness of a Flash of Lightning'.[8] To Wordsworth it came rather as the breaking of a storm that had been long gathering. But its impact on him was just as great and the estrangement intensified the pressure on a life already under strain.

Professionally Wordsworth was in limbo. He had a coterie reputation only. Though to devotees such as Lady Beaumont or Catherine Clarkson his poetic stature was beyond question, to reviewers and the poetry-buying public the author of *Lyrical Ballads* and *Poems, in Two Volumes* was still a figure of fun, fair game for the parodist and satirist, beneath the notice of the cultivated.[9] Lord Chesterfield, Farington reported, had been induced by Sir George Beaumont to buy the 1807 collection, much to the surprise of his bookseller. 'I gave seven shillings & Six pence for it, & anybody shall have it for the odd Sixpence', was his Lordship's verdict.[10] Wordsworth's sense of poetic identity, however, rested not only on the published poems, but on the grand design, as yet incomplete and unknown to the public. And Coleridge was inseparable from that project. Wordsworth seems to have been unaware how ambivalent Coleridge's assessment of his lyric achievement was and astonishingly impercipient about how a fellow-poet might feel, when he had promised so much and written so little. Crabb Robinson supposed 'that there was in Coleridge's mind a lurking literary jealousy of [him]', but Wordsworth had to reject the notion utterly.[11] It cast too long a shadow over recent years to be entertained. But he was justified in continuing to believe that Coleridge looked to him for the creation of the first true philosophic poem in the language. *The Recluse* had been conceived with Coleridge and *The Prelude* addressed to him. The one part of the plan which was at last coming to completion—*The Excursion*—opened with the narrative Coleridge had listened to so eagerly under the trees at Racedown. A potential breach with him threatened to erase the closing lines of *The Prelude* and to obliterate a fixed point in Wordsworth's sense of himself as a poet with a mission still to be accomplished.

Domestically, too, Wordsworth was under stress. In May 1811 the family had left Allan Bank for the disused rectory opposite Grasmere Church, but the house turned out to be cold, very smoky, and so badly drained that in wet weather they had to struggle through a bog to reach it. Often only one room was habitable because of poor chimneys—'It really is deplorable', Sara Hutchinson remarked, 'to think how much of William's time has been stolen from him by these petty inconveniences'.[12] They all began to dream of long visits away, but the cost of travelling seemed unjustifiable in what Wordsworth called 'our present poverty'.[13] Money worries pressed on him particularly as the head of an extended and growing family. Four adults—Mary, Dorothy, Sara, and himself—and five children had to be provided for and ever-present was the realization that he would almost certainly have to take even more responsibility, possibly financial, for Coleridge's sons, Hartley and Derwent, who were now at school in Ambleside. The education of his own children was a real concern. John was a fine and upright boy, but, his aunt Dorothy lamented, 'certainly the worst scholar of his age that I ever knew', and little Dorothy—'sharp enough but . . . too unsteady'—was making unsatisfactory progress.[14] An ardent convert to Dr Andrew Bell's new system of education—the so-called 'Madras' method—Wordsworth even started teaching a few hours daily in the local school and further set an example by taking his turn in regular church-going, as Dorothy put it, 'for the sake of the children'.* The poet who had celebrated the wisdom of children in *Lyrical Ballads* and the power of parental love in *Michael* was becoming a family man.

The middle-aged Wordsworth is often thought of as aloof, egotistical, impregnable, somehow less human than the obviously vulnerable Coleridge. The image has truth, but it is not the whole truth. Wordsworth was confident in his powers, but profoundly anxious about his ability to reach an audience now. He was absorbed in his poetry, but he was constantly concerned about the well-being, the health, and education of his children. None of them, especially the lamed Catherine and the new baby William, lacked his attention, time, or love. In one aspect of his life, however, Wordsworth was completely secure. After nearly a decade of marriage he had come to rely completely on his wife and, more important, he knew it. The love-letters of public figures are always surprising, but none more so than those between Wordsworth and Mary not discovered till 1977. Revealing his gratitude, admiration, affection, and above all his continuing sexual passion for his wife, Wordsworth writes as if realizing for the first time just how wholly his life is grounded in hers. One moment is particularly revealing:

I love thee so deeply and tenderly and constantly, and with such perfect satisfaction delight & happiness to my soul, that I scarcely can bring my pen to write of any thing else.—How blest was I to hear of those sweet thoughts of me which had flowed along thy dreams; sleeping & waking my Love let me be with thee as thou art with me![15]

'Flowed along thy dreams' echoes the tribute to the Derwent at the opening of *The Prelude* and folds Mary into one image of all that has made his life 'blest'.

### (3)

The quarrel with Coleridge came to a crisis in 1812. In February, his winter lecture programme over, Coleridge travelled north to see his family. He

---

* DW to CC, 12 May [1810]. *MY*, I. 487. In Bell's system monitors were selected after instruction to instruct the younger pupils, thus amplifying the effective capacity of each teacher. W and C strongly supported the system—'Next to the art of Printing it is the noblest invention for the improvement of the human species', W called it (*MY*, II. 210)—and Bell himself in his controversy with Joseph Lancaster, a rival educational reformer. Hill and Moorman refer to W's 'obsession' with the Madras system (*MY*, II. 210, n. 3). It was an obsession, but an understandable one. W rightly perceived that the education of the masses in a rapidly industrializing country was bound to become a vital national issue. As R. J. White has pointed out, in supporting Bell rather than Lancaster W and C were encouraging the Church of England to take control. Lancaster was favoured by the Dissenters. See C's *Lay Sermons*, ed. R. J. White (London and Princeton, 1972), 40–1.

picked up his sons in Ambleside, but then, to their astonishment, insisted on hastening through Grasmere to Keswick without stopping, even though the road passed the Wordsworths' door. Soon learning that he had arrived home, Dorothy sent messages to Greta Hall, urging him to visit them, but they were unheeded, and by 28 March it was known that he had left again for London. Wordsworth clearly could not sense that Coleridge might be timorous, or that in coming so near and yet remaining apart he was obviously pleading for a gesture, some sign that he was still welcome in the old domestic circle. To him Coleridge's behaviour seemed a considered insult, and it was the last straw. He had been planning a trip to London since early in the year. Now he acted and by late April was there, fired with '*determination* to confront Coleridge and Montagu upon this vile business'.[16]

Wordsworth's resolution was strengthened when Richard Sharp astonishingly showed him Coleridge's declaration that his recent visit to Keswick had confirmed beyond doubt that Wordsworth had become his 'bitterest Calumniator'.[17] That Coleridge was still writing this sort of letter some eighteen months after the event certainly explains Wordsworth's anger and why once he had got to London he would not let go. The truth would be reached, he thought, if Coleridge and Montagu would meet him in the presence of an arbitrator, say Josiah Wedgwood. Of course Coleridge refused to attend any such quasi-judicial tribunal, indeed, any meeting that included Montagu. The kindly and highly intelligent Henry Crabb Robinson began to act as go-between and, after a good deal of diplomatic point-scoring and manœuvring, Wordsworth was induced to send, and Coleridge to accept, a solemn denial that he had 'commissioned' Montagu to say anything whatever to Coleridge, and that though in 'some of the particulars enumerated by C. as having wounded his feelings there is something of the *form* of truth there is *absolutely nothing of the Spirit* in any of them'.[18]

The wound was healed, at least superficially, because both men chose that it should be. Wordsworth's defence was in part that he had been misreported—that it was 'morally impossible' that he could have used such an expression as 'rotten drunkard'—but he could not deny that he had warned Montagu against Coleridge, and whether the words 'absolute nuisance' were used or not, something had been said to give rise to their currency, and Coleridge knew it. But he, too, was prepared to be reconciled and Wordsworth's written statement enabled him to retain his dignity. Coleridge had been hurt, none the less, beyond mending. A year later he assured Poole that his feeling for Wordsworth could never return and in the years to come, despite some restoration of intimacy, he continued to speak of the breach as one of the greatest sorrows of his life.[19]

For the moment the bitter words fell silent and Wordsworth threw himself into London society. Like any husband on the loose in the city he reported back to his wife that parties were often tiresome, that the price of a haircut was outrageous, and that it was unfortunate he needed some new clothes, but the truth was that he was enjoying himself immensely. He was not a newcomer to London and now, though their fashionable address had earlier eased his entry into political and social circles, he was no longer regarded simply as the Beaumonts' protégé. He met again Rogers, Constable, Wilkie, Uvedale Price, Davy, lawyers, politicians, fringe literary figures, painters, possibly Haydon, certainly Washington Allston, some of Crabb Robinson's acquaintance, aristocrats and gentry, and, at the top of the tree, Lord Lonsdale, 'with a Star upon his breast and the Garter round his knee', and even Princess Caroline, wife of the Prince Regent.[20] On the night of 11 May Wordsworth was invited to one of Rogers's celebrated parties. In the hall he was met by the 22-year-old Byron—'a man', Wordsworth told Mary, 'who is now the rage in London, in consequence of his Late Poem Childe Haroldes pilgrimage'—who passed on the electrifying message that the Prime Minister, Spencer Perceval, had just been assassinated in the House of Commons.[21] To hear such news, so quickly, in such a way, and at such a place—Wordsworth knew that he was at the quick of national life.

Before a month was out his pleasure in being there was abruptly changed into anguish and unwarranted but entirely natural guilt. Over the night of 3–4 June 1812, after renewed convulsions, Catherine Wordsworth died. She was not yet 4, and what made it worse for her parents was that neither of them was by her side, either at her dying or her burial. Being in London Wordsworth had learned of Perceval's murder within hours, but, being still farther away from Grasmere on a visit to Christopher at Bocking in Essex, he did not even hear of the death of his own daughter until a week later, and by that time she was already lying in Grasmere churchyard. Mary was at Hindwell for a long visit, happily keeping in touch with Grasmere gossip through a triangular correspondence with her husband and sister-in-law. When he finally reached her, Wordsworth saw at once that being far away at the death of 'this beloved child endeared to her by such long and tender anxieties of maternal care and love' had intensified her grief with self-reproach.[22]

Wordsworth and Mary got through the summer, visiting and entertaining. On 1 December Thomas, their third child, died of measles and was buried alongside his sister. He was $6\frac{1}{2}$ years old.

The immediate effect of these blows registered visibly enough. Dorothy was convinced, probably rightly, that, after Thomas's death, only the exertion needed to save the other children, who also contracted the disease, kept Mary from total collapse. As it was she sank into deep depression, becoming thin, weary, and prey to uncontrollable fits of weeping. Publicly Wordsworth retained self-control—after Catherine's death his behaviour compared to De Quincey's was, according to Crabb Robinson, 'that which became a man both of feeling and strength of mind'.* The same words might also be applied to *Surprized by Joy*, the touching sonnet he wrote a year or so later about the loss of his 'heart's best treasure'. Wordsworth's private confession to Southey in December, however, movingly suggests a man only just in control and very much aware of his vulnerability: 'For myself dear Southey I dare not say in what state of mind I am; I loved the Boy with the utmost love of which my soul is capable, and he is taken from me—yet in the agony of my spirit in surrendering such a treasure I feel a thousand times richer than if I had never possessed it . . . O Southey feel for me!'[23]

The more penetrating impact of these shocks continued to register, deeply, for the rest of his life. In 1813 Wordsworth returned to the manuscripts of *The Excursion* and revised the Solitary's autobiographical narrative, pouring out, but through the dramatic voice, his sense of the enormity of the trial to which he had been subjected.[24] After the loss of all he has loved, the Solitary has retreated to the mountains to live a not-unhappy but minimalist existence, not trusting, not hoping, cautious of all feeling. Pain, disillusion, and fear have defeated him. In dramatizing this character Wordsworth identified the forces he knew he had to withstand, but like the Solitary he lived with an unfading sense of loss. Nearly forty years later he described to Aubrey De Vere the 'details of their illnesses with an exactness and impetuosity of troubled excitement, such as might have been expected if the bereavement had taken place but a few weeks before'.[25] Faced with the inexplicable, Dorothy trusted to the most familiar of Christian consolations: 'there is no comfort but in the firm belief that what God wills is best for all of us—though we are too blind to see in what way it is best', 'may we all . . . trust that our sufferings in this world are given to us in order that we may be perfected in a better world'.[26] Wordsworth returned to *The Excursion*, determined to complete this one section of his

---

* *HCR: Books*, 103. He records that 'Mr. De Quincey burst into tears on seeing Wordsworth and seemed to be more affected than the father'. De Quincy was distraught and in a letter to DW [13–15 June 1812] wrote open-heartedly about his love for Catherine: 'Many a time, when we were alone, she would put her sweet arms about my neck and kiss me with a transport that was even then quite affecting to me. Nobody can judge from her manner to me before others what love she shewed to me when we were playing or talking together alone.' Tactlessly he sought to identify himself as one of the family—as one of the three 'who doated so passionately upon her—her mother, her father, and I . . .'. *DQL*, 264–7. In Grasmere he repeatedly (according to his own account) 'passed the night upon her grave'. *Lindop*, 199–202 speculates perceptively about the 'element of hysteria in his sorrow' and its effect on the Wordsworths.

philosophic poem and in 1814 was able to issue his most evidently religious poem so far. It was rightly seen by some, however, as an uncertain and troubled work, for what Wordsworth offered—and continued to offer—was not a *confessio fidei* but an exploration of faith.

## (4)

In 1813 Wordsworth was under pressure from three connected demands: that he should save his wife's health; that he should, somehow, gain more money; that he should establish his reputation by published work, which would decisively refute the *Edinburgh Review's* most recent goading observations that he ought to be 'ashamed' of most of *Poems, in Two Volumes* and that Crabbe was 'the most original writer' of the age.[27]

What Mary needed immediately was clear. The shock of losing her children had stunned her, but the sight of their graves just across the road from her own front door threatened to push her into long-term decline. Thomas had tripped every day through the churchyard to school and now he was buried where he used to play with his friends. The family had to quit that house. After abortive negotiation about buying another Grasmere property, they eventually moved in May 1813 to Rydal Mount, a house recently acquired by Lady le Fleming of neighbouring Rydal Hall.[28]

It was, at last, a move that did not disappoint them. Substantial, well drained, comfortable, and situated on a hillside beneath a rock outcrop called Nab Scar, Rydal Mount could not have contrasted more pleasingly with the Rectory: '. . . surely this is the most beautiful and gay place you ever beheld', Sara enthused to her London-based cousin Thomas Monkhouse. 'I wish you could at this moment behold the splendor of Winandermere which lies before my eyes illuminated by the setting sun . . .'.[29] The actual inconvenience of moving, the cleaning, rehanging curtains, unpacking, and sorting, was just the distraction Mary and Dorothy needed. They fitted out the house from local auctions, benefiting as much from the excitement of bidding as from the purchases, and even plumped, for the first time in their lives, for 'a *Turkey*!!! carpet—in the dining-room, and a Brussels in William's study'. Though they were not, Dorothy assured Catherine Clarkson, 'setting up for fine Folks', they felt entitled to a little more comfort and were determined to make this place a real home.[30]

Dorothy's tone was jauntier than it had been because it looked as though their money worries were easing. Early in 1812 they had been so pinched that Wordsworth was forced to apply to Lord Lonsdale. Touching on his vocation, his independence from literary faction, and the connection between their two families, he did not whine in his letter of 6 February, but it was a begging letter none the less and Wordsworth must have hated writing it, especially if any memory flashed into his mind of how Calvert had pressed money on him so that he could be free to follow his genius. No office was immediately available, but in the summer, after getting confirmation of his financial difficulties from Rogers and Sir George Beaumont, Lonsdale generously offered Wordsworth £100 per year until a salaried post might come free. Grateful, yet reluctant, Wordsworth accepted because he really had no choice, but was very relieved when only two months later Lonsdale was able to offer him a proper job. By the end of April 1813 he had committed himself, through signing bonds and pledging sureties, to the honest conduct of his office: he was now Distributor of Stamps for Westmorland and the Penrith area of Cumberland, responsible for the distribution of and accounting for returns from the taxed, stamped paper used in legal transactions. Wordsworth became an agent of the national revenue-gathering service.

Was this defeat, a self-betraying compromise? Perhaps so. Certainly no act of Wordsworth's did his reputation more lasting harm. But these terms bear reconsideration. At the end of the decade Byron voiced the dismay of all the younger Romantics when he sneered at Wordsworth for making himself agreeable 'at dinner at Lord Lonsdale's'.[31] The poet of *Tintern Abbey*, it seemed, had become a Tory hireling. And Byron was certainly right to link the money and the politics. Had he known about *A Letter to the Bishop of Llandaff*, Lord Lonsdale would not have recommended its author for a government office. Nor would Wordsworth have proved himself so very willing to serve the noble lord and his interest in the next few years had he not felt extremely grateful to the man who, having honourably amended the wrong done to the father, was now favouring the son with striking evidence of friendship and respect.

But though Byron was right, from his point of view, the young Browning was not right enough. The opening to *The Lost Leader* is all too memorable:

> Just for a handful of silver he left us,
> Just for a riband to stick in his coat—[32]

but it is a vicious libel on Wordsworth in a way that Byron's comments are not. For Wordsworth's allegiance was not bought. He took the handful of silver because working for it seemed an honourable way of meeting both the claims of his poetic vocation and the needs of his family. Only someone much more Romantic than Wordsworth, or much more selfish, or more used to having money, would claim that the call of Art was inherently more important than the needs of his family.

What seems so striking in retrospect is that it was just a *handful* of silver. Wordsworth was too much the son of his father to treat his new responsibility lightly. He worried about procedures, rooted out inefficiency amongst sub-distributors, and worked much more conscientiously than he might have done. The Wordsworths' friend, Mrs Harden of Brathay Hall, had reckoned in 1806 that it was impossible to 'live at all comfortably in this country . . . under £1000 a year'.[33] Walter Scott would have agreed. Wordsworth and Southey mixed on equal terms with such people, but they could not afford, literally not afford, to adopt their standards. When the Border Minstrel declined the offer of the Laureateship in 1813, Southey accepted it, not only for the honour but for the paltry £90 a year that came with it. Wordsworth at first expected £400 a year from his Distributorship, but in practice it brought in much less and the 22 guineas for the Turkey carpet always did seem an extravagance.[34]

## (5)

It would be easy to over-dramatize these years, to play too strong a light on the farewell to Grasmere or on the acceptance of a salaried office. Facing up to possible necessity, Wordsworth told Daniel Stuart that he was ready to 'quit this part of the Country, provided the salary be adequate . . .' and that certainly would have been a significant move.[35] But Rydal Mount was only just down the road from Grasmere, connected to it by the line of Loughrigg Fell, by the Rothay flowing between the two lakes, and by a beautiful path which passes behind Rydal Mount and eventually joins a lane above the cottage at Town End. It was not for the first time that Wordsworth was associating with his social superiors, nor did he suddenly become wealthy or fêted. There was even a slight but pleasing connection between their new house and life and Wordsworth's past. Ann Tyson, his Hawkshead mother, had been in service to the wife of an earlier owner of Rydal Mount, Michael Knott, who had himself been a Distributor of Stamps.

None the less 1813–15 was a watershed as 1799–1800 had been. The move to Rydal Mount marked the beginning of a new phase of domestic life in which the family's pain over the breach with Coleridge and the loss of the children, even their most pressing worries about money, were eased. And on the base of domestic stability Wordsworth once more took the initiative in shaping his life as a writer, completing his major work, and arranging for various publications that would draw together the creative achievement of twenty years.

The clearest sign of renewed confidence was that in 1814 Wordsworth and Mary found both the time and the money for the kind of holiday she had been longing for. The old jaunting-car was overhauled and on 18 July 1814 Wordsworth, Mary, and Sara, escorted by John on a pony, set off north. To Wordsworth Scotland was, he had told Scott, 'the most poetical Country I ever travelled in' and this time he determined to push farther into it.[36] Following a straightforward clockwise route through Moffat, Glasgow,

Stirling, and Inverary, they reached Inverness on 14 August before turning southwards. Ten days later they were in Edinburgh. Here they spent a lot of time with John Wilson's mother in Queen Street and according to Sara met 'all the *wits* who were in town'. But even if the fine weather had not lured them into the country, Wordsworth would not have met them *all*. This was the citadel of the enemy and its wits ran the *Edinburgh Review*. He did, however, make one long-standing friend in Robert Pearce Gillies, a young literary aspirant whose admiration for Wordsworth's poetry immediately became veneration when he met the poet.[37]

On 1 September at Traquair, south of Edinburgh, they were joined by Dr Robert Anderson, compiler of the *British Poets* volumes which Wordsworth valued so highly, and by James Hogg, the 'Ettrick Shepherd', best known now for his powerful, dark novel, *The Private Memoirs and Confessions of a Justified Sinner* (1824), who guided them on a tour of the Yarrow.[38] Wordsworth was deeply stirred and at once began to draft *Yarrow Visited*. In 1803 he had delighted in suggesting in *Yarrow Unvisited* (published in 1807) that beauty left unseen retained a greater hold on the imagination. Now he saw the Yarrow and, revisiting his earlier poem, composed a sequel which celebrates the actual beauty of the place while recognizing how much its power to move depends on literary associations and the mind's play. It is not a joyous poem—Lamb rightly sensed its 'melancholy of imperfect satisfaction'—but it is amongst the most assured of the lyrics Wordsworth was able to add to his *Poems* (1815).[39]

Leaving the Yarrow they pushed on to Scott's home at Abbotsford. Scott himself was away, but his wife and daughter welcomed them with a warmth that Wordsworth never forgot.[40] On 9 September they arrived home.

The holiday in Scotland was the most immediate sign of the Wordsworths' more hopeful situation. The profounder significance, however, of the move to Rydal Mount cannot be identified by reference to any one event. Over the years both the place and the idea of Rydal Mount attracted a powerful cluster of feelings in all of the family, who cherished the house, the garden, and its atmosphere as a habitable domain. When it looked as if the lease would not be renewed in 1825–6, Wordsworth panicked, took emergency action, wrote about his plight, and mobilized influence. In view of his long tenure as the Sage of Rydal Mount his fluttering might look silly, but it was quite understandable. To lose Rydal Mount would have been to lose not just a house but a spot entwined with the reconstruction of their lives.

At Rydal Mount they restored in many ways the existence they had enjoyed in the cottage at Town End, relegating Allan Bank and the rectory to bad memories. They were comfortable in the house and it became, as the cottage had been, a domestic lodestone for friends, relatives, and the next generation of children—not a shrine but a home. As before at the cottage they worked hard to shape a garden, but this time they enjoyed a sense of historical continuity, as they planted and dug, designed and planned, where others had before them.[41] What they created had many uses, being big enough to allow one a little privacy, another some exercise along one of the terraces, but its emblematic significance was at least as important. In exploiting the levels of the hillside and both the near and the distant prospect, the garden was a re-declaration of what the smaller one at Town End had intimated—that this family was firmly, rootedly, there, but working with, not in the face of, the natural environment.

In an important respect, however, life at Rydal Mount was not a knitting together of what Allan Bank and the rectory had severed, but a regrouping and reshaping, almost, but not quite, a fresh start. The deaths of the children, and Mary's decline, following so fast on the break with Coleridge, had destabilized even Wordsworth's sense of domestic security and in the coming years he sought to re-establish it. Inevitably this meant, in personal terms, some reassessment of old friendships and a cautious fostering of the new.

The opportunity to complete one movement in his life presented itself with perfect timing. In 1812 the Wordsworth family had regained contact with Annette and Caroline in France. They learned much about their present situation from letters, but more from an unexpected source. A prisoner-of-war, Eustace Baudouin, contacted Wordsworth, having got his name from his brother Jean-Baptiste, who hoped to marry Caroline. With characteristic generosity and rectitude, Mary at once included her husband's first child in her anxieties about all of his family, hoping that 'something handsome' could be done for 'dear Caroline' if ever they were better off.[42] In 1816 Mary's wish was realized when Wordsworth settled £30 a year on Caroline at her marriage, a generous sum which continued until 1835, when it was ended with a capital settlement. But this was not a cold, merely financial gesture. The wedding had been planned for 1814 and Caroline and Annette were 'extremely anxious' that Dorothy at least should be there.[43] She was quite as keen, but Napoleon's escape from Elba halted all such plans. After Waterloo there was talk of Caroline travelling to London and though nothing came of it, the wedding taking place without Wordsworth or Dorothy in February 1816, it was clear that both families remained linked by genuine affection and concern. Mary's 'God bless her [Caroline] I should love her dearly & divide my last with her were it needful' was sincere.[44]

Caroline's marriage brought out the best in the Wordsworths. Awakening affectionate memories it enabled them all to feel a sense of rightness in this harmonious completion to what had begun so unpromisingly. De Quincey's marriage, in contrast, brought out the very worst, revealing just how raw-edged and prickly the adult Wordsworths could now be, if they sensed, however subliminally, that disorder threatened.

In November 1816 Margaret Simpson of the Nab, a farm between Grasmere and Rydal, gave birth to a son. She did not marry his father, De Quincey, until the following February. Clearly seeing no comparison with her own brother's youthful conduct, Dorothy sneered both at De Quincey's passion and its object, declaring—quite wrongly—that this 'stupid, heavy girl' would ruin him.[45] Wordsworth, too, was genuinely shocked at De Quincey's marrying beneath him, as he had been when his brother Richard had married his servant in 1814. Though Wordsworth had to admit that his sister-in-law was a 'very decent and comely person', he remained obdurate that such a connection was a 'disgrace'.[46]

These moral and social lapses precipitated the subsequent estrangement between the Wordsworths and De Quincey but they would not have done so had the baby and the marriage not confirmed fears about their one-time intimate which they were quite unable to cope with. For all his learning and intelligence, De Quincey seemed to be doing nothing very much. Moreover he procrastinated and could not be trusted to perform what he promised, despite the lavishness of the affection he displayed.[47] He was becoming addicted to opium and now had pursued gratification to the point of bringing into the world a child which it was not clear he could support. In short, De Quincey was beginning to resemble Coleridge. Tied to them as he was by the strongest feelings, even Coleridge had exhausted their readiness to be supportive and sympathetic. Now De Quincey seemed to be disintegrating in a Coleridgean fashion and they were not prepared a second time to become involved. Gradually he was pushed away.

(6)

When a number of equally important but very different events take place over the same period of time any narrative account risks separating what only existed in conjunction and assigning priorities to factors of equal weight. Was Mary's health more important to Wordsworth than completing *The Excursion*? Was the noise of his children invading the silence of his inner landscapes? It is difficult to assign priorities in anyone's spiritual, intellectual, and domestic life and especially so with Wordsworth, in whom an exalted sense of his poetic vocation was countered by an equally exalted sense of his duties as husband, brother, and parent. But there can be no doubt that amidst all the other pressures in the years 1812–15 what mattered intensely to him was the redeeming of his reputation.

Ever since his review of *Poems, in Two Volumes* Jeffrey had continued to snipe. The 'great captain' of the 'company of the lake poets' was in hiding, but he could still be got at and Jeffrey missed no opportunity.[48] Side-swipes in his article on Wilson's *The Isle of Palms* in 1812, for example, had been particularly vicious. The 'prosperity of Scott, or Campbell, or Crabbe', it had been pointed out, had not been won by 'ecstasies about spades or sparrows' eggs—or men gathering leeches—or women in duffle cloaks—or plates and porringers—or washing tubs'.[49] This was always the theme—that the lyrics of 1807 were ludicrous and that they epitomized Wordsworth. But even as Jeffrey was reopening the wounds, his victim was preparing an overwhelming rejoinder. By 1814 he was ready.

Wordsworth planned a two-pronged attack with an immediate follow-through. *The Excursion* had been completed over 1813–14. Another character, 'The Pastor', had been introduced but the loose dramatic structure had been retained in which each one—Wanderer, Solitary, Pastor, and poet—contributes from his own experience to a debate on major issues, such as public and private morality, rural and urban-industrial poverty, education. The Wanderer concludes with a reaffirmation of his faith in 'An active principle' in the universe, whose noblest seat is the human soul, but the poems ends with the friends promising to meet again for further discussion and the poet promising 'future Labours' in similar vein.[50]

This poem, in bulk if nothing else evidently a substantial work, was to be prefaced by an explanation of Wordsworth's further plans for *The Recluse* and of how this philosophical project was related to his other poems. Thus prepared, the reader was then to buy two more volumes which would include excerpts from the 1793 poems, the lyrical ballads, the lyrics published in 1807 onwards, and very recent work such as *Yarrow Visited* and *Laodamia*. But this was not to be a merely miscellaneous collection. The poems were grouped according to a classification Wordsworth had been pondering since 1809—'Poems of the Imagination', 'Poems Founded on the Affections', 'Poems of the Fancy', 'Poems Proceeding from Sentiment and Reflection', and more—which, drawing the whole *œuvre* together, was to demonstrate how the lyrical poems 'might be regarded . . . as composing an entire work within themselves, and as adjuncts to the philosophical Poem, "The Recluse"'.[51] These interdependent publications were to be followed by further evidence of Wordsworth's powers, the expanded *White Doe of Rylstone* and possibly even the other long narratives *Peter Bell* and *Benjamin the Waggoner*.

The versatility and power of Wordsworth's imagination were to be amply demonstrated. Even as books the volumes were meant to have an impact. *The Excursion* was a beautifully printed large quarto of 447 pages, prefaced by a dedicatory sonnet 'To The Right Honourable William, Earl of

Lonsdale, K.G. &c &c.' and a six-page summary of the contents of each of
the poem's nine books. After the text came six pages of notes and a sixteen-
page *Essay upon Epitaphs* accompanied by notes. *Poems by William
Wordsworth: Including Lyrical Ballads, and the Miscellaneous Pieces of the
Author* was dedicated, over three fulsome pages, to 'Sir George Howland
Beaumont, Bart.', each volume having a frontispiece engraving of Beau-
mont's pictures of the scene of *Lucy Gray* and *Peele Castle*. *The White Doe of
Rylstone* was equally grand, a generously spaced large quarto, prefaced by an
engraving of Beaumont's painting of Bolton Priory and an eight-stanza
Spenserian tribute to Mary, addressed by name as the poet's 'Beloved Wife!'
Purchasers—and Wordsworth eagerly expected sales—did not need to read
the poems to discern that their author thought of himself as in the line of
Spenser and Milton and that he was a friend of the great and the cultivated.

All aspects of this publishing venture were bold—the quantity of verse,
the timing of the publications, the format—but possibly the most important
was the Preface to *The Excursion*. Here, at last, Wordsworth revealed to the
public at large the grandeur of his self-conception. This poem, he declared,
was the philosophical first-fruits of a dedicated life and the harbinger of
more to come. Having retired to his native mountains 'with the hope of
being enabled to construct a literary Work that might live', he had
conducted a preliminary enquiry into his own powers (*The Prelude* at last
acknowledged), which had given rise 'to a determination to compose a
philosophical Poem, containing views of Man, Nature, and Society; and to
be entitled, The Recluse'. Transposing the actual chronology of *The Recluse*
and *The Prelude*, Wordsworth presents his life's work as proceeding to plan,
as a 'gothic Church' might slowly rise, the autobiographical poem being 'the
Anti-chapel' and the minor pieces 'little Cells, Oratories, and sepulchral
Recesses'. When completed, *The Recluse* would have three parts, whose
design and scope is suggested in the great 'Prospectus' with which the
Preface ends, where Wordsworth invokes Milton to assist him define his
own territory and the sources of his strength:

> . . . 'fit audience let me find though few!'
> So prayed, more gaining than he asked, the Bard,
> Holiest of Men.—Urania, I shall need
> Thy guidance, or a greater Muse, if such
> Descend to earth or dwell in highest heaven!
> For I must tread on shadowy ground, must sink
> Deep—and, aloft ascending, breathe in worlds
> To which the heaven of heavens is but a veil.
> All strength—all terror, single or in bands,
> That ever was put forth in personal form;
> Jehovah—with his thunder, and the choir

Of shouting Angels, and the empyreal thrones,
I pass them, unalarmed. Not Chaos, not
The darkest pit of lowest Erebus,
Nor aught of blinder vacancy—scooped out
By help of dreams, can breed such fear and awe
As fall upon us often when we look
Into our Minds, into the Mind of Man,
My haunt, and the main region of my Song.
—Beauty—a living Presence of the earth,
Surpassing the most fair ideal Forms
Which craft of delicate Spirits hath composed
From earth's materials—waits upon my steps;
Pitches her tents before me as I move,
An hourly neighbour. Paradise, and groves
Elysian, Fortunate Fields—like those of old
Sought in the Atlantic Main, why should they be
A history only of departed things,
Or a mere fiction of what never was?
For the discerning intellect of Man,
When wedded to this goodly universe
In love and holy passion, shall find these
A simple produce of the common day.
—I, long before the blissful hour arrives,
Would chaunt, in lonely peace, the spousal verse
Of this great consummation:—and, by words
Which speak of nothing more than what we are,
Would I arouse the sensual from their sleep
Of Death, and win the vacant and the vain
To noble raptures; while my voice proclaims
How exquisitely the individual Mind
(And the progressive powers perhaps no less
Of the whole species) to the external World
Is fitted:—and how exquisitely, too,
Theme this but little heard of among Men,
The external World is fitted to the Mind;
And the creation (by no lower name
Can it be called) which they with blended might
Accomplish:—this is our high argument.[52]

In this incalculably important Preface Wordsworth was doing many
things. He was keeping faith both with himself and Coleridge as they were at
Alfoxden, when *The Recluse* was first conceived, and with the sense of
blessedness he had celebrated in *Home at Grasmere*, from which these lines
are drawn. He was declaring that the 'Poet living in retirement' was not in
retreat from the world but engaged with it at the profoundest level. He was

affirming that all of his published work, the *Lyrical Ballads* and the despised lyrics of *Poems, in Two Volumes*, was part of an edifice whose significance was only now coming into view. It was a poet's manifesto and a prophet's utterance, the most important revelation of himself that Wordsworth was ever to publish. But it, and the volumes it introduced, failed in the short term to achieve any of his aims.

The *Excursion* was published in August 1814 in an edition of 500 copies. Reviewing it at once for Leigh Hunt's *Examiner*, Hazlitt too invoked Milton to suggest the nature of Wordsworth's art: 'He may be said to create his own materials; his thoughts are his real subject. His imagination broods over that which is "without form and void" and "makes it pregnant".' But his power, Hazlitt asserts, is at odds with the supposedly dramatic structure of the poem, for

the evident scope and tendency of Mr. Wordsworth's mind is the reverse of dramatic. It resists all change of character, all variety of scenery, all the bustle, machinery, and pantomime of the stage, or of real life,—whatever might relieve or relax or change the direction of its own activity, jealous of all competition. The power of his mind preys upon itself. It is as if there were nothing but himself and the universe. He lives in the busy solitude of his own heart; in the deep silence of thought.*

Hazlitt's characterization of Wordsworth's imagination was the most intelligent and perceptive criticism he had ever received, but the review rankled, partly because of its lament for the poet's failure to deal justly with the French Revolution, 'that bright dream of our youth; that glad dawn of the day-star of liberty', partly because of Hazlitt's petulant assertion that 'All country people hate each other', but most of all, perhaps, because praise of Wordsworth's 'refined and contemplative mind' was not likely to incite people to rush out to buy the book.[53] And Wordsworth was very anxious that he should, at last, reach a wide audience. Dorothy delighted in the news that the Duke of Devonshire had taken the poem on his travels and wished her brother to cultivate the good opinion of more eminent persons 'that they

---

* 'Character of Mr. Wordsworth's New Poem, *The Excursion*', *The Examiner*, 21 Aug., 28 Aug., 2 Oct. 1814. *Howe*, XIX. 10–11. The Wordsworth circle fostered the belief that Hazlitt was motivated by personal animosity born of embarrassment and shame. Something clearly happened to hasten Hazlitt's departure from the Lakes in 1803. In Jan. 1814 Southey claimed he helped him 'escape from Cumberland' (*Curry*, II. 93) and in Oct. MW alludes knowingly to DW about some affair (*MWL*, 24). But it is impossible to know what happened. Eleven years after the event the story had developed that Hazlitt had been helped to escape from enraged villagers after sexually assaulting a local girl, but the evidence is so flimsy that it is not worth repeating again at length here. Michael Foot has judiciously examined it in 'Hazlitt's Revenge on the Lakers', *Wordsworth Circle*, 14 (Winter 1983), 61–8. What is clear is that by 1814 all the Wordsworth circle believed that Hazlitt had behaved disgracefully in some sexual way and that what ought to have been gratitude had turned to spite.

may *talk* against the Writers [i.e. reviewers]',[54] and Wordsworth, too, comforted himself with commendations from high quarters—the Bishop of London's opinion, for example, transmitted by Sir George Beaumont. But he was realistic enough to recognize that unless this first edition sold quickly, a cheaper second edition would not be called for and his poem would founder, just an elegant acquisition for the libraries of the wealthy. What he needed was another major review.

It appeared in December. 'This will never do'—so began Jeffrey's article in the *Edinburgh Review*, an unforgettable opening to the most devastating critique Wordsworth was ever to suffer.[55] It is devastating because it is weighty, lucid, and in its own terms coherent. Jeffrey is so completely unsympathetic to Wordsworth that he is incapable of leaps of insight, those empathic identifications which make Hazlitt a critic of real power, but what he has to say against *The Excursion* is not self-evidently wrong, or cheap, or merely malicious. Much of it is very engaging, such as his mock-alarm, based on a clever misreading of the Preface, at the promise of more quartos of similar length, or his common-man's refusal to treat the Pedlar as a poetic fiction: 'A man who went about selling flannel and pocket-handkerchiefs in this lofty diction, would soon frighten away all his customers'.* But even the humour is controlled by a severe purpose. Jeffrey scorns Wordsworth's account of his dedicated life because he sees it as the desperate self-advertisement of a man who cannot now give up a doomed concern in which he has sunk so much capital. Once again he asserts that only a self-intoxicated recluse could continue to worship 'at the shrine of those paltry idols which he has set up for himself among his lakes and mountains', a lunatic entranced by 'the mystical verbiage of the methodist pulpit' into believing 'that he is the elected organ of divine truth and persuasion'. For the fact is, Jeffrey concludes, that the poem's message is a very commonplace one, but presented unintelligibly as a kind of 'mystical morality'.

What he can praise he does—notably the pathos of the story of Margaret in Book I[56]—but even his praise condemns, for he suggests that such evidence of poetic power can only make one resent all the more Wordsworth's 'perversion' of his talents, a perversion that must be ascribed

---

* Jeffrey on the Preface: 'What Mr Wordsworth's ideas of length are, we have no means of accurately judging; but we cannot help suspecting that they are liberal, to a degree that will alarm the weakness of most modern readers. As far as we can gather from the preface, the entire poem—or one of them, for we really are not sure whether there is to be one or two—is of a biographical nature; and is to contain the history of the author's mind, and of the origin and progress of his poetical powers, up to the period when they were sufficiently matured to qualify him for the great work on which he has been so long employed. Now, the quarto before us contains an account of one of his youthful rambles in the vales of Cumberland, and occupies precisely the period of three days; so that, by the use of a very powerful *calculus*, some estimate may be formed of the probable extent of the entire biography.'

to his own ludicrous 'system' and his incorrigible yearning for singularity. This poet, Jeffrey jocosely regrets, must be allowed to sink: 'The case of Mr Wordsworth, we perceive, is now manifestly hopeless'.

Jeffrey's review deftly reverses every claim Wordsworth's poems and prefaces have ever made. His retirement has cut him off from civilizing intercourse; his prophetic vision is a delusion; his theories of poetic imagination are nonsense; his style is prolix, his loftiness empty; his 'gothic Church' is built on sand; his whole output is not an unfolding of truth but a compounding of error.

Wordsworth affected to disdain the attack, but his language betrays his pain. 'You cannot scower a spot of this kind out of your mind', he told Catherine Clarkson, 'as you may a stain out of your clothes', and although he said he would not 'pollute [his] fingers with touching his [Jeffrey's] book', he hit back.[57] It was a major error of judgement. He had intended to reprint the Preface to *Lyrical Ballads* as an appendix to the new collection of poems, but since it was Jeffrey's argument that Wordsworth was lamentably stuck with his 'system', unable to move on, to do so might seem to confirm the justice of this repeated libel. In January 1815 therefore he hastily composed a new Preface, which justified the classification of the poems and, more importantly, defined in the loftiest terms the kind of imagination which he believed they displayed.[58] Although it contains some interesting criticism and many memorable formulations, such as 'Fancy is given to quicken and to beguile the temporal part of our nature, imagination to incite and support the eternal', it is neither, as the *Monthly Review* observed, 'remarkable for clearness of idea nor for humility of tone'.[59] On its own, however, the Preface would have done little harm. The mistake was to buttress it with an *Essay, Supplementary to the Preface*, in which Wordsworth hit out at critics 'of palsied imaginations and indurated hearts', and presented himself as one with Spenser and Milton, 'select Spirits for whom it is ordained that their fame shall be in the world an existence like that of Virtue, which owes its being to the struggles it makes and its vigour to the enemies whom it provokes'.[60]

Crabb Robinson feared that Wordsworth's betrayal of his pain and resentment would 'afford a triumph to his enemies', and he was right.[61] Summoning Chaucer, Spenser, Shakespeare, and Milton to his side, and , offering a definition of 'Genius' clearly to be tested against the poems it prefaced, Wordsworth presented himself as an easy target and Jeffrey did not delay. At the end of the year he reviewed *The White Doe of Rylstone*, beginning:

This, we think, has the merit of being the very worst poem we ever saw imprinted in a quarto volume; and though it was scarcely to be expected, we confess, that Mr

Wordsworth, with all his ambition, should so soon have attained to that distinction, the wonder may perhaps be diminished, when we state, that it seems to us to consist of a happy union of all the faults, without any of the beauties, which belong to his school of poetry. It is just such a work, in short, some wicked enemy of that school might be supposed to have devised, on purpose to make it ridiculous . . .[62]

Every barb is driven in. In the Preface Wordsworth had jokingly referred to himself as 'a water-drinker', so Jeffrey makes play with an image of the poet as intoxicated with self-admiration or 'unlucky in his choice of liquor— or of his bottle holder'. He mocks the pretension of such a story tricked out in quarto format, but concedes that Scott or Byron might have succeeded with even such poor materials—the most wounding comparison he could have made. The rest of the review subjects the poem canto by canto to witheringly reductive paraphrase.

Fought in this way, this was a battle Wordsworth could not hope to win. He fulminated about Jeffrey's 'stupidity', but Jeffrey was not stupid.[63] He was intelligent, witty, and licensed by the success of the *Edinburgh Review* to be as unfair as he chose. Nevertheless, Wordsworth struck back once more—it was another tactical mistake.

Late in 1815 it was suggested to him that Gilbert Burns would welcome advice on how best to present his brother Robert's life and work so as to vindicate it 'from the calumnies of Reviewers and pamphleteers'.[64] Wordsworth's response became an open *Letter to a Friend of Robert Burns*, published in 1816. It is an eloquent defence of the poet he had loved ever since his youth, which discriminates justly between the attention due to a poet as poet and the sympathy due to a poet as erring human being, but balance and good sense evaporate towards the end of the *Letter* as Wordsworth furiously assaults his tormentor. Malignant, depraved, an infatuated slanderer, Jeffrey is said to be motivated by 'vanity . . . restless, reckless, intractable, unappeasable, insatiable'. He is the Napoleon or Robespierre of letters. The disproportion between the concern for Burns's reputation and the language of the closing paragraphs is so great that Wordsworth could not but look foolish. 'Mr Wordsworth . . . with the voice and countenance of a maniac, fixes his teeth in the blue cover of the Edinburgh', his former disciple John Wilson chortled, but the 'world is not to be gulled by this hypocritical zeal in the defence of injured merit. It is not Robert Burns for whom he feels,—it is William Wordsworth.'[65] Jeffrey's reply was much cleverer. In the preamble to a review of Wilson's *The City of the Plague, and Other Poems*, he confessed to being in awe of true poets, ever ready to be indulgent to little faults, and therefore the more distressed whenever he saw in these superior beings 'traces of those meaner and more malignant vices which appear . . . inconsistent with the poetical character— the traces of paltry jealousy and envy of rival genius—of base servility and adulation to power and riches—of party profligacy or personal spite or rancour'.[66] Jeffrey's pained defence of his critical rectitude is long and tactically astute—it it not the work of a stupid man.

## (7)

During the early months of 1815 the Rydal household snatched at any encouragement about *The Excursion*: praise from 'A gentleman of Derby unknown to me', from 'A Lady of Liverpool, a Quaker', from Charles Lamb who 'calls it the best of Books', from 'Old Mrs Lloyd . . . enraptured with the Book', from De Quincey who reported the admiration of two Unitarians, and 'panegyrical letters' from 'Mary Ann and Letitia Hawkins'.[67] It was a pleasure to learn that Lady Beaumont was enthusiastic, though Dorothy shrewdly feared that 'her zeal will outrun her discretion, and prevent her from aiding the sale of the work as were she more moderate in her expressions she might do'.\* But there was, in fact, little comfort to be had. Lamb's essay for the *Quarterly Review*, in his opinion 'the prettiest piece of prose I ever writ', was so mutilated by the editor, Gifford, that Dorothy thought its 'feeble praise' would do more harm than the *Edinburgh*'s malignancy.[68] The *British Critic* undermined its positive remarks by judging that the poem was just too obscure: 'there are few who have music enough in their souls to unravel for themselves his abstruser harmonies'—'a very feeble composition', Dorothy loyally declared.[69]

'As to the Excursion I have ceased to have interest about it',[70] Wordsworth told Southey early in 1815, but no one believed him, least of all Catherine Clarkson who passed on criticism from her friend Patty Smith, only to receive by return of post a passionate rebuttal. Wordsworth defended the variety of the blank verse ('no Poem in the language furnishes a parallel'), the imagery, and the dramatic appropriateness of the various styles. Most passionately of all he rejected utterly the suggestion that *The Excursion* was doctrinally unsound. *Tintern Abbey* could be misinterpreted, he conceded, by someone 'reading in cold-heartedness and substituting the letter for the spirit', but not *The Excursion*:

She condemns me for not distinguishing between nature as the work of God and God himself. But where does she find this doctrine inculcated? Where does she gather that the Author of the Excursion looks upon nature and God as the same? He

---

\* *Ibid.*, 202. Uvedale Price wrote a long and sympathetic critique of the poem to Sir George and Lady Beaumont. He chooses his words very carefully, but one comic moment reveals how cautious he feels obliged to be over censure: 'If then it should not be popular, there must be some other reason besides it's being too contemplative—probably that which you suggested by saying "you perhaps may think it in some places too long". I did; & I will venture to say you did so likewise, or you would not have made the supposition'. Letter 18 March 1815. Pierpont Morgan Library.

does not indeed consider the Supreme Being as bearing the same relation to the universe as a watch-maker bears to a watch. In fact, there is nothing in the course of religious education adopted in this country and in the use made by us of the holy scriptures that appears to me so injurious as the perpetually talking about *making* by God—Oh! that your Correspondent had heard a conversation which I had in bed with my sweet little Boy, four and a half years old, upon this subject the other morning. 'How did God make me? Where is God? How does he speak? He never spoke to *me*'. I told him that God was a spirit, that he was not like his flesh which he could touch; but more like his thoughts in his mind which he could *not* touch.—The wind was tossing the fir trees, and the sky and light were dancing about in their dark branches, as seen through the window—Noting these fluctuations he exclaimed eagerly—'There's a bit of him I see it there!' This is not meant entirely for Father's prattle; but, for Heaven's sake, in your religious talk with children say as little as possible about *making*. One of the main objects of the Recluse is, to reduce the calculating understanding to its proper level among the human faculties.[71]

This is an engaging and yet sad moment. In 1798 Wordsworth would have made a lyrical ballad out of this conversation and the infant Willy would have joined the child of *We are Seven* as a subject for Victorian illustrators. But in 1815 Wordsworth was in a graver mood. Patty Smith's response and the similar reservations expressed by the devout James Montgomery in the *Eclectic Review* made him aware that for some with keener religious sensibilities than Jeffrey the doctrines of *The Excursion* were not common-place but objectionable.[72]

Wordsworth was being assailed from every quarter, but the worst was yet to come. On 3 April 1815 Coleridge gave Lady Beaumont his first impressions of *The Excursion*. Overall the poem was not as good as *The Prelude*; Book I, the story of the Ruined Cottage, was the best part of it; and there was something inherently wrong which he had not teased out, but, he mused, 'I have sometimes fancied, that having by the conjoint operation of his own experiences, feelings, and reason *himself* convinced *himself* of Truths, which the generality of persons have either taken for granted from their Infancy, or at least adopted in early life, he has attached all their own depth and weight to doctrines and words, which come almost as Truisms or Common-place to others'.[73] This was perceptive and generously sympathetic, but not intended for Wordsworth's eyes. None the less it reached him, provoking a plaintive and self-defensive request to Coleridge that he should provide chapter and verse for his censure. Wordsworth wrote that what he had learned from Lady Beaumont had 'perplexed' rather than 'enlightened' him.[74] Coleridge's reply would have enlightened a blind man.

Understandably apprehensive about another misunderstanding, Coleridge questioned whether it was ever wise to send criticism in a letter, qualified his remarks before he had made any, and generally tried to cushion the blow, but in the end he had to spell it out. He had believed Wordsworth to be deep in the genuinely philosophical part of *The Recluse*, and as he outlined what he thought it would cover, all of Coleridge's evolving thought from the 1790s to the present united in one great vision. Only a long quotation can convey the massiveness of his demonstration of what *The Excursion* was not:

I supposed you first to have meditated the faculties of Man in the abstract, in their correspondence with his Sphere of action, and first, in the Feeling, Touch, and Taste, then in the Eye, & last in the Ear, to have laid a solid and immovable foundation for the Edifice by removing the sandy Sophisms of Locke and the Mechanic Dogmatists, and demonstrating that the senses were living growths and developments of the Mind & Spirit in a much juster as well as higher sense, than the mind can be said to be formed by the Senses—. Next, I understood that you would take the Human Race in the concrete, have exploded the absurd notion of Pope's Essay on Man, Darwin, and all the countless Believers—even (strange to say) among Xtians of Man's having progressed from an Ouran Outang state—so contrary to all History, to all Religion, nay, to all Possibility—to have affirmed a Fall in some sense, as a fact, the possibility of which cannot be understood from the nature of the Will, but the reality of which is attested by Experience & Conscience—Fallen men contemplated in the different ages of the World, and in the different states—Savage—Barbarous—Civilized—the lonely Cot, or Borderer's Wigwam—the Village—the Manufacturing Town—Sea-port—City— Universities—and not disguising the sore evils, under which the whole Creation groans, to point out however a manifest Scheme of Redemption from this Slavery, of Reconciliation from this Enmity with Nature—what are the Obstacles, the *Antichrist* that must be & already is—and to conclude by a grand didactic swell on the necessary identity of a true Philosophy with true Religion, agreeing in the results and differing only as the analytic and synthetic process, as discursive from intuitive, the former chiefly useful as perfecting the latter—in short, the necessity of a general revolution in the modes of developing & disciplining the human mind by the substitution of Life, and Intelligence (considered in it's different powers from the Plant up to that state in which the difference of Degree becomes a new kind (man, self-consciousness) but yet not by essential opposition) for the philosophy of mechanism which in every thing that is most worthy of the human intellect strikes Death, and cheats itself by mistaking clear Images for distinct conceptions, and which idly demands Conceptions where Intuitions alone are possible or adequate to the majesty of the Truth.—In short, Facts elevated into Theory—Theory into Laws—& Laws into living & intelligent Powers—true Idealism necessarily perfecting itself in Realism, & Realism refining itself into Idealism.—[75]

It is easy enough to smile at this—the twice-repeated 'in short' is particularly winning—but it must have been impossible for Wordsworth. For this letter marks the most painfully ironic moment in his relationship with Coleridge. *The Recluse* had been conceived at Alfoxden in the exhilaration of talk, poetry, and mutual admiration. Uncertain as to his direction six years later, Wordsworth had exhorted Coleridge to send his 'notes for the Recluse. I cannot say how much importance I attach to this.'[76] Now, another decade on, Coleridge at last sent them—and they ended the long illusion. Years before Coleridge had said to his friend that 'you were a great Poet by inspirations, & in the Moments of revelation, but that you were a thinking feeling Philosopher habitually—that your Poetry was your Philosophy under the action of strong winds of Feeling—a sea rolling high', and he had been right.[77] But the poems sprang, in Lamb's phrase, 'from living and daily circumstances', and were valuable only in so far as they had the power 'to incorporate [themselves] with the blood & vital juices of our minds'.[78] Wordsworth could never have expounded Coleridge's philosophic system and he could not now. Although *The Recluse*, as a notion, lingered on for some years, its life, even as an idea, stopped in 1815.

Wordsworth was taking blows that would have crumpled the self-esteem of most writers. Seriously questioned when not actually ridiculed, his poetry was not selling.[79] He seemed to be reaching neither the fashionable who snapped up Scott or Byron, nor the middle-class readers whose growing appetite for serious literature was an increasing force in the market-place.[80] In February 1815 Dorothy tried to be optimistic—269 copies of *The Excursion* had been sold, they believed—but only six months later she gave up pretending: 'As to us *we* shall never grow rich; for I now perceive clearly that till my dear Brother is laid in his grave his writings will not produce any profit . . . however cheap his poems might be I am sure it will be very long before they have an extensive sale'.[81] Wordsworth did not crumple, partly because of the support given by his family, partly because he did have a coterie readership, a fit audience though few, but most of all because his faith in his own powers stubbornly survived. Regarding the final destiny of his work, he told Catherine Clarkson, 'I have neither care nor anxiety being assured that if it be of God—it must stand; and that if the spirit of truth, "The Vision and the Faculty divine" be not in it, and so do not pervade it, it must perish'.[82] But looking to posterity had to be a salve for much present hurt.

(8)

Explaining his response to Wordsworth's poetry W. J. Fox told Crabb Robinson that he supposed it was less than whole-hearted because he was not '*initiated* or *fraternized*'.[83] The implication that Wordsworth was only appreciated fully by a band of worshippers was not new. Twelve years earlier Coleridge had 'trembled' at the thought of him 'living wholly among *Devotees*', snug in what Keats, with characteristic suggestiveness, styled his 'fireside divan'.[84] But the knowledge that his work was valued by however small a circle had encouraged Wordsworth during his first, most creative period, 1798–1807, and had sustained him since then in the face of scorn. It continued to do so now in his darkest period and he welcomed, with revealing eagerness, evidence that his coterie was growing.

Early in May 1815 Wordsworth and Mary accompanied Hartley Coleridge to Oxford, saw him settled in at Merton College, and then carried on to London for a two-month visit.[85] As always, being in London meant energetically seeing people. Some were celebrities. He breakfasted with William Wilberforce and called on Leigh Hunt, co-editor of the *Examiner*, who had recently ended two years in prison for ridiculing the Prince Regent.[86] Most were old friends or acquaintances—the Lambs, the Beaumonts, Farington, Walter Scott, Godwin, Daniel Stuart, Rogers, Washington Allston, Richard Heber (Coleridge was not in town). As well as keeping these old friendships in repair, however, Wordsworth also made important new ones. On 23 May he took breakfast with Benjamin Robert Haydon, the painter (whom he had possibly met briefly in 1812), and soon, as friend introduced friend, he met Thomas Noon Talfourd and Barron Field, both fledgeling barristers, and the rising political journalist and editor John Scott.

Talfourd (b. 1795) and Field (b. 1786) were younger men whose long friendships with the poet were securely based on their devotion to his poetry. The word is not too strong, for they were disciples. When they met, Talfourd had just published *An Attempt to Estimate the Poetical Talent of the Present Age*, opening the relevant section: 'To the consideration of MR WORDSWORTH's sublimities we come with trembling steps, and feel, as we approach, that we are entering upon holy ground'.[87] The rest of the long assessment sustains the note of rapture and every word, especially the attack on the *Edinburgh Review*, must have been balm. Talfourd never wavered in his loyalty. In the 1837 Preface to his tragedy *Ion* he acknowledged that his becoming acquainted with Wordsworth's poetry, through Field, had transformed his own taste and feelings about literature and in 1844 he took a cottage in the Lake District to be near the poet in his old age.[88]

Field was equally enthusiastic and equally loyal. He later described himself as one who 'has cheered the rugged paths of professional studies with the Lyrical Ballads, and has carried the Excursion round his forensic circuit, at the hazard of ridicule from the whole Edinburgh-Review-blinded Bar'.[89] Their friendship had little chance to deepen, as Field left for New South Wales in 1816 and, after returning in 1824, went out again to Gibraltar in 1830. But even in 1815 Field demonstrated that he was the most welcome kind of disciple, one who really knew the poems in detail. Fascinated by the poet as technician, he noted all of Wordsworth's revisions after 1815, challenging and questioning when he was doubtful, and eventually aspired to be the first to write a full exposition and defence of the poetry and the aesthetic theory.[90]

John Scott's short friendship—he was killed in a duel in 1821—was differently based. Whereas Talfourd and Field believed that Wordsworth's demanding, elevated poetry would only one day win acclaim, Scott saw in Wordsworth the man for the hour. In *Cintra*, he wrote, 'the tone & the sentiment struck me as forming together the very voice that should now sound to animate the people of England to that high disposition of righteous independence, which takes the power of resistance from a submissive sense of duty'. As a political censor, who attacked corruption, profligacy, and tyranny in whatever quarter, but who was none the less a vigorous patriot, Scott welcomed Wordsworth as an ally and printed his two sonnets on Waterloo in the *Champion*, 4 February 1816, in the conviction that their tone was exactly right. 'Human nature', he wrote, 'demands to be vindicated from the slur that has been cast upon her, as if she had no resource from errors but in enormities,—and could not strip herself of certain prejudices without casting off all obligations and hardening her heart against all native affections & heavenly impulses.'[91]

Haydon was much the most exciting of Wordsworth's new friends—and the most difficult. Their closer acquaintance began in an extraordinary way. Searching for striking heads for his large painting *Christ's Entry into Jerusalem*, Haydon persuaded Wordsworth to submit to having a cast taken of his face.

He bore it like a philosopher. Scott was to meet him at Breakfast. Just as he came in the Plaister was covered over. Wordsworth was sitting in the other room in my dressing gown, with his hands folded, sedate, steady & solemn. I stepped in to Scott, & told him as a curiosity to take a peep, that he might say the first sight he ever had of so great a poet was such a singular one as this.

I opened the door slowly, & there he sat innocent & unconscious of our plot against his dignity, unable to see or to speak, with all the mysterious silence of a spirit.

When he was relieved he came into breakfast with his usual cheerfulness, and delighted & awed us by his illustrations & bursts of inspiration.[92]

The next day, still vibrating from their conversation, Haydon confided to his diary: 'I don't know any man I should be so inclined to worship as a purified being'.[93]

Wordsworth's feelings fell far short of worship, but he was drawn to Haydon. Impressed by the scope of the painter's ambition for his art, he described his own comparably elevated vision of *The Recluse* so excitingly that Haydon declared it 'as grand an intention as ever entered the

conception of any Poet'.[94] At the end of 1815 Wordsworth sent, as a 'little
offering of my regard', three sonnets, one of which allied poet and painter in
their sacred task:

> High is our calling, Friend!—Creative Art
> (Whether the instrument of words she use,
> Or pencil pregnant with etherial hues,)
> Demands the service of a mind and heart,
> Though sensitive, yet, in their weakest part,
> Heroically fashioned—to infuse
> Faith in the whispers of the lonely Muse,
> While the whole world seems adverse to desert:
> And, oh! when Nature sinks, as oft she may,
> Through long-lived pressure of obscure distress,
> Still to be strenuous for the bright reward,
> And in the Soul admit of no decay,—
> Brook no continuance of weak-mindedness:
> Great is the glory, for the strife is hard![95]

These heroic sentiments bonded the two artists in 1815, but they were
sadly prophetic of the strains that were to rupture their friendship later. For
Wordsworth and Haydon claimed kin just as their fortunes were diverging.
The poet slowly gained his 'bright reward', while the painter had still to
struggle against 'long-lived pressure of obscure distress'. In 1820 Wordsworth refused Haydon a loan, claiming reasonably that he could not afford
to put out money he knew would not be repaid. At the time Haydon
swallowed his disappointment, but four years later it fuelled a rancorous
letter to Mary Russell Mitford in which he returned bitterly to the poem
addressed to him: 'Depend on it Wordsworth has no heart he will write you
a Sonnet, & see you starve that he may write you another—but as to giving
you a loaf forbid it his *high calling*!—he has too *much regard* for you'.[96] The
two were reconciled in 1831 and Wordsworth did write another sonnet to
mark the resumption of their friendship, *To B. R. Haydon, on Seeing his
Picture of Napoleon Buonaparte on the Island of St Helena*, but by then it was
too late for them to offer each other very much. Wordsworth was about to
publish his most successful volume. Haydon was in the drawn-out decline
that ended in suicide in 1846.

During this 1815 London visit Wordsworth seemed at ease. 'Never did
any Man so beguile the time', Haydon wrote after a pleasant saunter to
Hampstead.[97] But he was touchy. Glancing into a new book by Godwin and
lighting on the words, 'All modern poetry is nothing but the old genuine
poetry, new vamped, and delivered to us at second, or twentieth hand', he
seized a pencil and, according to Lamb, the hapless owner of the volume, 'In
great wrath', wrote in the margin: ' "That is false, William Godwin. Signed

William Wordsworth" '.[98] And on one matter he was inflexible. He would not meet Hazlitt. Crabb Robinson was given a highly coloured account of how Hazlitt had made 'gross attacks on women' at Keswick in 1803, and so understood that Wordsworth's 'coolness' and Hazlitt's reciprocating bitterness were primarily personal in origin.[99] Haydon, too, heard the story and was convinced that the merest gesture from Wordsworth would have stopped the breach from widening: 'Had you condescended to visit him . . . his vanity would have been soothed and his virulence softened'.[100]

But though Hazlitt's comments on Wordsworth were bitingly *ad hominem*, as much contemporary journalism was, they were not born of personal spite. Hazlitt was a man of principle and to him Wordsworth now was one who had forsaken ideas, hopes, and an attitude to social affairs he believed they had once shared. What little Wordsworth published in 1816 was to confirm his dismay.

# 1816–1822

(1)

A HUGE bonfire on the top of Skiddaw on 21 August 1815 celebrated the victory of Waterloo. Blazing balls of tow and turpentine were rolled down the mountain as the revellers feasted on roast beef and boiled plum-puddings and got tipsy on punch. There was only one mishap. Wordsworth, grandly dressed 'like a Spanish Don' in a cloak of Edith Southey's, knocked over the kettle of boiling water for the punch and 'thought to slink off undiscovered', but bystanders identified the villain as 'the gentleman in red', to the delight of Southey, who led his party in a dance round him singing, ''Twas *you* that kicked the kettle down! 'twas you, Sir, you!' Southey does not record whether Mary and Dorothy joined in, but they probably did, for it was a mildly Bacchic festivity—at least one unnamed man from 'Messrs. Rag, Tag, and Bobtail' was too drunk to walk down at midnight and had to be led down, face to tail, on a horse.[1]

The picture of Wordsworth at a bonfire party, sharing the popular excitement amongst his family and friends, is one to linger on. Few readers, however, will want to linger over Wordsworth's public celebration of the nation's victory the following year, the volume *Thanksgiving Ode, January 18, 1816: With Other Short Pieces, Chiefly Referring to Recent Public Events.* Among the 'other short pieces' the three sonnets earlier sent to Haydon are attractive, but the *Thanksgiving Ode, Ode, Composed in January 1816,* and the *Ode,* 'Who rises on the banks of Seine' speak with the voice of the *Ode to Duty,* but amplified to a higher power.[2] 'Forced replicas of Abraham Cowley's plaster imitations of Pindar' one critic has called them and the judgement is not unfair.[3] But the volume is an important one and needs discussion, not because the odes can be reclaimed as enjoyable poetry— which much of the later work is—but because the volume is both a climax to a phase of Wordsworth's thought and a key to understanding his later years.

It opens with a convoluted 'Advertisement' that begins:

It is not to bespeak favour or indulgence, but to guard against misapprehension, that the author presumes to state that the present publication owes its existence to a patriotism, anxious to exert itself in commemorating that course of action, by which Great Britain has, for some time past, distinguished herself above all other countries.

Wholly unworthy of touching upon so momentous a subject would that Poet be, before whose eyes the present distresses under which this kingdom labours, could interpose a veil sufficiently thick to hide, or even to obscure, the splendor of this great moral triumph. If the author has given way to exultation, unchecked by these distresses, it might be sufficient to protect him from a charge of insensibility, should he state his own belief that these sufferings will be transitory. On the wisdom of a very large majority of the British nation, rested that generosity which poured out the treasures of this country for the deliverance of Europe: and in the same national wisdom, presiding in time of peace over an energy not inferior to that which has been displayed in war, *they* confide, who encourage a firm hope, that the cup of our wealth will be gradually replenished.[4]

What the 'present distresses' were did not need spelling out. That John Bellingham had assassinated the Prime Minister in May 1812 because he believed government economic policy to be the cause of his own ruin was emblematic of the state of the country. As he confronted Perceval in the House of Commons, other bemused sufferers were following 'Ned Ludd' in redressing their perceived wrongs. Frame-breaking in the northern industrial areas over 1810–12 terrified Parliament into creating yet another hanging offence, but fiercer attacks on mills followed and more machine-breaking in 1814. Food riots erupted sporadically and Southey was quick to see in a disturbance at Cockermouth 'something very like a Luddite spirit'. By 1816 he was certain that 'All imaginable causes which produce revolution are at work among us'.[5]

Wordsworth's response to these social portents was complex. He sought to face their meaning and yet also to efface it in the vision of a higher truth. That a collapse of social order was near in 1812 seemed certain: 'if much firmness be not displayed by the government confusion & havoc & murder will break out & spread terribly', he wrote to Mary, adding in another letter, from his own observation, that 'Nothing can be more deplorably ferocious & savage than the lowest orders in London'.[6] In the Preface to *Lyrical Ballads* (1800) he had pointed to the 'encreasing accumulation of men in cities' as one of the many forces combining 'to blunt the discriminating powers of the mind', but now he spoke more apocalyptically: 'the lower orders have been for upwards of thirty years accumulating in pestilential masses of ignorant population; the effects now begin to show themselves, and unthinking people cry out that the national character has been changed all at once, in fact the change has been silently going on ever since the time we were born; the disease has been growing, and now breaks out in all its danger and deformity'.[7] Uneducated, impoverished, febrile, the masses were, he believed, as the Paris mob had been in the early 1790s, prey to incendiaries. Opposition in Parliament from Brougham and Burdett, or outside it from Cobbett, struck him as likely to promote not liberty but insurrection in which all liberties would perish. Throughout the war, he fulminated to John Scott, the opposition 'blushed not to behave as if they had been retained by Buonaparte for his advocates'.[8]

And yet this distressed and divided country had triumphed over 'that audacious charlatan and remorseless desperado', Napoleon.[9] Even as social distress worsened, moreover, Wordsworth was guardedly optimistic about his country's capacity to defeat it too. How and why? To answer these questions Wordsworth drew on two convictions, one soundly based, the other questionable but potent enough to have sustained an empire on which the sun never set. Both are voiced in the 'Advertisement' and the odes of 1816.

Waterloo was won by guns, cavalry, and a disciplined infantry, testimony, Wordsworth claims, that a nation can only retain its freedom by 'an assiduous cultivation of military virtues'. But guns alone would not have been enough. In *The Convention of Cintra* and all of the Iberian sonnets which complemented it, Wordsworth had insisted on one truth:

> O'erweening Statesmen have full long relied
> On fleets and armies, and external wealth:
> But from within proceeds a Nation's health . . .[10]

Thanking Captain Charles Pasley for his *The Military Policy and Institutions of the British Empire* (1810), he had asserted in 1811 that the war would be won only if force were 'bottomed upon . . . notions of justice and right, and . . . knowledge of and reverence for the moral sentiments of mankind'. Ultimately it would be 'the mind of the Country' that would decide in the campaign against Napoleon.[11] And so, Wordsworth believed, it had proved. 'Providence' had placed 'the *exterminating sword*' in British hands, 'Dread mark of approbation',[12] but the *Thanksgiving Ode* was a celebration not only of the sword but of a 'great moral triumph'.

This conviction that his countrymen had displayed spiritual power was the basis for Wordsworth's optimism about the peace. Education for the ignorant masses would have to be a priority, but something more would be needed for the advance of the whole nation:

a new course of education, a higher tone of moral feeling, more of the grandeur of the imaginative faculties, and less of the petty processes of the unfeeling and purblind understanding, that would manage the concerns of nations in the same calculating spirit with which it would set about building a new house. Now a State ought to be governed (at least in these times)—the labours of the statesmen ought to advance—upon calculations and from impulses similar to those which give motion to the hand of a great Artist when he is preparing a picture, or of a mighty Poet when he is determining the proportions and march of a Poem. Much is to be done by rule; the great outline is previously to be conceived in distinctness, but the consummation of the work must be trusted to resources that are not tangible, though known to exist.[13]

The most intangible but most powerful of these resources is a nation's sense of its own nationhood—more specifically for Wordsworth now, England's sense of Englishness:

> Land of our fathers! precious unto me
> Since the first joys of thinking infancy:
> When of thy gallant chivalry I read,
> And hugged the volume on my sleepless bed!
> O England!—dearer far than life is dear,
> If I forget thy prowess, never more
> Be thy ungrateful son allowed to hear
> Thy green leaves rustle, or thy torrents roar![14]

It is a passage Burke would have applauded. Latent within it is a defence of the best of the established order, of the established Church, of the English landscape—of all that has evolved in the making of Englishness.[15]

Some exposition of Wordsworth's political views at the close of the war is necessary if much about his later life and writing is to be understood. But the poems to which one turns for an imaginative embodiment of them, the poems which were his public statement, are lifeless.[16] One might ascribe their failure to superficiality, or to the poet's ignorance, but while it is true that Wordsworth's vision of England would not have been shared by the frame-breakers of Nottingham or by most of the soldiers who actually fought at Waterloo, it is fair to say that he had thought about the significance of the war and its eventual outcome as seriously as any man and no one could impugn the sincerity of the emotions expressed in the 1816 odes. Are conservative views, or a reverence for the Church of England, inimical to poetry? Yeats and T. S. Eliot answer that. Was the ode form, though the obvious one for the occasion, a snare for Wordsworth, as it certainly was for Laureate Southey?[17] The *Ode: Intimations of Immortality*, or the *Vernal Ode*, or the *Ode on the Power of Sound* say not. Perhaps the most that can be said is that in attempting a generalizing utterance Wordsworth forsook the very ground of the success of most of his poems, which is that they are realized in and through the matter-of-fact, the everyday, the human. The *Westminster Bridge* sonnet, *St Paul's, Home at Grasmere*—these are celebrations of 'England!—dearer far than life is dear', whose substantiality rests on the local, the observed fact, transformed by imagination and love. *Michael* and *The Brothers* depict belonging, rootedness, loyalty, but not as abstractions, rather as forces expressed in daily living in a particularized place. The 1816 odes are empty of human beings, unanchored in specific place or event. Echoes of earlier poems, such as the phrase 'the bliss of gratitude', or 'Dear native regions', or the title *Elegiac Verses*, sadly remind the reader how far Wordsworth is from his own poetic terrain.[18]

(2)

Wordsworth was sensitive to the accusation that he was a political turncoat. To young radicals the evidence seemed overwhelming. 'Shelley . . . brings home Wordsworth's Excursion, of which we read a part; much disappointed. He is a slave', Mary Shelley noted in her journal. Her husband lamented his loss:

> Thou hast like to a rock-built refuge stood
> Above the blind and battling multitude:
> In honoured poverty thy voice did weave
> Songs consecrate to truth and liberty,—
> Deserting these, thou leavest me to grieve,
> Thus having been, that thou shouldst cease to be.[19]

Growingly conservative in religion and politics, the 'Poet of Nature' was no longer to Shelley like 'a lone star, whose light did shine / On some frail bark in winter's midnight roar'. But Wordsworth insisted, to the contrary, on the continuity of his views. 'In nothing are my *principles* changed', he told John Scott, and five years later he defended himself in the same vein to his old radical friend James Losh:

I should think that I had lived to little purpose if my notions on the subject of Government had undergone no modification—my youth must, in that case, have been without enthusiasm, and my manhood endued with small capability of profiting by reflexion. If I were addressing those who have dealt so liberally with the words Renegado, Apostate etc, I should retort the charge upon them, and say, *you* have been deluded by Places and Persons, while I have stuck to Principles . . .[20]

In fact Wordsworth had *published* nothing that would make this defence untenable. The politics of the *Thanksgiving Ode* volume could be traced through *The Excursion*, to the Iberian sonnets and *Cintra*, and back to the sonnets of 1802, but before that there had only been *Lyrical Ballads* and *An Evening Walk* and *Descriptive Sketches*.[21] But had he published all that he had written Wordsworth would have found it hard to deny that he had changed. *A Letter to the Bishop of Llandaff*, *Salisbury Plain* and *Adventures on Salisbury Plain*, the Juvenal imitation, not to mention the prospectus for the *Philanthropist* and the frank avowal of his political position sent to Mathews, would have testified against him.[22] This evidence was hidden. He had published nothing to be ashamed of, nothing to disavow. But his closest friends had, and when their past was dragged out unexpectedly in 1817, he too was implicated.

In December 1816 Coleridge published *The Statesman's Manual: or, The Bible the Best Guide to Political Skill and Foresight*, an essay, or *Lay Sermon*, on the present distresses directed at those most able to counteract them, 'the Higher Classes of Society'.[23] To Hazlitt, Coleridge had long appeared a Tory hireling, 'one whose daily prose is . . . dedicated to the support of all that courtiers think should be supported',[24] and he lost no time in pitching into this latest proof. Before *The Statesman's Manual* had actually been published, Hazlitt vilified its author as a windbag apostate and after publication he repeated the attack not once but three times, once in the *Edinburgh Review* and twice in the *Examiner*.[25] Indolent, capricious, vain, Coleridge is said to be a man of unfixed opinions, a metaphysical juggler, but he was not always so—and here is the explosive charge of Hazlitt's attack. He reminded readers of the *Edinburgh Review* of Coleridge's *Watchman* and *Conciones ad Populum* and in a letter to the *Examiner* drew on his memories of his first view of him preaching in 1798, nobly eloquent, fearless for the truth: 'That sermon like this Sermon was upon peace and war; upon church and state—not their alliance, but their separation—on the spirit of the world and the spirit of Christianity, not as the same, but as opposed to one another',

Hazlitt had written enough about *The Statesman's Manual* and it is possible that the warfare might have died down had the apostates not been delivered naked to their enemies. Social distress and political unrest worsened over the turn of the year 1816–17. Calls for reform grew more strident. Mass meetings in London's Spa Fields and an attack on the Prince Regent's carriage led to the suspension of Habeas Corpus and a clampdown on the press. Southey, Coleridge, and Wordsworth were in no doubt where they stood. In the *Quarterly Review* for October 1816 Southey called on the government to stamp out sedition and to suppress dissent in the pursuit of public order at all cost.[26] But in the 1790s, when it had been Thelwall and not 'Orator' Henry Hunt addressing mass meetings, when the Treason Trials had demonstrated the 'insolence and presumption of the aristo-cracy'[27] and the acquittals of Hardy, Horne Tooke, Thelwall, and their co-defendants the efficacy of reasoned protest, when the transports to Botany Bay and the Alfoxden spy showed what legislative and executive power could do when intent on order at all cost—then the poets had reacted very differently, and in 1817 that fact was uncovered in the most embarrassing way imaginable.

In 1794 Southey had preached defiance against tyranny in his tragedy *Wat Tyler*. Attempts to publish the play had foundered and the manuscript disappeared. In February 1817, coinciding neatly with the *Quarterly Review*, it was published.[28] Southey's application for an injunction was refused, but in fact no legal action could undo the damage. He was denounced by an opposition MP, in a debate on the Seditious Meetings Bill, as a malignant renegado, bent on suppressing liberties for which he had once fought, and in the *Examiner* for 9 March Hazlitt paraded Southey's apostasy in extracts from *Wat Tyler*.[29] Defending him at once in the *Courier*, 17 and 18 March, Coleridge reviewed Southey's early career and cleared him of all charges, first, by ascribing the ardour of Southey's early productions to the innocent zeal of a '*stripling* Bard', and, second, by insisting on Southey's integrity as a man.[30] It is difficult to imagine a more inept defence against this opponent at this moment. Seizing on the comical image of the stripling bard, Hazlitt, first in the *Morning Chronicle* and then in the *Examiner*,[31] surveyed Southey's publication history, laying out titles for inspection, and reminded readers that this innocent youth's productions had been sufficiently numerous and important for him to become a chief object of the *Anti-Jacobin* attack. But Southey had not been alone. Wordsworth and Coleridge had been Jacobins. What is more, Hazlitt insisted, all of their best work had been done under that flag:

All the authority that they have as poets and men of genius must be thrown into the scale of Revolution and Reform. Their Jacobin principles indeed gave rise to their Jacobin poetry. Since they gave up the first, their poetical powers have flagged . . . Their genius, their style, their versification, every thing down to their spelling, was revolutionary.

It was not Coleridge's fault that Hazlitt had been able to widen his attack to include all three poets. Facts were on his side and Hazlitt had a memory. None the less, his ironical advice to Southey to 'apply for an injunction against Mr Coleridge' was well aimed. As Dorothy remarked, 'of injudicious defenders [Coleridge] is surely the Master Leader'.[32] And, from Wordsworth's point of view, there was worse to come. In this year of publishing accidents, the timing of Coleridge's next book could not have been more unfortunate.

Coleridge had been overwhelmed by the Preface to Wordsworth's *Poems* (1815). If the Preface to *Lyrical Ballads* 1800 and 1802 had been 'half a child of [his] own Brain', the 1815 manifesto seemed to him even more dependent on theoretical ideas that he had nurtured.[33] Impelled by what his recent editor has called a 'near obsession with Wordsworth's new Preface', Coleridge at first thought to issue his own forthcoming poems, with preface, in exactly the same format as Wordsworth's volumes, but the preface expanded to become a book, an apologia for his own literary life and opinions.[34]

Planned for 1815, *Biographia Literaria* actually appeared in July 1817, and so it could not but seem a continuation of the battle being waged between the 'Lake Poets' on the one hand and Jeffrey and Hazlitt on the other. Coleridge's aim was to give an account of the development of his own philosophic, religious, and aesthetic principles, to establish in what ways he differed from Wordsworth on issues of poetic theory and practice, and to define more truly, against the calumny and misrepresentations of reviewers, the nature of his friend's greatness. What he achieved, given the barely healed wound of their estrangement and the duress of haste, illness, and anxiety, was remarkable—a revealing and very readable autobiography, a philosophical-religious treatise, and a critique of Wordsworth which is required reading to this day, on which the poet himself acted, despite initial reluctance, when he revised his work.[35] But, inevitably, in pursuing his aim Coleridge brought to light again the Jacobin years, *The Watchman*, the Alfoxden spy episode, and the long-drawn-out battle with Jeffrey. So vehement was his attack on the personal integrity of the despot of the *Edinburgh Review*, moreover, that Jeffrey took the unprecedented step of defending himself in a signed contribution when the work was reviewed later in the year.[36]

Throughout 1817 the radical Wordsworth, who had declared himself a foe to 'monarchical and aristocratical governments, however modified' and to 'Hereditary distinctions and privileged orders of every species',[37] and who had fathered a child in revolutionary France, was a hovering figure, a presence implicated in but not quite summoned by the literary warfare. But the threat that he would be summoned was real. Hazlitt had not forgotten his first meeting with the poets and every word that Coleridge wrote about his early years, his association with Southey, their persecution by the *Anti-Jacobin*, and the non-existence of the 'Lake Poets' as a sect recalled that time.

'I have no doubt, that Wordsworth will be displeased.' Coleridge was thinking of his proof in *Biographia Literaria* that Wordsworth's theory was false and that he had 'never acted on it except in particular Stanzas which are the Blots of his Compositions'.[38] There was another reason, however, why Wordsworth might find *Biographia Literaria* disturbing. In 1815 he had begged Coleridge not to publish *To William Wordsworth*, the tribute written on hearing the poem addressed to him, *The Prelude*, judging that 'the commendation would be injurious to us both, and my work when it appears, would labour under a great disadvantage in consequence of such a precursorship of Praise'.[39] The public had heard far too much from Jeffrey and others about the mutual admiration of the 'Lake Poets', and Wordsworth feared that Coleridge's rapturous poem would be further confirmation, making them both look foolish. He was also anxious that no further hints should be given to the public of great work yet to come. Coleridge suppressed the poem, but what he did publish quickened both of Wordsworth's anxieties. Throughout his discussion of the poetry up to 1815 Coleridge offered both close readings of particular lines and general observations about the whole *œuvre* which are so sharp, and so strikingly expressed, that they remain touchstones in Wordsworthian criticism. But he also invoked the unwritten, gesturing largely towards the future. 'What Mr. Wordsworth *will* produce, it is not for me to prophesy', he wrote, 'but I could pronounce with the liveliest convictions what he is capable of producing. It is the FIRST GENUINE PHILOSOPHIC POEM.'[40] Meant as the highest praise, every word of these two sentences was heavy with admonition. Wordsworth himself had prophesied *The Recluse* in the Preface to *The Excursion*, and Coleridge now publicly reaffirmed his faith in the project and in its architect. But his letter to Wordsworth on *The Recluse* had devastatingly revealed how far apart were their conceptions of philosophical poetry and, with *The Excursion* published, Wordsworth had no idea how to proceed.

Characteristically he turned from Coleridge's vision of philosophic poetry to his own. In 1817 he wrote a number of odes—*Ode: 1817* (later called *Vernal Ode*), *Ode, Composed upon an Evening of Extraordinary Splendor and Beauty*, *Ode: The Pass of Kirkstone*, *Ode to Lycoris, May, 1817*, and its companion *To the Same* ('Enough of climbing toil!'). Together they make up a very interesting group in which Wordsworth returns to the sources of his power as a lyric poet, after the more public utterance of *The Excursion* and the political sonnets and odes. Each is a meditation on a natural phenomenon—a bee at work, a sunset—or on an event—climbing Helvellyn, crossing the Kirkstone Pass—an intense exercise of the imagination to disclose meaning in an experience. Wordsworth's return to his lyric formulae, however, is a highly self-conscious one, which exploits, even indulges, a retrospective, autumnal tone. As always with Wordsworth, retrospection involves private allusion, a gathering together of past and present visible only to his intimates. The address to Dorothy in the second *Lycoris*, for example, includes tender lines that had been lying in manuscript for more than ten years.[41] But all of the poems dwell on the human being as a creature of time, on experience placed in the context of the aeons of the past and the unimaginable timelessness of the future, and the most striking of them all, *Composed upon an Evening of Extraordinary Splendor and Beauty*, actually invites the reader to consider the passing of time embodied in the poet's evolving canon. Moved by the spectacle of an irradiated earth,

Wordsworth invokes an earlier celebration of the world apparelled in celestial light by alluding, in a note and in the verse, to the *Ode: Intimations of Immortality*.[42] Both poems acknowledge the loss of primal vision, but whereas the earlier ode triumphantly asserts gain and growth, the later one is much more muted, a poignant hymn of gratitude for an unlooked-for 'glimpse of glory'.

Through the accomplishment of the verse all of the 1817 poems testify to Wordsworth's creative vigour, but their tone suggests a poet aware that a movement in his imaginative life is coming to a close. The ebullience of earlier lyrics is missing, the energy that suggested the limitless possibilities for poetry in the play of the imagination upon the everyday. In *Biographia Literaria* Coleridge reminded readers, and Wordsworth, of a poetic life governed by a long-term aim, the production of the first genuine philosophic poem. His words only have to be slightly rearranged, however, for the real issue to stand clear. It is a question: 'What *will* Mr. Wordsworth produce?'

(3)

The most significant thing about the poems of 1817 was that they had been written at all, for Wordsworth had been harassed throughout the previous year by unproductive worry. In April 1816 Richard Wordsworth fell seriously ill and all Wordsworth's latent fears about his stewardship of his and Dorothy's money surfaced. Richard was persuaded to make a will that secured the future, but his death in May revealed that his personal affairs were in such disarray that Wordsworth was engulfed in the correspondence and travelling necessary to sort them out. Worry nagged him, so much so that Dorothy wished he could have gone abroad with Southey, if only because 'the vexatious chain would have been broken, and a fresh stream of thoughts admitted into his mind'.[43] Some matters were still outstanding late in 1817, but when Wordsworth felt obliged to go to London in November to confer with Christopher he took Mary and Sara with him so that business could become a holiday.

The weather and the city were at their discouraging worst. Snow fell early in December and the London fog, Sara reported, lay on the narrow streets, 'not only thick but of a yellow color', making inside and out 'as dirty as smoke', and necessitating candles and lamps at midday.[44] But London was London and they enjoyed themselves, shopping, going to the theatre and opera, entertaining at Thomas Monkhouse's, or going out to see friends, so often that Sara sighed after a month, 'I *hope* we shall go out in the evenings no more'.[45]

The most memorable occasions were centred either on Monkhouse's place in Queen Anne Street or on Haydon's studio in Lisson Grove. The bachelor Monkhouse, hospitable and gregarious by nature, was determined to make his cousins' stay a festive one and Haydon was thrilled to have his revered friend back in town.

On 2 and 22 December Wordsworth sat for Haydon, the two artists enacting a tableau of 'High is our calling, Friend!', as Haydon drew and prepared to insert Wordsworth into *Christ's Entry into Jerusalem*, while his sitter read Milton, *Tintern Abbey*, *The Happy Warrior*, and Book IV of *The Excursion* out loud. 'He is a most eloquent power', Haydon recorded. 'He looked like a spirit of Nature, pure & elementary. His head is like as if it was carved out of a mossy rock, created before the flood! . . . That nose announces a wonder.' On Boxing Day 1817 Wordsworth was finally inserted to Haydon's satisfaction alongside Voltaire and Newton, 'a wonderful contrast',[46] and on 15 January 1818 he was sitting once again, this time for a chalk sketch, which was presented to Mary.[47]

It was Haydon who brought about the first meeting between Wordsworth and Keats. An infant when *Lyrical Ballads* was published, Keats had come of age artistically just as Wordsworth was making his great declaration in *The Excursion* and *Poems* (1815), and to him *The Excursion* seemed one of the 'three things to rejoice at in this Age', the others being Haydon's pictures and Hazlitt's depth of taste.[48] When he sent Wordsworth his own first volume, *Poems* (1817), the inscription, 'To W. Wordsworth with the Author's sincere Reverence', was not a formality but a genuine acknowledgement of indebtedness by one who was so steeped in Wordsworth's poetry that his own high conception of the poetic life was largely shaped by it.[49] Haydon arranged the meeting, not at his own home but at Tom Monkhouse's, and as they walked together towards Queen Anne Street he observed that Keats showed 'the greatest, the purest, the most unalloyed pleasure at the prospect'.[50]

Perhaps more than on any other occasion in Wordsworth's life one longs for a reliable witness to what actually happened. Nearly thirty years later Haydon reported that when, at his urging, Keats had recited his 'exquisite ode to Pan', Wordsworth had drily said, 'a Very pretty piece of Paganism', crushing the 'young Worshipper', who 'felt it *deeply*' and never forgave the slight.[51] Keats's biographer, Robert Gittings, is rightly cautious about accepting this late account from a man 'whose megalomaniac tendencies were tipping over into the insanity, in which he destroyed himself a few months later', and Mary Moorman argues, also rightly, that even if such words were spoken, 'pretty' was not in Wordsworth's mouth a derogatory term.[52] There is other evidence, however, not cited by either. In the 1824 letter to Mary Russell Mitford already mentioned (p.314), Haydon briefly touches on the occasion, apparently quoting Wordsworth verbatim after only six years. But this, too, is deeply tainted evidence. Haydon was recalling with great bitterness the poet's refusal to lend money in 1820. His letter is a diatribe against Wordsworth, which even descends to contrasting Mary Wordsworth, 'his squinting wife . . . his hideous wife', with Mrs Haydon, 'an acknowledged beautiful creature'. Wordsworth is described as 'an old satyr . . . lecherous, animal & devouring', 'an old beast, cloked in piety and verse', a snob, a sycophant, a hypocrite, not a patch on Coleridge or Hazlitt.[53] Haydon remembers Wordsworth's words to Keats because, like everything else about him now, they seem foul.

Something clearly was said, very possibly even what Haydon claimed so long after to have heard. But there is nothing to support the story in his diary, in which he noted day by day whatever struck him as of interest, nor in Keats's letters, and although Keats did move from being a worshipper to being a thoughtful and independent critic of Wordsworth both as man and poet, whatever happened at their first meeting did not stop him from reciting his poetry again in Wordsworth's presence at Haydon's on 28 December.

Dining in Haydon's painting room, Keats, Lamb, Thomas Monkhouse, the poet, and the painter grew uproarious over Homer, Shakespeare, Milton, Voltaire, and Newton. Wordsworth, Haydon recorded in his diary, was 'in fine and powerful cue', but his gravity was steadily undermined by Lamb's fooling, as he became more tipsy and more outrageous with every toast. Other visitors dropped in after dinner, including one John Kingston, a Comptroller of the Stamp Office, who came specifically to see Wordsworth. He must soon have wished he had set up a business meeting elsewhere. Really, so Haydon judged, 'a very mild & nice fellow', Kingston was at a loss in such a Bohemian company and when he tried to make what he took to be appropriate conversation it came out as, 'Pray, Sir, don't you think Milton a very great genius?' Keats was doubled up, Wordsworth was embarrassed, but Lamb, well the far side of sobriety, could not resist sending up this Jack-in-office: ' "What did you say, Sir?" "Why Sir," said the Comptroller, in his milk & water insipidity, "I was saying &c., &c., &c." "Do you say so, Sir?" "Yes, Sir," was the reply. "Why then, Sir, I say, hiccup, you are—you are a very silly fellow".' Embellishing the story later, but probably truthfully, Haydon recalled Lamb prancing around Kingston, trying to feel his bumps so as to assess the phrenology of one who could utter such 'very *deep* remarks'.[54]

As he wrote up his diary in the afterglow of this wonderful evening, Haydon tried to paint the scene overall.

There was something interesting in seeing Wordsworth sitting, & Keats & Lamb, & my picture of Christ's entry towering up behind them, occasionally brightened by the gleams of flame that sparkled from the fire, & hearing the voice of Wordsworth repeating Milton with an intonation like the funeral bell of St. Paul's & the music of Handel mingled, & then Lamb's wit came sparkling in between, & Keats's rich fancy of Satyrs & Fauns & doves & white clouds, wound up the stream of conversation. I never passed a more delightful day, & I am convinced that nothing in Boswell is quite equal to what came out from these Poets. Indeed there were no such Poets in his time. It was an evening worthy of the Elizabethan age, and will long flash upon 'that inward eye which is the bliss of Solitude'.

The conversation, the gaiety, the eager talk of poetry, even Lamb getting merry, everything recalls Alfoxden, save that Coleridge was missing. Wordsworth and he had been brought together, in fact, the night before by Monkhouse, but that party had not been a success. Coleridge had held forth on painting in what Crabb Robinson called his mystical style, but the stream of words that had once enchanted Wordsworth now merely irritated him to 'dry unfeeling contradiction'. Wordsworth needled Coleridge beyond politeness and afterwards Crabb Robinson had to admit to himself: 'I was for the first time in my life not pleased with Wordsworth.'[55]

For once this sensitive and intelligent observer's imagination failed him, for at the beginning of the month Wordsworth had given him the key to his behaviour on the twenty-seventh. Over breakfast at his brother Christopher's, Wordsworth had revealed how raw he felt about *Biographia Literaria*. Possibly he thought that for Coleridge to publish an autobiography at this stage of his life was an indulgence. Possibly he objected to its evasions and elisions. What was clear to Crabb Robinson was that he resented being involuntarily the centrepiece of what professed to be Coleridge's book about himself, and that he found both the praise and the censure distasteful—especially the censure. None of this could be said directly to Coleridge, but Wordsworth could not be at ease with him and at another party on 30 December Crabb Robinson noticed that both men, politely, kept apart.[56]

(4)

In December 1817 Wordsworth picked up some gossip from Tom Monkhouse which he relayed at once to Lord Lonsdale. Word had it that a candidate, possibly Henry Brougham, was planning to contest Westmorland in the forthcoming general election. This was, of course, 'a piece of absurdity'. The Lowthers always nominated the two county members and it was taken for granted that this time Lord Lonsdale's candidates—his two sons Viscount Lowther and Colonel Henry Lowther—would be returned unopposed. By early January this 'ridiculous business' had become a threatening reality.[57] By the time the Wordsworths reached home Brougham had already been adopted. Writing from Coleorton, where they broke the journey north, Mary told Tom Monkhouse, with the air of a wife humouring her husband's latest craze, 'William continues to imagine that he can be of use in Westmorland'.[58] She clearly had no inkling of just how obsessional he would become or of what reserves of energy he would find to devote to the Lowther cause.

Preparations in Kendal for Brougham's campaign astonished Wordsworth and convinced him that this was to be a real contest. But he never considered it a purely local affair. That certain freeholders were prepared to vote against the Lowthers was symptomatic of a wider malaise which Wordsworth diagnosed confidently. Since 1810 Brougham had been identified with most liberal causes.[59] He had defended John and Leigh Hunt against libel charges and Manchester radicals against the charge of sedition. He was in favour of the freedom of the Press and so, Wordsworth believed, was favoured by the Press, which was rapidly becoming a social and political solvent, as it had been in the early years of the French Revolution. Brougham stood for Dissent against Church, for urban and industrial against landed interest, for opposition against establishment. Whether Wordsworth's assessment of this brilliant and mercurial lawyer-politician was accurate is beside the point. If Brougham was not actually a Jacobin he was behaving like one and he had to be stopped. 'This attempt is no common affair of county Politics', Wordsworth assured Lord Lonsdale, 'but proceeds from dispositions and principles, which if not checked and discountenanced, would produce infinite mischief not to Westmoreland only, but to the whole kingdom.'[60] That Brougham had been a mainstay of the *Edinburgh Review* was to Wordsworth, of course, not the least of his sins.

For the next six months until the poll closed on 3 July Wordsworth worked tirelessly for the Tories. His family were with him—he even joked that poor Willy, who caught jaundice, was 'a complete Yellow', i.e. a Tory.[61] When Keats arrived in the Lakes in June he was staggered to hear from a waiter in Bowness that Wordsworth had been there canvassing in person for the Lowthers and was very disappointed when he called at Rydal Mount to learn that the poet was away at Lowther.[62] Had Keats called on almost any other day during the campaign he would have been disappointed, for Wordsworth was always at work. And the best that can be said is that having joined the battle he fought to win. Even-handedness, dignity, and propriety were abandoned. He gave the Lowthers a breakdown of the political allegiances of friends and acquaintances. He dined out, listened, and reported back. He attempted to browbeat the editor of the *Kendal Chronicle*, advised Lord Lonsdale about the possibility of suborning the paper entirely by buying it out, and finally assisted in setting up a rival paper, the *Westmorland Gazette*. When this faltered under its first editor brought up from London, De Quincey was installed in July. Not an entirely safe choice commercially, Wordsworth thought, but he recommended him as being firmly on the right side, and when his performance displeased the Lowthers did not scruple to lean on him heavily.[63]

Constantly monitoring the local mood, Wordsworth wrote to the *Kendal Chronicle* to protest against misrepresentation, signing himself 'A Friend to Consistency' and 'A Friend to Truth'. The opposition dubbed him 'Bombastes Furioso'. He also published *Two Addresses to the Freeholders of Westmorland*.[64] A part of the second of these is effectively *ad hominem*. Where is Brougham's money coming from, Wordsworth asks, raising the spectre of malignly anonymous paymasters. What about his past? In 1806 he had approached Lord Lonsdale for nomination as a candidate in the Lowther interest—behold, the hypocrite unmasked.[65] Brougham talks of the Rights of Man—so did Tom Paine, an acknowledged atheist revolutionary. But most of the *Two Addresses* concerns not this particular campaign but politics more generally and is of interest because it reveals very clearly the dominants in Wordsworth's thought. Compulsively reassessing his own past, Wordsworth returns repeatedly to the French Revolution, to the origins of the war with France, to its conduct, and to the state of the nation in peace, in order to show that the Opposition has remained set in an ideological stance that was, possibly, forgivable in 1790 but is demonstrably foolish, not to say unpatriotic, given all that has occurred since. Opposition in Parliament, which is legitimate and necessary, has shaded into support for radical agitation which would undo social cohesion. The freedom of the Press had been abused by such as Cobbett and more wickedly by such as William Hone, whose blasphemous satires, debauching the minds of the semi-literate, no wise authority could tolerate.[66] Legislation there must be against all these enemies who are nurtured by the very tolerance of a civilized society, but what is needed most of all is a recognition that in the 'power of large estates, continued from generation to generation in particular families', rests not tyranny but the surest guarantee of 'protection, succour, guidance, example, dissemination of knowledge, introduction of improvements, and all the benefits and blessings that among Freemen are diffused, where authority like the parental, from a sense of community of interest and the natural goodness of mankind, is softened into brotherly concern'.[67]

The election itself demonstrated that radical opposition disturbed social cohesion, as it was bound to. The Lowthers could rely on deference and self-interest to bring in the vote. Brougham had to make a big noise and flatter independent-minded freeholders that they were in the vanguard of history.

Dorothy fancied Brougham 'one of the French Demagogues of the Tribunal of Terror . . . He is very like a Frenchman.'[68] To the mass of the population who were not enfranchised he was someone who brought welcome excitement and its contemporary political corollary, beer. There was a riot in Kendal on 11 February and such an enthusiastic welcome for Brougham in late March that Dorothy was convinced that the 'majority of the Populace of Westmorland are ready for revolution'.[69] This was nonsense. In the poll at Appleby, the county town, Brougham was defeated and after a further break-out on 3 July the populace became quiet. But the Lowthers and their supporters did not relax. After the election Wordsworth advised Lord Lonsdale on how best to create more loyal freeholders and even organized a syndicate to buy land to ensure more safe votes. When Brougham stood again in 1820 he was again defeated and once more Wordsworth had been active in the campaign.

## (5)

Wordsworth was now so busy as executor of Richard's estate, and as political activist, that his family grew worried. It was 'pitiable that William should be thus diverted from his natural pursuits', Mary thought, and Sara feared that 'Poetry & all good & great things will be lost in Electioneering'.[70] Dorothy privately deplored the hours he spent tutoring John, but his brother Christopher remonstrated directly: 'I long to hear of your getting on with the Recluse—and grieve therefore to think of your time being taken up . . . Really your time is too valuable for such occupations.'[71] Their concern, which indicates how fully his family entered into Wordsworth's vision of himself and of his life's work, is understandable, but it was unfounded. From whatever cause, whether it was the pleasure of overcoming the difficulties of Richard's affairs or the thrill of being on the winning side in the election struggle, Wordsworth was full of energy and it was not deflected from poetry for very long. On the contrary, once the 1818 election was over he returned with renewed force and confidence to writing and to the business of publishing, that is, of marketing himself.

Wordsworth was writing new poetry, but he also had on hand old compositions which he had not abandoned. The *Salisbury Plain* poems and *The Borderers* remained hidden (more safely than *Wat Tyler*) and neither *The Prelude* nor *Home at Grasmere* could be published until *The Recluse* was completed. But *Peter Bell* and *Benjamin the Waggoner* continued to live in his imagination and in 1819 he issued both.

*Peter Bell* was something of a sensation. Alerted by pre-publication advertising, John Hamilton Reynolds dashed off *Peter Bell: A Lyrical Ballad*, in which he drew on his detailed knowledge of Wordsworth's earlier poetry to create a pastiche of the quintessential 'simple' style.[72] This 'ante-natal Peter', as Shelley called it,[73] was published on 15 April 1819, the real one about a week later, and literary circles buzzed with so much gossip about both that a second edition of Wordsworth's poem was called for a fortnight later. Reynolds had given Wordsworth his most immediate sales success. *Peter Bell* was presented aggressively. Wordsworth announced that the poem belonged to 1798 and in the dedication to Southey he not only allied himself proudly with the discredited Laureate, but also alluded to the hope he had first expressed years ago in the 1800 Preface to *Lyrical Ballads*, that such a poem might fill '*permanently* a station, however humble, in the Literature of my Country'.[74] Justifying the low subject matter of the poem Wordsworth also alluded unmistakably to *Biographia Literaria* in a manner which suggests that he did not think that Coleridge had said the last word on Imagination.

Faced with Wordsworth unregenerate and unrepentant about a poem that belonged to his *Lyrical Ballads* phase, many reviewers reacted in kind. Out came the well-worn lexicon of scurrility: 'gross perversion of intellect'; 'of all Mr. Wordsworth's poems, this is decidedly the worst'; 'another didactic little horror of Mr. Wordsworth's'; 'unequivocal marks of that tincture of imbecility which is the latent cause of the eccentric action of true genius'; 'daudling, impotent drivel'; 'so superlatively silly, as to be beneath . . . any expression of contempt contained in the idiom of the English language'.[75] But Crabb Robinson was wrong to fear that Wordsworth had 'set himself back ten years by the publication of this unfortunate work'.[76] The slashing review had become almost a ritual. Readers who scorned Wordsworth were satisfied to have their views reinforced, but on readers who had decided in his favour despite reviews ever since 1807, this kind of by now stale abuse could have little impact.

Far from being deterred, Wordsworth almost immediately published *The Waggoner*. The poem had been prepared for the press, *Peter Bell* was selling, and, as Sara Hutchinson put it, the reviewers might as well be given 'another bone to pick'.[77] Dedicating the poem to Lamb, Wordsworth once again reminded critics that this was the work of an earlier period, 1806. Since the publication of *Poems, in Two Volumes* in 1807 had destroyed what reputation he had had, this was a coolly defiant gesture. Lamb was delighted to be honoured and claimed in mock dismay that it was the fault of the binding that his copy seemed 'always to open at the dedication'.[78] But *The Waggoner* was not carried along on the success of its companion and a second edition was not required.[79]

While reviews of the 1819 publications were still appearing, Wordsworth was ready with his next volume. For some time he had been writing sonnets. In a letter to Sara in December 1818 Mary painted a picture she knew would gladden her: 'W. is at this moment sitting, as he has been all the morning . . . with his feet on the Fender, and his verses in his hand—nay now they have dropped upon his knee and he is asleep from sheer exhaustion—he has worked so long'.[80] He had been busy with four sonnets which were published with *Peter Bell*, twelve which appeared with *The Waggoner*, and on a sequence of thirty-three sonnets, some being earlier poems revised, which appeared in 1820 as *The River Duddon*.

Hidden away from the main tourist routes, the Duddon had been a special place for Wordsworth ever since he had first explored its upper stream as a schoolboy. In a note to *An Evening Walk* he had long ago pointed out that 'up the Duddon . . . may be found some of the most romantic scenery of these mountains',[81] and he now celebrated it over the course of an imagined walk from where it rises on Wrynose Fell to the estuary at Broughton. The whole sequence is competent, but it concludes magnificently as the poet draws back from particular scenes to contemplate why the river has such a hold on his imagination:

> I thought of Thee, my partner and my guide,
> As being past away.—Vain sympathies!
> For, *backward*, Duddon! as I cast my eyes,
> I see what was, and is, and will abide;
> Still glides the Stream, and shall for ever glide;
> The Form remains, the Function never dies;
> While *we*, the brave, the mighty, and the wise,
> We Men, who in our morn of youth defied
> The elements, must vanish;—be it so!
> Enough, if something from our hands have power
> To live, and act, and serve the future hour;
> And if, as tow'rd the silent tomb we go,
> Thro' love, thro' hope, and faith's transcendent dower,
> We feel that we are greater than we know.

The sonnet sequence was in future included in Wordsworth's volumes of *Miscellaneous Poems*, with the result that the make-up of the 1820 volume was effaced, recoverable only by those with access to rare books. But its identity as a discrete volume is of the greatest historical importance. It opens with a note on the geography of the Duddon and closes with a revised text of the *Topographical Description of the Country of the Lakes*, which had anonymously introduced Wilkinson's plates a decade before. The *Description* was published, a note explains, partly so that it might reach a wider audience, Wilkinson's work being expensive and of limited circulation, and partly 'from a consciousness of its having been written in the same spirit which dictated several of the poems, and from a belief that it will tend materially to illustrate them'. This mixture of prose and verse is maintained within the volume. Sonnet XVIII, 'Seathwaite Chapel', which refers to a 'Gospel Teacher',

> Whose good works formed an endless retinue:
> Such Priest as Chaucer sang in fervent lays;
> Such as the heaven-taught skill of Herbert drew;
> And tender Goldsmith crown'd with deathless praise!

is supported by a twenty-page 'Memoir of the Rev. Robert Walker', documenting the life of this model Christian, who for thirty-four years ministered to his obscure flock. In addition to the Duddon sonnets and the prose guide, Wordsworth also included the 1817 poems inspired by climbing Helvellyn, by crossing the Kirkstone pass, and by an evening of extraordinary splendour and beauty. None of these poems is exclusively local. The *Ode: The Pass of Kirkstone* no more requires a reader to know the road out of Ambleside than *Michael* calls for familiarity with Grasmere. But in 1820, the poems and the detailed *Topographical Description* which is their complement proclaimed once again Wordsworth as poet, celebrant, and interpreter of a particular, blessed region. In *The Prelude* he recalled the moment in youth that claimed him as a 'dedicated Spirit':

>                          Magnificent
> The morning was, a memorable pomp,
> More glorious than I ever had beheld.
> The Sea was laughing at a distance; all
> The solid Mountains were as bright as clouds,
> Grain-tinctured, drenched in empyrean light;
> And in the meadows and the lower grounds
> Was all the sweetness of a common dawn,
> Dews, vapours, and the melody of birds,
> And Labourers going forth into the fields.[82]

The 1820 *River Duddon*, as an entirety, confirmed that this vision was still Wordsworth's richest imaginative resource.

One more historically significant feature of this volume ought to be highlighted, as it too has been effaced by the passing of time and the inclusion of the *River Duddon* volume in the collected works. In *Biographia Literaria* Coleridge had described how while he was at Nether Stowey he had sought for a way of organizing in poetry his reflections on 'men, nature, and society'. A unifying principle suggested itself as he traced the progress of a stream, but 'Many circumstances, evil and good, intervened to prevent the completion of the poem, which was to have been entitled "THE BROOK".'[83] The echo in 'men, nature, and society' of Wordsworth's own words in the published Prospectus to *The Recluse* and, closer still, to his own letters about the poem in 1798[84] must have reminded him how inextricably linked were his early pretensions as a philosophic poet with Coleridge's fertilizing genius. But whereas he was ready to acknowledge Coleridge's role in *The Recluse* project, he was not prepared to concede any further indebtedness and in an unnecessarily long 'Postscript' he made his position clear. The sonnets were, he explained, composed on different occasions over many years:

In this manner I had proceeded insensibly, without perceiving that I was trespassing upon ground preoccupied, at least as far as intention went, by Mr. Coleridge; who, more than twenty years ago, used to speak of writing a rural Poem, to be entitled 'The Brook,' of which he has given a sketch in a recent publication. But a particular subject cannot, I think, much interfere with a general one; and I have been further kept from encroaching upon any right Mr. C. may still wish to exercise, by the restriction which the frame of the Sonnet imposed upon me . . . May I not venture, then, to hope, that instead of being a hinderance, by anticipation of any part of the subject, these Sonnets may remind Mr. Coleridge of his own more comprehensive design, and induce him to fulfil it?[85]

The sting here lies in 'at least as far as intention went'. Dedicating his recent collection to Coleridge, Lamb had admitted that his Muse had departed. But so, too, he feared, had Coleridge's: 'You yourself write no Christabels, nor Ancient Mariners, now'.[86] His tone, however, had been wistfully elegiac. Wordsworth's combined reproach, self-defence, and irritation.

The *River Duddon* appeared in April 1820 to reviews which could hardly have been more different from those of a year earlier. Only the *Eclectic Review* was grudging. The rest of the journals chimed in with the *European Magazine's* encomium: 'to us . . . he appears beyond all comparison the most truly sublime, the most touchingly pathetic, the most delightfully simple, the most profoundly philosophical, of all the poetical spirits of the age'.[87] The *Topographical Description* was praised. The 'Memoir of the Rev. Robert Walker' was praised and quoted at length. The 1817 odes were judged 'most exquisite' and 'singularly beautiful' and the Duddon sonnets themselves recognized as the 'gem of the volume . . . very beautiful'. Wordsworth, *Blackwood's* declared, had never been unpopular with those who really cared for poetry, but now there could be no doubt that the ascent of his reputation had 'triumphantly begun'.[88]

Before the year was out, as if to consolidate the grounds for this observation, Wordsworth had completed a period of astonishing activity by issuing five more volumes. They marked, as he recognized, the end of a phase of his life as a writer.

Before the 1830s publishers issued books not in durable casing but in flimsy boards, sometimes only in paper wrappers, which were discarded when the purchaser had the volume bound. It was thus possible, even usual, for volumes bought over a number of years to be bound uniformly to make a set. When *The River Duddon* was published purchasers were informed that 'This Publication, together with "The Thanksgiving Ode," Jan. 18. 1816, "The Tale of Peter Bell," and "The Waggoner," completes the third and last volume of the Author's Miscellaneous Poems', and an alternative title-page was included so that the book could be bound up into a uniform set, not as a separate volume, *The River Duddon etc.*, but as volume III of *Poems by William Wordsworth etc.*, volumes I and II being the *Poems* of 1815. In the same year Wordsworth issued a second edition of *The Excursion*, typographically similar to these other three volumes, so that a reader who had bought all of his poems as separate publications since 1815 could now have a uniform set, which would include the poem which had previously only been available as an expensive quarto.

1820 also saw a different four-volume edition, *The Miscellaneous Poems of William Wordsworth*. Encumbered with so much bibliographical information the reader could be forgiven at this point for being bewildered and possibly dismayed at what might look like opportunism on Wordsworth's part. The bewilderment is justified, but not the dismay. The 1820 four volumes were not a shrewd piece of marketing strategy, an attempt to get readers to part with their money for old wares in a fresh package, but a quite new edition in which Wordsworth presented all of the poetry he wanted to preserve, in a reconsidered order, in a fully revised text, complemented by the theoretical prose. Wordsworth was very consciously reviewing and re-presenting all that he had done.

It would be tedious to examine the edition in detail, but two features are important. The first is that the volumes display not only what Wordsworth now regarded as the canon of his miscellaneous poems, but how he wanted it seen. *An Evening Walk* and *Descriptive Sketches* were included in full, revised texts (only excerpts had been published in 1815), but this did not signal any softening towards the principle of chronological presentation. Although the contents page did indicate when poems were first published, the generic principle of classification introduced in 1815 remained. Perhaps the most significant detail of presentation of all is that the *Ode: Intimations of Immortality* stood apart, with its own title-page, as the last poem in volume IV, identified as the consummate lyric achievement.

The second feature is that the whole canon has been scrutinized and revised. Some of the changes reveal that, contrary to myth, Wordsworth did respond to criticism. In *Biographia Literaria* Coleridge had judged *Alice Fell* a failure—it was dropped. Lines in the *Ode: Intimations* appalled him—they were excised.[89] Reviewers and Crabb Robinson had objected to 'offensive passages' and 'over-coarse expressions' in *Peter Bell*—revised, even though the poem had only been in print a year. In 1807 the Blind Highland Boy had floated in 'A Household Tub'. In 1820 this stumbling-block to the fastidious had been transformed into a Turtle Shell. Most of the changes, however, reveal not that Wordsworth had 'resolved to make some concessions to public taste', as Crabb Robinson put it,[90] but that he regarded all of his poetry as existing in a continuum that knew no perfect tense. Whether a poem had been written in 1800 or in 1817 it was re-created and relived in 1820. Some of the results are very surprising. Few readers who are moved by the climax of *Michael*:

> There is a comfort in the strength of love;
> 'Twill make a thing endurable, which else
> Would overset the brain,—or break the heart:

would imagine that twenty years separated this last, beautifully cadenced, and entirely characteristic Wordsworthian line from the other two. Barron Field was probably not the only one to be shocked by the revision to *Elegiac Stanzas . . . Peele Castle*, in which

> and add the gleam,
> The light that never was, on sea or land,
> The consecration, and the Poet's dream

became

> and add a gleam,
> Of lustre, known to neither sea nor land,
> But borrowed from the youthful Poet's dream.[91]

It is impossible to overestimate the labour Wordsworth expended on such revision. Punctuation, capitalization, words, phrases, whole stanzas—all were reviewed. The whole body of his poetry became provisional until it had been rethought. For Wordsworth this was not a substitute for fresh composition: it *was* fresh composition, which entailed all of the usual anxiety and exhaustion. In 1820 Wordsworth presented his canon anew. Then, Sara Hutchinson reported, '*he says* he will never trouble himself with anything but the *Recluse*'.[92] Her emphasis indicates how much better she knew the poet than he knew himself, for this collection was only the forerunner of others and on them all he lavished comparable effort.

### (6)

Once the four volumes were in the press Wordsworth was free to satisfy at last a longing that had been growing more and more insistent. By the late morning of 11 July 1820 he was once again crossing the Channel to Calais.

His party was a large one—Mary and Dorothy, Thomas Monkhouse and his bride of only three days, Jane Horrocks, her sister, and the Horrocks maid. They had arranged to meet Henry Crabb Robinson at Lucerne, which they reached on 15 August—but they had also hoped for one more, Robert Jones, Wordsworth's companion on his first European tour in 1790. On their way south Mary and Wordsworth had stayed with him at his parsonage at Souldern in north Oxfordshire (Dorothy was already in London) and the sight of his old friend chafing to be off reminded Jones of their early rising and long days walking in France and Switzerland. But even if he had been fit enough—this 'good kind creature' had grown very fat[93]—parish and family responsibilities made it impossible for him to leave. Jones had to be content with vicarious revisiting. 'I wish particularly to know your Route', he wrote in 1821, 'and whether the things you saw in Switzerland in 1820 brought to your recollection sometimes . . . the objects you saw with far different eyes in 1790.'

Jones's question reveals why he ought to have been in the party. 'It would have been a singular and memorable incident in our lives to have gone over the same ground together after an interval of 30 years.'[94] Exactly. He recognized that for Wordsworth this tour was to be a re-enactment of formative experience. Superficially everything was different. Wordsworth was 50, not 20. He was responsible for his wife and sister. Jones and he had walked with knapsacks; now the party and luggage were transported from inn to inn. In 1790 the two had really to count their money, whereas in 1820 Wordsworth repeatedly haggled with innkeepers and carmen simply because he objected to being treated as if he were a wealthy Englishman ripe for fleecing. But in many ways Wordsworth was what he had been in 1790—energetic, remarkably tolerant of discomfort, open to experience, and determined.

Above all else, he was determined to return to the Alps. As Dorothy put it in her *Journal of a Tour on the Continent (1820)*, 'Switzerland was our end and aim'.[95] At first their journey was comfortable and leisurely. In Belgium they visited the battlefield of Waterloo. They saw Cologne Cathedral, the Rhine Gorge, the Falls at Schaffhausen, the usual tourist sights. Once they reached the mountains, however, Wordsworth threw off his years and clearly expected the others to do so too. Having shed the Horrocks sisters at Geneva—they could not face the rigours of this sort of travelling—the party carried on by charabanc, mule, and even on foot over the St Gotthard Pass into Italy as far as Milan and then back again over the Simplon Pass.

Although together day by day the three Wordsworths were, in fact, experiencing different tours. Mary was seeing the Alps and the Italian Lakes for the first time, enjoying what she had heard her husband talk about and what she had read about in his autobiographical poem. Dorothy, too, was seeing them for the first time, but her imaginative hold on these scenes reached far back before Mary Hutchinson had claimed her brother's love, back to the time when his first concern had been to share everything with his sister. She had kept his 1790 letter from the Alps and now she remembered 'the shapeless wishes of my youth—wishes without hope—my brother's wanderings thirty years ago, and the tales brought to me the following Christmas holidays at Forncett; and often repeated while we paced together on the gravel walk in the parsonage garden, by moon or star light'.[96] Repeatedly on this tour Dorothy's responses were registered through what her brother had told her or what he had written, as if even now that vicarious experience of thirty years before was dominant.

Mary and Dorothy both wrote accounts of their journey. Wordsworth produced only a series of tepid poems, published in 1822 as *Memorials of a Tour on the Continent, 1820*. But odd moments in Dorothy's *Journal*, and all of Wordsworth's previous writings, indicate what this tour meant to him. In 1790 he had been awed and exhilarated: 'My Spirits have been kept in a perpetual hurry of delight by the almost uninterrupted succession of sublime and beautiful objects which have passed before my eyes . . .'.[97] In 1804–5 he had relived the disappointments and discomforts as well as the elation, and found in his Alpine experiences forms and images for much of *The Prelude*'s richest poetry. In *The Excursion* he had exploited his memories afresh in his account of the Solitary's life. Now he was once again at their source. At Lake Como Dorothy was convinced they could make out 'The path which my Brother had travelled, when bewildered in the night thirty years ago' (*1805 Prelude*, VI. 617–57).[98] Wordsworth identified the Spittal at Gondo where he and Jones had passed a dreadful night, 'deafened and stunned / By noise of waters' (*1805 Prelude*, VI. 578–9), but despite Dorothy's entreaties he would not go inside.[99] The very track up the mountainside which had misled them on the Simplon Pass was discovered: 'It was impossible for me to say how much it had moved him', Dorothy wrote, 'when he discovered it was the very same which had tempted him in his youth. The feelings of that time came back with the freshness of yesterday, accompanied with a dim vision of thirty years of life between.'[100]

For Dorothy this often repeated 'thirty years' seems to intimate mortality, but at one moment she recognizes how profoundly Wordsworth was revelling in the collapse of yesterday into today. Describing the journey towards Chamonix she writes:

At the head of the hollow, having walked a while on the top of the hill, I, being then alone, looked suddenly down from the edge of the steep into a long, level, verdant, and narrow Dell, sprinkled with brown wood cottages. While standing on the brow of the precipice above this shady deep recess, the very image of pastoral life, stillness and seclusion Wm. came up to me, and, if my feelings had been moved before, how much more interesting did the spot become when he told me it was the same dell, that '*aboriginal vale*', that '*green recess*' so often mentioned by him—the first of the kind he had passed through in Switzerland, and 'now' said he, 'I find that my remembrance for thirty years has scarcely been less vivid than the reality now before my eyes!'[101]

This is a fascinating conjunction of the elements that make up Wordsworth's imaginative grasp of experience—past and present, primary sensation and remembered sensation, personal and vicarious involvement, living and writing. In 1790 the 20-year-old 'Enthusiast in . . . admiration of Nature in all her various forms' had declared his faith from the Alps that 'scarce a day of my life will pass [in] which I shall not derive some happiness from these images'.[102] Faced with the reality after thirty years the middle-aged man finds that his memory has been equal to the charge he laid upon it. But Dorothy's *Journal* demonstrates that the scene they gazed on was not an unmediated reality. Quoting from *The Prelude*, VI. 445–52, she recalls one of the passages in which, after a lapse of fourteen years, Wordsworth had 'enshrine[d] the spirit of the past / For future restoration'. In the 'thirty years of life' between first and second visiting, Wordsworth had retained experience in memory, but he had also fixed it in poetry.

The tour ended with further highly significant revisiting. On 30 September the party arrived in Paris and two days later Mary met Annette for the first time 'in the Louvre at one o'clock'.[103] Did Eustace Baudouin do all the talking or was Wordsworth's French adequate to introduce the mother of his first child to the mother of his later ones? We do not know. Dorothy's *Journal* is silent and Mary's notes little but dates and addresses. One important detail, however, was recorded. Throughout the visit, which lasted a month, Caroline always called Wordsworth 'Father'.[104] When he had last seen Annette, Wordsworth had been about to get married and Caroline had been a young girl. Now his daughter was married with children of her own. Wordsworth's relationship with Annette no longer had any vital connection to the present and, in a sense, he had recognized as much in the poetry of the past year. The *River Duddon* volume had included *Vaudracour and Julia*, the narrative of illicit love embedded in *The Prelude* as a surrogate for any more direct account of his own affair with Annette.[105] Excerpting it in this way Wordsworth extracted the poem from the autobiographical context which provided some of its meaning and effaced whatever connection it had had with his own experience. Reviewers who welcomed the poem as a moving tale of young, doomed love would have been amazed to learn that it obliquely registered the youthful passion of the two middle-aged grandparents strolling about the Louvre and Jardin des Plantes.

By the time they reached Paris the Wordsworths had endured vermin and bad food, outfaced rapacious innkeepers, and struggled in three languages with boatmen, stable-keepers, and mule owners. Before they reached home, however, they had to outface death itself. Impatient to be back, they took an alternative boat when the regular packet was cancelled because of contrary winds and threatening weather, but it went aground and broke up. Only the chance that they had struck before making deep water saved them, as they were able to stay with the wreck till rescued. After delay in Boulogne they finally reached England on 7 November 1820. In London they visited old friends, including Coleridge, and saw the Elgin Marbles. Crabb Robinson could not tell whether Wordsworth enjoyed them, but watching him on the tour had taught him '[Wordsworth] is a still man when he does enjoy himself and by no means ready to talk of his pleasure except to Miss Wordsworth'.[106] Dorothy went to the Clarksons for Christmas. Her brother and sister-in-law travelled north via Cambridge, where Christopher had just become Master of Trinity College, and Coleorton, arriving back just in time to spend Christmas at home.

In 1800 Wordsworth had written about the attraction of permanent forms, through whose sovereignty,

> still paramount to every change
> Which years can bring into the human heart
> Our feelings are indissolubly bound
> Together, and affinities preserved
> Between all stages of the life of man.[107]

No concept had a stronger hold on his imagination. 'The days gone by / Come back upon me . . .'; 'Did bind his feelings even as in a chain'; 'And I could wish my days to be / Bound each to each by natural piety'; '*backward, Duddon . . . I see what was, and is, and will abide*'; *Yarrow Unvisited, Yarrow Visited, Yarrow Revisited*.[108] The quotations and titles are only a tiny sample of what could be adduced to show Wordsworth's compulsion to trace affinities, to preserve wholeness, to recover and review the past. The 1820 tour was his greatest act of revisiting. Amongst the Alps and in Paris Wordsworth brought into conjunction his past and his present, tested memories, and made a shape of thirty years experience. In Paris his beginnings as a poet were recalled by Helen Maria Williams seeking him out. When his sonnet *On Seeing Miss Helen Maria Williams Weep at a Tale of Distress* had been published in the 1787 *European Magazine*, his first appearance in print, he was a schoolboy and she was an established poet. Now it was she who was honoured by a visit from one whom the same magazine had just acknowledged 'the most profoundly philosophical of the poetical spirits of the age'.[109]

This meeting is an emblem of the whole tour. As Wordsworth recited to the elderly lady her sonnet to Hope which had moved him when he was young, he was harmonizing his experience, completing a pattern.[110] One moment on the tour, however, could not be made harmonious and intelligible. It stood outside his experience, demanding yet resisting interpretation. On the first stage of their journey Wordsworth had insisted on visiting 'Peterloo', where a year before eleven people had been killed and hundreds injured when mounted yeomanry had cut through a crowd to arrest 'Orator' Hunt, as he addressed a mass meeting of Manchester radicals. The field of Waterloo made sense. Seeing it, Wordsworth wrote later, 'we felt as Men *should* feel'.[111] What the soldiers had died for there was not in doubt. The battle of 1815 closed a movement of history that had opened with the fall of the Bastille and the era had corresponded with Wordsworth's own development as an adult. He had lived through it and understood it. But the meaning of 'Peterloo' was still unfolding. On the Continent in 1820 Wordsworth established the coherence of his past life. Over the next twenty years his struggle was to understand the politics and social realities of a new era, whose grim portent was the battlefield in Manchester.

(7)

In 1821 Dorothy began to compose an account of the tour, as she had done after her visit to Scotland in 1803. Discussion of her hastily jotted memoranda prompted Wordsworth to his own re-creation and shaping, but what began as a complementary activity—'I will write some Poems for your journal'—soon engrossed him.[112] By November Sara was regularly sending transcripts to their travelling companion Tom Monkhouse, accepting with her usual tolerance that what the poet wrote one day he changed the next, 'altering and improving . . . to the no small *disfigurement* of my M.S.' and that whenever he declared he was finished, it was certain that 'there will be another batch . . . in a day or two'.[113] Dedicated to his 'Dear Fellow-travellers', the sequence was published in 1822 as *Memorials of a Tour on the Continent, 1820*. Simultaneously, however, Wordsworth was at work on a very different poem. It too was prompted by sights that had stirred him on their tour, but these were in England, not among the Alps.

On the journey out Wordsworth had been impressed by the situation of his old friend, the portly bachelor clergyman Robert Jones. Here was a man retired from the world, yet doing good, daily, in the most valuable way possible, ministering to the spiritual and temporal needs of his flock. To Wordsworth the parsonage at Souldern had seemed particularly striking, modest but practical, withdrawn yet visibly at one with the church and parish, an emblem of its incumbent's state, so striking that he had written a sonnet about it as their tour began, much to the annoyance of Mary who had looked forward to a holiday free from the grumpiness that usually accompanied the struggle with a poem.[114] On their way home they had experienced ecclesiastical life at the other end of the scale, when they stayed in Cambridge with the new Master of Trinity College, their brother Christopher, described by Southey as so 'red-hot' in orthodoxy that he believed 'in forty articles, thirty-nine not being enough for his capacious conscience'.[115] Since his time there, Wordsworth noted, Cambridge seemed to have shared in the spiritual renewal that had reinvigorated the Church of England. Now the grandeur of the chapels was matched by 'a great ardour of Study among the young Men' and the zeal of the new breed of Fellows. 'Judging from what one sees here', he told Lord Lonsdale, 'one cannot but augur well for the rising generation'.[116] After Cambridge they had visited the Beaumonts at Coleorton, where, discussing the site for a new church, Wordsworth and Sir George 'were naturally led to look back on past events with wonder and gratitude, and on the future with hope'.[117]

King's College chapel and Souldern parsonage, the Master of Trinity presiding over the past, Sir George Beaumont, the ideal English gentleman, acknowledging responsibility for the future—these images, overlaid perhaps on the threatening image of Peterloo, were the origin of *Ecclesiastical Sketches*, published in 1822. For his meditation in 102 sonnets on the history of Christianity in England, Wordsworth mined his extensive historical reading, but this sequence was not presented as the musings of a poetical antiquarian. It was, as *Cintra* and *The Excursion* and the *Thanksgiving Ode* had been, addressed to contemporary issues. In his prefatory advertisement Wordsworth acknowledged that while writing he had in mind the agitation for Catholic emancipation, and a long note, in which he contrives to print his sonnet on the Souldern parsonage, reflects on the importance of civilized, refined, comfortably endowed clergymen, who 'in many parts of England have long been, as they continue to be, the principal bulwark against barbarism, and the link which unites the sequestered Peasantry with the intellectual advancement of the age'.[118] In the 'Memoir of the Rev. Robert Walker' in the *River Duddon* volume two years before Wordsworth had exemplified the true spirit of Christianity in its human aspect. Now he ranged over the past to situate such a clergyman as Walker in the context of the evolving Church, tracing origins, and in the concluding sonnet, which parallels exactly the imagery of the last of the *River Duddon* sequence, looking hopefully to the future. The stream has flowed through centuries defiled by war, corruption, and dissension, but now,

> The living Waters, less and less by guilt
> Stained and polluted, brighten as they roll,
> Till they have reached the Eternal City—built
> For the perfected Spirits of the just!

Henry Crabb Robinson thought *Ecclesiastical Sketches* 'one of [Words-worth's] greatest publications', but this, the judgement of a self-confessed 'apostle' dedicated to the 'conversion' of 'scoffers', will not be the view of most readers.[119] There are some strong lines and *Mutability* is rightly anthologized as an example of Wordsworth's later manner at its most august, but for the most part the sonnets are dull.[120] Their composition, however, marked a very important moment in Wordsworth's intellectual life. The young radical who had scorned the idea of vegetating on a 'paltry curacy' and had arraigned the Bishop of Llandaff had always been moved by the fabric of the Church visible, the 'snow-white church' of Hawkshead, 'sending out a gracious look all over its domain', and by the idea of the Church as a force for cohesion and continuity.[121] *Ecclesiastical Sketches* brings together images of the Church as an evolving power in history, as a visible emblem of faith, and as a community of people, lay and ordained. Ten years earlier Wordsworth had confessed that he felt 'no need of a Redeemer', a sentiment which would have appalled the red-hot Master of Trinity—even for his diary Crabb Robinson thought it prudent to enter it in shorthand—and there is no evidence of the extent to which Wordsworth's beliefs had become more orthodox in the meantime.[122] He detested religious cant, mistrusted sectarians who pursued ideological purity, and declined to satisfy those who wanted assurance that the religion of *The Excursion* was four-square with the thirty-nine articles. But by 1822 he had become committed to the Church of England, and the necessity of defending it as *the* safeguard against anarchy and social retrogression was a constant in all of his future thinking about politics and national culture.

In 1822 Wordsworth also published the first separate edition of *A Description of the Scenery of the Lakes*. He was not to publish a new volume for thirteen years.

# PART III

'fame—a late though lasting consequence.'
(*Letter to 'Mathetes'.*)

# 1822–1832

## (1)

IN 1822 Jeffrey pronounced, 'The Lake School of Poetry . . . is now pretty nearly extinct'.[1] Seven years later, on the other hand, Parson and White in their invaluable *Directory* of the Lake District listed Wordsworth, amongst the 'Eminent Men' of Westmorland, as 'the father of the Lake School of Poetry'.[2] Both comments were right in a sense. 'The Lake School of Poetry' had always been a critics' label, but it had not been entirely foolish. There was a link, an obvious and strong one, between the *Lyrical Ballads* and the *River Duddon*. But by 1822 the vein seemed to have run out. *Memorials* and *Ecclesiastical Sketches* were not at all 'Lakeish', and they marked the beginning of a decade that was barren of significant poetry, 'Lake School' or not. Wordsworth's reputation, however, continued to grow despite the dearth of new poems. In Jeffrey's mouth 'Lake School' had been a taunt. By the end of the decade every Ambleside innkeeper knew that when tourists asked the way to Rydal they were hoping for at least a glimpse of the 'father of the Lake School of Poetry'.

Hostility and scepticism did not suddenly die out, of course, and Wordsworth remained as ever thin-skinned. He was deeply hurt by severe reviews of *Ecclesiastical Sketches* and *Memorials* in the *Literary Gazette*, the more so because he thought that his publisher Longman's part-ownership of the journal ought to have ensured favourable notices.[3] Although he generally refused to allow *Blackwood's Magazine* in the house, he did read John Wilson's attack in 1828 on the lack of specific Christian teaching in his poetry.[4] Wordsworth's response was surprisingly mild. He had long ago—and with justice—concluded that Wilson was unbalanced. 'He is a perverse Mortal' was his severest comment.[5] But no such tolerance was allowed to Chauncy Hare Townshend, an old friend of Southey's, who assaulted Wordsworth in *Blackwood's* a year later. 'Hugely belly-ached', as Hartley Coleridge coarsely but accurately put it, Wordsworth declared him 'a miserable maggot crawled out of the dead carcass of the Edinburgh review'.[6]

But these were minor checks to a reputation that was steadily growing. Wordsworth did not feel secure until the 1830s, but throughout the previous decade bad press had been more than countered by overwhelming evidence that the influence of the poetry was spreading and that the poet himself was now an honoured figure.

There was the evidence of fame, all gratifying but some of it silly and eventually very troublesome. In August 1820 Sara reported that a gentleman had called to ask 'in veneration of Wm.' whether he could 'see *the Study*'.[7] This Mr Irving was the bell-wether to what became a considerable flock of pilgrims who for the next thirty years trod the path to Rydal Mount. Other recognition, however, gave unmixed pleasure, such as the request in 1831 from the Master of his old college that the poet 'whose writings have uniformly and essentially tended to the promotion of virtue and religion',[8] should sit for his portrait by an 'eminent artist' of his own choice.[9]

There was the evidence, too, that he was increasingly honoured in America. Pirated editions of his poetry had been in circulation there since 1802, but now Wordsworth's anger at this theft was assuaged by proof that he had been contributing to the culture of an emerging nation. In 1822 he was visited by William Ellery Channing, the famous Boston minister, in 1824 by John Hobart, Bishop of New York, in 1825 by a law professor from Yale, Henry Dutton, and in 1828 by Andrew Norton, Professor of Sacred Literature at Harvard.[10] A letter from a pioneer educationalist, Elizabeth Peabody, in 1827 was particularly pleasing, as it revealed (as John Wilson's approach in 1802 had done) an ardent spirit in sympathy with what he believed to be the essence of his poetry:

When very young, and during the whole period of youth, I was dissatisfied with the manner in which the old communicated with the young—feeling especially that the system pursued in schools, the whole theory of education, was essentially defective, holding converse only with that part of human nature which may perhaps be denominated mechanical—and that the soul was neglected . . . The education I received was wanting in power to connect together the heart and the intellect . . . I have arrived to the conclusion that . . . *poetry* is the best means by which to develop the noble part of [children's] nature, and this conviction has been growing, although except *yours*, I never found any that would at all answer my purpose.[11]

In 1826 Wordsworth was pressed by Elliot Cresson, a Quaker merchant and philanthropist from Philadelphia, for a written memento of his visit to Rydal Mount. It is significant that he did not just dash off a quotation from one of his poems, as he was later to do on many such occasions. Into Cresson's album he entered a long statement about Anglo-American relations, which concluded:

It is my earnest wish that animosity may cease between us; that we may think of each other not for the purpose of inflicting reciprocal injuries, but with kindness and good will; and that Emulation may act only to make the two Nations, so closely connected by consanguinity, by institutions, customs and language, every day more and more worthy of each other's esteem. Policy requires this, Justice would infallibly produce it, and Nature sanctions it.[12]

These were not empty words. As Alan Hill has observed, in amassing through conversation and correspondence information about 'the problems and prospects of American society, the role of the Church as a unifying force, and the future of American literature', Wordsworth was in advance of most of his contemporaries, because his interest was 'not a side-line, but an extension of his central concerns'.[13]

Wordsworth's importance was also attested by those who were eager that his poetry should be more widely known. In 1825 Allan Cunningham urged him to agree to the publication of a selection of his work. Wordsworth was hostile to the idea at that moment. About to reissue the whole of his poetry, he feared any publication that might damage sales of the Collected Works—such as the cheap, unauthorized Galignani edition coming out of Paris in 1828—but he was not opposed to the idea as such.[14] This was significant. Since 1800 Wordsworth had controlled the dissemination of his own work, presenting each collected edition as a further stage in a still evolving corpus. For the first time he now accepted, at least in principle, that in his own lifetime an editor might have a role in promoting his work. Cunningham came close to succeeding in 1828, but in 1831 it was Joseph Hine who prevailed.[15] A schoolmaster in Brixton, passionately committed to the value of poetry in education, Hine was irresistible, and any doubts Wordsworth retained about the prudence of what he had agreed to were swept aside when he saw him in action. Edward Quillinan describes Wordsworth's visit to the school:

The boys rose and bowed, sate and gazed; pencils and slates were brought out at word of command; pedagogue gave out, line by line, the Sonnet supposed to be written on Westminster Bridge . . . When finished, several boys in turn read it out aloud: very well too. They were then called upon to explain the meaning of 'the river glideth at its own sweet will'. One boy . . . made a dissertation on the influence of the moon on the tides etc etc and seemed rather inclined to be critical; another said there was no wind, another that there were no water breaks in the Thames to prevent it gliding as it pleased; another that the arches of the bridge had no locks to shut the water in and out: and so forth. One boy said there were no boats—that was the nearest. Poet explained: was then called upon by Pedagogue to read his Sonnet himself; declined: Ped. entreated: Poet remonstrated: Ped. inexorable: Poet submitted. I never heard him read better. The Boys evidently felt it; a thunder of applause: Poet asked for a half-Holiday for them—granted—Thunders on Thunders . . .'[16]

*Selections from the Poems of William Wordsworth, Esq., Chiefly for the Use of Schools and Young Persons* was published by a new young publisher, Edward Moxon, in 1831.[17] It was prefaced by a defence of reading poetry aloud in schools, as 'a mode of culture profitable to health, to manners, to the understanding, and the social affections', which Dickens's Mr M'Choakumchild would have done well to read.[18] At this point Wordsworth entered the history not only of poetry but of educational theory and practice in nineteenth-century Britain.

Hine wanted to use Wordsworth's poetry for a noble end. This could not be said of other editors who badgered him. In the 1820s and 1830s publishers created a market for 'annuals', elegantly produced, illustrated compilations of poetry and prose—like today's 'coffee-table book', the ideal present.[19] High prices were paid for contributions to the *Amulet*, the *Keepsake*, the *Literary Souvenir*, the *Bijou*, and others with equally alluring names. Repeatedly approached, Wordsworth agreed to write for Frederic Mansel Reynolds of the *Keepsake*, whose offer of 100 guineas for twelve pages of verse was munificent and irresistible.[20] The details of how his commerce with this booth in the literary market-place led to recrimination, anger, and self-disgust are unimportant.[21] But the fact that he was being pursued by the editors of the annuals is not. These were entrepreneurs, making money. Their assiduity indicated that though his collected volumes might be selling sluggishly, his was now a famous, marketable name.

The growing reputation, however, was based on past achievement. Wordsworth's fame rested on what he had published up to 1815 and in the period 1822–35 he published nothing that materially affected it one way or the other.

This barrenness is not surprising. One need not subscribe to 'Romantic' notions about the ideal conditions for the production of poetry—suffering, solitude, imaginative possession, and so on—to see that during the fifth decade of Wordsworth's life many factors were working against it. 'I sought a theme and sought for it in vain', Yeats wrote in old age, laying bare the poet's deepest anxiety.[22] Wordsworth too was asking, 'what next?' and repeatedly feared that the answer might be, 'little or nothing'. In 1826 he confessed that he was 'haunted' by the idea that he had 'written too much'. Two years later he remarked, 'my vein, I fear is run out', and in 1831 he told Haydon that the Muse had forsaken him.[23] Throughout these years he was nagged by worry about his family and periodically acutely troubled by the condition of his eyes, which were now inflamed more frequently and more severely than ever before. An equally important enemy to poetry was simply that in middle age Wordsworth relaxed into social life and into the enjoyment of his fame.

(2)

Reflecting on the Wordsworths' situation after the death of Catherine and Thomas, Catherine Clarkson had shrewdly remarked to Crabb Robinson in 1813: 'Our friends have no *acquaintances*—They have neighbours—But in their present circumstances they need the sight of *equals* who are not intimate friends . . . by degrees from disliking these sort of visitors they wd. find the benefit of them'.[24] Fifteen years later she might well have lamented the opposite case. In the 1820s and 1830s, giving full rein to what Catherine Clarkson called 'the generous impulses of their nature', the Wordsworths entered whole-heartedly into social life, entertaining, travelling, enjoying themselves at breakfasts and dinners, theatres, and the opera. 'We are growing old and ought to make the best of our time to keep up long tried affections', Wordsworth wrote to Jones.[25] But he did not behave as though he were growing old. Aged 60, he rode Dora's pony from Lancaster to Cambridge, covering thirty-seven miles one day through torrential rain.[26] Nor did he only foster long-tried affections. Away from home for weeks, sometimes months, on end, Wordsworth found not only the physical energy for arduous journeys but also what is much rarer, the emotional energy required to reach out and hold on to new friends. By 1830 he seemed, and not only to Hartley Coleridge, 'yearly less of the Poet, and more of the respectable, talented, hospitable Country gentleman'.[27]

Rydal, London, Colcorton, where they had half-promised to pay an annual visit, and now Cambridge—these were the fixed points in Wordsworth's life, and if he was not to be found in one of these places he was probably at Lowther Castle. During the summers at Rydal they entertained non-stop. In August 1822, for example, Dorothy explained to Edward Quillinan how it was that 'the summer— past and to come—is wholly filled up'.[28] The Clarksons stayed a fortnight. They were followed by two aunts, Joanna Hutchinson, a Mrs Ellwood, and Colonel Henry Lowther. Christopher Wordsworth and his sons were lodging at Ivy Cottage, close by Rydal Mount, and soon Robert Jones was expected for a three-week stay. In future summers such welcome visitors were outnumbered by mere acquaintances or by total strangers who called, sometimes proffering a letter of introduction, but often with no more than their reverence for Wordsworth's poetry to recommend them.

At home in the Lakes there was much gaiety and some fashionable grandeur. In 1825 John Bolton of Storrs Hall laid on three days of festivities in honour of Canning and Sir Walter Scott. At dinner on 21 August Wordsworth was in the company of Scott, Canning, Lockhart, John Wilson (now Professor Wilson of Edinburgh University), Lord and Lady Frederick Bentinck, Sir James Graham, three prominent MPs, and several members of the Bar. Next day Wilson was master of ceremonies for a champagne dinner and a regatta in which fifty oared barges processed on the lake.[29] In 1826 they had 'a house-ful all the summer', Sara reported, adding that Wordsworth was 'only *agreeable by fits*', as he was 'busy among his verses'.[30] His tetchiness is understandable. In one helter-skelter paragraph Sara lists a large dinner party for Sir George Beaumont, Rogers, and 'some smaller folk', a musical evening, a wedding followed by a dinner, a christening, 'a huge picnic party into Easedale', a stream of guests, and the promise of more, 'so when our *season* is to end I know not'. A year later Sara was wryly calling their behaviour 'dissipation', as she described a summer which included a party of seventeen ascending Saddleback, a ball for sixty-five people, and 'the House . . . so full that we were obliged to have three beds of our Neighbours'.[31] At the end of the summer of 1831 Wordsworth wrote in high good humour to John Kenyon that they had been enjoying 'unexampled gaiety in Regattas, Balls, Dejeuners, Picnics by the Lake side, on the Islands, and on the Mountain tops—Fireworks by night—Dancing on the green sward by day . . . In the room where I am now dictating, we had, three days ago, a dance—forty beaus and belles, besides Matrons, ancient Spinsters, and Greybeards—and to-morrow in this same room we are to muster to a Venison feast.'[32]

In the same letter Wordsworth also suggested that unrest on the Continent was the reason why 'such multitudes of Pleasure Hunters have found their way this Summer to the Lakes', but in fact the region was becoming more and more fashionable and not the least famous of its sights was the poet himself. He did not always live up to expectations. In 1830 the Ruskin family on holiday 'went to Rydal Chapel in preference to Ambleside as we had heard that Mr Wordsworth went to Rydal . . . We were in luck', the 11-year-old John Ruskin noted, but 'We were rather disappointed in this gentleman's appearance as he seemed to be asleep the greater part of the time'.[33]

Wordsworth was also observed asleep in London. In April 1823 Crabb Robinson arranged a musical party and supper at which the guests included the Monkhouses, the Flaxmans, Rogers, Coleridge, and his friends the Gillmans. Promised 'first-rate music', Wordsworth declined all other invitations, but though he declared himself 'perfectly delighted and satisfied', he covered his face and fell asleep.[34] Wordsworth's letters and the many eye-witness accounts of his visits make it plain, however, that in London he rarely behaved like a man past 50. He indefatigably enjoyed everything that London had to offer—panoramas, museums, freakshows, the Italian opera, the theatre. William Jerdan recalled going with him to the 1830 Royal Academy exhibition. Before Turner's *Jessica* the poet growled, 'Did you ever see anything like that . . . it looks to me as if the painter had indulged in raw liver until he was very unwell'.[35] Other eye-witnesses, such as Rogers, Thomas Moore, and, of course, Crabb Robinson, record him revelling in breakfast parties, dinner parties, and excursions.

One evening in March 1831 Wordsworth at last met Francis Jeffrey at a party given by Sir James Mackintosh, at which John Lockhart was also a guest. Both men behaved decorously. Jeffrey asked to be introduced to the poet and he in return spoke to him, according to Henry Taylor, as 'a man of the world', appearing not to be 'conscious of anything having taken place between them before'. Jeffrey's comment that Wordsworth was not 'in any degree poetical, but rather a hard and sensible worldly sort of a man' perhaps betrays relief that nothing unseemly occurred.[36] Did Lockhart, one wonders, have in mind the very different way he had himself behaved in the literary feud that ended in the shooting of John Scott?*

Propriety had ruled, but on an earlier occasion it decidedly and embarrassingly had not. During Wordsworth's visit to London in March–April 1824 Haydon arranged that he should meet the exiled Italian poet Ugo Foscolo. 'Ugly as a baboon, and intolerably conceited,' in Scott's view,[37] Foscolo was notoriously volatile and Haydon was probably being mischievous in bringing the two poets together over tea one evening. If so, he was not disappointed. Foscolo, 'whirling round the room—twirling his quizzing glass rapidly in excitement, as if he were suffering under some galvanic influence', quarrelled with Wordsworth about the possibility of disinterestedness in human conduct. Wordsworth maintained that life afforded many examples of disinterested behaviour and cited cases such as he might have included among the stories told in *The Excursion*. Foscolo became enraged and ended the dispute by doubling his fist under Wordsworth's nose and bawling, 'Bah! It is all to satisfy self, Sir, to please self.' 'Wordsworth remained unmoved', Haydon's pupil William Bewick noted, and 'he shut both his eyes'.[38]

This was a literary-artistic party and there were many such. In April 1823, for example, Wordsworth went to Tom Monkhouse's with Coleridge,

---

* In 1820–1 journalistic warfare between *Blackwood's* and the *London Magazine* turned into an affair of guns and death. Lockhart and John Scott, driven by intense personal animosity, manoeuvred themselves into a position where a duel became inevitable. Lockhart made the running, but it was his friend Jonathan Christie who pulled the trigger. Scott died from his wound on 27 Feb. 1821. For a detailed account see Patrick O'Leary, *Regency Editor: Life of John Scott* (Aberdeen, 1983), 132–67.

Lamb, Moore, and Rogers—'the *most brilliant Thing* this Season' in the latter's judgement.[39] But this circle was not exclusively literary and artistic. On 23 December 1830 he dined at Lambeth Palace with the Archbishop of Canterbury and shortly after with Blomfield, Bishop of London, who was now a firm friend. By the end of January 1831 he was able to report, 'Five times have I dined . . . at the table of an Earl—and twice in the company of a Prince . . . prepare yourselves for something stately and august in my deportment and manners'.[40] In April he stayed at what was still the focus of London's intellectual-political élite, Holland House, and, according to rumour that was soon buzzing about the incident, gave Lord John Russell a dressing-down on the Reform Bill.

When in London, Henry Taylor observed, Wordsworth 'spends his time wholly in society, mixing with all manner of men, and delighting in various women'.[41] Taylor indicates exactly what was important to Wordsworth now. London offered diversion, political excitement, stimulation of all kinds, but most of all it offered the chance to sustain old friendships and to make new. He saw Crabb Robinson very often on most visits, met Rogers, Scott, and Talfourd, closed the rift with Coleridge, and renewed his relationship with Haydon which had cooled after 1824. He sought out Godwin and never failed to see Lamb, cherishing a friendship which now stretched back more than thirty years.

But Wordsworth was also establishing new connections. The civil-servant playwright Henry Taylor presided over a breakfast salon of young intellectuals and political aspirants. 'When Wordsworth happened to be in London', he recalled 'I got him to come; and though he was old, and the rest so young, and he was opposed to them in politics, yet the force and brightness of his conversation, his social geniality, and the philosophic as well as imaginative largeness of his intellect, delighted them all.'[42] The most famous of Taylor's 'Benthamites' was John Stuart Mill, who, as his *Autobiography* movingly records, had already been deeply touched by Wordsworth's poetry at a crisis in his intellectual development before he met the poet on 27 February 1831.[43] His visit to Rydal Mount later in the summer was an act of homage which did not disappoint the young disciple. Mill 'found [Wordsworth] still more admirable & delightful a person on nearer view than I had figured to myself from his writings; which is so seldom the case that it is impossible to see it without having one's faith in man greatly increased & being made greatly happier in consequence'.[44]

The young William Charles Macready, later the celebrated actor, was another who acknowledged in his *Reminiscences* a moment of conversion, when Wordsworth's poetry 'made me in some respects a wiser, and excited in me the aspiration to become a better man'.[45] He met the poet in London in June 1823 and called at Rydal later in the year. Unable to dine with him in 1831, but anxious not to miss him, Wordsworth invited Macready to breakfast.[46] John Kenyon, who, according to Sara, had a 'better verbal knowledge of [Wordsworth's poems] than the Author himself', cemented the friendship that had begun in 1819.[47] All of Kenyon's chatty, affectionate letters now at the Wordsworth Library confirm Southey's judgement that he was one of the best and pleasantest of men.[48] In 1825 a young woman, Maria Jane Jewsbury, sent her *Phantasmagoria*, dedicated to Wordsworth. He was already well disposed to one who wrote that she had been studying his work for three years, but when they met in the same year she won over the whole family.

From all of Wordsworth's more recent acquaintance, however, two were to become outstandingly important to him in different ways. One was William Rowan Hamilton, a mathematical genius who became Professor of Astronomy at Trinity College, Dublin, at the age of 22, and soon afterwards Astronomer Royal for Ireland.[49] Hamilton visited Wordsworth at home in September 1827 and conquered him completely. It was like meeting the young Coleridge again. As well as being a mathematical prodigy, Hamilton was an extraordinary linguist and very well read in English and European poetry. Wordsworth was dazzled, but he also had something to offer. Hamilton wrote poetry and he asked Wordsworth's advice with genuine humility. It was given, with a clarity, force, and copiousness which indicates just how impressed Wordsworth was by Hamilton's creative abundance.* United in their conviction that the pursuit of science needed the 'infusion' of the 'spirit of poetry' if it was to make for 'intellectual perfection', the young and the old man remained steadfast in their mutual admiration.[50] Hamilton recommended friends who visited Rydal Mount and regularly sent his poems, and his sister Eliza's, for the master's correction. Wordsworth, for his part, remained convinced that Hamilton was one of 'the two most wonderful men' he had ever met—the other being Coleridge.[51]

The other significant new friend was Edward Quillinan—a very different sort of man. An Irish lieutenant of dragoons on half pay, married to the daughter of the poet and bibliophile Sir Egerton Brydges, Quillinan had moved to near Rydal in 1821. In 1822 his wife was badly burnt in an accident at home and Quillinan was away in London when she worsened and died on

---

* W's letters to Hamilton ought to be as well known as his formal critical prose. While offering practical criticism, with a Johnsonian eye for slackness in diction and image, W also makes significant generalizations, e.g. 'the logical faculty has infinitely more to do with Poetry than the Young and the inexperienced, whether writer or critic, ever dreams of. Indeed, as the materials upon which that faculty is exercised in Poetry are so subtle, so plastic, so complex, the application of it requires an adroitness which can proceed from nothing but practice, a discernment, which emotion is so far from bestowing that at first it is ever in the way of it.' 24 Sept. 1827. *LY*, I. 545–7.

25 May, with only Dorothy Wordsworth at her side. He at once left Ivy Cottage for the Brydges seat, Lee Priory, in Kent, where the two small children, Jemima and Rotha, could be cared for. But the link with the Wordsworths remained strong. Himself a poet, Quillinan was devoted to Wordsworth and, though he differed in everything from the military, cigar-smoking, Roman Catholic Irishman, Wordsworth liked him too. The real bond, however, was with Wordsworth's family. Mary, Dorothy, Sara, and Dora looked upon Quillinan's motherless 'darlings' as an extension of their own family and he could not do enough to convey his gratitude for their attendance on his wife. Regular gossipy letters after he left, and meetings in London, brought them all closer and closer together.

All of these new friends—and more could be named—were important to Wordsworth in the coming years. They were, firstly, younger than he was. Wordsworth was approaching the period in which one's circle of real friends begins to diminish. Tom Monkhouse died in 1825 and in 1827 Sir George Beaumont. 'Nearly five and twenty years have I known him intimately', Wordsworth wrote to Rogers, 'and neither myself nor my family ever received a cold or unkind look from him.'[52] Within a decade Sir George was followed by Scott, Coleridge, Lamb, William Calvert, and Sara Hutchinson. Such friends could not in any sense be replaced, but the support they had given, the intellectual stimulus and friendly concern, could to some degree. Unlike many people, Wordsworth approached old age buttressed not just by his family, but by young friends made in middle age.

They were important, too, because they formed a link with the next generation of writers, artists, and intellectuals. Wordsworth had come to poetic and political consciousness when Cowper was the major poet, when Burke and Paine were powers, and when the fall of the Bastille signified the end of the old order in Europe. By 1830 he was a survivor from a past age. His new friends, however, ensured that he was not, and, more important, that he did not see himself as, just a monument to be wondered at. Talfourd, Macready, Taylor, Kenyon, these men were friends of Dickens, Thackeray, Elizabeth Barrett, and of the rising generation of editors, journalists, literary middlemen, and publishers, all creating and exploiting the growing mass market for literature. Wordsworth could not be of this world, but nor was he out of touch with it. In 1825 Hazlitt published a series of sketches called *The Spirit of the Age*. In 1844 Richard Hengist Horne tried to characterize the early Victorian scene with *A New Spirit of the Age*. Wordsworth appears in both, and he is treated in Horne's book not as a relic but as a constituent power of the new era.

That Wordsworth was ready to relax into social life, to indulge himself, in fact, is shown most clearly of all in the frequency with which he now yielded to his wanderlust. Given that travelling meant fatigue, expense, and the danger of drowning, as in 1820, one might have expected Wordsworth at 50 plus to settle down, but he remained, as he put it, 'as much a Peter Bell as ever'.[53] In 1823, after a round of visits to Coleorton, Oxford, London, and Lee Priory, Wordsworth and Mary toured Belgium and Holland in May and June. The following year, in August, they were guided round North Wales by Robert Jones, where they included in their sight-seeing the famous 'Ladies of Llangollen'.[54] In June 1828, seemingly on a whim, Wordsworth and Dora, with only a carpet-bag apiece, set off on a tour of Belgium, the Rhineland, and Holland. What was special about this tour was that Coleridge was persuaded to join them. Exactly twenty-five years before, Wordsworth, Coleridge, and a different Dorothy had set off together, only to separate with irritation and recrimination. At last that and all the subsequent wounds seemed to have healed. Two eye-witnesses who left attractive accounts of the party, Julian Charles Young and Thomas Colley Grattan, agree on one thing—that Coleridge was as loquacious as ever and that Wordsworth curbed himself in company, allowing Coleridge to dominate conversation, as if he conceded his friend's greater intellectual power.[55]

A year later he was off again, this time breaking new ground. Encouraged by Hamilton, Wordsworth and John Marshall, together with his son James, sailed on 30 August 1829 from Holyhead to Ireland, where for five weeks they followed a punishing itinerary that took them to all parts of the country save the far mid-west.[56] Wordsworth's account of just one part of the tour reveals what he was prepared to endure in the pursuit of first-hand experience and knowledge:

We left Kenmare each on a vile Irish Hack Horse at five in the morning, rode 3 hours, breakfasted and sailed on the bay of Glengariff upwards of two hours and called on Mr White, Brother to Lord Bantry, at his beautiful cottage or Castle upon Glengariff bay, walked about his charming grounds, lunched with Mrs White and her two interesting daughters . . . returned to Kenmare on the Hacks in three hours over vile roads; reached the place by eight—were up next morning between 4 and five—off on our hacks after a poor breakfast about half past six, rode 11 Irish miles (about 15 English) took to our feet, clomb and clomb till we reached the summit of a ridge, descended something less than 1,500 feet, mounted another ridge as high, descended and then took the mountain of Carranthouel the highest in Ireland, 3–4000 feet above the level of the sea—descended walked two hours—then two hours more—mounted our horses which we had sent round the mountain, and rode 4 Irish miles to Killarney which we reached at ten—having taken nothing all day but a bad breakfast—one crust of bread, and two basins of milk, and a glass of whiskey.[57]

And this was performed by a man who the following year could write lugubriously, 'My days are in the course of nature drawing towards a close . . .'.[58]

(3)

Balls and regattas, entertaining friends, long absences from home, and tours abroad—all of these did Wordsworth good, but they were not likely to inspire poetry, or rather, not the kind of poetry that might either add to his reputation or contribute to *The Recluse*. But even if Wordsworth had been living a less gregarious or more static life, it is not probable that he would have written more than he did, for though this was a period of much pleasure and frequent travel Wordsworth was assailed for much of the time by anxiety. Grief, pain, even intense anxiety, these can stimulate and get the imagination's adrenalin flowing. Wordsworth's anxieties were unproductive, but they demanded time and attention, and on occasions they plunged him into gloom—not Byronic despair or Arnoldian *Weltschmerz* from which poetry is made, just gloom.

Although Wordsworth's eyelids were often so inflamed that for long periods he could neither read nor write, he was otherwise in good health. 'He is still the crack skater on Rydal Lake', Dorothy boasted in 1830, 'and, as to climbing of mountains, the hardiest and the youngest are yet hardly a match for him.'[59] Eighteen months later, on the top of Helvellyn once more, Wordsworth proved that this was not just sisterly talk. But if he was strong, those dearest to him were not. Mary was attacked by lumbago and became increasingly lame.[60] Dora was sparky and sunny, but worryingly frail, subject to colds and infections which increased her father's already over-protective concern. And Dorothy was breaking down. In 1819, at 48 years of age, she told Catherine Clarkson that with only six teeth left (which were extracted shortly after) she had 'a true old woman's mouth and chin' and looked 70. Physically she seemed strong—'I was never leaner in my life', she reported in 1821, 'I can walk with as little fatigue as when I was twenty'[61]— but she, too, was increasingly prey to periods of malaise and in April 1829 she fell so dangerously ill that Wordsworth braced himself for her death. 'What a shock that was to our poor hearts', he wrote to Crabb Robinson. 'Were she to depart the Phasis of my Moon would be robbed of light to a degree that I have not courage to think of.' At the end of 1831 she collapsed again and was in bed for over ten weeks. Commending her to Christopher's prayers, Wordsworth admitted that what worried him most of all was that 'her recovery from each attack is slower and slower'.[62]

A different kind of threat unsettled them all in 1825. Wordsworth's relationship with Lady le Fleming, their landlady, had been as uncertain as such relationships generally are. In 1822 he had presented her with inscribed copies of *Memorials* and *Ecclesiastical Sketches* and the following year composed two poems honouring her generosity and piety in building a church at Rydal.[63] At the same time, however, Wordsworth as tenant was complaining about the state of the roof at Rydal Mount and insisting that she put in hand long-promised repairs. Irritated, and not a little capricious, Lady le Fleming indicated in 1825 that she wanted the Wordsworths to leave, ostensibly so that she could install an aunt in the house. Wordsworth knew how to be respectful to his betters, but he would not be bullied and he acted with impressive speed and aggression. Laying out 'an extravagant fancy price', he bought an adjoining field, commissioned a local architect, George Webster, to design a rather grand house in the picturesque-historic style (see Pl. 13), and negotiated for timber and materials.[64] Whether she liked it or not, Lady le Fleming was to have not just the Wordsworth family as neighbours, but a big new villa next to her church and her own home. Wordsworth's counter-threat worked and the aunt was anyway disinclined to move. By the end of the year the scare was over.

Wordsworth had been deeply stirred. Rydal Mount might have a leaky roof and poky back rooms, but it was the place where all of the family had remade their lives after the death of the children. Wordsworth had shaped the garden as thoughtfully as he had the winter garden at Coleorton and indoors three adults, with separate needs and quirks, had made an environment in which they lived in harmony. Lady le Fleming's whim struck not just at Wordsworth's rights as tenant, but much more profoundly at his need for order, continuity, and control over his life.

This external threat to family life at Rydal came, moreover, at a time when the family itself was under strain. Wordsworth was persistently anxious about his children. Having failed to get John into Charterhouse, Wordsworth tutored him himself—disastrously. John was slow and, as Sara Hutchinson observed, frightened of his father, who seemed to be despairing of him.[65] In 1820 he entered Sedbergh School, and in 1823, when his father was persuaded that he would be unable to cope with Cambridge mathematics, he matriculated at New College, Oxford. Wordsworth's letter to John Keble at Oriel, enlisting his help, reveals his state of mind.[66] He writes as a fond but over-anxious parent, whose concern to ease his son's path is inextricable from an insidious determination to control it. And so it continued. Subject to steady parental pressure, John moved towards the Church. His first curacy at Whitwick, near Coleorton, was only obtained through the Beaumont connection, and his first livings, Moresby, above

Whitehaven, and then nearby Brigham, were presented by his father's patron Lord Lonsdale. Hesitant, unsure of himself, passive, John Wordsworth became, as Hartley Coleridge unadmiringly put it, 'a truly respectable Clergyman',[67] his one independent act being to woo Isabella Curwen, daughter of Henry Curwen of Workington Hall, whom he married, with some pomp, in October 1830. 'The Father's allowance to his daughter', Wordsworth reported with relief, 'is so liberal as to remove every objection on prudential grounds.'[68]

Wordsworth's efforts for John at least succeeded. Nothing, it seemed, worked with Willy. 'Wants a Situation. A youth of about fifteen years of age. He is able to do any kind of work, but prefers sitting to standing, riding to walking, and lying in bed to anything in the world.' This spoof advertisement in the *Kent's Bank Mercury*, a newspaper concocted by Dora and Maria Jane Jewsbury while on holiday at the coast in August 1825, sums up the family's perception of him.[69] Having been to school in London and then at Charterhouse, Willy Wordsworth returned home in June 1822 extremely ill. His parents were stunned by his neglected state and after months of nervous watching over him decided that he should remain in Ambleside at Mr Dawes's school. The attractive but wayward adolescent, however, seemed fitted for nothing in particular. He wanted to go into the army and staggered everyone by clandestinely taking steps in 1828 to secure a commission. Utterly opposed to the idea, Wordsworth extinguished this one spark of independence and fell back on conventional expedients, ever more desperately. Should Willy go into business? Should his brother John tutor him up to University entry standard in Classics and maths? Perhaps Lord Lonsdale could find him a niche. 'He *must* go somewhere', Wordsworth sighed.[70] Eventually Willy was dispatched to Germany, to acquire languages of use in the commercial world, but in 1831 he returned home, unemployed and not obviously employable. Father manœuvred, son acquiesced, and in the same year William Wordsworth junior became his father's sub-distributor of stamps at Carlisle.

'Somewhere . . . he must go, whatever is done with him.'[71] It is a sad comment. In his own youth Wordsworth had strongly resisted attempts to 'do' something for him. Disdaining security he had insisted on following his own bent, existing on little, accepting help only when he saw no smack of compromise. And *The Prelude* had been his testimony to the conviction that everything—the planned and the adventitious, pleasure and fear, lassitude and energy, depression and stimulus, false and true—had combined to a mysterious but benevolent end. But with his own children Wordsworth evidently feared the unplanned. He fretted, sought advice, and pulled strings to organize their progress. Possibly the distress over Hartley Coleridge sharpened his concern. Dismissed from his Oriel Fellowship in

1820, Hartley had drifted back to Ambleside, where he taught for a while before becoming, in effect, a much-loved gentleman vagrant.* Every time Hartley called at Rydal Mount to pick up money or a parcel sent by his mother, Wordsworth was reminded of *Frost at Midnight* and his own poem *To H.C., Six Years Old*, with its prophetic lines:

> O blessed vision! happy child!
> Thou art so exquisitely wild,
> I think of thee with many fears
> For what may be thy lot in future years.

Wordsworth was certainly, too, simply worried about money, as the comment about Isabella Curwen's allowance reveals. Like many parents who have had to struggle, he wanted to shield his children from financial care. Well intentioned though it was, however, his loving control damaged both his children and himself. John Wordsworth distanced himself from his father, Willy became merely a shadow of him, and Wordsworth settled into a steady state of paternal anxiety whose focus now was Dora.

(4)

Anxiety about problems at home was compounded by concern at the course of national affairs. Although in both spheres Wordsworth was troubled by specific issues, there was a vital difference in the nature of his anxiety. As father or husband or brother he could act directly on domestic problems. But with national policy it was quite different. As an intelligent, educated, and well-travelled man Wordsworth had confidence in his capacity to analyse social and political trends, but as a poet he had no power to influence government policy, no privileged position whatsoever in relation to the affairs of state that engrossed him. The most he could do was attempt to influence them by proxy through supplying ideas to those who did have the power. He wrote many thousands of words to Lord Lonsdale and Viscount Lowther and to the fiercely Tory baronet Sir Harry Inglis about electoral reform, to Charles Blomfield, Bishop of London, on the issue of Catholic emancipation, to Hugh Rose of Cambridge about the state's role in education.[72] But although he thought he might 'possibly have occasion at some time or other to address the public', he did not do so.[73] Southey did in his *Sir Thomas More: or, Colloquies on the Progress and Prospects of Society*,

---

* The Wordsworths and Southey were at first opposed to Hartley's return. See *L Y*, I. 168–9 n. 7 for a particularly savage letter from RS, who feared that he would disrupt life at Greta Hall as his father had done. However the Wordsworths did all they could to help him, finding him lodgings, settling bills, holding letters, and so on, believing that if he were to lead an eccentric life it was best done where he was known and loved.

1829. Coleridge did in *On the Constitution of the Church and State*, also in 1829. But Wordsworth made no public contribution to the great debates which dominated English politics in the decade before the 1832 Reform Bill.

This reticence is worth stressing, for it reminds us that all of the evidence for Wordsworth's political views in this period has to be drawn from reports of his conversation and from private letters. This is historical evidence, of course, but it is of a different kind from a public utterance such as *The Convention of Cintra*. Advocacy was not called for in letters to Viscount Lowther or Bishop Blomfield, as it would have been in any address to an unknown public. Wordsworth's statements are not subtle, nor are they refined, and they are certainly not even-handed in their use of evidence and argument, for Wordsworth was not arguing. His intention was rather to share ideas with, and to stiffen the resolve of, influential people whose outlook he already knew he broadly shared.

Had he published an essay on Politics in Church and State it is unlikely that it would have added significantly to the arguments being propounded at Westminster and in the periodical press during the political manœuvring that led up to the Catholic Relief Bill of 1829 and the Reform Bill of 1832. Wordsworth was vehemently opposed to any concessions for the Roman Catholic Church on many grounds, but they amounted to one question: 'Are not the same Arguments that induced our Forefathers to withdraw from the Roman faith 300 years ago still applicable?' The papacy, he believed, was 'founded upon the overthrow of private judgement'. Since the Roman Church retained its claim to the property of the Anglican, it was dangerous, not to say absurd, even to think of 'allowing Catholics to legislate for the property of a protestant Church'. As long ago as 1809 Wordsworth had reasoned with the liberal Wrangham, 'with the Methodists on one side and the Catholics on the other, what is to become of the poor Church and people of England', but then Catholic emancipation had been little more than a debating issue.[74] Now it was a real threat and Wordsworth's antagonism was accordingly less measured. What he had seen of Catholics in Belgium and more especially in Ireland had moved him to wish that Protestants would display 'such devout reliance on the mercy of their Creator, so much resignation, so much piety', but his experience in Ireland of the power of 'Popery' alarmed him.[75] The established Church in an integral part of Great Britain was being overwhelmed. The evil had to be combated there, not freed by law to spread in the mother country.

Wordsworth was logical. He saw that if it was argued that the number of the Roman Catholic faithful legitimized concession, the same argument would have to apply to English Dissenters. The Church of England would survive, but its controlling influence on local and national life would have been sacrificed. And this hostility to the argument from numbers was the rock-bottom of his opposition to extension of the franchise. Although he could say that 'the Constitution of England which seems about to be destroyed, offers to my mind the sublimest contemplation which the History of Society and Govern[ment] have ever presented to it', or, less astonishingly, 'I now perceive many advantages in our present complex system of Representation, which formerly eluded my observation', he did wish that power was not so entirely 'in the hands of the large Proprietors' and could contemplate what he called '*tentative*' reform. But extension of the franchise could not but end 'in universal Suffrage' and, recognizing this, he entreated God's forgiveness for the authors of the 1832 Reform Bill, who 'have already gone so far towards committing a greater political crime than any recorded in History'.[76]

Many excuses might be made to extenuate this grotesque observation. Wordsworth was writing in bitter disappointment to Lord Lonsdale—intemperance might be expected. He was disgusted by the unprincipled strategems that ministers had to resort to to get the Bill passed. Major riots at Bristol indicated that malign forces were being unleashed. Many of the best and wisest of his generation thought as he did—and so on. But it is difficult to imagine a more wrong-headed judgement or one that could indicate more dismayingly how sterile Wordsworth's political imagination had become since 1818, when he had first taken an active part in electioneering.

In July 1831 Julius Hare described meeting the poet the previous April: 'I was very much grieved to find how much the state of the country and the ministerial Reform bill had preyed upon his health. Everybody said, he seemed to have grown three years older in the last three months.'[77] If added to the comment to Lord Lonsdale, this account suggests a possible reason why Wordsworth published nothing in prose or poetry about these great national events. At earlier crises he had poured out sonnets dedicated to independence and liberty and he had celebrated victory in the appropriate public genre, the ode. But those crises had not only been stirring in themselves, they had yielded up resources for the imagination. At the 1802 invasion threat, Milton and Shakespeare had been summoned to give resonance to an idea of Englishness threatened by Napoleon, himself an icon upon which imagination could play. Hofer, the Tyrolean innkeeper, William Tell, Palafox, the hero of Saragossa, Ferdinand Schill, and Gustavus IV, the 'Royal Swede', all of these figure in the 1809–10 sonnets which celebrate heroic resistance, that finest proof that 'from *within* proceeds a Nation's health'. The fate of Toussaint L'Ouverture, the death of Nelson, Clarkson's triumph at the Bill for the Abolition of the Slave Trade in 1807, the death of Charles James Fox—Wordsworth had been able to grasp each of these public events imaginatively and make something of them. But the decade 1822–32, though quite as important politically as the previous two, yielded nothing. To some of the younger generation the events of the age were heavy with meaning. Carlyle's *Signs of the Times* (1829) and Macaulay's trenchant critique of Southey's *Colloquies* (1830), for example, imperiously interpreted the circumstantial because they had an imaginative, prophetic vision of its larger significance.[78] But for Wordsworth social unrest, religious dissension, political chicanery, these obtrusive but confusing realities, eluded imagination's grasp. And he felt it to be so. 'The Muse has forsaken me', he told Haydon in 1831, 'being scared away by the villainous aspect of the Times.'[79]

## (5)

This was Wordsworth's gloomiest moment, but the Muse had not forsaken him. Perhaps insulted by his words, she visited him soon afterwards 'in the wood adjoining [the] garden' at Rydal Mount and within twenty minutes he was back indoors dictating a sonnet for Haydon.[80] She visited him, too, on another occasion which recalled a moment of communion nearly thirty years before. In 1802 Wordsworth had composed 'Among all lovely things my Love had been' while on horseback, concentrating so hard that he did not notice his fingers going numb with cold. In 1830, trotting astride Dora's pony between Lancaster and Cambridge, Wordsworth whiled away 'two days of tempestuous rain' by composing verses in memory of Sir George Beaumont and a sonnet to Chatsworth.[81] During their tour of North Wales in 1824 he had similarly defied the elements, addressing a sonnet *To the Torrent at the Devil's Bridge* as the rain poured down.

But the Muse's visits were fitful during this, the least productive period of Wordsworth's life. He wrote occasional pieces, such as the poems on the erection of Rydal Church, or on the 'Miserrimus' stone in Worcester Cathedral.[82] There were domestic lyrics, such as the lovely tribute to Mary, 'Let other bards of angels sing', *The Triad*, a celebration of Edith May Southey, Sara Coleridge, and Dora, and the sonnet to Sara Hutchinson, 'Excuse is needless when with love sincere'. In 1823–4 Wordsworth laboured at translating parts of the *Aeneid*, and in 1828–9 he even composed one substantial ode, *On the Power of Sound*, which he considered in parts 'equal to anything I have produced'.[83] But these, even the ode, were, by Wordsworth's standards, small-scale works, and so disparate that there could be no question of issuing them as a separate volume.

Two poems give an insight into the workings of Wordsworth's imagination now. One, *The Armenian Lady's Love*, is amongst his very worst poems, 'unenlivened', in Mary Moorman's words, 'by a single glimpse of imaginative power'.[84] But it has an intriguing dedication:

The subject of the following poem is from the Orlandus of the author's friend, Kenelm Henry Digby: and the liberty is taken of inscribing it to him as an acknowledgement, however unworthy, of pleasure and instruction derived from his numerous and valuable writings, illustrative of the piety and chivalry of the olden time.

*The Broad Stone of Honour*, to which this note refers, was the work of a young man who found 'The Middle Ages . . . more vivid . . . than the present, and a great deal preferable'.[85] A Catholic convert, Digby was obsessed with chivalry. He read everything, visited every European castle and site, and compiled in *The Broad Stone of Honour* a gallimaufry of chivalric lore as 'Rules for the Gentleman of England'. Reaching its third, greatly enlarged edition by 1828–9, this text-book of 'the olden-time' moved many an idealistic young man—Tennyson amongst them—and pointed the way for the early Victorian return to Camelot. What is striking is that Wordsworth should have been susceptible to it. At a time when it seemed that weak or base men dominated public life, when politics had become a business of concession and stratagem, when urban and agrarian unrest threatened social order while utilitarian legislators desperately tried palliative or repressive measures in turn, Wordsworth was touched by a book that transported readers to a realm where personal honour, inner purity, and outward valour were paramount.[86] *The Broad Stone of Honour* clad the ideals of *The Happy Warrior* in armour and spoke to Wordsworth's imagination. The most famous passage in Burke's *Reflections* was the lament for the passing of chivalry, and its author now struck Wordsworth as the 'wisest of the Moderns'.[87]

Haydon, too, touched him when he was feeling most barren. Seeing that the poet was impressed by his painting of *Napoleon on the Island of St Helena*, Haydon had urged him to honour the sentiment of 'High is our calling, Friend!', by composing a complementary poem. He could only manage prose, Wordsworth replied, 'for the Muse has forsaken me'.[88] What he eventually sent was this:

> Haydon! let worthier judges praise the skill
> Here by thy pencil shown in truth of lines
> And charm of colours; *I* applaud those signs
> Of thought, that give the true poetic thrill;
> That unencumbered whole of blank and still;
> Sky without cloud—ocean without a wave;
> And the one Man that laboured to enslave
> The World, sole-standing on the rocky hill—

With arms close folded and averted face
Tinged, as we may fancy, in this dreary place
With light reflected from the invisible sun
Set like his fortunes; but not set for aye
Like them. The unguilty Power pursues his way,
And dawn perpetual doth before him run.

Nine years later Wordsworth celebrated another Haydon picture in *On a Portrait of the Duke of Wellington upon the Field of Waterloo*. The later sonnet is perhaps inferior, but both are amongst the strongest poems Wordsworth wrote after 1822 and what their quality suggests is that in the titans of the Napoleonic war he continued to find poetic possibilities which eluded him in the unheroic age of Catholic emancipation and the Reform Bill.

In December 1822 Dorothy confided to Crabb Robinson her belief that her brother would not 'in his life-time, *publish* any more poems'.[89] This remark was probably not as unfounded as it might seem. Dejected by the slow sale of *Sketches* and *Memorials*, Wordsworth might well have said that he would never again put together a separate collection of new poems.[90] But this did not mean that he had lost interest in publication—here Dorothy was quite wrong. Maybe a new volume was unlikely, but Wordsworth's whole identity as a poet was vested in his Collected Works and he was as determined as ever that they should continue to be issued, that their format should be as he wished, and that each edition, through revision to the text and through additions to the contents, should be not a five-volume epitaph but fruit of a still-blossoming tree.

Not that the Collected Works sold well. After the first year of publication, for example, sales of the 1820 four-volume edition dwindled to double figures annually and it was not until 1825 that stock of the printing of 500 was low enough for Wordsworth to plan a further edition. Although he complained that profits were consumed in advertising, he also felt that Longman's marketing was inept and was tempted to abandon the firm, strongly so when the terms offered for a new edition were embarrassingly poor.[91] Alaric Watts was amazed by the discrepancy between Wordsworth's reputation and his receipts. 'You have been most grossly imposed upon . . . I do most sincerely hope you will have nothing further to do with them', he wrote, but as the firm he recommended, Hurst and Robinson, crashed, and as the greatest publisher of all, John Murray, seemed 'disposed to put on the airs of a Patron', to Wordsworth's disgust, no choice was left but to remain with Longman for the five-volume Collected Works which appeared in May 1827.[92]

This was Wordsworth's third collected edition (1815, 1820, 1827). *Memorials of a Tour* and *Ecclesiastical Sketches* were incorporated into the canon and every poem was freshly scrutinized, right down to the commas and semicolons. *The Excursion* was revised with particular care. Wordsworth was aware, however, that even his warmest admirers found his way of presenting his poems and his continual revision disconcerting. Lamb, Crabb Robinson reported, thought that there was only one good order for the poems, 'the order in which they were written—That is a history of the poet's mind', but he preferred a classification based on 'the great objects of human concern'—Nature—Infancy and Youth—Active Life—Old Age— Social Relations—the Contemporary World.[93] Wordsworth was troubled, but unmoved, and so positive that 'Lamb's order of time is the very worst that could be followed'[94] that he removed from the contents page such information as had previously been given about the chronology of his poems, as if to emphasize that these were emanations of the poetical mind, not a history of one poet's mind in particular. Newly revised, each collected edition was a re-presentation of the whole, still-evolving corpus, not a mere augmenting of the old by addition of recent work. Wordsworth's demand on his reader was inordinate. To keep up with the poet's current writing it was necessary to check every poem, not just run over the contents pages ticking off what was new. Crabb Robinson's 'The variations of the three editions I possess are a matter of very interesting remark' was a generous response.[95]

Walter Savage Landor acknowledged his presentation set equally warmly, but his letter of thanks contained one unintentionally piercing comment: 'The only thing that disappointed me, was, to see no continuation of the Recluse. And yet perhaps, if there is any one who wishes your happiness without any reference to his own, he would wish that a part of it should always remain unfinished. Nothing is so delightful to a man as the progress of a poem: when he has finished it his doubts and anxieties come in.'[96] In 1815 Wordsworth might have been receptive to these words from a brother-poet: in 1828 they only added to his misgivings. For everyone was waiting—and worrying. In 1821 Christopher welcomed *Ecclesiastical Sketches* but hoped that they 'do not interfere too much with the progress of the Recluse', just as Dorothy was confiding in Catherine Clarkson that 'William . . . has not looked at the Recluse or the poem on his own life; and this disturbs us. After fifty years of age there is no time to spare . . .'. Both Mary and Dorothy sensed that Wordsworth was frightened. Hopeful that he would get back to work in 1824, Mary admitted that she dared not mention her hope, 'lest he should be scared by the prospect', and Dorothy told Crabb Robinson that her brother felt 'the task so weighty that he shrinks from beginning with it'. 'How years roll away', she lamented to another friend in 1828, as she reported no progress on *The Recluse*. Dora joined in, impatient for recent lyrics to be published, 'for till they are out of the way we feel convinced, his great work will never be touched; every day he finds something to alter or new stanzas to add—or a fresh sonnet—or a fresh Poem growing out of one just finished—which he always promises shall be the last'.[97]

Such expectant anxiety was a heavy burden. Twenty years before only Coleridge had believed that Wordsworth's lyric writing was blocking *The Recluse*. Now all of his household did. Periodically Wordsworth entered into the fiction that the 'great work' was still in being. In 1822 he assured Landor that *The Recluse* lived in his thoughts, excusing its continued seclusion there by the explanation that his manuscripts were so messy that he could not face them just then. Four years later he told Crabb Robinson that he saw *Composed when a Probability Existed of our being Obliged to Quit Rydal Mount as a Residence* as 'an introduction to a portion of his great poem', and in 1831 he was promising that 'the Recluse shall be his winter's employment'. But Dora, who reported the promise, was close enough to her father to sense the truth: 'entre nous I think his courage will fail him when winter really arrives'.[98]

Wordsworth's courage did fail him, but not his energy nor his creativity. Only months later Dora could write: 'Father is particularly well and busier than *1000* bees'.[99] What had happened was a revisiting that had deeply affected him and moved him both to fresh composition and to a further imaginative engagement with his own past.

(6)

In August 1831 Sir Walter Scott urged Wordsworth to visit him before he left to spend the winter in Italy. Wordsworth was impatient to be off. He longed to see Scott in his own home again and hoped, too, that if Dora were to accompany him she would benefit from a tour into the Highlands, but a severe attack of eye-trouble delayed the start of their journey, so that they did not arrive at Abbotsford until 19 September, only five days before Scott's planned departure.

Two sick elderly men greeted each other. Wordsworth's eyelids were so inflamed that he wore a green protective shade—'There's a man wi' a veil, and a lass drivin' ', an urchin had shouted after them in Carlisle—and the dull headache that came with each flare-up wearied him.[100] But Scott's condition was much worse. Broken by overwork, he had suffered a minor stroke that had impaired his speech and movements and weakened him so much that his doctors forbade him to drink wine and insisted that he flee the Scottish winter. Wordsworth had known of Sir Walter's ill health, but not until he saw him did he realize the full gravity of his comment that 'if [Wordsworth] did not come soon . . . it might be too late'.[101]

Scott had gathered his family and friends round him, so there was little chance for quiet talk that evening or the next day when the party visited Newark Castle on the Yarrow. Wordsworth noted how gamely Scott walked when they left the carriage and what pleasure he took 'in revisiting those his favourite haunts', but as they crossed the Tweed on the way home, under 'a rich but sad light of rather a purple than a golden hue' spread over the Eildon hills, he sensed that the outing had been the Border Minstrel's farewell to the locality he had made so entirely his own.[102] Within a few days Wordsworth had memorialized the occasion and his fears:

> A trouble, not of clouds, or weeping rain,
> Nor of the setting sun's pathetic light
> Engendered, hangs o'er Eildon's triple height:
> Spirits of Power, assembled there, complain
> For kindred Power, departing from their sight;
> While Tweed, best pleased in chanting a blithe strain,
> Saddens his voice again, and yet again.
> Lift up your hearts, ye Mourners! for the might
> Of the whole world's good wishes with him goes;
> Blessings and prayers in nobler retinue
> Than sceptred King or laurelled Conqueror knows,
> Follow this wondrous Potentate. Be true,
> Ye winds of ocean, and the midland sea,
> Wafting your Charge to soft Parthenope![103]

On the morning of 22 September the two men at last had a private talk and Scott haltingly entered a poem into Dora's album (see p. 370). 'I should not have done anything of this kind but for your father's sake', he told her, 'they are probably the last verses I shall ever write.' What it had cost him was obvious. Scott, prolific poet and novelist, had not managed to write his own name properly.[104] But if Wordsworth was moved by this evidence of his old friend's physical impairment, he was overwhelmed by a farewell gesture. Taking their leave, Wordsworth said that he hoped Sir Walter would benefit from the Italian climate and from seeing the memorials of antiquity. Scott replied, smiling:

> When I am there, although 'tis fair,
> 'Twill be another Yarrow.[105]

Only a poet could have alluded so deftly as to draw together in a few words the whole of their affectionate relationship. Having passed the Yarrow unvisited the day after his first meeting with Scott in 1803, Wordsworth had composed his poem on that non-event, he later told him, 'not without a view of pleasing you'.[106] Now, in quoting Wordsworth's lines, Scott recalled

Sir Walter Scott's entry in Dora Wordsworth's album, 22 September 1831. Scott's declining state is revealed by the two misspellings in the last line of the poem and the omission of the S in his own name (the letter has been added by a later hand).

both the beginning of their friendship and Wordsworth's second tribute to him in *Yarrow Visited* with its allusion to *The Lay of the Last Minstrel.*

As he and Dora continued their journey northwards, Wordsworth shaped his farewell, not just to an old friend—'Dear Sir Walter! I love that Man', he had said, simply, a year before—but to a poet who had outfaced grief, loss, and sickness by drawing on the personal fortitude that Wordsworth himself had prayed for in *Resolution and Independence.*[107] The minstrel of heroic times, Scott had proved himself heroic and his image rightly dominates Wordsworth's last Yarrow poem, *Yarrow Revisited.* Gracefully weaving together past and present, their hopes and life's realities, the natural world and the play of imagination on it, the poem suggests that just as the Border Minstrel's imagination had created a complementary beauty to that of Tweed and Teviot, so it may do again with Vesuvio's vine-clad slopes, drawing and conferring strength as the poetic vision has always done. It is a tribute to Scott, but also to the great power both poets served:

> What were mighty Nature's self?
> Her features, could they win us,
> Unhelped by the poetic voice
> That hourly speaks within us?

Wordsworth believed that 'there is too much pressure of fact for these verses to harmonise with the two preceding poems', but he was mistaken.[108] It is the pressure of fact against the consolations of fancy which shapes the poem's meditation and makes it so poignant. The closing lines of *Yarrow Revisited* sum up all three poems and reaffirm the rewards both of art and friendship. It is a strong poem, a fine sequel to a sequel, but it did not end Wordsworth's imaginative engagement with Scott and the Yarrow. Twice more in the coming decade he drew on memories of them in the creation of moving elegiac poems.

If Wordsworth had composed nothing on this Scottish tour he could have said truly that his vein had run out, for the visit to Abbotsford and the weeks following offered, profusely, everything his imagination had always fed on—the past and the present, sensations remembered against sensations re-experienced, connection either with the recesses of his own being or with those dearest to him. The farewell to Scott set the retrospective mood and the rest of the journey intensified it, as Wordsworth travelled over ground he had covered with Mary in 1814 and Dorothy in 1803. Exhilarated by the exercise—he often walked twenty miles a day—isolated from news of 'the deplorable state of the country', Wordsworth was more creative than he had been at any time since 1822.[109] From Abbotsford they pushed on through Edinburgh and Stirling, into the Highlands and then west to Mull, before taking the familiar route home, Inverary—Glasgow—Lanark—Moffat—

Carlisle—Penrith, and 'dear daddy', Dora reported joyfully, 'was busy composing most of the time'.[110] On his return Wordsworth had the basis of the new collection he had feared he would never issue. The tour refreshed him as a poet and brought him, at age 65, unexpected success. *Yarrow Revisited, and Other Poems* sold better than any other single-title volume he had yet published.

Celebrating his renewed creativity in the last poem of *Yarrow Revisited*, Wordsworth none the less acknowledged its autumnal character and when he returned home in 1831 he acted as a man aware that, for all his fresh vigour, 'Life's three first seasons [were] passed away'.[111] Returning to 'mangled and also illegible MSS' over the winter 1831–2, he and Mary worked, according to Dora, 'like slaves from morning to night', the poet deciphering and revising while his long-suffering wife transcribed. What Wordsworth was 'so much occupied with . . . as to forget his meals and even his politics', however, was putting in order past poetry, so that, should he be afflicted like Scott, fair-copy manuscripts would be ready for the press.[112] He did, as promised, return to *The Recluse*, but only to the one unpublished part he had written long before, *Home at Grasmere*, seeming to accept that it would be issued posthumously. He turned also, inevitably, to *The Prelude*, the poem that had always been intended for publication after *The Recluse*, and with unremitting labour prepared a fresh copy. In December his eyes protested against long hours of poring over scrawl by candle-light and by February Wordsworth admitted to being 'very much tired', but his creative burst was not spent.[113] Acutely worried by Dorothy's illness, depressed by the progress of the Reform Bill, Wordsworth none the less continued to work and in June 1832 he published a further, four-volume, Collected Works.

# 1833–1839

## (1)

A T 65 years of age, with bad eyes, missing teeth, and a growth on a toe that might need surgery, Wordsworth applied to himself Shakespeare's lines,

> That time of year thou mayst in me behold
> When yellow leaves, or none, or few, do hang
> Upon those boughs . . .

He was preparing for death, even going so far as to close a letter to an old acquaintance, 'Wishing you ease and consolation for the remainder of your days, and a quiet passage to a happy Immortality . . .'.[1] Only two years before, however, this old man had travelled with Crabb Robinson to the Isle of Man, and then once again to Scotland, tolerating the new discomforts of the steamship as well as the familiar ones of carriages and bad inns in his determination to see Staffa with 'Fingal's Cave' and the Christian site, Iona.[2]

The last decades of Wordsworth's life are full of such ironies, reversals, and puzzles. Again and again in his letters he emphasizes his decrepitude, but he was strong enough in 1837 to get to Rome and Venice and to bear, as well as the usual strains of nearly five months of foreign travel, both snow and intense heat. When he was 70 he climbed Helvellyn again. He was afraid that the Muse was forsaking him, but he was able to celebrate his 1833 journey in a series of no fewer than 45 sonnets *Composed or Suggested during a Tour in Scotland . . . 1833*, he published new volumes or fully revised new editions in 1835, 1836, 1838, 1840, 1842, 1845, and 1849–50, and his Italian tour prompted yet another strong series of *Memorials*.[3]

Honours were bestowed on him, but the crown, the Laureate's wreath, did not come until he had fallen almost silent and it was only accepted on condition that nothing would be required of him. But nothing more was needed. As an old man Wordsworth was dismayed by many trends in contemporary life, but he lived to see his work influencing the spiritual and intellectual leaders of the new age. He lived long enough, moreover, to hear his poetry praised for just the qualities that had once exposed it to scorn. His retirement to the Lakes, formerly derided as the social and intellectual self-mutilation of a man sadly prey to devotional ravings, now seemed the spiritual way of a great religious poet. His personal vision had struck Jeffrey as proof that Wordsworth was a crazed egotist, but now the transfiguration of the ordinary, the daffodil or the celandine, indicated rather that Wordsworth was a poet of high imagination, a prophet and seer. Even his simplicity was revalued. Readers whose hearts skipped when Oliver Twist asked for more had no difficulty with the little girl in _We are Seven_ or with the sobbing of Alice Fell.[4]

The saddest irony, however, was that, just as Wordsworth's reputation became firm, fixed points in his life, which had underpinned his personal stability and strength, vanished.

(2)

Wordsworth's most famous line is probably, 'I wandered lonely as a Cloud'.* The words 'lonely', 'alone', 'solitary', take up column inches in the _Concordance_. But the poet of the lonely brooks and the high fells relied on the security of a family, a home, and a circle of friends, and ever since 1799 he had nurtured these with the sure instinct of someone acknowledging imperative needs. Life in the cottage at Grasmere had been hard, but no one who saw the Wordsworth family there ever doubted that it was the ground of the poet's assurance. After the deaths of Catherine and Thomas, Wordsworth, Mary, Dorothy, and Sara Hutchinson had carefully and deliberately rebuilt their life together at Rydal Mount. And in both homes Wordsworth fostered friendship. He tried to keep old friendships in repair and he welcomed new. But as Wordsworth entered his sixties and his years of fame this domestic stability collapsed.

In 1833 Dorothy fell seriously ill. Wracked by pain in her bowels and immobilized by swollen and discoloured legs, she lay in bed, increasingly dependent on brandy and opium as sedatives and pain-killers. At the first attack over the winter 1832–3 Wordsworth saw 'little or no hope of Recovery', but by September he was able to report to Christopher that 'She can walk a little without support, and has a good appetite . . . tho' subject to fits of pain'.[5] Dorothy emerged, however, a frightened invalid. The following spring she confessed that, though 'the sun shines so bright and the birds sing so sweetly that I have almost a painful longing to go out of doors', the threat of rain or the east wind cowed her.[6] By the end of the summer the

---

* It ought to be recorded for non-British readers that in 1986 this line featured in a television advertising campaign for Heineken beer. The little scene, which showed W being inspired to perfection after numerous failed attempts on the line, assumed that viewers would recognize a caricature of W _and_ know the correct wording.

gypsy Dorothy was only out of bed four to six hours a day and the following year she was once again so ill that only opium in increasing quantities made her suffering bearable.[7] But this was a further worry. Convinced that the drug was affecting her mind, Dorothy's family tried to wean her off the 'treacherous support'.[8]

By later 1835 it was clear that Dorothy was beyond the ministrations of either opium or the sunshine and fresh air. The diagnosis of her illness obtained by her most recent biographers is 'senile dementia of the type similar to Alzheimer's disease which is a genetically determined pre-senile dementia'.[9] One minute singing to herself, the next Dorothy was lashing out at her nurses in 'rage and fury'. Mary's restrained language about 'her uncomfortable *habits* . . . stomach a little disordered' only veils the reality of soiled clothing and bedclothes.[10] During the occasional periods of remission Dorothy was wheeled out on to the terrace in a bath-chair, but generally she remained in her room, by the fire that she insisted on at all times of the year. Nor was this confinement the only reversal of her old self. The lean and energetic Dorothy now ate compulsively and grew very fat.

The Rydal Mount household coped with what Wordsworth called 'my dear ruin of a Sister'.[11] Whereas at her similar collapse in October 1833 Edith Southey had to be confined for months in an institution for the insane, Dorothy could be nursed at home and she was, with unstinting love, for a further twenty years. But the cost was enormous, not financially, although an additional servant had to be engaged to help with the daily laundry and nursing, but in emotional terms. Dorothy's condition was not a secret—she was not the hidden madwoman in the attic of *Jane Eyre*—but there could be no pretence that life at Rydal Mount could continue as it had. 'She would terrify strangers to death', Mary commented in 1838, facing the truth, as always, unflinchingly and without rancour.[12]

Just as Dorothy's condition worsened, Sara Hutchinson died of rheumatic fever on 23 June 1835. For thirty years the Wordsworths had depended on her. She had been Wordsworth's amanuensis, an extra mother to his children, a companion for Mary and Dorothy. Witty, irreverently unawed by the poet, generous, and stable, she had defused tension and added gaiety to all of their lives. She had been, above all, a support for her sister and she died when Mary needed her help as never before.

'How a thought of the presence of living friends brightens particular spots, and what a shade falls over them when those friends have passed away!'[13] In the 1830s Wordsworth wrote variants on this observation many times. In 1829 William Calvert died. He was followed in 1833 by James Losh and in 1835 by an older friend still, John Fleming, who had shared Wordsworth's rambles round Esthwaite while they were at school. Richard

Sharp died in March 1835 and so the following month did Robert Jones, Wordsworth's companion amongst the Alps in 1790.

Wordsworth mourned all of these friends. One by one connections back to formative periods of his life—to school, Cambridge, the Alps, Windy Brow—were being severed. But the loss of three other friends affected him much more profoundly. Scott, who had not recovered in Italy, died shortly after his return home in 1832. On 25 July 1834 Coleridge died and at the end of the year, on 27 December, Lamb also died unexpectedly, after a fall in the street.

Wordsworth had already lamented Scott's decline in *Yarrow Revisited* and *On the Departure of Sir Walter Scott*, so that when the collection *Yarrow Revisited* was published in 1835 it had the appearance of a memorial volume. He made no immediate public tribute to Coleridge, but in private he was eloquent about the friend he had loved so deeply. Reporting his conversation in August 1834, Robert Perceval Graves wrote:

One of the first things we heard from him was the death of one who had been, he said, his friend for more than thirty years. He then continued to speak of him, called him the most *wonderful* man that he had ever known, wonderful for the originality of his mind & the power he possessed of throwing out in profusion grand central truths from which might be evolved the most comprehensive systems.[14]

Lamb was celebrated in a privately circulated *Epitaph*, which, dwelling on his conscientious labours, on his affectionate nature, and on his Christian resignation, concluded, 'O he was good, if e'er a good Man lived'.[15] But it took one more death to release Wordsworth's feelings in all their complexity and intensity. In November 1835 'the poet was much affected by reading in the newspaper the death of Hogg, the Ettrick Shepherd. Half an hour afterwards he came into the room . . . and asked Miss [Elizabeth] Hutchinson to write down some lines which he had just composed.' The lines were a version of the *Extempore Effusion upon the Death of James Hogg*—Wordsworth's last great poem and his finest elegy.[16]

Wordsworth had felt no affinity for Hogg personally, nor did he care for his writing.[17] His death was none the less a catalyst that activated a chain of associated memories and feelings that reached back over thirty years. The poem opens by contrasting Wordsworth's 1814 and 1831 visits to the Yarrow, the first when Hogg guided him, the second in the company of Scott, the 'border minstrel'. Both of these visits had been celebrated in *Yarrow Visited* and *Yarrow Revisited*. The lament that 'death upon the braes of Yarrow, / Has closed the Shepherd-poet's eyes', however, alludes directly to Wordsworth's first Yarrow poem, *Yarrow Unvisited*, which borrows the phrase 'winsome marrow' from Hamilton's 'exquisite Ballad'

*The Braes of Yarrow*, to allude to Dorothy.[18] And this recollection of the Yarrow unvisited during the Scottish tour of 1803 not only folds Scott still more firmly into the poem, but recalls their partner on the tour, Coleridge, and the anxiety and recrimination which, parting them then, marked the beginning of the deterioration of their friendship. Now Wordsworth's 'winsome marrow' was unrecognizable, Coleridge and Lamb were dead, and Scott, the poet whose life had most publicly exemplified the artist's struggle against adversity, was lying at Dryburgh Abbey. Wordsworth's tribute to them all is a friend's *ave atque vale*, a poet's lament for the makers, and a survivor's recognition of the imminence of his own death:

> The mighty Minstrel breathes no longer,
> 'Mid mouldering ruins low he lies;
> And death upon the braes of Yarrow,
> Has closed the Shepherd-poet's eyes:
>
> Nor has the rolling year twice measured
> From sign to sign, its stedfast course,
> Since every mortal power of Coleridge
> Was frozen at its marvellous source;
>
> The rapt One, of the godlike forehead,
> The heaven-eyed creature sleeps in earth:
> And Lamb, the frolic and the gentle,
> Has vanished from his lonely hearth.
>
> Like clouds that rake the mountain-summits,
> Or waves that own no curbing hand,
> How fast has brother followed brother,
> From sunshine to the sunless land!
>
> Yet I, whose lids from infant slumbers
> Were earlier raised, remain to hear
> A timid voice, that asks in whispers,
> 'Who next will drop and disappear?'

(3)

Had Wordsworth's memorial tribute been written only a few months earlier it could have been added to the collection *Yarrow Revisited, and Other Poems*, published in April 1835. It would have been an appropriate setting, for much of the poetry of this, Wordsworth's first separate volume for thirteen years, is retrospective and elegiac. Dedicated to an even older poet, Samuel Rogers (1763–1855), whose first important work dated from 1792, it opens with a note to *Yarrow Revisited* which describes the poem as a 'memorial' to a day spent with Scott and reminds the reader of 'the Author's previous poems suggested by that celebrated Stream', the Yarrow. With the backward glance already established, the opening stanza, which directly invokes the first poem in the series, dwells on the years that have passed between each of Wordsworth's visits. Next comes *On the Departure of Sir Walter Scott*, now given a meaning by Scott's death which it did not have in 1831 when it was composed. This poignant sonnet is followed by another, *A Place of Burial in the South of Scotland*, and by many other poems which maintain the retrospective mood, not just the obviously elegiac ones, such as *Elegiac Musings in the Grounds of Coleorton Hall* or the *Epitaph* ('By a blest Husband guided'), but the many which are suggested by a historical site or monument, *Composed in Roslin Chapel*, or *Bothwell Castle*, or *Roman Antiquities Discovered, at Bishopstone, Herefordshire*, or *Fancy and Tradition*, which meditates on our need for the human stories of the past:

> Were only History licensed to take note
> Of things gone by, her meagre monuments
> Would ill suffice for persons and events:
> There is an ampler page for man to quote,
> A readier book of manifold contents,
> Studied alike in palace and in cot.

To suggest that *Yarrow Revisited* is only elegiac or wistfully retrospective, however, would be to misrepresent the volume. The anthologist looking for the best of Wordsworth will, justifiably, light on the poems about Scott and one or two sonnets, but such a selection distorts what was important about *Yarrow Revisited* when it appeared in 1835 and sustains the myth that Wordsworth's late collections are uninteresting as collections. By the 1830s critics were already pushing the damaging notion that poetry's proper concern was states of mind, the imagination, and the inner being.[19] Wordsworth had never conceded such limitation of the poetic terrain. Much of his most eloquent writing had been political and, though in 1833 he doubted the efficacy of works of imagination at a time that called 'above everything' for 'patient examination and sober judgement', when he compiled his collection he issued his last important political statement.[20]

It was inevitable, for Wordsworth was still obsessed with politics. After the passing of the 1832 Reform Bill he took on the mantle of Jeremiah. The Bill was bad, but its progeny, already to be descried, would be terrifying. Filtering out much that he actually saw in France in the 1790s, the unity, the gaiety, the triumphal arches, Wordsworth now insisted that what he had witnessed were 'the calamities brought upon all classes, and especially the poor, by a Revolution'. 'My heart aches at the thought of what we are now threatened with', he wrote, apparently sharing Lord Lonsdale's conviction that 'as this reformed Parliament cannot be altered for the better, nothing can prevent an explosion and the entire overthrow of the Institutions of the Country'.[21]

Wordsworth in this mood is irresistibly comic. He sounds exactly like Sir Leicester Dedlock in *Bleak House*, always muttering about floodgates and Wat Tyler, but his apocalyptic gloom was also boring and on occasions his family told him so. Weary of taking down a political diatribe in what was supposed to be a letter to Crabb Robinson, Mary revolted and wrote into the paragraph, 'I M.W. *will not* write another word on this subject'.[22] But he would not be checked. *The Warning*, written in 1833, is Wordsworth-Jeremiah at his darkest. The poem is so bleak, in fact, that he wavered about publishing it, until the imminent general election of 1835 persuaded him that it was his duty 'to give this warning to my Countrymen, at this awful Crisis'.[23]

*The Warning* is an interesting document, if not an interesting poem, two features of which are worth comment. One is that Wordsworth bases his prediction of future turmoil on his interpretation of the French Revolution. This was commonplace. The fall of the Bastille and the fury of the Paris mob were still being evoked in the mid-century by those who feared the onset of anarchy. What is striking in *The Warning*, however, is how rigid Wordsworth's interpretation has become. In *The Prelude* he had recorded from first-hand experience something of the complexity of the event, particularly as it affected the aspirations of the young and idealistic, but by 1833 all sense of potential or actual gain had been eliminated in a one-sided retrospect. What Englishman can hope, Wordsworth asks:

> Not He, who from her [England's] mellowed practice drew
> His social sense of just, and fair, and true;
> And saw, thereafter, on the soil of France
> Rash Polity begin her maniac dance,
> Foundations broken up, the deeps run wild,
> Nor grieved to see, (himself not unbeguiled)—
> Woke from the dream, the dreamer to upbraid,
> And learn how sanguine expectations fade
> When novel trusts by folly are betrayed,—
> To see presumption, turning pale, refrain
> From further havoc, but repent in vain,—
> Good aims lie down, and perish in the road
> Where guilt had urged them on, with ceaseless goad,
> Till undiscriminating Ruin swept
> The Land, and Wrong perpetual vigils kept:
> With proof before her that on public ends
> Domestic virtue vitally depends.

The second feature worth note is that Wordsworth was alert enough to social portents to be afraid of something quite new. *The Warning* castigates national leaders for conceding radical demands, blind to the reality that the satisfaction of one claim only generates another. But the poem's most urgent warning is directed to the 'labouring multitude', driven by 'stress of real injuries' to enlist in battalions led by flatterers and deceivers:

> O for a bridle bitted with remorse
> To stop your Leaders in their headstrong course!
> Oh may the Almighty scatter with his grace
> These mists, and lead you to a safer place,
> By paths no human wisdom can foretrace!
> May He pour round you, from worlds far above
> Man's feverish passions, his pure light of love,
> That quietly restores the natural mien
> To hope, and makes truth willing to be seen!
> *Else* shall your blood-stained hands in frenzy reap
> Fields gaily sown when promises were cheap.[24]

Before Carlyle's *Chartism* (1839), or Dickens's vision of conspiratorial incendiaries in *The Old Curiosity Shop* (1840–1), or Disraeli's *Sybil* (1845), or Elizabeth Gaskell's *Mary Barton* (1848), Wordsworth had seized on what was to become a dread image in the coming years of Chartist unrest, the 'marshalled thousands, darkening street and moor'.

In *The Warning* the poet allied himself with the most timorous of his contemporaries. But not all of Wordsworth's responses to the Spirit of the Age or to the labouring multitude were grounded on fear, as another poem, *Humanity*, and the prose *Postscript* to the collection reveal. If *Yarrow Revisited* counts in the history of English poetry because it contains some of Wordsworth's best late work, this poem and the remarkable essay with which the volume concludes claim for it a small but honourable place in the history of the nineteenth-century working class.

In *Humanity* Wordsworth declaims:

> Shame that our laws at distance should protect
> Enormities, which they at home reject!
> 'Slaves cannot breathe in England'—a proud boast!
> And yet a mockery! if from coast to coast,
> Though *fettered* slave be none, her floors and soil
> Groan underneath a weight of slavish toil,
> For the poor Many, measured out by rules
> Fetched with cupidity from heartless schools,
> That to an Idol, falsely called 'the Wealth
> Of Nations,' sacrifice a People's health,

Body and mind and soul; a thirst so keen
Is ever urging on the vast machine
Of Sleepless Labour, 'mid whose dizzy wheels
The Power least prized is that which thinks and feels.[25]

When this passage was written in 1829 it was intended to heighten the poem's overall anti-slavery argument, but by 1835 recent revelations had given it particular topical relevance. The title, *Humanity*, must have disturbed readers who were still digesting the horrors catalogued in Sadler's 1832 enquiry into child labour in the factories, especially if they were among the humanitarian few who were not satisfied with the concessions wrested from the industrial interest by the 1833 Factory Act.* But another feature of the contemporary ethos troubled Wordsworth even more than this slavery. The exploitation of children was a social cancer, but it had arisen unplanned, an expedient response to continually changing economic conditions, and legislation, he trusted, would now alleviate it. The Poor Law Amendment Act of 1834, on the other hand, was a considered response to a social problem. It represented the best that commissioners of enquiry, statisticians, and analysts could devise. That was what was so worrying about it. Faced with the messy reality, not Poverty in the abstract, but masses of unemployed or unemployable people, Parliament had enacted a Bill which epitomized the Malthusian attitude to human distress which Wordsworth had always detested. Relief in future was to be available solely in workhouses and conditions in them were to be such that no one would voluntarily enter one if there were any alternative. As Carlyle sardonically observed: 'If paupers are made miserable, paupers will needs decline in multitude. It is a secret known to all rat-catchers.'[26]

Thirty years later in *Our Mutual Friend* Dickens depicted Betty Higden as less afraid of death than of entering the workhouse, the 'Bastille' for the poor, and in a *Postscript* he spelt out his view of the Poor Law: 'I believe there has been in England, since the days of the STUARTS, no law so often infamously administered, no law so often openly violated, no law habitually so ill-supervised'.[27] Many Victorian attacks on the workhouse system echo Dickens's argument: the law is brutally administered. In 1835, however, before any evidence of practice had accumulated, Wordsworth had to take a different stand. But even if he had been writing in 1865 his line of attack would have been the same, for the new Poor Law struck at two principles which he had adhered to throughout all changes in his political orientation. They were both simple, but fundamental. The first was that people ought to

---

* Under the 1833 Act children under 9 were to be excluded from factories; children under 13 were to work not more than 48 hours and no one under 18 more than 69 hours a week. It indicates how appalling were the revelations of Sadler's enquiry that this legislation seemed benign.

be treated by the state as if they mattered. Whatever encouraged the best human characteristics—self-respect, independence however lowly, hope, love of one's family and one's country—ought to be fostered, which meant that those who could not support themselves through no fault of their own ought to be able to claim, as a right, support which would not diminish their self-esteem. 'With all due deference to the particular experience, and general intelligence of the individuals who framed the Act . . . it may be said, that it proceeds too much upon the presumption that it is a labouring man's own fault if he be not, as the phrase is, beforehand with the world.'[28] All that needs to be said of this judgement is that it was right.

The second was that all legislation framed from a theory was suspect. Wordsworth recognized that some amendment of existing Poor Law practice was required, but he rightly feared that this solution conformed to 'theories of political economy' rather than to human realities. 'It is broadly asserted by many, that every man who endeavours to find work, *may* find it: were this assertion capable of being verified, there still would remain a question, what kind of work, and how far may the labourer be fit for it?' In 1792 the French Revolution had been made real to Wordsworth when Beaupuy had pointed to the hunger-bitten girl and said, "Tis against that / Which we are fighting'.[29] In 1835, when so many of his views had suffered a sea change, Wordsworth remained true to this conviction—that a theory stood or fell by its bearing on the individual case.

## (4)

In 1836 one Fitzjames Price sent Wordsworth his Latin rendering of *Yarrow Visited*—'Anne hac Arrovia est? an hocce flumen . . .'.[30] Wordsworth could afford to be amused that his work was being translated into a dead language, for by then he was enjoying less equivocal evidence of success. The first edition of 1,500 copies of *Yarrow Revisited* had sold out within nine months, confirming the impression already given by the increasing sales of the 1832 Collected Works that his reputation was taking off. In America the text of the 1820 collected edition had been available since 1824 in four beautifully printed volumes and *Yarrow Revisited* was issued in Boston and New York in the same year as in London. By 1837, moreover, Wordsworth had his American editor, Professor Henry Reed of the University of Pennsylvania, who won his co-operation, not only because he was responsible and intelligent but because he cared as much as the poet did about textual accuracy.[31] 'What do you think', Wordsworth wrote to Crabb Robinson, 'of an edition of 20,000 of my Poems being struck off at Boston . . . An Author in the English Language is becoming a great Power for good or evil—if he writes with spirit.'[32] In 1839 he learnt that his work had reached the other frontier when he received a copy of the Westminster Bridge sonnet translated 'into the Bengalese tongue . . . by a native Indian gentleman of Consideration'.[33]

Fame, the 'late but lasting consequence', had arrived, bringing with it celebrity. In September 1835 Wordsworth was elected Honorary Member of the Kendal Natural History and Scientific Society and two years later the Liverpool Royal Institution conferred on him a similar honour. In 1838 and 1839 he was awarded honorary degrees by Durham and Oxford Universities and in 1838 he was asked whether he would stand for election to the Rectorship of Glasgow University. The Dowager Queen Adelaide made a point of visiting Rydal Mount during her visit to the Lakes in July 1840 and three years later Wordsworth became Victoria's Poet Laureate. At 71 years of age he was even invited to stand as a Conservative candidate for the Ayr Burghs.

Every post brought further proof of fame. Some letters were embarrassingly fulsome. Thomas Powell, a shady literary adventurer, for example, having elicited a note from Wordsworth, rhapsodized over it in these terms:

While I was reading it a strange delight came over me—a sunbeam seemed to stir the inmost depths of my Soul—The thought that the Author of 'Peter Bell' and the 'Excursion' had held communion with me awoke in me, like the morning sunlight on the Memnon-Head, the music of [?Spring]—Life when I lived in the world of Idea.

And so on for four pages.[34] Some letters were puzzling. Thomas Forbes Kelsall wrote and asked for a manuscript copy of *Yarrow Revisited*. Impressed by the candour and directness of the request, Wordsworth complied, but then wondered, wrongly as it happened, whether he had been tricked.[35] Did he respond to this astonishing demand:

Mr Wordsworth,—Sir
    I have just finished an excellent tragedy, one of the best perhaps in existence,—& it will be still better on receiving a few finishing touches from your [?pen]. I shall take the liberty of sending it to you the next post,—also I request the loan of £20— till I get it published. I stand high, very high in the poetical world, and you must have heard of me ere this, let my reputation be sufficient Security & please to forward the money next post, *without fail*.
I remain Sir Your fervent / Admirer<br>Charles Swain.

Almost certainly not, but Swain, a prolific Manchester poet, must have received some courteous words, for in 1842 he presented a copy of his unutterably dull *The Mind, and Other Poems* to Wordsworth 'with every sentiment of respect and admiration'.[36]

Many letters, however, were of the most welcome kind, neither ingratiating nor intrusive, just sincere thank-yous for what his poetry had meant. Sir William Gomm, for example, described how he had turned to Wordsworth's poems at a time of great grief:

They were my Companions in a lonely Pilgrimage over the North of Germany;—undertaken mainly because I found rest intolerable;—and if you could see those Weather-worn Volumes:—how they are scarr'd about with my pencil marks where passages delighted me through immeasurable portions of them:—but particularly in that invaluable and most glorious portion of the Excursion 'Despondency Corrected':—you would there discover better than I shall ever find words to express to you whether I owe you a Debt or not.

The Reverend Henry Alford spoke for many when he said simply, sending his own volumes *The School of the Heart*, 'I thought it but due to send some acknowledgement to you to whom I owe so much'.[37]

Presentation volumes and bundles of manuscript began to pile up alarmingly. Wordsworth was almost invariably polite, astonishingly so, and he became adept at acknowledging a gift with variations on 'For this mark of attention I sincerely thank you, promising myself much pleasure from the perusal of your book at my early leisure'.[38] He was even forbearing with those who sent their own poems for his comment, but eventually he revolted against 'those abominable Albums and Autographs' with which he was 'cruelly pestered', and in 1840 he declared he was sinking beneath the 'inundation of complimentary Letters' which 'the penny-postage has let in . . . upon me'.[39]

One of the strangest letters to arrive at Rydal Mount in 1837 was an outpouring in childish handwriting from a 19-year-old:

Sir,

I most earnestly entreat you to read and pass your Judgement upon what I have sent you, because from the day of my birth to this the nineteenth year of my life, I have lived among wild and secluded hills where I could neither know what I was or what I could do.—I read for the same reason that I eat or drank—because it was a real craving of Nature. I wrote on the same principle as I spoke,—out of the impulse and feelings of the mind;—nor could I help it, for what came, came out and there was the end of it, for as to self conceit, that could not receive food from flattery, since to this hour not half a dozen people in the world know that I have ever penned a line.—But a change has taken place now, Sir, and I am arrived at an age wherein I must do something for myself—the powers I possess must be exercised to a definite end, and as I dont know them myself I must ask of others what they are worth,—yet there is no one here to tell me, and still, if they are worthless, time will henceforth be too precious to be wasted on them.

The writer was Branwell Brontë and what he sent was 'the prefatory scene of a much longer subject', in verse, entitled *The Struggles of Flesh with*

*Spirit*.[40] The letter was evidently the appeal of an anguished young man, but it was very gauche. To declare, 'Surely in this day when there is not a *writing* poet worth a sixpence the feild [*sic*] must be open if a better man can step forward', was not tactful, and Wordsworth did not reply. His silence is understandable. This was just one more letter from someone quite unknown, who sounded not a little unbalanced. 'But READ it Sir and as you would hold a light to one in utter darkness as you value your own ~~soul~~ kind heartedness *return* me an ANSWER if but one word telling me whether I should write on or write no more.' Anyone might be forgiven for deciding it would be prudent not to begin a correspondence with someone who could write like this. But one would swap a hundred of Wordsworth's later letters for the reply he might have sent.

In 1836 William Boxall wrote from Hardwick House in Suffolk: 'you have here a knot of true & sincere worshippers . . . & I believe nothing short of a pilgrimage to Rydal Mount will suffice them'.[41] The 'pilgrims' kept coming. Not all of them observed the rules of polite society. Edward Quillinan recorded in his diary a conversation between a couple outside the gate of Rydal Mount. The lady was heard to say, 'We must not go in; but do you get on the wall & snatch a sprig of laurel, or anything; we *must* take something away'.[42] Most of the hundreds whose names were entered in the Rydal Mount Visitors Book, however, arrived in proper form, bearing letters of introduction from mutual friends or from others who had already made the pilgrimage.

Wordsworth was becoming a national monument. In *England and the English* (1833), Bulwer Lytton assessed all of the factors that made for the unparalleled interest of contemporary English life and gave Wordsworth his due place.[43] For many, Rydal Mount was a must on the modern equivalent of the Grand Tour that generally included a visit to a northern industrial city as well. Americans continued to seek him out. Ralph Waldo Emerson called on his first visit to England in 1833 and described his reception later in *English Traits* (1856). He found the 'hard limits of [Wordsworth's] thought' distressing, though conceding that on 'his own beat', i.e. when talking about and reciting poetry, he was impressive.[44] In *The Old World and the New* (1836) Orville Dewey gave a long account of his visit, also in 1833. If he had been expecting poetic talk he was disappointed. For two evenings in succession Wordsworth talked mainly about politics and only when he walked Dewey to Grasmere, to see it after sunset, did he behave as a Lake poet. 'The mountain side had a softness of shadowing upon it, such as I never saw before, and such as no painting I ever saw approached in the remotest degree. It seemed, Mr W.— said, as if it were "*clothed* with the air".'[45] Charles Sumner visited in 1838 in an appropriately reverent frame of mind. 'How odd it seemed', he wrote, 'to knock at a neighbour's door, and inquire, "Where does Mr. Wordsworth live?" Think of rapping at Westminster Abbey, and asking for Mr. Shakespeare or Mr. Milton!' He was not disappointed in 'this great man'.[46]

Some were. Meeting Wordsworth in March 1835, not at Rydal Mount but at Henry Taylor's in London, Carlyle judged him 'A genuine kind of man, but intrinsically and extrinsically a *small* one'. But it is perhaps inaccurate to say that Carlyle was disappointed. Himself an embryonic sage, and very conscious of the fact, Carlyle had expected little and got, he wrote, 'mostly what I expected', naturalness and sincerity, yes, but also much self-conceit and half-wisdom.[47] Thomas Adolphus Trollope, brother of Anthony, had higher expectations dashed. In his autobiography, *What I Remember* (1887–9), Trollope recalled that on a visit with his mother in August 1839 he had felt that 'There was something in the manner in which [Wordsworth] almost perfunctorily, as it seemed, uttered his long mono-logue, that suggested the idea of the performance of a part got up to order, and repeated without much modification as often as lion-hunters, duly authorized for the sport in those localities, might call upon him for it'.[48] Trollope might have given more thought to the feelings of the lion, for what his account reveals is that, weary as he might have been, Wordsworth did entertain Mrs Trollope and make her welcome. And though she was a distinguished guest, she was only one of very many.

All of these visitors played some part in establishing Wordsworth's reputation, either privately through their letters and conversation or publicly through their memoirs, lectures, and essays. The one who was to have the greatest influence, however, as poet, critic, editor, and future President of the Wordsworth Society, was only a schoolboy when Wordsworth first met him—Matthew Arnold. After two summers of prospecting—during one of which they lived in Allan Bank—Dr Arnold of Rugby and his family determined to build a holiday home in the Lakes in 1833. Fox How, tucked in beneath Loughrigg Fell, looks across the river Rothay towards Nab Scar and Rydal and the two families soon became close. While Dr Arnold and the poet were arguing about politics, religion, and national education, the adolescent Matthew absorbed a presence which, as a writer, he had later to struggle to assess and, at least in part, throw off.[49]

By the 1840s adulation of Wordsworth was becoming absurd. One unidentified witness, who remembered 'Sir Geo. & Ly. Beaumont's bringing him to Grosvenor St . . . when their admiration was laughed at & his Poetry held very cheap', recorded seeing at a London party 'the Chair he had been sitting upon . . . put aside as *sacred*!' This kind of flattery Wordsworth soon found 'insupportable'.[50] But the unknown writer's comment that 'Few people ever *lived*, to *witness* the change of opinion, & enjoy their *triumph* as he has done', was certainly fair. One aspect of celebrity, however, Wordsworth strongly disliked—the public's appetite for information about the Poet as Man. His sensitivity is understandable, but his hope that he could enjoy fame yet be shielded from intrusion was unrealistic and in the 1830s he had to face the fact.

Coleridge's death in 1834 released a flood of biographical material. De Quincey's articles in *Tait's Edinburgh Magazine* from September 1834 to January 1835, which commented unflatteringly on Coleridge's marriage, his domestic habits, his drug-taking, and his plagiarism, provoked outrage. 'Seldom have I experienced more sorrow and anger than at the treacherous misrepresentations of De Quincey', Hartley Coleridge wrote, speaking for Southey, Wordsworth, and their families.[51] But from Wordsworth's point of view worse was to come. In 1835 Coleridge's nephew, Henry Nelson Coleridge, issued *Specimens of the Table Talk of the Late Samuel Taylor Coleridge.* In 1836 Thomas Allsop's *Letters, Conversations & Recollections of S. T. Coleridge* appeared, followed in 1837 by Joseph Cottle's *Early Recollections, Chiefly Relating to the Late Samuel Taylor Coleridge* and in 1838 by James Gillman's *Life of Samuel Taylor Coleridge.* Every one of these publications nettled Wordsworth. The *Table Talk* disclosed information about *The Recluse.*[52] Allsop printed a particularly unpleasant letter from Coleridge to himself about Wordsworth and his mingling of religion with worldly prudence.* Cottle, intent on highlighting his own part in the discovery of two geniuses, mangled evidence in a distorted account of the years when Wordsworth and Coleridge had been at their closest. He also alerted the world to the existence of the unpublished tragedy *The Borderers.*[53] Gillman, through slack writing, suggested that Wordsworth had been at one time a salaried journalist.[54]

While his life was still unfolding, Wordsworth had to recognize that its earlier phase was now being treated as history, a subject for scrutiny, investigation, comment, and interpretation. So far, he had only figured as an adjunct to Coleridge, but in 1839 De Quincey focused directly on him in a further series of articles for *Tait's.*[55] Observant, shrewd, by and large

---

* Allsop, p. 54, quoted the letter of 8 Aug. 1820 in which C attacked both W's 'vague misty, rather than mystic, Confusion of God with the World . . .' and his 'worldly prudence'. *CL*, V. 95. W expected to be pained by C's letters. In a very important statement to Moxon, 10 Dec. 1835, about the publication of private letters he said that 'poor C. . . . was subject to write or speak inconsiderately from the mere impression of the moment'. *LY*, III. 134. Southey was much more bitter and he feared what revelations might still be to come about C's attitude to W. In an unpublished letter to Joseph Cottle, 14 Apr. 1836, he wrote: 'Coleridge received from us such substantial service, as few men have received from those whose friendship they had forfeited: this indeed was not the case with W. as it was with me, for he knew not in what manner C. had latterly spoken of him. But he continued all possible offices of friendship to his children long after he regarded his own conduct with that utter disapprobation which alone it could call forth from any one who had any sense of duty & moral obligation.' MS Berg Collection, New York Public Library.

generous, De Quincey's essays are fascinating, but they broadcast exactly the kind of domestic detail that Wordsworth regarded as sacredly private. As early as 1829 the Wordsworths had begged Coleridge to destroy all their letters to him, since 'at this day such abominable use is made of every scrap of private anecdote, or transient or permanent sentiment, of every one whose name has ever been at all known by the publick', and in 1835 Wordsworth declared, 'I do most earnestly wish that not a single letter I ever wrote should survive me'.[56] There was nothing he could do to put this wish into effect, but when Barron Field submitted his *Memoirs of Wordsworth* to the poet its subject was adamant. 'I set my face *entirely* against the publication of Mr. Field's MSS', he told Moxon. To the author he wrote more gently, but equally firmly. 'In matter of authorship', he counselled Field, 'it is far better not to admit people so much behind the scenes as it has been lately fashionable to do.'[57]

(5)

The success of *Yarrow Revisited* put Wordsworth in a confident mood, so confident in fact that in 1836 he took what is a big step even for an established writer—he changed his publisher. Unconsciously he had been moving towards Edward Moxon ever since they had worked together on Hine's *Selections* in 1831. Impressed by the efficiency and tolerance the young publisher had displayed in his dealings over the printing of his *Epitaph* for Lamb and Talfourd's *Letters of Charles Lamb*,[58] Wordsworth began to ask Moxon's advice about the publication of his next collected edition and the second edition of *Yarrow Revisited* and was struck by the contrast between his readiness to write letters and Longman's costiveness. When it came, however, the break was sudden and decisive. In April 1836 Wordsworth was expecting Longman to proceed with an edition, but on 6 June he brusquely rejected their proposals and, ignoring protest, by 25 June had signed a declaration that 'Mr Wordsworth . . . considers Mr Moxon as entitled to especial consideration in preference to other Publishers [?for] any future edition which may be required of his works'.[59]

Securing Wordsworth was a coup for Moxon. It confirmed his ambition and commercial acumen, but it also indicated something else about him. Moxon, himself a poet, was poet-struck and he was determined to build up a publishing house that would be worthy of the Muse.[60] Economics had to be paramount, of course, and Moxon could be fierce in money matters, as an acerbic exchange of letters between him and Wordsworth in 1842 reveals, but his dealings with his authors were never confined to the ledger.[61] He accompanied Wordsworth to Paris in 1837, visited him in the Lakes, entertained him, and undertook little commissions, such as getting his spectacles and false teeth mended in London.

Wordsworth put Moxon to the test immediately. For the six-volume edition of 1836–7 he revised his corpus so thoroughly that he created 'essentially new versions of several poems, substantially revised versions of a hundred more, and pervasive changes in the details of presentation that alter dramatically their appearance before the reader's eye'.[62] As usual his family was conscripted, Mary, Dora, and Quillinan, who was surely wistful as he noted in his diary for 1 September 1836, 'Instead of partridge-shooting, better employed in helping Mr. W to "tinker", as he calls it . . .'.[63] And as usual the publisher and printer had to suffer for Wordsworth's obsessive pursuit of poetic finish. Revisions were entered into a copy of the 1832 edition, but he did not scruple to revise the revisions, in his own poor hand, or to send separate sheets with cross-references to the printed text. A surviving proof sheet contains a memo from Mary to the printer: 'Please to send a Revise. Mr. W. hopes this will be the last *revise* required.'[64] But it was not. As he had been since 1800, so Wordsworth remained, a printer's nightmare.

Revision on this scale, which lasted throughout the second half of 1836, invariably made Wordsworth irritable and unwell, and this time he was so tetchy that away from home the following year he was stricken with remorse. From Salzburg he sent this apology:

Dearest Mary, when I have felt how harshly I often demeaned myself to you, my inestimable fellow-labourer, while correcting the last Edition of my poems, I often pray to God that He would grant us both life, that I may make some amends to you for that, and all my unworthiness. But you know into what an irritable state this timed and overstrained labour often put my nerves. My impatience was ungovernable as I thought *then*, but now I feel that it ought to have been governed. You have forgiven me I know, as you did then, and perhaps that somehow troubles me the more.[65]

It may be, however, that Wordsworth's behaviour was due not just to the scope of the revision, 'hours of labour' in which 'progress bears no proportion to pains', but to its nature, for at 66 years old he thought of himself as revising 'for the last time'.[66] The whole of his life's work was brought under review. Looking coldly, perhaps too coldly, on the 'swagger and flourish' of his early poems, he heavily reworked *An Evening Walk* and *Descriptive Sketches*.[67] But it was not only the 'juvenile pieces' that were scrutinized. The whole corpus was 'tinkered' with and he even contemplated revision to so perfect a poem as the Westminster Bridge sonnet.[68] *Alice Fell* was reinstated in the canon, reversing, now that Coleridge was dead, a decision Wordsworth had made out of deference to the strictures on the poem in *Biographia Literaria*. And he was quite clear that 'the value of this Ed. in the eyes of the judicious . . . lies in the pains which has been taken in the revisal of so many old Poems, to the re-modelling, and often re-writing whole Paragraphs, which . . . have cost me great labour and I do not repent of it'.[69]

In 1838 another volume appeared which also had an air of finality about it, *The Sonnets of William Wordsworth: Collected in One Volume*. Words-worth claimed not to care about the book 'except for the money that it would bring', but this was affectation. He had long been in love with the sonnet form and in bringing together no fewer than 415, each handsomely printed on a separate page, Wordsworth knew that he was presenting an achievement which was, in its own way, quite as substantial artistically as *The Excursion*.[70] The acknowledgement to Milton, 'our great fellow-countryman', in the prefatory Advertisement, indicated where he thought his sonnets stood in literary history.

This considered presentation of his life's work entailed one further conscious decision—Wordsworth at last publicly abandoned *The Recluse*. On 17 December 1836 Barron Field gave Wordsworth his judgement of *Yarrow Revisited*: 'Your genius only mellows with age. Not the smallest spark of decay is visible yet.' And he added, 'Oh! continue "The Recluse".'[71] Field could not know that, as he wrote, the only part of *The Recluse* that would be published in Wordsworth's lifetime was going through the press with one change that outweighed all the others in significance. Since 1814 *The Excursion* had been described on every title-page as 'a Portion of the Recluse' and its Preface had begun, 'The Title-page announces that this is only a portion of a poem . . .'. From 1836 this sentence remained unchanged, but it no longer made sense, for the title-page now read simply, *The Excursion*, leaving the Preface, with its account of the 'long and laborious Work, which is to consist of three parts', as the memorial to *The Recluse*. Readers who did not buy the 1836–7 edition, or who did not bother to look at the title-page, continued to expect fulfilment of the promise Wordsworth had made for so many years. James Montgomery, for example, writing in 1838 about *The Excursion*, asked bluntly, 'Where is the rest?'[72] But Wordsworth had ended the long pretence. On 9 May 1838 the American George Ticknor asked Wordsworth—surely naïvely—why he did not finish *The Recluse*. The poet turned to him 'very decidedly, and said, "Why did not Gray finish the long poem he began on a similar subject? Because he found he had undertaken something beyond his powers to accomplish. And that is my case".'[73]

With his work published in a fully revised text and his mind rid at last of a phantom, Wordsworth had one task left, the final preparation of the poem that once had been inextricable from hopes for *The Recluse*, *The Prelude*.

The Preface to *The Excursion* had implied that as the biographical poem was 'preparatory' to the philosophical it could not be published until the latter was complete. Circumstances had changed, and the publication of Coleridge's long-suppressed poem on hearing *The Prelude* read out, and De Quincey's 1839 essays, had recently reminded the public of its existence, but Wordsworth remained disinclined to publish, on the grounds that the subject was too personal in character.[74] But he wanted it made public after his death. In August 1838 he began to read the whole poem to Isabella Fenwick and was soon, as she put it, so possessed by revision that although he laboured 'seldom less than six or seven hours in the day', the verse was never, in fact, out of his mind.[75] The 1832 manuscript was reviewed and frequently, often very messily, revised, before Dora and Elizabeth Cookson set to work to copy out all fourteen books afresh.[76]

As he worked on *The Prelude* Wordsworth was looking to posterity. He was also, however, engaging with posterity in a very different way. In 1837 Talfourd introduced a Bill which aimed to extend copyright from twenty-eight years from publication, or the term of the author's life, to sixty years from the date of publication. This was an issue which Wordsworth had long felt vehement about. 'The wrongs of literary men are crying out for redress on all sides', he had declared in 1819 and the progress of his own career had only intensified his passion.[77] Throughout the years in which his work was making headway his family had had to live sparsely and now that his fame was growing, justice demanded that they should enjoy its fruits. But under the meagre provision of the existing law they could hope for little. The law was bad for literature, in that it encouraged writers to look to instant returns by pandering to current taste and it bore heavily on him, as Wordsworth repeatedly pointed out, not ashamed to admit that a personal sense of injustice was the ground of his readiness to join fight.

Talfourd's Bill failed to become law despite repeated attempts and a new, modified, Act was not passed until 1842. But if effort alone had counted, Talfourd would have succeeded much earlier, for Wordsworth proved an indefatigable ally. He lobbied every influential person he had any connection with, however slight, including Gladstone and Peel; he wrote to the press; he drafted a petition to Parliament, under Talfourd's guidance. In Cornell University Library a large collection of letters survives from illustrious persons assuring him that they would attend readings in the House or otherwise support the Bill, together with letters from Talfourd keeping Wordsworth informed about developments and strategy. 'I am pretty sure', Wordsworth wrote in 1838 with justifiable self-satisfaction, 'that without my own endeavour . . . the Bill would not have proceeded so far.'[78] It is an indication of Wordsworth's current standing that, in first introducing the Bill, Talfourd pointed to him as a heroic victim of the copyright law, one who had been undeflected by years of scorn from his pursuit of enduring art which was only now, belatedly, recognized as a source of national pride.[79]

(6)

For someone who thought himself in the sere, the yellow leaf, Wordsworth continued to display remarkable energy. In May 1836 he set off south for what turned out to be one of his most hectic visits ever. Delayed by the death of one of the horses and the shedding of a metal tyre near Northampton, the coach did not pull into London until nearly 2 a.m. on 11 May, but by noon the same day Wordsworth had made his way to the house of his host, the philanthropist Joshua Watson, and was writing the first of a stream of letters to his family.

Eventually he flagged, but not until he had whirled through two months at a rate that would exhaust most people half his age. At breakfast parties, morning calls, dinner parties, and suppers Wordsworth met Henry Taylor and many of his circle (James Spedding, Edward Villiers, James Stephen, Carlyle), Crabb Robinson, John Kenyon and Talfourd, of course, Richard Monckton Milnes (later Lord Houghton), Gladstone, Lord Lonsdale, and Lord Liverpool. He talked business with Moxon, poetry with Rogers, Landor, and H. F. Cary, the translator of Dante, and Church matters with his brother Christopher and Joshua Watson. He went on outings to the Zoo, to the Dulwich Gallery, to the Elgin Marbles, to Windsor Castle, and to Chiswick House. He heard Constable lecture, after which the painter sent him a gift in memory of their friend Sir George Beaumont and a very warm letter, declaring his 'pride' that Wordsworth had joined his audience.[80] He was also in the audience at Covent Garden on 26 May for Macready's triumph in Talfourd's *Ion*. This, though 'the happiest day I have spent since I came to London', was a particularly demanding one.[81] Before the performance Wordsworth dined with Landor and Talfourd, and after it, at a celebration supper, he sat next to Macready and met Robert Browning, Mary Russell Mitford, the painters Clarkson Stanfield and John Lucas, John Forster, and others. Macready, elated, relieved at the reception of the play, and merry on toasts to the dramatist and the actors, winningly flattered Wordsworth over supper by suggesting that a passage in *Ion* owed something to *The Borderers*. Wordsworth was loud in praise of Talfourd's Muse, but, as the actor noted in his diary, he was pleased to be told that the priority of his own lines had been noticed.[82]

At a quite different kind of party two days later Wordsworth made a new friend—Elizabeth Barrett. John Kenyon had invited her to a reception to honour the poet, but she had refused, not wanting to be in a crowd. Her reluctance was fortunate. In a large gathering the two poets might have done little more than make polite noises at each other, whereas at the informal meeting Kenyon arranged they had a real conversation, which Elizabeth Barrett recorded at length.[83] Awed by the man she was later to call 'the king-poet of our times',[84] she was not overawed, and she held her own as they talked about Alfieri's life and poetry, Shakespeare, Spenser, Chaucer, Dante, and the nature of the poetic life, and eventually about whether genius was invariably attended by 'some great deficiency either intellectual or moral'. Wordsworth was decidedly of the opinion that moral deficiency proceeded 'more from want of genius than a redundancy of it'. Elizabeth Barrett was impressed. His voice was 'low & calm', she wrote, *as if with truth*'. Wordsworth was later to be 'pleased with the power and knowledge' her poems displayed (though they were 'too ideal' for his taste),[85] but there is no record of the impression the 30-year-old poet made on him at their first meeting. But we can be sure that he was not displeased to discover that she was in the group that was visiting Chiswick House on 2 June.

'My engagements are as follows', Wordsworth reported on 14 June: 'Tomorrow breakfast with Lord Northampton, dine at home. Thursday dine with Mr Courtney; Friday with Lord Liverpool, Saturday Sir Robert Inglis.' Suddenly Wordsworth could stand it no longer. He was 'much exhausted by these long London tete a tetes with people . . . who wish to hear me talk and never are at rest', and he was missing his family. 'In fact', he told them at the end of June, 'I am heartsick and homesick.'[86] A week later Wordsworth was back at Rydal Mount.

Returning home meant abandoning a plan to go on from London to Italy and Wordsworth's last letters from London are so homesick and plaintive that one might expect him never to have left Rydal again for more than a few days at a time. But the old appetite was still strong in him. In 1833 Sara Hutchinson had commented that Wordsworth thought 'travel the sovereign remedy for all things'. Perhaps that was not quite true, but it was certainly as true as ever that, as he put it, wandering was his 'passion', and there was one place he longed to see before he died.[87] On 19 March, accompanied by Crabb Robinson and Moxon, Wordsworth took the steamer out of London, *en route* for Calais on the first stage of his last great tour—to Italy.

The 1790 walking tour with Jones had been remarkable, but in some ways it was less remarkable than this one. Two elderly men (Moxon only went as far as Paris) travelled in a carriage bought for £70 from 19 March to 7 August 1837. Hindered by deep snow in France, scourged by the heat in Italy, checked by cholera from pressing on to Naples, they none the less carried through this ambitious itinerary: Paris—Cannes—Lucca— Sienna—Rome—Florence—Bologna—Milan—Venice—Salzburg— Munich—Heidelberg—Cologne—Brussels—Calais. In 1790 the young Wordsworth had moved on constantly, eager to reach the Alps and to pile sensation on sensation. Now he and Robinson took more time to absorb places and to meet people. In Paris they visited the Baudouins three times. In Rome they met William Collins (father of the novelist Wilkie Collins), and another painter, Keats's devoted friend Joseph Severn. The British were to be found everywhere—half of 'the fashionables of Florence' displaying themselves on horseback were, Wordsworth judged, English.[88] They bumped into Mr and Mrs George Ticknor repeatedly and at Milan found themselves in the same hotel as two sons of William Blackwood the publisher. Predictably the poet took the opportunity to harangue them about copyright.

Not surprisingly Alexander Blackwood was not pleased to be subjected for half an hour to 'another edition of Talfourd's oration'. The poet did impress him in one way, however. Blackwood could hardly believe that he was intent on setting off to Venice, 'for a man of sixty-eight in such hot weather . . . a bold undertaking'.[89] But if the journey was not noticeably taking its toll, it was, none the less, very demanding. Wordsworth was very anxious about his health and his nerves grew ragged over inconveniences, such as the Italian habit of locking up churches and public buildings seemingly at whim. The two companions were, moreover, very different from each other. Crabb Robinson was a clubbable bachelor, who took delight, Wordsworth complained, in 'loitering about towns, gossiping, and attending reading-rooms, and going to coffee-houses; and at *table d'hôtes*, etc, gabbling German, or any other tongue'. He did not like early rising either, Wordsworth moaned in the same letter, and he wanted to stay away from England as long as possible. Towards the end of the tour each man was sure that he had sacrificed himself to the interests of his friend, as a true English gentleman should. 'I have . . . made many sacrifices of which he has not been aware', Wordsworth confided to Mary.[90] It looked different to Crabb Robinson. 'I at once made up my mind to accede to his wishes as I have always done', is one revealing diary entry.[91] But on one issue—the length of their stay—Wordsworth certainly did get his own way and his fellow-traveller was justified in feeling that he had behaved impeccably.

Wordsworth insisted on not lingering in Austria and Germany because by July he was missing his family intensely. 'A man must travel alone, I mean without one of his family, to feel what his family is to him!'[92] But those at Rydal had been in his thoughts from the start of the tour. It was Mary's willingness to remain behind to look after Dorothy that made her husband's travels possible and it is clear from his long and frequent letters home that he knew it. Of course they contained complaints—Mary would not have trusted them if they had not—but essentially they were an attempt to convey to his family, in a spirit of gratitude, just how much their self-effacement had made available to him.

These letters, which are amongst Wordsworth's longest and most interesting, reveal that his capacity for delight was undiminished and that what he enjoyed he enjoyed at first, not second, hand. Even a critical anecdote told by Crabb Robinson demonstrates it. Wordsworth, he wrote to a lady they had met at Rome,

cares rather less than I wish for works of antiquity—he has a fine sense for the charms of colour, but is less susceptible to beauty of form either in Sculpture or Architecture. I overheard him exclaim with rapture at the sight of two children playing by the Amphitheatre at Nismes 'Oh that I could steal those children and carry them off to Rydal Mount!' And on top of the Colosseum he was admiring the rich verdure beyond as much as the sublime edifice below.[93]

Robinson was, however, surprised by how deeply Wordsworth was moved by the inside of St Peter's.

Wordsworth was most profoundly touched, as always, by a sight or sensation that was already endeared to him through personal or literary connection. Neither fatigue, nor loneliness, nor the stupidity of a guide could stop him making a very arduous journey to Vallombrosa—it was a pilgrimage in memory of Milton and a line of *Paradise Lost*.[94] Discovering in Rome that a pine tree he admired against the sunset had been saved from felling by Sir George Beaumont, Wordsworth was so moved that he clasped the trunk of the tree, honouring it as a 'monument of my departed friend's feelings for the beauties of nature . . .'.[95] At Lake Como memories of Robert Jones and of Mary and Dorothy on the 1820 tour 'came upon [him] as fresh as if they had happened the day before', and he kept to himself as much as possible, aware that tears were near.[96]

Wordsworth regretted that his journey had not been taken years before, for, though his mind had been 'enriched by innumerable images' and 'vivified by feelings', he was now too old, he thought, to make them answer 'noble purposes' in verse.[97] But once again he was lamenting departed powers prematurely. In the same letter to his family, 5 July 1837, he confessed what he knew would make Mary cross, that he had lost two or three nights' sleep trying to correct a first draft of what became *The Cuckoo at Laverna*. Other composition followed, and when Wordsworth published his last separate collection in 1842, it contained his final travel sequence, *Memorials of a Tour to Italy*, dedicated rightly, and touchingly, to Crabb Robinson,

> For the kindnesses that never ceased to flow,
> And prompt self-sacrifice to which I owe
> Far more than any heart but mine can know.

(7)

During the late 1830s Wordsworth's fame continued to increase. There were of course dissenting voices. In 1836 Landor unexpectedly and splenetically attacked him in *A Satire on Satirists*,[98] and in 1838 Henry Chorley warned against 'an idol-worship, extreme and trenching upon superstition!'[99] But these grumbles counted for nothing. In 1838 Wordsworth was awarded an honorary degree by Durham University and on 12 June 1839 he became an honorary Doctor of Civil Law in the University of Oxford.

The ceremony itself was a personal triumph. In his Creweian Oration to a packed Sheldonian Theatre John Keble praised Wordsworth as the poet of humanity and at the granting of the degree, as *Jackson's Oxford Journal* noted, 'the great poet . . . was enthusiastically cheered' by an audience who had greeted mention of Queen Victoria and her ministers with disdain. But there was also a symbolic significance to the occasion. Robed in his new honour, Wordsworth awarded the prize for the Newdigate Prize Poem to a 20-year-old Christ Church undergraduate—John Ruskin. For a moment the foremost poet of the age spoke to the shy young man who was to become the greatest prose writer of the Victorian period and one of the most important conduits for and interpreters of the Wordsworthian spirit.

This moment was an emblem of Wordsworth's position in his seventieth year, a position that was unique in the history of English poetry. His influence on his natural successors, Byron, Shelley, and Keats, had been ambivalent. Acknowledging the liberating power of his early poetry, they had all lived to lament what they saw as his political apostasy. Their early deaths, however, had coincided with the rise of his reputation, which was thus allowed to go unchallenged by the work the second-generation Romantics might have produced. Now Wordsworth's early poetry spoke again to a new generation, but in a quite different context. To the writers who came to maturity in the early Victorian period the social and political upheaval that had been the setting for his early work was just history and his political shift a matter of no concern.[100] Byron, Shelley, and Keats had actually witnessed the author of *Lyrical Ballads* become an intimate of Lord Lonsdale and an apologist for conservatism, but the next generation took what they needed from *Lyrical Ballads* and *The Excursion* and *Yarrow Revisited*, untroubled by the poet's progress that had dismayed their immediate predecessors, and only hazily aware of what the political situation had been like when Jeffrey had discerned in Wordsworth's simple lyrics a threat to the established order. And in taking what they needed the younger generation inevitably reinterpreted Wordsworth, not consciously or polemically, but simply by the emphasis they put on what they valued.

To some Wordsworth was pre-eminently the celebrant of unregarded lives. In his Sheldonian Oration Keble had spoken of him as 'one who alone among poets has set the manners, the pursuits, and the feelings, religious and traditional, of the poor not merely in a good but . . . even in a celestial light'.[101] Wordsworth was moved to ask Keble for a copy of his tribute, because he felt that he had penetrated to the essence of his poetry. Many others would have echoed Keble's words. In 1838 Elizabeth Gaskell divulged to a friend her conviction that even in the poorest part cf Manchester evidence of 'the Poetry of Humble Life . . . is met with on every hand', and to convey just what she meant she quoted the passage from *The Old Cumberland Beggar* which begins, '. . . man is dear to man', and ends, 'That we have all of us one human heart'.[102] Mrs Gaskell could not have known that only a few years before Wordsworth had himself singled out this last line as the ground of his trust that his poetry would last or that he would continue to insist that poems such as *The Idiot Boy* were fundamental to his achievement.[103] When Sir Henry Bunbury excused his unauthorized printing of Wordsworth's 1801 letter to Fox, he explained that he thought its message, that 'men who do not wear fine cloaths can feel deeply', now had a fresh relevance in the light of the deteriorating 'condition of our labouring classes'.[104] To these admirers—to whom must be added Dickens, Kingsley, and George Eliot—Wordsworth was the poet of the humble. His art, as the hero of Kingsley's *Alton Locke* puts it, was 'democratic art', and it spoke to those who were anxiously aware that even as the poet was receiving his DCL the first Chartist petition was being presented in London, a plea for redress from the new poor, the labouring masses of the industrial North.[105] Nor did it only speak to writers. When Southwood Smith, a passionate advocate of education for children in factories, corresponded with Wordsworth, he did so because he read the poetry as essentially humanitarian in tendency.[106]

Others, however, put a different emphasis on the value of Wordsworth's writings, which can be characterized by a glance at another moment on this Oxford visit which was quite as emblematic as Wordsworth face to face with Ruskin. The morning after the degree ceremony Wordsworth was guest of honour at a breakfast party in Magdalen College given by Francis Faber.[107] Here he met, among others, Faber's brother Frederick, John Keble, and John Henry Newman. Each of these men was soon to achieve distinction and notoriety, Newman and Faber by their conversion to and high service in the Roman Catholic Church, Keble by his equally significant adherence to the Anglican. But in June 1839 they represented the intellectual core of the movement for spiritual renewal within the Church of England, the Tractarian or Oxford Movement, and when they gathered in Faber's rooms it was to meet the poet whose influence they all acknowledged.

Frederick Faber had been a devotee of Wordsworth since he was a schoolboy. He had met him in 1831 and in 1837 had returned with a reading-party to Ambleside, where he also assisted the local clergyman. *The Cherwell Water-lily*, his first collection of poems, published in 1840, includes many with Ambleside settings, all of a Wordsworthian cast.[108] Keble was the author of the most popular volume of devotional verse published in the nineteenth century, *The Christian Year* (1827), and when he dedicated the lectures he had given as Professor of Poetry at Oxford to Wordsworth, he did so conscious that the poet was his great exemplar.[109] When Newman met Wordsworth in 1839 he had just singled him out in an article in the *British Critic* as a poet of 'philosophical meditation', whose works 'addressed themselves to . . . high principles and feelings', and he was to return to this essay as an important document in his intellectual development when he wrote *Apologia pro vita sua* (1864).[110]

This is not the place for an essay on Wordsworth and the Oxford Movement, but the fact that each of these men, the intellectual élite of the Anglican Church, acknowledged his indebtedness to Wordsworth's writings is worth highlighting.[111] It is equally important to note that he was at ease with these breakfast companions because he had become accustomed to being with Anglican clergymen of most persuasions. His brother was an eminent High Churchman. His son was a vicar. Amongst his older friends he counted bishops, Anglican philanthropists such as Joshua Watson, and the highly visible Dr Thomas Arnold of Rugby. His younger friends included the Reverend Robert Perceval Graves, who settled in the Lake District just to be near Wordsworth,[112] and Aubrey De Vere, an intensely devout young disciple, who converted to Rome in 1851. De Vere paid regular visits to the poet's grave until extreme old age.[113]

As poet, Wordsworth spoke to all of these men. It is certain, however, that as private individual he remained, as he always had been, reticent even with them about his personal faith. Amongst the seven volumes of his letters there are no statements of belief that would have satisfied even a Low Church vicar on all points and the numerous entries about religion in Crabb Robinson's diary only reveal how unavailing were his efforts to establish exactly what Wordsworth did profess.[114] But the devotion to the Church of England of the author of *Ecclesiastical Sketches* was not in doubt, and it was confirmed by such further witness as the long discussion of priesthood in the latter part of the *Postscript* to *Yarrow Revisited* and Wordsworth's persistence in the late 1830s over raising money for a new church at Cockermouth.[115]

His role as spiritual counsellor was also attested by many private testimonies. William Channing told him in 1835 that his poetry had long been 'a fountain of spiritual life'. Elizabeth Ogle wrote that seeking strength she had turned to the poems, 'And here she found it—here she first began to drink those waters of peace, of comfort, of quiet yet earnest joy, which (with reverence be it spoken) she has found no where else in such rich abundance, excepting at the Fount of Life itself'. John Simon summed up what Wordsworth's teaching had offered him: 'Instruction in all, which it chiefly behoves to know—humbler reliance in the Divine rule—fuller love of Man—deeplier & holier sympathies with Nature—in success, self-diffidence—in trial & suffering the stay and comfort of Religious wisdom—are lessons, which I, in common with thousands—owe to those works'. Thomas Pringle, poet, explorer, and anti-slavery activist, went even further in his *Poems* (1839). His sonnet *Poems are Nature's Priests* likens England to degenerate Israel and concludes:

> Yet Israel then had SAMUEL—we have WORDSWORTH still.[116]

In her letter, Elizabeth Ogle quoted from *Tintern Abbey*, a commonplace occurrence which indicates what was happening. Wordsworth's canon early and late was being absorbed into the early Victorian spiritual ethos. Precisely because, as he put it to a future Dean of Canterbury, he had always 'been averse to frequent mention of the mysteries of Christian faith', Wordsworth's evidently spiritual poetry was available to a wide range of readers, dogmatic and latitudinarian alike.[117] Aubrey De Vere had no difficulty in finding that the 'Christianity so zealousy asserted in Wordsworth's maturer poetry' was 'obviously implied in the whole of it'.

The transaction between writer and reader, however, is never one-way. As he entered his last decade Wordsworth knew from overwhelming evidence that his poetry had comforted, strengthened, and encouraged many people. But as testimony accumulated that it was treasured as a spiritual resource, he increasingly saw it with his readers' eyes. Valued not just as an explorer of 'the burthen of the mystery', but as a specifically Christian poet, he felt the responsibility of the role thrust upon him when he came to revise his work for his next collected edition.

# 1840–1850

AFTER Queen Adelaide's visit to Rydal Mount on 27 July 1840 Dora wrote to her brother Willy: 'Do you think Mammy will be able to sleep tonight after having been shaken by the hand at her own door by a Queen—having talked with the Queen in this very room—her old husband the old Poet having walked side by side & talked with her Majesty a full hour I am sure—the World and his Wife were assembled on our front to see the cortege—& Tommy Troughton with his band, & all the flags, & all the rushbearings placed in two lines from the high waterfall gate to our gate made as pretty as an avenue for the Queen to walk thro' roofed by the green trees & the bright blue sky as was ever seen'.[1] The World and his Wife saw a hale 70-year-old, attended by a loving wife and daughter, receive the latest tribute of many which had made him the region's most famous resident. Only those closest to him knew that the poet who coped so serenely with such high honour was, in his private life, a deeply troubled old man.

Wordsworth had married late, at 32, and had fathered his last child, Willy, when he was 40, with the result that he entered his seventies fretting over the future of his children in a way that most parents have stopped doing at least ten years earlier. He was, moreover, an obsessively anxious father.

His worry about Willy was clear. How was he to survive? Passive, lacking in self-confidence, Willy still looked to his parents for emotional and financial support. In March 1835, for example, his mother sent a letter to cheer him up, in which, mingled with hints about not wasting money on billiards, she wrote: 'We are quite delighted with your improved hand-writing—and also with the style of your letter. Cultivate conciseness of expression. As an exercise, your Father advises you to read any essays or letters that you think well or tersely composed . . .'.[2] It is an astonishing tone to adopt towards a 25-year-old. Wordsworth himself at that age would have torn such a letter up. But there is no sign that it ruffled the relationship into which son and parents had settled, a dependency that Wordsworth confirmed by sorting out his son's career for him.

Willy's future would be more secure if he could become Distributor of Stamps in his father's place. Wordsworth had been trying to effect this since

1835, but it was not until 1842 that the right configuration of friends with influence and power occurred that made the transfer possible, without loss of income to himself. With the support of Gladstone, now vice-president of the Board of Trade, and the Prime Minister himself, Sir Robert Peel, Wordsworth passed his office to his son in July and in October he accepted, 'as a mark of favor from the Crown consequent upon [Peel's] recommendation', an annual Civil List pension of £300 for life.[3]

In Willy's case the father's anxiety was focused not on the problem or its solution, both of which were identifiable, but on how to bring about the desired result. Over Dora, however, Wordsworth felt anxiety of an altogether different kind, anxiety compounded of fear, anger, jealousy, and self-doubt, which he could not bring into focus, because to do this would involve recognizing that he was himself the major part of the problem.

In 1837 the friendship between Dora and Edward Quillinan had moved into the stage in which bantering and the occasional insult become lovers' language and the following year Dora revealed to her father that she wanted to consider herself engaged.[4] His response is fascinating. In a letter of early April 1838 Wordsworth sermonized about Henry Taylor's pursuit of Theodosia Spring-Rice, nineteen years his junior, passed on to John, his son, whose marriage to Isabella Curwen was suspected to be unhappy, and only in one sentence did he address Dora's situation directly: 'I take no notice of the conclusion of your Letter; indeed part of it I could not make out. It turns upon a subject which I shall never touch more either by pen or voice. Whether I look back or forwards it is depressing and distressing to me, and will for the remainder of my life, continue to be so.'[5]

Wordsworth was not hostile to Quillinan as an individual. He had come to respect his literary judgement, which for him was always an indication of a person's morals and character, and even after they had quarrelled he was prepared to aver that he was 'a most honourable and upright man'.[6] But he was opposed to Quillinan marrying his daughter. He was thirteen years older than she was, with two daughters to support, no reliable income, no settled home, an uncertain temper, and a slightly shady past.[7] Dora was without an income or substantial expectations and, much more important, she was extremely frail. Wordsworth did smother his daughter with affectionate concern and he was, as Henry Taylor noted, 'passionately jealous', but Dora's health goes a long way to justify his protectiveness.[8] Though she was not at all valetudinarian, by 1836 pain in her back—on which a variety of medical advice was sought—had made the exercise recommended so difficult that she could not even face being rowed to the island on Rydal Lake, an outing of a few hundred yards there and back.[9]

Wordsworth's uncompromising declaration in April 1838, however, solved nothing. It simply created an intolerable situation. In 1830 Hartley

Coleridge had remarked that Dora 'would be a healthier matron than she is a Virgin', adding 'but strong indeed must be the love that could induce her to leave her father, whom she almost adores, and who quite dotes upon her'.[10] Now, at 34, Dora was torn as Hartley had foreseen. Willing neither to grieve her elderly father nor to renounce Quillinan, she began to show the strain. She is, Mary admitted early in 1839, 'looking ill and has lately been losing her appetite'.[11]

In 1839 the situation worsened. Dora revealed to her father that her suitor had asked her to '*dare* the rough chance' of marriage without absolutely secure financial provision. Wordsworth demanded to know on exactly what grounds Quillinan was optimistic about his ability to support a wife, in a letter which, though it closed with 'affectionate remembrances', was very frosty.[12] Quillinan's angry response further distanced them all. He reproached Dora, she reproached her father, her mother reproached her. Believing now that the 'hopelessness of the case is manifest', Quillinan spelt it out to Dora that at bottom the conflict was 'between your love for your father and your kindness for me'.[13] But that was not entirely fair either. Money was an issue, and it was his recognition of that fact in May which prepared the way for meetings in June at which Wordsworth conceded that 'the event is inevitable'. Quillinan was overjoyed and at once 'dismounted from [his] high horse', reporting to Dora, 'your Father and I are right good real friends'.[14] By the following year the two lovers were together in London, 'a sort of public annunciation', Crabb Robinson assumed, 'of the connection intended to be consummated between them'.[15]

Throughout this sad time the good angel to all of the family was Isabella Fenwick. First visiting Rydal Mount in 1833, when she was 50, she had become for the Wordsworths by 1836 'in the first rank of those whom we love and esteem'. Tributes to Isabella Fenwick are plentiful. Crabb Robinson called her 'A lady universally beloved for the rare union of the warmest religion with perfect liberality'. In his *Autobiography* Henry Taylor gave an account of her impact on him as a young man which was so ardent that he felt obliged to insist that his 'admiration was wholly unamorous'. To Mary Wordsworth she was 'that dear good woman who is a treasure to us all'.[16] But the most striking testimony to her kindliness, intelligence, and strength of character is found not in these descriptions of her personal qualities but in the letters Wordsworth wrote to her. In 1840 the joke was that he was sending a poem not *with* his love but *to* his love, and the women at Rydal Mount who made it were right.[17] Addressing her as 'my *dearest Friend*', 'my beloved Friend', 'my beloved Friend, and heart-sister', Wordsworth found in Miss Fenwick a substitute for Dorothy, Sara Hutchinson, and Dora after her marriage.[18] He wrote to her more revealingly than to anyone else and was so stimulated by her company that in 1839 he and Mary moved in with her in Ambleside for a few days, mainly, as Wordsworth candidly admitted to Crabb Robinson, 'because it may not be prudent for me to walk to see her so often as I could wish'.[19] Wordsworth was a very lucky man and it says a great deal for Mary that she loved his new 'heart-sister' as much as he did.

Isabella Fenwick was both a balm and an astringent. In 1838 she had moved to Ambleside to be near the Wordsworths and, through counsel to Dora, support for Mary, and a lot of discussion with the obdurate father, she eased them all towards the marriage, which took place from her house in Bath on 11 May 1841.[20] John Wordsworth performed the ceremony, but it was Willy who walked with Dora into St James's Church. As Quillinan explained to his daughter Rotha the following day:

Mr Wordsworth was so agitated at parting with his sole daughter that he said to me almost at the last moment, 'I have told Dora that I would accompany you to church if you wished it, but this interview with my child has already so upset me that I think I can hardly bear it.' We all then begged him *not* to come, & it was agreed that his son William should act for him; but he gave us his blessing very affectionately both before & after the wedding: nothing indeed could have been kinder than he & all have been.[21]

Did Mary or Wordsworth, one wonders, remember how Dorothy had similarly been unable to face their wedding in 1802?

(2)

With public recognition honouring his lifetime's work as a poet and domestic anxieties disturbing him as a private man, Wordsworth might have fallen silent. But the poet who welcomed the bright sunshine on his seventieth birthday 'upon the whole, in a chearful state of mind' continued to write.[22] In 1839 he composed a number of sonnets on subjects taken from his Italian tour, responding to what he described to Ticknor as the 'ghost or surviving Spirit of travelling . . . One enjoys objects while they are present but they are never truly endeared till they have been lodged some time in the memory.'[23] The August after his seventieth birthday he climbed Helvellyn for the last time—a remarkable feat in itself—and when he returned home a sonnet on Haydon's recent painting of *Wellington Musing upon the Field of Waterloo* was in first draft, as he put it, 'warm from the brain'.[24] In 1840 also he wrote a meditation on the legitimacy of capital punishment, in a sonnet sequence which Crabb Robinson thought admirable and Henry Taylor considered a substantial contribution to the current debate on the question.[25] Most important of all to his well-being, moreover, Wordsworth began to envisage what he had thought he would never do again, the publication of a completely new volume.

What prompted him was almost certainly serendipity. In 1839 Thomas Powell solicited contributions to a volume he and others were putting together, which eventually appeared as *The Poems of Geoffrey Chaucer, Modernized* (1841).[26] Wordsworth was keen to help—'My love and reverence for Chaucer are unbounded', he told Crabb Robinson—and he started to look for the translations he had made in 1801.[27] Finding what he wanted, however, proved not only more difficult than he expected (though he assured Powell that he and Mary had looked 'with great diligence . . . among my papers'), but also more interesting.[28] In manuscripts copied out many years ago he came across *Salisbury Plain* and *Adventures on Salisbury Plain*, his tragedy, *The Borderers*, elegies for a village schoolmaster, and verses in memory of his brother John—all unpublished. The Salisbury Plain poems had come into his mind recently when John Kenyon's blank verse *Moonlight* had stirred memories of his own experiences at Stonehenge in 1793. Disclosing that he had written 'a Poem of some length in the Spenserian Stanza', he remarked to Kenyon, 'I have it still in Mss and parts may perhaps be thought worth publishing after my death among the "juvenilia" '.[29] Wordsworth also knew that there was speculation about *The Borderers*. Learning of its existence from Cottle's materials for his *Early Recollections*, Crabb Robinson had urged in 1836 that it be 'preserved at all events as a curiosity'. It could not fail to be of interest, he thought, 'as the *dramatic experiment* of a great philosophic and lyric poet'.[30]

There was an additional reason for considering publication of these poems—they were still under his control. Wordsworth felt strongly that 'raking together every thing that may have dropped from a distinguished Author's pen' was an 'abuse', but the flurry of books and articles after the deaths of Coleridge and Lamb had demonstrated that the public had an appetite for it.[31] He decided to forestall any posthumous publication of what he had so far excluded from the canon and he did so in an entirely characteristic way. In March 1841 he told Moxon that he had been 'copying out about 2000 Lines of miscellaneous Poems, from Mss, some of which date so far back [as] 1793'.[32] What he did not say was that he was also revising them. When the Salisbury Plain poems were published in 1842 as *Guilt and Sorrow; or, Incidents upon Salisbury Plain*, a prefatory note placed the composition in 1793–4 and gave some details of its genesis, 'as a matter of literary biography'. A note appended to *The Borderers* similarly suggested that interest in the origins of the play was legitimate. It was, Wordsworth explained, an embodiment of what he had learnt about 'sin and crime' during his 'long residence in France, while the Revolution was rapidly advancing to its extreme of wickedness'. But both of these notes are

misleading. Wordsworth encouraged historical, even biographical, interpretation of the poems, while actually presenting revised, in the case of *Guilt
and Sorrow* transformed, texts.[33] As ever, he was determined to control the
image of his own intellectual development that emerged from the poetry.

The 1842 volume, however, was not just a gleaning of old material. Its
title was *Poems, Chiefly of Early and Late Years*. More recent poems
included the *Sonnets upon the Punishment of Death*, 28 miscellaneous
sonnets, a number of lyrics such as *Airey-Force Valley* and *Composed by the
Sea-shore*, and the sequence of blank verse meditation, sonnets, and lyrics,
*Memorials of a Tour in Italy*. And the most interesting of these memorials is
one which combines both impulses at work in the whole volume, the drive to
record youth's achievement and to celebrate experience in age—*Musings
near Aquapendente*.[34]

Wordsworth and Crabb Robinson had visited Aquapendente, between
Sienna and Rome, on 25 April 1837, but in *Musings*, written early in 1841,
the place serves only as a point from which the poet roams over all of the
tour, reflecting on history, the sources of poetic power, and the utilitarian-
ism of the present age. Few readers will persevere to the end, for the blank
verse is stiff, but the opening section is striking. Resting on a slope of the
Apennines, Wordsworth is prompted by a flowering broom to return in
thought to his own mountains, to Fairfield, Seat Sandal, Glenridding-
screes, and low Glencoign, and to the verse he had written in celebration of
these lonely places with magical names forty years before, when he had just
moved to Grasmere.[35] Memories of the Fairfield range introduce the figure
of Scott, who climbed Helvellyn with Wordsworth in 1805:

> Where once together, in his day of strength,
> We stood rejoicing, as if earth were free
> From sorrow, like the sky above our heads.

And the image of the ailing Scott, which now intrudes, inevitably recalls the
poets' last meeting at Abbotsford, in 1831, when Scott had quoted at
Wordsworth lines from *Yarrow Unvisited* in reference to his own impending
visit to Italy. 1841, 1837, 1831, 1805, 1800, the memories recess to
Wordsworth's first Grasmere poems, to the moment when he consciously
chose to live, whatever the cost, as a poet, and they return to the present in
Italy, when the survivor in old age is still

> free to rove where Nature's loveliest looks,
> Art's noblest relics, history's rich bequests,
> Failed to reanimate and but feebly cheered
> The whole world's Darling—free to rove at will
> O'er high and low, and if requiring rest,
> Rest from enjoyment only.

In this opening section of recollection enshrined in a fusion of old verse and new, and in its tone of sober joy, Wordsworth's most characteristic voice in blank verse is heard for the last time.

Wordsworth's attitude to the publication of this, his final discrete volume, was strange. Moxon was in difficulties. He had come through prosecution for issuing a blasphemous libel, Shelley's *Queen Mab*, and rumour reaching Rydal that 'Moxon may Crash' proved unfounded.[36] But times were hard, as Moxon told Wordsworth in a letter about the 'present wretched state of the publishing business'.[37] The poet none the less refused to allow copies of the new book to be sent out for review, despite protest from Moxon, and when sales did prove disappointing he fell back on his old defence—that public taste was at fault. 'Dr. Arnold told me that his lads seemed to care for nothing but Bozzy's [Dickens's] next number', he moaned. 'Can that Man's public and others of the like kind materially affect the Question.'[38]

Gloomy, truculent, and defensive, Wordsworth claimed that he was publishing 'Most reluctantly and merely to save trouble to my Successors'.[39] But whenever he had sung this tune in the past it had indicated anxiety, not indifference, and so it did now. Wordsworth worked very hard on this volume, as the surviving manuscripts reveal, and he presented it not as scraps from a writer's workshop but as a coherent collection, which completed all that had gone before. There was a biographical and historical interest—this the notes acknowledged—but the book was not *merely* of biographical interest. The prefatory poem, *Prelude*, insists that this work, whose forerunners 'through many a year / Have faithfully prepared each other's way', speaks with

> A Voice devoted to the love whose seeds
> Are sown in every human breast, to beauty
> Lodged within compass of the humblest sight,
> To cheerful intercourse with wood and field,
> And sympathy with man's substantial griefs

and that its message is urgently addressed to the Britain of the 'hungry-forties',

> When unforeseen distress spreads far and wide
> Among a People mournfully cast down,
> Or into anger roused by venal words
> In recklessness flung out to overturn
> The judgment, and divert the general heart
> From mutual good . . .

Compared with the grandeur and ambition of the earlier prefatory manifesto, the 'Prospectus' to *The Recluse*, this poem looks slight, but it is, none the less, an unequivocal assertion of what Wordsworth had maintained ever since 1800—that his poetry had a social, didactic function, that his volumes were bound each to each, and that his theme was 'Man . . . Nature, and . . . Human Life'. It was also his last declaration of this kind. A few strong poems were still to come: the sonnet, 'Wansfell! this Household has a favoured lot' (1842), which Wordsworth thought 'one of his most perfect as a work of art';[40] the sonnet *At Furness Abbey* (1845), and the elegy for his grandson Edward, 'Why should we weep' (1845–6); the pendant to *The Old Cumberland Beggar*, 'I know an aged Man . . .' (1846).[41] Wordsworth continued, even, to be surprised by the Muse's refusal to leave him. In 1845 he reported that 'only a few days ago . . . I was able to put into Verse the Matter of a Short Poem which had been in my mind with a determination and a strong desire to write upon it for more than thirty years'.[42] These poems were added to the collected editions, for which he continued to revise the canon, but *Poems, Chiefly of Early and Late Years* was the last collection with its own identity and it marked, for the public, the end of Wordsworth's creative life.

## (3)

*Poems, Chiefly of Early and Late Years* is a teasing volume. The notes accompanying the early poems gesture towards autobiographical disclosures, yet give very little away, and what little is given is subverted by the revision of the text. The poet of the 'egotistical sublime' remained reticent. But although the title suggests finality, this collection was not Wordsworth's last retrospect. He had consciously marked the beginning of his life as poet by assessing his past in a private autobiography that opened with a question: 'Was it for this . . .?' He signalled its close by another private autobiography, this time concentrating not on what had made him a poet but on what he had made as a poet. For the last time he interrogated his memory at length, as fascinated as ever by its power to resist and to give meaning to what Hardy called time's 'mindless rote'.[43]

In 1843 Wordsworth dictated to Isabella Fenwick notes about the origin and composition of his poems.[44] Christopher Wordsworth drew on them for his *Memoirs of William Wordsworth* (1851) and in 1857 John Carter printed them piecemeal, as later editors have done, in the six-volume Collected Works he prepared for Moxon. But although Alexander Grosart included them in the first collection of Wordsworth's prose in 1876, they were omitted from the one authoritative edition now in use, that by Owen and Smyser, with the result that they are assimilated by readers, if at all, only amongst the mass of other notes that accompany scholarly texts on the poems and, of course, only poem by poem. This is a pity, for the Fenwick

Notes, as they are usually called, are best read entire, not as a source of information merely, but as a document in Wordsworth's autobiography.

They originated in 1841. After Dora's wedding, Wordsworth and Mary, the Quillinans, and Isabella Fenwick had moved on from Bath to Wells and thence, as Wordsworth put it, 'to the old haunts of Mr Coleridge and myself and dear sister, about Alfoxden'.[45] In his returns to Wales, Scotland, and the Alps, Wordsworth had taken pleasure in aligning memory with present experience, but this revisiting was risky. He was returning to a sacred place, where change would have been profoundly upsetting.[46] But little had altered and, as Miss Fenwick told Henry Taylor, he 'was delighted to see again those scenes . . . where he had felt and thought so much',[47]—Alfoxden House, where little Basil Montagu had evaded his tiresome questions, giving rise to *Anecdote for Fathers*, the glen where he, Thelwall, and Coleridge had talked about escape from 'the jarrings and conflicts of the wide world', the brook running down Holford Combe, Wordsworth's 'chosen resort', where he had composed *Lines Written in Early Spring*.[48] 'He pointed out the spots where he had written many of his early poems', Isabella Fenwick reported, 'and told us how they had been suggested.' Every scene reminded Wordsworth, too, of what Dorothy had been—'the only painful feeling that moved in his mind', Miss Fenwick observed—but being able to recall so vividly her presence in this place was also to render her a kind of homage.

Memories—of Tom Poole and young Basil, of Hazlitt and Lamb, of Thelwall and the spy, above all, of Coleridge and *Lyrical Ballads*—stirred in Wordsworth and over the winter of 1842–3 they were augmented by whatever he could recollect that seemed worth recording about the poetry from Hawkshead days to the present. The Fenwick Notes are rich in information about his travels, his reading, his circle of friends, about his childhood, and his observation of local characters and customs. Many are memorable for decisive judgements on writers and books and some because they give glimpses of the Lake District as it was and as it had become—Wordsworth's waspish comment on neighbours who live in 'double-coach-house cottages' in the note on *Ode to Lycoris* is a good example of the latter. It is not the otherwise unknown information, however, nor the flashes of sharpness which give the Fenwick Notes their real value, but the insight provided by the whole body of the notes into Wordsworth's preoccupation and fundamental concern as a poet with specific places, with the lives of lowly people, with history, and with the relation between politics, individual morality, and religion, and into his struggle to integrate his desire to celebrate the local and actual with his reluctance 'to submit the poetic spirit to the chains of fact and real circumstance' (note to *An Evening Walk*). The Fenwick Notes need to be read alongside *The Prelude* and with *Biographia*

*Literaria* in mind. They matter because they are a great poet's last attempt at what had been his lifelong endeavour—to record, interpret, and harmonize disparate experience.

## (4)

As Wordsworth completed his reminiscences, the last of the friends who had peopled his recollections of Racedown, Alfoxden, and early years at Grasmere died. In 1839 Southey had married again, but his marriage to Caroline Bowles, over which his family split bitterly, was barely a year old before his mind gave way. When Wordsworth called on him in July 1840 Southey did not recognize his visitor until told his name. 'Then', Wordsworth sadly reported, 'his eyes flashed for a moment with their former brightness, but he sank into the state in which I had found him, patting with both hands his books affectionately, like a child.'[49] He died on 21 March 1843 and though the divided family did not invite Wordsworth to the funeral, he made his way there none the less, through the driving rain, with Quillinan, and at the end of the year he composed the *Inscription* ('Ye vales and Hills') for the monument in Crosthwaite Church.

Southey had been Poet Laureate since 1813. Now the honour was offered to his old friend. The Lord Chamberlain wrote that it gave him 'very peculiar gratification' to be able 'to propose this mark of distinction on an Individual whose acceptance of it would shed additional lustre upon an Office in itself highly honourable'.[50] Wordsworth declined, in similarly courtly terms, declaring himself too old for the duties of the Laureateship, but when the Lord Chamberlain assured him that these were now 'merely nominal' and Sir Robert Peel went further, insisting that the queen wanted Wordsworth to accept on the understanding that 'you shall have nothing *required* of you', he could no longer refuse.[51]

Wordsworth received this 'high Distinction' in April 1843 with 'unalloyed pleasure', but it made no difference to his pattern of living, which had been established over the last fifteen years. Its centre was, more firmly than ever, domestic life with Mary at Rydal Mount. Still vigorous, Wordsworth helped the gardener James Dixon in planting and thinning trees and until well into his seventies he lent a hand turning the grass at hay-making. And at all times of the year he walked. Having strained muscles 'from too much exercise and imprudently climbing styles and gates', he told Miss Fenwick that the pain had taught him 'that I must yield to the invisible changes which Time makes in one's constitution', but it is clear that he did not.[52] In December 1843, for example, Quillinan wrote to Crabb Robinson that he had been 'walking about a considerable part of the morning through the waters & the mists with the Bard who seems to defy all weathers; & who called this a beautiful, soft solemn day; & so it was; though somewhat insidiously soft, for a mackintosh was hardly proof against its insinuation'.[53]

Wordsworth also remained as active mentally—'He is in great force, & in great vigour of mind', his son-in-law noted.[54] Undoubtedly this continuing intellectual vitality was due to the stimulation provided by friends. In old age Wordsworth and Mary did not turn in on themselves. Isabella Fenwick continued to grow on them. In 1846 it was reported that '[Wordsworth] goes every day to Miss Fenwick . . . gives her a smacking kiss, & sits down before her fire to open his mind'.[55] Henry Crabb Robinson came almost every Christmas for a long stay and since he continued till the end of his life to read steadily in the best of contemporary writing his conversation was an enormous boon to Wordsworth, whose eyes prevented him from reading much. Crabb Robinson was companionable—he loved an evening's whist—but he was also an invaluable irritant, with decided views of his own.

There was also other stimulation close at hand, for by the 1840s the Grasmere–Rydal–Ambleside area had become a little constellation of talent. There were the Arnolds at Fox How, who kept open house to a wide range of friends.[56] In 1840 Wordsworth had helped Eliza Fletcher, the much-travelled and well-connected widow of an Edinburgh advocate, buy Lancrigg in Easedale, and as she and her family began to spend more time there he became a regular visitor. Mrs Fletcher, whom Wordsworth had known since 1833, was a friend of the Arnolds, Henry Taylor, and Isabella Fenwick, but her extensive acquaintance reached beyond Wordsworth's existing circle to, for example, William Rathbone Greg, one of the noted intellectual mill-owning family of Manchester, who had a house in Ambleside, and Elizabeth Gaskell, whom Wordsworth met in 1849, when she had become famous as the author of *Mary Barton*.[57]

Mrs Fletcher's *Autobiography* gives a fascinating account of this Lake District milieu.[58] The people Wordsworth could expect to meet at Lancrigg or Fox How or Wansfell, Greg's house, were intelligent, literate, travelled, and politically aware. A further addition to the circle had all of these attributes and one other—she was eccentric. Harriet Martineau, who built herself a house in Ambleside in 1846, was a writer, a proto-feminist controversialist, a health and hygiene faddist, and a proselytizing Mesmerist. In every way an independent, characterful woman, she burst into Ambleside society.[59] Privately she thought Wordsworth a dear old silly, as she revealed in a letter which says as much about her character as it does about his:

. . . I, deaf, can hardly conceive how he, with eyes & ears, & a heart which leads him to converse with the poor in his incessant walks, can be so unaware of their personal state. I dare say you [Elizabeth Barrett] need not be told how sensual vice abounds in rural districts. Here it is flagrant beyond anything I ever could have looked for: &

here, while every Justice of the peace is filled with disgust, and every clergyman with (almost) despair at the drunkenness, quarrelling & extreme licentiousness with women,—here is dear good old Wordsworth for ever talking of rural innocence, & deprecating any intercourse with towns, lest the purity of his neighbours should be corrupted![60]

Wordsworth for his part found her often tiresome, credulous, too quick to leap to conclusions, 'in many respects . . . a dangerous companion'.[61] But there was no doubt that Harriet Martineau had a mind and that she had stimulated him as someone overawed by the Laureate Bard could not have done.

Rydal Mount continued to attract friends, such as Aubrey De Vere and Macready, and the usual stream of pilgrims. Perhaps the most unexpected of these was Thomas Cooper, the Chartist activist, who had passed his time in Stafford gaol writing an extraordinary poem, *The Purgatory of Suicides*, which he managed to get published in 1845. Cooper turned up in September 1846, covered in dust, with no introduction, but Wordsworth received him, he recalled, 'with a smile so paternal, and such a hearty "How do you do? I am very happy to see you"—that the tears stood in my eyes for joy'. They discussed poetry, Byron, Southey, and Tennyson, and politics—the Tory poet staggered Cooper by saying that the Chartists were right in their aims, only blameable in their methods. Cooper was thrilled to be introduced to Dorothy 'as a poet!' and, noticing the 'kindest affection' with which Wordsworth talked to his sister in her wheelchair, he left Rydal Mount 'with a more intense feeling of having been in the presence of a good and great intelligence, than I have ever felt in any other moments of my life'.[62]

Occasional but stimulating visits to London still complemented the quieter existence at Rydal Mount. Wordsworth visited in 1842, 1845, and for the last time in 1847. In 1842 the city invigorated and excited him as much as it had when he was young, but now it was no longer a type of the 'blank confusion' he had imaged in *The Prelude*, but a hospitable place, whose map he knew well, not 'An undistinguishable world to men', but the home of many friends whose doors stood open.[63] Keyed up by the negotiation over the transfer of the Distributorship and by the renewed activity in the copyright campaign, Wordsworth seems to have found limitless energy, as an astonished Henry Taylor told Isabella Fenwick:

. . . yesterday I almost spent the day with him, and it was well for me that I could walk pretty stoutly, for, beginning by telling me that he had a lame leg and could not walk as well as usual, he walked from Upper Spring Street (which is just on the other side of the New Road) to Upper Grosvenor Street, from thence to the end of Grosvenor Place, thence to Belgrave Square, then to Cadogan Place, then to the Colonial Office (where he dined off some scraps and fragments of the office-keeper's dinner), then to the House of Lords, and when we came out of that (I having been long uneasy about the fatigue he was undergoing, not to mention the lameness) he proposed that we should take an omnibus to Baker Street, look in upon Mrs Wordsworth, and then take half an hour's walk in the Regent's Park! And it was done accordingly. And from the beginning of the day to the end never did he cease talking and for much of the time with his best vivacity.[64]

The 1845 visit was not much less strenuous. Summoned by an invitation to the Queen's Ball on 25 April, Wordsworth hastened to Samuel Rogers for a lesson in etiquette. Apparelled in Rogers's court dress and Sir Humphry Davy's sword, Wordsworth presented himself to his sovereign so becomingly that the wife of the American Minister to London had to dab her eyes. As Wordsworth explained to Henry Reed in Philadelphia, with much solemn enjoyment: 'To see a grey haired Man of 75 years of age kneeling down in a large assembly to kiss the hand of a young Woman is a sight for which institutions essentially democratic do not prepare a spectator of either sex . . . I am not therefore surprised that Mrs Everett was moved . . .'.[65]

That Wordsworth so relished explaining the symbolism of this encounter suggests that he would have been aware of the significance of another, a few days later. On 4 and 6 May the 'king-poet of our times', as Elizabeth Barrett called him, met his successor.[66] As long ago as 1830 Wordsworth had thought Alfred Tennyson 'not a little promising'.[67] Now, after a long silence, the younger man had proved himself to be a poet of exhilarating versatility and power. In 1842, as Wordsworth was publishing his valedictory *Poems, Chiefly of Early and Late Years*, Tennyson had brought out the collection that included *Ulysses*, *Morte d'Arthur* and *Dora* (which Wordsworth thought more essentially Wordsworthian than any pastoral he had written himself).[68] According to Tennyson, on one evening Wordsworth took his arm with 'Come, brother bard, to dinner', and when the younger man had 'at last, in the dark, said something about the pleasure he had taken from Mr Wordsworth's writings' the 'old poet had taken his hand, and replied with some expressions equally kind and complimentary'.[69] Five years later the man whom he now judged 'decidedly the first of our living Poets', became Poet Laureate on Wordsworth's death.[70]

Throughout this period testimonies to Wordsworth's fame continued to flood in. He was flattered to be nominated for election in 1846 as Rector of Glasgow University against Lord John Russell, though relieved that he was saved from the exertions of office by being defeated on a casting vote. Election to the Royal Irish Academy in 1846 was a notable honour. Fan letters accumulated at Rydal Mount, none more engaging than the one from Mrs Sara P. Green of Charlestown, Massachusetts, which enclosed an advertisement for the Rydal Mount Ladies Boarding School and her lecture entitled *Poetry of Nature*.[71] Dickens at his most inventive could hardly have bettered either. There was a surprising number of verse tributes, birthday odes, and musical settings. The Wordsworth Library has a collection of poems, for example, sent by Keats's friend Benjamin Bailey, now Senior Chaplain of Ceylon. Elizabeth Barrett, Wordsworth learned, borrowed Haydon's painting of him on Helvellyn and placed it at the foot of her sofa.[72] John Ruskin prefixed a quotation from *The Excursion* to the first volume of *Modern Painters* in 1843.[73]

But although Wordsworth's poetry was a force in national and international culture, his activity as a public figure was almost at an end. He was always ready to reinforce the teaching implicit in his poems—his letter of 16 December 1845 about value and methods in education is a splendid anticipation of *Hard Times*—but the poetry would do its work without further intervention from the Sage of Rydal Mount.[74] Only once more was he stirred to speak out directly and to lend what weight his name and Laureate's office carried to a public cause.

Wordsworth was not opposed to railways. 'O that there were a railway from Kendal', he had exclaimed in 1836, wishing Mary and Dora in London.[75] When, however, it was proposed in 1844 to push a line into the Lakes as far as Low Wood, just short of Ambleside (soon modified to a site above Bowness, the present Windermere station), he was appalled. His immediate form of protest was a sonnet, *On the Projected Kendal and Windermere Railway*, printed in the *Morning Post*, 16 October 1844, but this was followed up by two long letters in the same newspaper, 11 and 20 December, which sought to demonstrate that his was a principled and not a selfish objection, and a campaign in letters to those, such as Gladstone, with power to influence the decision on the line.[76] All his efforts—and his, of course, was not the only protest—were in vain.

The core of Wordsworth's argument was two persuasive points. First, since there was no demand from industry for the line, its purpose must be to exploit the area's one staple, its beauty, for tourism. But the incursion of the railway and the development that would follow would only destroy the beauty and peace the tourists were coming to enjoy. Second, people only benefit from what they see with a tutored eye. The appropriate tutoring can be gained from books, pictures, best of all from repeated personal exploration, from familiarization, but it cannot be gained by being pitched on a brief excursion into completely foreign terrain.

Both of these arguments are respectable and if Wordsworth had rested his case on them his letters (which were reprinted as a pamphlet) would have roused little ire. But he went further, expressing fears that 'the whole of Lancashire, and no small part of Yorkshire, pouring in upon us to meet the men of Durham, and the borderers from Cumberland and Northumberland' would, with their artisan taste for 'wrestling matches, horse and boat races . . . pot-houses and beer-shops', desecrate the region and debauch the already vulnerable 'lower class of inhabitants'.[77] Such a fear did not reveal simply the timorousness of old age. As long ago as the 1800 Preface to *Lyrical Ballads* Wordsworth had identified 'the encreasing accumulation of men in cities' as one of the causes working 'to blunt the discriminating powers of the mind'. For him the town–country opposition had never been merely a literary device. But the language of the *Morning Post* letters does in places suggest both fear of the mass and condescension, and it is easy to see why Barron Field, for example, though still a devoted admirer, wished he would fall silent and not expose himself to ridicule. 'Mr W[ordsworth] . . . can no more pretend to "retirement" than the Queen. They have both bartered it for fame. As for Mr W. he has himself been crying *Roast-meat* all his life. Has he not even published, beside his poems which have made the District classic-ground, an actual Guide?'[78] Field's arguments in his long and passionate remonstrance are not unanswerable, but they certainly represent the common-sense response and it prevailed. By the end of April 1847 trains were steaming into the station, giving Manchester labourers their first glimpse of the lake and the mountains beyond.[79]

## (5)

In 1845 an Inspector of Schools, Hugh Tremenheere, wanted Wordsworth to address his ideas on education to those 'whose positions, whether as Landlords or Manufacturers make them answerable to a great extent for the condition of the lower classes on their estates or in their neighbourhoods'. 'Happily', he added by way of encouragement, 'your voice is now more and more listened to.'[80] Others in the early 1840s were equally anxious that Wordsworth's voice should be heard, but their concern was with other orders of society. In 1841 Aubrey De Vere advocated a selection of his poems for the poor, suggesting that the principle of choice should be 'that of providing a continual ascent for the mind of the poor man, by beginning with subjects of familiar interest, advancing to those of more various & excursive interest, & concluding with those of a higher and more directly spiritual interest'.[81] Two years later a Manchester clergyman, Richard Parkinson, asked permission to prefix the 'Memoir of the Rev. Robert Walker' to his own *The Old Church-clock*: 'You would thus be instructing & delighting a humbler class of readers than can be expected to have access to the volumes in which the memoir now appears & striking into the low strata of society those sorts of sound church principles, which are now beginning to bear their proper fruit in the higher regions of the earth'.[82] James Burns, a bookseller who specialized in publishing Tractarian literature, likewise claimed a social justification for his *Select Pieces from the Poems of William*

*Wordsworth*: 'it is now high time to have recourse to his poetry as one of our direct instruments of education'.[83]

De Vere and Parkinson were genuinely altruistic. For all his high-toned sentiments, Burns was not and Moxon and Wordsworth were furious about his unauthorized publication.[84] But Moxon shared his fellow publisher's entrepreneurial instinct. Publishing—especially the publishing of poetry in the age of 'Boz'—needed to be innovative and aggressive. Soon after taking Wordsworth on he had wanted to issue a one-volume collected edition, but Wordsworth had resisted, afraid of a check to sales of the six-volume set. By 1843, however, the multi-volume set was looking all too familiar, the 1842 *Poems, Chiefly of Early and Late Years* needed to be incorporated in the canon, and Wordsworth was Poet Laureate. An attractive new edition was called for, and in 1845 it appeared—a single-volume, double-columned, but beautifully printed Collected Works, prefaced by an engraving of Wordsworth that makes him look like a poet from the antique world, and a picture of Rydal Mount.[85]

This edition mattered a great deal to Wordsworth and he controlled its making as tightly as ever, issuing detailed instructions about both engravings, the wording of the title-page, and the placing of the poem, 'If thou indeed derive thy light from Heaven', with which he wanted the volume to open. And, of course, for the last time, he revised the whole canon, tinkering yet again both with poems only recently published and with those that dated from the very beginning of his career.

Although the surviving evidence of Wordsworth's intense labour is fascinating, it would be tedious to list the revisions here, and unnecessary, for most are small and probably went unnoticed even by his most devoted readers. One change, however, could have been missed by no one, since it radically altered some of Wordsworth's finest verse in what contemporaries regarded as his most important poem.

At the end of the first book of *The Excursion* (formerly *The Ruined Cottage*), the Wanderer assuages the poet's sadness on hearing the story of Margaret's fatal decline by this passage of reconciling wisdom:

> 'My Friend! enough to sorrow you have given,
> The purposes of wisdom ask no more;
> Be wise and cheerful; and no longer read
> The forms of things with an unworthy eye.
> She sleeps in the calm earth, and peace is here.
> I well remember that those very plumes,
> Those weeds, and the high spear-grass on that wall,
> By mist and silent rain-drops silvered o'er,
> As once I passed, into my heart conveyed
> So still an image of tranquillity,

So calm and still, and looked so beautiful
Amid the uneasy thoughts which filled my mind,
That what we feel of sorrow and despair
From ruin and from change, and all the grief
The passing shows of Being leave behind,
Appeared an idle dream, that could not live
Where meditation was. I turned away,
And walked along my road in happiness.'

Although Wordsworth had never been happy with this narration—the rest of *The Excursion* grew, in part, out of attempts to explore further the questions about human suffering which it raised—this is essentially how the text stood from 1814 until the most recent reprint of the stereotyped edition in 1843, quoted above. But now he revised the climax totally, bringing both Margaret's death and the poet's grief within the aegis of the faith that transcends both:

'My Friend! enough to sorrow you have given,
The purposes of wisdom ask no more:
Nor more would she have craved as due to One
Who, in her worst distress, had ofttimes felt
The unbounded might of prayer; and learned, with soul
Fixed on the Cross, that consolation springs,
From sources deeper far than deepest pain
For the meek Sufferer. Why then should we read
The forms of things with an unworthy eye?

[as text above]

      . . . and all the grief
That passing shows of Being leave behind,
Appeared an idle dream, that could maintain
Nowhere, dominion o'er the enlightened spirit
Whose meditative sympathies repose
Upon the breast of Faith. I turned away
And walked along my road in happiness.'

Wordsworth had a fine ear for blank verse and he must have flinched as he scored out his original cadences for some of these rhythmically brutal lines. But the explicitly Christian statement had to be included. Why? It has been suggested that he was responding to doubts raised recently about his religious position. In 1842 John Wilson (under his pseudonym Christopher North) had asked, 'Was Margaret a Christian?', to point up his attack on the 'utter absence of Revealed Religion, where it ought to have been all-in-all', and the *Eclectic Review* in the same year had managed to suggest that Wordsworth was both a pantheist and a sentimental, High Church crypto-

Romanist.[86] But even without these goads it is likely that *The Excursion*, Book I, would have been revised, for in the early 1840s Wordsworth became much more devout, not devout enough to satisfy Isabella Fenwick, who nursed a 'great desire to see Mr. Wordsworth become a Catholic-minded man, and pass his evening of life under the shadow of some cathedral', but devout enough to have a cedar cross nailed above his bedroom window in 1842, so that his eye could rest on it as soon as he awoke.[87] And the strongest influence in fostering this kind of piety was the man who gave him the cross, Frederick William Faber.[88]

In 1840 Faber was living in Ambleside in the household of a distant relative of Wordsworth's, as tutor to the eldest son of Mr and Mrs Benson Harrison.[89] Although Crabb Robinson repudiated the views of this 'flaming zealot' entirely, he confessed that he could not resist his personal charm and it is clear that he was worried that Wordsworth was still more susceptible to the attraction of this 'very amiable and interesting young man'.[90] While abroad the following year Faber kept in touch by letter,[91] and over the turn of 1841–2 and 1842–3 he was once more in Ambleside, disputing with Wordsworth and Crabb Robinson on such topics as transubstantiation, as the two old men and their young companion walked together on Loughrigg or round Rydal Lake. Once settled in his living at Elton, near Peterborough, he treated his friends at Rydal Mount to a racy account of his warfare against local Dissenters and, even though a terse note of 17 November 1845 announcing his reception into the Roman Catholic Church ended the connection, he continued to write to Quillinan and in 1848 was still speaking warmly of 'what my feelings have always been & still are to all the Wordsworths'.[92]

Faber admired Wordsworth, but not like those readers whose grateful letters have already been quoted, who valued in *Tintern Abbey*, the *Ode: Intimations*, and much of *The Excursion* an inexplicit, undoctrinaire spirituality which meshed comfortably with their own religious belief. Faber suspected the undefined and rejected the quintessentially Wordsworthian *Tintern Abbey*, for example, because it smacked of pantheism, of which he had 'a great horror'.[93] Although, he told Keble, he recognized that for many Wordsworth had been 'the *Perirrhanterium*', i.e. the 'Sprinkler of Holy Water', he mourned 'over his not having known Cath[olic] Truth when he was young', and hoped that 'as his mind becomes more affectionately disposed towards authority & dogma' he would register his growing 'distaste' for Milton by removing from his text the reference to him as '*holiest of men*'.[94]

The arrogance and bigotry of these remarks about the poet who had believed he was Milton's heir are breathtaking, but Faber had his way. In 1845 'Holiest of Men' was excised from the 'Prospectus' to *The Recluse*, a remarkable testimony to Faber's persuasive powers. And what this letter to Keble reveals is quite clear. The young priest valued Wordsworth's poetry as a precursor of, and an agent in, the dissemination of Tractarian Christianity and what he wanted was that it, and the poet, should be more obviously identified with the cause. Entrusted by Wordsworth with writing a note to *Musings near Aquapendente*, he took the opportunity to extol the virtues of the Oxford Movement, 'as likely to restore among us a tone of piety more earnest and real than that produced by the mere formalities of the understanding, refusing, in a degree which I cannot but lament, that its own temper and judgement shall be controlled by those of antiquity'.[95] The note appeared in 1842, of course, as Wordsworth's. Faber claimed that it was at his urging that Wordsworth had added to the *Ecclesiastical Sonnets*, 'in order to do more justice to the Papal Church for the services which she actually did render to Christianity and humanity in the middle ages',[96] and when he dedicated his *Sights and Thoughts in Foreign Churches and among Foreign Peoples* (1842) to Wordsworth, he publicly drew attention to their 'many thoughtful conversations on the rites, prerogatives, and doctrines of the Holy Church'. In 1844 he printed Wordsworth's *Stanzas Suggested in a Steamboat off Saint Bees' Heads* in his Life of St Bega in Newman's *Lives of the English Saints*, hymning it as an 'instance of the remarkable way in which his poems did in diverse places anticipate the revival of catholic doctrines among us'.[97]

In November 1844 Wordsworth attended a meeting of the Cambridge Camden Society, only to hear himself eulogized as 'one of the founders of the Society', which was dedicated to ecclesiological renewal.[98] But this seems to have been the high-water mark of his Tractarian leanings. In January 1845 Crabb Robinson noted with relief that Wordsworth was 'no partisan of [the Society's] pro-papistical labours', and at the end of the year, in which Faber went over to the Roman Church, he recorded that the poet regretted that 'he had ever uttered a word favourable to Puseyism' and 'expressed himself strongly against Faber'.[99]

Faber was much the most interesting newcomer to the circle of the poet's late years, but his influence must not be over-emphasized. Wordsworth had many High Church acquaintances and his post-bag confirmed that many others besides Faber valued his poetry as an expression of Christian truth.[100] It is clear, however, that something very striking did occur in the early 1840s. As a result of private spiritual experience, about which we know nothing, and external influences, about which we know a good deal, Wordsworth not only became a markedly pious man but also accepted the identification of himself as a Christian poet. The revision of *Adventures on Salisbury Plain* for the 1842 volume rewrote the radical protest poems of 1793–5 for the Christian present. The sailor, who was formerly presented as a victim of 'violated' Justice, now dies declaring, 'My trust, Saviour! is in thy name'.[101] And as this was its first printing, readers were not to know that this conclusion to the poem really belonged not to Wordsworth's early but to his late years. What happened to *The Excursion* was slightly different, since the poet could not recall and eliminate all the editions since 1814. What he did do in revising the story of Margaret, however, was to make *The Excursion* of 1845 congruent with his current perception of it, which was also clearly that of his contemporaries. It became what it certainly had not been, an explicitly *Christian* poem.

(6)

The preparation of the 1845 volume was Wordsworth's last substantial act as a poet. Though alert enough to attend to details of the 1847 reissue of the one-volume edition and of the final collected edition in six volumes of 1849–50, he was never again capable of the work he put into the 1845 revision. In December 1845 he confessed to Crabb Robinson that 'he was at last quite tired' and six months later he was both exhausted and depressed.[102] At a very low moment he told Isabella Fenwick that he often thought his life had 'been in a great measure wasted', a thought which was too frequently entertained, Mary implied in a postscript to this letter, by the old man who now 'sits more over the fire in silence etc etc and is sooner tired on his walks'.[103] Over Christmas 1846–7 Crabb Robinson noted that he hardly spoke to anyone and that 'He allowed me uncontradicted to state heresies which would not have been tolerated a few years ago'.[104]

When someone at Rydal Mount remarked that he was silent, Wordsworth answered, 'Yes, the Silence of old age'.[105] But his loss of vivacity was not simply a symptom of age. It reflected less the stiffening of the joints than the numbing effects of a series of griefs. In 1843 Joanna Hutchinson, Mary's surviving sister, died. Over Christmas 1845 a message reached them from Rome that their grandson Edward, son of John and Isabella, had succumbed to fever, not quite 5 years old, and that two more of the children were in danger.[106] On 2 February 1846 Wordsworth's last brother, Christopher, died, as the family at Rydal were preparing themselves for another death, that of Richard Wordsworth's son John, who was lying in Ambleside, wasted by consumption. His aunt and uncle visited him daily until the end on 18 August 1846. To these deaths was added one other—in late June came the news that Haydon had committed suicide.

This is a terrible list. The Wordsworths were being shocked by sudden death and racked by John's drawn-out decline. Each death, moreover, revived memories that had never really faded. Aubrey De Vere recalled Wordsworth describing the loss of Catherine and Thomas with an 'impetuosity of troubled excitement, such as might have been expected if the bereavement had taken place but a few weeks before',[107] and in 1841 Wordsworth had re-enacted his grief over the death of his brother John in a poem created from contemporary verse but now published for the first time in the 1842 volume, *Elegiac Verses: In Memory of my Brother, John Wordsworth*. A subtitle pin-points where the brothers had said farewell almost forty years earlier.[108] But the impact of the family losses in 1845 and 1846 was intensified most of all by the culminating blow, the death of Dora.

In 1844 Dora had fallen alarmingly ill. The following year Quillinan took her to Portugal, where her health improved so markedly that when they returned home in 1846 to settle in Loughrigg Holme, a cottage across the valley from Rydal, her family allowed themselves to believe that the danger was over. During the winter of 1846–7, however, weakened once again by the Lake District weather, Dora caught a cold which soon reactivated her tuberculosis. Quillinan summoned her parents from London in May 1847 and for two months until 9 July all three watched over her, dying, in Rydal Mount.

This loss was insupportable and for some time it looked as if Wordsworth would follow his daughter to the grave. When Crabb Robinson came for his Christmas visit in 1847 he observed that neither parent could mention Dora's name or allude to her death. Wordsworth avoided being alone with his old friend—'whichever room I may happen to be in, he goes into the other'—and even their stand-by for companionable evenings, whist, was rejected 'with a shudder'. After a walk with Crabb Robinson he would, Mary confided, 'retire to his room sit alone & cry incessantly', and at the end of the visit Wordsworth was 'unable to take leave of [him] for sobbing'.[109]

During their vigil Dora's husband and her father had drawn closer together. Quillinan had even managed to write the Laureate's *Ode on the Installation of his Royal Highness Prince Albert as Chancellor of the University of Cambridge, July, 1847*.[110] But in his grief after her death Wordsworth could not suppress his resentment against the man whose fecklessness (as he unjustifiably saw it) had hastened her end.[111] Quillinan was suffering 'a *horrible desolation*', but, immured in his own pain, his father-in-law was incapable of reaching out to him. 'I cannot bear to cross the Bridge and Field that leads to his Abode', Wordsworth told Isabella Fenwick, 'and he does not come hither.'[112] It is an indication of Quillinan's good sense that, angry and hurt though he was, he did not allow what Crabb Robinson feared, 'a lasting estrangement which might widen and lead to an entire alienation'.[113]

After Dora's death Wordsworth consciously faced the imminence of his own and what it would entail. *The Prelude* lay ready for immediate posthumous publication, but as this clearly would not prevent further biographical probing, in November 1847 he dictated memoranda about his early life for his nephew Christopher to use after his death in whatever way might seem most appropriate.[114] It was hoped, as Mary put it, that word getting about that 'biographical notices' were 'intended to appear from that quarter, may prevent indifferent persons to take upon them to Publish—as poor Cottle and others have done for Coleridge'.[115] In the event, the family decided on a full-scale 'official life', Christopher's two-volume *Memoirs of William Wordsworth*, published by Moxon in 1851.*

(7)

At the beginning of 1848 Mary wrote to Kate Southey, 'This is a gloomy season with us—but what season *now* is not gloomy with us? . . . Mr. Wordsworth's spirits are so overwhelmed that I can fix upon nothing', but by June she was able to give Crabb Robinson a more cheering report. Though Wordsworth still shrank from walking towards Dora's home under Loughrigg, or into Grasmere where she lay buried, they were, she wrote, '*at home* more as we used to be'.[116] Once her husband was able to face company again, Mary's letters resume their recital of visits to friends and relatives, to John and Willy, now married, and of news and gossip about the neighbourhood, which indicates that Rydal Mount was no longer locked away in mourning from the outside world.

Newspaper rumours that Wordsworth had become imbecile would be, Henry Taylor thought, a boon if 'they tend to relieve Mr Wordsworth from the pressure of visitors during the season for making tours—a pressure which amounts to more than people have any conception of & which he is now not equal to'.[117] But Mary was wiser. Although she complained to Isabella Fenwick that she and her husband were only ever alone at breakfast and that it seemed 'as if America had broken loose, so many, especially from New York, of that country make their way to the Poet', she was glad that the tourists still came—'it does him good to talk to them'.[118] Those who did seek out a man in his late seventies were hoping, of course, to meet a Phenomenon and for the most part they were not disappointed. Ellis Yarnall, a friend of Henry Reed, for example, approached Rydal Mount in

---

* Despite surviving evidence in family letters at WL, it is not entirely clear how, why, or when this decision was reached. See *Moorman*, II. 609–10. It is clear, however, that EQ felt slighted. IF's letter to HCR, 17 Jan. 1848, *HCR*, II. 660, indicates their anxiety about whether EQ would co-operate over the IF notes. His letter of 25 July 1849 to Mrs H. N. Coleridge, WL, reveals that he certainly did feel that there had been an understanding that he and not Christopher was to be the poet's biographer. EQ, moreover, thought the poet's nephew unfitted for his task. In his diary for 11 July 1850 he recorded: 'Mrs W told me today that C.W. knew less of W's poetry than almost any of her acquaintance, & his wife nothing at all'. WL.

1849 in a spirit of 'reverential admiration and love', and was so awed by Wordsworth's solemnity, nobility, and 'moral elevation' that he departed feeling that he had talked with one 'living as if in the presence of God'.[119] Such attributes, however, were far too much for the 11-year-old Algernon Swinburne, when his parents took him to see the great poet in 1848. Wordsworth was rather stiff with the adults, but he was so very kind to Algernon, who was 'greatly interested at the thought of seeing the great poet', that when they parted and the poet said 'he did not think Algernon would forget him', the sensitive little boy left in tears.[120]

Rather to Crabb Robinson's surprise, Wordsworth's restored self-possession carried him through the grief he felt when Hartley Coleridge died on 6 January 1849. At the funeral, he observed, the poet's 'spirits were not as I feared they would be affected by the occurrence'.[121] Three days previously Wordsworth had unconsciously revealed why. With Derwent Coleridge and Crabb Robinson he had walked to Grasmere to arrange the details of Hartley's burial. 'Let him lie by us, he would have wished it', he had said to Derwent the previous day and now he pointed out to the sexton exactly where he and Mary were to be laid.[122] For all his puritanism, Wordsworth had remained very fond of Hartley—in contrast to Crabb Robinson who was censorious about his drunkenness and vagabond ways—but he had passed beyond grief.[123] Though he still took pleasure in attending to Dorothy—'almost the only enjoyment [he] seems to feel', according to Mary—in reality he was waiting for death.[124]

It came just a year later. For most of the year Wordsworth was in good health. Meeting him in June 1849 near Great Malvern, where the Wordsworths were visiting Tom and Mary Hutchinson, Mary's brother and sister-in-law, Crabb Robinson noted that while the '*strength* of his mind' had declined, his body's had not: 'On Sunday he crossed the Malvern Hill twice without suffering any inconvenience'.[125] And appropriately, it was walking that brought about his death. On 14 March 1850 Wordsworth 'complained of a pain in his side', but he ignored it and on the seventeenth he walked to Grasmere, not returning until after dark. 'A cold even[ing]— *& no* overcoat', Mary wrote in her Almanack.[126] He walked out the next day, but when he and Mary walked towards White Moss Common on the nineteenth it was for the last time. What Quillinan called 'this vile bright keen half-snowy cutting north-easterly weather' brought him down with pleurisy.[127]

For a month Wordsworth lay dying. Mr Fell and Mr Green from Ambleside gave unstinting medical attention, but there was nothing that could be done. Unfortunately, one of the doctors showed it. 'Unluckily (*entre nous*)', Quillinan wrote to Mrs Fletcher's daughter, Lady Richardson, '[Wordsworth] says he does not like the *dolorous* face of Green, whom we all understand to be a very able man. I ventured to tell Fell today and ask his partner not to look so *very* solemn.'[128] Suffering acute pain, and with some difficulty in breathing, Wordsworth soon passed beyond objecting, jokily or otherwise. He died at 12 noon on 23 April 1850. Everyone remembered the time because the cuckoo-clock, a gift from Miss Fenwick, was telling the hour.[129]

Dorothy Wordsworth died 25 January 1855. Mary, strong, wise, and steadfast, a heroine if ever there was one, remained 'the Solitary Lingerer' until 17 January 1859.[130] All three were buried at Grasmere, in the midst of great beauty. To the west and south are Silver How and Loughrigg and to the east the slopes of Stone Arthur, Seat Sandal, and the Fairfield mass. And Grasmere Churchyard can still be seen from the point at the end of Loughrigg where Wordsworth as a schoolboy, glimpsing the lake and the vale for the first time, exclaimed:

> What happy fortune were it here to live!
> And if I thought of dying, if a thought
> Of mortal separation could come in
> With paradise before me, here to die.

# NOTES

INTRODUCTION

1. John Keats to Richard Woodhouse, 27 Oct. 1818. *Keats*, I. 387.
2. W to Anne Taylor, 9 Apr. 1801; W to Samuel Carter Hall, 15 Jan. 1837. *EY*, 327; *LY*, III. 348.
3. Tim Hilton, *John Ruskin: The Early Years 1819–1859* (New Haven and London, 1985), 109.
4. W to James Tobin, 6 Mar. 1798. *EY*, 212.
5. Preface to *The Excursion* (1814). *PW*, V. 1–2.
6. John Keats to J. H. Reynolds, 3 May 1818. *Keats*, I. 282.
7. *TWT*, 127.
8. Jonathan Wordsworth, 'The Climbing of Snowdon', *BWS*, 451.
9. James Jackson, drowned 18 June 1779. *1799 Prelude*, I. 258–87.
10. *1805 Prelude*, V. 450–81.
11. Susan J. Wolfson, 'The Illusion of Mastery: Wordsworth's Revisions of "The Drowned Man of Esthwaite," 1799, 1805, 1850', *PMLA* 99 (1984), 917–35.
12. *1805 Prelude*, XII. 225.


CHAPTER I

1. *1799 Prelude*, II. 243–9.
2. Nikolaus Pevsner, *The Buildings of England: Cumberland and Westmorland* (Harmondsworth, 1967), 109. The house was built for Joshua Lucock, Sheriff of Cumberland, in 1745.
3. William Wilberforce, *Journey to the Lake District from Cambridge: A Summer Diary 1799*, ed. C. E. Wrangham (Stocksfield, 1983), 78.
4. Alexander Carlyle, *Anecdotes and Characters of the Times*, ed. James Kinsley (London, 1973), 213.
5. Brian Bonsall, *Sir James Lowther and Cumberland and Westmorland Elections, 1754–75* (Manchester, 1960), p. vi.
6. Joanne Dann, 'Some Notes on the Relationship between the Wordsworth and Lowther Families', *Wordsworth Circle*, 11 (1980), 80–2, gives further information, including evidence of John Wordsworth's part in Sir James's attempt to evict 400 tenants in Inglewood Forest.
7. *1799 Prelude*, I. 17–26.
8. See *The Sparrow's Nest* and the IF note, *Grosart*, III. 15.
9. *Reed*, I. 41.
10. See IF note to *On a High Part of the Coast of Cumberland*, *Grosart*, III. 145–6.
11. *Memoirs*, I. 9. W's autobiographical record is reprinted in *Prose*, III. 367–82 and future citation will be to this edition. The quotation is p. 372.
12. DW to Jane Marshall, 19 Mar. [1797]. *EY*, 179.
13. *1799 Prelude*, I. 288–327; *1805 Prelude*, XI. 257–315; *1850 Prelude*, XII. 208–61. At *1805 Prelude*, XI. 341–2 W defines his description of this scene as an attempt to 'enshrine the spirit of the past / for future restoration'.
14. For details of the site and a map see David McCracken, *Wordsworth and the Lake District: A Guide to the Poems and their Places* (Oxford, 1984), 151–2 and for readings of

the poetry which will be particularly helpful to those with an interest in the relation between the poetry and the life, see David Ellis, *Wordsworth, Freud and the Spots of Time: Interpretation in The Prelude* (Cambridge, 1985), esp. 62–83 and Jonathan Wordsworth, *William Wordsworth: The Borders of Vision* (Oxford, 1982), 55–60.

15. *Prose*, III. 372. The comment on teaching is found in W to Hugh James Rose, 11 Dec. 1828. *LY*, I. 684–6.

16. *Memoirs*, I. 34.

17. *Prose*, III. 371.

18. *1805 Prelude*, V. 259–60.

19. DW to LB [18 and 19] Mar. 1805. *EY*, 568.

20. *1799 Prelude*, II. 236; *1805 Prelude*, II. 202; ibid. I. 517.

21. Thomas West, *A Guide to the Lakes* (London, 1778), 61 and 57–8.

22. See Alfred Fell, *The Early Iron Industry of Furness and District* (Ulverston, 1908), J. D. Marshall, *Old Lakeland* (Newton Abbot, 1971), and William Rollinson, *Life and Tradition in the Lake District* (London, 1974). See also the pages on the work of miners and quarrymen in W's 1811–12 description of the lakes entitled, by the editors, *An Unpublished Tour*, *Prose*, II. 314–20.

23. *1805 Prelude*, IV. 14–15; *TWT*, 120 and photograph facing p. 45. In James Clarke's *Survey of the Lakes* (London, 1787), 146, the grammar school is mentioned at some length and said to be 'very beneficial both to the town and neighbourhood, by the number of gentlemen's sons boarded there'.

24. *Prose*, II. 330.

25. *1805 Prelude*, IV. 19–28.

26. For full details of Ann and Hugh Tyson and the life of their world see *TWT* throughout. My chapter is indebted to this marvellous labour of loving scholarship and I will only give citations in future on specific points of information.

27. See *TWT*, 58–60 for Robert Woof's assessment of the evidence for exactly where Ann Tyson lived at Colthouse and his judgement that it remains 'something of an open question'.

28. *1805 Prelude*, IV. 217–20.

29. In summer the boys were expected to be at school from 6 or 6.30 to 11 in the morning and then from 1 to 5 in the afternoon. In winter the hours were 7 or 7.30 to 11 a m and then 12.30 to 4 p.m. See *TWT*, 104–5.

30. *1799 Prelude*, I. 235–6 and the IF note to *Nutting*, *Grosart*, III. 39.

31. *1799 Prelude*, I. 57–66; *1805 Prelude*, I. 342–50.

32. *TWT*, 211–15. *1805 Prelude*, VIII. 217–18.

33. *1799 Prelude*, I. 279–83.

34. *1799 Prelude*, I. 275–9.

35. *1805 Prelude*, VIII. 398–9.

36. IF note to *River Duddon*, *Grosart*, III. 99. It has generally been accepted that W's fishing companion was a Hawkshead saddler called George Park. Pursuing a chain of evidence of a tenuousness that evidently delighted him, Thompson concludes that he was, in fact, one John Martin of Outgate, a weaver. *TWT*, 200–7.

37. *1799 Prelude*, II. 204–14; *1805 Prelude*, II. 170–80. The minstrel was Robert Greenwood, remembered by Ann Tyson as 't'lad wi't flute'. He went up to Cambridge at the same time as W. A man with 'much of Yorick in his disposition', according to W, 3 Aug. 1791, *EY*, 56–7, Greenwood became a Senior Fellow of Trinity and remained a lifelong friend of the Wordsworths. See *TWT*, 78–80 and 147.

38. *1799 Prelude*, II. 143–5.

39. DW to Mary Lamb, 9 Jan. 1830. *LY*, II. 191.

40. *1799 Prelude*, I. 150–69; *1805 Prelude*, I. 452–73. As with most, but not all, of the descriptions of childhood pleasures in *The Prelude* W is unspecific about dates in this passage and allows us to think that skating was a regular pastime. Thompson, however, draws attention to a 'prolonged, severe frost' in early spring 1785 and notes that a bill paid to George Park, saddler and ironmonger of Hawkshead (see n. 36 above), may have been for skates. Park's son Tom, a year older than W and a friend, was an outstanding skater, but drowned in Esthwaite 18 Dec. 1796 after falling through the ice. See *TWT*, 108–9. A pair of skates said to be W's are preserved in the Wordsworth Museum at Grasmere.

41. See *Reed*, I. 294 n. 9, and *Home at Grasmere*, 38. The quotation is from line 165.

42. *1799 Prelude*, II. 98–139; *1805 Prelude*, II. 99–144. Two late sonnets *At Furness Abbey* record how much 'the spirit of the place' continued to move W. See *PW*, III. 62–3.

43. IF note to *The Excursion. Grosart*, III. 198 and *PW*, V. 373.

44. *1799 Prelude*, I. 30–2; II. 379; II. 392–4; *1805 Prelude*, I. 313–15; II. 349; II. 362–4.

45. *TWT*, 247–9.

46. W to John Wilson, [7 June 1802]. *EY*, 355.

47. W's influence on George Eliot can be discerned in the stress placed in *Adam Bede* on 'sympathy', in the presentation of the community in *Silas Marner*, and in the meditations on memory and the past in *The Mill on the Floss*. It is evidenced quite specifically, though, throughout her work, in epigraphs and quotations. Of W's poems she wrote: 'I never before met with so many of my own feelings, expressed just as I could like them'. *The George Eliot Letters*, ed. Gordon S. Haight (9 vols., New Haven and London, 1954–78), I. 34. In 1838 Elizabeth Gaskell quoted from *The Old Cumberland Beggar* in a letter which announces the moral intention of her own early work: 'the beauty and poetry of many of the common things and daily events of life in its humblest aspect does not seem to me sufficiently appreciated'. *The Letters of Mrs Gaskell*, ed. J. A. V. Chapple and Arthur Pollard (Manchester, 1966), 33.

48. IF note to *Lines Left upon a Seat in a Yew-tree, Grosart*, III. 9. Quoted *TWT*, 258, where the conjuror is identified, 299–302, as one Bartholomew Purcel.

49. IF note to *The Two Thieves, Grosart*, III. 186–7.

50. See *TWT*, 152–66, 172–3, 186–90. The poems referred to will be found most conveniently in *Gill: Oxf. W.*, 'If Nature, for a Favorite Child', p. 137; *The Fountain*, p. 138; *Two April Mornings*, pp. 140–2; *Five Elegies*, pp. 142–7. W's declaration that his schoolmaster was drawn from life was made in a letter to Henry Reed, 27 Mar. 1843. quoted *TWT*, 151.

51. IF note to *The Excursion, Grosart*, III. 196–7. *TWT*, 234–46 discusses other possible sources for the figure in seven packmen.

52. MS B text of *The Ruined Cottage*, ll. 59–61. See *The Ruined Cottage*, 46.

53. Fell, op. cit. n. 22, pp. 390–414 gives an account of the industry at Bonaw. DW's entry for 1 Sept. 1803 in her *Recollections of a Tour Made in Scotland. DWJ*, I. 309.

54. *1799 Prelude*, I. 207. IF note to *The Excursion, Grosart*, III. 205. The real name of the Westons was Gilbert, according to Joseph Budworth, *A Fortnight's Ramble to the Lakes in Westmoreland, Lancashire, and Cumberland* (London, 1792), 130.

55. W used these stories in *The Excursion, Michael*, and *Peter Bell*. Quotations from *1799 Prelude*, I. 425, and *Peter Bell*, l. 1159, in *Peter Bell*, 132.

56. *1805 Prelude*, XIII. 98–9.

57. *TWT*, p. xvi.

58. Budworth was impressed that Lake District people he met 'even talk of their forefathers and carry an oral account for several generations of any one who has been out of the common way', op. cit. p. vii.

59. *Reflections*, 119. For an excellent account of the meaning of Burke for W and of the importance of the oral tradition noted by Budworth to the poet see *Chandler*.

60. When published in 1850, after W's death, *The Prelude* was subtitled 'Growth of a Poet's Mind'. W's vision of life was so clearly grounded in his experiences of the Lake District and has, in turn, so powerfully shaped readers' perception of the place that it is important to register the objection of an economic historian, J. V. Beckett, who insists that W's was a personal and idealized vision. Demonstrating the importance of industry and mobility to the Lake District in the 18th century, Beckett declares (arguably too sweepingly) that 'Wordsworth's view of Cumbria, outdated in 1700, was totally misleading by the later eighteenth century'. See his *Coal and Tobacco: The Lowthers and the Economic Development of West Cumberland, 1660–1760* (Cambridge, 1981), 4–6.

61. W's lifelong concern with the education of the young cannot be documented in a footnote. The reader unfamiliar with his letters and prose, however, should see: DW's letter on 19 Mar. [1797] about their rearing of little Basil Montagu, *E Y*, 180; W's *Reply to 'Mathetes'*, *Prose*, II. 3–41; W's letter emphasizing as late as 1845 the 'Knowledge . . . which comes, without being sought for, from intercourse with nature', *L Y*, IV. 732–4, and the very fruitful article by Alan G. Hill, 'Wordsworth, Comenius, and the Meaning of Education', *RES* NS 26 (1975), 301–12.

62. See Robert Woof's highly informative Appendix IV on Hawkshead Grammar School, *TWT*, 342–5.

63. IF note to *Ode to Lycoris*, *Grosart*, III. 168.

64. W translated Juvenal in 1795, making direct reference to the political and social events of the time. See also Jane Worthington, *Wordsworth's Reading of Roman Prose* (New Haven, 1946).

65. For good comment on W's response to Newton see *Sheats*, 4–5, and Stephen Prickett, *Coleridge and Wordsworth: The Poetry of Growth* (Cambridge, 1970), 6–12. The quotation is from *1805 Prelude*, VI. 186–7.

66. *TWT*, 344.

67. *Reed*, I. 296. *TWT*, 92.

68. *Prose*, III. 372. After John Wordsworth's death his books were removed by Richard Wordsworth of Branthwaite. That W remained concerned about his father's library is suggested by Richard Wordsworth's letter of 7 Oct. 1805 [WL], which gives a schedule of the books. As well as law and history books it includes volumes of Euclid, *Gil Blas*, Fielding, and, somewhat surprisingly, d'Holbach's *Système de la Nature*. Paul Kelley, who has worked to establish the extent of W's early reading, makes the contrast in his unpublished thesis between W's father and Southey's, who 'read nothing, except Felix Farley's Bristol Journal'. *SL*, I. 83.

69. *TWT*, 55 and 344.

70. *1805 Prelude*, X. 510.

71. Quoted Ben Ross Schneider, *Wordsworth's Cambridge Education* (Cambridge, 1957), 77. Schneider notes that the 'poets of our time' would have included Thomson, Young, Blair, Akenside, Collins, Beattie, Dyer, as well as Chatterton and that W's school verses *Dirge: Sung by a Minstrel* borrows the refrain from Chatterton's *Song from Aella*. See *PW*, I. 267–8.

72. *TWT*, 344.

73. *TWT*, 344. W first encountered Crabbe in extracts from *The Village* printed in the *Annual Register* of 1783, as he told Crabbe's son in 1834. See *L Y*, II. 691. As Carol Landon has pointed out, this volume also contains an extract from James Beattie's discussion of the sublime in his *Dissertations Moral and Critical* (1783), which influenced W's early poetic attempts. See 'Some Sidelights on *The Prelude*', *BWS*, 370.

74. For details of Bowman's activities for the library and a list of books donated see *TWT*, 343–68. The library catalogue lists an astonishingly comprehensive collection of 18th-century poetry in editions dating largely from 1779–87, as well as Chaucer and the major 17th-century poets.

75. *1805 Prelude*, V. 586–8. That memorizing for W implied a critical judgement is suggested by the form of this later remark recorded in *Grosart*, III. 460: 'I have been charged by some with disparaging Pope and Dryden. This is not so. I have committed much of both to memory.'

76. *1805 Prelude*, X. 512–14.

77. *1805 Prelude*, V. 575–81.

78. *1799 Prelude*, II. 156–78.

79. *The Idiot Boy*, 347–8: 'I to the muses have been bound / These fourteen years, by strong indentures'.

80. IF note to *An Evening Walk*, in *An Evening Walk*, 301. For a further note on the image itself see also p. 54.

81. See *Reed*, I. 298–301. Appendix III, 'Wordsworth's Earliest Poetic Composition'.

82. The manuscript of the poems of Charles Farish and of John Bernard Farish, who was not at Hawkshead School, is discussed *TWT*, 313–21. Two things stand out from this collection of verses dated 1780–4. One is that the poems dwell on locality, suggesting that the boys were encouraged to ground emotions and meditation in the local and known. The other is that it would seem that they were also encouraged to practise versification by rendering a subject in different forms and tones. The poems on 'Matilda', referred to but not printed in *TWT*, 313, are, in fact, exercises of this kind, as are John Bernard's verses printed *TWT*, 319–21. Charles was evidently proud enough of his brother's efforts to show them to his schoolfellow.

83. *TWT*, 80. W's *Sonnet on Seeing Miss Helen Maria Williams Weep at a Tale of Distress* was published in the *European Magazine*, 11 (1787), 202. James Averill, *Wordsworth and Human Suffering* (Ithaca, 1980), 33, points out that the *European Magazine* had reviewed Williams's *Poems, in Two Volumes* in 1786. His evidence that W knew this extensive notice is further indication that W was keeping up with contemporary writing.

84. *Reed*, I. 291.

85. For an account of the *Vale of Esthwaite* MSS see *Reed*, I. 18–19, 308. Keats's remarks on invention appear in a letter to Benjamin Bailey, 8 Oct. 1817. *Keats*, I. 170.

86. *The Vale of Esthwaite*, 95–102 and 194–9. *PW*, I. 272 and 274.

87. *Ode: Intimations of Immortality*, 144–8. The boat-stealing is *1799 Prelude*, I. 81–129; *1805 Prelude*, I. 372–426.

88. *1799 Prelude*, II. 435–64. The passage had originally been written to describe the experiences of the Pedlar in *The Ruined Cottage* of Feb.–Mar. 1798.

89. See *Reed*, I. 58–9 for details, including the fact that John Wordsworth is certified as having died of 'dropsy'.

90. *1799 Prelude*, I. 330–74.

91. *1805 Prelude*, XIII. 385.

92. References to 'Uncle Kit' can be confusing. Christopher Crackanthorpe Cookson (1745–99) changed his name in 1792 to Christopher Crackanthorpe Crackanthorpe on inheriting Newbiggin Hall.

93. For details of the money laid out see *TWT*, *passim*, but esp. 89–91, 134–5, 143–4, 372–4, and *Reed*, I, *passim*, 59–95.

94. DW to Jane Pollard [6 and 7 Aug. 1787]. *EY*, 7.

95. *Reed*, I. 59–60.
96. *Prose*, I. 46.
97. Robert Woof, *TWT*, 373–4, makes important corrections to *Reed*, I. 61 on the boys' movements, concluding that there is no 'evidence for the view that Wordsworth, later, in his long vacations, both before and at Cambridge, 1787–9, ever spent the period of the actual school holidays in Hawkshead'.
98. The words are spoken by the Female Vagrant in *Salisbury Plain*, l. 387. The poem was written in 1793, when W's own sense of alienation and homelessness was at its most intense.
99. *1805 Prelude*, VI. 208–60.
100. *1805 Prelude*, XI. 317.
101. DW to Jane Pollard [22 July 1787]. *EY*, 1–5.

CHAPTER 2

1. James Beattie, *The Minstrel: or, The Progress of Genius*, Book I (1771); Book II (1774). I. vi. 6–9.
2. DW to Jane Pollard [10 and 12 July 1793]. *EY*, 100–1.
3. W to William Mathews, 23 May [1794]. *EY*, 119. For Mathews see n. 65 below.
4. As already noted in Introduction, 8–9, the placing of the climbing of Snowdon is the most striking example of how W ignores chronology when it suits the purposes of the poem. The ascent took place after W had left London in 1791, before he went to France. In a chronological scheme, therefore, it would appear in Books VII to IX in *The Prelude*, not, as it does, at the end of the poem, *after* events of 1792–5.
5. 8 June 1831, WL.
6. *1805 Prelude*, III. 381–7.
7. Ibid. III. 80–1; VI. 33–4.
8. Ibid. III. 35–6; 295–322.
9. Ibid. III. 43. W's friends from school included John Fleming, William Penny, and Edward Birkett at Christ's, Fletcher Raincock at Pembroke, Charles Farish at Queen's, Robert Greenwood at Trinity, John Miller at Jesus, Thomas Gawthrop at St John's. His cousin John Myers entered St John's the same time as W, travelling up to Cambridge with him.
10. *1805 Prelude*, III. 437.
11. Henry Gunning, *Reminiscences of the University, Town and County of Cambridge, from the Year 1780* (2 vols., London, 1854), I. 14–15.
12. *1805 Prelude*, III. 41.
13. Ibid. III. 630–5.
14. Ibid. III. 65–8, 512–13, 627.
15. In *Wordsworth's Cambridge Education* (Cambridge, 1957), Ben Ross Schneider gives a detailed account of the teaching methods and examination requirements in Cambridge. His book should be supplemented by Christopher Wordsworth's two studies, *Social Life at the English Universities in the Eighteenth Century* (Cambridge, 1874) and *Scholae Academicae: Some Account of the Studies at the English Universities in the Eighteenth Century* (Cambridge, 1877), and Gunning, op. cit.
16. See Schneider, op. cit. 14, 30–8.
17. W's uncle William Cookson held one of the two Fellowships at St John's reserved for men from Cumberland. He vacated it on his marriage in 1788. At St John's, Cookson had become fast friends with William Wilberforce (1759–1833), the evangelical

philanthropist and slave-trade abolitionist, who was also a friend of Pitt. Cookson helped Wilberforce acquire a property on Windermere and in return was helped through Wilberforce's interest to the living at Forncett and eventually a canon's stall at Windsor. As Robert Woof remarks, *TWT*, p. xix, this friendship 'does remind us of the social class [W's] relatives moved in'. John Robinson (1727–1802) had a distinguished career. In 1760 he became sole steward of the Lowther estates and in 1764 MP for Westmorland. He was MP for Harwich from 1774 till his death. For an excellent account of him see Ian R. Christie, 'John Robinson, M.P. 1727–1802', *Myth and Reality in Late Eighteenth-century British Politics* (London, 1970), 145–82. Edward Christian was a Fellow of St John's 1780–89 and another friend of Cookson. He became Professor of Common Law in 1788 and, though later noted for his incapacity, he represented the Wordsworth cause in the Londsdale hearings of 1791 when he seemed to be a rising man.

18. Richard Watson (1737–1816) of Trinity College was appointed Professor of Chemistry in 1764 when, as he engagingly admitted, 'I knew nothing at all of Chemistry, had never read a syllable on the subject'. *Anecdotes of the Life of Richard Watson*, by his son Richard Watson (London, 1817), 28–9. By adroit manœuvring he became Regius Professor of Divinity in 1771 and in 1782 Bishop of Llandaff. He built Calgarth Park in 1789, where he resided after appointing a deputy for his professorial duties. Watson undoubtedly had an eye for the main chance and his attitude to his offices seems scandalous, but he was an able and industrious man of latitudinarian views, who was relied on by government circles in the 1790s to put the case against radicals in a measured and common-sense manner. For W's scathing rejection of all that he stood for in 1793 expressed in his *Letter to the Bishop of Llandaff* see ch. 3, 71–3.

19. Unitarian thinking had been gaining ground within the University through the activities of such men as John Jebb of Peterhouse, Robert Tyrwhitt and William Frend of Jesus, and Thomas Fyshe Palmer of Queen's, who all suffered because of their Dissenting opinions. Jebb and Palmer left Cambridge in 1776 and 1783, however, and the notorious trial of Frend by the University authorities did not take place until 1793. Scholars such as George McLean Harper, *William Wordsworth: His Life, Works, and Influence* (2 vols., London, 1916), 58–61 and Schneider, op. cit. 98–9, 113–52, dealing with these and other figures, have rightly emphasized that Cambridge was not intellectually somnolent, but Leslie Chard, *Dissenting Republican: Wordsworth's Early Life and Thought in their Political Context* (The Hague, 1972), 28–32, seems justified in his conclusion that W was not personally stirred by radical or Dissenting movements during his time at Cambridge. This is not to say that ideas may not have been registered then which surfaced from 1791 onwards.

20. *1805 Prelude*, VI. 41.

21. Ibid. III. 78–118.

22. Ibid. III. 339–41, 375–407.

23. 'When at school, I, with the other boys of the same standing, was put upon reading the first six books of Euclid, with the exception of the fifth; and also in algebra I learnt simple and quadratic equations; and this was for me unlucky, because I had a full twelve months' start of the freshmen of my year, and accordingly got into rather an idle way; reading nothing but classic authors according to my fancy, and Italian poetry.' *Memoirs*, I. 14.

24. See *PW*, I. 283–7 for W's translations from Virgil and Horace and *Sheats*, 44–7.

25. Agostino Isola (1713–97), a Milanese émigré and friend of the poet Gray, was retained by the Professor of Modern History. 'As I took to these studies with much interest', W says, 'he was proud of the progress I made'. *Memoirs*, I. 14. See June Sturrock,

'Wordsworth's Italian Teacher', *BJRL* 67 (Spring 1985), 797–812. Isola published editions of Tasso and Ariosto and may have influenced W when he and Greenwood, Gawthrop, and Millar gave a copy of Tasso's *Jerusalem Delivered* to Hawkshead School library in 1789. See *TWT*, 353–4. In 1796 W was encouraging DW to study Italian. See *EY*, 170. In later life W translated from Michelangelo, Ariosto, Metastasio, and Tasso, *PW*, III. 14–15, 408; IV. 367–72, and in 1847 was even consulted by Alexander Cunningham about his projected translation of Tasso (published 1853). W's late but richly rewarding tour is recorded in *Memorials of a Tour in Italy, 1837* (1842).

26. See *An Evening Walk*, 6.

27. Robert Arnold Aubin, *Topographical Poetry in Eighteenth-century England* (New York, 1936), remains the most comprehensive account of this very varied and important genre.

28. *An Evening Walk* (1793), 1–8.

29. Ibid. 51. William Cookson married on 17 Oct. 1788 and took up the living of Forncett St Peter in December.

30. DW to Jane Pollard [7 and 8 Dec. 1788]. *EY*, 19.

31. John Chevallier, Master of St John's, died 14 Mar. 1789. W refused to honour the custom of placing verses on the pall spread over the coffin in the college hall 'as I felt no interest in the deceased person, with whom I had had no intercourse, and whom I had never seen but during his walks in the college grounds'. *Memoirs*, I. 14. William Cookson was not impressed by this demonstration of a fledgeling Romantic integrity, telling his nephew, justly, that 'it would have been a fair opportunity for distinguishing yourself'.

32. DW to Jane Pollard, 16 Feb. [1793]; [10 and 12 July 1793]. *EY*, 87, 97.

33. Cited *An Evening Walk*, 9–10.

34. *1805 Prelude*, XII. 312; XI. 383–4.

35. Ibid. IV. 16–17. The evidence for W's vacation movements is incomplete but Robert Woof's detailed account, *TWT*, 134–5, which corrects Moorman and Reed, is the most advanced study of the problem to date.

36. *TWT*, 135.

37. John Robinson to W, 6 Apr. 1788. Quoted *EY*, 18.

38. In a letter of 6 Oct. [1790] DW admitted to Jane Pollard, 'I confess . . . that had he acquainted me with his scheme before its execution I should (as many of his other friends did) have looked upon it as mad and impracticable'. *EY*, 39. DW is, in fact, borrowing W's own terms from his letter to her of 6 [and 16] Sept. [1790] in which he explains, 'I did not call on [Richard] not so much because we were determined to hurry through London, but because he, as many of our friends at Cambridge did, would look upon our scheme as mad and impracticable'. *EY*, 37.

39. See letter of 6 [and 16] Sept. [1790] cited above.

40. For a full illustrated account of their journey see Donald E. Hayden, *Wordsworth's Walking Tour of 1790* (Tulsa, Okla., 1983).

41. 11 Oct. 1815. WL.

42. W to DW, 6 [and 16] Sept. [1790]. *EY*, 32 and 27. In the dedication to *Descriptive Sketches* (1793) W refers to himself and Jones 'each with his little knapsack of necessaries upon his shoulders'. *Descriptive Sketches*, 32.

43. Robert Jones to W, 23 Feb. 1821. WL.

44. W's copy of *Orlando Furioso* is in the Wordsworth Library.

45. W to DW, 6 [and 16] Sept. [1790]. *EY*, 37.

46. Ibid. *EY*, 36.

47. Thomas Gray to Mrs Gray, 13 Oct. 1739. *Gray*, I. 122. Gray's letters and his Journal of his 1769 visit to the Lake District were printed in William Mason's *The Poems of Mr Gray: To which are Prefixed Memoirs of his Life and Writings* (York, 1775), frequently reprinted. The catalogue of W's library records that he owned the 1776 edition. See Chester L. Shaver and Alice C. Shaver, *Wordsworth's Library: A Catalogue* (New York and London, 1979), 108.

48. *1805 Prelude*, VI. 456–8.

49. In his Sept. letter W confessed to DW, 'Magnificent as this fall certainly is I . . . was disappointed in it. I had raised my ideas too high.' In a fascinating illustrated article, 'Wordsworth and the Rhinefall', *SIR* 23 (1984), 61–79, Theresa M. Kelley accounts for W's disappointment in the fact that he viewed the spectacle from the wrong bank.

50. W to DW 6 [and 16] Sept. [1790]. *EY*, 37. *1805 Prelude*, VI. 578–9.

51. Andrew Varney, 'Wordsworth and "Those Italian Clocks"', *Notes and Queries*, NS 17 (1980), 69–70, explains how W and Jones could have made such a mistake in a way that justifies the testiness of W's recollection.

52. *1805 Prelude*, VI. 621–57.

53. W to DW, 6 [and 16] Sept. [1790]. *EY*, 33.

54. *1805 Prelude*, VI. 424. DW to HCR, 21 Dec. 1822. *LY*, I. 176.

55. W to DW, 6 [and 16] Sept. [1790]. *EY*, 34.

56. For a photograph of the building erected in the 17th century by Kaspar Stockalper, who controlled the trade route over the Simplon Pass, see Hayden, op. cit. n. 40, p. 51.

57. *1805 Prelude*, VI. 549–72. For an account of W's experience and photographs of the scenes the reader should see both Hayden, op. cit. n. 40, pp. 40–53 and Max Wildi, 'Wordsworth and the Simplon Pass', *English Studies*, 40 (1959), 224–32; and 43 (1962), 359–77.

58. *EY*, 33 and 34. *Gray*, I. 128.

59. On pp. 108–13 of his *An Excursion to the Lakes: In Westmorland and Cumberland, August 1773* (London, 1774), William Hutchinson prints 'Dr Brown's Letter on Keswick and Dovedale' (Newcastle, 1767). Dovedale is compared much to disadvantage with Keswick, but enough is praised to have incited W to a visit. It is noteworthy that in the letter cited in the note on p. 46 above Shelley refers to Matlock when searching for an analogue for the Alpine scenery.

60. W to DW, 6 [and 16] Sept. [1790]. *EY*, 35–6.

61. *Lines Written a Few Miles above Tintern Abbey*, 63–6.

62. 'Author's Voyage down the Rhine (Thirty Years Ago)', in *Memorials of a Tour on the Continent, 1820* (1822) 8. *PW*, III. 409–10.

63. For DW's very entertaining narrative see *DWJ*, II. 3–336. W's *Memorials* can most conveniently be read in *PW*, III. 164–201, but it should be noted that the text there is that of the last revised edition of 1849–50, by which time considerable changes had been made to the text of the first edition of 1822. The most notable is the excision of the sonnet on the Voyage down the Rhine.

64. W to DW, 6 [and 16] Sept. [1790]. *EY*, 35 and 37.

65. W to William Mathews, 17 June [1791]. *EY*, 49. Mathews (1769–1801) of Pembroke College, son of a London bookseller, reacted against the bigotry of his Methodist father's household. Resisting pressures towards the ministry, he first taught in Leicestershire and then attempted to make a living in London. Both as a journalist and in the law he was a disappointed man. In 1801 he went to the West Indies, where he died of yellow fever.

Mathews was a serious and scholarly man, remembered by his brother, the famous comic actor Charles, as 'devoted to profound and abstract studies, mathematics . . . an absolute thirst for languages, six of which he could speak or read before he was twenty'. He was not an atheist, but he was strongly opposed to the 'load of trumpery and ceremonies' characteristic of all organized religion. In the year of his death he wrote to his brother that, if there is any way to gratify the 'benevolent Author of all Beings', then it is to 'imitate His perfection by mutual benevolence and kindness'. See Mrs Anne Mathews, *Memoir of Charles Mathews, Comedian* (4 vols., London, 1838–9), I. 35 and 326–7.

66. DW to Jane Pollard, 23 May [1791]. *EY*, 47.

67. DW to Jane Pollard, 16 June [1793] and [10 and 12 July 1793]. *EY*, 96, 98.

68. *Memoirs*, I. 48.

69. DW to Jane Pollard, 26 June [1791]. *EY*, 51. She refers to three of Jones's five sisters.

70. Charlotte Smith (1749–1806) was separated from her feckless husband, who was the brother-in-law of John Robinson, MP. Her attempt to raise money by writing succeeded when her *Elegiac Sonnets* (1784) caught the public taste. She was a supporter of the French Revolution. Author of a number of novels (*Desmond* of 1792 declaring her French sympathies), she is remembered now only for the success of her poems. W quoted from her *To the South Downs* in *An Evening Walk*, 19, and in 1835 paid tribute to her as 'a lady to whom English verse is under greater obligations than are likely to be either acknowledged or remembered'. *PW*, IV. 403.

71. In 1778 Lord Lonsdale had been granted an injunction staying the proceedings initiated by the Wordsworth administrators. On 28 Feb. 1791 he was ordered to pay £4,000 into the court. He did not do so, the injunction was lifted, and the way cleared for a full hearing at the Carlisle assizes in Aug. There, on 26 Aug. an order was made that the heirs of John Wordsworth should receive damages of approximately £5,000 and in November arbitrators were named to fix on the exact sum. But nothing was settled, in fact, until the death of the earl in 1802.

72. W to William Mathews, 23 Nov. [1791]. *EY*, 62 and 23 Sept. [1791]. *EY*, 58–9.

73. Ibid. *EY*, 58.

74. RW to Richard Wordsworth, 7 Nov. 1791. *EY*, 61 n. 1.

75. W to William Mathews, 23 Nov. [1791]. *EY*, 62.

76. Cited n. 74.

77. *1805 Prelude*, IX. 36–7.

78. Anna Seward to Mrs Knowles, 25 July 1789. *The Letters of Anna Seward, Written between the Years 1784 and 1807* (6 vols., Edinburgh and London, 1811), II. 298–9. The letters of the 'Swan of Lichfield' are a barometer of English attitudes to events in France.

79. Ian R. Christie, *Stress and Stability in Late Eighteenth-century Britain* (Oxford, 1984), 157.

80. Richard Price, *A Discourse on the Love of our Country*. Delivered 4 Nov. 1789. Quoted from Marilyn Butler's very informative anthology *Burke, Paine, Godwin, and the Revolution Controversy* (Cambridge, 1984), 32. Butler's anthology should be consulted alongside Alfred Cobban, *The Debate on the French Revolution 1789–1800* (London, 1950).

81. Edmund Burke's *Reflections on the Revolution in France* was published on 1 Nov. 1790. As James T. Boulton points out in *The Language of Politics in the Age of Wilkes and Burke* (London, 1963), 77–8, Burke was warned that an 'unseemly "war of

pamphlets" . . . would follow publication, a prophecy which was amply realised'. Burke's polemic is subtitled 'And on the Proceedings of Certain Societies in London Relative to that Event', a reference to Richard Price's *Discourse* noted above.

82. *Letters to the Right Honourable Edmund Burke on Politics* (Oxford 1791), 2. See Vivian H. H. Green, *The Commonwealth of Lincoln College, 1427–1977* (Oxford, 1979), 363–9.

83. See Boulton, op. cit. 97–133 for an illuminating analysis of the rhetorical strategies of Burke and his opponents and (pp. 265–71) a bibliography of the pamphlet war precipitated by the *Reflections*.

84. *The Parliamentary History of England*, ed. William Cobbett, XXIX (London, 1817), col. 249.

85. Ibid. cols. 387–8. Quoted in John W. Derry, *Charles James Fox* (London, 1972), 303–4.

86. *1805 Prelude*, IX. 96–7.

87. IF note to *The Excursion. Grosart*, III. 197. Joseph Fawcett (*c.* 1758–1804), friend of Godwin and Hazlitt, drew large crowds to discourses, which were published as *Sermons Delivered at the Sunday-evening Lecture, for the Winter Season, the Old Jewry* (2 vols., London, 1795). The *Sermons*, which are uncontroversial, had little impact on W, but Fawcett's poem *The Art of War* (London, 1795), W said, 'made me think more about him than I should otherwise have done'. See Arthur Beatty, *Joseph Fawcett: The Art of War: Its Relation to the Early Development of William Wordsworth*, University of Wisconsin Studies in Language and Literature, II (1918), 224–69. In the IF notes W claimed that the Solitary in *The Excursion* was in part modelled on Fawcett.

88. *1805 Prelude*, IX. 26. W's link with Nicholson was almost certainly through his cousin Elizabeth Threlkeld, who managed a haberdasher's in Halifax and was a customer of the wholesaler Nicholson. Her father was a Unitarian minister. See *EY*, 2 n. 2 and 16 n. 4. W's recollection that he was befriended by Nicholson 'when I had not many acquaintances in London' makes it more likely that he was referring to 1791 and not, as *Moorman*, I. 219–20 seems to suggest, 1793.

89. See *Goodwin*, 83–98.

90. *Reflections*, 94.

91. *Roe*, 28–31. For an account of the Society see *Goodwin, passim*.

92. Joseph Johnson (1738–1809) was already a very important publisher by 1791. He championed the Unitarian cause, especially through the works of Joseph Priestley, published contemporary poetry of real stature in Cowper and Erasmus Darwin, and through his *Analytical Review*, founded in 1788, disseminated a high-toned but distinctly non-establishment critique of current affairs. His hospitality drew together dissenting spirits of many persuasions. During the 1790s, however, Johnson's willingness to entertain radical ideas and writings made him increasingly conspicuous, and in February 1799 he was sentenced to six months in King's Bench Prison for having published a seditious pamphlet by Gilbert Wakefield. For a full account of Johnson and his remarkable circle of radical acquaintance, see Gerald P. Tyson, *Joseph Johnson: A Liberal Publisher* (Univ. of Iowa Press, Iowa City, 1979).

93. The general reader can grasp the essentials of the debate by comparing E. P. Thompson, *The Making of the English Working Class* (London, 1963), with Ian R. Christie, *Stress and Stability in Late Eighteenth-century Britain* (Oxford, 1984).

94. *1805 Prelude*, IX. 88–100. Richard D. Altick's *The Shows of London* (Cambridge, Mass., 1978) is a wonderfully informative and entertaining account of the variety of public entertainment in London. It even includes (p. 41) a picture of the 'learned pig' mentioned *1805 Prelude*, VII. 682.

95. Joseph Priestley (1733–1804) was a Unitarian minister of considerable eminence as a

scientist, educational theorist, and controversial writer. For a brief account of his importance see Marilyn Butler, op. cit. 83–4. For the attack on his house, a major portent of the mood of reaction setting in, see R. B. Rose, 'The Priestley Riots of 1791', *Past and Present*, 18 (1960), 68–88.

96. Quoted John W. Derry, op. cit. 293. Burke, *Reflections*, 127.

97. *1805 Prelude*, IX. 15–17.

98. Ibid. X. 881.

99. Leslie Stephen, 'Wordsworth's Ethics', *Cornhill Magazine*, 34 (1876), 206–26; reprinted in *Hours in a Library: Third Series* (London, 1879), 178–229. Stephen treats Wordsworth's poetry as the exposition, in a manner appropriate to imaginative literature, of truths about life. Though now scorned, the essay seems to me to come closer than much criticism to an appreciation of the *value* of the writing of a poet who declared, 'Every great Poet is a Teacher: I wish either to be considered as a Teacher, or as nothing'. W to Sir George Beaumont, *c*. 20 Feb. 1808. *MY*, I. 195.

100. W to Anne Taylor, 9 Apr. 1801. *EY*, 327.

101. Jacques Pierre Brissot (1754–93), radical journalist and activist, founder of *Les Amis des Noirs*, a society for black emancipation, editor of the *Patriote Français*. Brissot was a leading figure in the Jacobin Club and an advocate in 1791 of severe measures to combat counter-revolution at home and swift military actions against the threat from beyond the frontier. Increasingly out-manœuvred by Robespierre, Brissot was expelled from the Jacobin Club on 10 Oct. 1792 and executed on 31 Oct. 1793, with others of his circle, early victims of 'the Terror'.

102. W to RW, 19 Dec. [1791]. *EY*, 70.

103. Ibid. 68–9. W's fussy calculations about money indicate how anxious he was to dispel suspicion that his stay abroad was an extravagance.

104. Ibid. 69. Missing Helen Maria Williams was a loss, as she would have been able to introduce W to a wider circle of sympathizers with the Revolution. Williams (1762–1827) was a successful poet and novelist who, becoming an ardent supporter of the Revolution in France, where she mostly lived after 1791, wrote numerous books interpreting French politics for the British public, beginning with *Letters Written in France in the Summer of 1790* (1790). She and W did not meet until 1820.

105. Ibid. 69. Shaver points out that W may have known Foxlow's half brother at St John's.

106. Ibid. 70.

107. For information about the Vallon family and circle I draw, as all commentators must, on G. M. Harper, *Wordsworth's French Daughter* (Princeton, 1921) and Émile Legouis, *William Wordsworth and Annette Vallon* (London, 1922). Questions regularly put to the guides at Dove Cottage and the Wordsworth Museum, Grasmere, indicate that it is still widely believed that Wordsworth behaved badly and hushed up his relationship with Annette. This is not the case. The facts were not kept from the poet's circle. The cover-up began with the *Memoirs* in 1851. Christopher Wordsworth wanted to tell the story, knowing that it could not be kept hidden indefinitely, but, overruled by Mary Wordsworth, he had to settle for the very broadest hint in *Memoirs*, I. 74–5: 'Wordsworth's condition in France was a very critical one: he was an orphan, young, inexperienced, impetuous, enthusiastic, with no friendly voices to guide him, in a foreign country, and that country in a state of revolution; and this revolution, it must be remembered, had not only taken up arms against the monarchy and other ancient institutions, but had declared war against Christianity. The most licentious theories were propounded; all restraints were broken; libertinism was law. He was encompassed with strong temptations; and although it is not the design of the present work to chronicle the events of his life except so far as they illustrate his writings, yet I could not

pass over this period without noticing the dangers which surround those who in an ardent emotion of enthusiasm put themselves in a position of peril without due consideration of the circumstances which ought to regulate their practice.' In a proof copy at the Wordsworth Library someone, possibly Edward Quillinan, Wordsworth's son-in-law, has written against this paragraph: 'passage much objected to by Mrs W'. None the less it stood.

108. W. to William Mathews, 19 May [1792]. *E Y*, 76.

109. W to RW, 3 Sept. [1792]. *E Y*, 80–1. The letter also indicates how volatile were W's plans at this time, as he assured Richard, 'I shall be in Town during the course of the month of October', whereas he did not get back to London until towards the end of Dec. See *Reed*, I. 137.

110. *Moorman*, I. 202; Hunter Davies, *William Wordsworth* (London, 1980), 55; F. M. Todd, *Politics and the Poet: A Study of Wordsworth* (London, 1957), 46–7.

111. *1805 Prelude*, X. 189–91: 'Reluctantly to England I returned / Compelled by nothing less than absolute want / Of funds for my support'.

112. *Moorman*, I. 181; Todd, op. cit. 41.

113. *1805 Prelude*, VI. 352–4.

114. The literature on the French Revolution is dauntingly complex and extensive. The literary reader can only rely on the professional historians, uneasily aware that they disagree, sometimes fundamentally, on important matters. It seems, therefore, right to acknowledge that I have particularly valued the following, and to suggest that the reader who wants more information about the actors and events of the Revolution should turn to them: J. M. Thompson, *The French Revolution* (Oxford, 1943; 2nd edn, 1944); M. J. Sydenham, *The French Revolution* (London, 1965); A. Goodwin, *The French Revolution* (London, 1953; 5th edn, 1970).

115. Sydenham, op. cit. 86.

116. *1805 Prelude*, IX. 93–5.

117. W to RW, 19 Dec. 1791. *E Y*, 70.

118. Jean Henri Gellet-Duvivier (1754–93) was, according to Legouis, op. cit. 7, a man 'whose mind had been deranged by his wife's recent death, and who showed imprudent exaltation in the expression of his hatred of the Revolution'. He was executed on 13 July 1793 for an assault on an Orléans deputy.

119. *1805 Prelude*, IX. 126–91; quotation line 200.

120. For a full account see Georges Bussière and Émile Legouis, *Le Général Michel Beaupuy 1755–1796* (Paris and Perigueux, 1891). W believed that Beaupuy died in the counter-revolutionary uprising in the Vendée in 1793, but in fact he was killed at Emmendingen on 19 Oct. 1796, fighting not against 'deluded man / His fellow countrymen' (*1805 Prelude*, IX. 433–4), but against the Austrians.

121. *1805 Prelude*, IX. 298–328.

122. Ibid. 511–24.

123. The club was not closed to foreigners, for its register reveals that in Feb. 1792 'A member asked for a hearing and proposed two Englishmen for membership'. Its politics were radical. On 25 June it petitioned the Legislative Assembly for the deposition of the king. Grégoire had been elected Constitutional Bishop of Blois in Feb. 1791 and he was in the town during W's stay. On 21 Sept. 1792 he moved in the National Convention the trial of the king and repeated the call on 15 Nov., the day on which he was elected President of the Convention. W referred to the bishop, 'a man of philosophy and humanity', and to his speech of 15 Nov., in his *A Letter to the Bishop of Llandaff* (1793), *Prose*, I. 32. *Roe*, 49–51, 66–9, which should be consulted for fuller detail, suggests that Grégoire was behind the petition of Les Amis presented on 25 June

1792, and points out that W must have read, if not actually heard, his speech of 15 Nov.

124. On W's return sometime in Sept. 1792 Orléans was a profoundly disturbed town. On 9 Sept. 53 political prisoners were removed from Orléans, where they were awaiting trial, to Paris, only to be murdered at Versailles. Between 16 and 18 Sept. riots broke out, ostensibly over food supplies, which had to be quelled by force.

125. W to William Mathews, 19 May [1792]. *EY*, 77.

126. J. Gilchrist and W. J. Murray, *The Press in the French Revolution* (Melbourne and London, 1971), 27.

127. 'I accuse you of having clearly aimed at supreme power.'

128. *1805 Prelude*, IX. 49–52.

129. Antoine Joseph Gorsas (1752–93) issued his *Courrier* from the opening of the States-General in 1789. An associate of Roland and Brissot, he was convinced of the necessity of the September Massacres and was strongly anti-monarchist. Elected to the Convention in Sept. 1792 he became one of its secretaries in Jan. 1793. An attack on Marat, however, led to the raiding of his printing works on 9 Mar. 1793. He fled, but returning to Paris from hiding in Normandy and Brittany he was arrested on 6 Oct. and executed the following day. Burke vilified Gorsas in his *Preface to the Address of M. Brissot to his Constituents* (1794) and in the margin of his own collected Burke (now at the Wordsworth library) W has written and initialled the comment: 'I knew this man' against one of Burke's references to Gorsas. See *The Works of the Right Honourable Edmund Burke: A New Edition* (16 vols., London, 1803–27), vol. VII (1815), 305.

130. See Eric Robinson, 'An English Jacobin: James Watt, Junior, 1769–1848', *Cambridge Historical Journal*, 11 (1953–5), 349–55. Watt, son of the great engineer, had certainly been active in Paris, presenting greetings to the Jacobin Club from the Manchester Constitutional Society in Apr. 1792, but he seems to have left Paris on 7 Oct. This fact conflicts with W's recollection shortly before his death: 'I went over to Paris . . . at the time of the revolution in 1792 or 1793, and so was *pretty hot in it*; but I found Mr J. Watt there before me, and *quite* as warm in the same cause'. For the most advanced discussion of the evidence so far, see *Reed*, I. 125–6. James Losh (1763–1833) of Carlisle, lawyer, remained a lifelong but not uncritical friend of W. See W's letter of 4 Dec. 1821 defending himself against Losh's charge that he had deserted the political principles they had shared in youth (*LY*, I. 96–9). There is no hard evidence that they did meet in Paris, but some to suggest that they travelled back to England together (see *Reed*, I. 139). See also John G. Alger, *Englishmen in the French Revolution* (London, 1889) and J. M. Thompson, *English Witnesses of the French Revolution* (Oxford, 1938).

131. Thomas Paine (1737–1809) was much the most famous Englishman in Paris at this time. Author of *The Rights of Man*, he had fled to France in Sept. 1792 to escape prosecution and had been elected a member of the National Convention. The text of the address from White's Hotel is reproduced in John G. Alger, *Paris in 1789–94* (London, 1902), 327–8. Charlotte Smith and Helen Maria Williams were also toasted.

132. W to William Mathews, 19 May [1792]. *EY*, 77–8.

133. *Descriptive Sketches* (1793), ll. 792–809.

134. See *Sheats*, 59–74 and *Roe*, 68–9.

135. *Prose*, I. 32.

136. DW to Jane Pollard, 16 Feb. [1793]. *EY*, 87.

137. *Moorman*, I. 180–1, where this translation of the letters is made. The originals, which W and DW never received because they were held up by the French authorities, are printed in Legouis, op. cit. 125–33.

138. See Chester L. Shaver, 'Wordsworth's Vaudracour and Wilkinson's *The Wanderer*', *RES* NS, 12 (1961), 55–7. In his travel diary Wilkinson, who shared chambers with

RW, speaks of the story of a chevalier near Blois and his love for a young woman of bourgeois origins, which he would have narrated, were it not that a gentleman of his acquaintance intends to put it into fiction. Todd, op. cit. 221–5, also points out similarities between the story of Vaudracour and Julia and the *Memoirs of Mons. and Madame du F . . .*, incorporated in Helen Maria Williams's *Letters Written in France* (1790). *Vaudracour and Julia* was published as a separate poem in the collected edition of 1820.

CHAPTER 3

1. George Eliot, *Felix Holt* (1866), ch. 3.
2. W to William Mathews, 19 May [1792]. *EY*, 76.
3. DW to Jane Pollard [10 and 12 July 1793]. *EY*, 100.
4. DW to RW [28 May 1792]. *EY*, 79.
5. W to William Mathews, 19 May [1792]. *EY*, 76.
6. W to William Mathews, 23 May [1794]. *EY*, 120.
7. For the entry in Christopher Wordsworth's Cambridge diary see *Descriptive Sketches*, 10.
8. Thomas De Quincey, 'William Wordsworth', *Tait's Edinburgh Magazine*, 4 (Apr. 1839), 248. *DQR*, 191–2.
9. *1805 Prelude*, IX. 124–5. For the literary genesis of *Descriptive Sketches* and in particular the influence of Ramond de Carbonnières's *Lettres sur l'état politique, civil, et naturel de la Suisse*, see *Sheats*, 59–74.
10. *1805 Prelude*, IX. 521–2. For the addresses see *Goodwin*, 244–62 and 501–12.
11. *Goodwin*, 253.
12. *Roe*, 119 cites Thomas Erskine's recognition that the 'spirit which . . . prepared the nation for war, was an absolute horror of everything connected with France . . . It confounded the casual intemperance of an enlarged and warm zeal for the freedom and happiness of mankind with a tendency to universal anarchy.' *A View of the Causes and Consequences of the Present War with Frnace* (1797), 18.
13. See *Goodwin*, 272–3 and Olivia Smith, *The Politics of Language 1791–1819* (Oxford, 1984), 62 for evidence of hysteria against Paine in 'several events in which Paine was ritualistically killed'.
14. W to William Mathews, 19 May [1792]. *EY*, 77.
15. *1805 Prelude*, X. 249–74.
16. The Appendix to Watson's *A Sermon Preached before the Stewards of the Westminster Dispensary* can be found in *Grosart*, I. 24–30.
17. *A Letter to the Bishop of Llandaff on the Extraordinary Avowal of his Political Principles Contained in the Appendix to his Late Sermon by a Republican. Prose*, I. 17–66. Quotation p. 48. Page references for the following summary of W's argument are not given.
18. *The Gentleman's Magazine; and Historical Chronicle*, 63 (1793), 648, reviewing John Cocks's *Short Treatise on the Dreadful Effects of Levelling Principles*.
19. William Calvert (1771–1829) and Raisley Calvert (1773–95) were sons of the steward to the Duke of Norfolk at Greystoke Castle, near Penrith. Their father had died in 1791.
20. *1805 Prelude*, X. 303–5.
21. DW to Jane Pollard, 30 Aug. [1793]. *EY*, 109.
22. IF note to *Guilt and Sorrow: or, Incidents upon Salisbury Plain*. See *Salisbury Plain Poems*, 221.
23. W to John Kenyon [summer 1838]. *LY*, III, 616.

24. *The Gentleman's Magazine; and Historical Chronicle*, 63 (1793), 856–7 describes the extent and ferocity of the storm at length.
25. Quoted from the MS version of the 'Advertisement' to *Guilt and Sorrow*. See *Salisbury Plain Poems*, 216.
26. *1805 Prelude*, XII. 318–36.
27. For W's reading in antiquarian accounts of Stonehenge and Druidic practices see *Salisbury Plain Poems*, 35. For Rousseau see n. 29. For Chatterton see Francis Celoria, 'Chatterton, Wordsworth and Stonehenge', *Notes and Queries*, NS 23 (Mar. 1976), 103–4. Paul Kelley has kindly drawn my attention to the record of a woman who died of exposure on Stainmore in 1791 in B. R. Alderson, *The Parish Register of Bowes 1670–1837* (Wakefield, 1964), 66.
28. As n. 25.
29. See Paul Kelley, 'Rousseau's "Discourse on the Origins of Inequality" and Wordsworth's "Salisbury Plain"', *Notes and Queries*, NS 24 (July–Aug. 1977), 323, and for a fuller demonstration of W's indebtedness see *Chandler*, 130–1.
30. See Z. S. Fink (ed.), *The Early Wordsworthian Milieu* (Oxford, 1958), 88–89 and 134–5.
31. As n. 22.
32. *Roe*, 157.
33. See Frida Knight, *University Rebel: The Life of William Frend, 1757–1841* (London, 1971).
34. See *Goodwin*, 286–9 and 303–6.
35. For W's knowledge of Gorsas see ch. 2. For a statement of the evidence about the possible visit to France see *Reed*, I. 147. For further consideration, with some additional information supporting conjecture that W did go, see David V. Erdman, 'Wordsworth as Heartsworth: or, Was Regicide the Prophetic Ground of Those "Moral Questions"?' in *The Evidence of the Imagination: Studies of Interactions between Life and Art in English Romantic Literature*, ed. Donald H. Reiman, Michael C. Jaye, and Betty T. Bennett (New York, 1978), 37.
36. Émile Legouis, *William Wordsworth and Annette Vallon* (London, 1922), 42–6.
37. *1805 Prelude*, X. 373–80.
38. W to William Mathews, 17 Feb. [1794]. *EY*, 112.
39. See *Reed*, I. 149–50.
40. W wrote to William Mathews from Halifax on 17 Feb. [1794]. His previous surviving letter is as distant as 3 Sept. [1792].
41. DW to Jane Pollard, 30 Aug. [1793]. *EY*, 108.
42. Ibid. 111, and DW to Jane Pollard [5 June 1793]. *EY*, 91.
43. DW to Jane Pollard [10 and 12 July 1793]. *EY*, 101.
44. Ibid. 97 and 101–2.
45. DW to Jane Pollard [21 Apr. 1794]. *EY*, 114–15. Gray's Journal, 1 Oct. 1769, *Correspondence of Thomas Gray*, ed. Paget Toynbee, Leonard Whibley, and H. W. Starr (3 vols., Oxford, 1971), III. 1079.
46. DW to Mrs Christopher Crackanthorpe, 21 Apr. [1794]. *EY*, 117.
47. For a description of the manuscript see *Salisbury Plain Poems*, 6–7.
48. W to William Mathews, 23 May [1794]. *EY*, 120.
49. For a description of the manuscripts see *An Evening Walk*, 12–13.
50. See Lamb's very funny letter to Thomas Manning, 15 Feb. 1801: 'I had need be cautious henceforward what opinion I give of the Lyrical Balads.—All the north of England are in a turmoil. Cumberland and Westmorland have already declared a state of war . . .' *Marrs*, I. 272–3.
51. In 1808 W reproved a friend of Lady Beaumont for careless reading of 'I wandered

lonely as a cloud': 'what shall we think of criticism or judgement founded upon and exemplified by a poem which must have been so inattentively perused? My Language is precise . . .' *MY*, I. 194.

52. DW to Jane Pollard, 16 Feb. [1793]. *EY*, 89.

53. Averill, *An Evening Walk*, discusses the 1794 work, 13–16, and presents the first ever continuous reading text as well as a transcription and photographs of the manuscript, 127–267.

54. *An Evening Walk* (1794), 330–40, p. 142.

55. *An Evening Walk* (1793), 379–84, p. 74.

56. *An Evening Walk* (1794), 125–32 and 203–6, pp. 135, 138.

57. *Sheats*, 96.

58. W to SGB [*c*.23] Feb. 1805. *EY*, 546.

59. See W to RW, 10 and 17 Oct. [1794]. *EY*, 130–4.

60. *1805 Prelude*, XIII. 360–1.

61. W to William Mathews, 17 Feb. [1794]. *EY*, 112. Also 23 May, *EY*, 118–20.

62. The Calvert money began to be released in Oct. 1795.

63. W to William Mathews, 23 May [1794]. *EY*, 119.

64. RW to W, 23 May 1794. *EY*, 121.

65. *Roe*, 176–7, points out that W's question to Mathews, 'What remarks do you make on the Portuguese?' suggests that he has been struck by Godwin's assertion that Portugal is subject to a high degree of depotism.

66. William Godwin, *An Enquiry Concerning Political Justice, and its Influence on General Virtue and Happiness* (2 vols., London, 1793), I. 9; II. 510–11; II. 804–5.

67. Ibid. II. 452–3.

68. Ibid. I. 71; I. 202.

69. W to William Mathews [8] June [1794]. *EY*, 124.

70. Ibid. 125.

71. Ibid. 124.

72. A weekly journal called the *Philanthropist* was published between Mar. 1795 and 18 Jan. 1796. There is no evidence that W participated in it, but it is tempting to believe that he may have contributed to its genesis. See *Roe*, 276–9 for a full discussion, 'Wordsworth and Daniel Isaac Eaton's *Philanthropist*'.

73. *1805 Prelude*, X. 539–52 and 580.

74. *Cursory Strictures on the Charge Delivered by Lord Chief Justice Eyre to the Grand Jury, Oct. 2 1794* (London, 1794), 24. Quoted *Goodwin*, 341.

75. W to William Mathews [*c*.24 Dec. 1794 and 7 Jan. 1795]. *EY*, 137.

76. *Political Justice*, II. 886.

77. As n. 75.

78. W to William Mathews, 7 Nov. 1794. *EY*, 136.

79. W to William Mathews [*c*.24 Dec. 1794 and 7 Jan. 1795]. *EY*, 138.

80. W to William Mathews [8] June [1794]. *EY*, 124.

81. RW to W, 13 Oct. 1794. *EY*, 132.

82. W to William Mathews [*c*.24 Dec. 1794 and 7 Jan. 1795]. *EY*, 139.

83. Henry Gunning, *Reminiscences of the University, Town and County of Cambridge, from the Year 1780* (2 vols., London, 1854), II. 87.

84. For succinct information about the Godwin circle see *Roe*, 159–75 and Peter H. Marshall, *William Godwin* (New Haven and London, 1984).

85. *Howe*, XI. 17.

86. Preface to *Caleb Williams*, ed. David McCracken (Oxford, 1970), 1.

87. Marshall, op. cit. 139.

88. See *Thoughts: Occasioned by the Perusal of Dr Parr's Spital Sermon* (London, 1801), in which, defending his own constancy against the attacks of apostates who once were 'friends of liberty', Godwin reveals his sense of intellectual isolation.

89. Marshall, op. cit. 140–3.

90. See *Roe*, 190–5.

91. The first comment, made by John Binns in his *Recollections of the Life of John Binns* (Philadelphia, 1854), 45, recalls Godwin's style in debate. For the second, see Marshall, op. cit. 172.

92. From Godwin's defence of his purpose in the novel, quoted Marilyn Butler, 'Godwin, Burke, and *Caleb Williams*', *EIC*, 32 (1982), 239.

93. *Political Justice*, I. 216.

94. Quoted *EY*, 147.

95. W. R. Hamilton to W, 6 Jan. 1831. [WL].

96. Quoted *EY*, 147.

97. DW to Jane Marshall (formerly Jane Pollard], 2 [and 3] Sept. [1795]. *EY*, 150.

98. Ibid. *EY*, 149.

99. RS to Grosvenor Charles Bedford, 1 June 1794. *Curry*, I. 54.

100. W to Francis Wrangham, 20 Nov. [1795]. *EY*, 156–9. The lines are 9–10 of 'Imitation of Juvenal-Satire VIII', *PW* I. 302.

101. For the clearest account to date of the evidence on the meeting see Robert Woof, 'Wordsworth and Coleridge: Some Early Matters', *BWS*, 76–91.

102. C to George Dyer, late Feb. 1795. *CL*, I. 152.

103. *Lectures*, 6.

104. See Woof, op. cit. 83–91 and James H. Averill, 'Another Early Coleridge Reference to *An Evening Walk*', *English Language Notes*, 13 (1976), 270–3.

105. *BL*, I. 78.

106. W to William Mathews [20 and] 24 Oct. [1795]. *EY*, 153.

CHAPTER 4

1. *Moorman*, I. 281.

2. W to Francis Wrangham, 20 Nov. [1795]. *EY*, 159.

3. W to William Mathews [t.24 Dec. 1794 and 7 Jan. 1795]. *EY*, 139.

4. For an account of the Bills see *Goodwin*, 387–8. The Seditious Meetings Bill was the more important, as it was clearly intended to stifle all grass-roots opposition to the government of the day.

5. Azariah Pinney to W, 26 Nov. 1795. Pinney Papers, Bristol University Library. Future citation to PP.

6. In the preface to his magisterial study, *The State of the Poor: or, A History of the Labouring Classes in England* (3 vols., London, 1797), I, p. i, Sir Frederick Morton Eden explained that what impelled him to begin his work was the 'difficulties, which the labouring classes experienced, from the high price of grain, and of provisions in general, as well as of clothing and fuel, during the years 1794 and 1795'. For further details about food riots see *Goodwin*, 360.

7. *Lectures*, 69.

8. W to William Mathews [20 and] 24 Oct. [1795]. *EY*, 154.

9. For a text of the poem see *PW*, I. 302–6. The topicality of the Juvenal is discussed in Stephen Gill, ' "Adventures on Salisbury Plain" and Wordsworth's Poetry of Protest 1795–97', *SIR* 11 (1972), 48–65.

10. DW to Jane Marshall, 30 Nov. [1795]. *EY*, 162.

11. For a text of the revisions see *Salisbury Plain Poems*, 109–17.
12. W to Francis Wrangham, 20 Nov. [1795]. *EY*, 159.
13. *Adventures on Salisbury Plain*, ll. 392–4. It should be noted that no manuscript of the 1795 poem exists and that the reading text above is taken from a manuscript of 1799.
14. *The Ruined Cottage*, MS D, 195. *Ruined Cottage*, 57.
15. For an account of the magazine poetry of the period see Robert Mayo, 'The Contemporaneity of *Lyrical Ballads*', *PMLA* 69 (1954), 486–522 and Mary Jacobus, *Tradition and Experiment in Wordsworth's Lyrical Ballads (1798)* (Oxford, 1976), especially chs. 6–10.
16. John Langhorne, *The Country Justice* (1774–1777), Part II (1775), pp. 25–6. In 1837 W remarked to S. C. Hall that 'As far as I know, it is the first Poem, unless perhaps Shenstone's Schoolmistress be excepted, that fairly brought the Muse into the Company of common life . . . upon which it looks with a tender and enlightened humanity'. *LY*, III. 348.
17. W to Francis Wrangham, 20 Nov. [1795]. *EY*, 159: 'Its object is partly to expose the vices of the penal law and the calamities of war as they affect individuals'. Southey's Eclogues were not published until 1797, but they circulated in manuscript after their composition in the first half of 1794. Their sharpness was much softened for Southey's collected edition of 1837, which is, unfortunately, the library edition in which they are most generally available.
18. Joseph Fawcett's *The Art of War* (1795) marvels at the paradox that civilized man has methodized in war the crime of Cain which all men abhor in ordinary life. W said in his note to *The Excursion* that Fawcett's poem 'had a good deal of merit, and made me think more about him than I should otherwise have done'. *PW*, V. 375. For a brief discussion of the poem's links to *Adventures on Salisbury Plain* and further references to scholarship see Gill article cited in n. 9.
19. [Joseph Cottle], *Poems* (Bristol, 1795). 'This small volume is presented to the Public, not from a fond persuasion of its merit, but from a belief, that it is the duty of every man to raise his feeble voice in support of sinking humanity, and not to be content with thanking God, that he feels indignant at the enormities of war, without labouring to inspire the same abhorrence in the breasts of others' (p. ii). The major poem is 'War A Fragment' and Cottle's long Preface denounces modern warfare (as opposed to the chivalric combats of the past) and pleads for genuine Christianity, as man's only hope.
20. *Salisbury Plain Poems*, 111.
21. William Godwin, *An Enquiry concerning Political Justice, and its Influence on General Virtue and Happiness* (2 vols., London, 1793), II. 720.
22. *Adventures on Salisbury Plain*, l. 109.
23. Ibid. ll. 658–64.
24. Ibid. ll. 820–4.
25. *Salisbury Plain Poems*, pp. 281–2: W's revision is almost comically direct:

> His fate was pitied. Him in iron case
> (Reader, forgive the intolerable thought)
> They hung not:—no one on *his* form or face
> Could gaze, as on a show by idlers sought.

26. W to Francis Wrangham, 20 Nov. [1795]. *EY*, 159.
27. Azariah Pinney to W, 6 Mar. 1796. PP.
28. Charles Lamb to C [31 May 1796]. *Marrs*, I. 11.
29. W to William Mathews, 21 Mar. [1796]. *EY*, 169.

30. *Weekly Entertainer*, 21 Nov. 1796, 419. The magazine was subtitled 'Agreeable and Instructive Repository'. It was in fact a curious compilation of extracts from old numbers of the *Annual Register*, excerpts from recent publications, puzzles of various kinds, and a few poems. One can see why W longed for a London newspaper.

31. See *Salisbury Plain Poems*, 287–303 and *Borderers*, 746–809.

32. DW to ?, 24 Oct. 1796. *EY*, 172.

33. *1805 Prelude*, X. 874–6, 888–904.

34. Ibid. 922–6.

35. Ibid. 917.

36. DW to Jane Marshall, 19 Mar. [1797]. *EY*, 181.

37. W to William Mathews [20 and] 24 Oct. [1795]. *EY*, 155.

38. Ibid. 154.

39. William Crowe, *Lewesdon Hill* (Oxford, 1788). The poem also influenced C, who printed an extract from it in *The Watchman* for 2 Apr. 1796 and recalled in *BL*, I. 17–18, that it had given him the same kind of pleasure as the poems of Bowles.

40. For an account of domestic life at Racedown, drawn largely from Dorothy's letters, see Robert Gittings and Jo Manton, *Dorothy Wordsworth* (Oxford, 1985), and Bergen Evans and Hester Pinney, 'Racedown and the Wordsworths', *RES* 8 (1932), 1–18.

41. Azariah Pinney to James Tobin, 12 Apr. 1796. PP.

42. DW to Jane Marshall [7 Mar. 1796] and 19 Mar. [1797]. *EY*, 166, 180.

43. Ibid. 180.

44. DW to ?, 1799. *EY*, 281.

45. DW to Jane Marshall, 19 Mar. [1797]. *EY*, 181.

46. DW to Jane Marshall, 30 Nov. [1795]. *EY*, 161: 'William has had a letter from France since we came here. Annette mentions having despatched half a dozen none of which he has received.'

47. Charles Lamb to C [8–10 June 1796]. *Marrs*, I. 22.

48. Ibid.

49. The Preface was provocatively dated 12 May 1794, the day on which Thomas Hardy and other defendants in the Treason Trials were arrested. 'What is now presented to the public', Godwin declared, 'is no refined and abstract speculation; it is a study and delineation of things passing in the moral world.' *Caleb Williams*, ed. David McCracken (Oxford, 1970), 1. For an important essay on the novel's political significance, see Marilyn Butler, 'Godwin, Burke, and *Caleb Williams*', *EIC* 32 (1982), 237–57.

50. For a full edition and an account of the changes see *Enquiry Concerning Political Justice and its Influence on Morals and Happiness*, ed. F. E. L. Priestley (3 vols., Toronto, 1946).

51. *Monthly Magazine, and British Register*, 1 (Feb.–June 1796), 273–7.

52. William Godwin, *Enquiry Concerning Political Justice, and its Influence on Morals and Happiness* (2nd edn., 2 vols., London, 1796), I. 292.

53. In his pamphlet on the Two Acts, *Considerations on Lord Grenville's and Mr. Pitt's Bills* (1975), Godwin had actually criticized Thelwall for his impetuosity.

54. W to William Mathews, 21 Mar. [1796]. *EY*, 170.

55. Ibid. 169. As W said, 'This preface is indeed a very conceited performance'. Southey describes how he was struck by the suitability of the story of Joan of Arc for epic treatment: 'in the course of a few days I formed the rude outlines of a plan, and wrote the first three hundred lines; the remainder of the month was employed in travelling; and I made no progress even in idea. The subject was resumed on the 13th of August, and the original poem in TWELVE books, finished in six weeks from that time. My performance pleased myself . . .'.

56. Charles Lamb to Thomas Manning, [3 Nov. 1800]. *Marrs*, I. 244.

57. W to William Mathews, 21 Mar. [1796]. *EY*, 169.
58. The catalogue of the library, dated 2 May 1793, is in the Pinney Papers.
59. DW to Jane Marshall [7 Mar. 1796]. *EY*, 165.
60. W to William Mathews, 21 Mar. [1796]. *EY*, 169.
61. DW to Jane Marshall, 30 Nov. [1795]. *EY*, 160.
62. Ibid. 161.
63. DW to Jane Marshall [7 Mar. 1796]. *EY*, 165.
64. Reported by DW to Jane Marshall, 30 Nov. [1795]. *EY*, 162.
65. 'Advertisement' to *Guilt and Sorrow* in 1842. *Salisbury Plain Poems*, 215–7.
66. John-Baptist Louvet, *Narrative of the Dangers to which I have been Exposed, since the 31st of May 1793* (London, 1795); Citizeness Roland, *An Appeal to Impartial Posterity: A Collection of Pieces Written by her during her Confinement in the Prisons of the Abbey, and St Pélagie* (2 vols., London, 1795); Helen Maria Williams, *Letters: Containing a Sketch of the Politics of France from the Thirty-first of May 1793, till the Twenty-eighth of July 1794, and of the Scenes which have Passed in the Prisons of Paris* (2 vols., London, 1795). In its issues of 21, 28 Sept. and 5 Oct. 1795 the *Weekly Entertainer* carried long extracts from Williams's *Letters* under the heading 'Affecting Incidents in the Revolutionary Prisons of France'.
67. *1805 Prelude*, X. 610.
68. That Madame Roland and Louvet figure so strikingly in *The Prelude*'s account of the Revolution, far more than their historical importance warrants, may be due in part to W's familiarity with these books. Madame Roland's famous last words, 'O Liberty, how many crimes are committed in thy name', alluded to in *The Prelude*, X. 351–4, are to be found in the description of her execution added to *An Appeal*, II. 137–47.
69. Edmund Burke, *Three Letters Addressed to a Member of the Present Parliament, on the Proposals for Peace with the Regicide Directory of France* (London, 1796). Citation to the Bohn's Standard Library Edition of Burke's *Works* (6 vols., London, 1886), V. 152–433. Quotation p. 169.
70. In each issue from 31 Oct. to 5 Dec. 1796. W certainly knew these issues. His letter about Fletcher Christian, printed *EY*, 171, appeared in the number for 7 Nov. and his *Address to the Ocean* on 21 Nov.
71. Burke, op. cit. 163.
72. Thomas Erskine, *A View of the Causes and Consequences of the Present War with France* (London, 1797). Erskine, the counsel who had saved the defendants in the 1794 Treason Trials, was a notable Whig. In his review of British politics since the beginning of the French Revolution (which he had witnessed in Paris in 1790), Erskine attacks both the competence and the integrity of Pitt and tries to show that his government had always sought pretexts for war against the Revolutionaries on ideological grounds.
73. Burke, op. cit. 220.
74. *Weekly Entertainer*, 28 (21 Nov. 1796), 419.

75.               I mark the glow-worm as I pass,
              Move with 'green radiance' through the grass

*Lines Written at Shurton Bars . . .* ll. 4–5. First published in *Poems* (1796). The note reads: 'The expression "green radiance" is borrowed from Mr. Wordsworth, a Poet whose versification is occasionally harsh and his diction too frequently obscure; but whom I deem unrivalled among the writers of the present day in manly sentiment, novel imagery, and vivid colouring'. For an important detailed consideration of the dating of this note and its significance see Robert Woof, 'Wordsworth and Coleridge: Some Early Matters', *BWS*, 83–91.

76. C to George Coleridge, 6 Nov. 1794. *CL*, I. 125.
77. See *Lectures*, 21–74 and 277–318.
78. For a full account of C's work on the periodical see *Watchman*, pp. xxvii–lvi.
79. The volume included three poems by Charles Lamb and one, *Effusion XV*, which C acknowledged in the Preface as a joint production with Southey.
80. C to John Thelwall, 13 May 1796. *CL*, I. 215.
81. C to Joseph Cottle [6 Jan. 1797]. *CL*, I. 297.
82. C to RS [13] Nov. 1795. *CL*, I. 172.
83. C to John Thelwall, 19 Nov. [1796]: 'I am, & ever have been, a great reader— have read almost anything—a library-cormorant—I am *deep* in all out of the way books'.
84. *Lectures*, 70.
85. W to William Rowan Hamilton, 25 June 1832. *LY*, II. 536.
86. 2 Apr. 1796. *Watchman*, 196.
87. C was extremely hostile to Godwin's atheism, although there was much in *Political Justice* that attracted him. As early as [11 Sept. 1794] (*CL*, I. 102) he was inveighing against Godwin's unbelief and, although his refutation of *Political Justice* was never written, the 1795 lectures on religion 'constitute a considered Christian alternative to Godwin's atheistic radicalism' (*Lectures*, p. lxvii).
88. C to John Thelwall. 17 May 1796. *CL*, I. 216.
89. 'Fragments of Theological Lectures' printed in *Lectures*, 339.
90. *Effusion XXXV* was subjected to extensive revision. Manuscript versions are included in *CPW*, II. 1021–3. The text of 1796 is reprinted in Kelvin Everest, *Coleridge's Secret Ministry: The Context of the Conversation Poems 1795–1798* (Hassocks and New York, 1979), 198–9.
91. *Religious Musings*, ll. 42–5. *CPW*, I. 110–11. 'I rest for all my poetical credit on the *Religious Musings*.' C. to Benjamin Flower, 1 Apr. 1796. *CL*, I. 197. Lamb told Coleridge that he did not hesitate 'to pronounce it sublime'. *Marrs*, I. 10.
92. DW to ?, 24 Oct. 1796. *EY*, 172.
93. See *Borderers*, 302–3. W quotes 'Irritat mulcet falsis terroribus implet' from Horace's *Epistles*, II. i, *To Augustus*. Paul Kelley has pointed out to me that the immediate context of the epigraph is Horace's praise of great tragic playwrights, who can move an audience's feelings and imagination by poetic means alone.
94. See *Borderers*, introduction *passim*, especially 21, 27–33.
95. *The Borderers*, IV. ii. 103.
96. *The Borderers*, IV. ii. 143–5.
97. Ibid. l. 142.
98. *The Borderers*, III. v. 26–9, 30–3.
99. *Borderers*, p. 813.
100. *1805 Prelude*, X. 806–10.
101. Ibid. ll. 815, 835–6.
102. *Chandler*, ch. 9, argues that W was responding in *The Borderers* more to the French Ideologues than to Godwin. See p. 294 n. 29 and p. 295 n. 3.
103. *1805 Prelude*, X. 878–940; quotation ll. 896–7.
104. ll. 26–7. *The Works in Prose and Verse of Charles and Mary Lamb*, ed. Thomas Hutchinson (2 vols., Oxford, 1924), II. 540.
105. *Religious Musings*, ll. 362–4. *CPW*, I. 122.
106. *The Borderers*, III. iii. 95.
107. Ibid. ll. iii. 344.

108. Ibid. V. iii. 264–75.
109. W to Francis Wrangham, 25 Feb. 1797. *EY*, 178.
110. Noted in Gill's diary for 21 Nov. PP.
111. Azariah Pinney to W, 25 Mar. 1796. PP.
112. W to RW, 7 May [1797]. *EY*, 182–5.
113. Ibid. 184.
114. DW to RW, 28 May [1797]. *EY*, 185–6.
115. W to RW, 12 June [1797]. *EY*, 188.
116. Outstanding claims were met in 1812, 1814, and 1816. See W's letter of explanation to CW, 12 Jan. 1816. *MY*, II. 270–2.
117. See *Watchman*, p. xxxii, for a photograph.
118. George Dyer, *The Poet's Fate* (London, 1797), 26. For discussion and a photograph of the cartoon, see Burton R. Pollin, 'Charles Lamb and Charles Lloyd as Jacobins and Anti-Jacobins', *SIR* 12 (1973), 633–47.
119. Robert Southey, *Joan of Arc* (1796) and *Poems* (1797). Robert Southey and Robert Lovell, *Poems* (1795). *Poems, by S. T. Coleridge, Second Edition, to which are now Added Poems by Charles Lamb and Charles Lloyd* (1797). George Dyer, *Poems* (1792) and *The Poet's Fate* (1797). Francis Wrangham, *Poems* (1795; private printing, published *c*.1802). G. H. Noehden and John Stoddard, *Fiesco: or, The Genoese Conspiracy. A Tragedy* (1796).
120. C to John Prior Estlin, 4 July [1796], and to Thomas Poole [4 July 1796]. *CL*, I. 222 and 227.
121. See *CL*, I. 220 for the recommendation of C as 'of that description of persons, who fall within the notice of your benevolent Institution. He is a man of undoubted talents, though his works have been unproductive, and, though he will in future be able to support himself by his own industry, he is at present quite unprovided for, being of no profession.' For the foundation of the Fund in 1790, which was a sign of the increasing professionalization of literature, and for the grant of ten guineas to Coleridge, see Nigel Cross, *The Common Writer: Life in Nineteenth-century Grub Street* (Cambridge, 1985), 14, 21.
122. C to John Prior Estlin, 4 July [1796]. *CL*, I. 224: 'The Reviews have been wonderful— The Monthly has *cataracted* panegyric on my poems; the Critical has *cascaded* it; and the Analytical has *dribbled* it with very tolerable civility. The Monthly has at least done justice to my Religious Musings—They place it "on the very top of the scale of Sublimity."—!—!—!'
123. C to Richard Brinsley Sheridan, 6 Feb. 1797. *CL*, I. 304.
124. In the Preface to *Poems on Various Subjects* (1796) C justifies the egotism of so many of his poems: (1) the poet's own feelings and sufferings *are* subject-matter; (2) the act of composition actually helps, for 'by a benevolent law of our nature from intellectual activity a pleasure results which is gradually associated and mingles as a corrective with the painful subject of the description'; (3) the reader will benefit, for 'the public' is 'but a term for a number of scattered individuals of whom as many will be interested in these sorrows as have experienced the same or similar'. The Preface, which notably anticipates aspects of the Prefaces to *Lyrical Ballads* 1800 and 1802, shows C to be interested both in the nature of composition and in the moral efficacy of poetry.
125. Charles Lamb to C [17 Oct. 1796]. *Marrs*, I. 51.
126. C to Charles Lloyd, senior. 15 Oct. 1796. *CL*, I. 240.
127. C to George Coleridge [*c*.10 Mar. 1798]. *CL*, I. 397. See also C's explanation to Charles Lloyd, senior, of 14 Nov. [1796], that his planned retirement is in accord with the

dictates of Christianity, being both an active search for a virtuous way of life and a flight from temptation. *CL*, I. 255–6.

128. C to Joseph Cottle [early Apr. 1797]. *CL*, I. 319.

129. Ibid. 320–1. By contrast with Southey, who had advertised the speed of his epic composition (see n. 55), C declares: 'I would be a tolerable Mathematician, I would thoroughly know Mechanics, Hydrostatics, Optics and Astronomy, Botany, Metallurgy, Fossilism, Chemistry, Geology, Anatomy, Medicine—then the *mind of man*—then the *minds of men*—in all Travels, Voyages and Histories. So I would spend ten years—the next five to the composition of the poem—and the five last to the correction of it.'

130. *Critical Review*, 19 (Feb. 1797), 194–200.

131. *Monthly Magazine, and British Register*, 1 (Feb.–June 1796), 36.

132. Mary Wordsworth to Sara Coleridge, 7 Nov. 1845. *LY*, IV. 719. Mary quotes W's words. The 'we' refers to W and Dorothy, Mary having left Racedown at the beginning of June.

133. C to the Wordsworths, 8 Feb. 1804. *CL*, II. 1060.

134. DW to ? MH [June 1797]. *EY*, 189.

135. C to John Prior Estlin [9 June 1797]. *CL*, I. 326.

136. As n. 134, pp. 188–9.

137. C to John Prior Estlin [10 June 1797]. *CL*, I. 327.

CHAPTER 5

1. *1805 Prelude*, XIII. 390–3; 414.

2. Both pictures are in the National Portrait Gallery.

3. 'My First Acquaintance with Poets', *Howe*, XVII. 118.

4. See IF notes quoted *PW*, I. 360–?; II. 178.

5. C to Josiah Wade, 16 Mar. 1797. *CL*, I. 317.

6. Charles Lamb to C, 24 June 1797. *Marrs*, I. 113.

7. DW to ? MH [4 July] and 14 Aug. 1797. *EY*, 189, 190–1.

8. For Charlotte Poole see Mrs Henry Sandford, *Thomas Poole and his Friends* (2 vols., London, 1888), I. 79. For W's comments see IF note to *The Farmer of Tilsbury Vale*, *PW*, IV. 447 and W's letter 9 Apr. 1801, *EY*, 322.

9. W returned to Racedown in early August to fetch Peggy and little Basil. *Reed*, I. 203, 205.

10. DW, 14 Aug. 1797. As n. 7.

11. IF note to *Lines Written in Early Spring*, *PW*, IV. 411–12.

12. DW to Jane Marshall, 30 Nov. [1795]. *EY*, 161.

13. C to Joseph Cottle [*c*.3 July 1797]. *CL*, I. 330. See also C to Estlin, 18 May 1798 on W: 'His genius is most *apparent* in poetry—and rarely, except to me in tete a tete, breaks forth in conversational eloquence'. *CL*, I. 410.

14. *Journals*, 5–7.

15. DW to Mrs William Rawson [3 July 1798]. *EY*, 223.

16. C to Joseph Cottle [early Apr. 1798]. *CL*, I. 403. C to William Godwin [19 Nov. 1801]. *CL*, II. 775.

17. John Thelwall, *Lines written at Bridgewater, in Somersetshire, on the 27th of July, 1797; during a long excursion in quest of a peaceful retreat*, in *Poems, Chiefly Written in Retirement* (Hereford, 1801), 126–32.

18. For a more detailed account see *Goodwin*, 405–14. In his poem Thelwall declares:

> my soul
> Is sick of public turmoil—ah, most sick
> Of the vain effort to redeem a Race
> Enslav'd, because degenerate . . .

19. Entry for 27 July 1830 in *Specimens of the Table Talk of Samuel Taylor Coleridge*, ed. H. N. Coleridge (2 vols., London, 1835), I. 190–1.
20. C to Joseph Cottle as n. 13.
21. As n. 15.
22. *Journals*, 3.
23. For the fullest account of the spy episode, and conclusive identification of Walsh, see *Roe*, 248–62. In her *Selections from the Papers of the London Corresponding Society 1792–1799* (Cambridge, 1983), Mary Thale presents copious evidence of the vigilance of the spies who infiltrated the radical movement and identifies their controllers.
24. Mrs Henry Sandford, op. cit. n. 8, I. 235. See also C's letter to John Thelwall, 21 Aug. 1797, *CL*, I. 343–4, dissuading him from thinking of settling near Stowey: 'Very great odium T. Poole incurred by bringing *me* here . . . Wordsworth came & he likewise by T. Poole's agency settled here— / You cannot conceive the tumult, calumnies, & apparatus of threatened persecutions which this event has occasioned round about us. If *you* too should come, I am afraid, that even riots & dangerous riots might be the consequence . . .'.
25. See Roger Wells, *Insurrection: The British Experience 1795–1803* (Gloucester, 1983), esp. ch. 4.
26. C to John Thelwall, 30 Jan. 1798. *CL*, I. 382.
27. See Mrs Henry Sandford, op. cit. n. 8, I. 225–6, 241–2.
28. W to James Losh, 4 Dec. 1821. *LY*, I. 96–9.
29. C to Benjamin Flower, [11 Dec. 1796]. *CL*, I. 268. Poem published *Morning Post*, 16 Apr. 1798; title changed to *France: An Ode* for separate publication same year. C to John Prior Estlin [23 July 1797] and to George Coleridge [*c*.10 Mar. 1798]. *CL*, I. 338, 397–8.
30. William Godwin, *Thoughts: Occasioned by the Perusal of Dr Parr's Spital Sermon, Preached at Christ Church, April 15, 1800* (London, 1801), 9. Reprinted in Godwin's *Uncollected Writings*, ed. Jack W. Marken and Burton R. Pollin (Gainesville, 1968), 281–374.
31. For a fascinating account of Wedgwood's scheme see David V. Erdman, 'Coleridge, Wordsworth, and the Wedgwood Fund', *BNYPL* 60 (1956), 425–43, 487–507. My quotations are from Wedgwood's letter to Godwin, 31 July 1797.
32. DW to Mrs William Rawson, 13 June 1798. *EY*, 222. Note also that on 16 Oct. 1797 C was explaining to Poole why he believed children should be permitted 'to read Romances, & Relations of Giants & Magicians, & Genii'. *CL*, I. 354.
33. The passage in DC MS 16 begins:

> There are who tell us that in recent times
> We have been great discoverers, that by dint
> Of nice experience we have lately given
> To education principles as fixed
> And plain as those of a mechanic trade.
>       . . . it is maintained
> We now have rules and theories so precise

That by th' inspection of unwearied eyes
We can secure infallible results.

Its climax is the description of the boy hooting to the owls. See *1805 Prelude*, V. 290–449.

34. For full evidence and thoughtful analysis see Stephen Maxfield Parrish, *The Art of the Lyrical Ballads* (Cambridge, Mass., 1973), esp. ch. 2; Thomas McFarland, *Romanticism and the Forms of Ruin* (Princeton, 1981), esp. chs. 1 and 2; Lucy Newlyn, *Coleridge, Wordsworth, and the Language of Allusion* (Oxford, 1986).

35. Note to *The Wanderings of Cain*, *CPW*, I. 285–7.

36. IF note to *We are Seven*, *PW*, I. 361.

37. DW to MH, 20 Nov. 1797. *EY*, 194.

38. DW to CW, 8 Dec. [1797] and W to Joseph Cottle, 13 Dec. [1797]. *EY*, 195, 196.

39. See *EY*, 197 n. 1.

40. C to W [23] Jan. 1798. *CL*, I. 379. After reading the play W told James Tobin on 6 Mar. [1798] that 'The Castle Spectre is a Spectre indeed'. *EY*, 210. W saw it in Bristol around 21–3 May. His chagrin is understandable. As Shaver notes, *EY*, 211, 'During the first three months of its London run the play is said to have earned £18,000'.

41. From the 1800 Preface to *Lyrical Ballads*. *Prose*, I. 128.

42. Entry for 21 July 1832 in C's *Table Talk*, op. cit. n. 19, II. 69.

43. In the IF note W said that 'for several passages describing the employment & demeanour of Margaret during her affliction I was indebted to observations made in Dorsetshire & afterwards at Alfoxden'. *The Ruined Cottage*, 476. For the striking passage from Southey, which C included in *The Watchman*, 1 Mar. 1796, and for reference to other literary analogues, see ibid. 5–6 and Jonathan Wordsworth, *The Music of Humanity* (London, 1969), esp. chs. 1 and 2.

44. MS B, ll. 74–5, 83–5, 246–56, 526–9.

45. John Keats to John Taylor, 30 Jan. 1818.

46. *The Ruined Cottage*, 155.

47. Michael C. Jaye analyses the fragments in 'William Wordsworth's Alfoxden Notebook: 1798', *The Evidence of the Imagination: Studies of Interactions between Life and Art in English Romantic Literature*, ed. Donald H. Reiman, Michael C. Jaye, and Betty T. Bennett (New York, 1978), 42–85.

48. Jonathan Wordsworth, op. cit. 201.

49. C to John Prior Estlin [18] May [1798]. *CL*, I. 410.

50. W to William Rowan Hamilton, 25 June 1832. *LY*, II. 536.

51. C to Thomas Poole, 24 Sept. 1796. *CL*, I. 236.

52. *Frost at Midnight*, ll. 54–64; *This Lime-tree Bower my Prison*, ll. 60–4. *CPW*, I. 242, 181.

53. *The Ruined Cottage*, 159.

54. DW to MH, 5 Mar. [1798]. *EY*, 200.

55. *Howe*, XVII. 118.

56. See *The Ruined Cottage*, p. 269.

57. *Lines: Written at a Small Distance from my House*, ll. 33–4; *Lines Written in Early Spring*, ll. 13–16. Text of 1798, as *Gill: Oxf. W.*, 55, 81.

58. 'Advertisement' to *Lyrical Ballads* (1798). For Hazlitt, *Howe*, XVII. 119. For a fine account of Hazlitt's intellectual precocity see David Bromwich, *Hazlitt: The Mind of a Critic* (New York and Oxford, 1983).

59. *The Tables Turned*, ll. 17–32. *Gill: Oxf. W.*, 131.

60. C to RS, 14 Aug. 1870. *CL*, II. 977.

61. *Monthly Review*, 29 (June 1799), 207. Quoted in a very useful discussion by Mary Jacobus, *Tradition and Experiment in Wordsworth's Lyrical Ballads (1798)* (Oxford, 1976), 237.

62. See Parrish, op. cit. n. 34 and Jacobus, op. cit., above, who prints two of William Taylor's popular translations of Bürger, pp. 277–88.

63. Quoted from C's very lovely words in *BL*, II. 7, on how W was to affect readers: 'by awakening the mind's attention from the lethargy of custom, and directing it to the loveliness and the wonders of the world before us; an inexhaustible treasure, but for which in consequence of the film of familiarity and selfish solicitude we have eyes, yet see not, ears that hear not, and hearts that neither feel nor understand'.

64. C to LB, 3 Apr. 1815. *CL*, IV. 564.

65. Elizabeth Gaskell to Mary Howitt, [18 Aug. 1838]. *The Letters of Mrs Gaskell*, ed. J. A. V. Chapple and Arthur Pollard (Manchester, 1966), 33.

66. *CPW*, I. 106–8, ll. 61–2. First published in the *Monthly Magazine*, Oct. 1796, the poem was titled *Reflections on Having Left a Place of Retirement* when published in *Poems* (1797).

67. C to Charles Lloyd, senior, 14 Nov. [1796] and Thomas Poole [11 Dec. 1796]. *CL*, I. 255, 266.

68. See *CL*, I. 360–74 for the letters that passed between C and his benefactors. Quotation in text from C's letter to Estlin [16 Jan. 1798]. *CL*, I. 370.

69. C to Josiah Wedgwood, 17 Jan. 1798. *CL*, I. 374.

70. C to TP [27 Jan. 1798]. *CL*, I. 381.

71. C to George Coleridge [*c*.10 Mar. 1798]. *CL*, I. 397.

72. C to RS [13] Nov. 1795. *CL*, I. 173.

73. C to Joseph Cottle [7 Mar. 1798]: 'Poole (whom I feel so consolidated with myself that I seem to have no occasion to speak of him out of myself) thinks . . .' *CL*, I. 391.

74. C to RS [*c*.17 July 1797]; to Joseph Cottle [7 Mar. 1798]; to John Prior Estlin [18] May [1798]. *CL*, I. 334, 391, 410.

75. C to George Coleridge [*c*.10 Mar. 1798]. *CL*, I. 397–8.

76. *Howe*, XVII. 117.

77. In 1817 (after the publication of *The Excursion* in 1814) C made public in *Biographia Literaria* the conviction he had held for twenty years: 'What Mr. Wordsworth *will* produce it is not for me to prophesy: but I could pronounce with the liveliest conviction what he is capable of producing. It is the FIRST GENUINE PHILOSOPHIC POEM.' *BL*, I. 155–6. W's letters to Tobin and Losh, *EY*, 212, 214.

78. For a full discussion see *Johnston*.

79. C to W, 30 May 1815. *CL*, IV. 571–6.

80. Entry for 21 July 1832, C's *Table Talk*, op. cit. n. 19, II. 70.

81. C to John Thelwall, 22 June 1796; C to George Dyer [late Feb. 1795]. *CL*, I. 221, 152.

82. TP to C, 8 Oct. 1798. Mrs Henry Sandford, op. cit. n. 8, I. 278.

83. C to TP, 6 May 1799. *CL*, I. 491.

84. C to TP, 31 Mar. 1800. *CL*, I. 584.

85. Entry for 3 Nov. 1810. *CN*, III. 4006.

86. C to Joseph Cottle [*c*.20 Nov. 1797]. *CL*, I. 357.

87. For a particularly sympathetic account of what Lamb was suffering during these years see Winifred F. Courtney, *Young Charles Lamb 1775–1802* (London, 1982), esp. chs. 9 to 14.

88. Charles Lamb to C [*c*.23 May–6 June 1798]. *Marrs*, I. 128–9.

89. See R. S. Woof, 'Wordsworth's Poetry and Stuart's Newspapers: 1797–1803', *SIB* 15 (1962), 149–89, and for further confirmatory evidence Appendix I to *Descriptive Sketches*.

90. W to James Losh, 11 Mar. [1798]. *EY*, 213.

91. They had heard travellers' tales from Tom Wedgwood, who had already followed the route they eventually took. See R. B. Litchfield, *Tom Wedgwood: The First Photographer* (London, 1903), 62. On 11 Mar. 1798 W begged Losh to extract from John Tweddell, who had gone to Germany in Sept. 1795, 'any information respecting the prices of board, lodging, house-rent, provisions &c'. *EY*, 213–14.

92. C to Joseph Cottle [*c*.13 Mar. 1798]. *CL*, I. 399–400.

93. W to Joseph Cottle, 12 Apr. 1798. *EY*, 215.

94. DW to RW, 30 Apr. [1798]. *EY*, 216.

95. W to Joseph Cottle, 9 May 1798. *EY*, 218.

96. Coleridge's account in ch. 14 of *Biographia Literaria* of the origin of *Lyrical Ballads* is very attractive, because it posits such a coherent order from discussion and shared ideas, to the 'plan', to composition, and finally to publication. Mark L. Reed, 'Wordsworth, Coleridge, and the "Plan" of the *Lyrical Ballads*', *UTQ* 34 (1965), 238–53, shows how far C was, in fact, retrospectively tidying up the history of the volume.

97. C to Joseph Cottle [probably 4 June] 1798. *CL*, I. 411–12.

98. Joseph Cottle, *Early Recollections, Chiefly Relating to the Late Samuel Taylor Coleridge . . .* (2 vols., London, 1837), I. 309.

99. C to Joseph Cottle [28 May 1798]. *CL*, I. 412. For the 'lash of the *Anti-Jacobin*' see the informative Appendix to *Essays*, III. 269–73.

100. D. F. Foxon brilliantly untangles the complexities of 'The Printing of *Lyrical Ballads*, 1798', in *Library*, 5th ser. 9 (1954), 221–41. The non-bibliographical reader will find W. J. B. Owen's account in his edition of *Lyrical Ballads 1798* (Oxford, 1967; 2nd edn. 1969), pp. xvi–xx more accessible. As late as mid-Sept. *Lyrical Ballads*, though printed, lacked a publisher. Cottle tried to deal with Longman, but eventually settled with J. and A. Arch. W independently dealt with Johnson. In *Why the Lyrical Ballads?* (Berkeley, 1976), 47, John E. Jordan remarks that W's behaviour 'smacks of a certain disingenuousness'. To me it suggests that W had become impatient with Cottle—who clearly was dithering—or genuinely anxious that the volume would die. On either reading, W's behaviour certainly signals a strong proprietary interest in the book.

101. W to James Tobin. 6 Mar. [1798]. *EY*, 211.

102. DW to Mrs William Rawson [3 July 1798]. *EY*, 223.

103. DW to RW, 31 May 1798. *EY*, 219.

104. See W to Joseph Cottle, 28 [Aug. 1798] and to William Mathews, 21 Mar. [1796]. *EY*, 227 and 170.

105. DW to RW, 31 May [1798]. *EY*, 219. Once again, as usual in letters to Richard, DW puts their financial situation in as favourable a light as possible and stresses William's productive activity.

106. In *Wordsworth's Travels in Wales and Ireland* (Tulsa, 1985), 17–37, Donald E. Hayden draws together existing scholarship in an illustrated account of W's travels in the Wye area in 1793 and 1798.

107. W to Henry Gardiner, 3 Oct. 1798. *EY*, 231.

108. Note added for 1800 edition of *Lyrical Ballads*. W echoes C's definition of the '*essential* excellencies of the sublimer Ode', given in the Dedication to his *Ode on the Departing Year*. *CPW*, II. 1113.

109. William Gilpin, *Observations on the River Wye . . . Relative Chiefly to Picturesque Beauty: Made in the Summer of the Year 1770* (London, 1782), 12 and 35–7. In 'The Politics of "Tintern Abbey" ', *Wordsworth Circle*, 14 (1983), 6–14, Kenneth R. Johnston probes particularly well the meaning of what Gilpin and W actually saw and how each wrote about it.

110. *Lines . . . Tintern Abbey*, ll. 77–84. Text of 1798 as *Gill: Oxf. W.*, 133. Further references will not be given in the discussion of this very well-known poem.

111. *Expostulation and Reply*, ll. 23–4. 1798 text, as *Gill: Oxf. W.*, 130.

CHAPTER 6

1. C to Sara Coleridge, 18 Sept. 1798. *CL*, I. 416.
2. See all of C's letters between 18 Sept. and 26 Nov. 1798. *CL*, I. 415–49.
3. For W's account of his meetings see *Prose*, I. 87–98. For C's rather more racy one see his letter to Thomas Poole, 20 Nov. 1798. *CL*, I. 441–5. Klopstock gave W Johann Ebert's *Episteln und vermischte Gedichte* (1795), which is now in WL.
4. C to Sara Coleridge, 18 Sept. 1798. *CL*, I. 417.
5. C to TP, 26 Oct. 1798. *CL*, I. 435.
6. C to Sara Coleridge, 8 Nov. and 26 Nov. 1798. *CL*, I. 439, 445.
7. C to Sara Coleridge, 10 Mar. 1799. *CL*, I. 475.
8. C's description of Lessing to Benjamin Flower, 1 Apr. 1796. *CL*, I. 197.
9. E. S. Shaffer, *'Kubla Khan' and the Fall of Jerusalem: The Mythological School in Biblical Criticism and Secular Literature 1770–1880* (Cambridge, 1975), 33. For complementary information about the importance of Göttingen to C see Trevor H. Levere, *Poetry Realized in Nature: Samuel Taylor Coleridge and Early Nineteenth-century Science* (Cambridge, 1981), esp. ch. 1.
10. W to Josiah Wedgwood, 5 Feb. 1799. *EY*, 249.
11. Ibid.
12. W to C, 27 Feb. [1799]. *EY*, 254.
13. DW to C, 27 Feb. [1799]. *EY*, 252. Their movements, which are unknown, may have been recorded in the journal, now lost, which is mentioned by C in a letter to Thomas Longman, 15 Dec. 1800. *CL*, I. 654.
14. *Reed*, I. 264–5 examines the slender evidence and inclines to believe that the Wordsworths visited C twice in Göttingen during this period.
15. C to Sara Coleridge, 23 Apr. 1799. *CL*, I. 484.
16. W to Josiah Wedgwood, 5 Feb. 1799. *EY*, 249.
17. DW and W to C [14 or 21 Dec. 1798]. *EY*, 242.
18. C to W [early Dec. 1798]. *CL*, I. 451. W and DW to C [14 or 21 Dec. 1798]. *EY*, 236.
19. C to Sara Coleridge, 14 Jan. 1799. *CL*, I. 459–60.
20. C to TP, 6 Apr. 1799. *CL*, I. 479.
21. W and DW to C [14 or 21 Dec. 1798] and DW to ? [c.3 Feb. 1799]. *EY*, 236, 247.
22. *Prose*, I. 99–107.
23. *Reflections*, 156.
24. W to Josiah Wedgwood, 5 Feb. 1799. *EY*, 249.
25. W to C, 27 Feb. [1799]. *EY*, 255. In her journal for 1 Oct. 1798 DW records that in addition to Bürger they also bought Percy's *Reliques of Ancient English Poetry*. *DWJ*, I. 31.
26. The poems are: 'If Nature, for a favorite child'; *The Fountain*; *The Two April Mornings*; 'A slumber did my spirit seal'; *Song* ('She dwelt among th'untrodden ways'); 'Strange

fits of passion I have known'; all published in 1800. Five elegies related to the 'Mathew poems, but not published with the others, are printed in *Gill: Oxf. W.*, 142–7.

27. For a description of the manuscript, discussion, and transcription of the entries see *1799 Prelude*, 3–9, 71–119. Quotations will be taken from the 'Reading Text', pp. 121–30, without further reference. Quotations not from this manuscript will be identified by line reference to the 'Reading Text' of the *1799 Prelude*, pp. 39–67, or by page reference elsewhere in the volume. A text of both the earliest manuscript and the completed poem is also available in the *Norton Prelude*.

28. *1799 Prelude*, I. 288–94.

29. Ibid. I. 450–64.

30. RW to Basil Montagu, 14 May 1799, *EY*, 678.

31. W to Joseph Cottle [*c.*20 May 1799]. *EY*, 259.

32. RW to W, 15 May 1799. *EY*, 674.

33. W to Joseph Cottle, 27 July [1799]. *EY*, 267.

34. Nigel Cross, *The Common Writer: Life in Nineteenth-century Grub Street* (Cambridge, 1985), 126.

35. W to C, 27 Feb. and DW to CW, 3 Feb. 1799. *EY*, 256, 246.

36. W to Henry Gardiner, 3 Oct. 1798. *EY*, 232.

37. W to Joseph Cottle, 2 June and 24 June [1799]. *EY*, 263, 264.

38. W to Cottle [date uncertain 1799]. *EY*, 267–8. Southey's review appeared in the *Critical Review*, 24 (Oct. 1798), 197–204.

39. W to Cottle, 24 June [1799]. *EY*, 264.

40. W and DW to C, 24 [and 27] Dec. [1799]. *EY*, 281.

41. C to TP, 4 Jan. 1799. *CL*, I. 454. Sadly many letters seem to have been lost. On 14 Jan. 1799, *CL*, I. 459, C told Sara: 'I hear as often from Wordsworth as letters can go backward & forward in a country where 50 miles in a day & night is *expeditious* Travelling!'

42. C to TP, 4 Jan. 1799, *CL*, I. 455. DW and W to C, 14 or 21 Dec. 1798, *EY*, 238: 'You speak in raptures of the pleasure of skaiting—It must be a delightful exercise, and in the North of England amongst the mountains whither we wish to decoy you, you might enjoy it with every possible advantage'.

43. C to TP, 6 May 1799. *CL*, I. 490.

44. Ibid. 491.

45. DW to TP, 4 July 1799. *EY*, 266.

46. 'Your Uncle has left you £100, nobody else is named in his Will', W told DW on 8 Nov. 1799. *EY*, 271. The continuing strength of W's feelings about his Uncle Christopher is attested by the fact that while John and Christopher Wordsworth attended the funeral, he did not.

47. W to DW [8 Nov. 1799]. *EY*, 271. For C's reactions to the whole tour see *CN*, I, entries 510–55.

48. C to DW [*c.*10 Nov. 1799]. *CL*, I. 543. C's reaction to John was very positive: 'Your Br. John is one of you; a man who hath solitary usings of his own Intellect, deep in feeling, with a subtle Tact, a swift instinct of Truth & Beauty. He interests me much.'

49. Quoted *Reed*, I. 281.

50. C to DW [*c.*10 Nov. 1799]. *CL*, I. 545.

51. W to DW [8 Nov. 1799]. *EY*, 271. 'Mr Law's White palace—a bitch! . . . damned White washing', C exclaimed in his notebook entries 511 and 514. For W's response to Braithwaite's pleasure house see *TWT*, 378.

52. *1799 Prelude*, II. 37–9.

53. W to Joseph Cottle [*c.* 20 May 1799]. *EY*, 259.

54. Carl H. Ketcham gives a sympathetic account of John Wordsworth's life in *JWL*.
55. W to DW [8 Nov. 1799]. *EY*, 272: '. . . you will think my plan a mad one, but I have thought of building a house there [Grasmere] by the Lake side. John would give me £40 to buy the ground . . .'.
56. Ibid.
57. The 'glad preamble', as W calls it in *1805 Prelude*, VII. 4, consists of the first 54 lines of Book I. The date of its composition or utterance (as opposed to the date on which it was incorporated into the *1805 Prelude*) was for a long time disputed. I accept, as most scholars now do, the conclusion reached in John A. Finch's argument, 'Wordsworth's Two-handed Engine', *BWS*, 1–13.
58. W and DW to C, 24 [and 27] Dec. [1799]. *EY*, 280.
59. Ibid. 274. The cottage, once an inn called the Dove and Olive Branch, was rented from John Benson of Tail End (now Dale End).
60. For discussion of the shaping of the poem and a description of the manuscripts see *1799 Prelude*, pp. 20–34.
61. C to W, 10 Dec. 1798. *CL*, I. 453.
62. *1799 Prelude*, II. 242–9, 317–20. The 'Bless'd the infant Babe' passage is 267–310.
63. Quotation from *1799 Prelude*, II. 243, 409, 410.
64. C to TP, 6 Apr. and to Sara Coleridge, 8 Apr. 1799. *CL*, I. 479, 482.
65. *1799 Prelude*, II. 249–56.
66. C to W, 12 Oct. 1799. *CL*, I. 538.
67. See *1799 Prelude*, p. 27 and Jonathan Wordsworth and Stephen Gill, 'The Two-part *Prelude* of 1798–99', *JEGP* 72 (1973), 517–18.
68. *1799 Prelude*, II. 448–60.
69. W's announcement to James Tobin, 6 Mar. [1798]. *EY*, 212.
70. Mackintosh, who was knighted in 1803, only published a schedule of his proposed series in *A Discourse on the Study of the Law of Nature and Nations* in Jan. 1799. For an account of the actual lectures in Lincoln's Inn see Robert James Mackintosh, *Memoirs of the Life of the Right Honourable Sir James Mackintosh*, 2 vols. (London, 1835), 99–123. The editor admits that his father's 'ardour' gave some individuals cause for complaint. He defends his father's apparent reversal of view by arguing that Sir James remained true to his principles as the French Revolution changed its course. It is notable that this is the argument W was to use in his own defence to James Losh, 4 Dec. 1821. *LY*, II. 96–9.
71. William Hazlitt, 'Sir James Mackintosh' in *The Spirit of the Age* (1825). *Howe*, XI. 98.
72. C to W [*c*.10 Sept. 1799]. *CL*, I. 527.
73. *1799 Prelude*, II. 478–96.
74. William Cowper, *The Task* (1785), III. 108–11:

> I was a stricken deer that left the herd
> Long since; with many an arrow deep infixt
> My panting side was charged when I withdrew
> To seek a tranquil death in distant shades.

75. The quotation is from the Preface to *The Excursion* (1814). It is impossible to date the composition of the 'Prospectus' with certainty. For the most advanced discussion and text of the earliest manuscript see *Home at Grasmere*, 19–22, 255–63. See also *Reed*, II. 656–65 and Jonathan Wordsworth, 'On Man, on Nature, and on Human Life', *RES* 31 (1980), 2–29. I accept the latter's conclusion that the 'Prospectus' was written *c*.Jan.

1800. It has been illuminated by Thomas McFarland, 'Wordsworth on Man, on Nature, and on Human Life', *SIR* 21 (1982), 601–18 and is the corner-stone of M. H. Abrams's wide-ranging study *Natural Supernaturalism* (New York, 1971).

### CHAPTER 7

1. William Wilberforce, *Journey to the Lake District from Cambridge: A Summer Diary 1779*, ed. C. E. Wrangham (Stocksfield, 1983), 48. For Gray and further helpful references see *Home at Grasmere*, 38 n. On 9 Apr. 1801 W described Grasmere to Anne Taylor as 'a very beautiful spot of which almost every body has heard'. *EY*, 327. In the exhibition catalogue *The Discovery of the Lake District 1750–1810* (Grasmere, 1982), Peter Bicknell and Robert Woof give an excellent brief account of the many artists who were drawn to the happy valley.
2. Visitors now generally approach Grasmere from the south along the main road which keeps to the level of the lake. The old road referred to here diverges at the quarry below White Moss, now a car park.
3. *DQR*, 128.
4. Details given W and DW to C, 24 [and 27] Dec. [1799]. *EY*, 273–81.
5. 'Prospectus' to *The Recluse*, MS 1, ll. 39–40. *Home at Grasmere*, 259.
6. All quotation from *Home at Grasmere*, MS B. The dating of *Home at Grasmere* is problematic. In addition to Darlington's full discussion, the reader should see Jonathan Wordsworth, 'On Man, on Nature, and on Human Life', *RES* NS 31 (1980), 2–29, who concludes that '*Home at Grasmere* is, almost in its entirety, a poem of 1800', p. 28.
7. 'It was an April Morning . . .', ll. 17–30. *Gill: Oxf. W.*, 200.
8. See *PW*, II. 479–84.
9. *Home at Grasmere*, MS B, ll. 620–8.
10. 'A Discourse on Pastoral Poetry', *The Poems of Alexander Pope*, ed. John Butt (London, 1963), 120.
11. MS B, ll. 109–13.
12. The description of John is *Home at Grasmere*, MS B, ll. 866–72. DW's recollection is in a letter to Lady Beaumont, 29 Nov. 1805. *EY*, 649.
13. *MWL*, 3.
14. W to James Losh, 16 Mar. 1805. *EY*, 563. The reader who can visit Grasmere will find helpful maps to this and other named spots in David McCracken, *Wordsworth and the Lake District: A Guide to the Poems and their Places* (Oxford, 1984).
15. 'When first I journeyed hither', ll. 88–91. *Gill: Oxf. W.*, 223. DW to Jane Marshall [15 and 17] Mar. [1805]. *EY*, 559. W to James Losh, 16 Mar. 1805. *EY*, 563.
16. C to TP [21 Mar. 1800]. *CL*, I. 582.
17. C to Humphry Davy, 25 July 1800. *CL*, I. 612.
18. C to William Godwin [8 Sept. 1800]. *CL*, 620. For the description of Hartley, C to Samuel Purkis, 29 July 1800. *CL*, I. 615.
19. *Home at Grasmere*, MS B, ll. 81–2.
20. This account refers to W's letters of 8 [June], [mid-July], [29] July, [*c.*1 Aug.], [*c.*4 Aug.], [*c.*13 Aug], 15 Sept., [*c.*27 Sept.], [*c.*2 Oct.], [*c.*6 or 7 Oct.], [*c.*15 Oct.], [18 Dec.], [19 Dec. 1800], and 9 Apr. [1801]. Publication details for this and later editions are presented in W. J. B. Owen, 'Costs, Sales, and Profits of Longman's Editions of Wordsworth', *Library*, 5th ser. 12 (1957), 93–107.
21. C to TP, 24 July 1800, and to Daniel Stuart [*c.*30 Sept. 1800]. *CL*, I. 608, 627.
22. This note is printed at length here as it was omitted from the *Prose*.

23. Note to *The Thorn*. Gill: *Oxf. W.*, 593–4.

24. *CL*, I. 602. n. 1.

25. W to Biggs and Cottle [*c*.6 or 7 Oct. 1800]. *EY*, 305.

26. W to Longman and Rees, 18 Dec. 1800. *EY*, 309. C to Humphry Davy, 9 Oct. and to Josiah Wedgwood, 1 Nov. 1800. *CL*, I. 631, 643. To Davy C mentions a plan to publish W's *The Pedlar* and *Christabel* together. It is doubtful whether this was ever more than a sop for C. It is hard to imagine a more unlikely pairing of poems.

27. See *CL*, I. 631, n. 2 and C to Francis Wrangham, 19 Dec. 1800. *CL*, I. 658.

28. RS to C, 4 Aug. 1802. *SL*, II. 190. See also R. S. Woof, 'Wordsworth's Poetry and Stuart's Newspapers: 1797–1803', *SIB* 15 (1962), 149–89.

29. W's MS note quoted *Prose*, I. 167.

30. C to Daniel Stuart [*c*.30 Sept. 1800]. *CL*, I. 627.

31. Charles Lamb to W [30 Jan. 1801]. *Marrs*, I. 266–7.

32. Preface to *Lyrical Ballads* 1800. *Prose*, I. 120. Further quotations are taken from this source and will not be referenced separately.

33. Hazlitt's 'William Wordsworth' in *The Spirit of the Age. Howe*, XI. 87. In *Burke, Paine, Godwin, and the Revolution Controversy* (Cambridge, 1984), Marilyn Butler argues, pp. 226–9, that the essence of the theory behind *Lyrical Ballads* and the Preface 'seems to emanate from the radical tradition'. In *The Politics of Language 1791–1819* (Oxford, 1984), Olivia Smith discusses in detail the radical concern to establish the legitimacy of egalitarian writing.

34. W to Charles James Fox, 14 Jan. 1801. *EY*, 315.

35. Charles Lamb to Thomas Manning [15 Feb. 1801]. *Marrs*, I. 272–3.

36. JW to DW, 21 Feb. [1801]. *JWL*, 92. W to RW [*c*.23 June 1801]. *EY*, 337.

37. W to Longman and Rees, 18 Dec. 1800. *EY*, 310.

38. W to Anne Taylor, 9 Apr. 1801. *EY*, 328, referring to Preface to *Lyrical Ballads* 1800. *Prose*, I. 132.

39. For some account of W's revisions, publishing practice, and attitudes to his text see Stephen Gill, 'Wordsworth's Poems: The Question of Text', *RES* NS 34 (1983), 172–90 and ' "Affinities Preserved": Poetic Self-reference in Wordsworth', *SIR* 24 (1985), 531–49.

40. 28 Oct. 1800: '. . . I was carrying some cold meat to Wm in the Fir-grove'. *Journals*, 48.

41. Robert Anderson, *The Works of the British Poets, with Prefaces, Biographical and Critical* (13 vols., London and Edinburgh, 1792–5). In the IF note to *Yarrow Visited* W acknowledged the importance of this anthology to him: 'Through these volumes I became first familiar with Chaucer; and so little money had I then to spare for books, that, in all probability, but for this same work, I should have known little of Drayton, Daniel, and other distinguished poets of the Elizabethan age and their immediate successors, till a much later period of my life'. *Grosart*, III. 70.

42. For details see *Peter Bell*, 12–14.

43. See *Norton Prelude*, 516.

44. See *The Ruined Cottage*, introduction 24–30 and text 327–67.

45. DW's journal entries for 26 Jan., 30 Jan., 2 Feb., 11 Feb. 1802.

46. *To the Small Celandine*, 57–64.

47. *Written in March: While Resting on the Bridge at the Foot of Brother's Water*, 1–10.

48. DW journal entry 20 Apr. 1802.

49. For a sensitive account of the art of these poems see Jared R. Curtis, *Wordsworth's Experiments with Tradition: The Lyric Poems of 1802* (Ithaca and London, 1971).

50. Preface to *Lyrical Ballads* 1802. Gill: *Oxf. W.*, 609. See n. 52.

51. Gerard Manley Hopkins to Robert Bridges, 15 Feb. 1879. *The Letters of Gerard Manley Hopkins to Robert Bridges*, ed. Claude Colleer Abbott (London, 1935; 2nd edn. 1955), 66.

52. All quotation from the 1802 Preface will be taken from the text published in *Gill: Oxf. W.* and not referenced further. That text marks off the major additions of 1802. Paul M. Zall in his edition of *Literary Criticism of William Wordsworth* (Lincoln, Nebr., 1966) prints, as editors ideally should, both 1800 and 1802 Prefaces in full.

53. John Wilson's letter of 24 May 1802 is reprinted in Mary Gordon, *Memoir of Christopher North* (2 vols., Edinburgh, 1862), I. 38–48. It is worth noting that whereas a letter from Mary Hutchinson might be answered the day it was received, W delayed a week before replying to Wilson and then took two days to complete a considered response. See *Journals*, 129 and 131–2.

54. W to John Wilson [7 June 1802]. *EY*, 355.

55. C to TP, 17 May 1801. *CL*, II. 732.

56. See C's letter of 3 Feb. 1801 to Humphry Davy and the letters on philosophy to Josiah Wedgwood of 18 Feb., 24 Feb., and two undated of Feb. 1801. *CL*, II. 670–2, 677–703.

57. See *CN*, I. 1575, in which C recalls how on 24 Nov. 1799, on his way back to London from his tour of the Lakes with W, he had pressed Sara's hand and felt love's arrow, 'poisoned alas! and hopeless'.

58. C to TP, 7 Sept., 5 Oct., and 21 Oct. 1801. *CL*, II. 755–7, 763–6; 769–71.

59. DW to MH, 16 Apr. and to MH and SH, 14 June [1802]. *EY*, 351 and 363.

60. DW journal entry 10 Oct. 1801.

61. DW's journal entries for 21 Dec., 22 Dec., 25 Dec. 1801, 29 Jan., 6 Feb., 19 Mar. 1802.

62. DW journal entry 21 Apr. 1802. Quotation from the poem is to the text in *CL*, II. 790–8.

63. For texts of both versions see *P2V: Curtis*, 123–9, 317–23, and for discussion, with texts, the same author's op. cit. n. 49, pp. 97–113, 186–95.

64. Reference to 'Prospectus' to *The Recluse*. *Home at Grasmere*, MS B, l. 1013; and *1805 Prelude*, XII. 376–7.

65. C to W [c.10 Sept. 1799]. *CL*, I. 527.

66. C to RS, 29 July 1802. *CL*, II. 830.

67. C to TP, 14 Oct. 1803. *CL*, II. 1013.

68. *1805 Prelude*, I. 229.

69. DW journal entries 11 Feb. and 9 Mar. 1802. For a seminal discussion of Wordsworth and Jonson see Anne Barton, 'The Road from Penshurst: Wordsworth, Ben Jonson and Coleridge in 1802', *EIC* 37 (1987), 209–33.

70. *Home at Grasmere*, MS B, ll. 171–3.

71. DW journal entry 17 Mar. 1802.

72. DW to Mary Hutchinson, 29 Apr. 1801. *EY*, 331–2.

73. Thomas McFarland, *Romanticism and the Forms of Ruin: Wordsworth, Coleridge, and Modalities of Fragmentation* (Princeton, 1981), ch. 3.

74. As n. 72, p. 330. 'Sara's Rock' has been restored and now stands in the grounds of the Wordsworth Museum at Grasmere.

75. W. B. Yeats, *A Prayer for my Daughter*, 47–8:

> O may she live like some green laurel
> Rooted in one dear perpetual place.

76. DW journal entry 29 May 1802. Published in 1807 as *A Farewell*. *Gill. Oxf. W.*, 278–9.

77. DW to RW, 10 June [1802]. *EY*, 359.
78. C to RS, 2 Sept. 1802. *CL*, II. 860.
79. C to RS, 31 Dec. 1801. *CL*, II. 778.
80. For the most readable account of the circumstances of C's marriage see John Cornwell, *Coleridge: Poet and Revolutionary 1772–1804* (London, 1973), ch. 3.
81. *CPW*, II. 969.
82. *MWL*, n. 13, p. xxv.
83. See *Reed*, II. 197 and *EY*, 368–73, 382–4, 686–92 for correspondence between W and RW.
84. DW journal entry 30 June 1802.
85. DW entry for 10 July 1820, *Journal of a Tour of the Continent* (1820), *DWJ*, II. 8.
86. *To a Friend, Composed near Calais: On the Road Leading to Ardres, August 7th, 1802.*
87. W to ?, ? Nov. 1802. *EY*, 378. See also the IF note quoted *Gill: Oxf. W.*, 706 in which W recalls taking fire as DW read him Milton's sonnets on 21 May 1802.
88. Quoted Woof, op. cit. n. 28. p. 155.
89. Charles Lamb to W [30 Jan. 1801]. *Marrs*, I. 267.
90. Charles Lamb to Thomas Manning, 24 Sept. 1802. *Marrs*, II. 69. On W, Lamb, and London see Lucy Newlyn, '"In City Pent": Echo and Allusion in Wordsworth, Coleridge, and Lamb, 1797–1801', *RES* NS 32 (1981), 408–28.
91. *1805 Prelude*, VII. 682.
92. For details see *JWL*, 30–3.
93. DW to Jane Marshall, 29 Sept. 1802. *EY*, 377.
94. DW journal entry 4 Oct. 1802.

CHAPTER 8

1. C to Richard Sharp, 15 Jan. 1804. *CL*, II. 1032.
2. DW to CC [7 or 14 June 1803]. *EY*, 391.
3. DW to CC, 17 July [1803]. *EY*, 396.
4. MW to W, 1 Aug. 1810. *WLL*, 46.
5. *MWL*, p. xxi.
6. As n. 4, p. 49.
7. As n. 1.
8. Reported by Barron Field in his *Memoirs of Wordsworth*, ed. Geoffrey Little, Australian Academy of the Humanities: Monograph 3 (Sydney, 1975), 100.
9. Ketcham, *JWL*, 34–5, 37, gives a fuller account of John's money-raising and the strain it imposed.
10. W and DW to RW [17 July] 1803. *EY*, 398–9.
11. W to DW, 6 [and 16 Sept.] 1790. *EY*, 36.
12. DW to CC, 17 July [1803]. *EY*, 397.
13. DW to LB, 7 Aug. 1805. *EY*, 617. MW to W, as n. 4, p. 49.
14. *DWJ*, I. 255. For an illustrated account of the tour see Donald E. Hayden, *Wordsworth's Travels in Scotland* (Tulsa, 1985), 9–30.
15. *DWJ*, I. 286.
16. According to Aubrey De Vere W used this expression in a conversation on Scott's methods of composition. See *Grosart*, III. 487.
17. 'self-sufficing . . . solitude': *1805 Prelude*, II. 78. Hazlitt quotation: *Howe*, XIX. 11.
18. W to Thomas De Quincey, 29 July 1803. *EY*, 400. W to C [May or June 1808]. *MY*, I. 245.

19. *DWJ*, I. 406.
20. J. G. Lockhart, *Memoirs of the Life of Sir Walter Scott* (7 vols., Edinburgh and London, 1837–8), I. 404. DW quotation, *DWJ*, I. 395.
21. DW to LB, 4 May 1805. *EY*, 590.
22. The first 2-volume edition of *The Minstrelsy* appeared in Feb. 1802, and the second, in 3 volumes, in May 1803. Richard Sharp made W a present of the second in Apr. 1804. See *EY*, 469.
23. *Minstrelsy of the Scottish Border* (2 vols., Kelso, 1802), I, pp. xcv–xcvi.
24. W to SGB, 31 Aug. 1804. *EY*, 499.
25. W to Walter Scott, 16 Oct. 1803. *EY*, 413–14.
26. Lockhart, op. cit. I. 407. W to Walter Scott, 16 Jan. [1805]. *EY*, 530.
27. Lockhart, op. cit. I. 405.
28. HCR records that in 1812 W 'assented to the observation "that the secret of Scott's popularity is the vulgarity of his conceptions, which the million can at once comprehend" '. *HCR*, I. 82. To Scott himself W wrote of *Marmion* that he had read it with pleasure, but: 'I think your end has been attained; that it is not in every respect the end which I should wish you to propose to yourself, you will be well aware from what you know of my notions of composition, both as to matter and manner'. 4 Aug. [1808]. *MY*, I. 264. For Scott's comment quoted see *The Journal of Sir Walter Scott*, ed. W. E. K. Anderson (Oxford, 1972); 259; entry 1 Jan. 1827.
29. W to William Rowan Hamilton, 27 Oct. [1831]. *LY*, II. 441.
30. IF note to *Yarrow Revisited*. Grosart, III. 138. The poems are *Yarrow Revisited, On the Departure of Sir Walter Scott from Abbotsford, for Naples*, and *Musings near Aquapendente*. Scott is also a powerful presence in *Extempore Effusion upon the Death of James Hogg*.
31. Scott, *Journal*. Anderson, op. cit. 278. For a well-documented life of Beaumont (1753–1827) see Felicity Owen and David Blayney Brown, *Collector of Genius: A Life of Sir George Beaumont* (New Haven and London, 1988).
32. W to SGB, 14 Oct. 1803. *EY*, 406–11.
33. Ibid. p. 407.
34. SGB to W, 24 Oct. 1803. WL.
35. W to SGB, 31 Aug. 1804. *EY*, 499.
36. W to SGB, 25 Dec. 1804. *EY*, 517.
37. *Farington*, VI. 2271; entry 21 Mar. 1804.
38. C to RS, 12 Mar. [1803]. *CL*, II. 937.
39. W to Walter Scott, 16 Oct. 1803. *EY*, 412–13.
40. RS to John Rickman [mid-Apr. 1807]. *Curry*, I. 449.
41. John Keats to Benjamin Bailey, 23 Jan. 1818. *Keats*, I. 210.
42. W to SGB, 3 June 1805. *EY*, 595.
43. *A Complaint*, 9–10. Gill: *Oxf. W.*, 330.
44. C to RS, 14 Aug. 1803. *CL*, II. 974–5.
45. *CN*, I. 1463: 'What? tho' the World praise me, I have no dear Heart that loves my Verses—I never hear them in snatches from a beloved Voice, fitted to some sweet occasion, of natural Prospect, in Winds at Night—.' Quotation in text is entry 1606.
46. C to TP, 14 Oct. 1803. *CL*, II. 1013.
47. *CN*, I. 1616.
48. C to TP, 15 Jan. 1804. *CL*, II. 1036.
49. DW to CC, 15 Jan. 1804. *EY*, 430.
50. C to TP, 15 Jan. 1804. *CL*, II. 1035.
51. As n. 1, p. 1034.

52. *CN*, I. 1825 and 1826.
53. C to the Wordsworths, 4 Apr. 1804. *CL*, II. 1115–17.
54. Ibid. p. 1116.
55. W to James Losh, 16 Mar. 1805. *EY*, 566.
56. C to TP, 14 Oct. 1803. *CL*, II. 1013.
57. *CN*, I. 1616.
58. *Monthly Mirror*, 11 (June 1801), 389.
59. *Edinburgh Review*, 1 (Oct. 1802), 63–83.
60. W to John Thelwall [mid-Jan. 1804]. *EY*, 432. A lengthy note on p. 431 gives details of the attack on Thelwall.
61. Ibid. 433. Details of one of Bayley's offences in his *Poems* (London, 1803) are given *EY*, 413. Another was surely the Preface to his volume, which claims that 'a Preface is but the acknowledgment of a fraud committed by the writer upon the purchaser of his book—an apology for having entrapped the reader into the purchase of that which is unworthy of the price paid for it'.
62. DW and W to C [9 Dec. 1803]; W to Walter Scott, 16 Oct. 1803; W to Thomas De Quincey; 6 Mar. [1804]. *EY*, 424, 413, 455.
63. C to Joseph Cottle [28 May 1798]. *CL*, I. 412.
64. C to RS [8] Jan. 1803. *CL*, II. 913.
65. C to Richard Sharp, 15 Jan. 1804. *CL*, II. 1034.
66. *CN*, I. 1801.
67. *1799 Prelude*, II. 473–96, 509–14.
68. *1799 Prelude*, I. 453.
69. DW to CC, 21 Nov. [1803]. *EY*, 423.
70. The poem can be read as the MS E version in *The Ruined Cottage*, 382–448.
71. W to Thomas De Quincey, 6 Mar. [1804]. *EY*, 454.
72. Both poems have a complicated textual history. For details see *P2V: Curtis*, introduction *passim* and 104–10, 269–77. All quotations represent the poems as copied into MS 44, the volume prepared for Coleridge in the spring of 1804.
73. See *Gill: Oxf. W.*, 713–14 and article cited there on p. xxx for details of printing. When published in 1807 the poem was simply titled *Ode*. The more elaborate title and epigraph were added in 1815, at the suggestion, according to a late claim, of HCR. *HCR*, II. 838–9.
74. C to the Wordsworths, 8 Feb. 1804. *CL*, II. 1060.
75. *CN*, I. 1705, 1717.
76. *Chandler*, 249. The whole argument of Chandler's book supports his reading of the *Ode to Duty* and I am much indebted to it.
77. W to SGB, 20 July 1804. *EY*, 491.
78. For an account of the work see *Norton Prelude*, 516–20.
79. W's description of the themes of *The Recluse* to James Tobin, 6 Mar. [1798]. *EY*, 212.
80. W to C, 29 Mar. [1804]. *EY*, 464.
81. W to SGB, 1 May 1805. *EY*, 586.
82. C to the Wordsworths, 8 Feb. 1804. *CL* II. 1060.
83. The manuscript is MS 44 of the Wordsworth Library. DW to C, 6 Mar. 1804. *EY*, 448. DW to CC [25] Mar. 1804. *EY*, 459.
84. DW to LB, 25 [and *c*.30] May 1804. *EY*, 477.
85. W to Francis Wrangham [24 Jan.–7 Feb. 1804]. *EY*, 436.
86. DW to LB, 29 Nov. [1805]. *EY*, 650.
87. W to SGB, 3 June 1805. *EY*, 594.

88. DW to CC, 9 Oct. [1803]. *EY*, 403. Under the threat of invasion the Addington government appealed for Volunteers, organized locally, to defend the country. Beaumont raised a corps and in his letter to W of 24 Oct. 1803 wrote: 'I give you the highest credit for your military exertions[,] such things suit not Poets or Painters, but I am afraid we must all come to it at last'. WL.
89. W to SGB, 14 Oct. 1803. *EY*, 409.
90. *Essays*, I, p. cviii.
91. C to SGB, 1 Oct. 1803. *CL*, II. 998–1005.
92. Written in 1794, *Wat Tyler* remained in manuscript until published, without Southey's knowledge, in 1817. For a succinct account of the publication and ensuing controversy see Jack Simmons, *Southey* (London, 1945), 158–61.
93. W to Francis Wrangham [24 Jan.–7 Feb. 1804]. *EY*, 436.
94. William Frend, *Patriotism: or, The Love of our Country: An Essay* (London, 1804), 208. The book is now in WL.
95. *Anticipation* was published in the *Courier*, 28 Oct. 1803 and reprinted in the newly founded patriotic magazine the *Anti-Gallican*, 11 (1804), 426, forwarded to the press by Sir George Beaumont at W's suggestion. See *EY*, 411.
96. W to ?, Nov. 1802. *EY*, 379. It was assumed throughout the period of the invasion threat that the rebellious Irish would give assistance to the French if occasion arose, despite the new political situation brought about by the Act of Union of 1800.
97. *1805 Prelude*, IX. 123–5:

> [I] thus did soon
> Become a patriot—and my heart was all
> Given to the people, and my love was theirs.

98. *1805 Prelude*, IX. 511–26.
99. *Edinburgh Review*, 1 (1802), 66.
100. *The Old Cumberland Beggar*, l. 146.
101. *1805 Prelude*, X. 645–56.
102. RS to Thomas Southey, 22 Aug. 1805. *Curry*, I. 392. Southey described Somerville as 'a nondescript mulish compound of butcher and courtier, both bad breeds, and the mixture worse than either'.
103. *1805 Prelude*, X. 883–8.
104. *1805 Prelude*, X. 835–43.
105. Note to *The Thorn* published *Lyrical Ballads* 1800. *Gill: Oxf. W.*, 593.
106. W to SGB, 3 June 1805. *EY*, 595.
107. Preface of 1815. *Prose*, III. 37.
108. An adequate bibliography on Coleridge and Imagination would run to hundreds of titles. The interested reader should consult James Engell, *The Creative Imagination: Enlightenment to Romanticism* (Cambridge, Mass. and London, 1981) and Thomas McFarland, *Originality and Imagination* (Baltimore and London, 1985).
109. *1805 Prelude*, VI. 154–7.
110. *1805 Prelude*, XIII. 103–5.
111. *1805 Prelude*, XIII. 106–19.
112. JW to W, 24 Jan. [1805]. *JWL*, 155.
113. W to RS [12 Feb.] 1805. *EY*, 542.
114. W to James Losh, 16 Mar. 1805; to RW, 11 Feb. 1805. *EY*, 566, 540.
115. W to SGB [c.23] Feb. 1805. *EY*, 547–8.
116. W to Walter Scott, 7 Mar. 1803. *EY*, 553.

117. W to SGB, 12 Mar. 1805. *EY*, 556.
118. W to James Losh, 16 Mar. 1805. *EY*, 565.
119. Ibid.
120. W to CW [13 Feb. 1805]. *EY*, 543.
121. W to SGB, 12 Mar. 1803. *EY*, 556.
122. Ibid. 557.
123. W to SGB [*c*.23] Feb. 1805. *EY*, 547.
124. W to SGB, 1 May 1805. *EY*, 586.
125. *1805 Prelude*, XIII. 149–52.
126. *1805 Prelude*, XIII. 424–7.
127. *1805 Prelude*, XIII. 446–52.
128. W to SGB, 3 June 1805. *EY*, 594.
129. DW to LB, 4 May 1805. *EY*, 592.
130. DW to LB, 11 June 1805. *EY*, 598.
131. Ibid. 598. Also IF note to *Elegiac Verses in Memory of My Brother, John Wordsworth*, quoted *P2V: Curtis*, 682.
132. As n. 130, p. 599.
133. Printed from manuscript in *P2V: Curtis*, 608–14 and *Gill: Oxf. W.*, 307–12.
134. John's body was recovered on 20 Mar. 1805 and buried at Wyke Regis. *JWL*, 50–1.
135. W to James Losh, 16 Mar. 1805. *EY*, 565.
136. *Essays upon Epitaphs*, I. *Prose*, II. 58.
137. Having lost the tenancy of Gallow Hill, Tom Hutchinson moved into Park House farm, about two miles above the northern end of Ullswater, in 1804. Sara lived with her brother there until she joined the Wordsworths for an extended visit in early 1806 which heralded her eventual permanent residence with them.
138. RS, to Charles Wynn, 16 Apr. 1805. *SL*, II. 328.
139. The 750 copies of the quarto edition sold so rapidly that a second edition was called for and exhausted in the same year. Nearly 15,000 copies had been sold after five years. See Edgar Johnson, *Sir Walter Scott: The Great Unknown* (2 vols., London, 1970), I. 225.
140. On 10 Apr. 1806. Scott described W to Anna Seward as 'virtuous, simple, and unaffectedly restricting every want & wish to the bounds of a very narrow income'. *The Letters of Sir Walter Scott*, ed. H. J. C. Grierson (12 vols., London, 1932–7), I. 287.
141. IF note to *Musings near Aquapendente*. Grosart, III. 86. W also recalls that Davy grew bored by the literary emphasis of the conversation and left the two poets on the mountain top, making his way to Grasmere alone.
142. Twice to LB, 27 Oct. and 4 Nov. 1805. *EY*, 634, 636, DW indicates that W has been pondering publication of short poems, but decided against it. Within two years he had published such a collection, *Poems, in Two Volumes*.
143. Noted in *PW*, III. 444.
144. *P2V, Curtis*, 415. W acknowledged his indebtedness in a note in 1807. For a particularly valuable memoir see Hilton Kelliher, 'Thomas Wilkinson of Yanwath, Friend of Wordsworth and Coleridge', *British Library Journal*, 8 (1982), 147–67.
145. *1805 Prelude*, XIII. 98–102.

CHAPTER 9

1. DW to CC, 25 Dec. 1805. *EY*, 659.
2. *1805 Prelude*, I. 649. *Tintern Abbey*, 74 and 83.
3. DW to LB, 25 Dec. 1805. *EY*, 664.

4. W to Hans Busk, 6 July 1819. *MY*, II. 547. Quoted *Benjamin*, 3. Quotation will be given, without further reference, from the reading text of MS 1.

5. W to SGB, 17 and 24 Oct. 1805. *EY*, 628. DW to LB, 19 Jan. 1806. *MY*, I. 2.

6. DW to CC, 2 Mar. 1806. *MY*, I. 10, 12.

7. W to CC, 28 Mar. 1806. *MY*, I. 19.

8. Reports of the occasion differ. Rogers remembered a less dramatic encounter—see *Recollections of the Table-talk of Samuel Rogers: First Collected by the Revd. Alexander Dyce*, ed. Morchard Bishop (London, 1952), 61. W's is the account he was giving in old age, according to Mrs John Davy, quoted George McLean Harper, *William Wordsworth: His Life, Works, and Influence*, 2 vols. (London, 1916), II. 113.

9. The picture, now privately owned, is reproduced in colour as frontispiece to Hugh Sykes Davies, *Wordsworth and the Worth of Words*, ed. John Kerrigan and Jonathan Wordsworth (Cambridge, 1987).

10. In a letter of 29 June 1806 SGB explained: 'I did not show you Peele Castle tho' it was in the room, because I thought it might raise painful sensations in your mind . . .'. Quoted *Reed*, II. 321. The picture W probably saw (SGB also made a larger oil) is reproduced in colour in *William Wordsworth and the Age of English Romanticism*, ed. Jonathan Wordsworth, Michael C. Jaye, and Robert Woof (New Brunswick, London, Grasmere, 1987), 177.

11. W to Francis Wrangham. 7 Nov. 1806. *MY*, I. 89.

12. W to LB, 3 June 1806. *MY*, I. 35.

13. W to SGB, 1 Aug. 1806. *MY*, I. 64.

14. *Home at Grasmere*, p. 100.

15. W to SGB, 8 Sept. 1806. *MY*, I. 78-9.

16. DW to CC, 6 Nov. 1806. *MY*, I. 86-7.

17. W to C, 18 Sept. 1806. *MY*, I. 80.

18. DW to LB [late Sept. 1806]. *MY*, I. 84.

19. W to SGB, 8 Sept. 1806. *MY*, I. 79.

20. W to Francis Wrangham, 7 Nov. 1806. *MY*, I. 88.

21. W to SGB, 5 Aug. 1806. *MY*. I. 68.

22. W to Lord Lowther, 19 Aug. 1806. *MY*, I. 74-5.

23. SGB to W, 6 Nov. 1806. Quoted with W's reply of 10 Nov. *MY*, I. 92.

24. W to SGB, 17 and 24 Oct. 1805. *EY*, 627.

25. W to LB [? Dec. 1806]. *MY*, I. 112-20. For an illustrated account of the garden see Russell Noyes, *Wordsworth and the Art of Landscape* (Bloomington, 1968).

26. As n. 25. p. 268.

27. Author of *Essays on the Picturesque* (Hereford, 1794), Uvedale Price (1747-1829) contributed significantly to the later development of landscape aesthetics. Lady Beaumont won him over to Wordsworth. The two men met at Price's seat at Foxley in Herefordshire in 1810. Price's hobby-horse was the correct pronunciation of Greek and Latin and in later years he repeatedly sought the poet's advice on the topic. (MS letters, Pierpont Morgan Library.)

28. *Murdoch*, 81. Murdoch's is a brief but seminal discussion.

29. DW to LB, 23 Dec. 1806. *MY*, I. 121.

30. *CPW*, II. 1081-4. I quote from the MS version printed in the *Norton Prelude*, 542-5.

31. *CN*, II, entries 2938 and 2998.

32. In 1806 W declared 'the subject' of his *Address to the Sons of Burns* as 'too private and sacred a nature for the publick eye'. It is revealing that he seems to have had no such reservations about *A Complaint*. See *P2V: Curtis*, p. xxvii.

33. DW to CC, 16 Feb. 1807. *MY*, I. 137. C to Daniel Stuart [c.5 May 1807]. *CL*, III. 14.

34. DW to LB, 4 Nov. 1805. *EY*, 636.
35. *P2V: Curtis* gives a full account of the extremely complicated passage from manuscript to print.
36. Not published in 1807. Printed *P2V: Curtis*, 527.
37. Ibid. 36.
38. Ibid. 56.
39. C to RS, 29 July 1802. *CL*, II. 830.
40. C to TP, 14 Oct. 1803. *CL*, II, 1013.
41. John Harden was a comfortably off gentleman artist. From 1804 onwards he and his family maintained a steady friendship with the Wordsworths. For a lively account see Daphne Foskett, *John Harden of Brathay Hall, 1772–1847* (Kendal, 1974).

    Farington noted that 'Constable remarked upon the high opinion Wordsworth entertains of Himself'. *Farington*, VIII. 3164, entry 12 Dec. 1807. For rest of entry see p. 33 n.
42. DW to CC, 19 July 1807. *MY*, I. 156.
43. For details see Howard Colvin, J. Mordaunt Crook, Terry Friedman, *Architectural Drawings from Lowther Castle Westmorland*, Architectural History Monographs, 2 (London, 1980). For photographs of what is now one of the most spectacular ruins in the country see Geoffrey Beard, *The Greater House in Cumbria* (Kendal, 1978).
44. Lady Holland found W 'much superior to his writings, and his conversation is even beyond his abilities'. She gathered that he was 'preparing a manual to guide travellers in their tour amongst the Lakes' and found that W did not hesitate to insist that he was right when they differed 'as to the effects produced by *white* houses on the sides of the hills'. *The Journal of Elizabeth Lady Holland (1791–1811)*, ed. the Earl of Ilchester (2 vols., London, 1908), II. 231.
45. DW to Jane Marshall, 19 Sept. 1807. *MY*, I. 165.
46. T. Percy, *Reliques of Ancient English Poetry* (3 vols., London, 1765). Joseph Nicholson and Richard Burn, *The History and Antiquities of the Counties of Westmorland and Cumberland* (2 vols., London, 1777). Thomas Dunham Whitaker, *The History and Antiquities of the Deanery of Craven* (London, 1805).
47. See IF note, *PW*, III. 543. Also W's letter about the poem to Wrangham, 18 Jan. 1816.
48. W to Walter Scott [before 15 June 1806]. *MY*, I. 41.
49. In late life W was at pains to emphasize that comparison of his poem with any of Scott's was 'inconsiderate'. In the IF note cited above he declares that their approach to historical materials was 'entirely different'. But in 1808 C confessed to W: 'I cannot get rid of the Fear, that it will be talked of as an imitation of Walter Scott'. 21 May 1808. *CL*, III. 111.
50. W to LB, 21 May 1807. *MY*, I. 145–51.
51. W to C, 19 Apr. 1808. *MY*, I. 222–3.
52. W to Francis Wrangham, 18 Jan. 1816. *MY*, II. 276.
53. DW to Jane Marshall [23 Feb. 1808]. *MY*, I. 198.
54. *CN*, III, entry 3304.
55. W to C [late May or early June 1808]. *MY*, I. 239–45. The turmoil of C's feelings can be gauged from the fact that on 9 Mar. 1808 he had confided to Catherine Clarkson that Wordsworth's 'friendship and that of his Sister Dorothy's are the only eminent Events, or *Passages*, of my Life . . . in which I have not been cruelly deceived or deluded'. *CL*, III. 79.
56. C to W [21 May 1808]. *CL*, III. 107–15.

57. Deirdre Colman prints Jeffrey's replies and discusses the significance of this very important exchange in 'Jeffrey and Coleridge: Four Unpublished Letters', *Wordsworth Circle*, 18 (Winter 1987), 39–45.
58. W to SGB, 8 Apr. 1808. *MY*, I. 209.
59. Ibid. 208.
60. DW to CC [about 18 Apr. 1808]. *MY*, I. 214–16.
61. *A Narrative Concerning George and Sarah Green of the Parish of Grasmere Addressed to a Friend* was edited with a useful introduction by E. De Selincourt (Oxford, 1936). It has been reissued, with additional notes and illustrations, as *The Greens of Grasmere*, ed. Hilary Clark (Wolverhampton, 1987).
62. DW to CC, 19 July 1807 and 28 Mar. 1808. *MY*, I. 156 and 203.
63. DW to W, 31 Mar. 1808. *MY*, I. 207.
64. C to W, 21 May 1808. *CL*, III. 110.
65. W to Richard Sharp, [*c*.7 Feb. 1805]. *EY*, 534.
66. RS to Mary Barker, 2 Feb. 1808. Quoted *Reed*, II. 372. HCR to Thomas Robinson [Mar. 1808]. *HCR*, I. 52.
67. *Monthly Literary Recreations*, 3 (July 1807), 65–6; *Critical Review*, 3rd ser. 11 (Aug. 1807), 399–403; *Satirist*, 1 (Nov. 1807), 188–91; *Edinburgh Review*, 11 (Oct. 1807), 214–31; *Eclectic Review*, 4 (Jan. 1808), 35–43; *Cabinet*, 3 (Apr. 1808), 249–52.
68. Authorship ascribed to Richard Mant, later Bishop of Down and Connor. See W's letter to EQ, 10 Sept. 1830. *LY*, II. 324.
69. *Examiner*, 28 Aug. 1808. *British Critic*, 33 (Mar. 1809), 298–9.
70. W to Francis Wrangham, 12 July and 4 Nov. 1807. *MY*, I. 155 and 174. Southey is quoted in the second letter.
71. *Edinburgh Review*, 12 (Apr. 1808), 133. Jeffrey's zeal in harrying the 'Lakers' was considerable, but given his political and cultural milieu not unintelligible. For a thoughtful discussion see L. G. Mitchell, 'The *Edinburgh Review* and the Lake Poets 1802–1810', in *Essays Presented to C. M. Bowra* (Oxford, 1970), 24–38. Also Peter F. Morgan, *Literary Critics and Reviewers in Early Nineteenth Century Britain* (London, 1983), and John Clive, *Scotch Reviewers: The Edinburgh Review, 1805–1815* (London, 1957).
72. W to Samuel Rogers, 29 Sept. 1808. *MY*, I. 268.
73. Jeffrey returned to the attack while writing on Burns, *Edinburgh Review*, 13 (Jan. 1809), 249–76 contrasting his 'manly lines' with W's 'affectation of babyish interjections, and all the puling expletives of an old nurserymaid's vocabulary' (p. 276). He ridicules a number of poems specifically in what Catherine Clarkson called 'a paragraph [which] for insolence & malice exceeds all that I ever read'. Quoted *Reed*, II. 423.
74. W to LB, 21 May 1807. *MY*, I. 145–51.
75. W to C, 19 Apr. 1808. *MY*, I. 222–3.
76. W to RS [Jan. 1808]. *MY*, I. 162.
77. DW to Jane Marshall, 11 May 1808. *MY*, I. 236.
78. Preface to *Lyrical Ballads* (1800). *Prose*, I. 126–7. It is very revealing that in the letter to C, 19 Apr. 1808, *MY*, I. 223–4, W said he wanted to prefix to *The White Doe* lines from Samuel Daniel's *Musophilus* (1599), where the poet, defending poetry and humane learning against the scorn of the world, declares himself satisfied if he find only one fit reader in the present age.
79. W to SGB [Feb. 1808]. *MY*, I. 195.
80. See *Tuft of Primroses*, pp. 39–56 for 'reading text'.
81. W to Samuel Rogers, 29 Sept. 1808. *MY*, I. 269.

82. DW to Jane Marshall, 4 Dec. 1808. *MY*, I. 280.

83. DW to CC, 28 Dec. [1807]. *MY*, I. 183.

84. As n. 82.

85. DW to Thomas De Quincey, 1 May 1809. *MY*, I. 325.

86. See *Lindop*, esp. 134–55 and for De Quincey's own account of his approach to Grasmere *DQR*, 119–206.

87. DW to CC, 8 Dec. 1808. *MY*, I. 283.

88. *Memoir and Letters of Sara Coleridge*, ed. [Edith Coleridge] (2 vols., London, 1873), I. 18–19.

89. Ibid. 19.

90. W to LB, 21 May 1807. *MY*, I. 147.

91. See *Lindop*, 154. On 17 June 1806 Farington had noted that a mutual friend had reported that W's conversation proved him 'strongly disposed to Republicanism. His notions are that it is the duty of every Administration to do as much as possible to give consideration to the people at large, and to have *equality* always in view; which though not perfectly attainable, yet much has been gained towards it and more may be.' *Farington*, VII. 2785.

92. *Prose*, I. 352. All quotation in the following section is drawn from *The Convention of Cintra* presented in this fully edited text, pp. 193–415.

93. Ibid. 196.

94. DW to Jane Marshall, 4 Dec. 1808. *MY*, I. 280–1. C to Daniel Stuart, 3 Jan. 1809. *CL*, III. 160.

95. C to Daniel Stuart, 2 May 1809. *CL*, III. 205.

96. *DQL*, 132; letter 1 Apr. 1809. W's reply is [7 Apr. 1809]. *MY*, I. 317–19.

97. W and Sara Hutchinson to De Quincey, 5 May 1809. *MY*, I. 330.

98. W to Walter Scott, 14 May 1808. *MY*, I. 237.

99. W to Francis Wrangham [end Mar. 1809]. *MY*, I. 312.

100. C to Daniel Stuart, 13 June 1809. *CL*, III. 214.

101. For discussion of *Cintra* see Gordon Kent Thomas, *Wordsworth's Dirge and Promise* (Lincoln, Nebr., 1971) and *Chandler*.

102. *Farington*, IX. 3478, entry for 6 June 1809.

103. Ibid. 3482.

104. From the pamphlet's title-page. A facsimile is printed *Prose*, I. 221.

105. *Friend*, II. 13.

106. W to TP, 30 Mar. and 30 May 1809. *MY*, I. 310 and 352.

107. DW to CC, 15 June and W to Daniel Stuart [14 June] 1809. *MY*, I. 356 and 359.

108. DW to CC, 28 Mar. 1808. *MY*, I. 206. For a very early photograph of Wilson's now demolished house, Elleray, see *Murdoch*, 37.

109. The expedition was commemorated in a dreadful poem *The Angler's Tent*, which is introduced by a Wordsworth epigraph, is heavy with Wordsworthian echoes, and which honours Wordsworth and his family by direct mention. Published in *The Isle of Palms and Other Poems* (Edinburgh, 1812). For biography see Mrs Gordon, *Memoir of Christopher North: By his Daughter* (2 vols., Edinburgh, 1862); Elsie Swann, *Christopher North (John Wilson)* (Edinburgh, 1934).

110. *Friend*, No. 17 (14 Dec. 1809). *Friend*, II. 222–9. The letter was composed jointly with Wilson's friend Alexander Blair. See *Prose*, II. 3–5, 26–34 for introduction and text.

111. W's reply is found with introduction and commentary in *Prose*, II. 6–41; quotation p. 15.

112. Ibid. 21. The *Friend* was much concerned with Truth won from Error. On 4 Dec. 1808 Richard Watson, Bishop of Llandaff (the object of W's polemic in 1793), had reminded

C that he was identified with 'democratic principles' and urged him to consider 'whether, in the outset of your undertaking, it would not be of use publickly to abandon those principles . . .' C devoted early numbers to doing just that and, most significantly, in no. 11 (26 Oct. 1809), printed the now-famous passage from *The Prelude*, X. 689–727, 'Bliss was it in that dawn to be alive', in a context that makes it unambiguously a declaration of how easily youth is betrayed into folly by generous ideals. See *Friend*, II. 147–8 and 472.

113. DW to LB, 28 Feb. 1810. *MY*, I. 391.

114. The *Essays upon Epitaphs* are found *Prose*, II. 45–119. Further page references will not be given.

115. In a letter to Wrangham of [end Mar. 1809] W declares how 'tenderly attached' he is to the Church of England, which is identified in his vision with the 'people of England'. *MY*, I. 313.

116. The vital phrase from the 1802 Preface to *Lyrical Ballads*: '[the Poet] is the rock of defence of human nature; an upholder and preserver, carrying every where with him relationship and love'. *Gill: Oxf. W.*, 606.

117. *Friend*, 10 Aug. 1809; 28 Sept. 1809; 26 Oct. 1809; 16 Nov. 1809; 21 Dec. 1809; 28 Dec. 1809.

118. W to TP, 30 May 1809. *MY*, I. 352.

119. DW to CC, 12 Apr. 1810. *MY*, I. 399–400. On 16 Aug. 1808 and 22 Feb. 1809 Joanna Hutchinson reported how ill Sara seemed. Quoted *Reed*, II. 394 and 409.

120. DW to CC, 12 Nov. 1810. *MY*, I. 450.

121. C to W [*c*.10 Sept. 1799]. *CL*, I. 527.

122. There is some uncertainty about the dating of W's work on the developing *Excursion*. In placing it as essentially 1809 I agree with *Johnston*, 263 and note.

123. *The Excursion*, III. 383–7. *PW*, V. 86. Quotations are from the first edition of 1814. Since that text does not number lines, however, references are given to *PW* to help the reader find quoted passages.

124. *The Excursion*, II. 853–61. *PW*, V. 72.

125. *The Excursion*, IV. 10–11; 22. *PW*, V. 110. The argument unfolds throughout Book IV.

126. Most evidently at IV. 1206–75. W also incorporates verse written during composition of *The Prelude*, notably the passage beginning 763, 'We live by Admiration, Hope, and Love'. See *Norton Prelude*, 500–5.

127. John Keats to BH, 10 Jan. 1818. *Keats*, I. 203.

128. W to J. Pering, 2 Oct. 1808. *MY*, I. 271–2. But see n. 44.

129. For an important and finely illustrated account of Green, his work, and his local friendships see M. E. Burkett and J. D. G. Sloss, *William Green of Ambleside: A Lake District Artist (1760–1823)* (Kendal, 1984). W esteemed Green as an artist and valued him greatly as a friend. On his death in 1823 W composed the epitaph for his tombstone in Grasmere Churchyard.

130. For text, introduction, and commentary see *Prose*, II. 123–465. The Wordsworth Library has recently acquired Wilkinson's drawings for the engravings by William Wells.

131. See Peter Bicknell and Robert Woof, *The Discovery of the Lake District 1750–1810* (Grasmere, 1982), 38–9. Quoting from a manuscript diary, they reveal that in July 1799 James Plumptre of Cambridge thought of going out of his way up the Duddon solely on account of W's note to *An Evening Walk* (1793), 171: 'Mr. Wordsworth recommends the scenery on the Duddon: a Poet's word in scenes of nature is great'. Lack of time prevented Plumptre from following the note up.

132. The work was first acknowledged when published as *A Topographical Description of the Country of the Lakes, in the North of England*, annexed to *The River Duddon* (1820). It was reissued with slightly varied title separately in 1822 and 1823. For the fifth edition of 1835 it was titled *A Guide through the District of the Lakes in the North of England*. The reader should attempt to find the very fine *Illustrated Wordsworth's Guide to the Lakes*, ed. Peter Bicknell (Exeter, 1984).
133. 'Glad sight wherever new with old', *PW*, II. 154–5.
134. DW to RW, 9 Jan., and to CC, 12 Apr. [1810]. *MY*, I. 385 and 399.
135. W was first disabled by inflammation of the eyelids in Jan. 1805. The attacks, which recurred throughout his life, prevented reading or writing and made him hypersensitive to light. From 1820 he regularly wore a green eye-shade to alleviate the attacks.

CHAPTER 10

1. DW to CC, 12 May [1811]. *MY*, I. 488. C to Richard Sharp, 24 Apr. [1812]. *CL*, III. 389.
2. RS to W [Apr. 1812]. *Curry*, II. 33.
3. It is clear from C's notebook entry 3991 and his letter to J. J. Morgan [27 Mar. 1812] that, shattered as he was by W's reported comments on his conduct, he was more deeply wounded by Montagu's assertion that he had been 'commissioned' or 'authorised' to transmit them.
4. C to J. J. Morgan [12 Oct. 1811]. *CL*, III. 338.
5. *CN*, III, entry 3991.
6. *CN*, III, entry 4006.
7. DW to CC, 12 May [1811], *MY*, I. 490; DW to MW and WW, 3 May [1812], *MY*, II. 14.
8. As n. 1.
9. For example, W was parodied in *Rejected Addresses* (1812) [James and Horace Smith]; *Leaves of Laurel: or, New Probationary Odes, for the Vacant Laureateship* (1813) [John Hamilton Reynolds]; *Rejected Odes: or, Poetical Hops, Steps, and Jumps of a Dozen Popular Bards* (1813) [John Agg].
10. *Farington*, X. 3829. Entry for 20 Dec. 1810.
11. W to MW, 7–9 May 1812. *WLL*, 136.
12. SH to John Monkhouse, 28 Mar. [1812]. *SHL*, 45.
13. W to Basil Montagu, 16 Nov. [1811]. *MY*, I. 515.
14. DW to CC, 16 June 1811. *MY*, I. 497.
15. As n. 11, p. 134.
16. W to CC, 6 May [1812]. *MY*, II. 16.
17. As n. 1. W was so upset by this letter that he copied out the pertinent section. See DW's letter of 3 May 1812, *MY*, II. 16.
18. Crabb Robinson's record of the statement is found *HCR: Books*, I. 74–5. W's memorandum for DW, quoted here, is *WLL*, 139.
19. C to TP [13 Feb. 1813). *CL*, III. 437. In a bitter and self-pitying letter of 8 Oct. 1822 to Thomas Allsop C even adds a further accusation to his charge against W, the cause of one of the 'four griping and grasping Sorrows' of his life. *CL*, V. 249–50.
20. W to MW, 1 June 1812. *WLL*, 213. W's letters from London are amongst his most attractive. What he saw at parties repelled but fascinated him, especially one woman, whose 'Breasts were like two great hay-cocks or rather hay stacks, protruding themselves upon the Spectator . . .'.

21. W to MW, 9–13 May 1812. *WLL*, 147.

22. W to CC, 18 June [1812]. *MY*, II. 26. MW's letter to W, 29–31 May 1812, contains a most moving annotation, added in later years by Mary, as she read over a happy letter to her husband, written in ignorance of her daughter's death. See *WLL*, 198.

23. W to RS [2 Dec. 1812]. *MY*, II. 51. Four years later W was offering comfort in return on the death of Southey's 9-year-old son Herbert. See *MY*, II. 305–7.

24. See Book III, 584–679 and app. crit., *PW*, V. 94–9. W drew on this composition, and on his observation on how Mary and the children behaved, for *Maternal Grief*, a poem not published until 1842. *PW*, II. 51–4, 477.

25. 'Recollections of Wordsworth', *Grosart*, III. 489. Understandably W worried all the more about his surviving children. Both DW and SH thought he spoiled Willy: 'it would distress you to see how a pale look of that childs has the power to disturb his father . . . he will scarcely suffer the wind of heaven to come near him & he watches him the day through', SH reported to her sister Joanna, 24 Nov. 1815. *SHL*, 87. DW was brisker: 'Oh! Sara it is ten thousand pities he should be so spoiled'. To SH, 8 Apr. 1815. *MY*, II. 225.

26. DW to Mrs Cookson [31 Dec. 1812]; DW to CC, 6 Apr. [1813]. *MY*, II. 59, 88.

27. *Edinburgh Review*, 20 (Nov. 1812), 438 (review of *Rejected Addresses*) and 304 (review of Crabbe's *Tales*).

28. Looking for a Grasmere purchase W had dealings with a schoolfellow, William Pearson, who had made good. For W's far from charitable note about him and further details see *TWT*, 359–60, and for the earlier history of Rydal Mount, *TWT*, 26 n.

29. SH to Thomas Monkhouse [16 May 1813]. *SHL*, 53.

30. DW to CC [about 14 Sept. 1813]. *MY*, II. 114.

31. Unpublished Preface to *Don Juan. Lord Byron: The Complete Poetical Works*, ed. Jerome J. McGann (5 vols., continuing, Oxford, 1980–), V. 82.

32. Published in *Dramatic Romances and Lyrics* (1845). The young Browning most probably had in mind W's Civil List pension of 1842 and the Laureateship the following year. By then, however, most people did not mind honours done to the elderly poet and those who would have minded, Shelley and Byron for example, were dead. But taking on the Distributorship affected his reputation *at once*. In 1814 Peacock (writing as 'P M O'Donovan') attacked Byron, Southey, *et al.* in *Sir Proteus: A Satirical Ballad*. The poem is throughout a parody of W's 'simple' style, of a by now familiar kind. What is new is the attack on political turncoat language heard 'in the *receipts* of the *stamp-commissioners* for the county of *Westmorland*'.

33. Jessy Harden in 1806. Daphne Foskett, *John Harden of Brathay Hall, 1772–1847* (Kendal, 1974), 32.

34. With his clerk John Carter's salary and £100 a year to his predecessor, Mr Wilkin, to pay, W at first made about £200 a year. For a fuller account of his duties than is possible here, see *Moorman*, II. 244–53.

35. W to Daniel Stuart, 13 Oct. 1812. *MY*, II. 48.

36. W to Walter Scott, 7 Nov. 1805. *EY*, 641.

37. SH to Mrs Hutchinson, 2 Sept. [1814]. *SHL*, 79. Gillies gives an account of his first meeting and conversation with Wordsworth about the nature of the poetic life in his *Memoirs of a Literary Veteran* (3 vols., London, 1851), II. 139–44.

38. Edith C. Batho, *The Ettrick Shepherd* (Cambridge, 1927), is still the best brief account of Hogg. In 1816 he parodied W's blank verse very finely in three pieces in his collection *The Poetic Mirror*.

39. Charles Lamb to W [28 Apr. 1815]. *Marrs*, III. 147.

40. After the death of Scott's daughter Sophia W wrote to her husband John Lockhart about his clear memory of how charmingly she showed them round Abbotsford. 27 Apr. [1838]. *L Y*, III. 562.

41. The garden, which is still delightful, is open to visitors. For its earlier history and for W's gardening see *Murdoch*, 83–7 and Ken Lemmon, 'Poet's Hands on the Landscape: Wordsworth's Garden at Rydal Mount, Cumbria', *Country Life*, 3 May 1984, 1240–2. W was assisted in his work as gardener and Distributor of Stamps by John Carter, who, taken on as clerk and general assistant, became W's right-hand man for the rest of his life.

42. MW to W, 6 June 1812. *WLL*, 238.

43. DW to CC, 9 Oct. [1814]. *MY*, II. 158.

44. As n. 42, p. 239.

45. DW to CC, 2 Mar. [1817]. *MY*, II. 372.

46. W to CW, 26 Nov. [1814]. *MY*, II. 171: 'he has done a foolish thing in marrying one so young; not to speak of the disgrace of forming such a connection with a servant, and that, one of his own'.

47. Comments from MW, DW, and SH from 1811 onwards reveal progressive disenchantment. See e.g. *SHL*, 36–7 and 88; *MY*, II. 80–1; *MWL*, 24–5. For a full account see *Lindop*, 203–20 and *DQL*, 203–36.

48. *Edinburgh Review*, 19 (Feb. 1812), 373.

49. Ibid. 374–5.

50. For an excellent discussion of the later books of *The Excursion* see *Johnston*, 285–329.

51. W's plans for classification were outlined in some detail to C [5 May 1809]. *MY*, I. 334–6. Quotation from the Preface of 1815, *Prose*, III. 28.

52. The lines form the triumphant conclusion to MS B of *Home at Grasmere*, the first book of the first part of *The Recluse*.

53. In a letter to CC, 9 Oct. [1814], DW makes the best of it. Her argument goes: Hazlitt rhapsodizes about the philosophical parts but thinks the narratives 'a dead weight'; ordinary readers will, of course, prefer the narratives; therefore Hazlitt's review must do good, because it will bolster what would flag unaided. *MY*, II. 160.

54. DW to CC, 11 Nov. [1814]. *MY*, II. 165.

55. *Edinburgh Review*, 24 (Nov. 1814), 1–31. Published 6 Dec. 1814.

56. Most of the reviewers added, unknowingly, to the sharpness of their criticism by praising what had been written 16 years earlier, the narrative of *The Ruined Cottage*.

57. W to CC [Jan. 1815]. *MY*, II. 191.

58. For the Preface of 1815 see *Prose*, III. 23–52.

59. *Monthly Review*, 78 (Nov. 1815), 225. For a discussion of the 1815 Preface see W. J. B. Owen, *Wordsworth as Critic* (Toronto and London, 1969), 151–87; for the classification and arrangement, James Scoggins, *Imagination and Fancy: Complementary Modes in the Poetry of Wordsworth* (Lincoln, Nebr., 1966).

60. For the *Essay* see *Prose*, III. 55–107. Quotation p. 67. On 7 May 1815 James Hogg told John Murray that he heard that the literary world was 'laughing immoderately at Mr Wordsworth's new prefaces which certainly excell all that ever was written in this world in egotism vanity and absurdity'. Alan Lang Strout, *The Life and Letters of James Hogg, the Ettrick Shepherd* (Lubbock, Tex., 1946), 103.

61. *HCR: Books*, I. 165.

62. *Edinburgh Review*, 25 (Oct. 1815), 355–63.

63. For Jeffrey and his circle see refs. in ch. 9 n. 71.

64. *Prose*, III. 111–36. The introduction and commentary explain the complicated circumstances of composition. Quotation from a letter of James Gray to W, cited 111.

Gray endeared himself by fulsome praise of *The Excursion*: 'I question if ever there was a creation of genius that contained so many profound views of the intellectual nature of man and so many simple, pathetic and enchanting pictures of life. The pathos of the story of Margaret and the Solitary is really quite intolerable'. Letter 28 Nov. 1815. WL.

65. *Edinburgh Monthly Magazine* [afterwards *Blackwood's Edinburgh Magazine*], I (June, 1817), 265. Wilson, writing anonymously, also claims that W 'is in all respects, immeasurably inferior, as an intellectual being, to the distinguished person [Jeffrey] whom he so foolishly libels' (266). Wilson contributed a further highly laudatory article and another violent attack. The explanation of this bizarre behaviour is unknown, but it certainly helped the new magazine acquire a reputation for vigorous journalism.

66. *Edinburgh Review*, XXVI (June, 1816), 460.

67. W and DW to CC [31 December 1814]; W and DW to SH, 18 February [1815]. *MY*, II, 182, 202, 205.

68. Charles Lamb to W [7 January 1815]. *Marrs*, III, 129. DW to Priscilla Wordsworth, [27 February 1815]. *MY*, II, 207.

69. *British Critic*, 3 (May 1815), 450. DW to CC, 28 June [1815], 243.

70. W to RS [Jan. 1815]. *MY*, II. 187.

71. W to CC [Jan. 1815]. *MY*, II. 188–9.

72. James Montgomery's review in the *Eclectic Review*, 2nd ser. III (Jan. 1815), 13–39, is astonishing. There is much praise, but the core of the piece is the demand to know whether the poet is saved. Montgomery paraphrases W's 'ideas' about salvation and declares them true but decidedly not enough. 'We do not mean to infer, that Mr. Wordsworth excludes from his system the salvation of man, as revealed in the Scriptures, but it is evident that he has not made "Jesus Christ the chief corner-stone" of it.' There is much more in this vein. It is an indication of how hungry the Wordsworths were for a crumb of comfort that they took it from this review. In an unpublished letter of 29 May 1815 (Berg Collection, New York Public Library) Southey wrote to Montgomery that W wanted him to be told how gratified he was 'by the full & liberal praise which it awarded him,—and by the amiability & discrimination which were shown, but above all by the spirit which is breathed, which is so unlike the prevailing tone of criticism'. Unlike Montgomery, William Cookson did not feel obliged to put *The Excursion*'s religion to too rigorous an examination. On 20 Aug. 1814 he wrote to the nephew he had once so disapproved of: 'For my own Part I am peculiarly gratified . . . on account of the amiable and cheering light in which you have represented revealed religion'. WL.

73. C to LB, 3 Apr. 1815. *CL*, IV. 564.

74. W to C, 22 May 1815. *MY*, II. 238.

75. C to W, 30 May 1815, *CL*, IV. 574–5.

76. W to C, 6 Mar. [1804]. *EY*, 452.

77. C to W [28 July 1803]. *CL*, II. 957.

78. Lamb's phrase is found in his explanation of why he thought it an error to preface the *Lyrical Ballads* themselves with a polemical manifesto. W's phrase comes from his explanation in 1798 of why systematic expositions of moral philosophy fail to achieve a beneficial end. Charles Lamb to W, [30 Jan. 1801]. *Marrs*, I. 266–7. W [*Essay on Morals*], *Prose*, I. 103.

79. By June 1816 only 331 copies of *The Excursion* had been sold. The remaining 36 copies of the edition of 500 were divided with the author in 1834. *Poems* was a little more successful, the edition of 500 selling out by 1820. But by the end of 1817 only 352 copies had been sold. See W. J. B. Owen, 'Costs, Sales, and Profits of Longman's Editions of Wordsworth', *Library*, 5th ser. 12 (1957), 93–107. On 5 May 1814 W compared his

likely sales with those of Scott and Byron. *MY*, II. 148. He had cause to be rueful. Scott's *The Lay of the Last Minstrel* went to 15 editions by 1815 and 1,800 quartos of *The Lord of the Isles* sold in the first month of publication in 1815. Murray sold 25,000 copies of Byron's *The Corsair* (1814) in little over a month and paid £2,000 for the copyright of *Childe Harold* and *The Prisoner of Chillon*.

80. In 1812 the *Edinburgh Review*, 20, p. 280, had commented on Crabbe's audience: 'In this country, there probably are not less than two hundred thousand persons who read for amusement or instruction among the middling classes of society'. The accuracy of this figure is unimportant. What is significant is that this comment, in a review of poetry, registers awareness of a new readership. Hard evidence that it was 'Eager for information and instruction, conservative in so far as [its] taste for poetry was concerned' is to be found in the 40 editions of Cowper published between 1817 and 1825. 'No other poet, with the exception of Scott and Byron, was so frequently reprinted and none had such a sustained run of popularity.' Norma Russell, *A Bibliography of William Cowper to 1837* (Oxford, 1963), p. xvi.

81. DW to SH, 18 Feb. [1815]; DW to C C, 15 Aug. [1815]. *MY*, II. 202, 247.

82. W to CC, 31 Dec. [1814]. *MY*, II. 181.

83. W. J. Fox to HCR [6 Feb. 1815]. *HCR*, I. 83.

84. C to TP, 14 Oct. 1803. *CL*, II. 1013. John Keats to BH, 8 Apr. 1818. *Keats*, I. 265.

85. W was anxious to see Lord Lonsdale, who had recently offered him the Collectorship of Customs at Whitehaven. This substantial office would have meant more work and removal, yet again, to Whitehaven. W was clear that he did not want the post but felt that the offer was so splendid that he ought to present his refusal in person.

86. Hunt's attitude to W was and remained unsettled. He had ridiculed him in *The Feast of the Poets*, published in the *Reflector*, 2 (1811), 313–23, republished 1814, but in response to W's gift of *Poems* (1815) had affirmed that he was 'one of the most ardent of [W's] general admirers'. The 3rd edition of *The Feast* ( July 1815) reversed most of the poem's earlier judgements and the meeting on 11 June 1815 seems to have been cordial. See *HCR: Books*, I. 169. Hunt's account of it in his *Autobiography* (1850) was captious. See *The Autobiography of Leigh Hunt*, ed. J. E. Morpurgo (London, 1949), 252–6.

87. *Pamphleteer*, 5 (Feb. 1815), 462. Talfourd named one of his sons William Wordsworth Talfourd.

88. *Ion* circulated in private publication in 1835, was performed in 1836, and thereafter published.

89. Barron Field, *Memoirs of Wordsworth*, ed. Geoffrey Little (Sydney, 1975), 122.

90. W annotated much of Field's manuscript, but troubled both by its inaccuracies and by the fear that it would revive old controversies, he told Field on 16 Jan. 1840 that he was 'decidedly against' publication. Little, ed. cit. 17.

91. Both quotations from a letter of John Scott to W, 7 Feb. 1816. WL. For Scott see Patrick O'Leary, *Regency Editor: Life of John Scott* (Aberdeen, 1983).

92. *Haydon*, I. 450, entry for 13 June. The cast was taken on 11 June. See Reed, II. 606. For a life see Eric George, *The Life and Death of Benjamin Robert Haydon* (Oxford, 1948; 2nd edn. with additions by Dorothy George, 1967).

93. *Haydon*, I. 451. Haydon too named a son after the poet—Frederic Wordsworth Haydon.

94. BRH to W, 18 Nov. 1816. WL.

95. W to BRH, 21 Dec. 1815. *MY*, II. 259. The poem was published in the *Champion*, 1 Apr. 1816. W had been inspired by Haydon's letter of 27 Nov. 1815: 'I shall ever remember with secret delight the friendship with which you honour me, and the interest you take in my success. God grant it ultimately be assured! I will bear want,

pain, misery and blindness, but I will never yield one step I have gained on the road I am determined to travel over.' *Haydon: Corr.*, II. 19. On receiving the sonnet Haydon wrote in his diary, 'It is impossible to tell how I felt, after the first blaze of joy, feeling as it were lifted up in the great eye of the World, and feeling nothing more could be said of one . . .'. *Haydon*, I. 491–2. To W he wrote, 'You are the first English poet who has ever done complete justice to my delightful Art'. 29 Dec. 1815. *Haydon: Corr.*, II. 20–2.

96. For an account of the refused loan and Haydon's very interesting letter in full see Stanley Jones, 'B. R. Haydon on Some Contemporaries: A New Letter', *RES* NS 26 (1975), 183–9.

97. *Haydon*, I. 451.

98. Mary and Charles Lamb to Mrs Morgan and Charlotte Brent [22 May 1815]. *Marrs*, III. 161, 167 n.

99. 15 June 1815 HCR noted down what he understood Hazlitt to have done: 'It appears that Hazlitt, when at Keswick, narrowly escaped being ducked by the populace, and probably sent to prison for some gross attacks on women . . .'. *HCR: Books*, I. 169. On 10 Feb. 1816 he noted after a party: 'Hazlitt was bitter, as he always is, against Wordsworth'. Ibid. 179.

100. BRH to W, 15 Apr. 1817. WL. Quoted *Moorman*, II. 281.

## CHAPTER 11

1. RS to Henry Southey, 23 Aug. 1815. *SL*, IV. 121–2.

2. W substantially revised the poems for his 1845 volume. See *PW*, III. 151–63 and notes. I refer to the 1816 first edition by line and page, as line numbers are not given in that volume.

3. Carl Woodring, *Politics in English Romantic Poetry* (Cambridge, Mass., 1970), 141.

4. *Thanksgiving Ode . . .* (1816), pp. iii–iv. This important 'Advertisement' is omitted from *Prose*.

5. RS to General William Peachey, 22 Jan. 1813. *Curry*, II. 45. RS to Neville White, 8 Jan. 1816. *SL*, IV. 147.

6. W to MW, 9–13 May 1812; 23 May 1812. *WLL*, 148, 179.

7. W to CC, 4 June [1812]. *MY*, II. 21.

8. W to John Scott, 22 Feb. 1816. *MY*, II. 281.

9. Ibid.

10. *1810*, 1–3. Published in *Poems*, 1815, as XXVII of the second series of *Sonnets Dedicated to Liberty*. A note in the *Thanksgiving Ode* volume declares it 'a sequel' to the sonnet series.

11. W to Charles Pasley, 28 Mar. 1811. *MY*, I. 477–8. The whole letter, pp. 473–82, is astonishing, nearly 4,000 words long. To Southey's mind, Pasley's book 'ought to be not only in the hands but in the heart of every Englishman'. RS to Ebenezer Elliott, 7 Feb. 1811. *SL*, III. 298.

12. *Thanksgiving Ode*, 160–1. First edn. p. 11.

13. As n. 11, pp. 481–2. The 'very animated exhortation to the more general diffusion of education among the lower orders' in *Excursion*, IX. 336–62, 1814 edn., p. 402, had been one of the few passages quoted with approbation by Jeffrey. *Edinburgh Review*, 24 (Nov. 1814), 27.

14. *Thanksgiving Ode*, 137–44. First edn., p. 10.

15. For a passionate letter about Englishness see W to John Scott, 18 Apr. 1816. *MY*, II. 304.

16. The *Thanksgiving Ode* sold so badly that in 1834 almost half of the edition of 500 remained. As Longman handled the publication on a commission basis this time, W lost money, as the costs fell to him. See W. J. B. Owen, 'Costs, Sales, and Profits of Longman's Editions of Wordsworth', *Library*, 5th ser. 12 (1957), 98–9.

17. Southey the Laureate had published *Carmen Triumphale: For the Commencement of the Year 1814* and *Carmen Aulica: Written in 1814, on the Arival of the Allied Sovereigns in England*. Ascribing the badness of the first to the numbing effect of the Laureate's wreath, the *Edinburgh Review*, 22 (Jan. 1814) had called it 'a strange farrago of bad psalmody and stupid newspapers . . . a base imitation of Sternhold and the Daily Advertiser' (p. 448).

18. The volume is full of echoes; these are only the most striking examples. In order: *Thanksgiving Ode*, 2, echoes 'I wandered lonely as a Cloud'; *Ode, Composed in January 1816*, 105, echoes *Extract from the Conclusion of a Poem, Composed upon Leaving School*, published *Poems* (1815); *Elegiac Verses*, the final poem in the 1816 volume, recalls *Elegiac Stanzas . . . Peele Castle*.

19. *Journals of Mary Shelley*, ed. Paula R. Feldman and Diana Scott-Kilvert (2 vols., Oxford, 1987), I. 25. Quotation from Shelley's sonnet *To Wordsworth*.

20. W to John Scott, 25 Feb. [1816]. *MY*, II. 282. W to James Losh, 4 Dec. 1821. *LY*, I. 97.

21. *Descriptive Sketches* was a political poem, but its generalized zeal for liberty was neither seditious nor sanguinary enough to have embarrassed W had it been spotlighted in 1817. Excerpts from both poems had been printed in the 1815 collection headed 'Juvenile Pieces'.

22. W to William Mathews, 23 May and 8 June [1794]. *EY*, 118–20, 123–9.

23. Samuel Taylor Coleridge, *Lay Sermons*, ed. R. J. White (Princeton and London, 1972). *The Statesman's Manual* was followed in Mar. 1817 by *A Lay Sermon*.

24. Review of *Christabel*, *Edinburgh Review*, 27 (Sept. 1816), 67.

25. *Examiner*, 8 Sept. 1816; 29 Dec. 1816; 12 Jan. 1817. *Edinburgh Review*, 27 (Dec. 1816). *Howe*, VII. 114–18, 119–28, 128–9, XVI. 99–114.

26. 'Parliamentary Reform', *Quarterly Review*, 16 (Oct. 1816), 225–78. RS calls on the government to 'curb sedition in time; lest it should be called upon to crush rebellion and to punish treason' (p. 276).

27. W to William Mathews [*c*.24 Dec. 1794 and 7 Jan. 1795]. *EY*, 137.

28. For details see *Curry*, II. 150–1.

29. Southey defended himself in *A Letter to William Smith, Esq., M.P.*, which provoked a further literary flare-up in May. W's use of 'Renegado' in his letter to Losh recalls Smith's description of Southey. For Hazlitt see *Howe*, VII. 168–76.

30. *Essays*, II. 449–60.

31. *Morning Chronicle*, 22 Mar. 1817. *Essays*, III. 277–9. *Examiner*, 30 Mar. 1817. *Howe*, VII. 176–86.

32. DW to CC, 13 Apr. 1817. *MY*, II. 380.

33. C to RS, 29 July 1802. *CL*, II. 830.

34. *BL*, I. 1. This edition gives a full account of composition.

35. W told R. P. Gillies, 19 [Sept.] 1817 (*MY*, II. 399), that he had only skimmed parts of *BL*. Revisions made for his collection of 1820, however, reveal that W had absorbed C's comments.

36. *Edinburgh Review*, 28 (Aug. 1817), 488–515. Jeffrey's defence is 507–12. There is some dispute as to whether this review was by Hazlitt, but what matters here is that it was certainly thought to be his doing.

37. W to William Mathews [8] June [1794]. *EY*, 123.

38. C to R. H. Brabant, 29 July 1815. *CL*, IV. 579. Cited *BL*, I. p. liv.
39. W to C, 22 May 1815. *MY*, II. 238.
40. *BL*, II. 156.
41. For details see *PW*, IV. 97–8 and 423–4.
42. The 1817 poems were published in 1820 in *The River Duddon . . . and Other Poems*. W referred to the *Ode: Intimations* in a note printed immediately after *Composed . . . Beauty* (p. 197).
43. DW to CC, 13 Apr. [1817]. *MY*, II. 379.
44. SH to Dora Wordsworth, 4 Jan. 1818. *SHL*, 115.
45. Ibid. 114.
46. *Haydon*, II. 147–8, 171, 173.
47. Ibid. 182. SH told Dora on 4 Jan. 1818, 'Mr Haydon intends to make a chalk drawing of your Father for your Mother', and Haydon insisted to W, 12 Sept. [1818], 'I consider the drawing *hers* & *hers* only'. WL. See *Blanshard*, 55–60, 149–50.
48. John Keats to BRH, 10 Jan. 1818. *Keats*, I. 203. Haydon's copy of *The Excursion* is now in Cornell University Library. Against Book IV, 851ff., Haydon noted: 'Poor Keats used always to prefer this passage to all others'.
49. The volume is now in Princeton University Library. The inscribed title-page is reproduced in the *Princeton University Library Chronicle*, 38 (Winter–Spring 1977), plate 40.
50. BRH to Edward Moxon, 29 Nov. 1845. *The Keats Circle*, ed. Hyder Edward Rollins (2 vols., Cambridge, Mass., 1948), II. 143–4. For a fuller account, published after this chapter was written, see Jack Stillinger, 'Wordsworth and Keats', in *The Age of William Wordsworth: Critical Essays on the Romantic Tradition*, ed. Kenneth R. Johnston and Gene W. Ruoff (New Brunswick and London, 1987), 172–6.
51. Ibid.
52. Robert Gittings, *John Keats* (London, 1968), 167. *Moorman*, II. 318. In her *Recollections of a Tour Made in Scotland A.D. 1803* DW notes an occasion when W's use of 'pretty' in praise was mistaken for 'a half-censure'. *DWJ*, I. 320.
53. Stanley Jones, 'B. R. Haydon on Some Contemporaries: A New Letter', *RES* NS 26 (1975), 183–9.
54. *Haydon*, II. 173–6. The phrenological embellishment comes in Haydon's autobiography in *Life of Benjamin Robert Haydon, Historical Painter: From his Autobiography and Journals*, ed. Tom Taylor (3 vols., London, 1853), I. 353–6.
55. *HCR: Books*, I. 214.
56. Ibid. 213, 215.
57. W to Lord Lonsdale, 13 Dec. [1817]. *MY*, II. 404–5.
58. MW to Thomas Monkhouse, 23 Jan. 1818. *MWL*, 32–3.
59. Henry (later Lord) Brougham (1778–1868). The best account is still Arthur Aspinall, *Lord Brougham and the Whig Party* (Manchester, 1927).
60. W to Lord Lonsdale, 18 Jan. 1818. *MY*, II. 411.
61. W to Viscount Lowther, 16 Mar. 1818. *MY*, II. 441.
62. John Keats to Tom Keats, 25–7 June, and to George and Georgiana Keats, 27, 28 June 1818. *Keats*, I. 299, 302–3. 'What think you of that—Wordsworth versus Brougham!! Sad—sad—sad—and yet the family has been his friend always. What can we say?' It is a curious fact of literary history that, as Keats was travelling north via the Lakes, the young Thomas Carlyle was going south. He wandered about Grasmere in August 1818.
63. See *Lindop*, 224–37 and *DQL*, 278–327. W sought advice about the practicality of setting up a newspaper. Stuart warned of all the difficulties, but agreed that a new organ was needed. He wrote, 9 Mar. 1818, 'I recollect seeing the Kendal Paper about 15

months ago & thinking it among the most furiously jacobinical in the Kingdom'. WL. Stuart's grotesque judgement is a good indication of how polarized opinion had become. For evidence of how the Lowthers influenced the local press see Arthur Aspinall, *Politics and the Press 1780–1850* (London, 1949), 354–60.

64. For texts and annotation which gives details of the whole campaign see *Prose*, III. 139–228. 'Bombastes Furioso', see *MY*, II. 471 n. 2.

65. See Aspinall, op. cit. n. 59, 13–14. For W's verse squib on this topic, which plays on the pronunciation of Brougham as 'Broom', i.e. yellow, see *PW*, IV. 377–8.

66. Hone specialized in pamphlet satire which made a striking appeal visually, through illustration and typographical variety, as well as through the boldness of its assault on topical issues and personalities. He was notorious for having parodied the Creed and the Litany. When prosecution on charges of blasphemous libel failed, DW declared that 'The acquittal of Hone is enough to make one out of love with English Juries'. *MY*, II. 410. W agreed. He was strongly in favour of the Blasphemous and Seditious Libels Bill enacted in Dec. 1819. Hone was dangerous because he appealed to the lower orders. See Olivia Smith, *The Politics of Language 1791–1819* (Oxford, 1984), 154–201: 'The Power of the Press and the Trials of William Hone'.

67. *Prose*, III. 160, 186.

68. DW's eye-witness account of Brougham's entry to Kendal on 23 Mar. 1818. *MY*, II. 443.

69. DW to CC, 29 Mar. [1818]. *MY*, II. 454.

70. SH to Thomas Monkhouse, 13 Apr. 1818; 10 Apr. 1820. *SHL*, 132, 180.

71. CW to W, 17 Apr. 1819. WL. Cited *MY*, II. 532–3. CW was particularly anxious that W should not accept Lord Lonsdale's recent offer to make him a magistrate.

72. Reynolds was a sincere admirer of W. As a young man he had sent him a poem and thanked him for the 'deep pleasure your Poems have given me' (12 Nov. 1814). WL. In 1816 he presented his *The Naiad* through Haydon, to whom he also sent a rapturous letter, 'He has twined the pillars of the Temple of Philosophy with the loveliest flowers of Poetry' etc., 28 Sept. 1816. *The Letters of John Hamilton Reynolds*, ed. Leonidas M. Jones (Lincoln, Nebr., 1973), 5. Reynolds's parody was not the only one. In 1819 also appeared *The Dead Asses: A Lyrical Ballad*, ascribed to Thomas Boyles Murray. Both parodies were reviewed alongside W's *Peter Bell*. N. Stephen Bauer, 'Early Burlesques and Parodies of Wordsworth', *JEGP* 74 (1975), 553–69, includes a checklist 1801–36.

73. Line 3 of 'Prologue' to Shelley's *Peter Bell the Third*, composed 1819 but not published till 1839.

74. *Peter Bell*, 41. In 1800 W had hoped that if 'the views with which [*Lyrical Ballads*] were composed were indeed realized, a class of Poetry would be produced, well adapted to interest mankind permanently'. *Prose*, I. 120.

75. *Literary Gazette*, 1 May 1819, 275; *Literary Chronicle*, 29 May 1819, 21; *Examiner*, 2 May 1819, 282; *Eclectic Review*, 2nd ser. 12 (July 1819), 73; *Monthly Review*, 2nd ser. 89 (Aug. 1819), 421; *Monthly Magazine*, 47 (June 1819), 442.

76. *HCR: Books*, I. 230.

77. SH to John Monkhouse, 7 May 1819. Cited *Benjamin*, 24. In 1819 the poem was published as *The Waggoner*.

78. CL to W [7 June 1819]. *The Letters of Charles Lamb, to which are Added those of his Sister Mary Lamb*, ed. E. V. Lucas (3 vols., London, 1935), II. 250.

79. *The Waggoner* elicited its parody *Benjamin the Waggoner: A Ryghte Merrie and Conceitede Tale in Verse*. Possibly by Reynolds, probably by J. G. Lockhart, the poem

actually parodies W's egotistical book-making through spoof Preface, Notes, list of engravings, and finally advertisements. The whole is rich with allusion and echo. Whoever the author was, he knew W's work very well. See *Benjamin*, 26.

80. MW to SH, 1 Dec. 1818. *MWL*, 41.

81. *An Evening Walk*, 50. The note is to line 171 of the 1793 first edition.

82. *1805 Prelude*, IV. 330–9.

83. *BL*, I. 196.

84. 'On Man, on Nature, and on Human Life . . .', printed in Preface to *The Excursion* (1814); 'My object is to give pictures of Nature, Man, and Society'. W to James Tobin, 6 Mar. 1798. *EY*, 212. See also W to James Losh, 11 Mar. 1798, *EY*, 214.

85. *The River Duddon, a Series of Sonnets: Vaudracour and Julia: And Other Poems. To which is Annexed, A Topographical Description of the Country of the Lakes, in the North of England* (London, 1820), 38.

86. *The Works of Charles Lamb* (2 vols., London, 1818), I. p. vii.

87. *European Magazine*, 77 (June 1820), 523.

88. *British Review*, 16 (Sept. 1820), 47, 49; *British Critic*, 2nd ser. 15 (Feb. 1821), 134; *Blackwood's Edinburgh Magazine*, 7 (May 1820), 206. Uvedale Price told Lady Beaumont that the *Topographical Description* 'should be in every house all round them; not only as so well describing their characteristic beauties, but as pointing out in the most impressive manner all that ought not, & all that ought to have been done: the whole appears to be dictated by the finest taste & feeling; & the principles are so just, & comprehensive, that it should be the *manual* of Improvers in every part of the Kingdom'. 6 Aug. 1820. MS Pierpont Morgan Library.

89. *BL*, I. 74; II. 68, on *Alice Fell*. *BL*, II. 140–1, on *Ode*. *Alice Fell* was restored to the canon after C's death.

90. *HCR: Books*, I. 241.

91. See W's important letters to Field about revision, 16 Apr. and 24 Oct. 1828. *LY*, I. 600–3 and 640–7. Speaking of the *Peele Castle* lines Field had forthrightly told W: 'I don't see what right you have to reclaim and clip the wings of the words and tame them thus'. WL. Cited *LY*, I. 645. The original reading was restored in 1832.

92. SH to John Monkhouse [Nov –Dec. 1819]. *SHL*, 165.

93. MW to SH, 30 May 1820. *MWL*, 58.

94. Both quotations from Jones's letter of 23 Feb. 1821. WL.

95. *DWJ*, II. 23.

96. Ibid. 86.

97. W to DW, [6 and 16] Sept. [1790]. *EY*, 32.

98. *DWJ*, II. 244. The *Prelude* refs. are to the relevant accounts in the poem.

99. Ibid. 258–9.

100. Ibid. 260–1.

101. Ibid. 280.

102. As n. 97, pp. 35–6.

103. MW *Journal*. WL.

104. Recorded by HCR, who thought Caroline's open acknowledgement of her father 'indelicate'. *HCR: Books*, I. 248.

105. *1805 Prelude*, IX. 556–935.

106. *HCR: Books*, I. 257.

107. Verse connected with *Michael*. See *PW*, II. 481.

108. Quotations from *1805 Prelude*, XI. 33–334; *1805 Prelude*, III. 167; 'My heart leaps up', *Gill: Oxf. W.*, 246; *River Duddon*, 'Conclusion', ibid. 351.

109. *European Magazine*, 77 (June 1820), 523. Two notes from Williams now in the Wordsworth Library reveal how warmly she pressed for a visit, for which HCR had prepared her. He had introduced her to W's poetry in 1814. See *HCR: Books*, I. 148.

110. *Moorman*, II. 387 notes that Williams gracefully alluded to W's recitation in the 1823 edition of her poems.

111. *Sonnet: After Visiting the Field of Waterloo*, 12. Pub. *Memorials of a Tour on the Continent, 1820* (1822), 4.

112. DW to CC, 16 Jan. [1822]. *LY*, I. 104.

113. SH to Thomas Monkhouse, 23 Nov. [1821] and [26 Nov. 1821]. *SHL*, 225, 228.

114. MW to SH and Dora Wordsworth, 13 July 1820. *MY*, II. 616. For the sonnet *A Parsonage in Oxfordshire* see *PW*, III. 41–2.

115. *HCR: Books*, II. 641, recording Southey's opinion in 1807.

116. W to Lord Lonsdale, 4 Dec. 1820. *MY*, II. 648.

117. 'Advertisement' to *Ecclesiastical Sketches* (1822), p. v.

118. *Ecclesiastical Sketches* (1822), note p. 120.

119. *HCR: Books*, I. 282 and 268.

120. Line 14 of *Mutability* is a fine example of W's total recall of his own verse. He had written, but not published, the line 'Or the unimaginable touch of Time' in 1796 in a 'Gothic Tale', of which only a fragment survives. See *Borderers*, p. 752, l. 68.

121. W to William Mathews, 23 Sept. [1791]. *EY*, 59. *1805 Prelude* quotation: IV. 13–15.

122. *HCR: Books*, I. 87 and 158. In the latter entry HCR, reflecting on W's 'sentimental and metaphysical mysticism', observes: 'Wordsworth is too upright a man to be guilty of any wilful deception; but perhaps he is himself not perfectly clear on the subjects on which his mode of thinking and feeling is anxiously inquired after by his religious admirers'.

CHAPTER 12

1. *Edinburgh Review*, 37 (Nov. 1822), 449.

2. William Parson and William White, *History, Directory, and Gazetteer, of the Counties of Cumberland, and Westmorland . . . Furness* (Leeds, 1829), 57 and 617.

3. The reviews appeared on 30 Mar. and 6 Apr. 1822. Longman told W that it had been stipulated that the paper should be 'free from bookselling influence'. See *LY*, I. 127 n. 4 and 128 n. 1 and DW's letter to HCR, 21 Apr. [1822], expressing their anger at being robbed 'of the little profit which might have arisen from a first flush of sale'.

4. In an article on 'Sacred Poetry', *Blackwood's Magazine*, 24 (1828), 917–38. HCR drew W's attention to it. The evidence is not clear, but it seems that W's refusal to take *Blackwood's* shielded him from a much deeper hurt. In Sept. 1820 Lockhart published a private letter to him from C, which included an attack on W. In the subsequent furore over Lockhart's ethics, the fact that C's attack was itself reprehensible was lost sight of. For full details see *CL*, IV. 966–74; *CL*, V. 123–8. In a letter 23 Nov. [1871] SH told Tom Monkhouse that W would not allow the *London Magazine* or *Blackwood's* into the house. *SHL*, 227. SH, however, clearly did see them.

5. W to HCR, 27 Jan. [1829]. *LY*, II. 17.

6. *Blackwood's Magazine*, 26 (Sept.–Dec. 1829), 453–63, 593–609, 774–88, 894–910. The 'Essay on the Theory and on the Writings of Wordsworth' was as much an attack on W's 'partisans' as on the poetry itself. See W's letters to RS [late Jan. 1830] and to EQ, 4 Feb. 1830. *LY*, II. 198–200. For Hartley Coleridge's comment see *HCL*, 111.

7. SH to MW, 16 Aug. [1820]. *SHL*, 189.

8. James Wood to W, 8 June 1831. WL.

9. After taking advice from Rogers, W settled on Henry William Pickersgill. His sonnet 'Go faithful Portrait' honours the painting (*PW*, III. 50), which became the best-known likeness of the poet, through the engraving of it by W. H. Watt which appeared as a frontispiece to the collected poems of 1836 and subsequent editions. W disliked the engraving. In 1840 Pickersgill was commissioned by Sir Robert Peel to produce another oil. See *Blanshard*, 74–9, 88.

10. Alan G. Hill gives details in a most informative article, 'Wordsworth and his American Friends', *BRH* 81 (1978), 146–60.

11. Elizabeth Palmer Peabody to W, 9 Dec. 1825 [not sent until 17 June 1827]. Quoted *LY*, I. 565.

12. Dated 11 Sept. 1826. MS Berg Collection, New York Public Library.

13. As n. 10, p. 148.

14. See W to Allan Cunningham, 23 Nov. [1825]. Galignani published handsome one-volume editions of contemporary English poets. They were, of course, piracies and W believed that 'the Paris Edition will much hurt a Sale sufficiently languid'. He was pleased, however, that the edition was printed 'with admirable accuracy'. W to HCR [15 Dec. 1828]. *LY*, I. 690–1.

15. For details see *LY*, I. 653–4 and Appendix, giving Cunningham's proposed Preface and Table of Contents, 703–4.

16. EQ to Dora W, 3 Mar. 1831. Quoted, with additional information, *LY*, II. 395.

17. Edward Moxon, once of Longman, had started his own business. W transferred to him in 1836. Quotation p. x of Hine's Preface. A second edition was issued in 1834.

18. A year before *Hard Times* Dickens was insisting on the importance of imagination to a nation's health. It is striking that in a letter of 27 July 1853 to W. H. Wills he actually quotes from W's sonnet, 'The world is too much with us . . .'.

19. In ch. 27 of *Middlemarch* (1871–2) Ned Plymdale thinks the *Keepsake* 'the very thing to please a girl' George Eliot describes it ironically, as 'the gorgeous watered-silk publication which marked modern progress at that time'.

20. W also felt personally obliged to Reynolds for having recommended a successful treatment for his eyes in 1826. See W to Frederic Mansel Reynolds, 24 Oct. [1826], *LY*, I. 489–90.

21. For W's account see *LY*, II. 14–15, 27–8, 90.

22. W. B. Yeats, *The Circus Animals' Desertion*.

23. W to John Kenyon, 25 July [1826]; to EQ [11 Nov. 1828]; to BH, 23 Apr. [1831]. *LY*, I. 473, 656; II. 378.

24. CC to HCR [29 Mar. 1813]. *HCR*, I. 77.

25. W to Robert Jones, 18 May [1826]. *LY*, I. 448.

26. W's lively account to William Rowan Hamilton of 26 Nov. 1830 suggests that he was aware that his performance was very creditable.

27. Hartley to Derwent Coleridge, 30 Aug. [1830]. *HCL*, 111.

28. DW to EQ, 6 Aug. 1822. *LY*, I. 149.

29. See *LY*, I. 381 n. 1 for further details. For Storrs and the Temple built to celebrate naval heroes, see *Murdoch*, 30.

30. SH to EQ, 23 Aug. [1826]; to John Monkhouse, 19 Sept. [1826]. *SHL* 320, 324.

31. SH to EQ, 12 Sept. [1827]. *SHL*, 351–2.

32. W to John Kenyon, 9 Sept. [1831]. *LY*, II. 425–6.

33. Tim Hilton, *John Ruskin: The Early Years* (New Haven and London, 1985), 19.

34. *HCR: Books*, I. 293.

35. *Autobiography of William Jerdan* (4 vols., London, 1852–3), IV. 240. The *Morning Chronicle*, 3 May 1830, tried a different image, claiming that the picture resembled 'a lady jumping out of a mustard-pot'.

36. *Taylor*, 38. Lord Cockburn, *Life of Lord Jeffrey* (2 vols., London, 1852), I. 322.

37. E. R. Vincent, *Ugo Foscolo: An Italian in Regency England* (Cambridge, 1953), 22, quoting Scott's journal 24 Nov. 1825.

38. Thomas Landseer (ed.), *Life and Letters of William Bewick (Artist)* (2 vols., London, 1871), I. 74–94, 100–1.

39. Thomas Monkhouse to Miss Horrocks [22 Apr. 1823]. *HCR*, I. 125.

40. W to John Kenyon [late Jan.–early Feb. 1831]. *LY*, II. 366.

41. As n. 36, p. 39.

42. *Taylor: Autobiography*, I. 83.

43. John Stuart Mill, *Autobiography and Literary Essays*, ed. John M. Robson and Jack Stillinger (Toronto, 1981), 136–63: W's poems, Mill writes, 'seemed to be the very culture of the feelings, which I was in quest of. In them I seemed to draw from a source of inward joy, of sympathetic and imaginative pleasure, which could be shared in by all human beings . . .'.

44. John Stuart Mill to John Sterling, 20–2 Oct. 1831. *The Earlier Letters of John Stuart Mill 1812–1848*, ed. Francis E. Mineka (2 vols., Toronto and London, 1963), I. 82.

45. *The Diaries of William Charles Macready 1833–1851*, ed. William Toynbee (2 vols., London, 1912), I. 318–20. Entry 26 May 1836.

46. W to William Charles Macready [*c*.14 Mar. 1831]. *LY*, II. 372.

47. SH to John Monkhouse [Nov.–Dec. 1819]. *SHL*, 167.

48. RS to C. W. Wynn, 11 Jan. 1827. 'Kenyon is . . . one of the very best and pleasantest men whom I have ever known; one whom everybody likes at first sight, and likes better the longer he is known'. *Selections from the Letters of Robert Southey*, ed. John Wood Warter (4 vols., London, 1856), IV. 41–2.

49. The standard life is Robert Perceval Graves, *Life of Sir William Rowan Hamilton* (3 vols., Dublin and London, 1882–9). Much additional information is provided in Thomas L. Hankins, *Sir William Rowan Hamilton* (Baltimore and London, 1980).

50. Quotation from a letter of Hamilton to W, 1 Feb. 1830, in which he explains his attitude to poetry and science as the great pursuits of his life. MS Cornell University Library.

51. Graves, op. cit. I. 269.

52. W to Samuel Rogers, 10 Mar. 1827. *LY*, I. 518.

53. W to Basil Montagu [19 Oct. 1831]. *LY*, II. 439.

54. Lady Eleanor Butler and the Hon. Miss Ponsonby, whose attachment to one another and reclusive life became the object of admiration and curiosity. See Elizabeth Mavor, *The Ladies of Llangollen* (London, 1971).

55. Julian Charles Young, *Memoir of Charles Mayne Young* (2 vols., London, 1871). I. 170–85; Thomas Colley Grattan, *Beaten Paths; And Those Who Trod Them* (2 vols., London, 1862), II. 107–45.

56. For an illustrated account see Donald E. Hayden, *Wordsworth's Travels in Wales and Ireland* (Tulsa, 1985), 53–75. The party visited Edgeworthstown on 20–1 September, but a meeting between the poet and the novelist Maria Edgeworth was a disaster. She found him prosy, self-centred, and boring. See Marilyn Butler, *Maria Edgeworth: A Literary Biography* (Oxford, 1972), 443.

57. W to his family at Rydal, 17 Sept. [1829]. *LY*, II. 135–6.

58. W to John Gardner, 19 May 1830. *LY*, II. 265.

59. DW to Mary Lamb, 9 Jan. 1830. *LY*, II. 191.

60. On the way home from Cambridge in Apr. 1831 Mary was attacked so severely at Nottingham that she could not move. William and Mary Howitt, Quaker poets who had presented their first volume to W in 1827, came to their rescue, arranging that Mary, wrapped in a blanket, should be chaired to their house. W described his wife's 'tortures' as 'almost insupportable'. See W to EQ [29 Apr. 1831] and to DW and CW junior, 9 May [1831]. *LY*, II. 380–1 and 383.

61. DW to CC, 19 Dec. [1819] and [31 May 1821]. *MY*, II. 572; *LY*, I. 62.

62. W to HCR, 26 Apr. 1829. W to CW, 5 May [1832]. *LY*, II. 69 and 521.

63. *To the Lady Fleming: On Seeing the Foundation Preparing for the Erection of Rydal Chapel, Westmorland* and *On the Same Occasion*, both published 1827.

64. The entry 'Wordsworth as Builder' in *Murdoch*, 88, from which 'picturesque-historic' is taken, interestingly places the design in the context of 1820s Lake District building and points out that its 'rich eclecticism' had 'precise local antecedents'. 'Webster's house seems designed as a visual catalogue of motifs borrowed from the seventeenth and eighteenth century developments at Rydal Hall and Rydal Mount.'

65. SH to Thomas Monkhouse, 11 Jan. [1822]. *SHL*, 230.

66. Keble had met W in 1815 and, like Mill, was thrilled that W in person more than matched his expectations of him. See W to John Keble, 18 Dec. [1822], *LY*, I. 174 and n. 1 for Keble's enthusiastic letter.

67. Hartley to Derwent Coleridge, Aug. 1830. *HCL*, 112.

68. W to CW [12 June 1830). *LY*, II. 282.

69. The *Kent's Bank Mercury*. WL. W, MW, Dora, and Willy had been at Kent's Bank, on the north side of Morecambe Bay, throughout July, for the sake of Dora's health. For DW's record of her one-day visit, see *LY*, I. 376.

70. W to William Jackson [early Oct. 1828] *LY*, I. 620.
Gibson, John, 25

71. Ibid.
Gilbanks, Mr, 16

72. The most important letter: Gill, Joseph, 103, 116        *LY*, I. 309–15. W to Lord Lonsdale [c.23 Dec. 1831], 17 Feb. 1832, 24 Feb. 1832. *LY*, II. 468–9, 488–91, 496–501. W to Sir Robert Inglis, 11 June 1825. *LY*, I. 358–65. W to Hugh James Rose, 11 Dec. 1828 [late Jan. 1829]. *LY*, I. 684–6; II. 18–25. W to Charles James Blomfield, 3 Mar. 1829. *LY*, II. 34–46.

73. W to William Jackson, 10 Apr. 1829. *LY*, II. 65.

74. Quotations from W to Sir Robert Inglis, 11 June 1825; to Benjamin Dockray, 2 Dec. 1828; to Francis Wrangham [end Mar. 1809]. *LY*, I. 359–60, 679; *MY*, I. 313.

75. W to CW, 5 Sept. [1829]. *LY*, II. 122.

76. Quotations from W to William Rowan Hamilton, 22 Nov. [1831]; to James Losh, 4 Dec. 1821; to BH [c.8 July 1831]; to Lord Lonsdale, 24 Feb. 1832. *LY*, II. 455; I. 98; II. 408, 500.

77. Julius Charles Hare to Walter Savage Landor [July 1831]. MS Cornell University Library.

78. Thomas Carlyle, *Signs of the Times*, first published as a review article *Edinburgh Review*, 49 (June 1829), 439–59. Thomas Babington Macaulay, review of Southey's *Sir Thomas More: or, Colloquies on the Progress and Prospects of Society*, *Edinburgh Review*, 50 (Jan. 1830), 528–65.

79. W to BH, 23 Apr. [1831]. *LY*, II. 378.

80. W to BH, 11 June 1831. *LY*, II. 396. The sonnet was *To B. R. Haydon, on Seeing his Picture of Napoleon Buonaparte on the Island of St. Helena*.

81. W to William Rowan Hamilton, 26 Nov. 1830. *Elegiac Musings*, 'with copious elegy . . .' and 'Chatsworth! thy stately mansion . . .'. Also: 'as I passed through the tame and

manufacture-disfigured country of Lancashire I was reminded by the faded leaves, of Spring, and threw off a few stanzas of an ode to May'.

82. *A Gravestone upon the Floor in the Cloisters of Worcester Cathedral*, published Nov. 1828 in the *Keepsake*. In Dec. 1827 W had seen the gravestone with the one word 'Miserrimus' and assumed it was the epitaph for a vile and contrite man. After publication W learnt its real history: 'I have had a Worcester paper sent me that gives, what it calls the *real* history of Miserrimus—spoiling, as *real* Histories generally do, the Poem altogether'. W to Barron Field, 20 Dec. 1828. 'Miserrimus' was actually a non-juring clergyman and the word on the stone was his own choice.

83. W to Alexander Dyce, 23 Dec. 1837. *LY*, III. 502.

84. *Moorman*, II. 461.

85. Mark Girouard, *The Return to Camelot: Chivalry and the English Gentleman* (New Haven and London, 1981), 56. Girouard's finely illustrated book places Digby in context and sympathetically brings out the quixotic nobility as well as the dottiness of the 19th-century love affair with chivalry.

86. W met Digby at Cambridge. SH recommended the book in Feb. 1827 (*SHL*, 339) and on 29 May 1828 HCR noted: 'Wordsworth made honourable mention of Digby's Broad Stone of Honour'. *HCR: Books*, I. 357. W did not find Digby's analysis of the contemporary situation, however, entirely persuasive. See his thoughtful letter to CW junior, 27 Nov. [1828]. *LY*, I. 668–9.

87. W to BH [*c*.8 July 1831]. *LY*, II. 408. 'But the age of chivalry is gone.—That of sophisters, oeconomists, and calculators, has succeeded; and the glory of Europe is extinguished for ever.' *Reflections*, 70.

88. W to BH, 23 Apr. [1831]. *LY*, II. 377–8. For BRH's answer—'I cant let you off in dull prose . . .'—and W's letter about Napoleon and contemporary England, see W to BRH, 11 June 1831. *LY*, II. 396–7.

89. DW to HCR, 21 Dec. 1822. *LY*, I. 178.

90. After initial small sale—*Memorials* 172 copies in 1822–23, *Sketches* 145—sales dwindled and both editions were eventually remaindered, *Sketches* not even having covered costs.

91. For details and Watt's comment see W to Alaric Watts, 18 Oct. 1825. *LY*, I. 390–1.

92. W to Samuel Rogers, 23 Mar. [1825]. Rogers acted energetically as intermediary with Murray, but to no avail. W comically revealed his pique: 'I assure you that I would a thousand times rather that not a verse of mine should ever enter the Press again, than to allow any of them [booksellers] to say that I was to the amount of the strength of a hair dependent upon their countenance, consideration, Patronage, or by whatever term they may dignify their ostentation and selfish vanity'.

93. HCR to DW [20 Feb. 1826]. *HCR*, I. 151–3.

94. W to HCR, 27 Apr. [1826]. *LY*, I. 444.

95. HCR to DW [21 May 1827]. *HCR*, I. 183.

96. Walter Savage Landor to W. Undated letter, which reached England 3 June 1828. Published R. H. Super, 'Landor's Letters to Wordsworth and Coleridge', *MP* 55 (1957), 73–83.

97. CW to W, 5 Aug. 1821. WL. DW to CC, 27 Mar. [1821]. *LY*, I. 50–1. MW to EQ, 26 Oct. [1824]. *MWL*, 119. DW to HCR, 13 Dec. [1824]. *LY*, I. 292. DW to William Jackson, 12 Feb. [1828]. *LY*, I. 582. DW to EQ, 19 Dec. 1829. WL.

98. W to Walter Savage Landor, 20 Apr. [1822]. *LY*, I. 126. Entry 6 Oct. 1826. *HCR: Books*, I. 339–40. Dora W to Mrs Fletcher, 20 Oct. 1831. *The Letters of Dora Wordsworth*, ed. Howard P. Vincent (Chicago, 1944), 91.

99. Dora W to Maria Kinnaird, 17 Feb. 1832. Quoted *1850 Prelude*, 5.

100. W to Sir Walter Scott, 16 Sept. [1831]. *LY*, II. 434.
101. W to EQ, 23 Aug. [1831]. *LY*, II. 421.
102. IF note to *Yarrow Revisited, and Other Poems. PW*, III. 524–6; *Grosart*, III. 138–41.
103. *On the Departure of Sir Walter Scott from Abbotsford, for Naples*, published in *Yarrow Revisited, and Other Poems* (1835).
104. See IF note and F. V. Morley, *Dora Wordsworth her Book* (London, 1924), 73–80.
105. Mentioned in IF note. This allusion to *Yarrow Unvisited* quoted from *Musings near Aquapendente*, 76–7.
106. W to Walter Scott, 16 Jan. 1805. *EY*, 530.
107. W to Samuel Rogers [30 July 1830]. *LY*, II. 310.
108. IF note. See also W to William Rowan Hamilton, 27 Oct. [1831]. *LY*, II. 441: 'It is in the same measure and as much in the same Spirit as matter of fact would allow. You are artist enough to know, that it is next to impossible entirely to harmonize things that rest upon their poetic credibility, and are idealized by distance of time and space, with those that rest upon the evidence of the hour and have about them the thorny points [of] actual life.'
109. W to Lady Frederick Bentinck, 9 Nov. [1831]: 'During this time we almost forgot . . . the deplorable state of the country'.
110. Dora W to Mrs Fletcher, 20 Oct. 1831. Quoted *LY*, II. 439 n. 1.
111. *Apology: For the Foregoing Poems*, 26. The poem declares that though the 'several lays' of *Yarrow Revisited* were 'without preconceived design', they are bound to each other by a common origin, Scott and Abbotsford:

> that sorrow-stricken door,
> Whence, as a current from its fountain-head,
> Our thoughts have issued . . .

112. Quotations from W to Joseph Kirkham Miller, 17 Dec. 1831. *LY*, II. 463. Dora W to Maria Kinnaird, 17 Feb. 1832, as n. 99. Robert Perceval Graves, quoting W's nephew Charles, cited *Home at Grasmere*, 28.
113. W to John Gardner [*c*.2 Feb. 1832]. *LY*, II. 487.

CHAPTER 13

1. W to Francis Wrangham, 2 Feb. [1835]; W to George Dyer, 6 June 1835. *LY*, III. 19, 56.
2. The tour lasted 12–25 July 1833. For an illustrated account, with maps, see Donald E. Hayden, *Wordsworth's Travels in Scotland* (Tulsa, 1985).
3. The sonnets were published in 1835 in *Yarrow Revisited* and the *Memorials of a Tour in Italy* in 1842 in *Poems, Chiefly of Early and Late Years*.
4. *Oliver Twist* was published 1837–8. One might note, wryly, that Francis Jeffrey wept copiously over the death of Little Nell in *The Old Curiosity Shop*. Edgar Johnson, *Charles Dickens: His Tragedy and Triumph* (2 vols., London, 1952), I. 304.
5. W to John Spedding, 2 Feb. 1833; W to CW, 25 Sept. 1833. *LY*, II. 586, 644.
6. DW to Anne Pollard, 12 Apr. [1834]. *LY*, II. 701.
7. DW had always measured her health in terms of her capacity to walk. See her report to CC [31 May 1821], 'Not long ago my Brother and I spent a whole day on the mountains, went by a circuitous road to the top of Fairfield, walking certainly not *less* than 14 miles; and I was not the *least tired*'. *LY*, I. 62.
8. MW to Jane Marshall [mid-Dec. 1835]. *LY*, III. 140.

9. Robert Gittings and Jo Manton, *Dorothy Wordsworth* (Oxford, 1985), 282.

10. W to HCR [15 Dec. 1835]; MW to Jane Marshall, 26 Dec. [1838]. *LY*, III. 144, 653.

11. W to BRH [late Nov. 1840]. *LY*, IV. 146.

12. MW to Mary Hutchinson, 8 Oct. [1838]. *MWL*, 218. Mary Hutchinson was married to Thomas Hutchinson, brother of Mary, wife of the poet. Their daughter Elizabeth is mentioned in the passage from *Kilvert's Diary* quoted in the text.

13. W to Samuel Rogers, 5 Apr. [1835]. *LY*, III. 41.

14. Robert Perceval Graves to Felicia Hemans, 12 Aug. 1834. Transcript WL. Published *Memoirs*, II. 288–90.

15. *PW*, IV. 272–6. The first part of the poem, ll. 1–38, was privately printed as *Epitaph* in 1835. The expanded version was included in the Collected Works of 1836-7.

16. The poem was expanded and revised, but there is no reason to doubt the accuracy of this account of its extempore origin. *Kilvert's Diary*, ed. William Plomer (3 vols., London, 1938), I. 318. The *Effusion*'s earliest published version appeared in the *Newcastle Journal* for 5 Dec. 1835.

17. W thought Hogg 'undoubtedly a man of original genius', but of 'coarse manners and low offensive opinions', whose writing was disfigured by 'insupportable slovenliness and neglect of syntax and grammar'. IF note to *Extempore Effusion*, *PW*, IV. 459 and W to R. P. Gillies, 14 Feb. 1815. *MY*, II. 196.

18. W had acknowledged the borrowing from William Hamilton in a note to *Yarrow Unvisited* from 1807 on. Hamilton's poem also provides the stanza form for the *Extempore Effusion*.

19. See, for example, A. H. Hallam's very important review article on Tennyson's *Poems, Chiefly Lyrical* (1830), 'On Some of the Characteristics of Modern Poetry', *Englishman's Magazine*, I (Aug. 1831), 616–28, conveniently reprinted in Isobel Armstrong, *Victorian Scrutinies: Reviews of Poetry 1830–1870* (London, 1972), 84–101. Hallam charges W (and his admirers) with overvaluing the philosophical and reflective.

20. W to Mary Ann Rawson [? May 1833]. *LY*, II. 615.

21. W to Eliza Hamilton, 10 Jan. 1833. W to his family [1 Apr. 1833]. *LY*, 581, 601.

22. W to HCR [*c*.14 Nov. 1833]. *LY*, II. 657. HCR splendidly described W in 1835 as 'in the dolefuls'. HCR to J. Masquerier [1835]. *HCR*, I. 255.

23. W to Thomas Noon Talfourd, 1 Jan. 1835. *LY*, III. 3.

24. Quotations from *The Warning* are, of course, from the text of 1835. They correspond to ll. 61–75, 122, 129–39 of the last revised text, *PW*, IV. 110–14.

25. Text of 1835. Corresponds to ll. 81–94 of last text, *PW*, IV. 102–6.

26. Thomas Carlyle, *Chartism* (1839), ch. 3: 'New Poor-law'.

27. Dickens's first attack on inhumanity in workhouses was, of course, *Oliver Twist* (1837–8). The new Union workhouses were immediately dubbed 'Bastilles', and were still so called as late as 1910 in Arnold Bennett's *Clayhanger*.

28. *Postscript* to *Yarrow Revisited*. *Prose*, III. 246. Following quotations are p. 244.

29. *1805 Prelude*, IX. 519–20.

30. 28 May 1836. WL. In the extraordinary covering letter Price wrote: 'In venturing to submit the following ... I am actuated by a wish to show you what to the greatest poet of his age must be a particularly insignificant scribble'. 'There is a pleasure', he added, 'in connecting one's self, however slightly, with one whose greatness one *feels*.'

31. For a portrait of Reed see *LY*, III. 444. See also L. N. Broughton (ed.), *Wordsworth and Reed: The Poet's Correspondence with his American Editor: 1836–1850* (Ithaca, 1933).

32. W to HCR, 28 Jan. [1837]. *LY*, III. 355.

33. W to IF [3 Nov. 1839]. *LY*, III. 738.

34. Thomas Powell to W, 10 Oct. 1836. WL. Quoted in part *L Y*, III. 461, in an informative note about Powell.

35. See W to Thomas Forbes Kelsall [*c*.30 Oct. 1833] and his query about him to HCR [*c*.14 Nov. 1833]. *L Y*, III. 655–9.

36. Charles Swain to W, 10 Oct. 1833. WL. Swain's inscription quoted from a catalogue of B. H. Blackwell Antiquarian Books, 1985.

37. Sir William Maynard Gomm to W, 24 Feb. 1835. WL. For a note on Gomm, in which another passage from this letter is quoted, see *L Y*, II. 704. For Alford see *L Y*, III. 94.

38. W to unknown correspondent, 19 May [? 1835]. *L Y*, III. 52.

39. W to HCR, 15 Dec. [1837]. *L Y*, III. 493. W to Edward Moxon [? 18 Feb. 1840]. *L Y*, IV. 20.

40. Winifred Gérin, *Branwell Brontë* (London, 1961), 127–8. In *The Poems of Patrick Branwell Brontë*, ed. Tom Winnifrith (Oxford, 1983), 281, the mistake (started by Elizabeth Gaskell in her *Life of Charlotte Brontë*) is repeated, that Branwell Brontë only enclosed a part of his poem 'Still, and bright in twilight shining'. In fact he sent a copy of the whole, which is now in WL.

41. William (later Sir William) Boxall to W, 29 Aug. 1836. For information on Boxall and his portrait of W, see *L Y*, II. 376.

42. EQ diary entry 1 Sept. 1836. WL. On 18 Aug. 1838 IF lamented the erosion of W's time: 'Some days there are in the course of the day between twenty and thirty people at the Mount . . .'. *Taylor*, 94.

43. Edward Lytton Bulwer, *England and the English* (2 vols., London, 1833), ed. Standish Meacham (Chicago and London, 1970).

44. Ralph Waldo Emerson, *English Traits* (1856). *Essays and Lectures*, ed. Joel Porte [The Library of America] (New York, 1983), 775–8. Emerson's account follows very closely his journal entry of 28 Aug. 1833. For a brief but useful study of W's growing influence see Linden Peach, *British Influence on the Birth of American Literature* (London, 1982), 29–57, 'Man, Nature and Wordsworth: American Versions'.

45. Orville Dewey, *The Old World and the New: or, A Journal of Reflections and Observations Made on a Tour in Europe* (2 vols., New York, 1836), I. 104–12.

46. Charles Sumner to George S. Hillard, 8 Sept. 1838. *Memoir and Letters of Charles Sumner*, ed. Edward L. Pierce (3 vols., London, 1878–93), I. 355–6.

47. Carlyle's *Journal* entry, 17 Mar. 1835 and letter to his brother John, 23 Mar. 1835. Cited in Charles Richard Sanders, 'Carlyle and Wordsworth'. *Browning Institute Studies*, 9 (1981), 115–22. See also Fred Kaplan, *Thomas Carlyle: A Biography* (Cambridge, 1983), 223–5.

48. Thomas Adolphus Trollope, *What I Remember* (3 vols., London, 1887–9), II. 15–17.

49. It would be inappropriate to cite here the many studies which touch on Arnold's long tussle with W's influence. The best overall account of Arnold's life is Park Honan, *Matthew Arnold: A Life* (London, 1981).

50. ? to Anne Hayman, 2 Oct. [? 1842]. MS Beinecke Library, Yale. W to IF, 29 June 1841. *L Y*, IV. 210.

51. *Tait's Edinburgh Magazine*, NS 1 (Sept., Oct., Nov. 1834), 509–20, 588–96, 685–90; and 2 (Jan. 1835), 2–10. These essays, and those in n. 55, are most conveniently available in *DQR*. Hartley's comment is in a letter to Joseph Henry Green, 7 June 1836. Berg Collection, New York Public Library.

52. Entry 21 July 1832 outlines what C recalled as the plan for W's philosophic poem.

53. W was very hostile to the idea that 'the interests of literature' demand publication of what the author had discarded. See his statement to David Laing, 11 Dec. 1835. *L Y*, III. 137. This attitude explains why MW satisfied HCR's curiosity about *The*

*Borderers*, but added, 'say nothing about it, lest its destruction should follow'. 1 Nov. [1836]. *L Y*, III. 314.

54. Daniel Stuart added to the confusion. W wrote to him firmly on 17 May 1838 to set the record straight. *L Y*, III. 589.

55. 'Lake Reminiscences: From 1807 to 1830', *Tait's Edinburgh Magazine*, 6 (Jan., Feb., Apr. 1839), 1-12, 90-103, 246-54.

56. DW to C, 14 Nov. [1829]. MS Berg Collection, New York Public Library. W to Edward Moxon, 10 Dec. 1835. *L Y*, III. 134. In 1838 W was staggered when his letter to Fox of 14 Jan. 1801 surfaced in the *Correspondence of Sir Thomas Hanmer . . .*, ed. Sir Henry Bunbury, who had acquired it through his first wife, Fox's niece. W's remonstrance of 30 July [1838] is polite, but his anger is barely concealed. *L Y*, III. 624-5.

57. W to Edward Moxon, 10 Jan. 1840. W to Barron Field 16 Jan. 1840. *L Y*, IV. 5, 7. W had been deeply distressed by much that he learnt about Scott from Lockhart's *Life*. See W to Thomas Noon Talfourd, 8 Jan. [1838]. *L Y*, III. 511-12 and important n. 2.

58. W's letters to Moxon of 20 Nov. and 10 Dec. 1835 about his anxieties over Talfourd's proposed *Letters* are very important, not only because W spells out his attitude to the publication of correspondence but because they indicate that W felt that Moxon was a publisher with whom he could discuss matters of principle.

59. MS Berg Collection, New York Public Library. W seems to have behaved high-handedly, choosing to regard as proposals what Longman claimed were only estimates. See W to Messrs Longman and Co., 6 June 1836. *L Y*, III. 242 and n. 1 for Longman's reply.

60. See Harold G. Merriam, *Edward Moxon: Publisher of Poets* (New York, 1939). Moxon had dedicated the second volume of his *Sonnets* (1835) to W.

61. W thought that a letter of 2 Feb. 1842 indicated that Moxon regretted their dealings. His immediate reply of 3 Feb. (*L Y*, IV. 289-90) produced an equally swift and equally firm response. Moxon's letters are in the Wordsworth Library.

62. Jared R. Curtis, 'The Wellesley Copy of Wordsworth's *Poetical Works*, 1832', *Harvard Library Bulletin*, 28 (1980), 5.

63. WL. Cited in Curtis, op. cit. above, p. 8.

64. Cited *An Evening Walk*, 17.

65. W to his family [5 July 1837]; 'timed' refers to the race against time for the publication of the 6 volumes of the 1836-7 edition, which were issued monthly.

66. W to Edward Moxon [late Dec. 1836]. *L Y*, III. 337.

67. EQ Diary, cited *Descriptive Sketches*, 19. Birdsall and Averill (n. 64) print the texts of 1836.

68. W was attempting to meet the objection of Mrs John Kenyon that London could not be 'bare' and 'clothed'. His suggested rewording was not an improvement. See W to John Kenyon [c.24 Sept. 1836]. *L Y*, III. 292-4.

69. W to Edward Moxon, 28 Jan. [1837]. *L Y*, III. 353.

70. W had welcomed Moxon's concern about the appearance of a book, as he had disliked the format of his 1832 edition, but he was reluctant to agree to Moxon making the *Sonnets* 'a book of luxury', although he said that he would bow 'to [his] superior judgement'. W to Edward Moxon [c.3 Feb. 1838]. *L Y*, III. 518-19.

71. Barron Field to W, 17 Dec. 1836. Cited *L Y*, III. 355.

72. James Montgomery, 12 Jan. 1838. WL.

73. *The Life, Letters, and Journals of George Ticknor*, ed. G. S. Hillard (2 vols., London, 1876), II. 167. Cited *L Y*, III. 583.

74. C's *To William Wordsworth*, first published in *Sibylline Leaves* (1817), had recently reappeared in the 1834 3-volume *Poetical Works*. W to Thomas Noon Talfourd [*c*.10 Apr. 1839]. *LY*, III. 680: 'Its publication has been prevented merely by the personal character of the subject'. W also points out to Talfourd, however, that given the state of the present copyright law, the longer he delays publication the better it will be for his family.

75. IF to Henry Taylor, 28 Mar. 1839. *Taylor*, 117–18.

76. For an account of the manuscripts, with photographs, see *1850 Prelude*.

77. W to J. Forbes Mitchell, 21 Apr. 1819. *MY*, II. 534.

78. W to John Gibson Lockhart, 4 May [1838]. *LY*, III. 577–8. W's efforts were reinforced by his learning from Lockhart that despite Sir Walter Scott's prodigious output it seemed unlikely that his home, Abbotsford, could be saved if the law of copyright were not changed.

79. Talfourd's reference to W is quoted at length *LY*, III. 407.

80. John Constable to W, 15 June 1836. WL. Writing of his indebtedness to Beaumont, Constable said to W: 'it was from his hands that I first saw a volume of your poems—how then can I ever be sufficiently grateful . . .'.

81. W to his family [*c*.28 May 1836]. *LY*, III. 229.

82. *The Diaries of William Charles Macready . . . 1833–1851*, ed. William Toynbee (2 vols., London, 1912), I. 318–20. The lines, 'Action is transitory . . .' appeared as epigraph to the *White Doe of Rylstone* for the first time in the collected edition of 1836–7, but Macready recalled that W had recited this passage to him on an earlier occasion.

83. MS Berg Collection, New York Public Library.

84. Letter 7 July 1842 to H. S. Boyd, in *Elizabeth Barrett to Mr. Boyd*, ed. Barbara P. McCarthy (London, 1955), 247.

85. *HCR: Books*, II. 562. 3 Jan. 1839. On receiving a copy of her *The Seraphim, and Other Poems* (1838), W told the sender, John Kenyon, 17 Aug. [1838], that he would like to see her *Prometheus Bound* (1833). Kenyon arranged the gift and the volume, inscribed not by the poet but by her father, is now in the Berg Collection of the New York Public Library.

86. W to his family [14 June 1836]; [*c*.17 June 1836]; [?29 June 1836]. *LY*, III. 251, 254, 269.

87. SH to EQ, 27 May [1833]. *SHL*, 393. IF note to *The Excursion*, *PW*, V. 373.

88. W to Dora Wordsworth, 4 June [1837]. *LY*, III. 412.

89. Alexander to Robert Blackwood, 21 June 1837. Mrs [Margaret] Oliphant, *Annals of a Publishing House: William Blackwood and his Sons* (2 vols., Edinburgh and London, 1897), II. 158.

90. Both quotations, W to MW, 17 July [1837]. *LY*, III. 425–30.

91. *HCR: Books*, II. 531. 25 July 1837.

92. As n. 90, p. 429.

93. HCR to Frances Mackenzie, 17 Nov. 1837 [an addition to a W letter]. *LY*, III. 438.

94. See W to Dora Wordsworth, 30 May [1837]. *LY*, III. 404–9. Milton was thought to have lodged in the monastery at Vallombrosa. The line of *Paradise Lost* is Book II, 302–3: 'Thick as autumnal leaves that strew the brooks / In Vallombrosa . . .'.

95. IF note to *The Pine of Monte Mario at Rome. PW*, III. 494.

96. W to MW and Dora Wordsworth, 21 June [1837]. *LY*, III. 417. See also *HCR: Books*, II. 524. 12 June 1837. 'The view of this most beautiful of lakes was in itself to me an unmixed pleasure. Wordsworth blended with it painfully pleasing recollections of his old friend Jones . . . He also had a still more tender recollection of his journey here in 1820 . . .'.

97. W to his family [5 July 1837]. *L Y*, III. 423.
98. For a long and excellent note on Landor's attack see *L Y*, III. 374–5. The two poets had corresponded cordially in the 1820s and in 1831 HCR wrote to DW that what united him and Landor 'was our common love and admiration of the works of your brother—I never met with any one who is so warm and eloquent in the expression of his judgement in favour of Mr Wordsworth's poetry'. *HCR*, I. 223. Landor and W had seen much of each other during W's 1836 visit to London. See R. H. Super's authoritative *Walter Savage Landor: A Biography* (London, 1957), 276–7 and his 'Landor's Letters to Wordsworth and Coleridge', *MP* 55 (1957), 73–83. For HCR's two very full letters on the matter of 7 and 17 Dec. [1836] see *HCR*, I. 326–33.
99. Chorley's warning looks odd in context, as it appears in a celebratory coffee-table volume by Achille Collas called *The Authors of England* (1838), in which handsome reproductions of celebrated writers are followed by 'Illustrative Notices' by Chorley. For text of the warning and portrait see *Blanshard*, 84 and plate 45a.
100. It might have mattered more had they known more about it. In 1844 Keble hesitated about dedicating his lectures to W when his wife 'started a doubt on account of his having begun life as a Radical'. Letter 23 Jan. 1844 quoted Brian W. Martin, *John Keble: Priest, Professor and Poet* (London, 1976), 81.
101. Keble's Oration was in Latin (MS now in Keble College, Oxford). I use the translation in Sir J. T. Coleridge, *A Memoir of the Rev. John Keble* (Oxford and London, 1869), 249. Christopher Wordsworth printed the Latin in *Memoirs*, II. 355–6.
102. Elizabeth Gaskell to Mary Howitt [18 Aug. 1838]. *The Letters of Mrs Gaskell*, ed. J. A. V. Chapple and Arthur Pollard (Manchester, 1966), 33.
103. W to HCR [*c*.27 Apr. 1385]. *L Y*, III. 44: 'If my writings are to last, it will I myself believe, be mainly owing to this characteristic. They will please for the single cause, "That we have all of us one human heart!" '
104. Sir Henry Edward Bunbury to W, 8 June 1838. WL.
105. 'This is what I call democratic art—the revelation of the poetry which lies in common things. And surely all the age is tending in that direction . . . the great tide sets ever onward, outward, towards that which is common to the many, not that which is exclusive to the few.' Charles Kingsley, *Alton Locke* (1850), ch. 9.
106. Thomas Southwood Smith (1788–1861), a Unitarian minister who became a doctor. Famous for his work on the prevention of epidemic fever, he was involved in the 1830s and 1840s in most movements concerned with the health, housing, and education of the poor.
107. It was Francis Faber who wrote to W 17 Apr. 1839 asking whether he would accept an Honorary DCL. WL.
108. For a modern biography of Faber see Ronald Chapman, *Father Faber* (London, 1961).
109. John Keble, *De poeticae Vi Medica: Praelectiones Academicae* (2 vols., Oxford, 1844), translated as *Keble's Lectures on Poetry 1832–1841* by Edward Kershaw Francis (2 vols., Oxford, 1912). Dedication, I. 8: 'To William Wordsworth / True Philosopher and Inspired Poet'.
110. *The British Critic, and Quarterly Theological Review*, 25 (Apr. 1839), 400. John Henry Newman, *Apologia Pro Vita Sua*, ed. Martin J. Svaglic (Oxford, 1967), 94.
111. G. B. Tennyson's *Victorian Devotional Poetry: The Tractarian Mode* (Cambridge, Mass., and London, 1981) is dense with information and insights, particularly on Keble and Wordsworth.
112. W assisted Graves to obtain in 1835 the curacy of Bowness. The WL has a touching sonnet, dated 14 Jan. 1840, beginning:

> They call me poor: and, truly, little store
> Of this world's gold or luxury is mine.

Amongst his treasures Graves lists

> . . . two, whose love is dear as life,
> Are Rydal's Poet and his holy wife.

113. Son of Sir Aubrey De Vere, Bart., who visited Rydal Mount in 1833 and dedicated *A Song of Faith, Devout Exercises and Sonnets* (1842) to W. Aubrey De Vere (son) first visited W in 1841. His *Recollections* (1897) reveal his devotion to the poet. Passing a night under his roof he declared 'the greatest honour of his life' (p. 125). See also Wilfrid Ward, *Aubrey De Vere: A Memoir* (London, 1904), which draws on his diaries. To this very selective list ought to be added Julius Charles Hare (later Archdeacon of Lewes) and his brother Augustus (vicar of Alton, Wilts., died 1834). J. C. Hare fulsomely dedicated the second edition of their joint *Guesses at Truth* (1838) to W. See W's important letter of thanks, 28 May [1838]. *LY*, III. 592–5.

114. Crabb Robinson was frequently called upon to defend W's beliefs. In 1826 he sent Blake *Ecclesiastical Sketches*, hoping to refute his conviction that 'Wordsworth worships Nature and is not a Bible Christian'. Ten years later he was warmly denying that *The Excursion* could possibly be read as '*anti*-Christian', and in 1838 he had an argument with a man who claimed that Coleridge had told him that W 'was not a Christian'. Privately, however, in 1836, HCR noted: 'Wordsworth's own religion, by the bye, would not satisfy either a religionist or a sceptic'. *HCR: Books*, I. 335; II. 490, 550, 481.

115. Convinced that 'ours is at present truly a Church Militant, and it becomes every Soldier to be faithful to his duty', W made his campaign the erection of a new church at Cockermouth, which he regarded in 1836 as 'a desperate stronghold of Radicalism'. See W to Francis Merewether, 7 Mar. [18]36. *LY*, III. 180–2.

116. William Ellery Channing to W, 4 Mar. 1835; Elizabeth Frances Ogle to W, ?5 May 1840; John Simon to W, 2 July 1841. WL. Thomas Pringle, *Poems* (1839), 186.

117. W to Henry Alford [c.20 Feb. 1840]. *LY*, IV. 23. Aubrey De Vere, *Essays Chiefly on Poetry* (2 vols., London, 1887), I. 263.

CHAPTER 14

1. Dora to William Wordsworth jun. [27] July 1840. WL.
2. MW to William Wordsworth jun., 28 [Mar. 1835]. *MWL*, 140.
3. W to Sir Robert Peel, 17 Oct. 1842. *LY*, IV. 378.
4. See letters in late 1837 between Dora and EQ quoted *LY*, III. 497 and 549–50.
5. W to Dora Wordsworth [c.5 Apr. 1838]. *LY*, III. 548–50.
6. See for W's trust in EQ's literary judgement his letter 20 Sept. [1837]. *LY*, III. 464–5. Next quotation W to Dora Wordsworth [c.24 Apr. 1839]. *LY*, III. 686–7.
7. Sir Samuel Egerton Brydges, mired in financial complications, executed a land deal in 1830–1 which involved sharp practice, if not fraud. As one of the intended beneficiaries of the complex arrangement, EQ was implicated in the Chancery proceedings, which dragged on until 1842. See Mary Katherine Woodworth, *The Literary Career of Sir Samuel Egerton Brydges* (Oxford, 1935), especially 28–30.
8. *Taylor: Autobiography*, I. 337.

9. For W's search for medical advice see W to his family [?29 May 1836] and to Sir Charles Bell [Nov. 1836]. *LY*, III. 230–1 and 310–11. For the rowing see W to Dora Wordsworth, 2 June [1836]. *LY*, III. 235.

10. Hartley to Derwent Coleridge [Aug. 1830]. *HCL*, 112.

11. MW to EQ [early Feb. 1839]. *LY*, III. 660.

12. W to EQ, 13 Apr. [1839]. *LY*, III. 681–3.

13. EQ to Dora Wordsworth, 7 Apr. 1839. Quoted *LY*, III. 686.

14. WW to MW, 8 June [1839]; EQ to Dora Wordsworth, 10 June 1839. *LY*, III. 702–3 and n. 2.

15. *HCR: Books*, II. 580. Entry for 22 Feb. 1840.

16. W and MW to IF, 18 Jan. [1836]. *LY*, III. 157; *HCR*, II. 673; *Taylor: Autobiography*, I. 52; MW to Mrs S. T. Coleridge, 21 Nov. [1839]. *LY*, III. 742.

17. W and MW to IF [24 Mar. 1840]. *LY*, IV. 53.

18. W to IF, [3 Nov. 1840] and 10 July 1841. *LY*, IV. 134 and 215. HCR observed, 'Miss Fenwick . . . is a treasure to Wordsworth, and by the resources her society supplies, he is enabled to live without seeking for intercourse out of his own house. Two such women as Miss Fenwick and Mrs Wordsworth seem, indeed, enough for any one.' *HCR: Books*, II. 611.

19. W to HCR, 19 Feb. [1839]. *LY*, III. 664.

20. Shortly before the wedding CW had settled £1,000 on Dora in trust, the interest to be hers for life. For details see W to CW [3 or 4 May 1841]. *LY*, IV. 195–6 and n. 2.

21. EQ to Rotha Quillinan, 12 May 1841. WL.

22. W to Dora Wordsworth and IF, 7 Apr. 1840. *LY*, IV. 57.

23. W to George Ticknor [Dec. 1842]. *LY*, IV. 396.

24. W to BRH, 2 Sept. 1840. *LY*, IV. 100. For further details of painting and poem see Bishop C. Hunt jun., 'Wordsworth, Haydon, and the "Wellington" Sonnet', *Princeton University Library Chronicle*, 36 (1974–5), 111–32.

25. *HCR: Books*, II. 606. Henry Taylor, 'The Sonnets of William Wordsworth', *Quarterly Review*, 69 (Dec. 1841), 1–51.

26. W contributed *The Cuckoo and the Nightingale* (*PW*, IV. 217–28) and the extract *Troilus and Cressida* (*PW*, IV. 228–33).

27. W to HCR [23 Jan. 1840]. *LY*, IV. 11. W became very disenchanted when he began to suspect that Powell was hoping to float the book on W's name.

28. W to Thomas Powell, 18 Jan. [1840]. *LY*, IV. 8.

29. W to John Kenyon [summer 1838]. *LY*, III. 616.

30. HCR to W, 12 Sept. 1836. *HCR*, 316.

31. W to David Laing, 11 Dec. 1835. *LY*, III. 137.

32. W to Edward Moxon, 4 Mar. 1841. *LY*, IV. 183.

33. Full details of the revision, and texts, will be found in *Salisbury Plain Poems* and *Borderers*.

34. *PW*, III. 202–12. Quotations below are from the text of 1842.

35. See *PW*, II. 479, for the lines which W incorporates into *Musings*, 47–52.

36. Moxon was defended by Talfourd. He was found guilty, but not sentenced. W to HCR [late Nov. 1841]. *LY*, IV. 265.

37. Edward Moxon to W, 26 Jan. 1842. WL.

38. W to Edward Moxon [1 Apr. 1842]. *LY*, IV. 314.

39. W to Sir Aubrey De Vere, 31 Mar. [18]42. *LY*, IV. 312.

40. *HCR: Books*, II. 628. Entry 1 Jan. 1843.

41. *PW*, III. 63; IV. 266, 160–1.

42. W to George Huntly Gordon, 24 June [18]45. *LY*, IV. 680. The poem was 'Forth from a jutting ridge', *PW*, II. 123.

43. Thomas Hardy, *At Castle Boterel*—a poem about revisiting in age and a 'spot of time' that defies 'Time's unflinching rigour'.

44. IF's transcription is not extant. A copy by Dora and Edward Quillinan is now in the WL.

45. W to John Peace, 11 May 1841. *LY*, IV. 198.

46. It is worth noting that the Ws were dismayed by change on Salisbury Plain, which they saw as their tour continued: 'cultivation going on in many parts of the Plain takes sadly from the poetical feelings we had so *elaborately* attached to that region', MW told IF, 2 June [1841]. *MWL*, 246.

47. This and quotations following are IF to Henry Taylor, 20 May 1841. Quoted *LY*, IV. 198.

48. See notes to *Anecdote for Fathers*, and *Lines Written in Early Spring. Grosart*, III. 19–20, 159.

49. W to Lady Frederick Bentinck [30 July 1841]. *LY*, IV. 97.

50. Earl De La Warr to W, 30 Mar. 1843. *LY*, IV. 421 n. 1.

51. Earl De La Warr and Sir Robert Peel to W, both 3 Apr. 1843. Quoted *LY*, IV. 423–4. W's letter of acceptance (quotation next paragraph) is dated 4 Apr.

52. W to IF [5 Aug. 1841]. *LY*, IV. 221.

53. EQ to HCR, 9 Dec. 1843. *HCR*, I. 532.

54. Ibid.

55. Harriet Martineau to Elizabeth Barrett, 8 Feb. [1846]. *HCR*, II. 621.

56. Dr Arnold died 12 June 1842.

57. Elizabeth Fletcher's holiday log-book, 4–23 Sept. 1833, is now in WL. It reveals that she did not care for W on first meeting, but that after dining with him she decided that he and Mary were very pleasant. Elizabeth Gaskell met W in July 1849. EQ wrote to Mrs H. N. Coleridge, 25 July 1849, that she was 'As nice a person as possible . . , "a great pet" with the Arnolds, Davys, Miss Martineau & Mrs Fletcher'. WL.

58. *Autobiography of Mrs. Fletcher*, ed. the Survivor of her Family [Lady Richardson] (Edinburgh, 1875). H. A. L. Rice, 'Wordsworth in Easedale', *Ariel*, I (1970), 31–8 gives an attractive account of the Fletcher circle and W's place in it, quoting extensively from the diary of Mrs Fletcher's daughter Margaret, wife of Dr John Davy, Sir Humphry's brother. Much of this material had already been printed in *Grosart*, III. 435–58.

59. Full accounts of Martineau's life and writing will be found in R. K. Webb, *Harriet Martineau: A Radical Victorian* (London, 1960) and Valerie K. Pichanik, *Harriet Martineau: The Woman and her Work 1802–76* (Ann Arbor, 1980).

60. As n. 55. My reading of the MS in the Beinecke Library, Yale University, differs slightly from HCR's.

61. W to HCR, 7 Aug. [18]45. W was intolerant of Martineau's zeal for Mesmerism, to which she attributed her recovery from prolonged illness. See *HCR: Books*, II. 650 for an account of a grand dinner on 16 Jan. 1845, at which he was conscious that everyone was avoiding Mesmerism, 'by tacit consent. This was better than controversy.'

62. *The Life of Thomas Cooper: Written by Himself* (London, 1872), ed. John Saville (Leicester, 1971), 287–95.

63. *1805 Prelude*, VII. 695, 700.

64. Henry Taylor to IF, 11 May 1842. *Taylor*, 133–4.

65. W to Henry Reed, 1 July [18]45. *LY*, IV. 687.

66. Elizabeth Barrett to H. S. Boyd, 7 July 1842. *Elizabeth Barrett to Mr. Boyd*, ed. Barbara P. McCarthy (London, 1955), 247.

67. W to William Rowan Hamilton, 26 Nov. 1830. *LY*, II. 354.

68. *Poems* (2 vols., London, 1842). According to one account W said to Tennyson, 'I have been endeavouring all my life to write a pastoral like your "Dora" and have not succeeded'. Hallam Tennyson, *Alfred Lord Tennyson: A Memoir* (2 vols., London, 1897), I. 265.

69. Wilfrid Ward, *Aubrey De Vere: A Memoir* (London, 1904), 73–4.

70. W to Henry Reed, 1 July [18]45. *LY*, IV. 688.

71. Now in WL.

72. John Kenyon to W, 29 Mar. 1843. WL. Elizabeth Barrett wrote a sonnet inspired by the painting. It is entirely characteristic of W that, while gratefully acknowledging it, 26 Oct. 1842, he also suggested alterations. *LY*, IV. 384–5.

73. *The Excursion*, IV. 978–92.

74. W was responding to a request from Hugh Seymour Tremenheere, an Inspector of Schools, that he should contribute to the reform of education by writing an essay 'embodying your present impression on the subject of elementary education for the lower classes'. *LY*, IV. 732–4. Tremenheere had met W through Harriet Martineau.

75. W to his family, 4 [June 1836]. *LY*, III. 241.

76. For texts and excellent annotation see *Prose*, III. 331–66.

77. *Prose*, III. 346 and 350–1.

78. Barron Field to HCR, 16 Feb. 1845. *HCR*, II. 591–3.

79. Readers of this book will enjoy J. D. Marshall and John K. Walton, *The Lake Counties: From 1830 to the Mid-twentieth Century* (Manchester, 1981), which gives a fascinating and attractively illustrated account of industrial and agricultural change. Discussing the growth of tourism, the authors observe that W's arguments were resurrected later in the century, when defence of the Lake District became a priority. See especially 205–7.

80. As n. 74.

81. Aubrey De Vere to W, 3 Sept. [1841]. Quoted *LY*, IV. 256.

82. Richard Parkinson to W, 14 Mar. 1843. WL.

83. For Burns and a very suggestive account of the impact on publishing of identifiably sectarian readerships see Patrick Scott, 'The Business of Belief: The Emergence of "Religious Publishing"', in *Sanctity and Secularity: The Church and the World*, ed. Derek Baker (Oxford, 1973).

84. Some time later (the date, 1845 or 1847, is uncertain), Moxon issued an edition that was superficially identical to Burns's. Exactly how Burns came to publish his selection, and what passed between them before Moxon published his, remains obscure.

85. The engraving by W. Finden was of the bust of W executed in 1820 by Sir Francis Chantrey. W disliked Finden's engraving of Rydal Mount after G. Howse and when the volume was reissued in 1847 it was replaced by an engraving by T. H. Ellis after an attractive picture by Thomas Creswick. W's letter to Moxon, 17 Nov. 1845, *LY*, IV. 723, shows the control he wished to exercise over all aspects of the appearance of the book.

86. *The Recreations of Christopher North* (3 vols., 1842), II. 349–50. *Eclectic Review*, NS 12 (1842), 568–79. The significance of Wilson's questioning was pointed out by Jonathan Wordsworth, *The Music of Humanity* (London, 1969), 26.

87. Diary entry quoted Wilfrid Ward, *Aubrey De Vere* (London, 1904), 69. IF's piety clearly awed W. See his letter to her of [17 July 1844], *LY*, IV. 575, in which, astoundingly, he declares himself 'unworthy of being constantly in your sight'.

88. In a letter of 25 Nov. 1842 Faber told J. B. Morris that he had given his cedar cross to W. See *Faber Poet and Priest: Selected Letters of Frederick William Faber*, ed. Raleigh Addington (Cowbridge, 1974), 92.

89. Mrs Benson Harrison was Dorothy Wordsworth, daughter of W's cousin Robinson Wordsworth, who was the son of W's uncle Richard of Whitehaven.
90. HCR to Thomas Robinson, 29 [Dec. 1842]. *HCR*, I. 473 and diary entry 27 Dec. 1841. *HCR: Books*, II. 605.
91. The Wordsworth Library has a letter of Faber's sent from Vienna, 26 June 1841, which gives a vivid account of how he tried to smuggle a copy of the Galignani edition of Wordsworth, bought in Athens, past the guards on the Turkish–Hungarian border and how it was impounded until declared safe by the Austrian censor.
92. F. W. Faber to W, 31 Oct. 1843. Faber to EQ, 18 Feb. 1848. WL.
93. *Letters* as n. 88, p. 95.
94. F. W. Faber to John Keble, 12 Nov. 1842. Printed B. W. Martin, 'Wordsworth, Faber, and Keble: Commentary on a Triangular Relationship', *RES* NS 26 (1975), 436–42.
95. *Poems, Chiefly of Early and Late Years* (1842), p. 402. Printed *PW*, III. 493.
96. W to Henry Reed, 4 Sept. 1842. The sonnets were II, IX, X, of Part Two as the sequence appeared in 1845. Faber's claim is in the letter to Keble, as n. 94.
97. *Lives of the English Saints* [ed. J. H. Newman] (4 vols., London, 1844), II. 181–2.
98. *LY*, IV. 626. n. 2, quotes the President's words.
99. HCR to Thomas Robinson, 2 Jan. 1845. *HCR*, II. 582 and *HCR: Books*, II. 655, entry 19 Dec. 1845.
100. In 1841 W corresponded with an editor who wanted to make a selection of the poetry, showing its contribution to the Revival of Catholic Truth, and in 1844 with Henry Alford who wanted him to write hymns. See *LY*, IV. 353–4 and 527–8.
101. *Adventures on Salisbury Plain*, 819; *Guilt and Sorrow: or, Incidents upon Salisbury Plain*, 657. *Salisbury Plain Poems*, 154 and 281.
102. *HCR: Books*, II. 655, entry 19 Dec. 1845.
103. W to IF [13 May 1846]. *LY*, IV. 776.
104. HCR to Thomas Robinson, 5 Feb. 1847. *HCR*, II. 639–40.
105. Ibid.
106. W's sonnet elegy for Edward, 'Why should we weep or mourn, Angelic boy', was published in the last collected edition, 1849–50. *PW*, IV. 266.
107. *Grosart*, III. 489.
108. For the original elegies see *Gill: Oxf. W.*, 307–12 and note. The subtitle in 1842 reads: 'Composed near the Mountain track, that leads from Grasmere through Grisdale Hawes, where it descends towards Patterdale'. For a photograph of the spot see *JWL*, 36.
109. HCR to Thomas Robinson, 23 Dec. 1847 and to IF, 10 Jan. [18]48. *HCR*, II. 654, 657–8.
110. *PW*, IV. 392–4. On the day of Dora's death C. B. Phipps wrote to express the Royal pleasure. His words were sadly ironic: 'The force and beauty of the ideas, and the elegance of the Versification fully proved to Her Majesty and the Prince that Time had been powerless over the Mind or Skill of the Poet'. *LY*, IV. 852.
111. For expression of W's simmering anger about Quillinan, see his letter [19 Sept. 1844] to IF. *LY*, IV. 597.
112. EQ to IF, 13 Oct. 1847 and W to IF, 6 Dec. [1847]. Both *LY*, IV. 859.
113. HCR to IF, 24 Dec. [18]47. *HCR*, II. 656.
114. *Prose*, III. 369–82. A notebook now in the Northwestern University Library, Special Collections, contains some notes Christopher also made of his uncle's conversation.
115. MW to IF, 27 Dec. [1847]. *MWL*, 291.
116. MW to Kate Southey 23 Feb. [?1848] and to HCR, 7 June 1848. *LY*, IV. 865 and 869.
117. Henry Taylor to William Bradford Reed, 7 June 1848. WL.

118. MW to IF, 2 Aug. 1848. *MWL*, 299.
119. *Grosart*, III. 476–85. Yarnall later included this recollection in *Wordsworth and the Coleridges, with Other Memories Literary and Political* (New York, 1899).
120. Elizabeth M. Sewell, diary entry 8 Sept. 1849. *The Autobiography of Elizabeth M. Sewell*, ed. Eleanor L. Sewell (London, 1907), 106–10.
121. HCR to Thomas Robinson, 12 Jan. [18]49. *HCR*, II. 683.
122. [Derwent Coleridge], 'Memoir of Hartley Coleridge', prefixed to *Poems* by Hartley Coleridge (2 vols., London, 1851), pp. clxxxv–clxxxvii.
123. See HCR to Thomas Robinson [4–5 Jan. 1849] and 12 Jan. [18]49: 'a more worthless life cannot be imagined than his'; 'a life of intense sottishness'; 'The best that can be said of him is that he was a kind hearted man—Nobodys enemy but his own'. *HCR*, II. 681 and 684.
124. Reported by HCR to IF, 15 Jan. [1849]. HCR adds three exclamation marks to indicate his incomprehension that to W, DW's death 'would be . . . a sad calamity'. *HCR*, II. 685. For all his frequent visits, HCR did not understand the dynamics of Rydal Mount.
125. HCR to Thomas Robinson, 27 June 1849. *HCR*, II. 698.
126. Jemima Quillinan's diary, 14 Mar. 1850. MW's 1850 Almanack. WL. On 10 Mar. EQ had noted in his diary: 'Very keen cold weather—Mr W in the evening proposed to join us on our walk towards Grasmere . . . I remonstrated with him on being so thinly clad. "I care nothing about it" was his answer as if poor man, he were invulnerable.' WL.
127. EQ to Lady Richardson, 24 Mar. 1850. WL.
128. Ibid.
129. 'Mr Wordsworth breathed his last calmly, passing away almost insensibly exactly at twelve o'clock (this midday), while the cuckoo-clock at his bedroom door was striking the hour. In the Even[ing] to Grasmere Church Yard with John and Wm Wordsworth.' EQ diary, 23 Apr. 1850. WL.
130. MW's phrase in a letter to Susan Wordsworth [Christopher's wife], 7 Feb. 1855. *MWL*, 353. Closing quotation *Home at Grasmere*, 9–12.

# APPENDIX

THE philosophical verse discussed in Chapter 5, written in spring 1798 as a possible conclusion to *The Ruined Cottage*.

                          Not useless do I deem
These quiet sympathies with things that hold
An inarticulate language, for the man
Once taught to love such objects as excite
No morbid passions, no disquietude,
No vengeance and no hatred, needs must feel
The joy of that pure principle of love
So deeply that, unsatisfied with aught
Less pure and exquisite, he cannot choose
But seek for objects of a kindred love
In fellow-natures, and a kindred joy.
Accordingly he by degrees perceives
His feelings of aversion softened down,
A holy tenderness pervade his frame,
His sanity of reason not impaired,
Say rather all his thoughts now flowing clear
—From a clear fountain flowing—he looks round,
He seeks for good and finds the good he seeks;
Till execration and contempt are things
He only knows by name, and if he hears
From other mouths the language which they speak
He is compassionate, and has no thought,
No feeling, which can overcome his love.
And further, by contemplating these forms
In the relations which they bear to man
We shall discover what a power is theirs
To stimulate our minds, and multiply
The spiritual presences of absent things.
Then weariness will cease—We shall acquire
The [        ] habit by which sense is made
Subservient still to moral purposes,
A vital essence and a saving power;
Nor shall we meet an object but may read
Some sweet and tender lesson to our minds
Of human suffering or of human joy.
All things shall speak of man, and we shall read
Our duties in all forms, and general laws
And local accidents shall tend alike
To quicken and to rouze, and give the will

And power which by a [          ] chain of good
Shall link us to our kind. No naked hearts,
No naked minds, shall then be left to mourn
The burthen of existence. Science then
Shall be a precious visitant; and then,
And only then, be worthy of her name.
For then her heart shall kindle, her dull eye,
Dull and inanimate, nor more shall hang
Chained to its object in brute slavery,
But better taught and mindful of its use
Legitimate, and its peculiar power,
While with a patient interest it shall watch
The processes of things, and serve the cause
Of order and distinctness; not for this
Shall it forget that its most noble end,
Its most illustrious province, must be found
In ministering to the excursive power
Of Intellect and thought. So build we up
The being that we are. For was it meant
That we should pore, and dwindle as we pore,
Forever dimly pore on things minute,
On solitary objects, still beheld
In disconnection, dead and spiritless,
And still dividing, and dividing still,
Break down all grandeur, still unsatisfied
With our unnatural toil, while littleness
May yet become more little, waging thus
An impious warfare with the very life
Of our own souls? Or was it ever meant
That this majestic imagery, the clouds,
The ocean, and the firmament of heaven,
Should be a barren picture on the mind?
Never for ends of vanity and pain
And sickly wretchedness were we endued
Amid this world of feeling and of life
With apprehension, reason, will and thought,
Affections, organs, passions. Let us rise
From this oblivious sleep, these fretful dreams
Of feverish nothingness. Thus disciplined
All things shall live in us, and we shall live
In all things that surround us. This I deem
Our tendency, and thus shall every day
Enlarge our sphere of pleasure and of pain.
For thus the senses and the intellect
Shall each to each supply a mutual aid,

Invigorate and sharpen and refine
Each other with a power that knows no bound,
And forms and feelings acting thus, and thus
Reacting, they shall each acquire
A living spirit and a character
Till then unfelt, and each be multiplied,
With a variety that knows no end.
Thus deeply drinking in the soul of things
We shall be wise perforce, and we shall move
From strict necessity along the path
Of order and of good. Whate'er we see,
Whate'er we feel, by agency direct
Or indirect, shall tend to feed and nurse
Our faculties and raise to loftier heights
Our intellectual soul. The old man ceased.
The words he uttered shall not pass away.
They had sunk into me, but not as sounds
To be expressed by visible characters;
For while he spake my spirit had obeyed
The presence of his eye, my ear had drunk
The meanings of his voice. He had discoursed
Like one who in the slow and silent works,
The manifold conclusions of his thought,
Had brooded till Imagination's power
Condensed them to a passion whence she drew
Herself new energies, resistless force.

# SELECT BIBLIOGRAPHY

THIS is not a full bibliography of the subject, but a list of sources used, cited, or quoted. Place of publication is London, unless otherwise noted.

## I

### STANDARD EDITIONS OF WORDSWORTH

*The Poetical Works of William Wordsworth*, ed. Ernest De Selincourt and Helen Darbishire (5 vols., Oxford, 1940–9).
*The Cornell Wordsworth*. General editor Stephen Parrish. Volumes in order of date of publication:

*The Salisbury Plain Poems*, ed. Stephen Gill (Ithaca, 1975).
*The Prelude, 1798–99*, ed. Stephen Parrish (Ithaca, 1977).
*Home at Grasmere*, ed. Beth Darlington (Ithaca, 1977).
*The Ruined Cottage and The Pedlar*, ed. James Butler (Ithaca, 1979).
*Benjamin the Waggoner*, ed. Paul F. Betz (Ithaca, 1981).
*The Borderers*, ed. Robert Osborn (Ithaca, 1982).
*Poems, in Two Volumes*, ed. Jared R. Curtis (Ithaca, 1983).
*An Evening Walk*, ed. James Averill (Ithaca, 1984).
*Descriptive Sketches*, ed. Eric Birdsall (Ithaca, 1984).
*Peter Bell*, ed. John E. Jordan (Ithaca, 1985).
*The Fourteen-Book Prelude*, ed. W. J. B. Owen (Ithaca, 1985).
*The Tuft of Primroses with Other Late Poems for The Recluse*, ed. Joseph Kishel (Ithaca, 1986).
*The White Doe of Rylstone*, ed. Kristine Dugas (Ithaca, 1988).
*Shorter Poems 1807–1820*, ed. Carl H. Ketcham (Ithaca, 1989).

*The Prelude 1799, 1805, 1850*, ed. Jonathan Wordsworth, M. H. Abrams, and Stephen Gill (New York, 1979).
*William Wordsworth*, ed. Stephen Gill (Oxford, 1984).
*Lyrical Ballads 1798*, ed. W. J. B. Owen (Oxford, 1967; 2nd edn. 1969).
*The Prose Works of William Wordsworth*, ed. Alexander B. Grosart (3 vols., 1876).
*The Prose Works of William Wordsworth*, ed. W. J. B. Owen and Jane Worthington Smyser (3 vols., Oxford, 1974).
*Literary Criticism of William Wordsworth*, ed. Paul M. Zall (Lincoln, Nebr., 1966).
*The Illustrated Wordsworth's Guide to the Lakes*, ed. Peter Bicknell (Exeter, 1984).
*Letters of William and Dorothy Wordsworth*, ed. E. De Selincourt; *The Early Years, 1787–1805*, revised Chester L. Shaver (Oxford, 1967); *The Middle Years, 1806–11*, revised Mary Moorman (Oxford, 1969); *The Middle Years, 1812–1820*, revised Mary Moorman and Alan G. Hill (Oxford, 1970); *The Later Years, 1821–53*, revised Alan G. Hill (4 vols., Oxford, 1978–88).

*The Love Letters of William and Mary Wordsworth*, ed. Beth Darlington (Ithaca, 1981).

*Wordsworth and Reed: The Poet's Correspondence with his American Editor: 1836–1850*, ed. L. N. Broughton (Ithaca, 1933).


STANDARD EDITIONS OF COLERIDGE


*The Poetical Works of Samuel Taylor Coleridge*, ed. Ernest Hartley Coleridge (2 vols., Oxford, 1912).

*Poems*, ed. John Beer (1963); 2nd revised edn. (1974).

*Collected Letters*, ed. Earl Leslie Griggs (6 vols., Oxford, 1956–71).

*The Notebooks*, ed. Kathleen Coburn (6 vols., continuing, 1957–).


*The Collected Works of Samuel Taylor Coleridge*, general editor, Kathleen Coburn. Volumes used in order of date of publication:

*The Friend*, ed. Barbara E. Rooke (2 vols., 1969).

*The Watchman*, ed. Lewis Patton (1970).

*Lectures 1795 on Politics and Religion*, ed. Lewis Patton and Peter Mann (1971).

*Lay Sermons*, ed. R. J. White (1972).

*On the Constitution of the Church and State*, ed. John Colmer (1976).

*Essays on his Times*, ed. David V. Erdman (3 vols., 1978).

*Biographia Literaria*, ed. James Engell and W. Jackson Bate (2 vols., 1983).


*Specimens of the Table Talk*, ed. H. N. Coleridge (2 vols., 1835).


II

WORKS BY MEMBERS OF THE WORDSWORTH–COLERIDGE FAMILY CIRCLE


COLERIDGE, HARTLEY, *Letters*, ed. Grace Evelyn Griggs and Earl Leslie Griggs (1936).

—— *The Hartley Coleridge Letters: A Calendar and Index*, ed. Fran Carlock Stephens (Austin, 1978).

—— *Poems: With a Memoir of his Life by his Brother* [Derwent Coleridge] (2 vols., 1851).

COLERIDGE, SARA, *Memoir and Letters of Sara Coleridge*, ed. Edith Coleridge (2 vols., 1873).

HUTCHINSON, SARA, *Letters*, ed. Kathleen Coburn (1954).

WORDSWORTH, DORA, *The Letters*, ed. Howard P. Vincent (Chicago, 1944).

—— *Dora Wordsworth her Book*, ed. F. V. Morley (1924).

WORDSWORTH, DOROTHY, *Journals*, ed. E. De Selincourt (2 vols., 1941).

—— *Journals*, ed. Mary Moorman (1971).

—— *A Narrative Concerning George and Sarah Green*, ed. E. De Selincourt

(Oxford, 1936); reissued with additional material as *The Greens of Grasmere*, ed. Hilary Clark (Wolverhampton, 1987).

WORDSWORTH, JOHN, *Letters*, ed. Carl H. Ketcham (Ithaca, 1969).

WORDSWORTH, MARY, *The Letters . . . 1800–1855*, ed. Mary E. Burton (Oxford, 1958).

## III

### OTHER SOURCE MATERIAL PUBLISHED UP TO 1900

ALGER, JOHN, G., *Englishmen in the French Revolution* (1889).

ANDERSON, ROBERT (ed.), *The Works of the British Poets, with Prefaces, Biographical and Critical* (13 vols., London and Edinburgh, 1792–5).

BEWICK, WILLIAM, *Life and Letters of William Bewick (Artist)*, ed. Thomas Landseer (2 vols., 1871).

BINNS, JOHN, *Recollections of the Life of John Binns* (Philadelphia, 1854).

BROUGHAM, HENRY, Lord, *The Life and Times of Henry Lord Brougham* (3 vols., 1871).

BUDWORTH, JOSEPH, *A Fortnight's Ramble to the Lakes in Westmoreland, Lancashire, and Cumberland* (1792).

BURKE, EDMUND, *Reflections on the Revolution in France* (1790) ed. Conor Cruise O'Brien (Harmondsworth, 1968).

—— *Three Letters Addressed to a Member of the Present Parliament, on the Proposals for Peace with the Regicide Directory of France* (1796).

—— *The Works . . . A New Edition* (16 vols., 1803–27).

BUSSIÈRE, GEORGES, and LEGOUIS, ÉMILE, *Le Général Michel Beaupuy 1755–1796* (Paris and Perigueux, 1891).

CLARKE, JAMES, *Survey of the Lakes* (1797).

CLAYDEN, P. W., *Rogers and his Contemporaries* (2 vols., 1889).

COCKBURN, Lord [HENRY], *Life of Lord Jeffrey with a Selection from his Correspondence* (2 vols., 1852).

COLERIDGE, Sir J. T., *A Memoir of the Rev. John Keble* (Oxford and London, 1869).

COOPER, THOMAS, *The Life of Thomas Cooper* (1872), ed. John Saville (Leicester, 1971).

COTTLE, JOSEPH, *Poems* (Bristol, 1795).

—— *Early Recollections, Chiefly Relating to the Late Samuel Taylor Coleridge* (2 vols., 1837).

COXE, WILLIAM, *Sketches of the Natural, Civil, and Political State of Swisserland: In a Series of Letters to William Melmoth, Esq.* (1779).

—— *Travels in Switzerland: In a Series of Letters to William Melmoth, Esq.* (3 vols., 1789).

DE VERE, AUBREY, *Essays Chiefly on Poetry* (2 vols., 1887).

—— *Recollections* (1897).

DEWEY, ORVILLE, *The Old World and the New* (2 vols., New York, 1836).

DYER, GEORGE, *The Poet's Fate* (1797).

EDEN, Sir FREDERICK MORTON, *The State of the Poor: or, A History of the Labouring Classes in England* (3 vols., 1797).

EMERSON, RALPH WALDO, *English Traits* (Boston and London, 1856).

ERSKINE, THOMAS, *A View of the Causes and Consequences of the Present War with France* (1797).

FAWCETT, JOSEPH, *The Art of War* (1795).

—— *Sermons Delivered at the Sunday-evening Lecture, for the Winter Season, the Old Jewry* (2 vols., 1795).

FLETCHER, ELIZABETH, *Autobiography of Mrs Fletcher*, ed. the Survivor of her Family [Lady Richardson] (Edinburgh, 1875).

FREND, WILLIAM, *Patriotism: or, The Love of our Country: An Essay* (1804).

GILLIES, ROBERT PEARCE, *Memoirs of a Literary Veteran* (3 vols., 1851).

GILPIN, WILLIAM, *Observations on the River Wye . . . Relative Chiefly to Picturesque Beauty* (1782).

GODWIN, WILLIAM, *An Enquiry Concerning Political Justice, and its Influence on General Virtue and Happiness* (2 vols., 1793).

—— *Enquiry Concerning Political Justice and its Influence on Morals and Happiness*, ed. F. E. L. Priestley (3 vols., Toronto, 1946).

—— *Things as They Are: or, The Adventures of Caleb Williams* (3 vols., 1794); ed. David McCracken (Oxford, 1970).

GORDON, Mrs [MARY], *Memoir of Christopher North: By his Daughter* (2 vols., Edinburgh, 1862).

GRATTAN, THOMAS COLLEY, *Beaten Paths; And Those Who Trod Them* (2 vols., 1862).

GRAVES, ROBERT PERCEVAL, *Life of Sir William Rowan Hamilton* (3 vols., Dublin and London, 1882–9).

GRAY, THOMAS, *The Poems of Mr Gray: To which are Prefixed Memoirs of his Life and Writings*, ed. William Mason (York, 1775).

GUNNING, HENRY, *Reminiscences of the University, Town and County of Cambridge, from the Year 1780* (2 vols., 1854).

HANMER, Sir THOMAS, *Correspondence*, ed. Sir Henry Bunbury (1838).

HAYDON, BENJAMIN ROBERT, *Correspondence and Table-talk*, ed. Frederic Wordsworth Haydon (2 vols., 1876).

——*Life of Benjamin Robert Haydon, Historical Painter: From his Autobiography and Journals*, ed. Tom Taylor (3 vols., 1853).

HILLARD, G. S., *Life, Letters, and Journals of George Ticknor* (2 vols., 1876).

HUTCHINSON, WILLIAM, *An Excursion to the Lakes: In Westmoreland and Cumberland, August 1773* (1774).

JERDAN, WILLIAM, *Autobiography* (4 vols., 1852–3).

LAMB, CHARLES, *The Works* (2 vols., 1818).

LOCKHART, J. G., *Memoirs of the Life of Sir Walter Scott, Bart.* (7 vols., Edinburgh and London, 1837–8).

LOUVET, JOHN-BAPTIST, *Narrative of the Dangers to which I have been Exposed, since the 31st of May 1793* (1795).

MACKINTOSH, ROBERT JAMES, *Memoirs of the Life of the Right Honourable Sir James Mackintosh* (2 vols., 1835).

MATHEWS, Mrs ANNE, *Memoir of Charles Mathews, Comedian* (4 vols., 1838–9).

NICOLSON, JOSEPH, and BURN, RICHARD, *The History and Antiquities of the Counties of Westmorland and Cumberland* (2 vols., 1777).

OLIPHANT, Mrs [MARGARET], *Annals of a Publishing House: William Blackwood and his Sons* (2 vols., Edinburgh and London, 1897).

OVERTON, JOHN HENRY, and WORDSWORTH, ELIZABETH, *Christopher Wordsworth: Bishop of Lincoln 1807–1885* (1888).

PARSON, WILLIAM, and WHITE, WILLIAM, *History, Directory, and Gazetteer, of the Counties of Cumberland, and Westmorland . . . Furness* (Leeds, 1829).

PENNANT, THOMAS, *A Tour in Wales* (2 vols., 1784).

PIERCE, EDWARD, L., *Memoir and Letters of Charles Sumner* (3 vols., 1878–93).

ROLAND, Madame, *An Appeal to Impartial Posterity* (2 vols., 1795).

SANDFORD, Mrs HENRY, *Thomas Poole and his Friends* (2 vols., 1888).

SEWARD, ANNA, *The Letters . . . Written between the Years 1784 and 1807* (6 vols., Edinburgh and London, 1811).

SOUTHEY, ROBERT, *Selections from the Letters of Robert Southey*, ed John Wood Warter (4 vols., 1856).

—— *The Life and Correspondence*, ed. Charles Cuthbert Southey (6 vols., 1849–50).

TAYLOR, HENRY, *Autobiography* (2 vols., 1885).

—— *Correspondence of Henry Taylor*, ed. Edward Dowden (1888).

TENNYSON, HALLAM, *Alfred Lord Tennyson: A Memoir* (2 vols., 1897).

THELWALL, JOHN, *Poems, Chiefly Written in Retirement* (Hereford, 1801).

TROLLOPE, THOMAS ADOLPHUS, *What I Remember* (3 vols., 1887–9).

WATSON, RICHARD, *Anecdotes of the Life of Richard Watson* [by his son] (1817).

WEST, THOMAS, *A Guide to the Lakes* (1778).

WHITAKER, THOMAS DUNHAM, *The History and Antiquities of the Deanery of Craven* (1805).

WILLIAMS, HELEN MARIA, *Letters Containing a Sketch of the Politics of France from the Thirty-first of May 1793, till the Twenty-eighth of July 1794, and of the Scenes which have Passed in the Prisons of Paris* (2 vols., 1795).

WILSON, JOHN, *The Recreations of Christopher North* (3 vols., Edinburgh and London, 1842).

WORDSWORTH, CHRISTOPHER, *Memoirs of William Wordsworth* (2 vols., 1851).

—— *Social Life at the English Universities in the Eighteenth Century* (Cambridge, 1874).

—— *Scholae Academicae: Some Account of the Studies at the English Universities in the Eighteenth Century* (Cambridge, 1877).

YARNALL, ELLIS, *Wordsworth and the Coleridges, with Other Memories Literary and Political* (New York, 1899).

YOUNG, Julian Charles, *Memoir of Charles Mayne Young* (2 vols., 1871).

IV

OTHER SOURCE MATERIAL, SCHOLARSHIP, AND CRITICISM, PUBLISHED AFTER
1900

ABRAMS, M. H., *Natural Supernaturalism* (New York, 1971).
ALDERSON, B. R., *The Parish Register of Bowes 1670–1837* (Wakefield, 1964).
ALGER, JOHN G., *Paris in 1789–94* (1902).
ALTICK, RICHARD, D., *The Shows of London* (Cambridge, Mass., 1978).
ARMSTRONG, ISOBEL, *Victorian Scrutinies: Reviews of Poetry 1830–1870* (1972).
ASPINALL, ARTHUR, *Lord Brougham and the Whig Party* (Manchester, 1927).
—— *Politics and the Press 1780–1850* (1949).
AUBIN, ROBERT ARNOLD, *Topographical Poetry in Eighteenth-century England* (New York, 1936).
AVERILL, JAMES, *Wordsworth and Human Suffering* (Ithaca, 1980).
—— 'Another Early Coleridge Reference to *An Evening Walk*', *English Language Notes*, 13 (1976), 270–3.
BARRETT, ELIZABETH, *Elizabeth Barrett to Mr. Boyd*, ed. Barbara P. McCarthy (1955).
BARTON, ANNE, 'The Road from Penshurst: Wordsworth, Ben Jonson and Coleridge in 1802', *EIC* 37 (1987), 209–33.
BATHO, EDITH C., *The Later Wordsworth* (Cambridge, 1933).
—— *The Ettrick Shepherd* (Cambridge, 1927).
BAUER, JOSEPHINE, *The London Magazine 1820–29* (Copenhagen, 1953).
BAUER, N. STEPHEN, 'Early Burlesques and Parodies of Wordsworth', *JEGP* 74 (1975), 553–69.
BEARD, GEOFFREY, *The Greater House in Cumbria* (Kendal, 1978).
BEATTY, ARTHUR, *Joseph Fawcett: The Art of War: Its Relation to the Early Development of William Wordsworth*, University of Wisconsin Studies in Language and Literature, 2 (1918), 224–69.
BECKETT, J. V., *Coal and Tobacco: The Lowthers and the Economic Development of West Cumberland, 1660–1760* (Cambridge, 1981).
BICKNELL, PETER, *Beauty Horror and Immensity: Picturesque Landscape in Britain 1750–1850* (Cambridge, 1981).
—— and WOOF, ROBERT, *The Discovery of the Lake District 1750–1810* (Grasmere, 1982).
BLANSHARD, FRANCES, *Portraits of Wordsworth* (1959).
BONSALL, BRIAN, *Sir James Lowther and Cumberland and Westmorland Elections, 1754–75* (Manchester, 1960).
BOULTON, JAMES T., *The Language of Politics in the Age of Wilkes and Burke* (1963).
BROMWICH, DAVID, *Hazlitt: The Mind of a Critic* (New York and Oxford, 1983).
BRONTË, PATRICK BRANWELL, *The Poems*, ed. Tom Winnifrith (Oxford, 1983).
BULWER, EDWARD LYTTON, *England and the English* (1833), ed. Standish Meacham (Chicago and London, 1970).
BURKETT, M. E., and SLOSS, J. D. G., *William Green of Ambleside: A Lake District Artist (1760–1823)* (Kendal, 1984).
BUTLER, MARILYN, 'Godwin, Burke, and *Caleb Williams*', *EIC* 32 (1982), 237–57.

—— *Burke, Paine, Godwin, and the Revolution Controversy* (Cambridge, 1984).

CARLYLE, ALEXANDER, *Anecdotes and Characters of the Times*, ed. James Kinsley (1973).

CELORIA, FRANCIS, 'Chatterton, Wordsworth and Stonehenge', *Notes and Queries*, NS 23 (Mar. 1976), 103–4.

CHANDLER, JAMES K., *Wordsworth's Second Nature: A Study of the Poetry and Politics* (Chicago, 1984).

CHARD, LESLIE, *Dissenting Republican: Wordsworth's Early Life and Thought in their Political Context* (The Hague, 1972).

CHRISTIE, IAN R., *Myth and Reality in Late Eighteenth-century British Politics* (1970).

—— *Stress and Stability in Late Eighteenth-century Britain* (Oxford, 1984).

CHRISTIE, WILLIAM, 'Francis Jeffrey, Samuel Taylor Coleridge's *Biographia Literaria*, and Contemporary Criticism of William Wordsworth', D.Phil. thesis (Oxford, 1982).

CLIVE, JOHN, *Scotch Reviewers: The Edinburgh Review, 1802–1815* (1957).

COBBAN, ALFRED, *The Debate on the French Revolution 1789–1800* (1950).

COLEMAN, Deirdre, 'Jeffrey and Coleridge: Four Unpublished Letters', *Wordsworth Circle*, 18 (winter 1987), 39–45.

COLVIN, HOWARD, CROOK, J. MORDAUNT, and FRIEDMAN, TERRY, *Architectural Drawings from Lowther Castle Westmorland*, Architectural History Monographs, 2 (1980).

CORNWELL, JOHN, *Coleridge: Poet and Revolutionary 1772–1804* (1973).

COURTNEY, WINIFRED F., *Young Charles Lamb 1775–1802* (1982).

CRABBE, GEORGE, *Selected Letters and Journals*, ed. Thomas C. Faulkner (Oxford, 1985).

CROSS, NIGEL, *The Common Writer: Life in Nineteenth-century Grub Street* (Cambridge, 1985).

CURTIS, JARED, R., *Wordsworth's Experiments with Tradition: The Lyric Poems of 1802* (Ithaca and London, 1971).

—— 'The Wellesley Copy of Wordsworth's *Poetical Works*, 1832'. *Harvard Library Bulletin*, 28 (1980), 5–15.

DANN, JOANNE, 'Some Notes on the Relationship between the Wordsworth and Lowther Families', *Wordsworth Circle*, 11 (1980), 80–2.

DAVIES, HUGH SYKES, *Wordsworth and the Worth of Words*, ed. John Kerrigan and Jonathan Wordsworth (Cambridge, 1987).

DAVIES, HUNTER, *William Wordsworth* (1980).

DE QUINCEY, THOMAS, *De Quincey to Wordsworth: A Biography of a Relationship. With the Letters of Thomas De Quincey to the Wordsworth Family*, ed. John E. Jordan (Berkeley and Los Angeles, 1962).

—— *Recollections of the Lakes and the Lake Poets*, ed. David Wright (Harmondsworth, 1970).

DE SELINCOURT, ERNEST, *Dorothy Wordsworth: A Biography* (Oxford, 1933).

EDGEWORTH, MARIA, *Letters from England 1813–1844*, ed. Christina Colvin (Oxford, 1971).

ELIOT, GEORGE, *Letters*, ed. Gordon S. Haight (9 vols., New Haven and London, 1954–78).

ELLIS, DAVID, *Wordsworth, Freud and the Spots of Time: Interpretation in The Prelude* (Cambridge, 1985).

ENGELL, JAMES, *The Creative Imagination: Englightenment to Romanticism* (Cambridge, Mass., and London, 1981).

ERDMAN, DAVID, V., 'Coleridge, Wordsworth, and the Wedgwood Fund', *BNYPL* 60 (1956), 425–43; 487–507.

—— 'Wordsworth as Heartsworth: or, Was Regicide the Prophetic Ground of Those "Moral Questions"?', *The Evidence of the Imagination: Studies of Interactions between Life and Art in English Romantic Literature*, ed. Donald H. Reiman, Michael C. Jaye, and Betty T. Bennett (New York, 1978).

EVANS, BERGEN, and PINNEY, HESTER, 'Racedown and the Wordsworths', *RES* 8 (1932), 1–18.

EVEREST, KELVIN, *Coleridge's Secret Ministry: The Context of the Conversation Poems 1795–1798* (Hassocks and New York, 1979).

FABER, FREDERICK WILLIAM, *Faber Poet and Priest: Selected Letters*, ed. Raleigh Addington (Cowbridge, 1974).

FARINGTON, JOSEPH, *The Diary*, vols. I–VI ed. Kenneth Garlick and Angus Macintyre; vols. VII–XVI, continuing, ed. Kathryn Cave (New Haven and London, 1978–).

FELL, ALFRED, *The Early Iron Industry of Furness and District* (Ulverston, 1908).

FIELD, BARRON, *Memoirs of Wordsworth*, ed. Geoffrey Little (Sydney, 1975).

FINCH, JOHN A., 'Wordsworth's Two-handed Engine', *Bicentenary Wordsworth Studies*, ed. Jonathan Wordsworth (Ithaca, 1970), 1–13.

FINK, Z. S., *The Early Wordsworthian Milieu* (Oxford, 1958).

FOOT, MICHAEL, 'Hazlitt's Revenge on the Lakers', *Wordsworth Circle*, 14 (Winter 1983), 61–8.

FOSKETT, DAPHNE, *John Harden of Brathay Hall, 1772–1847* (Kendal, 1974).

FOXON, D. F., 'The Printing of *Lyrical Ballads*, 1798', *Library*, 5th ser. 9 (1954), 221–41.

FRIEDMAN, MICHAEL, H., *The Making of a Tory Humanist* (New York, 1979).

GASKELL, ELIZABETH, *The Letters of Mrs Gaskell*, ed. J. A. V. Chapple and Arthur Pollard (Manchester, 1966).

GEORGE, ERIC, *The Life and Death of Benjamin Robert Haydon* (Oxford, 1948); 2nd edn. with additions by Dorothy George (Oxford, 1967).

GÉRIN, WINIFRED, *Branwell Brontë* (1961).

GILCHRIST, J., and MURRAY, W. J., *The Press in the French Revolution* (Melbourne and London, 1971).

GILL, STEPHEN, '"Adventures on Salisbury Plain" and Wordsworth's Poetry of Protest 1795–97', *SIR* 11 (1972), 48–65.

—— 'Wordsworth's Poems: The Question of Text', *RES* NS 34 (1983), 172–90.

—— ' "Affinities Preserved": Poetic Self-reference in Wordsworth', *SIR* 24 (1985), 531–49.

GIROUARD, MARK, *The Return to Camelot: Chivalry and the English Gentleman* (New Haven and London, 1981).

GITTINGS, ROBERT, *John Keats* (1968).

——and MANTON, JO, *Dorothy Wordsworth* (1985).

GLEN, HEATHER, *Vision and Disenchantment: Blake's Songs and Wordsworth's Lyrical Ballads* (Cambridge, 1983).

GODWIN, WILLIAM, *Uncollected Writings*, ed. Jack W. Marken and Burton R. Pollin (Gainesville, 1968).

GOODWIN, A., *The French Revolution* (1953; 5th edn. 1970).

—— *The Friends of Liberty: The English Democratic Movement in the Age of the French Revolution* (1979).

GRAY, THOMAS, *Correspondence*, ed. Paget Toynbee and Leonard Whibley (3 vols., Oxford, 1935); with corrections and additions by H. W. Starr (3 vols., Oxford, 1971).

GREAVES, MARGARET, *Regency Patron: Sir George Beaumont* (1966).

GREEN, VIVIAN H. H., *The Commonwealth of Lincoln College, 1427–1977* (Oxford, 1979).

GRIGGS, EARL LESLIE, *Coleridge Fille: A Biography of Sara Coleridge* (Oxford, 1940).

HANKINS, THOMAS L., *Sir William Rowan Hamilton* (Baltimore and London, 1980).

HARPER, GEORGE MCLEAN, *William Wordsworth: His Life, Works, and Influence* (2 vols., 1916).

—— *Wordsworth's French Daughter* (Princeton, 1921).

HAYDEN, DONALD E., *Wordsworth's Walking Tour of 1790* (Tulsa, Okla., 1983).

—— *Wordsworth's Travels in Scotland* (Tulsa, Okla., 1985).

—— *Wordsworth's Travels in Wales and Ireland* (Tulsa, Okla., 1985).

HAYDEN, JOHN O., *The Romantic Reviewers 1802–1824* (1969).

—— 'William Wordsworth's Letter to John Wilson (1802)', *Wordsworth Circle*, 18 (1987), 33 8.

HAYDON, BENJAMIN ROBERT, *The Diary*, ed. Willard Bissell Pope (5 vols., Cambridge, Mass., 1960–3).

HAZLITT, WILLIAM, *The Complete Works*, ed. P. P. Howe (21 vols., 1930–4).

—— *The Letters*, ed. Herschel Moreland Sikes, assisted by Willard Hallam Bonner and Gerald Lahey (1978).

HEATH, WILLIAM, *Wordsworth and Coleridge: A Study of their Literary Relations in 1801–1802* (Oxford, 1970).

HILL, ALAN G., 'Wordsworth, Comenius, and the Meaning of Education', *RES* NS 26 (1975), 301–12.

—— 'Wordsworth and his American Friends', *BRH* 81 (1978), 146–60.

HILTON, TIM, *John Ruskin: The Early Years 1819–1859* (New Haven and London, 1985).

HOLLAND, ELIZABETH, Lady, *The Journal . . . (1791–1811)*, ed. the Earl of Ilchester (2 vols., 1908).

HONAN, PARK, *Matthew Arnold: A Life* (1981).

HONE, J. ANN, *For the Cause of Truth: Radicalism in London 1796–1821* (Oxford, 1982).

HOPKINS, GERARD MANLEY, *The Letters . . . to Robert Bridges*, ed. Claude Colleer Abbott (1935; 2nd edn. 1955).

HUNT, BISHOP, C. jun., 'Wordsworth, Haydon, and the "Wellington" Sonnet', *Princeton University Library Chronicle*, 36 (1974–5), 111–32.

HUNT, LEIGH, *Autobiography*, ed. J. E. Morpurgo (1949).

JACOBUS, MARY, *Tradition and Experiment in Wordsworth's Lyrical Ballads (1798)* (Oxford, 1976).

JAYE, MICHAEL C., 'William Wordsworth's Alfoxden Notebook: 1798', *The Evidence of the Imagination: Studies of Interactions between Life and Art in English Romantic Literature*, ed. Donald H. Reiman, Michael C. Jaye, and Betty T. Bennett (New York, 1978).

JOHNSON, EDGAR, *Charles Dickens: His Tragedy and Triumph* (2 vols., 1952).

—— *Sir Walter Scott: The Great Unknown* (2 vols., 1970).

JOHNSTON, KENNETH R., *Wordsworth and The Recluse* (New Haven and London, 1984).

JONES, STANLEY, 'B. R. Haydon on Some Contemporaries: A New Letter', *RES* NS 26 (1975), 183–9.

JORDAN, JOHN E., *Why the Lyrical Ballads?* (Berkeley, Los Angeles, London, 1976).

KAPLAN, FRED, *Thomas Carlyle: A Biography* (Cambridge, 1983).

KEATS, JOHN, *The Letters . . . 1814–1821*, ed. Hyder Edward Rollins (2 vols., Cambridge, Mass., 1958).

KEBLE, JOHN, *Lectures on Poetry 1832–1841*, trans. Edward Kershaw Francis (2 vols., Oxford, 1912).

KELLEY, PAUL, 'Rousseau's "Discourse on the Origins of Inequality" and Wordsworth's "Salisbury Plain"', *Notes and Queries*, NS 24 (July–Aug. 1977), 323.

KELLEY, THERESA M., 'Wordsworth and the Rhinefall', *SIR* 23 (1984), 61–79.

KELLIHER, HILTON, 'Thomas Wilkinson of Yanwath, Friend of Wordsworth and Coleridge', *British Library Journal*, 8 (1982), 147–67.

KNIGHT, FRIDA, *University Rebel: The Life of William Frend, 1757–1841* (1971).

LAMB, CHARLES, *The Letters . . . to which are Added those of his Sister Mary Lamb*, ed. E. V. Lucas (3 vols., 1935).

—— *The Letters of Charles and Mary Lamb*, ed. Edwin W. Marrs (3 vols., continuing, Ithaca and London, 1975–).

—— *The Works in Prose and Verse of Charles and Mary Lamb*, ed. Thomas Hutchinson (2 vols., Oxford, 1924).

LANDON, CAROL, 'Some Sidelights on *The Prelude*', *Bicentenary Wordsworth Studies*, ed. Jonathan Wordsworth (Ithaca, 1970), 359–76.

LAWRENCE, BERTA, *Coleridge and Wordsworth in Somerset* (Newton Abbot, 1970).

LEGOUIS, ÉMILE, *William Wordsworth and Annette Vallon* (1922).

LEMMON, KEN, 'Poet's Hands on the Landscape: Wordsworth's Garden at Rydal Mount, Cumbria', *Country Life*, 3 May 1984, 1240–2.

LEVERE, TREVOR H., *Poetry Realized in Nature: Samuel Taylor Coleridge and Early Nineteenth-century Science* (Cambridge, 1981).

LINDOP, GREVEL, *The Opium-eater: A Life of Thomas De Quincey* (1981).

LITCHFIELD, R. B., *Tom Wedgwood: The First Photographer* (1903).

LOSH, JAMES, *The Diaries and Correspondence*, ed. Edward Hughes (Surtees Soc. 171, 174) (2 vols., Durham and London, 1962, 1963).

McCRACKEN, DAVID, *Wordsworth and the Lake District: A Guide to the Poems and their Places* (Oxford, 1984).

McFARLAND, THOMAS, *Romanticism and the Forms of Ruin: Wordsworth, Coleridge, and Modalities of Fragmentation* (Princeton, 1981).

—— 'Wordsworth on Man, on Nature, and on Human Life', *SIR* 21 (1982), 601–18.

—— *Originality and Imagination* (Baltimore and London, 1985).

MACREADY, WILLIAM CHARLES, *The Diaries . . . 1833–1851*, ed. William Toynbee (2 vols., 1912).

MARSHALL, J. D., *Old Lakeland* (Newton Abbot, 1971).

—— and WALTON, JOHN K., *The Lake Counties from 1830 to the Mid-twentieth Century* (Manchester, 1981).

MARSHALL, PETER H., *William Godwin* (New Haven and London, 1984).

MARTIN, BRIAN W., 'Wordsworth, Faber, and Keble: Commentary on a Triangular Relationship', *RES* NS 26 (1975), 436–42.

—— *John Keble: Priest, Professor and Poet* (1976).

MAVOR, ELIZABETH, *The Ladies of Llangollen* (1971).

MAYO, ROBERT, 'The Contemporaneity of *Lyrical Ballads*', *PMLA* 69 (1954), 486–522.

MERRIAM, HAROLD G., *Edward Moxon: Publisher of Poets* (New York, 1939).

MILL, JOHN STUART, *Autobiography and Literary Essays*, ed. John M. Robson and Jack Stillinger (Toronto, 1981).

—— *The Earlier Letters . . . 1812–1848*, ed. Francis E. Mineka (2 vols., Toronto and London, 1963).

MITCHELL, L. G., 'The *Edinburgh Review* and the Lake Poets 1802–1810', *Essays Presented to C. M. Bowra* (Oxford, 1970), 24–38.

MOORE, THOMAS, *The Journal*, ed. Peter Quennell (1964).

MOORMAN, MARY, *William Wordsworth: A Biography; The Early Years: 1770–1803* (Oxford, 1957); *The Later Years: 1803–1850* (Oxford, 1965).

MORGAN, PETER, F., *Jeffrey's Criticism: A Selection* (Edinburgh, 1983).

—— *Literary Critics and Reviewers in Early Nineteenth Century Britain* (1983).

MORLEY, EDITH J., *The Life and Times of Henry Crabb Robinson* (1935).

MURDOCH, JOHN (ed.), *The Discovery of the Lake District* (1984).

NEW, CHESTER W., *The Life of Henry Brougham to 1830* (Oxford, 1961).

NEWLYN, LUCY, '"In City Pent": Echo and Allusion in Wordsworth, Coleridge, and Lamb, 1797–1801', *RES* NS 32 (1981), 408–28.

—— *Coleridge, Wordsworth, and the Language of Allusion* (Oxford, 1986).

NEWMAN, JOHN HENRY, *Apologia pro vita sua*, ed. Martin J. Svaglic (Oxford, 1967).

NOYES, RUSSELL, *Wordsworth and the Art of Landscape* (Bloomington, 1968).

O'LEARY, PATRICK, *Regency Editor: Life of John Scott* (Aberdeen, 1983).

OWEN, FELICITY, AND BROWN, DAVID BLAYNEY, *Collector of Genius: A Life of Sir George Beaumont* (New Haven and London, 1988).

OWEN, W. J. B., 'Costs, Sales, and Profits of Longman's Editions of Wordsworth', *Library*, 5th ser. 12 (1957), 93–107.

—— 'Letters of Longman & Co. to Wordsworth, 1814–36', *Library*, 5th ser. 9 (1954), 25–34.

—— *Wordsworth as Critic* (Toronto and London, 1969).

PARRISH, STEPHEN MAXFIELD, *The Art of the Lyrical Ballads* (Cambridge, Mass., 1973).

PEACH, LINDEN, *British Influence on the Birth of American Literature* (1982).

PEACOCK, MARKHAM L. (ed.), *The Critical Opinions of William Wordsworth* (Baltimore, 1950).

PEEK, KATHERINE MAY, *Wordsworth in England: Studies in the History of his Fame* (Bryn Mawr, 1943).

PEVSNER, NIKOLAUS, *The Buildings of England: Cumberland and Westmorland* (Harmondsworth, 1967).

PICHANIK, VALERIE K., *Harriet Martineau: The Woman and her Work 1802–76* (Ann Arbor, 1980).

PIPER, H. W., *The Active Universe: Pantheism and the Concept of Imagination in the English Romantic Poets* (1962).

POLLIN, BURTON R., 'Charles Lamb and Charles Lloyd as Jacobins and Anti-Jacobins', *SIR* 12 (1973), 633–47.

PRICKETT, STEPHEN, *Coleridge and Wordsworth: The Poetry of Growth* (Cambridge, 1970).

REED, MARK., 'Wordsworth, Coleridge, and the "Plan" of the *Lyrical Ballads*', *UTQ* 34 (1965), 238–53.

—— *Wordsworth: The Chronology of the Early Years 1770–1799* (Cambridge, Mass., 1967); *The Middle Years 1800–1815* (Cambridge, Mass., 1975).

REIMAN, DONALD H., *The Romantics Reviewed. Part A: The Lake Poets* (2 vols., New York and London, 1972).

REYNOLDS, JOHN HAMILTON, *The Letters*, ed. Leonidas M. Jones (Lincoln, Nebr., 1973).

RICE, H. A. L., 'Wordsworth in Easedale', *Ariel*, 1 (1970), 31–8.

ROBINSON, ERIC, 'An English Jacobin: James Watt, Junior, 1769–1848', *Cambridge Historical Journal*, 11 (1953–5), 349–55.

ROBINSON, HENRY CRABB, *Henry Crabb Robinson on Books and their Writers*, ed. Edith J. Morley (3 vols., 1938).

—— *The Correspondence . . . with the Wordsworth Circle*, ed. Edith J. Morley (2 vols., Oxford, 1927).

ROE, NICHOLAS, *Wordsworth and Coleridge: The Radical Years* (Oxford, 1988).

ROGERS, SAMUEL, *Recollections of the Table-talk of Samuel Rogers: First Collected by the Revd. Alexander Dyce*, ed. Morchard Bishop (1952).

ROLLINS, HYDER EDWARD (ed.), *The Keats Circle* (2 vols., Cambridge, Mass., 1948).

ROLLINSON, WILLIAM, *Life and Tradition in the Lake District* (1974).

ROSE, R. B., 'The Priestley Riots of 1791', *Past and Present*, 18 (1960), 68–88.

RUSSELL, NORMA, *A Bibliography of William Cowper to 1837* (Oxford, 1963).

SANDERS, CHARLES RICHARD, 'Carlyle and Wordsworth', *Browning Institute Studies*, 9 (1981), 115–22.

SCHNEIDER, BEN ROSS, *Wordsworth's Cambridge Education* (Cambridge, 1957).

SCOGGINS, JAMES, *Imagination and Fancy: Complementary Modes in the Poetry of Wordsworth* (Lincoln, Nebr., 1966).

SCOTT, PATRICK, 'The Business of Belief: The Emergence of "Religious Publishing"', *Sanctity and Secularity: The Church and the World*, ed. Derek Baker (Oxford, 1973).

SCOTT, Sir WALTER, *The Journal*, ed. W. E. K. Anderson (Oxford, 1972).

—— *The Letters*, ed. H. J. C. Grierson (12 vols., 1932–7).

SEWELL, ELIZABETH M., *Autobiography*, ed. Eleanor L. Sewell (1907).

SHAFFER, E. S., '*Kubla Khan' and the Fall of Jerusalem: The Mythological School in Biblical Criticism and Secular Literature 1770–1880* (Cambridge, 1975).

SHAVER, CHESTER L., 'Wordsworth's Vaudracour and Wilkinson's *The Wanderer*', *RES* NS 12 (1961), 55–7.

—— and ALICE C., *Wordsworth's Library: A Catalogue* (New York and London, 1979).

SHEATS, PAUL D., *The Making of Wordsworth's Poetry, 1785–1798* (Cambridge, Mass., 1973).

SHELLEY, MARY, *Journals*, ed. Paula R. Feldman and Diana Scott-Kilvert (2 vols., Oxford, 1987).

SHELLEY, PERCY BYSSHE, *Letters*, ed. Frederick L. Jones (2 vols., Oxford, 1964).

SIMMONS, JACK, *Southey* (1945).

SMITH, OLIVIA, *The Politics of Language 1791–1819* (Oxford, 1984).

SOUTHEY, ROBERT, *New Letters*, ed. Kenneth Curry (2 vols., New York and London, 1965).

STEPHEN, LESLIE, 'Wordsworth's Ethics', *Cornhill Magazine*, 34 (1876), 206–226. Reprinted *Hours in a Library: Third Series* (1879), 178–229.

STILLINGER, JACK, 'Wordsworth and Keats', in *The Age of William Wordsworth: Critical Essays on the Romantic Tradition*, ed. Kenneth R. Johnston and Gene W. Ruoff (New Brunswick and London, 1987), 172–6.

STROUT, ALAN LANG, *The Life and Letters of James Hogg, the Ettrick Shepherd* (Lubbock, Tex., 1946).

STURROCK, JUNE, 'Wordsworth's Italian Teacher', *BJRL* 67 (1985), 797–812.

SUPER, R. H., *Walter Savage Landor: A Biography* (1957).

—— 'Landor's Letters to Wordsworth and Coleridge', *MP* 55 (1957), 73–83.

SWANN, ELSIE, *Christopher North (John Wilson)* (Edinburgh and London, 1934).

SYDENHAM, M. J., *The French Revolution* (1965).

TAPLIN, GARDNER B., *The Life of Elizabeth Barrett Browning* (New Haven and London, 1957).

TENNYSON, G. B., *Victorian Devotional Poetry: The Tractarian Mode* (Cambridge, Mass., 1981).

THALE, MARY (ed.), *Selections from the Papers of the London Corresponding Society 1792–1799* (Cambridge, 1983).

THOMAS, GORDON KENT, *Wordsworth's Dirge and Promise* (Lincoln, Nebr., 1971).

THOMPSON, E. P., *The Making of the English Working Class* (1963).

THOMPSON, J. M., *English Witnesses of the French Revolution* (Oxford, 1938).

—— *The French Revolution* (Oxford, 1943).

THOMPSON, T. W., *Wordsworth's Hawkshead*, ed. Robert Woof (1970).

TODD, F. M., *Politics and the Poet: A Study of Wordsworth* (1957).

TYSON, GERALD P., *Joseph Johnson: A Liberal Publisher* (Iowa City, 1979).

VARNEY, ANDREW, 'Wordsworth and "Those Italian Clocks"', *Notes and Queries*, NS 17 (1980), 69–70.

VINCENT, E. R., *Ugo Foscolo: An Italian in Regency England* (Cambridge, 1953).

WARD, WILFRID, *Aubrey De Vere: A Memoir* (1904).

WARD, WILLIAM S., *Literary Reviews in British Periodicals 1798–1820: A Bibliography* (2 vols., 1972).

WEBB, R. K., *Harriet Martineau: A Radical Victorian* (1960).

WELLS, ROGER, *Insurrection: The British Experience 1795–1803* (Gloucester, 1983).

WILBERFORCE, WILLIAM, *Journey to the Lake District from Cambridge: A Summer Diary 1779*, ed. C. E. Wrangham (Stocksfield, 1983).

WILDI, MAX, 'Wordsworth and the Simplon Pass', *English Studies*, 40 (1959), 224–32, and 43 (1962), 359–77.

WOLFSON, SUSAN J., 'The Illusion of Mastery: Wordsworth's Revisions of "The Drowned Man of Esthwaite," 1799, 1805, 1850', *PMLA* 99 (1984), 917–35.

WOODRING, CARL, *Victorian Samplers: William and Mary Howitt* (Lawrence, Kansas, 1952).

—— *Politics in English Romantic Poetry* (Cambridge, Mass., 1970).

WOODWORTH, MARY KATHERINE, *The Literary Career of Sir Samuel Egerton Brydges* (Oxford, 1935).

WOOF, ROBERT, 'Wordsworth's Poetry and Stuart's Newspapers: 1797–1803', *SIB* 15 (1962), 149–89.

—— 'Wordsworth and Coleridge: Some Early Matters', *Bicentenary Wordsworth Studies*, ed. Jonathan Wordsworth (Ithaca, 1970), 76–91.

—— *The Wordsworth Circle* (Grasmere, 1979).

WORDSWORTH, JONATHAN, *The Music of Humanity* (1969).

—— (ed.), *Bicentenary Wordsworth Studies* (Ithaca, 1970).

—— '"The Climbing of Snowdon"' in above, 449–74.

—— 'The Five-book *Prelude* of Early Spring 1804', *JEGP* 76 (1977), 1–25.

—— 'On Man, on Nature, and on Human Life', *RES* NS 31 (1980), 2–29.

—— *William Wordsworth: The Borders of Vision* (Oxford, 1982).

—— and GILL, STEPHEN, 'The Two-part *Prelude* of 1798–99', *JEGP* 72 (1973), 503–25.

—— JAYE, MICHAEL C., and WOOF, ROBERT, *William Wordsworth and the Age of English Romanticism* (New Brunswick, London, Grasmere, 1987).

WORTHINGTON, JANE, *Wordsworth's Reading of Roman Prose* (New Haven, 1946).

# SKELETAL FAMILY TREE OF WILLIAM WORDSWORTH

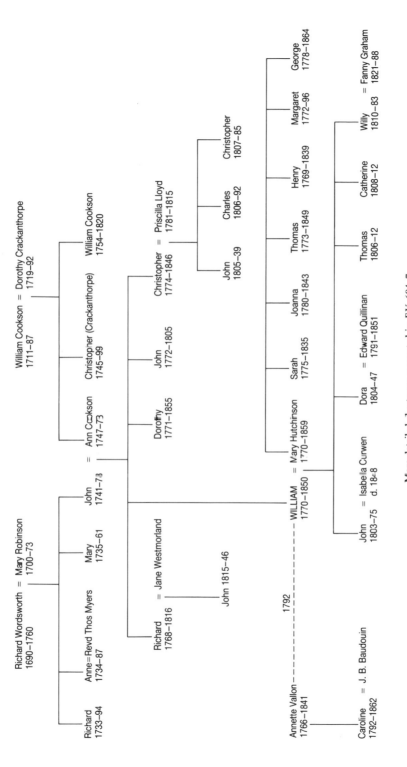

More detailed charts are presented in *EY*, 694–7.

# INDEX